D1525193

The Theology of Pope Benedict XVI

The Theology of Pope Benedict XVI

The Christocentric Shift

Emery de Gaál

THE THEOLOGY OF POPE BENEDICT XVI

First published in 2010 by
PALGRAVE MACMILLAN®
in the United States—a division of St. Martin's Press LLC,
175 Fifth Avenue, New York, NY 10010.

Where this book is distributed in the UK, Europe and the rest of the world,
this is by Palgrave Macmillan, a division of Macmillan Publishers Limited,
registered in England, company number 785998, of Houndmills,
Basingstoke, Hampshire RG21 6XS.

Palgrave Macmillan is the global academic imprint of the above companies
and has companies and representatives throughout the world.

Palgrave® and Macmillan® are registered trademarks in the United States,
the United Kingdom, Europe and other countries.

ISBN: 978–0–230–10540–9

Library of Congress Cataloging-in-Publication Data

Gaál Gyulai, Emery de.
    The theology of Pope Benedict XVI : the christocentric shift / Emery
de Gaál.
        p. cm.
    ISBN 978–0–230–10540–9 (hardback)
        1. Benedict XVI, Pope, 1927– I. Title.
BX1378.6.G33 2010
230′.2092—dc22   2010013068

A catalogue record of the book is available from the British Library.

Design by Newgen Imaging Systems (P) Ltd., Chennai, India.

First edition: November 2010

10 9 8 7 6 5 4 3 2 1

Printed in the United States of America.

In gratitude
Leo Cardinal Scheffczyk (1920–2005)
"Evangelizare investigabiles divitias Christi" (Eph 3:8)
Preach the unsearchable riches of Christ

If we draw near to him [Jesus Christ] with humble trust, we encounter in his gaze the response to the deepest longings of our heart: to know God and establish a living relationship with him in an authentic communion of love that can fill our lives and our interpersonal and social relations with the same love. For this reason, humanity needs Christ: In him, our hope, "we have been saved." (cf. Rom 8:24)[1]

—Benedict XVI, Easter Homily, 2008

Christ...is truly the origin of our harmony, the true David who has restored the lyre of our body which had long lain idle, its frame crumbling. The Lord has restored it, making it His own....God our Master Himself sought to renew this lyre, and so He hung His own lyre, nailed to the wood of His tree, and gave it fresh life when the cross destroyed all sins. Thus He ordered mortal man from the different nations into a single lyre, and tuned it for heavenly music, drawing peoples of all races into a single body. Then he struck the cords with the pelcrum of the Word, and the sound of the Gospel fills all creation with the praise of God.

—St. Paulinus of Nola (355–431), Poema XX

CONTENTS

Illustrations appear between 187 and 188

FOREWORD

The calling of a Christian is not, first and foremost, to be justified (Reformation), or to be a morally good citizen (Enlightenment), or even to enjoy heavenly bliss one day. Our beautiful vocation on earth is to partake sacramentally in Christ's eternal life and to make God visible to this world. By leading a holy life, Christians enable others to receive life's profound meaning, which they could never discover or produce on their own: "we should be holy and blameless before him...his sons through Jesus Christ...to the praise of his glorious grace..." so that others may know the hope to which he has called all (Eph 1). Through the fragility of human existence, may others behold the Divine. What a wonderful cause for which to exist! In his homily at the mass inaugurating his pontificate, Pope Benedict XVI observed: "And only where God is seen does life truly begin. Only when we meet the living God in Christ do we know what life is. We are not some casual and meaningless product of evolution. Each of us is the result of a thought of God.... There is nothing more beautiful than to be surprised by the gospel, by the encounter with Christ. There is nothing more beautiful than to know him and to speak to others of our friendship with him."[2] Establishing the identity and mission of Jesus Christ is of overriding, crucial importance for such a positively intrepid enterprise. Regarding this endeavor, it is of no small significance to examine Pope Benedict XVI's understanding of Jesus as he is one of the most outstanding theologians the Catholic Church has recently produced. As Joseph Cardinal Ratzinger, he served as Prefect of the Congregation for the Doctrine of the Faith for twenty-three years, and he is now Supreme Pontiff of a church numbering some 1.2 billion members worldwide.

In a sense one can state that Pope Benedict XVI is the "anti-Nietzsche," as the German author Botho Strauß formulated in the German daily newspaper *Frankfurter Allgemeine Zeitung* on October 20, 1994. Nietzsche's fateful "*Umwertung aller Werte*"[3] (revaluation of all values) is being reversed. Benedict XVI is challenging modernity to a revision of the suppositions and assumptions Nietzsche had instilled in such a sustained and lasting manner. A loss of purpose and of values has become the norm for many people. Nihilism has become the practical worldview, altering all areas of life. Nietzsche claimed, "Christianity is the greatest misfortune that had befallen humankind." Benedict XVI's response is, "Jesus Christ is the greatest fortune imaginable for humankind!" As Christians and as disciples of Christ, human beings experience the fact that they are not the product of a faceless law of nature, but rather they are personally willed by God. In Jesus Christ, God receives a face, a living vis-à-vis, who enters our history and never tires of turning the numerous peoples into the one chosen people.

The author's intention is to convey an appreciation for the understanding Pope Benedict XVI, as a believer and theologian, has for the person of Christ. In order to better illuminate the pope's supremely Christocentric motivation, this study will briefly present, as a background to his own significant theological contributions, the thought and concepts of the thinkers who formed and informed Pope Benedict XVI's own mind. Therefore, less attention will be given to his official work as prefect and pontiff and the documents and decrees that bear his signature. By a fortunate coincidence, this present work offers a background for Pope Benedict XVI's book on Jesus Christ *Jesus of Nazareth*.

The threefold intention of this study is to demonstrate that Pope Benedict's theology can only be understood if one grasps:

1. its overriding Christological concern;
2. its unification with the greater intellectual current within which it operates, namely, that of the *Ressourcement* movement (a return to patristic sources in order to live in the spirit of early Christianity); and,
3. its consonance with Christian faith, that is, with the testimony of scripture, the teaching of the councils, and the living faith of all the Catholic faithful throughout the Church's history.

While he is in general agreement with Ressourcement theology, Pope Benedict is not part of a movement or school of theology, but rather he is committed to the whole of the faith as expressed in scripture, the liturgy, the Church fathers, the saints, and the teaching office of the Church.

An often used Thomistic axiom states "*omnia quae recipiuntur recepta sunt secundum modum recipientis*" ("Everything received is received according to the mode of the one who receives"). As they received the message of Vatican II, some societies were engulfed in a profound cultural upheaval: a previously unheard of period of peace and prosperity was disturbed by radical questioning of the very foundations Europe and North America had been built upon for millennia. Simultaneously, in various locations, discontent was expressed about inherited, and what were seen to be no longer verifiable, customs and traditions. Some societies with these dispositions could not always appreciate the two central impelling forces behind the theological minds and intellectual currents giving shape and content to the documents of that great council. (Exacerbating the problem was the fact that most societies received news concerning Vatican II through the filter of a mass media altogether unfamiliar with theological terminology.) John XXIII's intention when announcing Vatican II was pastoral renewal. The central intellectual systematic currents giving shape and content to the work of the council's *periti* (advisors) were (a) the retrieval of Thomas Aquinas (neo-Thomism), and (b) the fathers of the Church (patrology) as enablers of a credible discipleship of Christ in the *hic et nunc* (here and now). The second current was a movement called Ressourcement, a French term meaning "going back to the living and life-giving wellsprings of Christian belief and existence: early writings of the Church fathers, councils, traditions and creeds." Instead of the Council being understood in light of these two central concerns that were present and influential during it, the vague term "spirit of the council" was adopted and seems to have been interpreted by the media in terms of an outside, wholly unchristian context, that is, in terms of a naïve optimism regarding humanity's ability for self-improvement unaided by grace or a good and caring God. At the time, the profound crisis of the Western identity in general—of which the upheavals of 1968, such as the student unrest at Berkeley and in Paris, are emblematic—influenced the reception of the Council. Perhaps future generations might call it a crude variation of Hegelianism (history produces truth on its own). The age that received the message of the council often could not behold the Holy Spirit at work in the council—as He had also been at work in previous councils—but rather was consumed with the temperament and spirit of its own age that came bursting forth: the self-becoming of the absolute spirit in time and space à la Hegel? It was an age that could not see God's offer of grace or appreciate humanity's need to embrace God's mercy as the positive basis for establishing a healthy rapport with the numinous. In short, the context was on the whole not conducive to a favorable reception of the council's teachings, wrought for the faithful by the same Holy Spirit present in Genesis, the Annunciation, Pentecost, and each prior council. Despite such powerful outside vectors, Joseph Ratzinger did not shy away from patiently spelling out another perspective. He was motivated not by faith in his own superior intellect but by his supreme confidence in the Truth revealed definitively by Jesus Christ and handed down by the power of the Holy Spirit through the liturgy and the reality of apostolic succession, upon which the Church is founded.[4] This is the basis for apprehending a correlation between reason and revelation, between scripture and tradition, and between truth and freedom.

It is to no small degree that this lack of appreciation for the abiding presence of the Holy Spirit in the Church—despite the rather recent pioneering and magisterial works on the Holy Spirit by theologians such as Heribert Mühlen and Yves Congar[5]—explains the negative public image of Cardinal Ratzinger since the late 1960s, leading to such caricatures as "Grand Inquisitor" and *Panzerkardinal* (*Panzer* is the German word for a military tank). This is aggravated by the fact that the Pope's association with Ressourcement theology is ignored by the mass media. Following upon the intellectualistic understanding of faith that dominated the age of neoscholastic manuals, a rationalistic understanding of theology, now a more social understanding of the nature of the Church, set in. Ever since the Middle Ages, there has gradually been less and less of an appreciation for the Holy Spirit's indispensable sustaining presence in the Church. The spiritual dimension of the Church—as an institution not made by human beings, but as God's gift and presence among people—has been lost sight of. This was perhaps exacerbated by Ratzinger's self-effacement and good humor in that he did not take offense easily and therefore did not rebuff negative perceptions. An additional factor adding to his negative image was that Ratzinger's skepticism regarding the hasty implementation of the Council's call for liturgical renewal was misinterpreted as an invitation to return to the Roman Rite of 1962.

Yet another contributing factor was his shyness in defending his own person both in public and within academia. This is only partially explained in terms of his temperament. In an age of mass culture, where people are formed and informed by an abstract/virtual reality concretized in the mass media, disregard for one's public image comes close to suicide. The question arises whether a Christian can care about the media's perception and still remain a disciple of Christ.

The truth shines on its own conditions. It requires our words in order to be conveyed, but it does not need human cosmetics in order to convince. Were one to clad the truth in appealing trappings, one would betray the truth. Provocatively for the postmodern mind, Jesus is not *a* way, but *the* Way, and *the* Truth for all people of all ages.

Indeed, for Ratzinger one criterion of a healthy Christian spirituality is the willingness to suffer a lack of understanding and appreciation, and even be subjected to malice, with good humor and without resistance, very much like Our Lord in "The Legend of the Grand Inquisitor" in Fyodor Dostoyevsky's (1821–1881) classic novel *The Brothers Karamazov*. Much in the vein of Augustine, the inner logic of creation by God and that of sin allow the opposing, sinful person (the other) full well to recognize truth. No matter how many words lies might employ, the sovereign reality of truth cannot be denied.

During his years as a student, Ratzinger was exposed to Romano Guardini's[6] (1885–1968) memorable interpretation of Dostoyevsky's writings in light of the ascendance of anti-Christian National Socialism.[7] As a young professor giving retreats, Ratzinger would have the participants read the parable of the Grand Inquisitor with the intention that they would thus cultivate an appreciation for the Christian genius amid a superficial world. In Dostoyevsky's masterful parable, the masses prefer the benign but ultimately cruel reign of the Grand Inquisitor to the truth of the defaced—and unrecognized by everyone but the Grand Inquisitor—Savior. The Russian novelist presents Jesus Christ, who returns to the Spanish city of Seville at the time of the Inquisition, as a provocation for the people led under the seemingly benign, but actually totalitarian, guidance of the aged Grand Inquisitor. After a long period of deception in which they have become accustomed to a life in which only earthly, material needs are sought after and met, the people have come to prefer ignorance to truth. The old man drives Jesus into the dark night after Jesus has kissed him rather than defend himself with words. This parallels Jesus' behavior before Pontius Pilate. Hatred-filled blindness is met by Jesus with kenotic humility. The reader is left with a clear impression: had Jesus defended himself before a man who knew him to be the way, the truth, and the life, he would have betrayed his divine sonship. With rhetorical elegance, the Grand Inquisitor argues that people value bread and material well-being more than freedom, which ultimately leads to the disturbance of their relationship with God. In the depths of their hearts, people opt for a world that is dedivinized, and the Inquisitor is "nonjudgmental" and "humane" enough to bring this about.

The visionary Dostoyevsky argued that people in the future would cheerfully surrender their conscience to a faceless society and turn to it as their deity of choice. (Forty years later this would come to pass in the forms of communism, National Socialism, and consumerist societies.) In place of the individual, society would henceforth determine what is good and evil, sinful and holy.

Along the same lines a friend of Dostoyevsky, the Russian philosopher and later convert to Catholicism Vladimir Soloviev (1853–1900), in the sobering *A Short Narrative of the Anti-Christ*, his last and most celebrated book, prophetically foretells a "new Jesus" appearing as savior on the stage of history as a global harbinger of peace who will lead all to embrace humanism and this world.[8] Following the impressions of totalitarianism and World War II, both books were rather widely read by European intellectuals during Ratzinger's adolescence and well into the 1960s. The common basis for these two Russian classics is the three temptations of Jesus by Satan in Matthew 4:1–11. There Jesus is tempted to change stone into bread, throw himself down from a pinnacle, and finally to worship the world and its dross. Ratzinger refers often to these temptations in his homilies.

There is one additional factor contributing to a misinterpretation of Ratzinger. Due to no fault of its own, the public at large is unable to differentiate between neoscholasticism—a long bygone effort marred by rationalism and transcendental Thomism—and modern-day Ressourcement theology. Support, however vague, for transcendental Thomism (vulgo: anthropocentric shift) is considered "modern," while everything else is considered preconciliar, at best, or neoscholastic and therefore "conservative." In keeping with the Bologna School of Church Councils, the Second Vatican Council has popularly been considered a watershed council dividing all of Church history into pre- and post-Vatican II eras. This unscientific "hermeneutics of discontinuity" explains the rise of irresponsibly superficial, black-and-white categories according to which certain individuals are considered either "preconciliar" or "postconciliar." Such a view is unable to apprehend the Church as a spiritual reality transcending political or social interests, and it cannot grasp the legitimate and healthy plurality of different theological currents arising from the one Church, which remains the point of reference for all balanced theologies. Thus, the anthropocentric shift tends to despiritualize and politicize religion. It has lost sight of two realities that vouch for the self-same identity of the Church of 2000 with herself in 2000, 2010, 1965, and 27 AD: the abiding presence of the Holy Spirit by virtue of: the charism of apostolic succession; and the Eucharistic presence of the risen Lord Jesus. As a consequence, popular perception never considered labeling Ratzinger as anything but "preconciliar," "conservative," or "traditionalist."

If it was the tragedy of the past forty years to divorce the major theological developments leading up to the Vatican III Council from its message (especially from that of the Ressourcement movement), is it an overstatement to claim that the recovery of patristic thought will, by overcoming this artificial divorce, offer proper access to Vatican II *and* do greater justice to the singular inner coherence of the theology of Pope Benedict XVI?

Please note: every generalization is an injustice. Karl Rahner and Bernard Lonergan should not be seen as mere precursors to the anthropocentric shift. The two would certainly not advocate a reduction of Christology into anthropology—as likewise many representatives of the anthropocentric shift would not. Lonergan's epistemology, Trinitarian theology, and Christology are valuable achievements. Gustavo Gutiérrez's liberation theology accentuates the need to apply Catholic social teaching also to Latin America.

The myth of a progressive, pre-Vatican II Ratzinger and a conservative, post-Vatican II Ratzinger is fairly easy to explain in an age of oversimplification. In the public square, the anthropocentric shift implicitly became the exclusive lens through which the conciliar documents were interpreted. This has led to Ratzinger incorrectly and retroactively (that is, it is a classification of him that began around 1965 and afterward) being associated with this camp prior to and during the council. In fact, however, he has throughout his adult life, right up until the present time, belonged to the currents of Ressourcement and Christian personalism. The erroneous interpretation of his positions is exacerbated by Vatican II's general and unspecific treatments. In addition, he enjoyed a classical education in the humanities (*humanistische Bildung*) in his formative teen years, which is almost unknown and therefore inaccessible nowadays to people living in North America and what is culturally post-Christian Western Europe. But it is this very "living from the vivifying sources" of occidental culture and the Christian faith that make him appear—even in advanced age—to the unprejudiced observer as still youthful and on fire, not complacent and inert. The gleam in his eyes seeks to tell people that something fresh, bold, and noble is awaiting them; something that holds the promise of breaking away from the stale ways of ordinary life: Jesus is different and his disciples are original. Far more than being merely an indispensable basis for culture, Jesus Christ is a personal path to knowledge and happiness.

It is a joy reading Pope Benedict XVI's vast opus because of his sovereign command of the Western heritage and his genuine theological concern, which is characterized by being humble, nonpolemical, and removed from the slightest suspicion of vanity. It is doubtful whether our age will produce anyone similarly educated and erudite.

It must be pointed out that on November 6, 1992, Cardinal Joseph Ratzinger was appointed (the first German bishop ever to receive this honor) an associate member of the prestigious French *Académie des Sciences Morales et Politiques*, succeeding the Russian dissident, nuclear physicist, and human rights activist Andrei Sakharov. It is no exaggeration to call the Académie one of the most illustrious circles for intellectual discourse. It was founded in 1795 and is one of five academies belonging to the *Institut Français*, one of which is the *Académie Française*. It has included or includes members as varied as Albert Einstein, Václav Havel, and Prince Charles. His appointment illustrates how the Catholic faith, as expounded by someone of Ratzinger's intellectual caliber, is attractive to human rationality even in modern times.[9]

It is hoped that this study will contribute to the recognition that the facile application of categories such as "liberal" or "conservative" are political predications ill-suited to capturing the existential and intellectual struggle every Christian takes up in following the one Christ and joining his Church in the one symphony of praise to the triune God. Jesus Christ not only grants the gift of the future as eternal Redemption, but he liberates the present from the cold grip of a faceless, crude mass culture.

ACKNOWLEDGMENTS

Over the past years I have had the opportunity to teach regularly a course on Joseph Ratzinger's/Pope Benedict XVI's theology to seminarians at the University of St. Mary of the Lake/Mundelein Seminary. Father Raymond Webb, the academic dean, suggested I give the course a Christological perspective. My students' contributions, critiques, idealism, and joy in anticipation of ordination to the priesthood have motivated me to see this *scriptum* mature into a publishable book.

I am much indebted to Father Charles R. Meyer, professor emeritus of systematic theology, for painstakingly proofreading the text, discovering mistakes, and suggesting improvements. Words of gratitude also go to Father Thomas A. Baima, provost and professor of systematic theology, for suggesting the publisher. Mrs. Laura Malashanko from Ave Maria University meticulously edited the first draft. Last but not least, Mrs. Lorraine Olley, director of the Feehan Memorial Library, as well Mrs. Marian Johnson and Mrs. Anna Kielian, ingeniously discovered titles even in faraway lands. Also, I benefited from the lively discussions on the mind of Benedict XVI at the informal gatherings of scholars hosted by the Lumen Christi Institute at the University of Chicago. Tracey Rowland made valuable suggestions. At the vibrant Catholic-Jewish Scholars Dialogue in Chicago I shared some of my insights into the thoughts of Pope Benedict XVI.

I thank Chris Chappell, associate editor, and Samantha Hasey, editorial assistant, from Palgrave Macmillan for their kind patience and suggestions.

With much competence and enthusiasm Father Paul Stemn undertook the final editing and supplied the ready-for-print version. This investigation would not have come about without his reliable and always cheerful assistance.

This study is dedicated to Leo Cardinal Scheffczyk. I studied theology under him in Munich and he was so gracious to be the homilist during my first holy mass at Ingolstadt's splendid Münster cathedral. He and Pope Benedict XVI have much in common. He lived, as the pope does, exemplarily charitable independence from passing fashions when proclaiming gently and joyfully the unsearchable riches of Christ's gospel.

Never did the scholar Ratzinger enjoy sufficient leisure to share with the public square a fully developed structure of his theological vision. May this study suggest its possible contours. The Holy Father lives constantly in the presence of the Eucharist. St. Gregory the Great relates in the second book of the *Dialogues* concerning the Pope's patron: the Abbot St. Benedict "lived with himself under the eyes of God."

Fr. EMERY DE GAÁL
Mundelein, Solemnity of
Saints Peter and Paul, 2010

ABBREVIATIONS

CA   *Confessio Augustana*, Lutheran Confession of Faith, Augsburg 1530.

CSEL   *Corpus Scriptorum Ecclesiasticorum Latinorum*, 95 vols. Vienna, 1866–present.

DH   Heinrich Denzinger, rev. *Enchiridion Symbolorum, Definitionum et Declarationum de rebus Fidei et Morum.* 40th ed. Edited by Peter Hünermann. Freiburg i. Br.: Herder, 2005.

ND   J. Neuner, SJ, and J. Dupuis, SJ. *The Christian Faith in the Doctrinal Documents of the Catholic Church.* 7th ed. New York: Alba House, 2001.

PG   *Patrologiae cursus completus: series graeca.* 162 vols. Edited by J.-P. Migne. Paris, 1857–1886.

PL   *Patrologiae cursus completus: series latina.* 217 vols. Edited by J.-P. Migne. Paris, 1844–1864.

Documents of Vatican II

DH   *Dignitatis Humanae*, Declaration on Religious Freedom

DV   *Dei Verbum*, Dogmatic Constitution on Divine Revelation

GS   *Gaudium et Spes*, Pastoral Constitution on the Church in the Modern World

LG   *Lumen Gentium*, Dogmatic Constitution on the Church

SC   *Sacrosanctum Concilium*, Constitution on the Sacred Liturgy

Introduction: The Christocentric Shift

It is a commonly held opinion that Joseph Ratzinger's theological contributions are essentially ecclesiological in nature. While it is true that he dedicated his dissertation and *Habilitationsschrift* (habilitation, that is, his post-doctoral thesis) to ecclesiological themes, the inner motivation and fulcrum of his theology is supremely Christological. His concern is not primarily an academic or cerebral one but is rather the result of a personal encounter with Jesus Christ as a believer living the sacramental life of the Catholic Church. For Ratzinger, God is the reality of charity that constitutes a human being in freedom. God's invitation to covenantal relationality actuates full freedom in the individual human being. "Christian belief in God means that things are the being-thought of a creative consciousness, of a creative freedom, and that the creative consciousness that bears up all things has released what has been thought into the freedom of its own, independent existence."[1] In the Christian Redeemer, the unity and the whole of reality become tangible. God's only begotten Son, Jesus Christ, demonstrates for every age again what genuinely fulfilled human existence is. Ratzinger perceives this as a predicatory figuration of the central call of human beings, namely, as being *called to freedom*. Jesus Christ points to the central reality that every human being is called to consciously conform himself or herself to and find fulfillment in the acceptance of oneself as proexistence, that is, as existing "for" others. The proexistence of Jesus Christ's crucifixion makes concrete charity possible. Thus, genuine and edifying change in this world occurs not by modifying structures but by transforming human persons toward genuine freedom. In this sense, Ratzinger subscribes to a personalist Christology. It is also in this sense that one is either a structuralist or a Christian; *tertium non daretur* (no other alternative exists). Every distance from Christ is a distance from the source of meaning and unity. The various facets of reality, the different academic disciplines of philosophy and faith, partake in a whole that becomes apparent in Christ.[2] Only the God-man Jesus Christ, as the eternal Son of God, grants unity, comprehension of the whole, and the world's deepest meaning. With singular coherence this expresses itself in Ratzinger's oeuvre.[3]

Paradoxical only to the uninformed modern bystander, the personal encounter with Jesus Christ, and, therefore, with the concrete Church, is not a limitation on freedom but the very thing that makes freedom possible. In light of Christ, the mystery of the Incarnation is the unsurpassable climax of the human spirit's quest for freedom. "Today in broad circles, even among believers, an image has prevailed of a Jesus who demands nothing, never scolds, who accepts everyone and everything, who no longer does anything but affirm us."[4] Yet, in contrast, the Jesus of the gospels is demanding and bold and certainly does not have convenient expectations. The early Church was not full of scholastic explanations or shallow, appeasing platitudes but rather of Christians living and dying in the charity of the Lord.

The present age is marked by a sense of optimism in humanity's capacity to build a better society. "In reality ideological optimism is merely the façade of a world without hope trying to hide from its own despair with this deceptive sham."[5] In contrast to the optimism of a self-perfecting world, Christian optimism is based on the supernatural virtue of hope, a hope not trusting in the perfection of immanence but seeking, already in the here and now, union with God. This union is brought about by God, not by human capabilities. Realistic human hope is anchored in the person of Jesus Christ, for he is proof of God's presence in the brokenness of humanity. In fact, in Christ this hoped for union of humanity with God has already begun. This dignifies human existence beyond all imagination. In accord with Bonaventure (1217–1274), Ratzinger argues that Christian hope is not stagnant but organizes the here and now in preparation for the kingdom of God. He thereby makes clear that Christian hope rests not on a state or condition but on a person: "Thus all our hopes are at bottom hope in the great and boundless love: they are hope in paradise, the kingdom of God, being with God and like God, sharing his nature (2 Pt 1:4)."[6] If, however, people lose sight of "God's standard, the standard of eternity, then all that remains as guiding thread is nothing but egoism."[7] He continues: "[T]he justification of Christian hope is the Incarnation of God's Word and love in Jesus Christ." Liberating individuals from the subjective experience of the recipient, Jesus answers the deepest questions of human existence offering "a gratification that is limitless, for the infinite." The utter uniqueness of Jesus lies in the fact that he is the God-man. "Only he who is both man and God can be the ontological bridge leading from the one to the other. And therefore he is this for everyone, not only for some."[8]

While outside manifestations of faith may and in fact should undergo change over time, all developments, higher viewpoints, and new understandings are legitimate as they give expression to a renewed commitment to the one Jesus Christ. In that qualified sense Ratzinger is Platonic. But in contrast to that philosopher, he will insist that outward change is indicative of a healthy life.

In Ratzinger's estimation, modern defenselessness vis-à-vis various forms of intellectual dictatorships and human spiritual inner turmoil is grounded in the fact that wisdom is not, in the strict sense, scientific. It is erroneously believed that only scientific knowledge grants insight, and that wisdom and truth represent unenlightened naïveté. Thus, in the age of technical rationality humankind becomes its own creator with the world subject to its mastery, constructing a reality relentlessly transparent to all but that which is exclusively the product of humankind's own rationality. A predefined essence of the human person is not countenanced. Such a human being is free and strangely driven by this very freedom to invent what the human being must be. Everything is at his and her disposal and mercy, the environment, animals, and humankind itself. All that is could equally be disposed of, including the differences between men and women and animals and human beings. This modern frame of mind lacks the ability for critical self-reflection. Only faith can demarcate the limits of technical rationality by showing that the truth of humankind is grounded in a personally willed creation. Human beings discover this truth about themselves by going outside themselves to the tradition of humanism as it is preserved by Jesus of Nazareth.[9] Amid the confusing multitude of traditions and philosophies, nothing exists beyond them to adjudicate right from wrong, good from evil.

As Vatican II reiterates: "it is only in the mystery of the Word made flesh that the mystery of man truly becomes clear" (*Gaudium et Spes* [GS] 22). Thus, the Christian perceives in Jesus the breakthrough to the center of a humanistic tradition leading to the origin of humanity and the basis of humanism. This origin does not oppose reason but rather supplies reason with its very foundation. Thus, humankind is protected against fallacious traditions or a complete lack of tradition. By sharing in Jesus' relationship with his Father, one gains an interior acquaintance with God and is able to make sense of life, death, and oneself. This path is not abstract, but one of prayer, thereby emulating Jesus. God is not a Plotinian, impersonal One, but a personal Thou, and humankind may thus address him. In contrast to all other relationships, addressing God in this manner allows access to the deepest recesses of one's self, without which no human being is whole. In the process of this discovery, Ratzinger reminds us, one recognizes oneself, because one is being recognized; I can cherish, because I am being cherished.[10]

Prior to the Second Vatican Council, theologians such as Karl Adam, Josef Andreas Jungmann, and Karl Rahner had spoken of "a factual monotheism" (that is, a denial of the Christian triune God). Nowadays, the danger comes from the diametrically opposed position. There is a new Arianism (denial of the full divinity of Jesus Christ) or Nestorianism (two separate persons in the incarnate Christ) threatening the faith, either by negating outright the divine nature of Jesus or by separating the divine and human in Jesus. At the core, the contentious issues are not epistemology, ecclesiology, or social matters but a proper understanding of Christology. The hypothesis of a Christ is left for the Church or idiosyncratic theologians to ponder. The overwhelming majority are concerned with the much reduced and quite manageable figure of Jesus. Often this limited, horizontal perspective is imposed upon liturgy as its governing tenor. In Ratzinger's estimation, all crises within Christianity are only secondarily institutional in nature. Primarily, the question is one of Jesus Christ's divinity and the Incarnation's relationship to the praxis of faith. Invariably, the foundational understanding of faith and discipleship becomes one-sided and confusing as the believer follows only the human Jesus and no longer also the divine Christ. One thereby reduces faith to an imitation (if not a mimicry) of a human exemplar. Christ's divinity is not addressed and is perhaps even downright negated. This clashes with the New Testament's bold call to all Christians to "be imitators of God" (Eph 5:1).

Consonant with the Christian faith, and along with the theologian and
later cardinal Henri de Lubac (1896–1991) and the larger part of Christians
living today, Ratzinger insists that the deeds of Jesus are also the deeds of a
divine person. In the life of Jesus' human existence, God becomes tangible.
Certainly the words of Jesus contain irreplaceable significance, but his ministry may not be reduced to mere words. The flesh as lived Word, up to and
including the cross, is equally important. The vital connection with the spiritual figure (*Gestalt* in German, *eidos* for Plato) of Jesus enables the words to
speak with their indwelling power. It is the spiritual figure that permits access
to the essence of a human being. Both the unfolding and destiny of humankind is imaged in Jesus Christ and his terrestrial life. Human life should not
be limited to an exterior imitation of Jesus' life. The inner figure of Jesus
Christ contains, in its history and self-immolation on the cross, the measure
for future, self-confident humanity. In every Christian, something like the
unfolding of this prototype occurs, and in this the individual human being
comes to be his or her true self:

> At first sight it may seem to be a rather parochial, merely internal
> Christian matter, when we speak of the prayer of Jesus as the New
> Testament's basic affirmation regarding his person. In reality this is pre-
> cisely the point which concerns us existentially, i.e., it is what is central
> to humanity. For the New Testament designates it as the place where
> man may actually become God, where his liberation may take place; it is
> the place where he touches his own truth and becomes true to himself.
> The question of Jesus' filial relation to the Father gets to the very root
> of the question of man's freedom and liberation, and unless this is done
> everything else is futile.[11]

In his book *The Nature and Mission of Theology*, Ratzinger observes rather
apodictically: "There is only one bearer of the promise, outside of which is
the chaotic world of self-realization where men compete with one another
and desire to compete with God but succeed merely in working right past
their true hope."[12] Jesus Christ frees humankind from being reified, from
ulterior motives, and from being objectivified.

It seems that Ratzinger presupposes something quite unheard of in ages
past: he assumes the preponderance of technology and the sciences enjoyed in
everyday modern life unintentionally suppresses any appreciation for meditation and contemplation. Thus, natural revelation becomes inaccessible to
the postmodern human being. Inevitably, the consequence is a loss of access
to the natural law (aside from the Reformation's unambiguous opposition
to it in the sixteenth century). That the *lex divina* (divine law) and the *lex
naturalis* (natural law) no longer meet as the *desiderium naturale ad videndum
Deum*—usually rendered as *desiderium naturale videndi Deum* (the natural desire
for the vision of God)—is lost sight of amid the constant fleeting impressions
and surrogate satisfactions of a consumerist society.

This Christological statement is not an isolated spiritual observation but
one indebted to the history of Christian spirituality and the recent encyc-
licals of John Paul II. It was eloquently expressed in the Second Vatican

Council: "In reality, it is only in the mystery of the Word made flesh that the mystery of man truly becomes clear" (GS 22). God entered into the history of humanity as a human being, one subject among billions of individuals. The Son of Man entered the history of every human being so that each one might discover his or her singular greatness and dignity before God. This had been a *cantus firmus* with John Paul II as well. Human life hinges on these questions: Is Jesus also the Christ? Is he one of the dead or living? The answers determine both proclamation and sacramental life. If Jesus as Eternal Son of God and His saving Resurrection are the merely wishful expressions of the last will of the historic Jesus, then the liturgy, including the Eucharist, is solely a ritual and the expression of some vague togetherness, reducing faith to a chance event and sentiment. Yet in the liturgy the Church proclaims the presence of a divine triune mystery, which entered history in the Incarnation of the God-man and reached its unsurpassable perfection in his Resurrection.

Faith does not rest on an authoritarian fixation, but on Jesus Christ's gift of self to his Church and a life of discipleship. Only such a perception renders the correlation of authority (*auctoritas*) and infallibility (*infallibilitas*) comprehensible. Jesus Christ delegates the authority with which he spoke to the Twelve (Mk 3:14f; 6:7–13, par.). Genuine Christian authority is a concretion of the Incarnation. Authority within the Church is an outgrowth of Christ's birth and of Pentecost. No sociological or political interpretation can reach the meaning of the Church's hierarchical nature. It requires belief to be reached and understood. Knowing God, and experiencing God within the context of a Church constituted in this manner, is for both Benedict XVI and Bonaventure not a question of theory but of everyday prayer life. The eternal Son's obedience to the Father becomes incarnate in both the concrete life of the Church and the individual Christian, insofar as each is prayerful. One of Ratzinger's theses is, "Since the center of the person of Jesus is prayer, it is essential to participate in his prayer if we are to know and understand him." In other words, immersing oneself in the prayer of Jesus is to know the person of Jesus himself. This is *the* indispensable heuristic principle for Christology and indeed for all of the Christian faith.

Perhaps vaguely inspired by the nineteenth-century theologian Johann Adam Möhler, the overriding term is no longer "hearing" or "understanding" but "Incarnation." The eternal inner-Trinitarian, self-surrender of the Son to the Father enters the world. The humanity of Jesus is a result of the Son's eternal obedience to the Father, a sign of the Son's responding in charity. Thus, his humanity—possessing the fullness of grace—is wholly directed toward the divine. This serves to illustrate that Jesus' humanity cannot be reduced to mere human subjectivity. In the same way, the realm of matter is not subject to independent laws. The second person of the Blessed Trinity becoming flesh frees humankind from either taunting the body in a libertarian fashion or abusing it ascetically. Of course, asceticism is a legitimate and indispensible component of Christian spirituality. Incarnation sheds new dignity on the human body and thereby argues against extreme views of the human body. Accepting the human body, as well as protecting the environment, are made possible by Jesus having lived among people.[13] The art of

Christian existence consists in worshipping and serving God while in the world with a body. This is the beauty of everyday spirituality. Becoming the body of Christ and offering the human body as a home to the Word of God is the great theme. There is an anabatic and katabatic (ascending and descending) aspect to it. This movement from the Word to body and again to the Word means true appropriation.[14]

These are *in nuce* (in a nutshell) "the new 'aesthetics' of faith" and "the arrow of beauty" that serve as correctives for some distortions of Jesus Christ—and therefore of the human person. Quoting the Byzantine mystical writer Nicholas Cabasilas (death c. 1322),[15] Ratzinger describes true knowledge as "being touched by reality, 'by the personal presence of Christ himself.' "[16] Encountering the beauty of Christ is to encounter "a more real, more profound knowledge than mere rational deduction.... For faith to grow today we must lead ourselves and the persons we meet to encounter the saints and to come in contact with the beautiful." This, however, imposes upon us a task: it is a task to oppose "the cult of the ugly" and to "withstand the deceptive beauty that diminishes man instead of making him great and that, for that reason, is false."[17] Ultimately, the Church must present to the world the face of Christ crucified, a "face that is so disfigured [that] there appears the genuine, the ultimate beauty: the beauty of love that goes 'to the very end' and thus proves to be mightier than falsehood and violence."[18]

PART I

Establishing the Christocentric Vision

CHAPTER 1

Highlights of a Lifelong Ministry

The life of Joseph Ratzinger reads to the outsider like a singularly remarkable career. He had already begun teaching fundamental theology one year after his ordination to the priesthood in the archdiocesan seminary of Freising. By 1957 he had earned the habilitation, the German terminal degree allowing one to teach as a full professor at university level. Thereafter, he became a star theologian and sought-after professor in the departments of Catholic theology at the respective universities of Bonn (1959–1963), Münster (1963–1966), Tübingen (1966–1969), and Regensburg (1969–1977). At the young age of thirty-six, he was appointed *peritus*, that is, theological advisor, to the highly respected and influential archbishop of Cologne, Joseph Cardinal Frings, during the Second Vatican Council. It was also "the projectile" of the person of Joseph Ratzinger that had intercepted the curial schemata for the Council, designed under the supervision of Alfredo Cardinal Ottaviani (1890–1979), then head of the Holy Office. Perhaps rather symptomatic of some representatives of neoscholasticism, Ottaviani's motto had been *Semper Idem* (Always the same, referring to Christ's immutability and constancy). In contrast to Ottaviani, Ratzinger had opposed the notion of a "Catholic state," supported the *Declaration on Religious Freedom: Dignitatis Humanae* (*DH*), and, out of consideration for Protestants, opposed a separate document on Our Lady, "lest the adoption of such a text imperil the effects of the Council."[1]

In March 1977, on beautiful Marienplatz in the heart of Munich, the capital of predominantly Catholic Bavaria, where a baroque column to Our Lady stands in the center of the city square, Ratzinger's "enthronement"[2] as archbishop was joyfully celebrated by the people. Established by Boniface in AD 739, this archdiocese looks back on a long legacy. Yet, today it is also a major center for culture, commerce, and technology. Automotive (BMW) and computer industries are located there, as is a sizable portion of Germany's mass media. The archdiocese is one of the largest in Europe and a center for theological and intellectual discourse. Ratzinger was archbishop of Munich until 1981, when he was called to Rome to serve as Prefect of the Congregation for the Doctrine of the Faith, succeeding the Croatian Cardinal Franjo Šeper. He was also appointed president of both the Papal Biblical Commission and the International Theological Commission (which he had been a member of since 1969). Earlier, Pope John Paul II had offered him the position of Prefect of the Congregation for Catholic Education, which he had declined as he had been then for too short a time ordinary of Munich. Now he had become the chief theological advisor to and collaborator with the charismatic philosopher Pope John Paul II, a relationship that would last for twenty-three years. In 1993 he became Cardinal Bishop and in 2002 Dean of the College of Cardinals.

On April 19, 2005, the conclave elected Ratzinger successor to the Chair of Peter and to the unforgettable Pope John Paul II. As the entire world looked on, he was enthroned as Pope Benedict XVI in St. Peter's Square on April 24, 2005. Pope Benedict XVI is the first German pontiff of recent history, following Gregory V (996–999), Clement II (1046–1047), Damasus II (1048), Victor II (1055–1057), and Stephan IX (1057–1058).[3] The theologian Eberhard Jüngel summarized well the attitude of German-speaking Lutherans: "We shall accompany the pope from the country of Luther with critical sympathy, but when necessary also with sympathetic criticism."[4]

When Ratzinger became archbishop of Munich in 1977, he had chosen as his motto *Cooperatores Veritatis* (Coworkers of Truth, from 3 Jn 8). In his election to the papacy, while he certainly chose the name Benedict in order to emphasize his understanding of himself as a successor to Pope Benedict XV (1914–1922), who labored tirelessly to bring about peace during World War I, thus underlining his own peacemaking mission, his choice of Benedict also signified a long-term vision. In the sixth century the monk St. Benedict (ca. 480–550), the founder of Western monasticism, had fashioned the basis for a new, Christian Europe that would come about after the Dark Ages (that is, the migration of peoples from around 500–800) and would lead to the high culture of the Middle Ages.

In addition to the motto he chose as archbishop and the significance behind the name Benedict, Pope Benedict's papal coat of arms is also enlightening. The coat of arms contains images of a bear, a crowned Moor, and a shell. The bear refers to a story surrounding St. Corbinian (ca. 720–730). St. Corbinian was the founding bishop of Freising (and Munich, Ratzinger's home archdiocese and archbishopric). While crossing the Alps on his way to Rome at one point, St. Corbinian's horse was torn apart by a bear. Corbinian then commanded the bear to carry his load as punishment. The bear, therefore, represents the "draft animal" pulling God's cart in this world, an animal rather ill-suited for this task. The crowned Moor is a symbol of the city of Freising and for Ratzinger "a sign of the universality of the Church." The shell points to earthly life as a pilgrimage and the moral of Augustine's story of a boy trying to scoop all of the water in the ocean into a hole using a shell: the human intellect cannot exhaust the mystery of God.[5]

According to his own statements, Pope Benedict intends to continue on the path laid out by his charismatic predecessor: proclaim the gospel message to the contemporary world, promote ecumenical efforts to bring about Christian unity, foster peaceful dialogue among the world religions, advocate for the defense of human rights, and work for peace in the world. In the words of Cardinal Ottaviani, former Prefect of the Congregation for the Doctrine of the Faith, a prefect "is an old carabiniere guarding gold reserves."

As Pontifex Maximus, Benedict XVI is not only entrusted with the preservation and defense of this gold, namely, the faith, but with proclaiming it to the world and renewing the Christian faith so that the face of the earth may in turn be renewed. Undoubtedly, Benedict XVI is uniquely gifted for this task. No previous pope has written as profound and seminal theological works as he; and certainly no pope has influenced the direction of theology over the course of half a century more than Pope Benedict XVI.

CHAPTER 2

Personality and Temperament

Behind this litany of impressive data stands a surprisingly inconspicuous and humble, even shy, human being. He is the second son of a Bavarian gendarme of modest means, with an older brother and sister as his siblings. Joseph Aloysius Ratzinger was born in the hamlet of Marktl am Inn on April 16, 1927. He was christened in a six-sided, white limestone baptismal font in St. Oswald Parish Church during the Easter Vigil Mass on the very day he was born.[1] His native country, characterized by a gently undulating landscape, is one of wooded hills, small lakes, and winding roads and trails, dotted by countless little white chapels and onion-domed church towers. Visitors will invariably notice that the chapels and churches seem to form the inseparable ingredients of a preconceived (divine) grand design. They are a constitutive part of picture-book, idyllic Catholic Bavaria. One senses that the Catholic faith belongs to life as much as plain air does. At noon the farmers would pause working to pray the Angelus. Such *liberalitas Bavariae* enjoyed both the prospect of heaven and the natural beauties of Bavaria. He has written: "The Catholicism of my Bavarian homeland...has been able to find a place for everything that is human: prayer, but also celebration; repentance, but also joyfulness.... In the faith of my parents I found the confirmation that Catholicism had been a bulwark of truth and justice against that regime of atheism and lies represented by National Socialism."[2] The town of Altötting is located in some proximity to Marktl, and it is home to the major Marian shrine in southern Germany. In essentially baroque Old Bavaria (Altbayern), almost every town has as its center a column honoring Our Lady.

The evident baroque exuberance of Bavaria is earthly and heavenly at the same time: "Faith gives joy. When God is not there, the world becomes desolate, and everything becomes boring, and everything is unsatisfactory. It's easy to see today how a world empty of God is also increasingly consuming itself, how it has become a wholly joyless world."[3] Influenced by the joyous effulgence of baroque churches in Bavaria with their numerous statues and paintings of saints—sometimes in hauntingly ethereal beauty—it is understandable that Ratzinger correlates beauty and truth: "I have often said that I am convinced that the true apologetics for the Christian message, the most persuasive proof of its truth, offsetting everything that may appear negative, are the saints on the one hand, and the beauty that the faith has generated, on the other."[4]

He is firmly convinced that "beauty will save us," as Dostoyevsky wrote famously in *The Brothers Karamazov*. Spiritual music by Mozart, baroque architecture, and the beauty of the Bavarian landside have inspired Ratzinger. This Bavarian legacy explains his theological hermeneutics: "beauty is knowledge, a higher form of knowledge, since it strikes man with all the grandeur of truth."[5] Even amid a sea of banalities and ugliness in the world today, beauty can be found in Jesus Christ, who is infinite and true beauty. It becomes visible through people touched by God; thus Ratzinger's affinity with John the evangelist, Augustine, Bonaventure, and von Balthasar.

As beauty illumines the mind, his is an unambiguous option for the *analogia fidei* (analogy of faith)—without necessarily negating the *analogia entis* (analogy of being), as long as it has a healthy dose of Bonaventure's *humilitas* (humility)—*Demut des Denkens* (a phrase coined by Ratzinger, meaning humility of thought).[6] Mindful of the limits of rationality, one does not have to leave rationality behind when entering into faith in Jesus Christ. Reason truly actualized is a dimension of faith. Thus, for instance, non-Christians may think they are free, but only through Jesus Christ can they realize true freedom in the Father, and Son, and Holy Spirit; the freedom within the Blessed Trinity to selflessly receive and give. Sacramental life thus becomes the realm of full freedom. The "yes" uttered to God's revelation becomes reason's chance to mature into participatory existence with the Divine. The voluntary, self-imposed restraint of reason sets Ratzinger apart from almost all significant modern theologians, including Schleiermacher, Kierkegaard, Harnack, Troeltsch, Pannenberg, K. Rahner, and so forth.

The claim has been made that Ratzinger outright rejects the analogy of being. Yet, he argued in his inaugural lecture in 1959 that "it is a necessary dimension of Christian reality." Otherwise, Christ as the Logos would be irrelevant. Along with Augustine he reminds one of the need for a *ratio purificata* (purified reason), as reason left to its own devices can be turned in many directions. The true thinker is the one in discipleship with the One on the cross.[7]

As a five-year-old boy, Ratzinger was impressed by the regalia of Cardinal Michael von Faulhaber (1869–1952) and expressed the wish to become a priest.[8] In 1937 Faulhaber would administer confirmation to him. Born in Lower Franconia, Faulhaber had been professor of Old Testament studies at the University of Strasbourg before becoming the bishop of Speyer (1910) and subsequently archbishop of Munich (1917–1952). A product of Wilhemine Germany, he would be considered a bit authoritarian today. This, however, served the Church well in a time of turmoil (World War I and the political confusion of the 1920s) and helped rally Catholics in distancing themselves interiorly from National Socialism. Anti-Catholic demonstrations by Nazis were part of everyday life for the Ratzinger brothers. The archbishop belonged to a group called *Amici Israel* (Friends of Israel), committed to combating anti-Semitism. He suggested and contributed to Pope Pius XI's anti-Nazi encyclical *Mit brennender Sorge* (*With Burning Anxiety*) of 1937. Faulhaber would frequently visit the minor and major seminaries.

Ratzinger has described how impressive Cardinal Faulhaber's homilies were to everyone. He admired his "*festliche Gebärde*" (festive demeanor), "*Disziplin des Glaubens*" (discipline of faith), and "*souveräne Güte*" (sovereign gentleness). With glowing words, he has displayed respect for Faulhaber's scholarly positions and persistence in preaching despite massive ideological and political attacks concerning the presence of God. On June 29, 1951, Cardinal Faulhaber ordained Joseph Ratzinger, along with forty-four other candidates, to the priesthood. On June 17, 1952, Joseph Ratzinger participated in the funeral procession for Cardinal Faulhaber. Based on the cardinal's motto, *Vox temporis, vox Dei* (Voice of the age, voice of God), in the homily in commemoration of Faulhaber's death in 1977 Ratzinger stressed his predecessor's understanding of the presentic nature of faith, speaking to every age in a fresh way. Faulhaber had felicitously conjoined the Holy Spirit hovering over the menorah by protesting "against enslaving people to a faith in race and people."[9]

All of Upper Bavaria breathes the baroque exuberance of the Catholic faith. To this day, Bavarians greet each other with *Grüß Gott*, or may God greet or bless you. The Church's feast day celebrations are never restricted to the confines of the Church. All of society, and one is tempted to say even all of nature, joins in. This joy is particularly evident in the *Primizmesse* and subsequent *Primizsegen*, the first mass and the following first blessings, administered by a newly ordained priest. The townsfolk are willing to walk miles and actually wear out the soles of their shoes to receive the blessing of a newly ordained priest. Ratzinger highlights the proper Christocentric interpretation of this event:

> We [the Ratzinger brothers] were invited to bring the first blessing into people's homes, and everywhere we were received even by total strangers with a warmth and affection I had not thought possible until that day. In this way I learned first-hand how earnestly people wait for a priest, how much they long for the blessing that flows from the power of the sacrament. The point was not my own or my brother's person.... In us they saw persons who had been touched by Christ's mission and had been empowered to bring his nearness to men. Precisely because we ourselves were not the point, a friendly human relationship could develop very quickly.[10]

When asked once by a student in St. Peter's Square why he became a priest, Pope Benedict responded: "There was the Nazi regime. We were told very loudly that in the new Germany 'there will not be any more priests, there will be no more consecrated life, we don't need this anymore, find another profession.' But actually hearing these loud voices, I understood that in confronting the brutality of this system, this inhuman face, that there is a need for priests, precisely as a contrast to this inhuman culture."[11]

One of his cousins had Down syndrome. The Nazis brought him to a concentration camp, and shortly thereafter, his relatives were informed that the cousin had died of "pneumonia." When hearing that other people with mental disabilities had also been delivered to concentration camps and died there of the same "sickness," it became clear to young Joseph that in the eyes of the totalitarian regime it made no economic sense to offer patience and love to the weak or the disabled.[12]

His parents reared their children in dignified, but modest circumstances. His father retired from the police force as early as possible so that he might not be compelled one day to collaborate in future National Socialist atrocities. In order to enable his family to survive Hitler's reign of brown terror, Ratzinger's father bought a farmer's old home on the outskirts of an insignificant town. His mother worked diligently. "My father... with unfailing clairvoyance saw that a victory of Hitler's would not be a victory for Germany but rather a victory of the Antichrist that would surely usher in apocalyptic times for all believers, and not only for them."[13]

Regarding the atmosphere in their home, Seewald observes: "In the Ratzinger household, pretentiousness was considered something like a mortal sin. True greatness, they believed, shows itself in little things. And real 'personalities' are to be recognized, not in magnificence but in humility." Fellow intellectual Josef Pieper (1904–1997), to whom Ratzinger is much indebted, often quoted a native Westphalian proverb: *ein Schuft, der mehr verkauft als er ist* (a scoundrel is he, who sells more than he is). The abbot St. Benedict wrote: "Through exalting ourselves, we go downward, but by humility, upward."[14] In 1977 a German newspaper concluded: "Joseph Ratzinger has the merit of all great persons. They cannot be classed or categorized. They are themselves."[15] Is this not the case because he trusts in the Catholic genius, the figure of Christ, more than his own talents or the applause the public may shower upon him?

For many years his confessor was Fr. Frumentius Renner, of the Order of St. Benedict (OSB), a monk at the missionary Benedictine archabbey of St. Ottilien, east of Augsburg. Fr. Renner guided Ratzinger into a Christ-centered mystical life, one measured, tempered, and balanced by the teachings of the Rule of Benedict. "He resembled in many ways the early Christians... who saw in all the blows of earthly fate and all historical changes the heralds of the end times. In this advent attitude he lived, always relaxed, never fanatical or doctrinaire, but with eyes alert for anything threatening in the Church or the world."[16]

Ratzinger's youth was spent in the twelve years the Nazi regime was in power (1933–1945). The *Zentrumspartei*, the Catholic Center Party, was ruling in Bavaria at the beginning of that era, and the Bavarian population had overwhelmingly voted against the National Socialist Party of German in the fateful election of 1933, and therefore the deleterious effects of National Socialist ideology were not felt as strongly in Bavaria as elsewhere in the Reich. Nevertheless, all were aware of the utter disregard for human rights and the subsequent indiscriminate incarceration of Jews, opposition politicians, gypsies, the mentally retarded, and Catholics—lay people, priests, and religious alike—in concentration camps. This violence certainly sensitized Ratzinger to the perils of a materialistic worldview seemingly autarkic from God. He and his family must have been grateful for members of the clergy in their ancestry, such as the much-respected Dr. Georg Ratzinger, who was a priest and innovative social reformer. Up until 1899 he had been elected a representative to the Berlin *Reichstag* for the Bavarian *Patriotenpartei*.[17] This priest and great-uncle of the family had been a parliamentarian both in the Bavarian *Landtag* (state legislature) in Munich and later in the *Reichstag* (federal parliament) in Berlin. Having written his doctoral dissertation on how the Church can help the poor, as a politician he advocated the abolition of child labor and promoted farmers' rights.

Ratzinger's father, trained as a constable under the Bavarian King Ludwig III, had been a member of the *Marianische Männerkongregation* (Men's Marian Sodality) of Altötting. From the very onset, he opposed Hitler and refused to join the Nazi organization. Smoking a cigarette, he would read the oppositional periodical *Der Gerade Weg* (*The Straight Path*). By 1933 he had bought a rundown farmer's house in order to live in greatest possible independence from the political cacophony of the day. In 1937 the family moved into it as a home.[18] In his father's home, "resistance to an atheistic system was understood to be an attribute of Christian existence."[19]

Very much like Karl Rahner's (1904–1984) parents in Freiburg im Breisgau,[20] Ratzinger's parents in bucolic Hufschlag, located near Traunstein, also offered room and board to students, planted a wide variety of vegetables in the garden, and enjoyed the fruits from a few orchard trees in order to make ends meet.

In 1943 Ratzinger was forcibly conscripted as an underage helper in the German air defenses and served without firing one shot. In September of the following year he was released home, directly after which he was called to serve through November in the Austrian Legion along the Austro-Hungarian border. There he witnessed an untold number of people, including Jews, led off to death camps. Then he was drafted to join the infantry. After deserting from the *Wehrmacht* and narrowly escaping summary execution, he was relieved and grateful to be an American-held prisoner of war until the bloodshed ended. He was briefly interned in a sizable open-air POW camp near Ulm. He returned home in a milk truck in June 1945. The horrors and deprivations of war would leave a lasting impression on young Joseph Ratzinger. They would enable him to retain an acute sense of the truly important things in life, for the things money cannot buy and prestige cannot grant access to.

His home country, Bavaria, has a long, well-documented history characterized by remarkable political, social, and cultural continuity. The Agilolfinger dynasty ruled this territory from the sixth century AD until 788. For more than seven hundred years, descendents of Otto von Wittelsbach ruled the country, from 1180 until 1918. In this perspective, the Third Reich appears to Bavarians as a brief spook. The young boy conversing with his father and elder brother during extended walks (*Spaziergänge*) on the course and nature of contemporary politics must have been instilled with the awareness that positive powers ultimately prevail in history. The forceful sermons against National Socialist ideology delivered by Cardinal Faulhaber must have further formed him.

Receiving a classical education in a *humanistisches Gymnasium*, a type of secondary school emphasizing the liberal arts with formative exposure to the languages and cultures of Greek and Latin antiquity, reinforced his critical distance from the prevailing crude and simplistic dominant brown zeitgeist. It proved to be an immunization against the "seduction of a total-itarian ideology."[21] Someone trained in the humanities as a young person understands the relative strengths and weaknesses of the present situation in light of history and is thus able to discern a meaningful future. Attempts by the Nazis and more recent attempts by other groups[22] to do away with the classical languages in the secondary school curricula have amounted to nothing short of a *damnatio memoriae*, that is, the eradication of one's own identity.

Both Ratzinger boys attended the modern archdiocesan preparatory sem-inary (*Erzbischöfliches Studienseminar St. Michael*) in Traunstein. Joseph was there from April 16, 1939, until 1945. He scored A's and B's in all subjects except gymnastics. His spiritual and intellectual efforts were consistently de-scribed as "*höchst lobenswert*" (most laudable). His teachers considered him conscientious, independent, and comrade-like.[23]

Later, his education would prove valuable to his theological studies, when he would be able to read the Church fathers in the original, and even pio-neer the translation of a text written by St. Thomas Aquinas. Access to the thoughts and personality of the Angelic Doctor was difficult for him: " 'His crystal-clear logic' seemed to him 'too firmly enclosed within itself, too impersonal and ready-made.' In Augustine's case, by contrast 'the passionate, suffering, and questioning man' was 'always directly present,' says Ratzinger, someone 'with whom one can identify.' "[24]

In late 1945 he entered the major seminary in Freising. He was received as a seminarian by the priest and rector Dr. Michael Höck, who had recently been released from the Dachau concentration camp. About 1,000 Catholic priests had perished in that Nazi death camp. As a novice seminarian, Ratzinger translated the first German version of Thomas Aquinas's treatise *Quaestio disputata de caritate* (*Disputation on Charity*), which would prove foundational for his encyclical as pope, *Deus Caritas Est*. The then prefect of studies, Father Alfred Läpple, summarized well Ratzinger's worldview as a diligent theol-ogy student: "Life as a gift from God is more than a well-balanced story. It is quite different from a life according to Kant's categorical imperative of duty. The story of a life should become one of faith. You are not the property of the state. You are not the property of your parents, but you belong to God and to God alone. Every human being is the image of God, everyone, includ-ing the unbaptized. It is God who searches with you for the path that your steps should follow."[25] Christian personalism was engrained in the young seminarian.

After two years in the archdiocesan seminary on the *Domberg* of Freising, Ratzinger pursued theological studies at Munich's venerable *Ludwig-Maximilians-Universität*, founded in 1471. Such great minds as Johann Michael Sailer, Franz Xaver von Baader, Johann Adam Möhler, Joseph Görres, Ignaz von Döllinger, Otto Bardenhewer, and Martin Grabmann had taught theology at this university. This group cultivated a particular interest in the Church fathers, history in general, the social dimensions of ecclesial life, metaphysics, and mysticism. Having resisted the Bismarckian anti-Catholic *Kulturkampf* (1871–1888), the department of theology was sup-pressed by the National Socialists in 1941. During the days of Ratzinger's own studies in Munich, Romano Guardini (1885–1968), Gottlieb Söhngen (1892–1971), and Michael Schmaus (1897–1992) were the university's theological luminaries.

The most important date in Ratzinger's life, according to his own estimation, was his ordination to the priesthood. He was ordained together with his brother, Georg Ratzinger, who is three years his elder, on June 29, 1951, in the venerable *"Dom"* of Freising from the hands of the towering personality of Cardinal Faulhaber on the Feast of Saints Peter and Paul.[26] "We were more than forty candidates, who, at the solemn call on that radiant summer day, which I remember as the high point of my life, responded 'Adsum,' 'here I am.' We should not be superstitious; but, at the moment when the elderly archbishop laid his hands on me, a little bird—perhaps a lark—flew up from the high altar in the cathedral and trilled a little joyful song."[27]

Considering this background, one sees that the word "career" is totally unsuitable to describe the curriculum vitae of Joseph Ratzinger. It would be equally incorrect to perceive in the Ratzinger boys' decision to join the priesthood a craving for "upward mobility." In fact, since both brothers refused to join the *Hitlerjugend* (Hitler Youth Movement), their parents had to pay a rather high school tuition at first.[28]

Tellingly, after ordination he served for one year as parochial vicar (that is, associate pastor) in the Munich parish of *Heilig Blut* (Precious Blood), in the borough of Bogenhausen. This was, incidentally, the same parish the Jesuit priest and martyr Alfred Delp had served in. Delph had been hanged by the Nazis in Berlin's *Plötzensee*. He was executed for his collaboration in the failed assassination plot of Hitler by Graf Stauffenberg and the *Kreisauer Kreis* on July 20, 1944. The Protestant theologian Dietrich Bonhoeffer had also belonged to this group. The resistance fighter Ludwig Baron von Leonrod, the politician Franz Sperr, and the priest Hermann Wehrle had also lived there before being executed by the Nazis. Both Ratzinger's upbringing by his father and the martyrdom of these four heroic men reminded him of the incalculable cost of Christian discipleship. This explains in no small degree the good humor and equanimity with which Joseph Ratzinger has borne numerous cases of misunderstanding, instances of disrespect, and even occasional invectives during his ministry.

Delp had authored *Der Mensch und die Geschichte* (*Man and History*).[29] This prescient Jesuit priest saw far deeper than the ugly grimace of National Socialism. He warned that into the twentieth-century man, left to his own resources, would enter a dense phalanx of lies and threats bent on humiliating him. Atheism is deeper than the Nazi or Communist ideologies. It negates the eternity of the individual human soul and corrupts his conscience, rendering him unable to discern right from wrong. Because man is created in the image and likeness of God, man will free himself from materialist totalitarianism only by relating to the God-man Jesus Christ and by living sacramentally in this relationship. In a way, it is the lifelong central concern of Ratzinger to enable all human beings to overcome oppressive materialism, be it in the form of a political ideology, consumerism, or economic pragmatism, and to liberate them in Jesus Christ and therefore liberate them to be their true selves.

One of his great teachers was the priest and scholar Romano Guardini. Asked once what it means to be a priest, Guardini responded "ministry"— (in German *Seelsorge*, which translates literally as "care of souls")—"for me [it] means helping through the truth."[30] Indeed, one must constantly be reminded that the priestly charism means the unconditional willingness to suffer all imaginable and unimaginable consequences of discipleship. Only someone living the evangelical counsels (sometimes called "the counsels of perfection," that is, poverty, chastity, and obedience) can do this radically and, precisely for this reason, cheerfully.

While parochial vicar in Munich's *Heilig Blut* parish, his pastor Max Blumschein (1884–1965) repeatedly told him, alluding to Augustine, that a priest must glow from within. He was given an overwhelming workload: sixteen hours of religious instruction in five classes, two Sunday masses, one hour daily of hearing confessions, four hours of confession on Saturday afternoons, responsibility for all areas of youth ministry, and in addition countless funerals, weddings, and baptisms.[31] Ratzinger was conspicuous for his naturalness, humility, and lack of an intellectual air. Pastor Blumschein had experienced firsthand the Nazi's arrests of two soon-to-be martyred priests, the parochial vicar Hermann Wehrle and the Jesuit Alfred Delp.[32] Father Delp had made numerous statements both as a homilist and in prison, which would leave an indelible mark on many a priest, last but not least on the young priest Ratzinger: "Bread is important. Freedom is more important. Most important, however, is unbroken loyalty and unbetrayed adoration"[33]; "The hour of the birth of human freedom is the hour of encounter with God"; "The bent knee and empty hands held forth are the two primordial gestures of a free human being."[34]

Reflecting Delp's conviction that National Socialism was but an epiphenomenon of the long-lasting struggle of Christianity against materialist nihilism, he wrote in the *Poesiealbum* (autograph book) belonging to a little girl in one of his religion classes in Sacred Heart Parish:

> However the winds blow
> You should stand against them
> When the world falls apart
> Your brave heart (may) not despair.
> Without the heart's bravery which
> Has the courage to withstand unshakably
> The spirits of the time and the masses,
> We cannot find the way to God
> And the true way of Our Lord.[35]

CHAPTER 3

Formative Early Encounters as a Seminarian: Personal Existentialism Grounded in Jesus Christ

In 1998, Pope John Paul II observed: "The more distinguished of the Catholic theologians of this century, to whose reflections and researches Vatican II owes so much [were] educated in the school of the Angelic Doctor [Thomas Aquinas]"[1] Ironically, this does not include the most preeminent collaborator of Pope John Paul II, Joseph Ratzinger.

Theology was undergoing profound changes in the first half of the twentieth century that would become public in a special way with the promulgation of Pius XII's encyclical, *Humani Generis*, in 1950 and with the Second Vatican Council (1962–1965). It is still too early to assess this age without the necessary historic distance; yet, to begin to understand it, it is sufficient to highlight the deeper concern that motivated the more creative minds.

The Dominican Marie-Dominique Chenu (1895–1990) well summarized the sense of unease theology students felt when subjected to the rigidity of neoscholastic curriculum, based on propositional truths. While profiting immensely from the astute and cultured lectures at the Angelicum in Rome given by the preeminent Thomist of his day, Réginald Garrigou-Lagrange (1877–1964), he could not help discerning a divided personality in the lecturer. While a master of spirituality, deeply influenced by Spanish mysticism, particularly by John of the Cross, Garrigou-Lagrange taught a purely cerebral Aristotelianism and an arid form of Thomism. According to Chenu, true to Aristotle, he saw Thomas as understood by the Jesuit Luis de Molina (1535–1600), arguing only from an effect to a cause. No human being has an innate knowledge of God; nor is there knowledge of human consciousness prior to an engagement with the empirical world (i.e., as neoscholasticism held).[2] Réginald Garrigou-Lagrange taught dogmatic and spiritual theology for fifty years (1909–1959) and almost became the very definition of theology in Rome, so much so that the French novelist François Mauriac memorably called him *le monstre sacré* of Thomism.[3]

In this intellectualistic ambience, spirituality and theology never met for some young thinkers. While the past idiom spoke eloquently to past generations of Catholics and in fact produced numerous saints, its language and approach seemed to have become worn out. The younger generation, such as Chenu, Romano Guardini, Yves Congar, Henri de Lubac, Hans Urs von Balthasar, Hugo and Karl Rahner, Jacques Maritain, Karol Wojtyla, and Josef Pieper, could not live and teach Catholic philosophy and theology without repeated reference to the personification of God's goodness among humankind: the Incarnate Word, Jesus Christ. Jesus Christ overcomes the split between scholarship and spirituality. A split they considered characteristic of the impersonal, abstract, neoscholastic frame of mind, perceived by some as akin to an eighteenth-century rationalist "Wolffian (comprehensive) metaphysics."[4] They called for a Christocentric integration of scholarship and spirituality, of ascetic contemplation and preaching, of theology and liturgy. Representative of Catholic thinkers for his generation and the next, in 1931 Chenu summarized this "religious crisis" in the following words:

> Those who enclose themselves in a scholastic Thomism, hardened by generations of textbooks and manuals [and marginalized by the intrusion of a massive dose of Baroque scholasticism] oblige themselves thereby to summary condemnations of positions of which they are largely ignorant. This would certainly not be the path for disciples of Thomas Aquinas. And less helpful is the way of those who, colluding strangely with anti-modernism, hand the memory of the medieval doctor over to a positivist intellectualism, keeping for themselves a Thomism which is only a paragon of their own pseudo-religious integrist position. But this exploitation of Thomism [which some naïvely view to be salutary] cannot hide the real intentions of others, penetrated with the spirit of Thomas and with the highest requirements of scientific or theological work. They meet honestly the problems legitimately posed by the philosophy of religion, biblical exegesis, and the history of dogma. Illumined by the experience of their teacher, they know how to discern in new terrain the relationships of reason and faith. Precisely this is the intellectual regime of Catholicism.[5]

Ratzinger himself faults neoscholasticism for bringing too much order into Thomas's still inchoate terminology. Too numerous distinctions were made in subsequent centuries between philosophy and theology. He concludes:

> The exclusion of ontology from theology does not emancipate philosophical thinking but paralyzes it. The extinction of ontology in the sphere of philosophy, far from purifying theology, actually deprives it of its solid basis. Contrary to the common hostility toward ontology, which is apparently becoming the sole link between contemporary philosophers and theologians, we held that both disciplines need this dimension of thought and that it is here that they find themselves indissolubly linked.[6]

As pure nature is a *fata morgana*, so likewise pure reason à la Kant does not exist. Only in recognizing this can one appreciate Thomas's position of an effective harmony between faith and reason. When faith and reason support each other the human spirit rises up to knowledge of God, is able to worship him, and partakes in divine life. A faith without reason may end in fundamentalism, while reason without faith may end in despair. A neoscholastic Thomism priding itself over time will not come to terms with "the mediation of history within the realm of ontology."[7] It is not intellectual defects that lead to unbelief, as many theologians held at the time when Ratzinger was preparing for the priesthood, but an inability to correlate time and ontology, as the philosopher Martin Heidegger would formulate. This group of neoscholatics is associated with Joseph Kleutgen, who influenced Leo XIII to encourage a revival of Thomism in 1879 in his encyclical *Aeterni Patris*. In retrospect, one must consider this encyclical a blessing. It inspired Désiré-Joseph Cardinal Mercier of Bruxelles to found *Le Revue Néo-Scholastique de Philosophie* at Leuven University. In fact, the famous Leonine critical edition of Thomas's writings under the direction of the Dominican Tommaso Maria Francesco Zigliara (1833–1893) would later occasion a rediscovery of the original Thomas. But well into the 1940s the ahistorical thinkers Descartes and Kant were considered Thomas's primary interlocutors. The beauty and glory of faith was lost despite Thomas's notion of the *desiderium naturale ad videndum Deum* (the natural desire for the vision of God) and his defining *pulchritudo* (beauty) as one of the transcendentals.

A group in agreement with the essence of the Ressourcement critique of neoscholasticism, but offering another antidote, is transcendental Thomism. It places more emphasis on the relative autonomy of nature à la Aristotle and integrates a Kantian understanding of knowledge: the human being as a self-reflecting agent invariably experiences the a priori of grace. Thus, something like a continuum between nature and grace, being and existence, is postulated and is captured in the concept of the "supernatural existential." Rahner's thought, as it was subsequently popularized, runs the danger of collapsing grace into nature. Rahner himself was acutely aware of this danger and postulated a remainder theory. For Rahner and transcendental Thomism, which led to an anthropocentric shift, nature itself is gifted (apart from Christ's salvific actions) with indwelling grace to such a degree that the sacraments are often considered by some today as mere additions. The Church and the sacraments then seem as explicit articulations of what already implicitly exists in nature all along.[8] Jointly with luminaries such as Rahner, Congar, Hans Küng, Johann Baptist Metz, Gustavo Gutiérrez, and Edward Schillebeeckx, Ratzinger belonged at first to the editorial board of the journal *Concilium*. Perhaps, at its core, this journal is too much occupied with system, just as neoscholasticism had been, and too little indebted to the patristic heritage of Thomism and the historic nature of revelation. As in the case of neoscholasticism, the drama of the inner self, of the human soul and God, was left unaddressed in transcendental Thomism. This gave impetus to the congeniality between Ratzinger and Wojtyla, who were from different biographical trajectories so very intrigued by personalism, phenomenology, patristics, and French Thomism.

Turning back to the seminarian Ratzinger, the rigid neoscholastic Thomism of his teacher Arnold Wilmsen was to him unable to address existentialism and the godless materialist ideologies of communism and National Socialism. There was a disconnection between theology and life and spirituality. In fact, the two-tiered (nature/grace) approach to reality unwittingly fostered "a total secularization that would banish God not only from social life but from culture and even from the relationships of private life" as de Lubac would formulate in drastic terms in the 1960s.[9] Turning to the texts of the Church fathers, the Tübingen School of Theology, and John Henry Cardinal Newman had a liberating effect on young Ratzinger, who had just experienced firsthand the horrors of National Socialism and war. In a way, he may have felt Jesus Christ had been his loyal companion during the harrowing war experiences; a personal experience with Christ such as this, however, did not match the style of neoscholasticism's approach. In contrast, the nineteenth-century Tübingen School held that the truth is alive and the Church is the grace-filled, vivacious vessel transmitting this truth as person—not as a sterile *societas perfecta*—but as the continuation of Jesus Christ's Incarnation. In the Church, the Logos and Holy Spirit are present as active participants. To the minds of many then, the critical correlation between faith's experiential moment and its intelligibility had to be recalibrated.

This explains the conflict that early on almost jeopardized Ratzinger's future ministry as an academic teacher. The two renowned Munich dogmaticians, Michael Schmaus and Gottlieb Söhngen, had argued over the proper understanding of revelation—the former perhaps rather vaguely still echoing the neoscholastic theologian Francisco Suárez. Schmaus considered revelation a perennial truth communicated to the mind through definitive and unchanging concepts accessible to human rationality. In contrast, Söhngen, who was Ratzinger's dissertation director, insisted that faith is communicated through history as a mystery accessible to the heart and mind.[10]

Excursus

Earlier, Chenu and a number of other young theologians had, without rejecting the content of Catholic teaching, rejected abstract presentations of it in the form of pseudo-Thomistic theses. They, like the tragic former Jesuit George Tyrrell (1861–1909)[11] before them, desired a more convincing presentation of the faith, connecting theory and praxis. The undeniable merit of the neoscholastic method was in demonstrating that the Catholic faith not only rejects superstition but is thoroughly intelligible. It was an attempt to solve the modern crisis of theology by picking up the thread of high scholasticism, thereby providing a timeless, unified theology. However, many thought there must be a better way to do justice to Thomas's own axiom: "Grace does not obliterate nature but perfects it, just as natural reason serves faith and the natural inclination of the will yields to charity."[12]

The Swiss theologian Hans Urs von Balthasar (1905–1988) provided a similar analysis in 1965. In his *The Glory of the Lord: A Theological Aesthetics V*, he detects in the Spanish Jesuit Francisco Suárez (1548–1617) the father of both Baroque scholasticism (seventeenth and eighteenth centuries) and of neoscholasticism (nineteenth and early twentieth centuries). His notion of the univocity of being (that stated that both God and the created order belong to the order of being) adduced a principle over and beyond both God and the world. As a result, Suárez's systematic theology could not reflect his Christ-centered Jesuit spirituality. St. Ignatius of Loyola's rich piety did not receive its commensurate expression in Suárez's theology. An analogical understanding of being is sacrificed. In the eyes of Balthasar, this led the Jesuit Luis de Molina to argue that man is able to reach a state of ultimate freedom that is independent from God's will. This leveling of the difference between grace and nature, while simultaneously leveling nature's orientation to grace, leads to a loss of the philosophical mystery, which in turn causes a loss of appreciation of theological mysteries and the ineffable mystery of divine glory. In the process, the sense of awe in front of the glory of creation dissolves into intellectualism. Alas, in the absence of the theologians' appreciation, "the sensorium for the glory of Creation" passed to the poets and artists such as Dante, Petrarch, Milton, Herder, Goethe, Hölderlin, and Keats and natural scientists such as Kepler, Newton, Kant, and Teilhard de Chardin.[13] Such neoscholastic aridity does not invite discipleship.

Reflecting back on the twentieth century, in 1987 Walter Kasper would declare: "There is no doubt that the outstanding event in the Catholic theology of our century is the surmounting of Neo-scholasticism."[14] Joseph Ratzinger was a part of this struggle for the integration of spirituality and theology. The discovery of the living Jesus of the gospels is the key concern. Significantly, Ratzinger began his studies in the midst of this climate of the intellectual transition to a different theological sensibility and "paradigm."

During his days in the archdiocesan seminary from November 1945 through July 1947 at the historic *Domberg* of Freising, which was the former see of the archbishop of Munich,[15] Ratzinger encountered the thought of significant minds. There the prefect of studies, Father Alfred Läpple (b. 1915),[16] acquainted him with Newman's concept of conscience, which would become Läpple's dissertation topic under the guidance of the Munich moral theologian Theodor Steinbüchel (1888–1949).[17] Thus, Ratzinger also read two volumes of Steinbüchel's philosophical foundations of moral theology. In his memoirs Ratzinger writes: "I found a first-rate introduction to the thought of Heidegger and Jaspers as well as to the philosophies of Nietzsche, Klages, and Bergson. Almost more important for me was Steinbüchel's book *Umbruch des Denkens (The Upheaval of Thought)*: here I read how, just as now we could affirm that physics was abandoning the mechanistic world view and turning toward a new openness to the unknown—and hence also to the Unknown, namely God—so, too, in philosophy we could detect a return to metaphysics, which had become inaccessible since Kant."[18] The New Testament is the paradigm for the design of one's personal life. The question regarding life is neither an abstract one, nor one that has the individual, contingent "I" as the point of departure, but rather Christ. What does Christ expect me to do? What would Christ do in my case? Oftentimes, Ratzinger would quote scripture to underline his point: "I have been crucified with Christ; it is no longer I who live, but Christ, who lives in me" (Gal 2:20a) and "in my flesh I complete what is lacking in Christ's afflictions for the sake of his body, that is, the church"

(Col 1:24b). In an age relentlessly stressing the collective, the masses, and the nation or race, Steinbüchel placed the emphasis on the individual living out a commitment. This was for him the inevitable consequence of the human person's being created in the image of God (Gn 1:26f).

The arid moralism generally associated with Kantian rationalism and Jansenist piety, but not unknown to neoscholasticism, clashes with the Christian faith. Steinbüchel's liberating vision was echoed in Cardinal Ratzinger's funeral eulogy for Luigi Giussani (1922–2005), the founder of the Italian movement *Communione e Liberazione* (Communion and Liberation) and professor at the *Università Cattolica del Sacro Cuore* in Milan: "Christianity is not an intellectual system, a collection of dogmas, or a moralism. Christianity is instead an encounter, a love story; it is an event."[19] Moralizing always smacks of Pelagianism, that is acting good and pleasing to God without the aid of divine grace. It denies the reality of grace. The Catholic faith, however, essentially involves a relationship with Jesus Christ. Ratzinger would use this as the opening salvo for his pontificate, that is, as the theme for his first encyclical as pope, *Deus Caritas Est*.[20] The Suárezean overemphasis on doctrinal clarity obfuscated the spiritual and existential dimensions of the Catholic faith. The affective, often dazzling beauty of Baroque architecture and theology frequently obscured the biblical realism of the here and now and preferred to emphasize eschatological perfection.

The partial weakening of the Christian understanding of the Bible's moral message within a short time span (1965–1970) can only be comprehended in light of this background. The extreme external, oftentimes casuistic, observance of moral precepts was sometimes replaced by a supposedly personal understanding of the good life that, in fact, frequently amounted to merely an uncritical surrender to prevailing outside tastes. Christians do not follow precepts in blind obedience, and they also do not self-generate the good life as various self-help movements (such as New Age groups) propagate. Both approaches miss the mark: one is good like Jesus is good.

Responding to objections raised by the British politician William Gladstone, Newman famously argued in his *Letter Addressed to His Grace the Duke of Norfolk* that he would first give a toast to his conscience and then to the pope. To Ratzinger, this meant that the objective papal ministry vouches for the sovereignty of the individual's conscience. The pope is bound to enunciate the material integrity of scripture and tradition, thus giving the individual believer the possibility of responding to God's charity.[21]

The charity of God toward a believer impels the believer to respond in kind to the highest degree humanly possible (1 Jn 4:16: "God is love, and he who abides in love abides in God and God abides in him"). In this perspective, the Ten Commandments become a divine gift. Without any ulterior motive—in contrast to Dostoyevsky's old woman in "An Onion" from *The Brothers Karamazov*, who was selfishly seeking merely liberation from hell—the Christian seeks the good for its own sake. As St. Ignatius of Loyola so timelessly phrased it:

> To give, and not to count the cost,
> To fight, and not to heed the wounds,

To toil, and not to seek for rest,
To labor, and not to ask for any reward
Save that of knowing that we do thy will.[22]

In reference to Cardinal Frings's speeches at the Vatican II Council, Ratzinger affirms this view a fortiori when citing the following passage from St. Gregory of Nyssa:

> This is true perfection: not to avoid a wicked life because like slaves we servilely fear punishment; nor to do good because we hope for rewards.... On the contrary, disregarding all those things for which we hope and which have been reserved by promise, we regard falling from God's friendship as the only thing dreadful and we consider becoming God's friend the only thing worthy of honor and desire.[23]

In particular, Ratzinger was impressed by Steinbüchel's discovery of personalism as a way to overcome the abstractions of Kant, Hegel, socialism, and National Socialism. In a time when politics was dictated by a dehumanizing ideology of the masses, Steinbüchel published a much noted article on the basic personalistic position of the Christian ethos.[24] This led Ratzinger as a young seminarian to the Jewish philosopher of religion and representative of mystical Chassidism, Martin Buber (1878–1965), who had written the small but epochal book *I and Thou* in 1923.[25] Early on, this thin treatise exerted a profound and lasting influence on Christian theologians and on the German Youth Movement, then still in its prime. In poetic language it illustrates how in the "I-Thou relationship" everyone is granted his or her full reality. It explains the difference between a person-thing relationship and one between two free persons. The latter finds its culmination in the personal relationship of a human being with God. The former, called the "I-It relationship," merely instrumentalizes human beings for one's needs and purposes. As a consequence, in the eyes of many of his contemporaries, Buber liberated the individual person from the cage of pathological individualism and constant monologues. He informed Ratzinger, and numerous other readers, that human existence is intrinsically one of dialogue. It quickly became a favorite topic for priests and educators in homilies and in giving religious instruction to numerous succeeding generations. The "I and Thou" as personal relationship comes about in this world because the "I" only exists in relationship to a "Thou." There are always givers and receivers. The riddle or enigma about who man the human being is can only be approximated by apprehending his/her essence as dialogical in a foundational way. The one realizes, actuates, and recognizes him/HERself in the encounter with another, and vice versa.[26] In this context he/she experiences him/herself respected as an end/purpose unto him/herself (*Zweck an sich selbst*) and is able to approach others likewise. Buber arrived at these insights via a critical analysis of Western and oriental mystical currents and their relationship to the world at large. He appreciated afresh Jewish spirituality and intellectualism in a conscious demarcation from the Enlightenment, German Idealism, and

Romanticism. In particular, Buber's grappling with the thought of the Jewish philosopher Franz Rosenzweig (1886–1929) must be considered key to his own dialogical *point d'appui*. He came to develop a vital, scripture-based existentialist view of the Jewish faith. Buber radically grounds the totality of creation in a triadic basis. From the outset of creation, God co-intends a personal relationality as an "I and Thou."[27] While there is the *Verhärtungsgestalt* (the form of a hardening of one's heart) of the "I-It" relationship, that is, an instrumentalized reality, as encountered in numerous instances within the purely natural realm, in Buber's judgment there always remains an openness to the more radical and primordial relationship of the "I and Thou." Thus, a human being possesses the dynamic potential to reconvalesce to an "I-Thou." This permits Buber to observe: "the human being becomes an I in confrontation with a Thou." There is no denying Buber is much indebted to Platonic cognitional structures.[28] Nonetheless, in contrast to pantheism and panpsychism—views negating an ultimate Thou—Buber attempts to make fecund a foundational Jewish affirmation regarding life and the world. The possibility always remains of a (divine) Thou speaking a word or utterance.[29] "Reading the Jewish thinker Martin Buber was 'a spiritual experience that left an essential mark' which he [Ratzinger] later compared with reading Augustine's *Confessions*."[30]

End of Excursus

These readings explain to no small degree Ratzinger's sympathies for Augustine and Bonaventure. Ratzinger confesses: "This encounter with personalism was for me a spiritual experience that left an essential mark, especially since I spontaneously associated such personalism with the thought of Saint Augustine, who in his *Confessions* had struck me with the power of all his human passion and depth" (Ratzinger, *Milestones*, 40) Ratzinger's sympathies for Augustine and Bonaventure were reinforced by the fact that the professor of Thomism at the Freising seminary, Father Arnold Wilmsen, was an arid, cocksure rationalist.[31] Even theologians not in agreement with Ratzinger on all matters—such as Francis Schüssler Fiorenza and Joseph Komonchak—admit that from his early studies to his first homily as pope, Ratzinger has displayed remarkable consistency. He has remained faithful to an Augustinian-Bonaventurian vision that does not trust philosophy or the sciences to save men but only the gospel.[32] "[W]ithout the light of Christ, the light of the world is not sufficient to enlighten the world," Benedict XVI stated in a Christmas message.[33]

In 1998 Ratzinger acknowledged that the moral theology of August Adam, *Das Primat der Liebe* (*The Primacy of Love*), had been "a key reading" for him during his youth.[34] This best seller placed the virtue of charity at the center of human existence and virtues, thus freeing moral theology from a rigorous, psychologically unhealthy fixation on sins. In this perspective, monogamous marriage corresponds best to the monotheist God of Christianity.[35] Much like August Adam, in the encyclical *Deus Caritas Est* Benedict XVI places charity at the center of the proclamation of the gospel: "God has made himself visible: in Jesus we are able to see the Father...since he has 'loved us first,' love can also blossom within us" (*Deus Caritas Est*, 17).

Ratzinger considered the personalist perspective the key source for the moral fortitude required in opposing National Socialism head-on, as had been done by his seminary rector Michael Höck. Höck, along with Munich Auxiliary Bishop Johannes Neuhäusler and the abbot of the Benedictine monastery of Metten, Korbinian Hofmeister, had been incarcerated in the Dachau concentration camp. In contrast, the heavily Thomistically inclined Michael Schmaus, Ratzinger's second and very critical reader of his habilitation, was accused of sympathizing with the Nazi regime.[36] Undoubtedly, the difficult military service the Ratzinger brothers experienced, constantly facing death, shaped and confirmed their personalist view early on and allowed them to develop a maturity well beyond their years. In Cardinal von Faulhaber's pontifical requiem for the fallen priests and seminarians of Munich, the archbishop described Nazi ideology as originating "either in a mental asylum or in hell."[37] He argued that the rights of individuals were brought into contradiction with the natural law by way of a hypertrophy of state laws. It was an accusation Ratzinger would often repeat. Only by living for and in the Lord can a priest overcome such inhumane humiliation for the betterment of general society. In the Lord one is called to be a pure hero in a moral and spiritual combat. The personal conversion to Christ, the wellspring of genuine humanism, is the key to overcoming degrading ideologies. One must detect in this a central motivation for Ratzinger becoming a priest and academic. It also explains the inner motivation for his occasionally critical observations regarding some current developments that are often more motivated by a functionalist view than a personalist one.

In view of the indisputable cruelties of war, the self-assured apologetics practiced in theology up to World War II did not prove unshakeable. It could no longer be taken for granted that an intellectualistic theology would survive. What sustained men such as Ratzinger on the battlefield was not abstract, neutral statements but the prayers of loved ones at home and one's inner self, namely, what the French philosopher Blaise Pascal (1623–1662) called "heart" and what Newman would associate with the notion of "conscience." In contrast, for the majority of younger men of their generation in Germany this would develop in such a way that *Angst* would be a central topos in any reflection on one's being. As a consequence, in the 1950s existentialism became in vogue in Germany. The icy cold of Nietzsche's "seven solitudes" became a sad reality. A modern Promethean attitude appeared that was altogether unaware of God's presence. Monological existence was the inevitable consequence for the majority in the 1960s. An unusual blending of German Idealism, Enlightenment thought, liberalism, and materialism took shape in Europe. Christianity was relegated to the dreamy realm of fairy tales. Only a minority still chose a personalist approach. It is certainly not by chance that in his first encyclical, *Deus Caritas Est*, Benedict XVI mentions Nietzsche as his first nonbiblical author.

The general intellectual climate was such that the positive quality of human existence was put into question and a Christian one was in the line of fire. Theology survived not because it retreated into a supposedly secure

intellectual sphere but because it was perceived by the seminarians as the
hazardous business of a daring life with Christ. Here the scholarly study of
theology became an ascetic exercise for men matured in war. It was a painful formation toward a Christian and priestly existence that the seminarian
Ratzinger underwent. The preceding modernist controversy (1898–1910)
had given too much emphasis to the scientific character of theology and lost
sight of the reality that theology always involves the totality of the human
person. One significant concern for the men returning from the battlefields
was that there should not be a rift between life and thought, between meditation and theology. This requires humility on the part of the human being.
God's Eternal Word, Jesus Christ, does not call for human elaborations and
adornments but should be at the very center of theology and proclamation.
This insight has formed Ratzinger's disposition as priest, professor, cardinal,
and pope to this very day.

There is no disinterested objectivity when pursuing theology. The theol-
ogizing human being is fully involved. The Latin words *inter* and *esse* (*inter
esse* = being in between) form the basis for the English word "interest,"
which means "being in the midst of it all as person," precisely because it
concerns one existentially. This insight was often pondered by Ratzinger
in his days of seminary training. The daring heart must be engaged. In the
wake of Cardinal Newman and Henri Bremond (1865–1933), theologians at
that time spoke of theology in terms of permitting the Holy Spirit to guide
one in having both revelation and dogma become an existential and affective
form of living. This corresponds well with modern Christian existentialist
philosophy as developed especially by Søren Kierkegaard.[38] The Danish philosopher had already argued in the first half of the nineteenth century that
Christianity is not first and foremost a teaching but an existence that needs to
be communicated to others so that this form of existence can be lived. Thus,
Christ did not institute docents but disciples. This concern is both biblical
and attested to by early Christianity.

The Benedictine theologian Anselm Stolz spoke in this context of
Denzingertheologie (an intellectualistic understanding of faith based exclusively on understanding conciliar and magisterial documents as compiled
in the *Enchiridion Symbolorum et Definitionum* by Heinrich Joseph Denzinger
[1819–1883], which, published beginning in 1854, has since had over forty
editions[39]). At that time, one derided such impersonal language as "one"
(third-person singular, in German *man*) thinking. All knowledge is acquired
in vain by the mind if one does not meditate over it and pray for the divine
charism. Very much like Jacob struggling with the angel in Genesis 32:25,
the theologian and priest must also struggle to acquire the proper inner disposition. Dogma is not merely a learned formula, but must be personally
acquired, prayed for, and affirmed as the existential *leitmotiv* of one's life.
Whoever practices faith on a daily basis and realizes the spirit of Christ gains
freedom.

The German priest and poet Peter Wust (1884–1940), another author popular among the Freising seminarians, observed that prayer is the human spirit's most sublime act of humility, granting insight into the central matters of
existence.[40] Concerning the philosophical definition of God as the impersonal

causa sui—as purpose unto itself—the philosopher Martin Heidegger notably formulated: "To this God man can neither pray nor can he sacrifice himself. In front of such a *causa sui* man can neither genuflect in reverence nor can he make music or dance for such a God."[41] In an almost ruthless bluntness, the Jesuit priest and martyr Alfred Delp (1907–1945) argued that the majority of society is no longer able to live in a relationship with God. It is as if an organ of the human body has wasted away.[42] This is the sad result of an intellectualistic understanding of faith.

Since René Descartes' (1596–1650) famous axiom *cogito, ergo sum* (I think, therefore I am) there has been a fateful turn toward the subject in European thought unintended by this believing French thinker. To personalist thinkers in the first half of the twentieth century, it became apparent that Christianity redeems humankind from being "a windowless monad"—as the Enlightenment thinker Leibniz (1646–1716) phrased it—by enabling humans to offer themselves to a divine Thou as their personal redeemer. A rather common way of putting this personalist shift at Ratzinger's time was: "The person gains himself by losing himself in God."[43] In loving God as a relational Thou, man and woman discover their own self. This is the most profound anthropological definition of humankind. Without God humankind is unable to acknowledge its gratuitous similarity with God. The Johannine insight, "He who does not love, does not know God," from 1 John 4:8 can also be read the other way around: (only) he/she who knows God, can love.

As stated earlier, Alfred Läpple introduced Ratzinger to the thought of the English convert and theologian John Henry Newman (1801–1890) and his concept of conscience. This was an important term as during the Third Reich one of its leaders—Hermann Göring—had grandiosely proclaimed: "I have no conscience. My conscience is the Führer." Newman showed Ratzinger—as Ratzinger would observe during a conference commemorating the centenary of Newman's death—that the human conscience is a dynamic entity developing to ever deeper degrees as the relationship of the human soul to God grows. In this perspective, conscience becomes the path of obedience to objective Christian truth.[44] The subjective evangelical position is overcome by discovering dogma's objectivity.[45] Thus, Ratzinger was often able to formulate sentences to this effect: "The I of the creed is the Church; the individual does not believe from his own competence, but rather with and in the Church."

With Läpple, Ratzinger also read Edith Stein's (1892–1942) translation of Thomas's *Quaestio disputata de veritate* in two volumes. The quality of this work encouraged Läpple to ask Ratzinger to translate Thomas's *Quaestio disputata de caritate* into German. At that time, the complete Thomistic corpus did not yet exist in German. Thus Ratzinger, from the very outset of his studies, gained an acute sensibility for the original reading of a text. Was perhaps this early work on a text by St. Thomas also cause for Ratzinger to write his first encyclical on charity?

CHAPTER 4

Graduate Studies in Munich

The University of Munich's department of theology was provisionally located in Fürstenried Castle, on the southern outskirts of Munich. Ratzinger was exposed there—and after its relocation in the city—to the teachings of four great local theological minds: Gottlieb Söhngen taught fundamental theology, Michael Schmaus taught dogmatics, Friedrich Wilhelm Maier taught New Testament, and Romano Guardini lectured on the Christian worldview. Parting ways with neoscholastic schemas, Schmaus attempted to reconstruct Thomistic dogmatics. Maier was one of the earliest Catholic scholars to embrace the hypothesis of a text "Q" (for "*Quelle*" in German, meaning "source") and a collection of sayings (*Logien*) stipulating that the synoptic gospels draw on unknown sources.[1] The writings of Henri de Lubac from faraway Lyon in France supplied a sweeping, symphonic vision of faith.

Gottlieb Söhngen

Of these four, Gottlieb Söhngen (1892–1971) exerted the greatest influence on Ratzinger.[2] This professor of fundamental theology was born in the old, cosmopolitan city of Cologne. He was lively, joyful, engaging, and extroverted. With the enthusiasm of a Rhinelander, he sensitized his students for the ecumenical cause. He considered faith essentially mystery and history as is history of salvation. His motto was "with Thomas beyond Aquinas, with Augustine beyond Augustine." God is not the abstract *summum bonum* (the highest good) of scholasticism, demonstrable via exact definitions or formulae. The mystery approaches us a *Du* (Thou). With Martin Buber, he believed the best human response is grateful praise of God. For this reason he was in agreement with Newman's motto *cor ad cor loquitur* (the heart speaks to the heart). Therefore he argued against any kind of ecclesiocentric hubris.

He taught Ratzinger to critically question neoscholastic ideas. He stressed the difference, but also the correlation between, theology as wisdom and as science.[3] Söhngen insisted on developing theology from primary texts: Plato, Aristotle, Clement of Alexandria, Augustine, Anselm, Bonaventure, and Thomas. Significantly, he also exposed Ratzinger to the Tübingen School of Theology. The attitude of *kenosis* (a self-imposed emptying of one's own ambition and will) preserves wisdom amid the vain bustle of the world. His concern was to assure that mystery was not reduced to a system. This, along with an interest in history, meant Augustine and Bonaventure appeared far more congenial to him in overcoming rationalism than the university teacher Thomas Aquinas. Treated within academia, Thomas must live from the bubbling "wisdom of God" lest he dry up into a rivulet of science. While at first disappointed by the infallible dogma on the bodily assumption of Our Lady into heaven, and even personally hurt by the attacks on de Lubac, Congar, and Teilhard de Chardin after Pope Pius XII issued *Humani Generis* in 1950, Söhngen was keen on not fostering an anti-Church or anti-Roman climate. In a way, his relationship to Ratzinger is comparable to that of Albert the Great to Thomas Aquinas. He considered Ratzinger his best and most promising student who would deepen and develop his own thought.[4]

In a memorable speech, Ratzinger recalled the emotional suffering at the hands of the Church (cf. Col 1:24) that his dissertation director endured with ecclesial loyalty and cheerful equanimity grounded in deep faith.[5] Söhngen had frequently stressed that theology is only properly understood when perceived as a unit.[6] This unity is preserved by acknowledging that dogmatic-systematic theology reigns supreme. Historic and exegetical areas serve as handmaids to systematic (dogmatic) theology (*Dienstmädchenstellung*).[7]

In *Die Einheit in der Theologie* (*The Unity in Theology*) Söhngen shows how theology occupies a particular position in the sciences as it is "the wisdom of faith through the path of science." Theology's formal object is God, or more precisely, the wisdom of God-become-man in Jesus. Since the days of Thomas Aquinas, theology's method had been that of the *intellectus fidei* (that is, the rational way in which faith perceives itself), which is defined as *scientia*. Central concepts informing theology—besides historic revelation— are memory (*memoria*) and participation (*participatio*), and also the pair of terms *analogia fidei* (analogy of faith) and *analogia entis* (analogy of being). In Söhngen's opinion, Thomistic epistemology's critical contribution consists of introducing the (for subsequent centuries definitive) distinction between philosophy and theology, that is, the distinction between the knowledge of reason and the knowledge of faith. Such a differentiation no longer allows the *intellectus fidei* to retreat to the Augustinian notion of spiritual insight as enabled by illumination. Historic human nature is never an autonomous entity à la *natura pura* (pure nature) but one that is, ever since its very beginning, open toward the supernatural. Nonetheless, the ability of humans to use unambiguous symbolic language and parables is darkened by sin. Thus, for the ultimate deciphering, human nature requires the language of parables and signs. This is the *modus operandi* of the *analogia entis*. Söhngen showed how natural knowledge of God is different from faith's knowledge but nonetheless cannot be divorced from it. The indivisibility of the two is grounded in the circumstance that natural knowledge of God is not abstract or metaphysical but a part of the divine economy. In other words, natural knowledge of God is part and parcel of the created order and of salvation history. In continuity with, but also in slightly nuanced difference to Söhngen,

Ratzinger would emphasize that an analogy of being approach may not be irresponsibly unrealistic. Such thinking implies a difference between subject and object, which does not actually exist as every human being is created in the image of God. No being can be thought of apart from God. God is the ground and measure of the human soul. Reason is also a divine attribute. Thus, there can be no measure outside the God and man relationship for Ratzinger. As Augustine wrote, "God is closer to me than myself" (*Confessions* 3, 6: "*Deus interior intimo me*").

In a critical demarcation from then contemporary Protestant theologians such as Karl Barth and Rudolf Bultmann, Söhngen did not tire of demonstrating that there exists no unbridgeable chasm between the *analogia entis* and the *analogia fidei*. The *analogia entis* is the natural constituent of the parable between God and humankind grounded in creation. The creator God is identical with the savior God. In contrast to that, the *analogia fidei* is the supernatural constituent of the parable between God and humankind grounded in the Divine Incarnate Word. There is no contradiction between the two as both are part of the one act of faith. Neither faith nor theology could come about if the two were not collaborators. Söhngen thus achieved the much discussed surmounting of an extrinsicistic understanding of revelation. Söhngen's seminal study *Die Einheit der Theologie* therefore not only impressed the young student Ratzinger but significantly impacted modern theological thought's shift toward a salvation-historic perspective.[8]

Theology in the second half of the twentieth century tended to define itself as scientific and considered itself called to bridge the modern day lifestyle and the Christian faith. It was thus often goal-oriented and problem-sensitive. This meant theology was concerned with justifying itself vis-à-vis other academic disciplines as equally academically rigorous. At the same time, it strove to legitimatize its relevance for everyday Christian life. As Laurence Paul Hemming has observed: "Thus—let us say—after a great natural disaster or even a vicious atrocity to hear the cry 'where was God in this?' they hear this not as a plea for understanding from those gripped by the pain of tragedy and who are seeking to understand it, but rather as a factual statement of disbelief."[9] The rhetorical figure collapses into a statement of fact. The biblical opposition and tension within a soul as expressed in the outcry "I believe; help my unbelief!" (Mk 9:24) is no longer appreciated. The spiritual dimension is lost sight of in many a theology.

Pope Benedict XVI is a man of unaffected and profound piety grounded in the immediate religiosity of Upper Bavaria and his family. His frequent references to the normativity of the piety of the simple and poor illustrate the egalitarian nature of faith. This critical nexus between scholarly theology and direct piety was affirmed in the person and theology of Söhngen. By following the premonitions, or better yet, intuitions of faith and the heart—in the vein of Blaise Pascal and Cardinal Newman—the believing heart not only enters deeper into divine love but unlocks a heretofore unknown level of knowing that remains accountable to human reason.

As eulogist at Söhngen's funeral on November 19, 1971, Ratzinger summed up the theology of his *Doktorvater* (doctoral thesis director) in the presence of cardinals Joseph Höffner and the blind archbishop emeritus of Cologne

Josef Frings. Ratzinger appreciated in Söhngen the fact that by posing such broad questions he never presented a closed synthesis of his thoughts. He observed that Söhngen was content contributing fragments to the theological enterprise. Nonetheless, he strove "to behold the whole in the fragment, to think fragments from the whole and to design them as reflections of the whole." He had the intrepidity "to pose radical questions" (*radix* in Latin means "root") and "to believe radically" (that is, from the root) at the same time. For this reason, he did not shy away from acknowledging that some ages remain helpless and sometimes even mired in contradictions. In unmistakably Ratzingerian language, he expressed his estimation of Söhngen in the following words: "We cannot ask for truth, if it has not first asked for us; we cannot seek truth, if we have not first been found by truth." He vouched for the Church's faith, which he never invented but received and lived in as a gift.[10] This combination of deep faith and not insisting on resolving all questions enabled Söhngen to retain his good humor in spite of the vicissitudes of his life.

Henri de Lubac

> Another circumstance came to my aid. In the fall of 1949, Alfred Läpple had given me *Catholicism*, perhaps Henri de Lubac's most significant work, in the masterful translation of Hans Urs von Balthasar. This book was for me a key reading event. It gave me not only a new and deeper connection with the thought of the Fathers but also a new way of looking at theology and faith as such. Faith had here become an interior contemplation and, precisely by thinking with the Fathers, a present reality....De Lubac was leading his readers out of a narrowly individualistic and moralistic mode of faith and into the freedom of an essentially social faith, conceived and lived as a *we*—a faith that, precisely as such and according to its nature, was also hope, affecting history as a whole, and not only the promise of a private blissfulness to individuals.[11]

This firm gaze on the spiritual end of human existence only grants "the happiest and most perfect form of social existence" lest it falls back into "a sort of refined egoism."[12] ("Refined egoism," in this context, refers to a sophisticated and socially accepted form of egoism that covers up its self-interest by feigning altruism, while the inner disposition is not honorable, as it is not assuming the mind of Jesus.)

Catholicism: Christ and the Common Destiny of Man, published in 1938, was de Lubac's first book. The French subtitle significantly reads: "The Social Dimensions of Dogma." In a reflection on the twentieth century, Fergus Kerr wrote: "Many, including Congar, Balthasar, Wojtyla and Ratzinger, regarded it as the key book of twentieth-century Catholic theology, the one indispensable text."[13] It may be considered a synopsis of the themes that would be addressed in greater detail in other books of this French Jesuit's significant oeuvre. It opposed an individualistic understanding of Christianity, which had prevailed in the West since the High Middle Ages.[14] Such an individualistic perspective is a departure from the biblical testimony, which emphasizes that Christ assumed and (potentially) redeemed the totality of humankind. Thus, since the second century the Church has been predicated as "Catholic" because she possesses the commission and the ability to bring all of humankind to the unity that the Church, from its very beginning, strives for by its very essence.[15] In language reminiscent of Augustine, de Lubac declared that the mysterious participation of individual human beings with God in the sacrament of the Church, and its system of sacraments, is the basis for genuine unity among humankind. He first established that sin and salvation, according to biblical and patristic testimony, have social ramifications. The Church is not a later, secondary gathering of faithful but the true and caring "mother" of the faithful. This allowed him to elaborate on the social dimensions of the sacraments. According to early Christian testimony, Christian hope is not individualistic but is aimed at the eternal perfection of all of humankind. There is a salutary quality to dogma: it allows true socialization. The dogma of the God-man places an infinite value on social interaction: in the other person one beholds always an *alter Christus* (another Christ).

While in all other instances, religious élan leads to a separation from the sensible realm and, therefore, to a flight from the world, in Christianity the opposite occurs. Through the Incarnation of Christ, God entered into history and thereby united himself to humankind. All of humankind is destined to become what Catholics already are: the Church, as "People of God" and as "Bride of Christ." De Lubac writes: "Amid the universal chorus, Christianity alone continues to assert the transcendent destiny of man and the common destiny of mankind. The whole history of the world is a preparation for this destiny."[16] This explains the tension between the universal salvific will of God and the concrete form of the Church as the locale of salvation. A similar tension exists, de Lubac acknowledges, between a humane disposition toward all human beings and the need to spread the gospel.

He further showed how individuality and sociality mutually enable one another. Only under the premise of unity with other human beings can the flourishing of the individual person come about. No human being could achieve such equilibrium on his or her own. This can only be granted by the spirit of God as a gift. Solely in God is such overarching unity conceivable. This divine overarching unity in turn enables the imagination to conceive of a similar human unity, without favoring the present age or a future one. Thus, the idea of the unity of humankind cannot be grounded otherwise than in the one mystical body of Christ. It is precisely the Church that is this mystical body of Christ; the Christian believing and living humanity as fraternity in the historic here and now.[17] The Church is essentially a Christological category: "In the likeness of Christ, who is her founder and her head, she is at the same time both the way and the goal; at the same time visible and invisible; in time and in eternity; she is at once the bride and the widow, the sinner and the saint."[18] Ecclesiology and Christology are intimately interwoven. Yet the manner is one in which the former serves as secondary truth to the latter. The Church's purpose is Christological, but Christ references the

Father: "By revealing the Father and being revealed by him, Christ completes the revelation of man to himself."[19] While Christian faith contains a number of paradoxes, none is greater than that of the vision of God as a free and completely unmerited gift. Nonetheless, it belongs to the very nature of the human soul to desire this grace.

While Ratzinger was completing his studies in Munich, de Lubac was banned from teaching theology in Lyon. (It is likely de Lubac was banned upon the instigation of the famous Dominican Thomist, the "monstre sacré," Réginald Garrigou-Lagrange. It is a well-known fact that Garrigou-Lagrange had opposed the *Nouvelle Théologie*.) In the person of de Lubac, Ratzinger discovered a selflessly heroic theologian, willing to be marginalized without becoming embittered or losing his love for the Church. Many thought the encyclical *Humani Generis*, issued on August 12, 1950, by Pope Pius XII, attacked de Lubac's contributions. In general language, the encyclical condemned various modern currents in theology: existentialism, emphasis on the Word vis-à-vis reason, discerning an opposition between scripture and dogma, considering the Roman Catholic Church as something less than the mystical body of Christ, and any distrust of scholastic theology. Quite the contrary, through the lens of de Lubac, Ratzinger began to comprehend the profound unity of faith, the Eucharist, and the Church in a new sacramental-mystical perspective.

Hans Urs von Balthasar

Another great mind Ratzinger would find enriching was the Swiss theologian Hans Urs von Balthasar (1905–1988). Gradually, the affinity between these two minds would grow. While Ratzinger turned to Augustine and Bonaventure, Balthasar left the Jesuit order in 1950 in shock and disappointment over the "desert and dreariness Neo-scholasticism had caused."[20] He could not reconcile this stale science with the new personalist approach to theology his licentiate thesis director, de Lubac, had shown him. The encounter with the living Christ ought to be the point of departure for any kind of theology. Further, the living Christ is none other than our neighbor: degraded people, whose faces have been trampled upon, reveal Jesus Christ. In this regard, Ratzinger and Balthasar are of a congenial mind frame. They were both influenced in central ways by Ressourcement—the one as a student of de Lubac, the other as a reader of him—and both expressed their sympathy with the *anawim* ("the poor," in Hebrew). It is little wonder that in 1972 they founded together the international theological periodical *Communio*, in which both published significant contributions.[21] Balthasar's observations paralleled those Ratzinger had heard earlier from Ferdinand Ebner and Theodor Steinbüchel. As Ratzinger once put it, "the task is to break through to the real, which stands behind the words," thereby opposing the linguistic turn and the theories of relativism. Shortly before Balthasar's death, Pope John Paul II created him a cardinal, thereby officially recognizing his major theological contributions. Alas, Balthasar passed away two days before the consistory was to convene. Thus, it may appear providential that during Balthasar's funeral in Lucerne on July 1, 1988, Ratzinger was able to speak the following words:

> Only with hesitation did Balthasar agree to receive the honor of the cardinalate, not by virtue of the coquetry of a great individual, but with an Ignatian spirit, which moulded his life. Somehow, this seems confirmed through the call to another life, which reached him at the eve of this honor. He was permitted to remain totally himself. But what the pope intended with this gesture of recognition remains valid: not only single and private individuals but the Church in her official responsibility tells us, that he is a just teacher of the faith, a signpost to the sources of living water, a witness to the Word, whence we learn Christ, whence we can learn life.[22]

Romano Guardini

In his autobiography Ratzinger makes only brief mention of Romano Guardini.[23] But this renowned priest and scholar was on the lips of many Catholics well into the 1970s. A number of themes that permeate Guardini's writings reappear in Ratzinger's oeuvre: the challenge of modernity, affirmation of the truly real, love, freedom, the creative dimension of God, liturgical renewal as renewal of humankind, and human life becoming meaningful in the encounter with the mystery and person of Jesus Christ. At first, one does not know who the author of the following lines might be: "The liturgy is based on the mystery of Easter; it is to be understood as the Lord's approach to us. In it he becomes our traveling companion, sets our dull hearts aflame, and opens our sealed eyes. He still walks with us, still finds us worried and downhearted, and still has the power to make us see."[24] Ratzinger penned these lines, but they could just as easily have originated from Guardini's quill.

Guardini was not a Thomist and found the neoscholastic textbooks insufferable. It does not come as a surprise that he wrote his doctoral thesis on Bonaventure's understanding of Redemption.[25] Particularly during his Munich years, Ratzinger must have been impressed by the lectures Guardini gave at Munich University—attended by sometimes more than a thousand students—and by the homilies he gave at the local university Church St. Ludwig (St. Louis). During his time as associate pastor in Heiligen Blut, Romano Guardini moved into the parish and began preaching there, which was the very parish the newly ordained priest Ratzinger would serve in. Additional surprising parallels exist between both men. Guardini wrote his splendid book *The Essence of Christianity* in 1938, and thirty years later Ratzinger would write the classic *Introduction to Christianity*. They shared a common concern for the Church as pivotal to understanding and following Christ. While in 1921 Guardini could state, "A process of great consequence has begun: the conscience of the Church is awakening in the souls of believers," fifty years later Ratzinger had to note: "The process of great consequence is that the Church is being extinguished in souls and scattered in communities." As the Church is the Eucharistic reality, serious theology is only made possible by thinking in harmony with the Church. Without the Church there is no encounter with Jesus Christ. Only then are the Church and her product, dogma, beheld not as limitations and restrictions on freedom and well-reasoned judgments but as the conditions for the possibility of the highest degree of freedom and the most sublime heights reason can reach.

An additional crucial point of agreement between the two men is the liturgy. Paralleling Guardini's classic *The Spirit of the Liturgy* (1918), eighty years later, in 1998, Ratzinger published his own *The Spirit of the Liturgy* in which he wrote:

> One of the first books I read after starting my theological studies at the beginning of 1946 was Romano Guardini's first little book, *The Spirit of the Liturgy*. It was published at Easter 1918 as the opening volume in the *Ecclesia Orans* series edited by Abbot Herwegen, and from then until 1957 it was constantly reprinted. This slim volume may rightly be said to have inaugurated the Liturgical Movement in Germany. Its contribution was decisive. It helped us to rediscover the liturgy in all its beauty, hidden wealth, and time-transcending grandeur, to see it as the animating center of the Church, the very center of Christian life. It led to a striving for a celebration of the liturgy that would be "more substantial" [*wesentlicher*, one of Guardini's favorite words]. We were now willing to see the liturgy—in its inner demands and form—as the prayer of the Church, a prayer moved and guided by the Holy Spirit himself, a prayer in which Christ unceasingly becomes contemporary with us, enters into our lives.[26]

Both men also shared a preoccupation with the destiny of Europe and feared it was in the process of repudiating its Christian heritage. Little wonder then that Ratzinger wrote an introduction to the English reprint of Guardini's classic book *The Lord*.[27] This book was first printed in German in 1937. It is a biblical meditation on the person and life of Jesus Christ. The dogma of the incarnate God allows for a fruitful ordering of theological thought. The experience of conversion allows a transcendence of the modern mind that overcomes the subjectivist post-Kantian mindset. Jesus Christ restores the relationship between thought and being. Modern thought can thereby take up the thread of the patristic and medieval thinkers. This conformity or "obedience" to being brings about an alignment with truth—a position that was also held by various philosophers such as Nicolai Hartmann, Edmund Husserl, and Max Scheler—and reveals the primacy of Logos over ethos. All subjective truthfulness runs the danger of making compromises. But the relationship to the objective Logos is a relationship with the innermost truth of every human being; thus the priority of being over doing. Both men repeatedly insisted on this aspect. "Concrete living" is the figure of Jesus Christ. In this figure, all contradictions and opposites are united, such as silence and Word and the individual and community. In Christ Jesus all forms of extremism—as they are exclusive and intolerant—are abandoned as humans discover the essence of their being. As Guardini prophetically warned while still teaching at the University of Berlin, the primacy of doing invariably brings about some form of tyranny. In Germany, this came about under the guise of National Socialism. Like Guardini, Ratzinger also feared the quest for truth lacked a recognized place in the methodological canon of universities.

The main connecting thread between the two is that Christianity is not an abstract idea but a concrete person.[28] In an age of industrialization, Guardini observed the depersonalization of the individual. This expressed itself in the phenomenon of the anonymous, depersonalized masses. It is an age that grants existence "only [to] impersonal [abstract] reality, [and] impersonal norms."[29] The attendant result is that "the modern world is complete in itself and self-isolated from its Creator and Sustainer." While showing that Jesus Christ transcends all human categories, he can nonetheless only be encountered in historic concretions whereby he is able to form and transform human existence. Guardini demonstrates this in the discipleship narration and the story of the transfiguration in the famous central fourth part of his classic *The Lord*. The essence of Christianity is only beheld in the person of Jesus. The author intends to enable the reader to encounter God in Jesus Christ from person to person. Earthly human existence can be touched by the divine. Both Guardini and Ratzinger could have stated, "We must confront all men, doctrines, epochs with Christ Himself."[30]

A brief reflection on factors that led up to Guardini's classic *The Lord* is appropriate. Shortly before World War I, in 1912, the painter Franz Marc spoke of how "Mysticism awakens in souls and along with it its primordial elements act."[31] One trusts in a transcendental experience of reality that forms everyday life. This hope or trust soon becomes a yearning, not only for the artistic avant-garde but for a great number of cultured people. Via the Mainz circle, gathered around the couple Wilhelm and Josefine Schleußner, Guardini was exposed early on to this mind frame as a student. This view of a pure, unadulterated but somewhat inchoate interiority did not, however, satisfy him. He searched for "another mysticism, in which the fervor of the secret is connected with the greatness of objective persons [Gestalten]."[32] As Augustine formulated it, "God and my soul, and nothing else in this world" (*Deum et animam scire cupio. Nihil plus? Nihil omnino*).[33] In 1922 Guardini envisioned a process involving all of popular culture in which "the Church awakens in souls."[34] Ten years after the painter Franz Marc's statement, modern humankind's soul seemed to have found its actual home again.

In the Tübingen theologian Wilhelm Koch, Guardini encountered someone able to teach him "the life-value of Catholic dogma."[35] This allowed him to appreciate the unconditional nature of the Catholic faith and its attendant intellectual edifice.[36] He began to criticize a theology that allows outside, rationalistic criteria to dictate the content of the faith. His attempt to fall neither for integralism nor for liberalism led him to discover a mediating objective concept in the figure of "obedience." The connecting link between himself and Jesus Christ is this concept of ecclesial obedience.[37] In 1929 he stated that it is exclusively the historic Jesus who allows people to apprehend Christian destiny. All of Christian culture is bound to the person of Christ.[38] All of the faith, the liturgy, and the Church hinges on the Savior's personhood. The Church can only be alive in souls if Christ is present in them, he "who steps out of the Father's mission to human beings."[39]

In his trial lecture at the University of Bonn on "Anselm of Canterbury and the Essence of Theology" in 1922, the young teacher stated emphatically: "The Church alone recognizes God, insofar as finitude is able to recognize infinitude. . . . What appeared upon first sight as a violation of all scientific thinking, is upon closer examination the unique possible basis of theological science: the actual subject of theology is the thinking community of the Church."[40] On this point, as Ratzinger did not tire of pointing out,[41] Guardini remained consistent through old age. In a diary entry dated September 28, 1954, Guardini reiterates that the actual norm for faith is not scripture but the Church. He describes the Church as "prophet." "In the hands of the Church," scripture becomes relevant.[42]

In Guardini's age, it was altogether uncommon for one to turn directly to Christ. Yet, it was his overriding intention to go beyond the conventional devotional customs, doctrinal definitions, or historic or psychological relativisms then in vogue, which ran the danger of dissolving the figure ("*Gestalt*," in German) of Christ. The realization that "the essence of Christianity is a person: Jesus Christ Himself" is at the heart of his thought.[43] To his mind, even the subtlest nuances in dogmatic Christology enunciating the *unio hypostatica* (the union of the divine and human in the one person of Jesus Christ) are insufficient.[44] This is the premise of his epochal *The Lord*. He wanted at all costs to avoid a dogmatic or psychological narrowing of the figure of the Lord.[45] In the encounter with Christ's figure or form (*Gestalt*), one apprehends not accidental features but the essence, the very heart, of a person. Therefore, preconceived terms or images should be avoided. This evolved from simple meditations and homilies that were written and distributed to subscribers under the heading "From the Life of the Lord." Later, these papers were edited and revised under the pregnant title, *The Lord*: "strictly speaking, a biography of Christ is another contradiction in terms. . . . Neither his personality nor his works are immediately traceable to the conditions of the times, for he came to us out of the fullness of time contained in the mystery of God, and it was to this mystery that he returned after he had 'moved among us' "[46]—as Ratzinger wrote in the English preface. The key to understanding Christ is his "Father's will," a realm no mortal can ever reach in this world. The meditations "do not attempt to recount Jesus' life in any chronological order or logical sequence; rather they select from it this or that teaching, event, trait, miracle, or thought, as it happens to warm to life."[47] Therefore, what should be drawn out is not an abstract idea of Christ's identity but a concrete reality; the unity of an overpowering being should come to the fore. The author's intention is not a distant reflection but a personal encounter with Jesus Christ. This is not to say the precise and exact sciences have lost their legitimacy, but that they also are subservient to a mystagogical concern, which is not limited to the liturgy but addresses the whole of life.

In consonance with Guardini's worldview, Ratzinger discerns the unity of all of reality in liturgical work, conjoining the spiritual and material spheres. In his contribution to a collection of articles commemorating the hundredth anniversary of Guardini's birth, Ratzinger reminds the reader of the foundational statement this precursor of liturgical renewal made: "Infinitely precious is the element of every gospel reality, but we apprehend it only properly in light of essential truth, as it speaks to our present [age] through the Church."[48] In Ratzinger's estimation, this constitutes Guardini's "Christological synthesis," uniting his understanding of liturgy with his philosophy. Truth, as Ratzinger states, to which human beings are oriented by their very nature, is not found somewhere at random or by chance, but in the living-concrete, in the *Gestalt* (form) of Jesus Christ. This living-concrete evidences itself as truth, which is the unity of seeming contradictions, combining "*Logos* and *Alogon*" (intelligible meaning and its unreasonable negation), that which makes sense and that which transcends human rationality. Under this consideration the *Alogon* is not absurd. Therefore, one must not reduce the images of Christ to a specific number. Whoever wishes to apprehend Christ must "convert," "must step out of the autonomy of high-handed thinking" and assume the disposition of "listening willingness."[49] Ratzinger summarizes this:

> This synthesis of cognition, which never surrenders its philosophical earnestness and breadth of search for the whole, but precisely in the radicality of such query goes beyond all mere theorizing, becomes in a moving way apparent in sentences, standing at the beginning of a small book on the image of Jesus the Christ in the New Testament, expressing the inner direction of all of Guardini's Christological statements: perhaps in the search for the image of Jesus we will even reach a "Gestalt," but arrive only at a row of lines, stepping out of our horizon. Perhaps we experience that the ascension not only means a singular event in Jesus' life, but is the manner in which He is given to us: as the heaven, vanishing into God's reserve. But the lines are also precious: they are signposts for faith's stepping beyond; and the circumstance that they are taken from our view, explaining that failure that instructs us to pray.[50]

As Guardini wrote: "The greatest of all graces is to love the Lord with a heart fully conscious of what it is about; to love...Christ himself, corporeally and spiritually, as one loves an irreplaceable person to whom one is bound through thick and thin."[51] The consequences of such love are not abstract but concrete: this love unleashes genuine human freedom and creativity, which includes forgiving others in light of the experienced divine forgiveness.[52] The densest encounter with the heart of the world occurs in transubstantiation: "Where is the impenetrability of divine mystery more apparent than here?"[53] Guardini stresses that in spite of the Savior's Eucharistic presence, he remains shrouded in the *mysterium fidei* (mystery of faith),[54] indicatively spoken by the celebrant immediately following the elevations of the paten and chalice. To further this concern of Guardini is the intention of Ratzinger's book *Jesus of Nazareth*.

Summary

Philosophically, Ratzinger's thinking, faith, and prayer life were inspired by philosophical personalism (Ferdinand Ebner and Martin Buber). This took on a concrete shape in the Christology of Romano Guardini. Gottlieb Söhngen added the dimension of mystery. Hans Urs von Balthasar and, particularly, Henri de Lubac gave impulses bringing forth a close correlation in the areas of Christology and ecclesiology. Both disciplines enable and explicate one another. Thus, for Ratzinger as well as for Guardini, faith is essentially believing along with the Church. In turn, the Church cannot be properly apprehended and lived by the believer without first being touched by the mystery of Christ. These various and varied factors blend into an unmistakable, inseverable unit that marks Ratzinger as a priest, theologian, and pope.

Pope Benedict organizes his life, prays, and works in a fervent and direct spirit much akin to that of Augustine, Bonaventure, Pascal, Newman, and de Lubac. The key to understanding this spirit is to appreciate that first the heart and then reason are employed; note well the expanding of the range of human intelligibility. The nature of this mystery is only heightened if human beings can "lift up their hearts to this mystery." "To be nothing in oneself, everything in Christ; to be obliged to contain such tremendous contents in so small a vessel; to be a constant herald with no life of one's own; to forego once and forever the happy unity of blood and heart and spirit in all one does and is."[55]

A biographer of Ratzinger, Aidan Nichols, has described theology especially in the second half of the twentieth century as tending to rely exclusively on historical science, thereby limiting the meaning of scripture and other religious texts. The testimonies of personal encounters, of a Spirit-sustained tradition, and of Church history as primarily salvation history played no role in the hermeneutical process. This seems an ironic overreaction to neoscholasticism, which was inclined to theologize with little reference to history.[56] In Ratzinger's view, God is not worshipped and cherished because he can be grasped in exact formulas and demonstrated beyond doubt as the *summum bonum*, or highest good. If this were so, then the consequences of being either an atheist, agnostic, or theist would be rather inconsequential. Rather, it is thrilling and life-altering to encounter God as a living Thou who is recognizable as personal and who encourages one to recognize him. The very Augustinian and Pascalian phrase *cor ad cor loquitur* ("heart speaking to heart," or, more figuratively, "having a heart to heart talk with God"), which was adopted by Cardinal Newman as his motto, best captures the highest drama imaginable in human existence.

CHAPTER 5

His Language and Style

While teaching seminarians at Freising's *Domberg* (cathedral hill), Ratzinger already displayed a linguistic mastery that fascinated and captivated people. To the students his approach was both brilliant and altogether novel. His lectures were methodical in structure and "meditative-reflective" in style. Shortly after his arrival in the parish of Heiligen Blut after ordination, his pastor, Father Blumschein, asked him to preach at the 7:30 a.m. Sunday mass, and Ratzinger even outperformed, as regards the quality of his homilies, the famous Jesuit homilists Fathers Friedrich Wulf and Franz Hillig.[1]

In Ratzinger's spoken and written language, there is something unmistakably distinctive. While precise, it is also pleasing and unassumingly elegant. It altogether lacks anything artificial or forced. A professorial tone is never detectable. His is a narrative style that expresses itself delightfully as is the case, for instance, in his *Introduction to Christianity*, now considered a theological classic of the twentieth century. As the former occupant of the Munich Guardini chair, Hans Meier astutely observed at one point, Ratzinger's literary style "has the flow of the Danube countries that captivates the reader."[2] While his style often employs argument, and certainly does not shy away from controversies, Ratzinger never acquired the polemical tenor or scathing irony of men such as Hans Urs von Balthasar, Karl Rahner, or Karl Barth.

Indeed, there is an effortless levity and clarity in his language that is beguiling, but only upon second sight: the speaker almost recedes, if not vanishes, behind the spoken message. Reminding one of the Salzburg *Wunderkind* composer, Wolfgang Amadeus Mozart, Ratzinger's thoughts seem to be generated as "one single stroke, as one coherent whole from his heart and intellect at the same time." The Cologne archbishop Cardinal Meißner calls him "the Mozart of theology." Like Mozart, he does not delight in dark problematizations. He is charming and always cheerful in a quiet way.

Ratzinger's education was that of the classical German *Humanistisches Gymnasium* within the context of the high school seminary of Traunstein, which exists to this day. He enjoyed reading Albert Einstein, Werner Heisenberg, Fyodor Dostoyevsky, Max Planck, Gertrud von Le Fort, Josef Pieper, Theodor Häcker, and Peter Wust. His language is inspired by the austere, formal precision of Latin; the elegant, melodious flow of classical Greek;

and the luminaries of German literature, Johann Wolfgang von Goethe, Adalbert Stifter, Joseph von Eichendorff, and Eduard Mörike,[3] whose writings are void of expressive pathos, metaphors, or hyperbole but are characterized by an unaffected earnestness. The jargon of existentialism à la Sartre or of the Group 47 (a group of German intellectuals founded in 1947, which would prove most influential for German culture until most recently), fashionable in the 1950s, did not affect his style. As regards linguistic discipline and the inner disposition of his language, there are also some remarkable parallels with Hans Carossa (1878–1956)—doctor, lyricist, and author—detectable in Ratzinger's writings and thoughts. Carossa had lived in the same general area of southern Bavaria as Ratzinger, namely in Bad Tölz, Munich, and Passau. Both experienced life during times of historical confusion and both reacted to their times by pointing, in their writings, to a concept of inner harmony. For Carossa this harmony was discernible from nature and the cosmos, whereas for Ratzinger it arises from living in Jesus Christ and looking at the form of Christ, the Church. Confronted with National Socialism and resisting the call to accommodate it, Carossa opted for "an inner emigration" rather than collaborating with the regime. The line "from the low evening a luminous star shines forth" is characteristic of Carossa's temperament.[4]

Theology as the conscious reflection on faith in Jesus Christ, held accountable to reason, is not exclusive to any single language. In contrast to common professorial language, Ratzinger avoids enigmatic and ponderous obscurity in favor of transparency, luminosity, and clarity. Citing medieval theologians, he often refers to "reason's waxen nose" (that is, reason is not the final arbiter in all matters). The rationalists who attacked the churches during the French Revolution gave warning of the antireligious excesses to which (secular) reason left to its own devices is capable of.[5] The clarity of Ratzinger's expression explains the ease with which his writings can be translated into all of the major languages: Italian, French, English, Russian, Spanish, Portuguese, Greek, Polish, Dutch, Czech, Croatian, Hungarian, and Slovenian; and even Korean, Chinese, and Japanese. In fact, sometimes his books or articles appear first in other languages, and only subsequently in German. Indeed, Italian has supplanted German as his language of everyday parlance. This is no wonder since, after the loss of Latin's preeminence even in ecclesiastical documents, Italian has now become the de facto official language of the Roman curia. The development of his language and style was aided by the circumstance that, from the beginning of his academic ministry, he intended to address a large audience as well as by the fact that he has always had an artistic vein as a consummate private musician and as an avid reader of literature. He never delighted in the esoteric or technical. After the purifying experience of World War I, Nazi rule, and World War II, many Germans sought simple, but authentic ways of expression in the arts, language, and in life. All of these factors contributed to the unassuming, but precisely for this reason credible and convincing, style of Benedict XVI that in turn endears him to numerous people of all cultures and walks of life.

Very much as in the case of the Church fathers and the bishops of early Christendom, his writings reflect a kerygmatic concern. While constantly struggling to achieve necessary distinctions and nuances, he insists the academy not be a solipsistic exercise according to the modern trend of "publish or perish," the expression of an unreflective dependence on the prevailing temper, or the obsequious adherence to a worldview sanctioned by a state or an academic community; rather, it serves the edification of the kingdom of God in the concrete here and now.

CHAPTER 6

Academic Teacher: Truth as Person

In 1952, at just twenty-five years of age, Ratzinger began teaching fundamental theology on the *Domberg* overlooking the old town of Freising, the
then seminary for priestly candidates for the archdiocese of Munich-Freising
and the place of his own seminary training. In his inaugural lecture he spoke
of truth as person; truth is encountered through charity. The theological *leitmotiv* is thus personal: in encountering Jesus as the Christ, the whole of life
receives its formative center. This Christocentric understanding of the priesthood elucidated by Ratzinger became the guiding and supporting motif for
numerous priests. He would deliver his lectures without notes, employing
signs, symbols, and metaphors to illustrate his thoughts, formulated in crystal
clear, reflective, and meditative language. Thus, he could inspire the students
and address "both [their] spirit and emotion."[1]

Only roughly half of his students in Bonn, and later in Münster, would
be actually enrolled in the theology program. The lecture halls he talked
in were usually filled to capacity. Refraining from employing a dramatic
manner or rhetorical skills, he convinced serious students by virtue of the
content and beauty of his lectures. He would prepare his talks with his sister
Maria as his listener. The moment she displayed pleasure, he knew he was
succeeding as an academic teacher. But his personality was also congenial to
the content conveyed: unpretentious, uncomplicated, generous, and always
willing to help. While in Münster, he would invite small groups of students
to his home.[2]

During the Second Vatican Council, he sent brief articles to Germany
detailing its progress. He then contributed to and edited a significant commentary on the documents of the Second Vatican Council.[3] In 1968 he
authored the best-selling *Introduction to Christianity*,[4] which influenced quite
a number of educated men and women to remain in the Church during the
tumultuous times between 1968 and 1980. During the *Katholikentag* (German
Catholic Diet) of 1966 in Bamberg, Ratzinger voiced critical words of caution. He warned against a naïve postconciliar triumphalism: "As long as the
Church is a pilgrim on earth, she has no reason to pride herself on her own
works. Such boasting could become more dangerous than a peacock feather
duster and a tiara [that is, pompous items of the papal court], which anyway

have caused us more to smile than to take pride in ourselves." He continues in the same speech: "A turning of the Church toward the world, which would entail turning away from the cross, cannot lead to the Church's renewal, but [only] to her demise. The purpose of the Church's turning toward the world cannot be to dispense with the scandal of the cross, but exclusively to render its nakedness accessible anew, by removing all secondary scandals [that is, sins committed by members of the Church], which have been interposed and have unfortunately oftentimes covered up the folly of the love of God with the folly of human self-love...."[5] It is erroneous to view the council as a democratic forum or the Church as essentially subject to the hidden laws of evolution.

Hans Küng (b. 1927), a Swiss religious thinker and former colleague of Ratzinger in Tübingen, portrays the unconfirmed image of Ratzinger being shouted down by students during the student revolt. Whether or not this single event occurred as Küng maintains, Ratzinger seems overall to have been quite popular among students during those heady times. During a podium discussion with professors Seckler, Küng, and Neumann, students demanded: "Ratzinger must speak! Ratzinger must speak!"[6]

A former student confirms his popularity:

> The lectures that I heard in Bonn from professors of neo-scholastic bent appeared arid and cold, a list of precise doctrinal definitions and that was it. When I listened in Tübingen to Ratzinger speaking about Jesus or of the Holy Spirit, it seemed at times that his words had the accent of prayer.[7]

Students of all walks of life would attend Ratzinger's lectures at the universities he taught. For instance, 850 copies of his lectures on the Eucharist were sold in one semester in Münster. At a conference at Münster University Ratzinger received ovations while Metz and Balthasar earned only respectful applause.[8] Beginning in Münster and continuing in Tübingen and Regensburg, he increasingly attracted students from all over the world.

While in Tübingen, holding one of two chairs reserved for dogmatic theology, he was scandalized by the subordination of religion in general to socialist utopian thinking. Romano Guardini's memorable expression *Unterscheidung des Christlichen* (distinguishing what is Christian) had alerted him early in life to possible threats to the Christian faith.[9] There, in this picturesque but restive town, he was reminded that Christ must remain at the center and the Church is the definitive place of his revelation and presence. The demonstrations of 1968—advocating a better and more just world—intended to achieve this without God. They became for Ratzinger "Manifestations of a brutal, cruel, tyrannical ideology.... Even Christians stopped talking about redemption through the cross, about the resurrection of Jesus Christ, and about our hope in eternal life. They, too, came to speak almost only of our society, of the better civilization that would be born. Utopia became the only dogma that inspired thought and action."[10]

Following his earlier, enthusiastic collaboration in the newly founded theological periodical *Concilium*, in 1972 he founded, along with Hans

Urs von Balthasar (1905–1988), Karl Lehmann, and others, the theological journal *Communio*.[11] Published in a multitude of editions in numerous languages to this day, this publication attempts to continue the legacy of the Second Vatican Council. While the periodical *Concilium* is also committed to the legacy of the Second Vatican Council—but emphasizing the Church as something akin to a parliament constantly in session, its counterpart *Communio* interprets the Vatican II Council and translates it into the underlying Eucharistic communion with Jesus Christ, which is the Church. It relates the doctrines of the Church to the saints and Church fathers and attempts to bring the Church's faith to bear in modern theology as an independent and central discipline. It is broadly inspired by the *Nouvelle Théologie* movement, also called Ressourcement,[12] which places emphasis on historical scholarship, a retrieval of the patristic spirit, and critiques neoscholasticism. It is associated with such notable French theologians as Henri de Lubac (1896–1991), Marie-Dominique Chenu (1895–1990), and Yves Congar (1904–1995). This means the periodical appreciates the Vatican II Council's novelty and optimistic mood as well as the continuity of salvation guaranteed by the abiding presence of the Holy Spirit in the Church. It therefore also consciously reflects on Church history and patristic scholarship. While welcoming new developments within the Church and theology, *Communio* emphasizes the even more important continuity of the constant self-identity of the Church enduring in time and space.

CHAPTER 7

Pastor to "Radical Christians": The Catholic Integrated Community

Ratzinger made a significant, but little known, acquaintance with the Catholic Integrated Community (*Katholische Integrierte Gemeinde*, abbreviated KIG), formally founded in1968 in Munich by the couple Herbert and Traudl Waldbrecher and headquartered in the Upper Bavarian town of Bad Tölz. The community draws its inspiration from the Second Vatican Council and attempts to live out the notion of "the people of God" in the visible forms of secular society and in the Catholic Church. More specifically, it was inspired by sections 18 and 19 of the *Decree on the Apostolate of the Laity* (*Apostolicam Actuositatem*).[1] In a world alienated from the gospel, it offers people a fresh way to God. It does not subscribe to a special or esoteric spirituality. Its intention is merely to contribute to calling together dispersed brothers and sisters as the people of God. The center of its life is belief in the presence and effectiveness of God in human history, the climax of which is found in the crucified and resurrected Lord Jesus.[2] The kibbutzim in Israel inspired one of its founders, Traudl Wallbrecher. Differing from a mere cult movement, she envisioned a community of shared life within the Catholic Church, where private property and personal responsibility are retained as preconditions for the free contributions of individuals to the whole of the Integrated Community. Soon after World War II, questions arose as to how such heinous crimes could be perpetrated within a state in which the majority of people were at least nominally baptized Christians. How could something like this occur in the Christian West?[3]

The group around Mrs. Wallbrecherpose the question: how could God have two brides, the *synagoge* (Judaism) and the *ecclesia* (Christian Church)? Is this split not at the root of strife? Need not Christianity be rooted in the Old Testament in order to be universal, that is, Catholic?

The Catholic Integrated Community comprises about 1,000 Catholics from all walks of life who attempt to live an authentic testimony to the faith of the early Christians, especially "the strength of faith of the early community."[4] A rose is used to symbolize the joint efforts of its members. The general public would not necessarily associate Ratzinger's name with this group.

Two major theologians have joined the community. Based on the Torah and the Prophets, Norbert Lohfink, SJ (Society of Jesus), professor of Old Testament studies at the Jesuit college of St. Georgen near Frankfurt am Main, demonstrated how the covenantal people of God (Israel) considered themselves "an alternative society" to their environment. His brother, the Tübingen New Testament scholar Gerhard Lohfink, distilled what is the true mark of a Christian community: the exercise of reciprocal charity. His exegetical findings led him to discover in the Church "a society of contrast" that thereby becomes "light to the world" and "salt of the earth."[5] If it was the mission of Jesus, as a Jew, to gather the people of Israel and reorient them to the will of God, then a Bible-based reform of the Church would likewise need to gather together the people of God.

To this end, the Integrated Community lives independently from ecclesial institutions as it does not accept Church taxes, which is a remarkable and telling exception in Germany. Its members strive for a *vita communis*—a communal life—and develop initiatives in the areas of the arts and craftsmanship, economics, medicine, and pedagogy. All contribute to building the discipleship of Christ and the Church as individuals, priests, religious, married couples, and families.

Revealingly, the prominent agnostic and opponent to Christianity, Gerhard Szczesny (1918–2002), encountered the Integrated Community in the early 1970s, just prior to authoring *The Misery of Christianity or a Plea for a Humanism without God*.[6] He later admitted that in this group he encountered, for the first time, people who lived their faith uninhibited by pretentions. Tellingly, he remarked: "I know how coffee tastes in church houses; in your case it tastes differently."

Amid some public controversy over whether this new group was Catholic or merely a sect, the then Professor Ratzinger visited the group in 1976. He seems to have found Christianity there as a form of life. He encountered a community of believers willing to live the gospel not merely in comfortable circumstances, as for instance in a club, but who were allowing Jesus Christ and the gospel to touch the depths of their lives and deaths. Indeed, coming from the arid climate of academia, Ratzinger the theologian seems to have encountered in the Integrated Community an orthopraxis congenial to his orthodoxy. The abstract theory of the conciliar document *Dei Verbum* (*DV*)—stating that revelation is always historical and thus contextual—received affirmation in this group. In the 1969 issue of its periodical *HEUTE in Kirche und Welt* (*TODAY in the Church and the World*), the group bemoaned the separation between academic theology and lived faith. In the isolation of academia, Christianity is given a historical context, but it fails to be salt of the earth and bread for the people, as it has become cerebral.[7] This fateful bifurcation is traced back to the foundation of universities in the Middle Ages. Ratzinger strives to overcome it by a recovery of the patristic genius.

Repeatedly, Ratzinger emphasized that early Christianity drew its primordial strength from transforming Greek philosophy and not from accommodating the then existing pagan religions. Thus, Christianity was able to create a singular synthesis of reason, faith, and life. Frequently, he called upon his fellow scholars to look up from their desks and to integrate the faith of nonacademically trained Christians. Inspired by Bonaventure, Ratzinger refers positively to the "*simplex et idiota*" (that is, "the simple of heart," and oftentimes, "the unschooled"). In his habilitation, Ratzinger describes the terminal point of earthly existence thus: "It is only in the Church of the final age that St. Francis' manner of life will triumph. As a *simplex et idiota*, Francis knew more about God than all the learned men of his time, because he loved him more."[8] His discovery in 1955 of a Bonaventurian anti-intellectualism would become a recurring theme in Ratzinger's oeuvre. He could not but interpret the bursting forth of a revolutionized academia in 1968 as the hypotrophy of barren intellectualism. Much earlier, thinkers such as Paul Natrop, Rudolf Eucken, Ernst Troeltsch, and Max Scheler had warned of an intellectualism carried too far. According to Ratzinger, positivism and materialism can be overcome by rediscovering a Christian wholesomeness where interiority is the constitutive inner core. The disorders found in the world—such as pollution, the depletion of natural resources, desertification, and climate change—are reflections of an interior disorder.[9] As he stressed in his first homily as pope, Christ must be the center of all things. He therefore argues in his habilitation for the "*Ende der Vernunfttheologie*" ("end of the [purely academic] theology of reason"). Precisely due to this, the second reader of his habilitation, the renowned theologian Michael Schmaus, rejected it in its original version, which he perceived as at times arguing against Aristotle and St. Thomas.

In his lecture at the Pontifical Biblical Commission in 2003, Ratzinger focused attention on Catholic theologians at the beginning of the twentieth century who favored intellectualism in order to overcome their sense of inferiority vis-à-vis Protestant scholarship. In writings such as Adolf von Harnack's classic *What Is Christianity?* (1900),[10] the superiority of the Protestant mind seemed to be manifested beyond any doubt. In his lecture, Ratzinger countered that no such thing as pure scientific objectivity exists. The proper perspective regarding scripture and history may only be a Christocentric one. The Lord's *Parousia* (the second coming of the Lord) is the decisive interpretation for both the Bible and history. In this lecture, Ratzinger argued by way of a Christological reduction of the creed: (1) the birth of Jesus from Mary, (2) the actual institution of the Eucharist through Jesus, and (3) his bodily Resurrection from the dead. This last point includes the empty tomb. These indispensable essentials of the Christian faith are distilled from the gospel narratives and are not based on historic conjectures or abstract intellectual deductions. If the historical-critical method were ascribed sole authority in this matter, then one would have a case of the self-overestimation of a method. The Catholic Integrated Community is in Ratzinger's estimation a helpful corrective to an overly intellectualized Christianity. Members of the Integrated Community frequently visited Cardinal Ratzinger in Rome. In return, Ratzinger often paid a visit to the community's house in Colle Romito during his years in Rome as prefect of the Congregation for the Doctrine of the Faith.

This community is also keenly interested in Christian-Jewish dialogue. Ratzinger visited the Holy Land with this group and while there, he engaged in discussions with numerous Jews. Encouraged by Ratzinger, this group had their foundation in Villa Cavaletti, a former Jesuit house located near Grottaferrata and tellingly named "The Academy for the Theology of the People of God," elevated to the status of a college. Perhaps by chance or by providence, the college is situated not too far from the papal summer residence in Castel Gandolfo. Cardinal Ratzinger celebrated the Eucharist in commemoration of the community's fiftieth anniversary of its founding in 1999 at the cathedral in nearby Frascati.[11] According to one of its leading thinkers, Father Ludwig Weimer, this college should institutionalize a constant renewal of the Church from her self-inflicted wounds, and as he maintains, "Christians are critics of Christianity for the sake of preserving the gospel." Just like Christianity as a whole, theology ought to preach God rather than its own wisdom. The authors of scripture were, according to Pseudo-Dionysius (Dionysius the Pseudo-Areopagite, a fifth-century theologian), the first theologians. According to Weimer, the college should be a place where humility and modesty are acquired and where theologians are formed to be prayerful and to live from the strength gained through meditation. The experience of the total Church as community should be foundational for the theological discourse at this college, rather than a theology solely engaged in the academic method of argument and counterargument.

Such a disposition empowers the people of God to free themselves from the preconceived notions society invariably imposes on the individual. Freedom thus acquired enables the individual to consciously celebrate the Eucharist as *Catholica*, that is, as all peoples of the human race unified as the "community of the sacramental body of Christ." While Jews do not belong to this community, Ratzinger reiterates there would be no Church without the Jews.[12] This touches the college's second mission: the unity of the Old and New Testaments; or, as its members put it, "re-rooting Christianity in its Jewish identity." In this manner, faith should again become a world-forming reality. Aesthetics plays a significant role, as "truth is beauty." Each human community is called to take on a form commensurate with the dignity of the human person and God's plan.

With this goal in mind, beginning in the winter semester of 2008–2009, a chair at Rome's Lateran University was dedicated to "The Theology of the People of God."[13] It is part of The Pontifical Pastoral Institute *Redemptor Hominis*. Father Ludwig Weimer is the chairperson. He has belonged to the Integrated Community since 1968 and received his terminal degree from Joseph Ratzinger in 1979.

At first Church authorities did not look favorably upon the Catholic Integrated Community. There was a period of misunderstanding until Cardinal Julius Döpfner (1913–1976), then archbishop of Munich, declared the community was not a sect but "a free group within the Church."[14] For both Ratzinger and the Integrated Community, apart from examining structural questions, the reform of the Church hinges on reconsidering the essence of its being: Jesus Christ. Strategies are secondary since the actual subject of all activity is God. In 1982, Gerhard Lohfink wrote the bestseller *Does God Need the Church?*[15] The author demonstrates that in scripture the gathering of the people of God occurred without human planning. The Church also "occurs" if people experience a call beyond human design and accept it: "You are my people."

Attempting to realize *agape* (lived Christian charity)on a broader scale, the Integrated Community runs a parish in Mikese, Tanzania, with a kindergarten and school that also accepts Muslim children. In Dar-es-Salaam, Tanzania, it operates a butchery, a bakery, a carpenter's shop, and even a metalworking shop. In addition, in Münster, Germany, it operates a boarding school and several additional schools near Munich. The underlying program is simple and clear: "The Christian message of fraternity realizes its obligation for the whole especially through mission, agape and suffering."[16] The group also runs a publishing house called Verlag Urfeld, which has published some of Cardinal Ratzinger's texts.

A central tenet of this community is its belief that the Church fulfills her task in the world only if she is a community in contrast to the world—for the sake of the world; if she is "salt for the world" and does not conform to the world. This group consciously seeks to live like the early Christians. It is likely this fraternal community reminded Ratzinger of a book he read as a seminarian in Freising, de Lubac's epochal *Catholicism*. Ratzinger may have discovered his own deeply personal theological method translated into reality when he encountered the communitarian way of life of this group. Morality invariably suffers shipwreck when it is treated merely intellectually. Faced with the modern individualization of all aspects of life, the Integrated Community "integrates" these aspects into a holistic whole.[17] The academy, and now college, that took up residence in the Villa Cavalletti serves to promote such an understanding of the people of God, that is, as a small, free community serving the whole of the Church. The aim of the college is that the laypeople and priests studying there will be kept from succumbing to inertia, the temptations of structures, and the fateful features of an institution. This also contributes to overcoming the crisis of conventional, university-based theology. A prayerful and humble theology is encouraged. Only such a perspective drawn from the living Lord, Jesus Christ, does justice to the meaning of the term "People of God." The community members attempt to live the gospel in a secularized society so that even people not connected with them gain access to the faith of the Church.

A central characteristic of the Catholic Integrated Community, as previously mentioned, is its relationship to Israel. The concept of the "People of God" defines the Church, composed of members from all peoples. The Church is the community constituted by the sacramental body of Christ. This community comes about by celebrating the Eucharist. Jews are not included in this social reality but, crucially, without the people of Yahweh there would be no Church. Reflecting upon this fact, as this group points out, is necessary so that one is mindful of one's heritage. At the suggestion and through the organization of the Catholic Integrated Community, Cardinal Ratzinger gave a paper in 1994 at a Jewish-Catholic conference in Jerusalem on the image of Israel contained in the *Catechism of the Catholic Church*.

PART II

Jesus Christ: God's Self-Disclosure

CHAPTER 8

The Beginnings of His Theology

In a congratulatory note on the occasion of the opening of the Academy of Villa Cavaletti on October 23, 2003, Ratzinger pondered the meaning of theology. He mentioned that the unknown fifth-century theologian Dionysius the Pseudo-Areopagite (Pseudo-Dionysius) had bequeathed to Western thought the notion that the primary subject of theology is God. Not only is he the object, but he is also the true agent of theology. With great intensity did Bonaventure and Thomas Aquinas struggle with this in the thirteenth century. For Pseudo-Dionysius, the point of departure for his reflections had been the fact that a human being who had written a part of scripture had opened his mind and heart to God. Therefore, the author of scripture does not speak from his own viewpoint but from God's perspective. Through a human being God has entered history as a speaking subject! Hence, the divine word exists in human words. As a consequence, one can state that one becomes a theologian to the degree in which one nears the sacred authors in their relationship with God and in the manner in which human and divine words collaborate. For Ratzinger, the result of this reflection is that theology must first and foremost be listening, believing, and praying; it must be listening to God. In the course of his message, he reminded the audience of Hans Urs von Balthasar's distinction between a kneeling and a sitting theology. The Academy of Plato did not believe it could approximate truth without venerating the muses in a cultic fashion. How much more, he asks, must theology be nourished from the theologian's conversation with the living God, receiving in the liturgy the tangible reality of God? God taught humankind to pray the "Our Father." Human beings become wholesome when they acknowledge they are his children and he is their Father. Thus, human beings and theologians are freed from reducing God to the interiority of human subjectivity.[1]

Dissertations and postdoctoral habilitations, the latter serving as the qualifying step for becoming a professor in Central Europe, serve a specific purpose within the course of academic studies. While the dissertation is usually dedicated to a rather narrow area—often presenting a novel discovery for scholarly debate—the habilitation analyzes a broad issue. Both demonstrate the author as an independent and even original academic scholar. While

often demarcating a particular viewpoint—by virtue of their topics and execution—they may also address a specific state of affairs in a particular discipline. The latter is undoubtedly the case with the dissertation and habilitation
Ratzinger submitted to Munich's much respected Ludwig-Maximilians-
Universität (founded in 1471).

At that time, it was customary in the theology department of Munich
University to challenge students to anonymously submit a thesis within nine
months on a topic chosen by a member of the faculty. That year it was Söhngen's
turn. He assigned the topic, "The People and House of God in Augustine's
Doctrine of the Church." Intrigued by the encyclical *Mystici Corporis Christi*
(1943), he wanted to see how Augustine differentiated between Christ and
his physical body vis-à-vis the Church, while remaining her head.

Ratzinger was urged by Söhngen to join the competition. Thus, Ratzinger
wrote his doctoral dissertation on this topic—and carried away the coveted
prize—*summa cum laude*![2] He limited his investigation to Augustine's early
writings. In a way this topic was timely in Germany after the ravages of World
War II. The German Protestant and Prussian Hermann Reuter had authored
a profound collection of Augustinian studies at the height of the Second
Reich, that is, the Wilhelmine Empire (1871–1918).[3] On the other end of
the geographic and confessional spectrum, the Bavarian Catholic theologian
Fritz Hofmann penned, in the year of Hitler's ascendance to power, a seminal book on Augustine's ecclesiology.[4] Both are recognized by Ratzinger
in his introduction as the central inspirations for his own study. The concept of *Volk*, or people, had taken on a peculiar flavor in the Third Reich.
Oddly, Erich Przywara's noteworthy synthesis of Augustinian thought goes
unmentioned.[5]

No doubt this topic was a *Sternstunde* (a unique, great opportunity) for
Ratzinger, and Söhngen was his "switchman" for a lifelong intellectual
ministry. Henceforth, he followed a path influenced by Augustine, characterized by a love for the Church and a predilection for disseminating the
Church's teaching. The parallels are quite striking. Both Augustine and
Ratzinger learned easily and possessed acute minds.[6] Both had a calling
to enter into dialogue and intellectual discussion with the contemporary
culture. Augustine passionately defended his conversion to Christianity.
For Ratzinger, the Christian faith includes rationality and intelligibility,
while Augustine counsels a critical mind not to hold the intellect in low
esteem when reflecting on the Blessed Trinity, "*intellectum vero valde ama*"
(greatly love the intellect).[7] Each of them commands a remarkable elo-
quence. Augustine was a professor of grammar and rhetoric. He expected
an accomplished orator to be keen on teaching truth (*docere*), to motivate to
the good (*movere*), and finally to delight in well-crafted sentences (*delectare*).[8]
While Augustine does dwell much on grace, his actual platform and theological culmination is the Church. The starting points of his ecclesiology are
the concept of *fides* (faith), which aids in his understanding of the "people
of God," and his concept of *amor* (love), which aids in his understanding
of "the house of God." While the Church consists of saints and sinners,
charity is the unifying bond of the Blessed Trinity and the Church. As
Nichols observes, "Augustine's 'charity' is, in the ecclesiological context,

what Ratzinger helpfully terms 'objective charity.' It does not betoken a subjective attitude, but rather belonging to the Church, and more specifically to that Church which itself lives in charity, that is, 'in Eucharistic love-relationship with [the Christians in] the whole world.'[9] This establishes the congeniality between Augustine and de Lubac's *Catholicism*.

This ecclesiological investigation brings together several significant areas: the Old and New Testaments and the relationship of Christianity to a pagan state. To Ratzinger's mind, Augustinian ecclesiality, or *Kirchlichkeit*, has its own characteristics and is marked off from both the Christian fourth-century donatist sect (a North African movement that considered sacraments administered by lapsed priests and bishops as invalid) and the pagan Roman culture still surrounding Christians. Ratzinger begins his inquiry with the question of whether the Augustine of the *Confessions* had embraced a concrete church or simply a philosophical outlook. Ratzinger admits that for Augustine, Christianity was at first glance a surrogate form of philosophy, which, however, offered him access to the Christian religion.[10] In Augustine's mind, Christianity was exclusive in the sense of offering a truth and lifestyle befitting the sophisticated and cultured person of his age as a *via regia* (in German, *Königsweg*, meaning "a regal way"), and yet it also spoke powerfully to the common man and woman as *salus populi* (salvation of the people). It was a synthesis of the elite and universal. Ratzinger gleans all of this from the *Confessions*. There exist brief moments in human life when wisdom and truth become tangible realities in the form of a vision. Aside from such grace-filled moments, a human must be perpetually reminded (cf. *memoria*) of divine wisdom because he or she suffers from *infirmitas*. Both scripture and the Church are reliable guides, and they are in fact the sole cures for such a postlapsarian forgetfulness. In the visible church, God offers us invisible nourishment.[11] The surety of having found truth rests on discovering the Church and living in it as the *people of God* in the *house of God* (the later term does not occur in Augustine's early writings). Passing through the triad of having faith, accepting authority, and practicing humility (*credere, auctoritas,* and *humilitas*), human beings shed childlike behavior and become adults in the Church as they approach divine wisdom and share in it. Augustine's mother, Monica, had sacrificed immeasurably so that Augustine might find the faith. For Augustine, the Church becomes the supernatural mother to Christians. Ratzinger also notes that Monica was an important dialogue partner for Augustine. Analogously, to Augustine's mind the Church becomes the forming and informing agent for the individual Christian.[12] In *De Magistro* Augustine stresses that in order for this reality to take hold of one, an interior life must be cultivated.[13]

Ratzinger cautions the reader not to dismiss Augustine's Platonic understanding of the world as the reflection of a more valuable reality beyond itself. He does acknowledge a lack of appreciation on the part of the young Augustine for the intimate involvement of God with and in the world. Ratzinger also acknowledges the fruitful tension in Augustine between *sarx* and *pneuma*, between the flesh and the spirit, as described by St. Paul (Rom 8:54; Gal 5:16). Not appreciating this Pauline tension of the world and spirit not only leads to a naïve view of life but also to an undervaluation of the birth of God in human form. At this time of his faith history, he did not yet appreciate fully the mystery of Christ's Incarnation. Only later would Augustine become more nuanced and speak of worldly life *secundum Deum*, that is, in keeping with divine precepts. The radical neo-Platonic separation of the world and God is overcome or fails to be overcome by accepting or rejecting the divine will and the joy of Bethlehem.

However primary the philosophical incentive may have been, Augustine was "torn from philosophical contemplation and silent meditation in the circle of friends"[14] and thrust into the already existing ecclesial pattern of the North African Church, which had been formed by Optatus of Milevis and Cyprian of Carthage and was ultimately traceable to Tertullian. His was not only an intensely private decision, but one with public and social ramifications: "It is the whole man, body and soul, who puts on Christ."[15] Via the Tertullian categories of "discipline" and "sacraments," as well as the "church" as image of God, the connection between Christ, the individual believer, and the Church was firmly established in North Africa, particularly by virtue of receiving the Eucharist. Jesus Christ is communicated to Christians, who in turn communicate him to the world. The Church as *disciplina* in Tertullian's understanding is just one logical step away from Augustine's ecclesiological understanding of the Church as *populus Dei* (the people of God). Challenged by Tertullian's pneumatic ecclesiology dissolving the visible church, Augustine would go so far as to affirm the *sacramenta* even if the *disciplina* fails.[16] Therefore, Ratzinger repeatedly stressed the dimension of communion, in order to overcome the Tertullian split between the institutional and spiritual Church.

In the Augustinian concepts of "house of God" and "people of God," Ratzinger apprehended the continuation of Cyprian of Carthage's terms *ordo, mater ecclesia,* and *fraternitas Christianorum* (order, mother Church, and the fraternity of Christians). For all North African theologians, these terms expressed the reality of Christ's Eucharistic presence in his, the Redeemer's, Church. This would resurface later in Ratzinger's theology as the category of Christian brotherhood.

In the mature Augustine, sharpened by struggles with the donatists, the Christological foundations of his ecclesiology become more apparent. Simultaneously, Augustine discovered the universality (*catholica*) of the Church and Christ by reading Luke:

"These are my words which I spoke to you, while I was still with you, that everything written about me in the law of Moses and the prophets and the psalms must be fulfilled." Then he opened their minds to understand the scriptures and said to them "Thus it is written, that Christ should suffer and on the third day rise from the dead, and that repentance and forgiveness of sins should be preached in his name to all nations, beginning from Jerusalem."[17]

The multitudes of nations are brought together by Jesus Christ as the one Abrahamic people in an inner unity. In Augustine's judgment, the donatists were bound to lose this catholicity because they no longer practiced charity, which is Christ's entire frame of mind. In the subsequent chapter, Ratzinger emphasizes that this charity is circumscribed as objective by predicating the *ecclesia* as *catholica*.[18] Only to the degree that the Church practices universal charity does she remain the faithful bride of Christ. Discerning who is a true member of the holy Church, within the larger Catholic Church, is the Lord's task alone.[19]

As Nichols remarks, "It is a change of emphasis—no more, but certainly no less—from the truth of God to the love of God. *Caritas* now appears as the 'power of God's inner unity of essence, become person in the Holy Spirit.' This unity is mirrored in that of the Church where through the unifying force of love, which the Holy Spirit, *vinculum amoris* (bond of love), personally is, the many believers are ushered into the unity of the body of Christ."[20] Here one also senses an affinity between Ratzinger and Henri de Lubac. Both subscribe to a consistently held Eucharistic ecclesiology with the presentic Christ in the center. Christ's charity abides in a mysterious way in his Church. One can only abide in the Church if one lives Christ's charity; however, finitely imperfect human charity will always remain. As with Augustine, for Ratzinger ecclesiology is essentially Christology.

Ratzinger shares the Augustinian emphasis on faith as the hermeneutical a priori: *Credo ut intelligam* (I believe so that I may understand). In a qualified sense, Ratzinger considers himself a Platonist: "A kind of memory, of recollection of God is, as it were, etched in man, though it needs to be awakened."[21] Precisely because Augustine is a counterweight to the towering Thomas Aquinas, Ratzinger opted to study the African Church father. The epistemology of Augustine seemed to him far more profound, and—more importantly—a closer approximation of human existence. The *ratio naturalis* (natural reason) is always personal and is never *ratio pura* (pure reason)— which does not in fact exist—but rather *ratio purificata* (purified reason). Only the individual believer can be the bearer of a *cor purum* (pure heart).[22]

Parallel to writing his thesis, Ratzinger read de Lubac's magisterial *Corpus Mysticum* (completed in 1939 and published in 1944) on the nature of the Church, which was yet another profound engagement with the writings of the Church fathers of the East and West. As Hemming has correctly observed: "It was de Lubac's invigorating influence that fed Benedict's emerging theological mind, and he won the prize."[23] Ratzinger discovers that God for Augustine does not communicate himself via a secretive *gnosis* (insight) in an "individualistic *thiasos*" (Bacchanal feast), indifferent to the private lives of the other participants in the cult. The concepts "People of God" and "mystical body of Christ" form one unit.[24] The one Holy Spirit affects such unity by way of realizing charity in both. As *ecclesia contemplativa*, as contemplative Church, she becomes ever again conscious of her identity.

In his study, de Lubac retraced the correlation of the concept of the Eucharist with that of the Church (this is evident in his work *Catholicism*).[25] He demonstrated that the term *soma mystikon* (mystical body) first occurred with Hesychius (sometime after 451 AD) and entered Western Christendom in the ninth century (translated as *corpus mysticum* by Ratramnus, Paschasius Radbertus, and Hrabanus Maurus). At that time, the term referred to the Eucharistic body and not to the Church. In contrast, Augustine had referred to the Church as the *Corpus Christi verum* (the true body of Christ). In reaction to Berengar of Tours' (c. 999–1088) symbolistic interpretation of the Eucharist, the Lord's real presence came to be vigorously emphasized. In the twelfth century, a significant change occurred: *Corpus Christi mysticum* (the mystical body of Christ) now referred to the Church, while *Corpus Christi verum* (the true body of Christ) referred to the Eucharist. This is evident for the first time around 1170 with Magister Simon's *Tractatus de sacramentis*. The Church as mystery then gradually vanished from the awareness of the faithful. The recovery of the intrinsic connection between the Eucharist and the Church, following 1 Corinthians 10:16—"The cup of blessing which we bless, is it not a participation in the blood of Christ?"—is, in de Lubac's estimation, *the* great challenge for contemporary theology. His celebrated axiom is: "The Church makes the Eucharist and the Eucharist makes the Church." In the celebration of the Eucharist, the Church receives herself anew as *corpus Christi*; thus, through the power of the Holy Spirit, the Church is Christ's real presence in the world.[26] In this seminal study, along with his work *Méditation sur l'Église* (1953), de Lubac prepared central statements on the Church that the Second Vatican Council would incorporate in chapters two through four of *Lumen Gentium* (*LG*). These included a Christological definition of the Church contextualized within a comprehensive Trinitarian understanding of herself as "people of God," "body of Christ," and "temple of the Holy Spirit." "[T]he Church, in Christ, is a kind of sacrament, a sign and instrument, that is, of communion with God and of unity among all men" (*LG* 1). This retrieval of the Church's essential nature opened the gates for a heretofore unimaginable ecumenical dialogue.[27]

A mere four years after completing his doctoral dissertation, Ratzinger submitted his habilitation, *Die Geschichtstheologie des Heiligen Bonaventura* (*On the Theology of History of St. Bonaventure*).[28] The selection of these two theologians (Augustine and Bonaventure) and topics for his terminal papers shows the author's—and his theses director's—concern. One has to consider the intellectual context in which they were written. The transitional intellectual situation of the time explains the choice of topics. Though new approaches existed, the academia was still characterized by neoscholasticism. While producing significant theologians of a remarkably high caliber, the neoscholastic trend was tending toward ossifying the Christian faith into a system of timeless, seemingly eternally valid, abstract truths captured in precise sentences. In the process, the historic, existential, and personal-interior dimensions of faith were being neglected. The main inspiration was drawn from the great Dominican theologian Thomas Aquinas, unfortunately often interpreting his magnificent synthesis apart from its thirteenth-century context and without Thomas's own personal, inner dynamism.

Famously, the second reader of Ratzinger's habilitation, Michael Schmaus, judged it defective and containing a "dangerous modernism" that could lead to a "subjectivization of the concept of salvation."[29] Later, in order to prevent Ratzinger and others from becoming *periti* (theological advisors) during the Second Vatican Council, Schmaus addressed them disparagingly as "*Twen-Theologen*"[30] ("theologians in their twenties"). But it was precisely this "novel" understanding of revelation that would prove revolutionary at the beginning of the Second Vatican Council and set the tenor for the whole council. Importantly, against an intellectualist reading, Ratzinger demonstrated that for Bonaventure revelation is far wider and richer than merely that which the human intellect can comprehend or that which is contained in scripture. Revelation is historical and contextual: it *is* Jesus Christ. Ratzinger shortened his thesis in only two weeks.

Similar to Romano Guardini, Ratzinger also discovered in Augustine and Bonaventure two original theologians quite unlike the more cerebral, Aristotelian Thomas Aquinas and later formalistic, neoscholastic thinkers. Closer examination reveals that in the cases of both doctors of the Church—Augustine and Bonaventure—the gravitational center is not dogmatic systematization for the sake of university lectures, but the historicity of faith and its mystical interiorization by a concrete human being. Both Augustine and Bonaventure represent a decided salvation-historic perspective, which has its roots in the biblical narratives of the Old and New Testaments. Theological and religious renewal occurs by rediscovering and reawakening the wellsprings of faith.

In his dissertation, Ratzinger examined the ways in which Augustine's definition of the Church developed in critical contrast to both the pagan understanding of cult and the Old Testament circumscription of the Jewish faithful as *Qahal Jahwe* (God's holy assembly). To Augustine's mind, "house of God" (*Domus Dei*) no longer signified the Jewish temple as a liturgical space but rather the living assembly of Christians. The presence of God is thus transferred from external structures to the interiority of the faith of individual believers. Meditation on the Church as "house of God" led Augustine to develop a theology of the living "people of God." The new temple in which God resides is "the people of God" as the body of Jesus Christ. The Church, therefore, is the community of loving believers, united under the one head, Jesus Christ, on a pilgrimage to the one and eternal triune God. The concrete liturgical assembly is—like the total visible church—only a real-symbolic anticipation of the yet to be revealed full Church.

Analogously to the people of a political state developing and expressing its sense of unity in secular law, the believing people of God discover and dynamically experience their constituting center in the celebrated and lived sacraments. The interpretation of the Church as "the body of Christ" has its life source in the sacraments. The people of God acquire and actuate their unity and communion in the liturgical Eucharistic community. All those receiving the body of Christ become members of the one living body of Christ. The ancient, pagan, and Old Testament notions of house and the people of God are transposed by Augustine by virtue of the new sacrament of the Eucharist, defining the Church as *Corpus Christi*.

In the process of his survey, Ratzinger examined the proper understanding of the term "catholicity" as a predication for this new people of God. Augustine highlights Pentecost as the foundational, primordial, Church-forming event. The Holy Spirit granted the apostles the ability to overcome language barriers among the peoples. According to Ratzinger's interpretation of Augustine, the true and inner cause of this marvelous event is that, when preaching, the apostles are sustained by the gifts of charity and peace,

which are not of their own making. Ratzinger was thus able to uncover in
the Augustinian terms *pax* (peace) and *caritas* (charity) the deeper foundations
for the Church's catholicity.

Unwittingly, in his interpretation of Augustine in 1951 Ratzinger anticipated central elements of the Second Vatican Council's ecclesiology. The
Church is the historic "people of God" on a pilgrimage to eternal salvation
and possesses within itself a sacramental character. At the Vatican II Council,
Ratzinger would thus serve as one of the decisive *periti*.

In his habilitation *On the Theology of History of St. Bonaventure*, the salvation-
historic dimension of faith becomes the all–determining perspective.
Particularly due to the provocative thesis of the Calabrian Abbot Joachim
of Fiore (d. 1202), the relationship between history and Christianity became
virulent. Joachim applied the teaching on the Blessed Trinity to history. He
therefore distinguished an age of the Father, of the Son, and of the Holy
Spirit, respectively. According to him, within the immanence of this world,
they relieve one another successively. In the Franciscan community, a tendency existed to apply the age of the Spirit to that of the order, as the concrete
realization of immanent history's last phase. To counter this rather strong
movement in his order, Bonaventure attempted in his late work *Collationes
in Hexaëmeron* (*Collations on the Six Days*), a synthesis between Joachim's
historic-symbolic vision and scholasticism's abstract thought. Via contemplation in the microcosm of the soul, which mirrors the Blessed Trinity, humans
discover the sevenfold condition of creatures: wisdom, goodness, origin,
magnitude, multitude, beauty, plenitude, and operation. Focused on God,
"The wholly flaming fire…will bear them aloft to God with fullest unction
and burning affection."[31] The ideal condition for Christ to find Christians
on the day of last judgment is the *ecclesia contemplativa* (the Church meditating
on Jesus Christ). Thus, Christ should be at the heart of all human undertak-
ings and of all academic disciplines, always directed toward the *eschaton* (end
times).

In this regard, Bonaventure discovered a new theory of biblical hermeneutics. In contrast to the theory of God as immutable and ever static, as
was characteristic of numerous late ancient Byzantine Church fathers and
medieval scholastics, Bonaventure unearthed the historic dimension of biblical exegesis. Meditating on scripture is dynamic, as it refers prophetically
to the future. This engagement is indispensable in order to apprehend the
past as a part of salvation history. If one attempts to unlock the future with
the past, the whole of history unfolds as an uninterrupted trajectory full of
meaning. Hope for future renewal is viable as memory of a salvific past. The
supernatural virtue of *spes* (hope) cannot simply be the product of a philosophical reflection. It must be the lived memory of the saving works God
had wrought in times past in Jesus Christ. While revelation and scripture are
closed, their significance is constantly unfolding further. This process will
only come to an end on the Day of Judgment. Biblical meditation is not only
the exegesis of history but also the prophecy of coming salvation.

In Bonaventure, salvation history and metaphysics are intertwined. In critical contradistinction to Joachim, as Ratzinger discovered, Bonaventure saw
history not as a succession of three different persons of the Blessed Trinity but

strictly and exclusively as one Christocentric event. Scripture is complete as text and nevertheless its relevance to history is incomplete if it is not grasped from the perspective of *Parousia*,the second coming of the Lord. Not scripture by itself is revelation, but its spiritual meaning. For Bonaventure scripture and revelation produce the *visio intellectualis* (spirit-filled vision) of the human *mens* (mind), illuminated by God. Christ's communication in history is not superseded by that of the Holy Spirit. Bonaventure, therefore, does not identify the final days with the tangible institution of the Church or a particular terrestrial order. Eschatological existence in the here and now can only exist in grace breaking through to the individual until, by God's grace, the hour arrives that will transform everything into a different and final state. Ratzinger divined Bonaventure as striving to make the ecclesial and spiritual structures of this world conducive to one day realizing this final state. For the time between Jesus' Ascension to heaven and the consummation of history, Bonaventure consciously established a salvific time of "inner-historical transformation of the church."[32] Within *tempus*, the world has moved from synagogue to *ecclesia*. For Bonaventure, the stigmatized St. Francis (1181–1226) became the exemplar of a Christian awaiting the *visio beatifica* (beatific vision). Is Ratzinger not repeating Bonaventure's praise of St. Francis when writing the following in 2000 to a gathering of Communione e Liberazione (Communion and Liberation) in Rimini, Italy?

> True knowledge is being struck by the arrow of beauty that wounds man, moved by reality how it is Christ himself who is present and in an ineffable way disposes and forms the souls of men. Being struck and over(whelmed) through the beauty of Christ is a more real, more profound knowledge than mere rational deduction. Of course we must not underrate the importance of theological thought; it remains absolutely necessary. But to move from here to disdain or reject the impact produced by the response of the heart in the encounter with beauty as a true form of knowledge would impoverish us and dry up our faith and our theology. We must rediscover this form of knowledge; it is a pressing need of our time.[33]

Not experiencing beauty any longer in the technical-scientific age, people become unable to behold Jesus Christ and therefore become merely pragmatic in their outlook. They apply technical approaches to overcome issues requiring a spiritual vision. Reason on its own cannot provide integrity to the human person.

Fortified by St. Francis's experience on Monte Alverno when he received the stigmata, the Franciscans are a community of contemplatives peacefully awaiting the *Parousia* of Christ. Yet, Ratzinger is careful to point out that for Bonaventure this group of spiritual Franciscans is not identical with the Franciscan order. The historic force is not an inexorable axiom or an abstract principle but a person. The historic process of Christ impelling the world to its final consummation is not the accomplishment of Dominicans or Franciscans but rather of the Holy Spirit who guides humankind to comprehending "the fullness of the truth of Jesus Christ." Contemplation is the only fitting human mode of preparing oneself for the *Parousia*.[34] The God-man Jesus Christ is history's meaning and humankind's goal, who will be met by a contemplative church in history's final stage.

According to Ratzinger: "Bonaventure sees the entire phenomenon of scholasticism and of scientific thought in a new and different way. He does not cease to recognize its great value for the present time; he himself does not cease pursuing it and loving it; he does not give up his concern for its correctness. But at the same time, he sees that it is not final in and of itself. One day the form of life of St. Francis"—beholding, contemplating, and stigmatized like Christ—"will become the universal form of the Church—the *simplex et idiota* [simple of heart] will triumph over the greatest scholars, and the Church of the final age will breathe the spirit of his spirit."[35]

This is the Christological ground for Ratzinger's *ceterum censeo* (by the way, as I say: recurring theme), taking up the cudgels repeatedly on behalf of the poor in the church. Very much like Ferdinand van Steenberghen (1904–1993), whose writings Ratzinger consulted when penning his thesis, Ratzinger apprehended in this position, not an opposition to Thomas, but a neo-Platonic form of Aristotelianism. Certainly mindful of Michael Schmaus's (his second reader's) position in this regard, Ratzinger devoted the final fifteenth chapter of his work to the much contested issue of Aristotelianism. Bonaventure rejects Aristotle's understanding of the world's eternity, as surely any Christian would. In Ratzinger's judgment, Bonaventure is neither anti-Aristotelian nor "Augustinian."[36] It should be noted that he has expressed sympathy for Thomas quite frequently, both in his habilitation and later on.[37] Both St. Thomas at the end of his life and St. Francis would agree that attaining poverty of spirit and holiness by way of contemplation and charity are superior to theology and scientific knowledge. In general, Nichols summarizes Bonaventure's and Ratzinger's understanding of history as constant *Heilsgeschichte* (salvation history) in the following words:

> In reality...time is always saving time. History is a movement of *egressus* from God, and *regressus* to him through Jesus Christ who is the "centre that both divides and unites." Through Bonaventure's work, Ratzinger here encountered, and appropriated, the Christocentricity which was being discovered anew by Catholic dogmaticians in the 1950s. Indeed, Bonaventure pressed Christocentricism to the point of making Christ who is the centre of all, the centre, even, of all of the sciences. In each case, he urges us to press beyond the "literal sense" of any given discipline to its ultimate meaning: thus the *De reductione artium ad theologiam* [retracing the arts to theology]. More particularly, Christ is the *medium distantiae*, the defining centre, in his Crucifixion. "With his Cross he has uncovered the lost centre of the world's circle, thus giving their true dimensions and meaning to the movement both of individual lives and of human history as a whole."[38]

In Ratzinger's estimation, Bonaventure achieved a synthesis of the mystical, cosmic, hierarchical, and historic orders that is relevant to this day. In faith and the Church there exists not merely a tiered hierarchy but also a hierarchical unfolding in history. This dynamic unfolding in history corresponds to a heightened degree of insight, reaching from the lowest level of knowledge of God to the highest, supra-intellectual, affective vision of God. The historic ascent of the Church from the days of the Old Testament prophets entails an increase in God's being known. Bonaventure therefore historizes not only external hierarchical thinking but also mysticism. Mysticism is not outside the categoriality of temporality when grace is bestowed upon someone but is determined by the historic unfolding of divine revelation. This revelatory movement culminates in beholding Christ as the highest level of charity, as lived exemplarily by Francis of Assisi.[39]

The expectation of an inner-worldly state of perfect and full salvation in history was the *cantus firmus* of Joachim's theology. After the age of the Father and of the Son, Joachim anticipated the third age, that of the Spirit, would begin around the year 1260. In that age, the contemplative lifestyle of monks and friars like St. Francis would be determinative. This would come about quasi-automatically, without divine initiative. Thus, Joachim is considered the founder of a movement of thinkers hoping for a terrestrial paradise. Such secular Joachimites are, for instance, the French revolutionaries, Marxists, eugenicists, and National Socialists. It was Ratzinger's contribution that for the first time demonstrated Bonaventure had opposed Joachimite positions.[40] The Christian saint is called amid the aberrations and follies of the world to present the image of authentic Christian wisdom. This enormous theological ambition has been the underlying, lifelong concern of all of Ratzinger's theological and pastoral efforts. Eight hundred years after Joachim, he would perceive it his commission as theologian and prefect to steer humankind away from the abyss of missing its destiny by seeking a perfect social *hic et nunc* (here and now).[41]

The perspective unfolded here reaches beyond the world. The terminal point of earthly existence for the human being is not the absolutized condition of something belonging to this world, such as a classless society, designer children, economic efficiency, a healthy environment, or a racially pure nation, but rather the Sabbath rest granted by God alone. The present infatuation with such projects is not novel. According to Augustine, it is part of the postlapsarian state to think and act *"etsi Deus non daretur"* (as if God were inexistent). A study of significant German thinkers confirms this. Gotthold Ephraim Lessing (1729–1781) proposed an "age of the new Eternal Gospel." His compatriot Immanuel Kant (1724–1804) held that it must be the highest task of humankind to labor for "a perfectly just civil order." Karl Marx (1818–1883) considered the classless society humanity's final and highest goal. The poet Heinrich Heine wanted to establish "the celestial kingdom already here on earth." For Ratzinger, "the generation of 1968" (that is, the generation that radically questioned all the values heretofore adhered to by Western civilization and whose assumptions are now the officially accepted standards of public discourse in the West) merely repeats the errors of these thinkers: "The World is being redeemed through God's patience and devastated by human impatience."[42]

Every human attempt to do away with peace granted as a gift from God alone is fated to create a new Babel (a confusing multitude of languages and views that will desolidarize society). In the theology of Bonaventure, Ratzinger found the central formula: "From God through Christ to God." Every secular utopia must be corrected by this eschatological perspective. Only considering history in its finality (that is, considering history in terms of the day of last judgment) allows one to master the present age in a humane manner. Without acknowledging the epochal historic fact of the Incarnation, that is, the hominization of God in Jesus Christ, one will constantly oscillate between a seemingly infinite multitude of truths. Particularly in Western Europe and North America, the idea of a terrestrial paradise that is self-produced without divine intervention has seemed attractive to large segments of society for the past four decades.[43] This political hope has been imposed on peoples by dictators in Eastern Europe, Asia, and Latin America.

Ratzinger's extensive academic studies conducted in the 1950s, while highly specialized, contain theological positions that are not merely relevant and forward-looking; they may also be programmatic for the pontificate of Pope Benedict XVI.

CHAPTER 9

The Inaugural Lecture in 1959

Inaugural lectures are significant as they frequently set the tenor for the subsequent teaching and work of a newly appointed professor. This was the case for Ratzinger's inaugural lecture, "The God of Faith and the God of Philosophers: A Contribution to the Problem of Natural Theology,"[1] when he assumed his position as ordinary of fundamental theology at the University of Bonn. In it, he stresses the need for collaboration between faith and philosophy. The current relevance of this topic in his judgment cannot be overestimated. Not only is it as old as humanity, but were one to consider this question settled once and for all, then humanity would cease to be. Ratzinger considered this question significant in the dialogue among cultures and among religions. The more recent thoughts of Ratzinger, *Truth and Tolerance*,[2] his dialogue with the German philosopher Jürgen Habermas at the Catholic Academy in Bavaria on January 19, 2004, and the papal Regensburg Lecture in 2006, are cases in point. His central point is that human rationality cannot discount the possibility that truth meets us as person, indeed as the divine-human Logos, thus affirming the viability of a relationship between charity and truth, and between faith and reason. Were only an abstract concept of God to be granted, such as the Kantian notion of God as a regulative idea, this would not suffice to compel good human action.

Ratzinger outright rejects both a fideistic separation of faith and reason and a hypotrophy of reason's faculties. For this reason, nine years after his inaugural lecture at the University of Bonn, in *Introduction to Christianity* he would warn against taking a retreat from the truth of reason into the arena of mere faith and revelation. Similarly, turning to Augustine—"What is so much yours as yourself, and what is so little yourself as yourself?"—one must admit the nonexistence of human reason's autonomy. Reason lives in historic contexts.[3] John Paul II wrote in his encyclical *Fides et Ratio* (which Cardinal Ratzinger, as prefect of the Congregation for the Doctrine of the Faith, certainly contributed to): "Faith and reason are like two wings on which the human spirit rises to the contemplation of truth; and God has placed in the human heart a desire to know the truth—in a word, to know himself—so that, by knowing and loving God, men and women may also come to the truth about themselves."[4]

Faith and reason are materially opposed, but mutually conditioning, realities and are not excluding movements in the human person. In philosophy, humans seek God, while in biblical faith God establishes—within the context of creaturely freedom—the relationship between humans and God. Famously, Martin Heidegger stated that to a God perceived as a *causa sui*, as the ground of his own being, one can neither pray nor offer sacrifices. Following from this, Ratzinger refers to reason that is not mindful of God as "amputated reason."[5] One can neither genuflect in awe nor make music and dance before such a God.[6] In any philosophy not related to revelation, God remains solitary and unreachable as the distant absolute. Scripture enables human beings to invoke and address God. In Ratzinger's train of thought, it is important to note that the God of philosophers and of faith—that is, God as an object of human inquiry and as a subject of revelation—is one and the same. In his debate with Habermas, he stated: "I should speak . . . of a necessary correlativity between faith and reason, religion and reason, both called to a mutual purification and sanation, in need of one another and [they] must recognize one another."[7] For Ratzinger, Christianity is the harmonious synthesis of faith and reason. A theologian prepares the foundation for an ultimately Eucharistic joy in which reason and mystery meet in Jesus Christ.

His point of departure in his lecture delivered on June 24, 1959, was the French philosopher Blaise Pascal's *"Mémorial."* Written on parchment and found in the hem of a coat after the thinker's death, it reads: "Fire: 'God of Abraham, God of Isaac, God of Jacob' not of the philosophers and scholars." Profoundly different from Descartes, Pascal, introducing the distinction of an *"esprit de géometrie"* and an *"esprit de finesse"*(that is, the spirit of exact reason and the spirit of nuanced perception respectively), the mathematician and "amateur" philosopher Pascal had in awe and joy encountered the living God as a Thou. This served for the young Ratzinger to demonstrate that the answer to the questions of people—posited between misery and grandeur—probing the infinite, is the biblical God and not the one of metaphysics.[8] Confronted with Kant's shattering speculative metaphysics, the Protestant theologian Friedrich Schleiermacher opted to move everything religious into the realm of mere feeling: more precisely, according to him, the pious consciousness in every human being is but "the feeling of absolute dependence (*schlechthin abhängig*)."[9] While the cost for doing so is huge, Ratzinger welcomes the intensification of the issue on the academic level. As a result of Schleiermacher, theoretical reason and religion have been divorced ever since: *"theoretische Vernunft, hat keinen Zugang zu Gott"* ("theoretical reason cannot access God").[10] As theoretical reason cannot access God, religious experience is beyond the reach of the sciences. Religion cannot be rationalized, and therefore dogmas are rendered no longer plausible. These consequences have become commonplace in our day and age. How is one to overcome the gap between the God of religion and the God of philosophy?

Ratzinger first examines two diametrically opposed responses. First, he discusses the position of Thomas Aquinas. For the Dominican teacher, the God of the philosophers and the God of religion coincide. The God of faith exceeds that of philosophy. Apart from Christianity, natural religion(s) cannot reach a higher knowledge than that which philosophy already offers. Indeed, for Thomas, whatever goes beyond philosophy in a *religio naturalis* must be considered an aberration if not downright rubbish. The principal operative here is "*gratia non destruit, sed elevat et perficit naturam*" ("Grace does not destroy, but elevates and perfects, nature").[11] Thus, while higher than philosophy, faith does not contradict a philosophical understanding of God. A Christian understanding of God incorporates and perfects the philosopher's definition of God. The God of Aristotle and Jesus Christ are one and the same. While Aristotle recognized the true God, Christian revelation provides a more profound and purer comprehension of God's essence.[12] The Christian faith can be related to a philosophical knowledge of God in the same way the eschatological vision of God is related to the Christian faith. They constitute three levels of one, uniform path to God.

The Reformed theologian Emil Brunner (1889–1966) developed his position in radical opposition to Thomas.[13] Brunner's point of departure is that in scripture God has names, whereas philosophy is concerned merely with abstract terms. The biblical revelation of God reaches its climax in the gospel of John: "I have manifested thy name to the men whom thou gavest me out of the world; thine they were, and thou gavest them to me, and they have kept thy word" (Jn 17:6). A relationship, Brunner argued, is thereby established between God and humanity. Philosophy accesses God via causality, but the God who reveals himself in names imparts some knowledge of his essence, such as coexistence with humankind. The major mistake for Brunner—so argues Ratzinger in critiquing Brunner's argument—was on the part of the Greek Septuagint, which translated the "*aehaeh ašaer aehjae*" of Exodus 3:14 meaning "I am who I am," into Greek as "Εγώ ειμι ο ών," meaning "I am the Being One." This conflation of the biblical and Greek understandings of God is *the* decisive misunderstanding for Brunner. Brunner perceivesw this identity between scripture and philosophy as deleterious for subsequent Christianity. God was thus "defined" in abstract, impersonal terms, which scripture does not allow. Brunner condemns, for instance, the connection Augustine made between neo-Platonic ontology and the biblical understanding of God, even considering it *the* central distortion of scripture. For philosophy, naming God is nothing short of anthropomorphism, ultimately rejecting revelation. Subsequent generations of Church fathers and scholastic theologians fell victim to this misunderstanding. Instead of acknowledging the radical difference between scripture and philosophy, they falsified revelation.

In Ratzinger's estimation, the continuation of this view is evident in the Protestant rejection of the *analogia entis* (analogy of being), as he witnessed in the spirited exchanges on this topic between Karl Barth on the one side and Erich Przywara and later Hans Urs von Balthasar on the other.[14]

In the second chapter of his lecture, Ratzinger draws particularly on Varro (116–27 BC) to demonstrate that in ancient Greece the Stoa—founded by Zeno the Younger in 308 Bc, this school of philosophers (Chrysipp, Seneca, Epictet, and Emperor Marc Aurelius) held that obedience to natural law and the divine will grants freedom, justice, courage, and ultimately bliss—did differentiate between a *theologia mythica*, a *theologia civilis*, and a *theologia naturalis*.[15] Further, he argues, both Tertullian and Augustine build their arguments on Varro's nuanced distinctions.[16] While *theologia mythica* is the area for poets, the people, and "fables," and *theologia civilis* is for the people and religious services, *theologia naturalis* is reserved for the philosophers and the "*physici*," who inquire into who or what the gods are. While the former are preoccupied with the divine as instituted by human beings, the latter inquire into the nature of the gods. Varro therefore illustrates the radical gulf between *theologia mythica* and *theologia civilis* vis-à-vis *theologia naturalis*. It is natural theology that dares think the possibility of monotheism and of God possibly addressing humanity. He notes that, paradoxically, as philosophers Plato and Aristotle were monotheists, but in their religious practice they remained polytheists! This lends legitimacy to Ratzinger's judgment regarding Augustine's conjoining neo-Platonic ontology and biblical insight in God. Ratzinger sides with Augustine and states that the mute and indescribable God of the philosophers becomes the speaking and listening God in Jesus Christ.

The synthesis of biblical faith and the Hellenic spirit is thus not only legitimate but also necessary. Philosophical truth is nothing short of "constitutive" for the Christian faith. Denying it would amount to nothing less than canceling out Christianity. This is borne out by the fact that biblical faith is monotheist. Israel did not worship a multitude of gods but the primordial source of the world. This is illustrated by way of Isaiah 40:12–18. The singular God of creation turns, as the absolute One, to the people of Israel. While they are not identical, approximations exist: both Greek natural theology and scripture define God with terms such as eternal, omnipotent, unity, truth, goodness, and holiness. Scripture itself uses such terms to distinguish its God from the deities of the surrounding peoples. It employs a language comprehensible to everybody. Using the *theologia naturalis*, the Old Testament faith can even become proclamatory to the outside world. As Christianity is not meant to be an esoteric, secret religion, accessible only to the initiated few, it was quite logical for early Christians to use a vocabulary borrowed from natural theology in order to evangelize.[17]

Notwithstanding the justification for joining natural theology and faith, Ratzinger describes Brunner's thesis as a "thorn." The difference between philosophy and theology, between *theologia naturalis* and the *religio Christiana*, cannot be nullified; it must be constantly kept in mind. Philosophy remains the other to which faith relates itself and must give an account to. This in turn enables a profound purification and transformation of faith to occur. Ratzinger regrets that sometimes the Church fathers were not sufficiently critical in appropriating philosophical concepts. The principled neutrality of Greek natural theology enabled it to overcome polytheism. Christianity is called to spell out more clearly the consequences of a God who is person, an I and a Thou. He calls upon Protestant and Catholic theologians to undertake this jointly. Citing Richard of St. Victor (d. 1173) reflecting on Augustine and the psalms, he reminds theology of its proper task: "*Quaerite faciem eius semper*" ("seek always his countenance").[18] He argues in conclusion that this need always entail a growth in charity toward the One recognized. Thus, the task of theology remains incomplete in this world. Theology is a constant asking for and seeking after the face of God, until he comes, and who then becomes the answer to all questions.[19] One could say this is *the* agenda Ratzinger gave all of his theological endeavors, which culminated in his book *Jesus of Nazareth*.

CHAPTER 10

Jesus Christ, the Sovereign, Unsurpassable
Revealer of Revelation

In the homily for the election of a pope on April 18, 2005, Cardinal Ratzinger preached:

> [W]e have a different goal: the Son of God, true man. He is the measure of true humanism. Being an "adult" means having a faith that does not follow the waves of today's fashions or the latest novelties. A faith that is deeply rooted in friendship with Christ is adult and mature. It is this friendship that opens us up to all that is good and gives us the knowledge to judge true from false, and deceit from truth. We must become mature in this adult faith; we must guide the flock of Christ to this faith. And it is this faith—only faith—that creates unity and takes form in the loved. On this theme, St. Paul offers us some beautiful words—in contrast to the continual ups and downs of those who are like infants, tossed about by waves: [he says] make truth in love, as the basic formula of Christian existence. In Christ, truth and love coincide. To the extent that we draw near to Christ in our own life, truth and love merge. Love without truth would be blind; truth without love would be like "a resounding gong or a clashing cymbal" (1 Cor 13:1).[1]

Ratzinger's concern is not so much merely to share the rare man or person of Jesus with his readers but "the figure of Jesus of Nazareth" as he puts it in his book *Jesus of Nazareth*. By figure he means "*Gestalt*," or more precisely, the "*figura Christi*" to use Augustine's expression. Thus, his concern is to portray "the Jesus of the Gospels as the real, 'historical' Jesus in the strict sense of the word" and the essence of who he is.[2] This second element suggests the insistent reconstruction of a Jesus that is accountable to both one's personal faith and to the historical-critical method. One of his central theses expressed in *Theologische Prinzipienlehre* (Theological Principles) notes that the "I" of the creed includes the transition from a "private I" to an "ecclesial I."[3] Only in the communion of the Church does the believer discover his or her true self. The baptismal profession of faith is no longer the profession of an isolated individual but that of the Church as a supra-individual unity. The Christ of faith and the historical Jesus are not unrelated realities but circumscribe one person. Christology is not a Platonic discipline detached from the earthly Jesus. With this as his premise, Ratzinger probes into the viability of Christology. How is one to accept both the divinity of the historical Jesus and the historical method without limiting faith to the historical method's range? In this regard, Ratzinger exceeds even that which well-churched contemporary exegetes, such as the renowned and now deceased New Testament scholar Rudolf Schnackenburg, spell out.[4]

Let us recall: studying Bonaventure, Ratzinger discovered that revelation is not simply synonymous with sacred scripture. No one in the Middle Ages could imagine anything like the neoscholastic approach. Revelation is far greater than anything human language can express. Temporally, it predates scripture but also manifests itself in it. This led Ratzinger to conclude the theological impossibility of the Protestant *sola scriptura* (scripture alone).

Sharing the general direction of de Lubac's Augustinian Thomism, Ratzinger argues the issue of revelation is linked to the possibility of the epiphany of Divine Charity and whether there are vestiges of the triune God to be found in human cognition.[5] At the conclusion of an interview with Peter Seewald, Ratzinger summarized world history: "Augustine saw that...it is a struggle between two kinds of love, between the love of God unto sacrifice of self, and self-love unto the denial of God. Thus he depicted history as the drama of a struggle between two kinds of love."[6] In Ratzinger's estimation, self-love amounts to a refusal to love at all. The modern-day denial of God and divine revelation is not the result of plain stupidity or foolishness, as neoscholasticism would insinuate. It illustrates an age with the inability to love, rather than the inability to think vigorously. The true task of the Church is to live revelation as that which enables humankind to love to the fullest. In the person of Christ, human beings encounter the fullness of reality: their own personhood is woven into a Trinitarian reality. For this reason, there can be no pluralistic theology of religions—as Paul Knitter and John Hick advocate—but only a Christocentric theology of history and anthropology. Alarmed by an unnuanced reading of *Gaudium et Spes* (GS), Romano Guardini (one of the fathers of liturgical renewal and author of *The Lord*), in 1965 advised Paul VI against an overly optimistic understanding of the world's autonomy: "[W]hat can convince modern people is not a historical or a psychological or a continually ever modernizing Christianity but only the unrestricted and uninterrupted message of Revelation."[7] Ratzinger has repeated this same idea in various ways time and again. revelation is not "a construction" of the human intellect but a divine message entrusted to human beings.

He goes to great length to explain that Jesus did not concoct an idiosyncratic teaching on his own but one that originates from close contact with his heavenly Father. For Jesus, prayer is conversation with his Father, such as when Jesus prayed "on a mountain." This led Adolf von Harnack to the extreme claim that Jesus' message is only about his Father. This in turn had him conclude the term "Christology" is a misnomer.

The proper nature of Jesus as the Christ is revealed in his reference to his baptism as death. This is nothing short of theophanic, but it is only comprehensible from the view of Easter. By taking the place of sinners in his baptism in the Jordan, he anticipates his own vicarious death on the cross and victorious Resurrection from the dead (Mk 10:38; Lk 12:50). Ratzinger draws here on the exiled Russian lay theologian Paul Evdokimov (1900–1970).[8] This baptism concentrates history into one moment. Therefore, every subsequent baptism is a participation in "Jesus' world-transforming struggle in the conversion of life that took place in his descent and ascent."[9] This leads the Roman Rite believer to profess before receiving communion, "Behold, the Lamb of God, who takes away the sin of the world" (Jn 1:29). Drawing on the research of the Lutheran exegete Joachim Jeremias (1900–1979), Ratzinger illuminates this germane concept. The Hebrew word *talia* may mean "Lamb," "boy," or "servant." It reveals Jesus Christ as the true Passover Lamb, and in baptism the disciples enter into the state of being in, that is, part of the fate and body of, the victimal Lamb. Ratzinger indirectly rejects the quest of Jeremias and others for the *ipsissima verba* (the very words): one may not attempt to get back behind the text or to psychologize Jesus. The sought-after familiarity with Jesus is granted to those who enter into discipleship. This is the import of both Romano Guardini's *Das Wesen des Christentums* (*The Essence of Christianity*)[10] and Augustine's line that God is "more intimately present to me than my inmost being."[11]

The way Christians view Jesus determines their ability to follow Christ. However, there is also another dimension involved. The nonbaptized world is not neutral in matters of good and evil. It is faced, just as Christians are, with the alternative of either following a good shepherd or the great deceiver. This is the reason Ratzinger often returns to the motif of the Antichrist. The deist theorem that God does not interact with this world is one of the traps of the Antichrist. *The Antichrist*, a classic work by Vladimir Soloviev, probably the greatest of nineteenth-century Russian philosophers and a convert to Catholicism, is a crucial instrument in understanding the challenges evil poses to all of humanity.[12] If Jesus Christ is not the Messiah, the fulfiller of all human hope, can any human being or human idea claim to provide a terrestrial kingdom of eternal peace and well-being? Ratzinger reminds his readers that by virtue of his Resurrection from the dead only Jesus Christ can fulfill such a hope.[13] "What did Jesus actually bring, if not world peace, universal prosperity, and a better world? The answer is very simple: God....Jesus has brought God and with God the truth about our origin and destiny: faith, hope, and love."[14]

For the Christian, Jesus Christ is not a lofty, intangible Platonic idea, but in a unique sense is, as Son, the expression of God's fatherhood. The biblical witness is of decisive hermeneutic importance: Christ is the "image of God" (2 Cor 4:4; Col 1:15). Thus, as understood by the patristic inspiration, Jesus Christ as "the new Adam" is the paradigm for God creating humankind. Jesus Christ becomes the human being who is the summons for all human beings to live as children of God. "'All that is mine is thine,' Jesus says in his high-priestly prayer to the Father (Jn 17:10), and the father says the same thing to the elder brother of the Prodigal Son (Lk 15:31)."[15] Pope Benedict

reminds his readers of St. Benedict's Rule (19, 7) where one reads "*mens nostra concordet voci nostrae*" ("our minds must be in accord with our voice"), and
this is brought about if one understands Jesus' statement, "He who sees me
sees the Father" (Jn 14:8f).[16] Truly, God makes himself accessible to humankind in Jesus Christ and thereby liberates humankind from all the fallacious
proposals to fulfill humanity. Human wholeness is Jesus Christ (alone). This
is revealed at Jacob's well. There Jesus observes, "My food is to do the will of
him who sent me, and to accomplish his work" (Jn 4:34). By emulating this
unity of Jesus' volition with that of his Father, human beings find the foundation and core of their own being. Human freedom finds a goal.[17]

Following the Church fathers—who were mindful of Jewish customs—
and contemporary exegetes, especially Jean Daniélou, Ratzinger presupposes
a connection between the Jewish feasts of atonement and the weeklong celebration of the Feast of Tabernacles and the transfiguration of Jesus. Only once
during the year is God's name YHWH pronounced by the high priest in the
Temple's Holy of Holies.[18] In the context of this feast, Simon Peter confesses
Jesus is the Son of the living God at the foot of Mt. Hermon (Mt 16:16). The
correlation of the God of the Old Testament and Jesus of Nazareth is thereby
established. The locale confirms this: in the Old Testament, the preferred
places to demonstrate God's closeness to humankind are mountaintops.[19] The
cloud of holiness, the *Shekinah*, hovers over the Lord and mirrors that of
Jesus' baptism in the Jordan River: "You are my beloved Son; with you I am
well pleased" (Mk 1:11). As Ratzinger concludes, "Jesus himself is the living
Torah, the complete Word of God. On the mountain they see the 'power'
(*dynamis*) of the Kingdom that is coming in Christ."[20]

It is no longer possible to apply common biblical templates to Jesus.
New predicates emerge: Christ for Messiah, *Kyrios* (Lord), and Son of God.
Predication and the essence of Jesus' person are identical. Jesus is God. This
is the conclusion drawn from the collapse of descriptions and person of
Jesus Christ. Significantly, Ratzinger points out that the philosophical term
homoousios (or *consubstantialis*, that is, "of the same substance as the Father")
was adopted, not to mold Christology into something more palatable to the
pagan mind but to safeguard the biblical witness of Jesus as the Son of God.
Only in this light can all people acknowledge Jesus reigning from the cross:
indeed, "*Regnavit a ligno Deus*" ("God has reigned from the cross"), as early
Christendom sang.[21]

While the term "Son of Man" appears in Daniel, it is almost exclusively
Jesus who uses the phrase. As this expression at times implies poverty and
suffering, in Jesus one must apprehend both human forsakenness and divine
sovereignty, earthly imprisonment and divine freedom; one who is suffering his passion and glorification on the cross. In the one person of Jesus an
unheard of, and heretofore unknown, coincidence occurs. "The inner unity
between Jesus' lived kenosis (cf. Phil 2:5–11) and his coming in glory is the
constant motif of his words and actions; this is what is authentically new
about Jesus, it is no invention—on the contrary, it is the epitome of his figure
and his words."[22] His divine capacity to forgive sins is linked with his passion. Thus, he reveals himself as lived proexistence (living for his Father and
therefore for us) par excellence. As the true offering, he becomes not only

the true template for every human being but even more profoundly, "He is not just one individual, but rather he makes all of us 'one single person' [Gal 3:28] with himself, a new humanity."[23] Fundamental to this view is the unity between the Son, Jesus, and his divine Father (Mt 11:25–27; Lk 10:22). "No one has seen God; it is only the Son, who is nearest to the Father's heart, who has made him known" (Jn 1:18). The final and full disclosure of God is based upon this "filial dialogue."

The last title Ratzinger discusses in his book *Jesus of Nazareth* is "I am," a title used by Jesus himself. This title evidences a continuation of God's self-revelation in the burning bush (Ex 3:14). It is a manifestation of God's and Jesus' divine "indescribable oneness and singularity." It also states the inseparable relationality of Father and Son. Only in light of this background could Jesus assert, "Before Abraham came into existence, I am" (Jn 8:58). With these words, Jesus Christ sets himself apart from all other forms of being. Only the identity of Jesus with God in one person explains his consoling words uttered to those who fear life: "Take heart, it is I [I am he]; have no fear!" (Mk 6:50). While the enigmatic "*ego eimi*" (I am) is Johannine, in Mark the question is posed, "Who is this that even wind and water obey him?" (Mk 4:41). Other descriptions of Jesus second this: "I am the Bread of Life"; "the Light of the World"; "the Door"; "the Good Shepherd"; "the Resurrection and the Life"; "the Way, the Truth and the Life"; and "the True Vine." Along with Schnackenburg, Ratzinger views these images as "variations on the single theme, that Jesus has come so that human beings may have life, and have it in abundance (cf. Jn 10:10). His only gift is life, and he is able to give it because the divine life is present in him in original and inexhaustible fullness."[24] The complete response to all human questions, wishes, and hopes lies in Jesus Christ, who *is* life. This exhaustive definition of life as Jesus Christ is essentially proexistence. One can trust the information given by the God-man because only He can address the Father as "Abba." However, with him and in him we too are granted the ability to address God as "Father." Ratzinger closes his book on Jesus by stressing the consonance of ecclesial dogma with biblical testimony, as expressed in a representative way by Peter, "You are the Christ, the Son of the living God" (Mt 16:16).[25] The First Council of Nicaea in AD 325 did not Hellenize the Christian faith but rather it vouched for the unique way only Jesus could speak of his Father in heaven.

Ratzinger agrees with the majority of exegetes that the synoptic gospels emphasize the unity of Father and Son. The Johannine Jesus reveals his divinity. Although John's Gospel was written down in the later part of the first century, this does not discredit the gospel. Ratzinger rejects outright Rudolf Bultmann's claim that gnosticism is the basis for the Jesus found in John and the belief in the Incarnation.[26] He cites the Protestant scholar Martin Hengel as a source for more reliable exegesis. Hengel disparaged Bultmann's hypothesis as "a myth."[27] Ratzinger demonstrates how the attempt to discover the author of the fourth gospel reveals more about Jesus Christ. Not only is the author an eyewitness, as John 19:35 stresses, but just as only Jesus knows through close proximity who the Father is, so the disciple knows through intimacy who Jesus is (Jn 13:25). "Just as Jesus, the Son, knows about the mystery of the Father from resting in his heart, so too the evangelist has gained his intimate knowledge from his inward repose in Jesus' heart. However true the Lutheran theologian Ulrich Wilkens' claim is that 'the beloved disciple' serves as a paradigm for Christian faith, it need be asserted that the disciple is an actual, historic human being, lest the content of his gospel evaporates."[28]

Could the claim of Irenaeus of Lyon indeed be correct that the disciple in question is John, the son of Zebedee? It has struck many as improbable that a fisherman could be in command of the rich symbolic imagery of temple priests. Following Henri Cazelles, Ratzinger offers the suggestion that Zebedee was a fisherman in Galilee and rotated as a priest, a common practice in those days. Nonetheless, Ratzinger agrees this does not answer how the complexity of the gospel's redaction can be explained. For this, he turns to the Church historian Eusebius of Caesarea (ca. 260–340), who allows the inference that there was a Johannine school in Ephesus. This enables Ratzinger to agree with Peter Stuhlmacher that there must be a close connection between the literary author and the beloved disciple of the Johannine corpus.[29] The credibility of the fourth gospel can therefore be trusted.

Ratzinger mentions, for instance, the cleansing of the temple by Our Lord in John 2:17. Ratzinger finds it remarkable that Jesus' disciples recall the verse from Psalm 69:10: "Zeal for thy house will consume me." Not only does a correlation between Jesus and the Logos occur in this pericope, but the disciples recall the verse due to the fact that they are already living in the Spirit-filled realm that one day will be called the Church. Gradually, their collective memory gives them the piece that provides the picture of a large, heretofore unimaginable mosaic, a picture shattering all human imagination. The gospel itself is called "pneumatic": without doing violence to historic circumstances, it leads the reader to the full Jesus Christ. "'Before Abraham was, *I am*' (Jn 8:58). It shows us the real Jesus, and we can confidently make use of it as a source of information about him."[30] In order to properly appreciate Jesus' discourses, the liturgical context of the Johannine corpus must be born in mind. Liturgy is a heuristic source for John. Jesus' discourses are not intended as mere rebuttals or contributions to a philosophical discussion. They acquire their inner dynamic from the fact that they are part of God's rectification of creation. Salvation means, among other things, apprehending the "*ego eimi*" ("I am"): God in Jesus Christ. The sacrament of God's Eucharistic presence intends to address and include all.

As John instructs the reader, *Siloam* means, "the One sent" (Jn 9:7). The evangelist is not concerned about teaching Hebrew but rather in conveying a sense for who Jesus is: the one who in his divine authority wrought the miracle of healing the man who was born blind. The man is not only cleansed, but he is also made a seer in both the physical and spiritual realms. Water again becomes a topos at the Last Supper, when the Lord humbly washes the feet of his disciples. Moses gave the people of Israel water from a rock that would sustain them. John intimates that Jesus produces a yet deeper and more intimate miracle, when from Our Lord's side "rivers of living water" issue forth (Jn 7:38). Such a Johannine view of Christ's death is not idiosyncratic but seconded by the Church fathers such as Justin, Irenaeus, Hippolytus, Cyprian, and Ephrem the Syrian. "He is the source, the living rock, from which the new water comes."[31] The words Jesus uttered during the cleansing of the temple at the Feast of Tabernacles anticipate and prepare the reader for Jesus' own sacrifice on the cross (Jn 19:34). It is not here that the Johannine dynamic stops. It yearns to include the reader. John's writings intend to evangelize when being read, facilitating the entry of the reader into the mystery of Christ: "'Whoever drinks from my mouth shall become as I am' (Barrett, *Gospel*, p. 328). The believer becomes one with Christ and participates in his fruitfulness. The man who believes and loves with Christ becomes a well that gives life."[32] The law is no longer an abstract principle but is, in Jesus Christ, a person.

When Jesus produces a remarkable surplus of wine at the wedding feast of Cana, what is one to make of this? Ratzinger reminds us to contextualize this within the "third day" matrix (see Jn 2:1). During the Exodus, in the morning of the third day, the Lord descended in fire from on high (Ex 19:16–18) and John intends to convey that this, along with Cana, prefigures the final theophany of God on the cross and on Easter Sunday. Thus, in Jesus' actions nothing short of God's own revelation occurs. At this point, Ratzinger calls to mind the opinion of Philo (13 BC–AD 50), who was a contemporary of the evangelist John, that the true giver of wine is the divine Logos, and then of applying this to Melchizedek. For the exegete Barrett as well, Jesus Christ, the eternal Logos, is represented as the priest of a cosmic liturgy.[33] Thus, in John's mind Jesus becomes the extension of Melchizedek. In the Eucharistic bread and wine, he provides nourishment for the members of the New Covenant. Just as Jesus transforms the Old Testament motifs, he also alters the pagan myth of Dionysius. As Song 2:15 and Song 7:12f relate, the vineyard symbolizes a bride. Isaiah 5:1–7 seconds this view. Joining this to the *ego eimi* ("I am," alluding to the meaning of the term YHWH, where God reveals Himself as "the One who is" in the Old Testament) statement in John 15:1, "I am the true vine," permits the believer to see God in his Son joining the lot of humankind and forming the one body of Christ (cf. Jn 11:52). Thus, Ratzinger observes: "The vine is a Christological title that as such embodies a whole ecclesiology."[34] "I am the vine, you are the branches" (Jn 15:5a). At the very least, this certainly justifies a pristine Logos-Christology. The Logos is the vine and shepherd for all men. All have been created from eternity "through" the Logos so that they might be one in him. "However widely scattered they are, all people can become one through the true Shepherd, the Logos who became man in order to lay down his life and so to give life in abundance (cf. Jn 10:10)."[35]

In the preface to the new edition of *Introduction to Christianity*, Ratzinger writes: "If it is true that the term *Logos*—the Word in the beginning, creative reason, and love—is decisive for the Christian image of God, and if the concept of Logos simultaneously forms the core of Christology, of faith in Christ, then the indivisibility of faith in God and faith in his incarnate Son, Jesus Christ, is only confirmed once more."[36]

It is in this Johannine vein, deepened by Plato's and Augustine's[37] understanding of beauty as a manifestation of truth, that Ratzinger is able to say: "So it is not merely the external beauty of the Redeemer's appearance that is glorified: rather, the beauty of Truth appears in him, the beauty of God himself, who draws us to himself and at the same time captures us with the wound of Love, the holy passion (*eros*), that enables us to go forth together, with and in the church, his bride, to meet the Love who calls us.... Whoever believes in God, in the God who manifested himself precisely in the altered appearance of Christ crucified as Love 'to the end' (Jn 13:1), knows that beauty is truth and truth beauty; but in the suffering Christ he also learns that the beauty of truth also embraces offense, pain, and even the dark mystery of death, and that this can only be found in accepting suffering, not in ignoring it."[38]

A Recapitulation

Over and against a superficial understanding of God's infinite transcendence, which considers God incompatible with a Christ "in diapers" (Kelsos, the second-century pagan philosopher also known as Celsus), Ratzinger employs a quote at the beginning of Hölderlin's *Hyperion*: "*Non coerceri maximo, conteneri tamen a minimo, divinum est*" ("Not to be confined by the greatest, yet to be contained within the smallest, is divine"). This unlimited Spirit, containing the totality of being, reaches beyond the greatest, so that the cosmos becomes miniscule to him. Precisely transcending the greatest and reaching out to the smallest is the true nature of the absolute. Forcing God out of history actually limits God, rendering him finite.[39]

Amid the heady days of the early 1980s, Ratzinger participated in a congress on the Sacred Heart held in Toulouse and a congress on Christology in Rio de Janeiro. The papers he gave there resulted in the book *Behold the Pierced One: An Approach to a Spiritual Christology*.[40] Significantly, he dedicated this meditation to the great expert on Christology, fellow council *peritus* and later cardinal, Alois Grillmeier, SJ (1910–1998).[41] The starting point for this precious meditation is that "Christology is born of prayer or not all."[42] As shall be demonstrated next, this insight is juxtaposed with the following statement: "Only in the context of a spiritual Christology will the spirituality of the sacrament reveal itself to us."[43] Systematic theology and spirituality are interrelated, as are Christology and especially the liturgy of the Eucharist.

According to scripture, Christ reveals himself as both the Messiah (Mk 8:29; Lk 9:20) and "the Son of the living God" (Mt 16:16). Jesus' divine filiation is constitutive for his messiahship. As Son, it belongs to his essence to pray to his Father. The words and deeds of Jesus arise from his unique prayerful relationship with God, his Father. While he prays in keeping with Jewish traditions, he also prays often on his own. At every important phase of his life, such as his departure from his disciples and at his death, he prays. Ratzinger concludes that prayer constitutes the personhood of Jesus. Thus, he elsewhere observes that divineSonship "manifests itself in the Gospels primarily in the prayer of Jesus."[44] The indispensable key to comprehending the person of Jesus lies in this. Partaking in Christ's prayer entails community with him. The Church offers to the individual such prayer with Christ and enables ecclesial solidarity. Ratzinger even argues the Church as a whole, her creed and particularly the Eucharist, arise from Jesus Christ's prayer. In the Introduction to the reprint of his dissertation, he summarizes: as the Church is the mystical body of Christ, Christology is central to the essence of what it means to be the Church. Augustine and the other Church fathers apprehend the Church "the People of God" exclusively in direct dependence on Christ. The concept of "People of God" is defined by the Eucharistic body of Christ. Thus, one would commit a grave error if one were to divorce the episcopal and priestly offices from Christology and ecclesiology.[45] "According to Luke, Jesus had spent the night that preceded this event at prayer on the mountain: The calling of the Twelve proceeds from prayer, from the Son's conversing with the Father. The Church is born in that prayer in which Jesus gives himself back into the Father's hands and the Father commits everything to the Son. This most profound communication of Son and Father conceals the Church's true and ever-new origin, which is also her firm foundation (Lk 6:12–17)."[46] The actual, transcendental subject of tradition is the Church. The Church vouches for a genuine insight into Jesus Christ. For the outsider, something impossible occurs. The Church receives herself in the worship of God, and this includes the Eucharist she celebrates.[47] For both the believing individual and the community, Christology is primarily experiential in nature.

In this vein, the Church's creed becomes prayer. Thus, the Church is nothing less than the transcendental hermeneutic key to an authentic understanding of the person of Jesus. Ecclesially grounded entry into Christ's prayer is indispensable. This does not render scholarly work in the areas of exegesis and systematic theology superfluous. Rather, such academic pursuits require the experience of prayer. When the Council of Nicaea stated in AD 325 that Jesus Christ is consubstantial with the Father, this statement entails that in Christ, God does not remain hidden in a cloud.[48] Ratzinger has repeatedly warned against divining an artificial opposition between the Christ of faith and the historic Jesus. There is but one subject in Jesus Christ. In the sovereign "*ego eimi*" ("I am"), Jesus speaks the divine "I" as the Logos of God. A supposed division between the historic Jesus and the divine Christ is connected with the accusation of a Hellenization of Christianity that betrays the biblical narrative à la Harnack. In Ratzinger's estimation, something quite contrary occurs: a transformation of the Hellenistic perception of God takes place. In this sense, the encounter between the rationality of Greek philosophy and the Christian message of the Incarnation becomes a hermeneutic key of lasting relevance. As Greek rationality does not express esoteric and local principles, which are set apart and inaccessible to the rest of humanity, but rather the principles common to human cognition everywhere, the incarnate Logos can be received by all peoples and cultures. Memorably, Pope Benedict's 2006 lecture at the University of Regensburg spelled this out in clear terms.[49] It should be noted, however, that in this context the Pope did not advocate simply a repristination of a symbiosis of Greek philosophy and the Christian faith. Rather, he called for a new synthesis of faith and reason.

Significantly, Jesus' prayer also opens up the way to soteriology (the Christian understanding of salvation). In fact, his death becomes an act of prayer and thus one of adoration. Praising God, saying thanks, and distributing the gifts of bread and wine during the Last Supper are an anticipation of his self-immolation: "At the Last Supper he had anticipated his death by giving himself, thus transforming his death, from within, into an act of love, into the glorification of God."[50] His death is accompanied by Psalm 22, expressing the suffering and hope of ancient Israel. Both Mark 15:34 and Matthew 27:46 attest to this reading. Luke 23:46 and John 18:28f confirm the close relationship between the Last Supper and the crucifixion. Further, they also argue for understanding Our Lord as handing himself over to the Father as a sacrifice.

This reaches to the heart of revelation's meaning. It is not the mere communication of sentences to the human intellect, taking place within the gradual action of God in history. God's announcement requires a commensurate reception on the part of human beings in order for revelation to come about. If this is the case, then all texts, including scripture, are testimonies to revelation, but they are not revelation itself.[51] While researching Bonaventure, Ratzinger discovered that in the thirteenth century no term existed that corresponds to the modern understanding of "revelation." There existed no word for the totality of the divinely revealed content. For the High Middle Ages, Revelation refers to an act in which God shows himself to a particular receiving subject. Without an actual receiver, no revelation occurs. There must be someone who becomes aware of it.[52] This has ecclesiological ramifications. The Church is not identified as a teaching institution but is rather "the living expression of the perpetuation of the mystery of Christ" in the community of believers. Revelation is not limited to a particular canon apart from its living context. Ignoring ecclesial tradition and lived liturgy, the Reformist principle of *sola scriptura*, however well intentioned, is woefully inadequate to capture the dynamic nature of revelation—which is unimaginable apart from the Church. For good reason, *Dei Verbum* (*DV*) emphasizes the immediate connection among revelation, scripture, and the Catholic Church: "Thus it comes about that the Church does not draw her certainty about all revealed truths from the Holy scriptures alone. Hence, both scripture and Tradition must be accepted and honored with equal feelings of devotion and reverence" (*DV* 9). The unifying element is not an abstract principle or formula but rather Jesus Christ, the creative power of the Logos, of reason. Thus, every Christian must protest against any form of ideology (an ideology is the attempt to define reality and life's purpose exclusively and exhaustively by way of human definitions with no recourse to religion—such as Marxism, Fascism, etc.): scripture is "theo-logy," that is, "God-science." Ratzinger had already discovered this in reading Guardini: the Logos has primacy over and against the ethos.

Preliminaries to the Council

Cardinal Josef Frings, archbishop of Cologne, president of the Fulda (German) Bishops' Conference, and a member of the commission preparing the Vatican II Council, had known of Ratzinger since the latter's appointment as professor of theology at Bonn University in 1959. Ratzinger indicates their "uncomplicated and heartfelt" relationship began after he delivered a paper on the theology of the future council at the *Katholische Akademie* in Bensberg. Frings, himself a first-rate violinist, relates their first encounter at a concert in Gürzenich, in which he requested Ratzinger's assistance on a paper he was to deliver on November 20, 1961, at the *Teatro Duse* in Genoa, Italy. The paper was for the *Institutum Colombianum* lecture series, at an institute founded by Father Angelo d'Arpa, SJ, to address questions concerning issues to be developed in preparation for the council.[53] Afterwards, Cardinal Julius Döpfner remarked, "These are beautiful dreams for the future, but probably little will come of them."[54] Pope John XXIII praised Cardinal Frings quite vividly for his visionary lecture.[55]

The lecture was titled *"Über das Konzil vor dem Hintergrund der Zeitlage im Unterschied zum Ersten Vatikanischen Konzil"* ("On the Council: The Background of the Current Intellectual Climate Compared to the First Vatican Council").[56] In the opening lines, Frings (and, in fact, Ratzinger who had penned the paper for him) states that the ever valid truth becomes incarnate in the time-conditioned historic Word, and one is called to ponder the particularities of the hour in which this Word ought to speak. This has been entrusted to the Church forever. How is this word to address a world swayed to and fro by the extremes of rationalism and fideism? The question requires a four-point analysis.

1. The intellectual situation is marked by a world that has becoming increasingly smaller. In this, he discerns a decisive moment for the Church to become a *"Weltkirche"* (global Church). As this uniform, technical world takes shape, the Church is called to seek new forms of evangelization, "a new *koine*" (that is, a new common language), to translate the gospel to the world and thereby "capture" it for Jesus Christ.

The justification for this thesis sounds quite prophetic. It is unimaginable today to assume Europe's cultural superiority based on Christianity vis-à-vis other religions, as did still the Protestant dogmatician Ernst Troeltsch (1865–1923) at the turn of the last century. In addition, a paradox is evident. While European technical rationality is indeed spreading to the farthest points of the globe, at the same time, various non-European cultures and religions are rediscovering their own worth and even beginning to woo Western people. This has ramifications for the Western hemisphere, which since the nineteenth century has increasingly subscribed to the ideology of relativism; namely, one of the chief ramifications is its loss of self-confidence. This development offers a positive opportunity to the Church: the opportunity to rediscover the Church as the new people formed of a multitude of peoples. This wealth is reflected in her liturgy. It is both unifying and enables diversity.

2. In all previous cultures, human beings lived in a close relationship with, and were dependent upon, nature. By virtue of technological breakthroughs, this has been altered profoundly. The whole of life is now accessed through the medium, or filter, of human technological accomplishments. A human being no longer encounters God's creation but rather

human achievements, traces of his or her own mind and abilities, superimposed upon this foundational natural reality. Thus, modern humankind is divorced from the most primordial sources of religious experience. There is no denying that amid an industrial milieu godlessness became popular for the working class. The consequence is that the "self-divinization of humankind" replaces the divinization of human nature through divine grace with inner necessity.[57]

3. Frings discerns an uncritical trust in science as a third contemporary feature. The sciences are expected to provide solutions to the deepest anxieties and longings of human beings, hitherto reserved for religion. But such scientific changes do not fundamentally alter the human condition. Human beings remain "the unknown" creature (A. Carrel) and "the great abyss" (Augustine). No matter how many beneficial scientific advances there may be, an inexplicable "rest" remains, and it is precisely this "rest" (that is, the range of human reason is always shorter than that of all reality) that is proper to being human, that is the essence of being a human being. "Charity remains the great miracle, defying calculation, guilt remains the dark possibility, which cannot be flogged to death, and at the bottom of the human heart remains that loneliness, which calls for infinitude and ultimately cannot be satisfied through something other, because the word remains—'solo Dios basta' (God alone suffices)—infinitude alone suffices for man."[58] For this reason, modern human beings ought to realize that the Church fears no science, as all knowledge is gathered together in God.

4. The final point concerns ideologies: Marxism, existentialism, neoliberalism, and so forth. All these express the human heart's yearning for a great, sustaining hope. This promise may not be only for an individual; it should be one capturing the heart and imagination of all humankind. With this background, the upcoming council appears as one with an overriding pastoral concern, intending to point to Jesus Christ as the only object worthy of placing such hope in. It is in the Church, which is the Father's house, that human beings will find such hope not disappointed.

In his conclusion, Frings discerns the movement of the Holy Spirit during the past half century in two major charismatic movements. The first one is Mariological. Lourdes and Fatima gave impetus to this movement, and it was ecclesially sanctioned. The other significant charismatic development is liturgical. From monasteries such as Solesmes, Maredsous, Beuron, and Maria Laach, liturgical renewal took off. However, Frings notes the two movements are strangely alien to each other. While one subscribes to the formula *per Mariam ad Jesum* (to Jesus through Mary), the other states the law of piety *per Christum ad Patrem* (to the Father through Christ). These two intellectual outlooks must not be viewed in isolation from each other. Mary is the primordial image of the *Mater Ecclesia* (mother Church) per se. Frings closes his reflections by reminding the audience of the numerous martyrs the Church has brought forth in recent times. Such suffering is an indication of the Church's invincible life, and he notes it is the task of the upcoming council to spell out that such life is a life in Christ.

The Council

Probably the most historic event Ratzinger took part in was the Second Vatican Council. He delighted in the general tenor of Pope John XXIII's opening address. In particular, he was pleased to hear the Holy Father's intention to renew the whole of the faith and not certain isolated aspects of it. He was heartened to note bishops acting as one formative body. Here he could appreciate in a tangible way "the fruitful tension" between the universal and particular Church. He was filled with confidence as he sensed Pope John XXIII was by no means inhibited by an "antimodernist neurosis."[59] In Ratzinger's estimation, this would allow the documents to be genuinely pastoral and ecumenical.

The Dominican theologian, and later cardinal, Yves Congar related in his diary *Mon Journal du Concile* that Karl Rahner, Ratzinger, and Gustave Martelet were considered "dangerous" by the then prefect of the Holy Office, Cardinal Alfredo Ottaviani (1890–1979).[60] While working on *Ad Gentes* (the Vatican II Council's decree on the Church's mission work), Congar rejoiced to find Ratzinger on the drafting committee: "He is reasonable, modest, disinterested, a great help."[61] Ratzinger, on his part, appreciated the broad-based rejection of preparatory schemata reflecting abstract scholastic terms and little pastoral sensitivity. He also welcomed the council's freedom from curial domination and the candor of its discussions.

On November 14, 1962, the Second Vatican Council's General Congregation met in the conciliar aula of St. Peter's Basilica. Famously on the agenda was the prepared schema *De fontibus revelationis* (*On the Sources of Revelation*). After Cardinal Alfredo Ottaviani's relation, presented by Father Salvatore Garofalo, the bishop of the French city of Lille, Cardinal Achille Liénart, responded first. After him, the archbishop of Cologne, Cardinal Josef Frings, took the floor. Both roundly rejected the schema. Such frankness contrasts sharply with the atmosphere prevalent during the First Vatican Council (1869–1870).

Cardinal Frings advanced two arguments for declaring his unequivocal *non placet* (that is, negative vote). First, the schema's tenor was much too professorial for a conciliar document. Second, it suffered from material deficiencies. Frings argued that the notion of the two sources of revelation is not in keeping with tradition, but rather it is indebted to the age of historicism. Such a view is superficial because it relates only to human insight into the content of revelation. While Frings conceded one may speak of scripture and tradition as two "*fontes cognoscendi*" of revelation (sources of insight into revelation), on the ontological level one must acknowledge only one source (*fons essendi*) of revelation—Jesus Christ, the Logos. He deplored the fact that the schema hardly thematizes revelation per se.[62] These central critiques determined the subsequent development of the constitution on divine revelation, which later would be named *Dei Verbum*. It would take slightly over three years to approve the final version on November 18, 1965. In the introductory portion and the first chapter, "*De ipsa revelatione*," tradition and scripture are defined as two modes of handing down revelation: the former preceding the latter, the latter subservient to the former. As *verbum* is the Latin equivalent to the Greek term *Logos*, it was decided it should be capitalized, per Henri de Lubac's suggestion, because it refers to the Christocentric nature of Christian revelation.[63]

The young *peritus* Ratzinger had already aired these concerns on October 10, 1962, in front of all the German-speaking bishops meeting in the Collegio S. Maria dell'Anima to discuss the two dogmatic schemata *De depositione fidei pure custodienda* and *De fontibus revelationis*.[64] Together with Karl Rahner, he submitted an alternative schema titled *De revelatione Dei et hominis in Jesu Christo facta*.[65]

The image of the blind Cardinal Ottaviani and the almost blind Cardinal Frings engaged in "theological shadowboxing" well captures the drama of the council. Both would have been much reduced in their roles had they not had reliable collaborators. While it is still too early to definitively ascertain Ratzinger's share in composing the various documents, his decisive influence on Frings's nineteen conciliar interventions can be verified beyond any doubt. In 1973 Cardinal Frings recalled Ratzinger supplying him with a masterful draft that Frings only slightly modified in one spot. The published Italian version immediately caused quite a stir in Catholic circles. This motivated Frings, in April of 1962, to request all theological drafts and schemata from then on be sent to Ratzinger for review, suggestions, corrections, and improvements. Shortly thereafter, Frings asked Ratzinger to give a significant lecture at the Anima, the German seminary in Rome, on October 10, 1962, regarding the preliminary draft of the dogmatic constitution *De fontibus revelationis*, including suggestions for counterproposals. The German episcopacy met at the Anima every Monday at 5:00 p.m. during the council to prepare their strategy. Such noted theologians as the Germans Herrmann Volk, Alois Grillmeier, Bernhard Häring; the Swiss Hans Küng; the Frenchmen Yves Congar, Jean Daniélou, Marie-Dominique Chenu, Marie-Jean Le Guillou; the Belgian Gérard Philips; and the Dutch Edward Schillebeeckx would attend. By the end of the first session, Ratzinger was officially appointed *peritus*, that is, council theologian. As such, he could participate in all conciliar sessions and was permitted to speak upon request. The archbishop soon introduced his *peritus* to all of the significant theologians.[66]

Ratzinger faulted the draft of *De fontibus revelationis* for its doctrinal tenor and its lack of consistency, apologetic posture, and insensitivity to the biblical movement. He methodically critiqued the title. Scripture and tradition are not actually the source of revelation. Rather, he maintains God's revelation itself, the unveiling and speaking of God in Jesus Christ, is the *unus fons* (one source) of revelation, while he refers to scripture and tradition as revelation's *rivuli* (brooks).[67] Jesus Christ is not the mere courier of a corpus of teachings that require blind submission on the part of the faithful, but rather *he is* the message. From within the midst of humanity, God reveals himself. The Word of God is identical with God and thus is light and life. Instead of a list of abstract truths, there is a concrete truth: Jesus Christ is "truth in person." Thus, scripture is not revelation but witness to revelation: essentially, that which is attested to transcends scripture. Even the most solemn acts of the teaching office and creeds are not full explications of the Word. As Cardinal Döpfner, archbishop of Munich, expressed it: the human person surrenders himself to God in freedom (*homo se totum libere Deo committit*). All the words of scripture reference the one Word, Jesus Christ: "The Church is not the Word, but she is the locus of the Word's habitation." The Old Testament is not a definitive norm for faith, and the New Testament cannot be superseded by a third or fourth covenant. In the final consequence, the countenance of Jesus Christ shines forth in the Church calling all to emulate him.

Revelation is more than what is written. A personal and dialogical event precedes scripture and is attested to by scripture. This was Ratzinger's insight after reading Bonaventure. Revelation as an ongoing event requires a believing subject. Ratzinger discerns this believing subject is the Church, not an individual person. The Church is the living reality that brings about tradition. This living handing down of the content of revelation is called the Church; tradition is the Church's self-reflex. In this nuanced sense *Dei Verbum* 5 speaks of faith: it belongs constitutively to the nature of revelation to be brought forth by the Church as an act of faith. This occurred in a most primordial form when Peter responded: "You are the Messiah, the Son of the living God" (Mt 16:17). Here, revelation comes full circle: its content has reached and been embraced by its addressee. In an essay written in 1958, Ratzinger makes the noteworthy observation: "Scripture is the material principle of revelation, which remains behind Scripture and is never fully objectified therein." It is for this reason that scripture, in order to be apprehended as revelation, requires an interpretation proper to the nature of revelation.[68] Romano Guardini had argued in this same vein: religiously inclined people did not generate Jesus' divine nature after he lived. Rather, vice versa, the apostolic charism can never exhaust the original plenitude of the divine Logos' Incarnation.[69]

Therefore, the Second Vatican Council did not willy-nilly allow the historical-critical method. Quite the contrary, the Incarnation of God in Jesus necessitates the historical-critical method in order to do justice to its human and historic nature. The historical-critical exegesis corresponds connaturally to the structure and nature of Christianity.[70] Ratzinger learned this under his teacher of New Testament studies, Friedrich Wilhelm Maier, and it forms the center of his theological labors.[71]

Revelation is not subservient to scripture and tradition but is the actual divine speaking and acting, preceding all historic variations of such speech. In this sense, revelation is the source feeding scripture and tradition. Drawing on the process of forming canons, Ratzinger shows how scripture and tradition are mutually related to each other. In this sense, the Church does not offer a final statement concerning the list of canonical books by the John, last apostle. Only by reflecting on the Holy Spirit as efficacious in the Church, and struggling to obtain his assistance, does the Church know which books belong to the canon of apostolic writings. The Church inquires regarding which books the Holy Spirit was effective in, with the Church being able to recognize the Holy Spirit's works. This vivacious struggle for the Holy Spirit can be circumscribed as "trader" as he enables the Church and its members to recognize him and thereby to become Church. This expresses trust in the Holy Spirit's work in spelling out, over generations, the nature of the Incarnation. The process that discovers the essence of revelation requires struggle for and trust in the Holy Spirit. An appreciation for the process of spiritual acquisition and the unfolding of the mystery of the Incarnation of Jesus Christ was rejected by Michael Schmaus, who refused to acknowledge it, and even called it a form of subjectivism.

Preventing a decline into irrationality, creedal truths gain a new value: they refer to Jesus Christ. Perceived thus, creedal statements lose the quality of binding statutes. Jesus Christ becomes their hub. As John 14:9 states, "He who has seen me has seen the Father." Thus, the Vatican II Council calls upon Christians to live in communion with the divine Thou, a circumincession of faith, hope, and charity.

Dei Verbum liberated the Church from a fixation on herself: "If sometimes it might appear that the Council was tending towards an ecclesiological mirroring of itself, in which the Church moved completely within its own orbit, and made itself the central object of its own proclamation, instead of constantly pointing beyond itself, here the whole of the life of the Church is, as it were, opened upwards, and its whole being gathered together in the attitude of listening, which can be the only source of what it has to say."[72]

Ratzinger welcomed the *Dogmatic Constitution on Divine Revelation (Dei Verbum)* as revolutionizing the very systemics of Catholic theology. It focuses on God's self-revelation in Jesus. It places the Church in a position of reverent listening to the Divine Word of God. Ratzinger was also delighted by its recognition that scripture is an outgrowth of the people of God's history.[73] The document's perspective bridged revelation and natural knowledge of God. Thus, a rapport could be established between revelation and philosophical reflection. The documents on religious freedom and the Church's relationship to Judaism, ecumenism, and other religions are grounded in *Dei Verbum*'s understanding of a Christ-centered revelation. Ratzinger himself believed this departure from an instructive-theoretical approach typical of the First Vatican Council was indebted in part to the dialectical theology of Karl Barth and the personalist philosophy advocated by thinkers such as Ebner and Buber.[74] Revelation is more than supernatural utterances made in Jesus' time and completed with the death of the last apostle. Were that the case, faith would entail relating to something merely past. Such an intellectualistic and historistic understanding of revelation, as often subscribed to in the nineteenth century, is faulty. Revelation is not the sum total of sentences uttered; it is a person, namely, Jesus Christ—spanning the tension of "the altar of the word" and "the altar of the bread" (Augustine)—scriptural and Eucharistic presence of the Lord. Jesus Christ is the Logos, the all-encompassing revelation. Francisco Suárez, SJ (1548–1617) had underscored the propositional nature of revelation: "Whereas Thomas looked at faith from the 'inside' and focused on the change that faith brings about in the human being, Suárez looked at faith 'from outside' and described the way we can see it working."[75] While Suárez ceased to perceive the supernatural virtue of faith as bringing about participation in divine life, Thomas saw, in the symbolic nature of language, the possibility of entering into such participation. No amount of words can exhaust *the* all-embracing Word.[76] In light of this background, according to Thomas Söding, theology's ongoing hermeneutical task is to correlate the Word with the numerous human words.[77]

Revelation is essentially a person, Jesus Christ, not a cognitive process. This comes alive and is confirmed as true by the individual believer who surveys the history of salvation; this is what Ratzinger and Jean Daniélou, SJ (*peritus*, and later cardinal) maintain is Church history.

While *Dei Filius*, the Vatican I document on revelation, is concerned with combating *ad extram* (to the outside, the world) the errors of naturalism and rationalism, *Dei Verbum* attempts to describe *ad intram* (to the inside of the Church) the tension between scripture and tradition and spell out how revelation is related to history. *Begnadete Teilhabe*, "engraced participation," is God's intention in revelation. Thus, God evidences himself as different from the remote, changeless, and pure being the ancient Greeks or those living during the Enlightenment had imagined God to be. *Dei Verbum* attempts to capture this in words: "This economy of revelation is realized by deeds and words, which are intrinsically bound up with each other. As a result, the works performed by God in the history of salvation show forth and bear out the doctrine and realities signified by the words: the words, for their part, proclaim the works, and bring to light the mystery they contain. The most intimate truth which this revelation gives us about God and the salvation of man shines forth in Christ, who is himself both the mediator and the sum total of Revelation" (*DV* 2). God reveals himself as person. This is the point of departure for *Dei Verbum*, whereas in *Dei Filius* natural knowledge of God serves as the introduction to the theme. Using the expression "the eternal decree of his will," *Dei Filius* is quite legalistic in tenor. In contrast, *Dei Verbum* speaks of "the sacrament of his will." His will enables entering the mystery of Christ as a unity of word and deed, law and grace, person and utterance.[78] Taking up the language of *Theosis* or deification, revelation's purpose is the transformation of the human person in the life of the Trinity.

Dei Verbum 12 stresses that God speaks in scripture using human language. It quotes Augustine[79] but does not do full justice to Augustine's broad understanding of scripture. It does not acknowledge that God does not speak out of inner, ontic necessity, but also that as shepherd he is impelled in charity to seek the lost sheep (Lk 15). Augustine demonstrates that scripture not merely informs but also believes and attests to what it relates.

Dei Verbum succeeds in bearing out the difference between the numerous traditions and the one Tradition (that is, numerous traditions understood as the accidental religious customs and conventions that assist in understanding the one Tradition). Ratzinger considered this a significant shift vis-à-vis the Council of Trent.[80] However, he did consider it a deficit that the council did not better define the relationship between Tradition and traditions.[81] Consequently, some engaged in ecumenical dialogue with Protestants, erroneously construed a hermeneutical priority of scripture over tradition. This is what comes from an isolated reading of *Dei Verbum* 9: "Sacred scripture is the speech of God as it is put down in writing under the breath of the Holy Spirit. And Tradition transmits in its entirety the Word of God...." Ratzinger had anticipated this danger.[82] Tradition is not based exclusively on written texts but is based on both written and oral testimony. The potential for misunderstanding goes back to the Tübingen scholar Josef Rupert Geiselmann, who in the 1950s advocated in favor of a Catholic *sola scriptura* by introducing the concept of *totam in scriptura* (that is, that scripture contains the entire content of revelation). In the specific volume of the *Quaestiones Disputatae* (which relates a series of exchanges among theologians on a particular topic), Ratzinger wrote with Karl Rahner on revelation and tradition, addressing this thorny issue and suggested a Christological solution. In it, Ratzinger postulates a primacy of revelation over testimony. It is with and in Jesus Christ that one comprehends the Old Testament. The New Testament attests to God's openness in Jesus Christ to humankind and begins the life of the Church. In the Johannine sense, Christ is "in us" and "we are in him." Christians live in the presence of Christ. It is this perspective that makes scripture one whole narrative.[83] Fortunately, *Dei Verbum* 6 formulates that scripture attests to God's revelation through the apostles and prophets. Scripture not only narrates God's search for humanity, but more importantly is, at the same time, the product of this search.

Dei Verbum 7 describes Jesus Christ as "promulgating" and "fulfilling" the gospel. This conjures up the notions of "communication" and "gift," which are no longer Christ's divine activities that occurred in a distant past, as the Council of Trent had argued. Rather, they intimate living with and in Christ in a way that captures Thomas Aquinas. Here Ratzinger finds:

> A comprehensive view of Revelation, precisely because it is concerned with the whole of man, is founded not only in the Word that Christ preached, but in the whole of the living experience of his person, thus embracing what is said and what is unsaid, what the apostles in their turn are not able to express fully in words, but which is found in the whole reality of the Christian existence of which they speak, far transcending the framework of what has been explicitly formulated in words. And finally, the guidance of the Paraclete promised to the disciples is not a "dictatio" but "suggestio," the remembering and understanding of the unspoken in what was once spoken, which reaches down to the depth of a process that cannot be measured by the terms "praedicatio oralis," and the transmission of which cannot therefore be merely the process of the handing down of words.[84]

The vessel containing revelation is Tradition in the singular, which is the sacramental reality in the form of the Church celebrating and living the seven sacraments and actuating herself daily in the Eucharist. Such an ecclesial grounding of Tradition renders a plurality of traditions incorrect. Tradition is the plenitude of God's presence in Jesus Christ and does not refer to exterior customs. However, even after Vatican II, the term "tradition" has remained ambiguous. As Cardinal Albert Meyer from Chicago rightly observed during a speech to the council on September 30, 1964, in the Church there do exist traditions that are accidental and/or altogether distorting to the faith.[85] In other words, how is one to differentiate between accidental customs, revisable traditions, and Tradition? Ratzinger regretted that the council did not satisfactorily address these concerns. No account is given of how traditions come about and what criteria ought to be applied to evaluate and discern a genuine tradition and safeguard the integrity of the faith. Ratzinger suggests this corrective can be found in scripture. He reminds his readers that *Dei Verbum* 10 stresses that tradition and scripture form the one deposit of the Word of God.

This lack is all the more deplorable because the pragmatic and technical outlook of our age is unable to appreciate spiritual processes such as Tradition. As people lose an appreciation for history, a degree of *humanitas* is lost. The Church must counteract this development and free humanity from an unhealthy fixation on the moment. An esteem for history and the experience of oneself as being part of it is important precisely in order to master the *hic et nunc* (here and now). This task is incumbent on the Church as it is both responsible for humanity's identity and because the Church's very lifeline is Tradition. Without Tradition, the Church loses her connection with Christ and cannot enter into his filial relationship with God the Father.[86] As Rowland summarizes Ratzinger's thought: "According to his more classical understanding of Revelation, Revelation is fully present only when, in addition to the material statements which testify to it, its own inner reality is itself operative in the form of faith. Thus, 'it is only to one who has entered into the community of faith with all its practices that the word of faith reveals itself.'"[87]

This insight is the result of his Augustinian-Bonaventurian background, where *memoria* (memory), *intellectus* (intellect), and *voluntas* (will) are faculties of the human soul that engage revelation. In fact, for Bonaventure these faculties correlate to the processions of the Trinity. The Eucharistic *anamnesis* (recollection) is the core of memory, giving history a meaning and direction it could never generate on its own. Thus, in the deepest sense human beings acquire a full identity that perdures in history but is not lost at the end of time. In this vein, Ratzinger sees history and historicity as necessary corollaries of one reality that is revelation. An intellect exposed to memory invariably produces Tradition and Tradition in turn realizes itself in history: "...for without trans-temporal relationship of person to person, humanity cannot be awakened to itself, cannot express itself."[88] Tradition and history are interdependent entities in need of each other. This analogy may be carried further: would not the human spirit abolish itself, if it negated the Logos as a historic reality? From this perspective, one understands the dynamic nature of revelation: it must be gained, conquered by every human being on his or her own. Echoing Johann Adam Möhler, Johann Michael Sailer, Newman, de Lubac, Daniélou, and the best theologians of the twentieth century, Ratzinger insists the human spirit in every human being must be activated. Revelation is Jesus Christ, whom each person must behold directly, so that the individual can establish a personal relationship with him. This comes about by engaging scripture and by apprehending in the history of the Church not "a detective story" but, first and foremost, salvation history speaking to the individual believer and incorporating him or her into the movement of temporality toward the final judgment day. The *Catechism of the Catholic Church* wants to convey in number 66 precisely this: "The Christian economy, therefore, since it is the new and definitive Covenant, will never pass away.... Yet, even if Revelation is already complete, it has not been made completely explicit;

it remains for Christian faith gradually to grasp its full significance over the course of the centuries."

Ratzinger is keenly mindful of the need for exegetical work to investigate the literal meaning of a biblical text. This is not merely a question of intellectual veracity but reveals a deeply Christological aspect. Exegesis plays the role of a guardian. Investigating the literal meaning wards off a gnosis that attempts to sever the ties between the *sarx* (flesh) and the *Logos*, between Jesus and Christ, between the human being Jesus and Christ the second person in the Blessed Trinity. At the same time, the Church's teaching office is likewise put to the test by such exegetical labors. Such a close correlation of these four elements, *Logos*, *sarx*, scripture, and the Church, prevents presumptuously playing scripture against the Church.[89] If such a separation of scripture and the Church were ever to occur, Ratzinger argues in the Erasmus lecture of 1988 that scripture would be reduced to mere literature.* The respective biblical texts need to transcend into one whole. This illumines the individual text's revelatory character. Ratzinger seems to argue that scripture needs to transcend into the Church to find its whole (*Ganze*). Indeed, it was exclusively in the Church and sanctioned by the Church (and not apart from her) that the biblical canon came about. This ecclesial exegesis assures the unity of Word and event in the person of Jesus Christ.[90] On this point Ratzinger addresses a sensitive and crucial issue that *Dei Verbum* was unable to resolve. In faithful continuation of the hermeneutics of Vatican II, Söding argues biblical scholarship is called upon "to probe a response" to God's self-revelation in Jesus Christ.[91]

Along with the Protestant theologian Ernst Käsemann, Ratzinger seems to argue that the New Testament in isolation, by itself, would favor a plurality of confessions, rather than their unity.[92] All ecumenical efforts would then be but exercises in futility. Ratzinger thus succeeds in demonstrating that Jesus Christ keeps the Tridentine inclusive *et . . . et* (Latin for "inclusive" or "as well as") alive in all areas of theology. Theology's concern is to show time and again from Jesus Christ's own perspective that faith is the spirit bringing scripture forth and therefore the gate accessing the interior of scripture.[93]

In Ratzinger's judgment, the council reflected on dogmatic development and was a part of this process. Despite his overall positive evaluation, he faulted *Dei Verbum* for its optimism regarding the *mysterium iniquitatis* (the mystery of sin),[94] but he was quite delighted about the way scripture is integrated.[95] In his commentary, he reminds the reader of the danger of separating scripture from the Church, which would lead either to fundamentalist biblicism or subjectivism. He welcomed the Church fathers and the Vulgate as hermeneutic tools, as they are moments of tradition and manifestations of the sense of the Church. He considered, in principle, the use of the term "tradition" in the singular well suited but observed a lack of nuance when evaluating the elements of tradition.[96]

---

*The annually held Erasmus Lecture is delivered in New York City and is sponsored by the Institute on Religion and Public Life, which publishes the monthly journal *First Things*.

This prelude is significant as it sheds light on Ratzinger's own theological profile. Cardinal Frings was blind by this time and was dependent on his *peritus* to compose his interventions. Frings would then learn the Latin text by heart. Also in this regard, one can hardly overestimate the seminal role Ratzinger played in the genesis of *Dei Verbum*.[97]

It is Ratzinger's foundational hermeneutic premise that a difference always exists between revelation and scripture (that is, he maintains the nonidentity of revelation and scripture). Another of his basic assumptions is that biblical exegesis merits the predication "exegesis" only insofar as it is in conformity with revelation. Furthermore, he divines (1) a consonance and continuity between the revelation beginning in Abraham and the one culminating in Jesus Christ, (2) all biblical narratives are testimonies to the one narrative of salvation history, and (3) this understanding is captured in the concept of *"Concordia testamentorum"* (agreement among the two testaments). These three principles can be detected in all of Ratzinger's writings, beginning with his doctoral dissertation and continuing in his habilitation, his contributions to the council, and up to this very day.

The insurmountable difference between tradition and scripture testifies to the greater valence of tradition as a historic event vis-à-vis revelation's attestation in scripture. In the first part of his habilitation, Ratzinger seems to demonstrate this thesis. To the medieval mind, treating tradition and scripture as equivalent seemed quite unimaginable. Unfortunately, Michael Schmaus, the second reader and second dogmatician in the department, rejected Ratzinger's draft. As a result, only the second part was submitted for the defense. It is this part alone that has been published and translated. The essence of the unpublished portion was summarized in an article by Ratzinger published shortly thereafter.[98]

In the habilitation and his subsequent article, Ratzinger argues that the term "revelation" comprises far more than merely the objective process of imparting God's self-communication and its manifestation in scripture. It also comprises the subjective self-accessing of the message by the addressee. In Ratzinger's interpretation of Bonaventure's view on revelation, Schmaus perceived an unjustifiable modernist, subjectivist reinterpretation of revelation. As Ratzinger does not tire of demonstrating, Bonaventure's understanding of revelation contains the Augustinian and pre-Thomistic understanding of revelation. Ratzinger carefully avoids reinterpreting Bonaventure's definition of revelation existentialistically. In Bonaventure, he sees a vivacious process described; something rather akin to what Newman also apprehended, namely, the process of the development of doctrine. Revelation as God turning toward a human being occurs continually. This is an ongoing process, however much the objective self-communication of God has come to a definitive end.

Referring to the late Byzantine theologian Nicholas Cabasilas, Ratzinger observes: "He is not content to leave this assertion (that knowledge causes charity) in general terms. In his characteristically rigorous thought, he distinguishes between two kinds of knowledge. One is knowledge through instruction, which remains, so to speak, 'second-hand' and does not imply any direct contact with reality itself. The second type of knowledge is knowledge through personal experience, through a direct relationship with the reality.... True knowledge is being struck by the arrow of Beauty that wounds man, moved by reality, 'how it is Christ himself who is present and in an ineffable way disposes and forms the souls of men' (cf. *The Life of Christ*, Book II, p. 15)."[99] In this sense, revelation is mediated through human beings formed by Christ through the sacramental life of the Church. This may also occur through the medium of art. Life in Christ is far too powerful to be constrained by human logic or language. It becomes apparent in the greatness of human beings, "touched by the very humanity of God himself."[100] In accord with Guardini, Ratzinger perceives the essence of Christianity residing in a person, Jesus Christ, who transforms other persons.

Revelation occurs ever anew in ecclesial contexts of the most varied kinds. Yet the reader of scripture is never a singular, lonesome reader (*Einzelleser*) but lives and appropriates scripture within the context of "the Church's living understanding of scripture." Thus, Pope Benedict XVI can claim: "He, who believes, is not lonesome." There exists a communitarian dimension to biblical faith that both transposes the addressee into the context of the past (*Sitz im Leben*—place in life) of a particular pericope and redeems him from making sense of the concrete contemporary world on his own. Such ecclesiality is constitutive for Christian faith. This is facilitated by the ever selfsame Church that brought forth scripture and administers the sacraments today.[101] In ecclesial revelation, the Bonaventurian notion of the celestial realm breaking into the present is no longer wishful thinking. With Christ's death, Resurrection, and Ascension into heaven a new era of *crisis* (in the Greek meaning of the word "crisis" as "judgment, separation, and selection") has come about, which will last until the final judgment day: it is an era of glory and vileness, of Redemption and agony. In this historic process, the Church becomes *in nuce* the bearer of the foretaste of heaven. This is the profound cause for cherishing this world and yet not being arrested in it. It can be lived out to the fullest in the discipleship of Christ.

It was a relief for Ratzinger to hear Pope Paul VI's programmatic speech opening the second session of the Second Vatican Council. Nichols writes:

> While admitting that someone else might have a different account, Ratzinger took from it, above all, its Christocentrism. Presenting Christ as the only mediator and hope of the Church, the pope declared that the Saviour was the true "president" of the Council. And he evoked for his listeners the great apsidal mosaic at Saint Paul's outside the Walls, where Christ the Pantocrator dwarfs the tiny figure of Pope Honorius III who, bowed low in *proskunēsis* before him, touches his feet with a kiss. In his address, the pope, in Ratzinger's words, declared Christ the "interpreter of the present and the measure of all that is happening."[102]

Ratzinger subscribed to a "progressive" vision in the following sense: his position was not dictated by the wish for modernization or adaptation to a more palatable understanding of Christ and the Church but by a return to biblical, patristic, and high medieval explications. This defines him as a man of the Ressourcement movement. He was not so much interested in modernity but in Jesus' will. Genuine renewal can only come about by a reorientation toward Jesus: "Giving priority to the Liturgy was an inspired choice, a 'confession of the true center of the Church.' That center is the Church's celebration of her nuptial with her Lord in the Eucharistic mystery. In that sacramental share in the sacrifice of Christ, the Church receives her deepest mission: adoring the triune God."[103]

The main concern of this second session was the *Dogmatic Constitution on the Church (Lumen Gentium)*. The Church is divined as the product of the economies of both the eternal Son and the Holy Spirit. It is built on both a sacramental and charismatic pillar. Christ himself personally entrusted Peter and his successors with the Petrine office. This vertical catholicity is complemented by a horizontal catholicity. Ratzinger seemed to believe that, in view of Eastern Christendom, the latter must be strengthened in order to promote a communal ecclesiology.[104] He welcomed Cardinal König's intervention to incorporate Mariology into *Lumen Gentium*. Emphasis is laid on Mary's defenseless lowliness as the paradigm for the Church's own triumph.[105] Later, Ratzinger would lament that this led to yet another misunderstanding. Rather than appreciating Mary as *Theotokos*, Mother of God, as the paradigm for the Church, Mariology was subsequently neglected. Yet, only via Mary does one understand the truth about both Jesus Christ and the Church. A balanced appreciation of Mary's role in salvation history prevents one from reducing the Savior to a mere human and from perceiving the Church as a mere congregation. For this reason, Ratzinger is now more favorably disposed to Marian titles than he perhaps was during the council.[106] He argues, "The marriage of Mariology with ecclesiology emphasizes that the idea of the Church necessarily includes that of the 'heavenly Church,' *ecclesia caelestis*. The Church's reality extends into the mystery of the End, which eludes all human concepts and dispositions."[107]

The most contentious issue was and is the interpretation of the Church of Christ as it "subsists in" the Catholic Church (*LG* 8). This was considered by many to mean the true Church also exists outside the Catholic Church. For Ratzinger, however, this formula simply means the Church of Christ is fully realized in its integral existence in the Catholic Church but grants that other Christian denominations have ecclesial elements. It's not that these denominations are not churches, but they lack certain *ecclesia*-constituting elements.[108]

Preserving Jesus Christ against Traditionalist Intellectualism and Modernist Subjectivism

Ratzinger admits how his study of Bonaventure helped him contribute to the conciliar discussions on revelation, scripture, and tradition: "By definition, revelation requires someone who apprehends it. These insights, gained through my reading of Bonaventure, were later on very important for me at the time of the conciliar discussion on revelation, scripture, and tradition. Because, if Bonaventure is right, then revelation precedes scripture and becomes deposited in scripture but is not simply identical with it."[109] In revelation, the understanding subject is always involved. He further elaborated this perspective in his collaboration with Karl Rahner when they jointly edited the volume of *Quaestiones Disputatae* on "Revelation and Transmission." Ratzinger's contribution to it is based on his inaugural lecture, given in 1963, at the University of Münster.[110] Ratzinger develops his argument in a critical analysis of Josef Rupert Geiselmann's thesis of the supposed self-sufficiency of scripture for Catholic theology. Ratzinger warns that such a thesis is self-illusion. The dogmas of 1854 and 1950 are unsustainable if one subscribes to this hypothesis. From the days of early Christianity, Catholic doctrinal development clashes with the Protestant principle of *sola scriptura*, which was introduced in the sixteenth century. This issue can only be resolved if one broadens the question to reflect on the relationship between scripture and tradition.[111] An incongruity exists between the two terms. Revelation refers to the sum total of divine actions and speeches regarding human beings. It describes a reality that scripture may attest to but which can never be exhaustively reduced to scripture alone. As reality transcends the message, revelation likewise transcends scripture. Should Ratzinger's term "sufficient" be retained, in the sense that Christ is "sufficient" for revelation?[112] Such a position safeguards revelation against becoming reduced by a naïve fundamentalist temptation.

Taking up Geiselmann's hypothesis of scripture's self-sufficiency, but without mentioning Ratzinger's convincing critique of this position, Hermann Häring, in his study on the theology of Ratzinger, commits a gross error when claiming that in the middle of the previous century scripture was discovered by Catholics as the sole source of revelation. In his critique of the encyclical *Dominus Jesus*, and of Pope Benedict's theology in general, Häring claims no other material or hermeneutic source exists but scripture.[113] This is contradicted both by Ratzinger's own texts in this area and by the council's document *Dei Verbum:* "Sacred Tradition and scripture make up a single sacred deposit of the Word of God, which is entrusted to the Church" (*DV* 10).

While admittedly serious deficits exist in sufficiently appreciating the Second Vatican Council's positions, there is no denying that the council perceived Jesus Christ as the culminating agent for revelation. Christian faith occurs essentially in the human person as the *universale concretum* (the concrete universal every human being can encounter) of God's covenantal loyalty, in a living and personal encounter with Jesus Christ. Subscribing to a pluralistic paradigm, Häring latently disputes the uniqueness of Jesus Christ: "In the meantime, it is a common opinion in theology that he who speaks of God's definitive revelation of Jesus Christ's uniqueness or of the One who precedes Abraham does not reference theoretically developed convictions but the result of believing experience. He who acknowledges Jesus as 'the Way, Truth, and Life,' does not make an objective statement concerning the 'way, truth and life elsewhere.'"[114]

Ratzinger agrees with Häring concerning the need for a believing subject, as there cannot possibly be revelation without accepting it. Yet concerning the quality of revelation they do not see eye to eye. To Ratzinger's mind, revelation is a historic reality, established in Israel as God's people and coming to its unsurpassable culmination in Jesus Christ. Jesus Christ is the Father's Word. Therefore, revelation precedes scripture and the latter attests to it. The two never become identical. Thus, one is compelled to divine in scripture not revelation itself but a witness to revelation. For this reason, both the *Catechism of the Catholic Church*[115] and Ratzinger outright reject the notion of Christianity being a "religion of the book." Rather, a historic, personal encounter is captured in written form for posterity's sake. Ratzinger turns to one of Paul's expressions that faith does not come from reading but from hearing (Rom 10:17). Reading neither scripture nor the *Catechism* communicates faith per se because it is a personal encounter.[116] A historistic and intellectualistic definition of revelation as the communication of a certain number of sentences is incorrect:

> Revelation, which is to say, God's approach to man, is always greater than what can be contained in human words, greater even than the words of scripture. As I have already said in connection with my work on Bonaventure, both in the Middle Ages and at Trent it would have been impossible to refer to scripture simply as "revelation," as is the normal linguistic usage today. Scripture is essential, as witness of revelation, but revelation is something alive, something greater and more: proper to it is the fact that it arrives and is perceived—otherwise it could not have become revelation. Revelation is not a meteor fallen to earth that now lies around somewhere as a rock mass from which rock samples can be taken and submitted to laboratory analysis. Revelation has instruments; but it is not separable from the living God, and it always requires a living person to whom it is communicated.[117]

With this background, one sees that scripture is not relegated to some insignificant role but becomes "the material principle of revelation." On the other hand, however, revelation will never be completely objectified. Precisely due to this insurmountable difference between the two, scripture requires an interpretation consonant with revelation as revelation. The exegete must grant God the option to reveal himself under the conditions proper to a supremely sovereign (because he is divine) revealer. The historical-critical method per se is neither correct nor incorrect. What is required is that the manner in which this method is applied conforms to revelation's unique nature.[118] In his inaugural lecture at the University of Münster, Ratzinger referred to exegesis as exercising the role of a "guardian." It therefore parallels the Church's office as guardian of the truth. Exegesis' task of "researching the literal meaning, thereby protects the Logos' close ties to the *sarx* [flesh] against Gnosticism."[119] No purely human science can be as egalitarian as revelation, speaking likewise to both the unschooled (*anawim* in Hebrew, *simplex et idiota* in Bonaventure's language) and the educated.

In *An Essay in Aid of a Grammar of Assent*, Newman argues similarly but from a completely different point of departure.[120] Taking Aristotle's notion of *phronesis* (prudence, thought, intellect)—in contrast to *episteme* (insight, knowledge)—as his point of departure, Newman shows the dignity of an insight gained from life experience. He compares the "illative sense," as he terms it, to (abstract) notional insight, the preferred tool in the realm of the sciences and logic. The latter can be obtained without personal, biographical engagement. However, every human being, *qua* human being, is able to use his or her conscience to arrive at a real assent, which is the mark of faith. This allows the individual to utilize imagination in order to develop a picture of Jesus Christ. The human picture of Our Lord becomes nothing short of an actual vivification of the Word. This discovery represents a significant rehabilitation of nonscientific knowledge without denigrating academic discourse. It establishes the relative autonomy of science and faith and thereby liberates humankind from the relentless colonization of all aspects of life by scientific thinking.[121] For the nineteenth century Newman was the first to recognize and rehabilitate the faith of the simple as a locale of genuine theological insight. The illative sense is something like an *organum investigandi* (a human organ investigating reality) overcoming the separation of humankind into scientific and nonscientific segments. It restores a sense of solidarity among all people of good will. Unfortunately, as is the case with much of Ratzinger's thought, Newman's groundbreaking discovery of the illative sense still awaits wider appreciation and reception.

The fact that scientific rationality has a wide but limited range is further corroborated by Albert Schweitzer's investigation into the quest for the historic Jesus. In part, it demonstrates the futility of a search for the historic Jesus.[122]

The relative autonomy of scripture vis-à-vis the Church and the limits of the Church's magisterium are thus implicitly stated. One can even make out a certain agreement between Ratzinger and Luther in this regard. Even at the early stage of his thought, Ratzinger saw a reciprocal subordination of scripture and the Church, which anticipated *Dei Verbum* 10: the teaching office's "authority in this matter is exercised in the name of Jesus Christ. Yet, this magisterium is not superior to the Word of God, but is its servant." The teaching office does not stand above the Word of God but serves it. The historical-critical method's validity can be acknowledged because a new conception of revelation exists. Revelation is an event of divine-human communication—as described in *Dei Verbum* 2 through 6—and not the general proclamation of truths that transcend time and space and simply require an external acknowledgment.[123] Christian faith requires a personal assent from each believer. Thus, Christianity lives from interiority. This explains Ratzinger's reservations concerning traditionalists who subscribe to an ahistoric understanding of revelation and verbal inspiration. He refers to the "continuity of Vatican II with the previous Councils. It is a continuity that is not a rigid, external identification with what had gone before but a preservation of the old, established in the midst of progress."[124] This is the content of the expression *inhaerere vestigiis*, "as a perfect example of dogmatic development, of the inner *relecture* [re-reading] of dogma in dogmatic history."[125]

While some tension may seem to exist between the views expressed earlier in his 1967 commentary on *Dei Verbum* and his later understanding of revelation as formulated in his 1989 essay "*Schriftauslegung im Widerstreit*" ("Exegesis in Conflict"), his essay on "Christology in the Conflicting Areas of Early Christian Exegesis and Modern Scripture Interpretation" supplies the critical bridge between the two.[126] In this short article, he compares the ontological view of Chalcedonian Christology (that claimed that Jesus Christ was fully divine and fully human while on earth) with a purely modern, existentialist exegesis. He shows that opposition to the Chalcedonian formula for Jesus Christ is not grounded in exegetical research but is, first and foremost, a modern prejudice. Scripture and exegesis were not formulated with an anti-Hellenistic thesis.[127] Attempts are often taken to rid Christianity of a supposedly fateful "Hellenization." Ratzinger argues one frequently misses a complete reception of *Dei Verbum* for this very reason. While embracing the historical-critical method, one ignores a hermeneutics consonant with the actual nature of revelation. Thus, one frequently encounters a naïve and unreflective amalgam of the historical-critical method and randomly selected secular philosophies. The result is a confusing plurality of hypotheses that do not build up the people of God. The exegete may not approach scripture a priori with a modern or scientific prejudice, constraining and limiting God's actions and revelation. To do so would preclude God's independence from the respective "human state of the art" methods, methods which are conditioned by contingent time and space. In order to do justice to God as sovereign and self-revealing, the exegete must be willing to undergo thoroughgoing self-criticism. Conformity to revelation is by no means a dogmatic or institutional, heteronymous determination of biblical scholarship, but a necessity the text itself requires. A magisterium that ensures scripture is read in the same manner and spirit in which it was composed is far from an ideological, self-immunizing institution. The magisterium is a function of the ecclesial community and through its faith it enables revelation to become, time and again, revelation, thus allowing the act of faith to be in agreement with scripture as a testimony to revelation. A difference exists between exegesis per se and exegetical work. The latter is oftentimes subcutaneously informed by a philosophical a priori guiding it. Such a historic or philosophical presupposition as a firmly established a priori hinders the exegete from allowing God to speak in history in his own aseity (being in and of himself) and essence, which would supremely overcome the contingence and sins of the world.[128] Unwittingly subscribing to an unbridgeable bifurcation of reality into the known phenomenal and transcendent noumenal realms à la Kant,[129] a thus preconditioned dualist exegete would invariably deprive revelation and Christ of their world-transforming qualities.

Prior to 2000, in preparation for the new millennium, Ratzinger warned of the inherent limits of an exegesis that questions God's revelation in Christ due to the rigorous application of scientific methods external to the faith. Christ is not distilled from scripture, nor is he the result of philosophical presuppositions. If this were so, Jesus could never be apprehended as the eternal Son of God. He writes:

> For example, when the point of departure is the idea of Jesus as a revolutionary, the Jesus of "liberation theology," on the one hand, entire sequences of passages fall by the wayside, whereas other elements

suddenly become central, indeed, appear to suggest lost sources and categorically demand the reinterpretation of the existing texts. The preconceived ideas of what Jesus cannot be (the Son of God), and of what he should be, themselves become tools of interpretation and ultimately lend the appearance of rigorous historical findings to what in reality is merely the result of philosophical presuppositions.[130]

CHAPTER 11

The Question of Faith in the World

When reflecting on Pope Paul VI's opening remarks at the council's second session, Ratzinger noted with satisfaction: "You had to hear it to fully appreciate how movingly it integrated theological considerations with personal spiritual testimony. The accents can, of course, be variously placed. What most impressed me was how Christ-centric it was."[1] In marked contrast, he noted that accommodating the contemporary culture seemed to be the single most important characteristic of the council in the eyes of the majority of observers. They often seemed to perceive the council through the filters of the terms "progressive" and "conservative" rather than to behold "the inner aspects, the spiritual profile of the Church" and recognize that the Christ-filled reality of the Church transcends such clichés. All renewal is measured against Christ, to whom scripture is witness.[2] To understand the council's most central concern, one should turn to *Gaudium et Spes* (GS) 22, as both John Paul II and Ratzinger emphasized at the 1985 Bishops' Synod: "Christ the Lord, Christ the new Adam, in the very revelation of the mystery of the Father and of his love, fully reveals man to himself and brings to light his most high calling." It is a quote that could have been taken directly from de Lubac's magisterial *Catholicism*, which discussed the liberating nature of Catholic dogma. The new Adam, Jesus Christ, transforms people into actuating their personhood, which they have by virtue of their being created in the image and likeness of Christ. This comes about by establishing a relationship with him. This entails the fact that only by embracing the Church's understanding of Christ do men and women understand themselves. Ecclesially formed dogma reveals to humankind its own identity. Ratzinger saw the pastoral constitution as "a discussion between Christian and unbeliever on the question who and what man really is."[3] Christology is another term for anthropology. He regrets that the document lends itself to misunderstanding as it emphasizes the Old Testament account of creation too much and emphasizes too little the perfection of humanity in beholding Jesus Christ face to face on the final judgment day. A "deep-rooted extrinsicism," a dualist two-tier thinking, a separation between nature and grace and between philosophy and theology was operative in the formation of the document.[4] For this reason, Ratzinger argues, it would have been far better to start the document with revelation in Christ. This would have shown that even a construction such as "pure reason" ultimately depends on theological presuppositions. The mystery of the Incarnation is not a superfluous addition to the secular description of an otherwise perfectly self-sufficient humanity. This "separatist reading" seems confirmed when examining *Gaudium et Spes* 36 in isolation: it advocates in favor of "the autonomy of earthly affairs."

While Thomas Aquinas does state creation is endowed with stability, goodness, and order on its own, he cautions that varying degrees of stability, goodness, and order exist. Moreover, the natural inclination to virtue can be weakened by sin.[5] This relative goodness does not come about on its own but is created by the triune God. The world on its own evidences "*vestigia*," traces of the Trinity as Augustine had argued in *De Trinitate*.[6] While Thomas might on occasion be misunderstood as favoring extrinsicism (that grace and revelation are totally alien to the human being), in sum neither Augustine nor Thomas lend arguments in support of an extrinsicist position. Maurice Blondel's epochal work *L'Action* (1893), on the self-execution of human thinking, which was much opposed by the author's secularist contemporaries, was not taken up explicitly by the council. This book attempted to overcome a too rigid separation of earthly and divine realms.

Ratzinger's criticism of the document includes its unqualified notion of "human autonomy" joined to an undifferentiated use of the term "freedom." It does not consider the lack of freedom humanity can suffer, as attested to by psychology and sociology. Neither does it integrate biblical testimony regarding discordant freedom, such as that found in Job, Ecclesiastes 15, and the Pauline description in Romans 7:13–25. Nor does it countenance Luther's (albeit one-sided) use of the notion "*servum arbitrium*" (man's enslaved will). Ratzinger even faults the document for its "downright Pelagian terminology."[7]

This detached reading of particular passages of the document was easier to accomplish for Ratzinger, who was used to stressing historical events as attested to in scripture and lived by the Church fathers, than it was for his fellow *peritus* during the council, Karl Rahner, who considered salvation and Redemption to occur ideationally in "the inward movements of the human spirit."[8]

Unfortunately, public perception of the council in the 1960s was that it was more concerned with reforming the institutional Church or welcoming the ways of the world into the Catholic faith than with a foundational recommitment to Jesus Christ. The Western hemisphere at the time was undergoing a profound period of cultural upheavals: student unrest, the Vietnam War, the casting aside of conventional mores, and so on. The differing circumstances in each country, when coupled with isolated readings of certain passages in the document, had various consequences. In France, for instance, some thought the *séparation* (severing of all ties between Church and state) proclaimed unilaterally by the French government in 1905 had been recognized by Vatican II. In Germany, the *Zentralrat der Deutschen Katholiken* (ZDK, that is, the German Catholic Church Council), a lay organization founded to defend the Catholic Church during the anti-Catholic *Kulturkampf* (1871–1887) suddenly defined its role in a novel way: as a mediator between the prevailing zeitgeist and the Church, thereby guaranteeing the Church would not lose touch with, and would even learn from, "the signs of the times." To this day, this goal is pursued every two years during the *Katholikentag* (a festival-like gathering organized by German Catholic laity) when Catholics, bishops, the major politicians of all parties, and intellectuals of different stripes gather in a particular city. In Eastern Europe, some leading Catholic bishops and theologians thought communism had a certain value for the betterment of society, and they interpreted the Vatican's *Ostpolitik* (that is, the policy of appeasement toward communist countries during the Cold War) under Cardinal Casaroli as recognizing the merits of Marxist ideology. The fact that many believers were suffering persecution for the sake of their faith was not appreciated by some Catholics.

The elusive term *aggiornamento* proved conducive to a superficial understanding of reform: reform understood, not as conversion to Jesus, but as the reorganization or redefinition of the nature of the Catholic faith. The general public was not sure what *aggiornamento* meant: accommodation, updating, radical change, and so forth. The term—heretofore unknown in theological discourse—had never before been used to define the purpose of a council. Quite tellingly, the Swiss theologian Karl Barth asked Paul VI during an audience in 1966 what the concept *aggiornamento* might mean.[9] Pope John Paul II's first encyclical, *Redemptor Hominis*, intended to bring about a Christocentric reorientation within the Church at large. *Redemptor Hominis* avoided stoic language when speaking of inter-human relationships, but it failed to follow the inspiration of personalism advocated by French and German philosophers. Pope Benedict's *Deus Caritas Est* attempts to introduce a more vigorous personalist perspective that the more intellectualist *Gaudium et Spes* had failed to integrate. In 1969, Ratzinger observed that were the Church "to accommodate herself to the world in any way that would entail a turning away from the Cross, this would not lead to a renewal of the Church, but only to her death."[10] This turning to the cross is, in his estimation, only possible by concentrating on Jesus.

CHAPTER 12

The Unity of the Old and New Testaments

In 1988 at St. Peter's Church in New York, Ratzinger gave a little noted description of the challenges contemporary biblical scholarship faces:

> In Vladimir Soloviev's *History of the Antichrist*, the eschatological enemy of the Redeemer recommended himself to believers, among other things, by the fact that he had earned his doctorate in theology at Tübingen [the German university town, known as one of the most rigorous places to study theology] and had written an exegetical work that was recognized as pioneering in the field. The Antichrist, a famous exegete! With this paradox Soloviev sought to shed light on the ambivalence inherent in biblical exegetical methodology for almost a hundred years now. To speak of the crisis of the historical-critical method today is practically a truism. This, despite the fact that it had gotten off to so optimistic a start.[1]

Ratzinger is far from belittling the numerous contributions the historical-critical method has made to understanding scripture and early Christianity—quite the contrary. He does argue, however, for a critical examination of the criteria used in interpreting the biblical witness. The historical-critical method is not the "court of last appeal" in understanding scripture. It must be used properly lest it draw one away from the revealer's intentions. "The word *interpretation* gives us a clue to the question itself: Every exegesis requires an 'inter'—an entering in and being 'inter,' or between, things—this is the involvement of the interpreter himself. Pure objectivity is an absurd abstraction. It is not the disinterested person who comes to knowledge; rather, interest [in the sense of an existential insertion of a person into the text] is itself a requirement for the possibility of coming to know." It is quite impossible to assume knowledge of something *Geistiges* (intellectual or spiritual) without being part of it. Even in the realm of the natural sciences, the noted nuclear physicist Werner Heisenberg enunciated the importance of the subject-object relationship. One cannot come to terms with an object other than as subject. The two cannot be neatly separated.[2] While remarkable insights into particular aspects and elements of scripture can be gleaned by an "outsider" who is not a believer, it is the believer as scholar who is able to integrate these insights into a greater whole. This is not an isolated or idiosyncratic view. Philosophers such as Paul Ricoeur, theologians such as René Laurentin and Ignace de la Potterie, and scripture scholars such as Peter Stuhlmacher are in agreement on this.[3]

If one discounts the heuristic value of such involvement, then scholarly efforts amount to something similar to pulling oneself up by one's own boot-straps. Ratzinger cites Bultmann, who argued that the Bible unfolds from proclamation. Only the Word is original to scripture. It is the Word that generates the only valid scene. All human words remain deficient vis-à-vis the Word. In fact, Bultmann tends to emphasize this to such an extent that he is unable to discern continuity between the pre-Easter Jesus and the community of believers that formed after the Lord's Resurrection.[4] Such discontinuity, Ratzinger seems to grant, would be observable if the sacramental reality of the Church and its seven sacraments did not form the binding link between Jesus and his believers over time and space. The Church as the reality celebrating the Eucharist vouches for its own continuity. This is a sacramental reality Bultmann had not experienced.

Only with this background is one able to comprehend the priority of the Word in Luther's understanding, his antithesis between Judaism and Christianity, his dialectic between the law and the gospel, and his polarizing the relationship between the Old and New Testaments. Disregarding the possibility of such a sacramental system, one does indeed reduce Christian existence to mere principled openness and alertness to the Word of God in the sense of a verbal message, as Martin Heidegger formulated in classic fashion in the twentieth century.

This is, in Ratzinger's judgment, a rather abstract and "philosophical" understanding of scripture. It is indebted to the philosopher Immanuel Kant (1724–1804), who claimed no human ear can ever hear the voice of "being-in-itself." Following this intellectual trajectory, modern exegesis is the victim of the reduction of history to philosophy. This is precisely Hellenization. Ratzinger poses the question of how one is to escape this situation:

> In the midst of the theological, methodological debate of his day, Gregory of Nyssa called upon the rationalist Eunomius not to confuse theology with the science of nature (theologein is not physiologein). "The mystery of theology is one thing," he said, "the scientific investigation of nature is quite another." One cannot then "encompass the unembraceable nature of God in the palm of a child's hand." Gregory was here alluding to the famous saying of Zeno: "The open hand is perception, the clapping hand is the agreement of the intellect, the hand fully closed upon something is the recording of judgment, the one hand clasped by the other is systematic science."[5]

He continues to cite Gregory: "These gliding and glittering lights of God's word which sparkle over the eyes of the soul...but now let what we hear from Elijah rise up to our soul and would that our thoughts too, might be snatched up into the fiery chariot...so that we would not have to abandon hope of drawing close to these stars, by which I mean the thoughts of God."[6] The overarching importance of scripture is lost if one specializes in particularities. The text calls for "sym-pathy" (that is, Greek for "suffering along with") or an understanding that is open toward the incalculable. It requires that the text address one, which for many would mean allowing an event of an irrational element to enter in. This, however, is precisely the crux of the matter: Protestant exegesis has no appreciation for the relationship between faith and reason because it does not appreciate the analogy of being. Faith allows reason to find much more reasonableness in scripture than reasonable scholarship would on its own. By being "biased" toward faith, reason extends its range and finds its fulfillment. Thomas Aquinas argued this: "The duty of every good interpreter is to contemplate not the words, but the sense of the words."[7] Otherwise, Ratzinger insists, one ultimately subscribes to a docetic Christology (according to which it merely seems as if the second person of the blessed Trinity, Jesus Christ, assumed human nature). Neither Jesus Christ nor human beings are elevated to a neutral area outside of history and the Church. Good exegesis will always give an account of the concrete *Sitz im Leben* (life context) generating a particular text.

Doing otherwise would amount to nothing short of a denial of the reader's creatureliness. The interpreter must accept the limitations implicit in it, as God did. On another occasion, Ratzinger quotes the French Jewish philosopher Simone Weil, who stated, "We experience the good only by doing it.... When we do evil we do not know it, because evil flies from the light."[8] Only when free from a mistake do human beings recognize it as such. Conversely, the good is recognized only when it is being done. Only God's charity can purify a damaged human heart and overcome the alienation suffered by the lack of a relationship with God. He quotes Paul's letter to the Philippians 2:5–8: "Jesus Christ, who, though he was in the form of God, did not count equality with God a thing to be grasped, but emptied himself, taking the form of a servant, being born in the likeness of men. And being found in human form he humbled himself and became obedient unto death, even death on a cross." In the *kenosis* of emptying himself, Jesus remained faithful to God as his eternal and obedient Son. In contrast to Adam, Jesus Christ goes Adam's way but "like God": "I do nothing on my own authority" (Jn 8:28). Therefore, the one who is truly like God does not grasp his autonomy, to the limitlessness of his ability and his willing. He does the contrary: he becomes completely dependent; he becomes a slave."[9] It is into such freedom—which is the most intense form of relationality—that the Bible scholar must enter in order to fully understand, as a scholar and as a human being, the biblical text.

In 1994, Ratzinger delivered a paper at a Jewish-Christian conference in Jerusalem in which he observed how difficult it had been for him as child to imagine Jesus condemning Jews. Jesus is free from any feelings of retribution. Christians and Jews should live in reconciliation for the sake of world peace so that the kingdom of the one God—of the Old and New Testaments— might come.[10] "Can the Christian faith, in its inner resoluteness and integrity, not only tolerate Judaism but accept it in its historic mission, or can it not? Can there be genuine reconciliation without surrendering the faith, or does reconciliation mean surrender? In the New Testament there are not two effects of the cross, one that condemns and one that saves, but only one that saves and reconciles."[11]

As close examination of its historic development illustrates, a profound interrelation exists between scripture and tradition. If one were to consider the Bible solely as a historic fact, one would miss its essence. This deeper understanding comes about by living in the Church, in its Eucharistic and sacramental life. As the Old Testament is an indissoluble part of this tradition, Ratzinger argues there exists but one covenant in which Jews and Christians pursue different paths.

Ratzinger based the central thesis of his doctoral dissertation on Augustine's teaching of the nature of the Church and on Henri de Lubac's discovery of the hermeneutic significance of the *concordia testamentorum* (material agreement in the two testaments) in the writings of the Church fathers. Augustine had cast this into the classic formula: "*Novum in Vetere latet, Vetus in Novo patet*" ("The New Testament lies hidden in the Old, and the Old Testament is opened up in the New").[12] *Dei Verbum* 16 quotes this. The unity between the two testaments is not a static unity but a unity that Christ conveys and enacts in the Holy Spirit. This allows one to apprehend a living unity between the Old and New Testaments, brought about by Jesus Christ and the Holy Spirit. What at first glance may seem various unrelated promises is sustained by a single fulfillment in Christ.[13]

In Ratzinger's theological vision, one cannot enter into the real presence of the Lord without beholding the presence of the divine in history in general and specifically as revealed in the Old Testament. Scripture and exegesis must be the soul of theology. Theology must apprehend itself as the interpretation of scripture within the Church. Otherwise, theology loses its foundations. Here one can make out a significant difference between Ratzinger and Karl Rahner as Ratzinger states: "I, on the contrary, precisely through my formation was marked above all by scripture and by the Fathers, by a form of thought that was essentially historical."[14] Ratzinger continuously strives to integrate scripture, patristics, liturgy, and history in order to spell out the spiritual message of a particular pericope. In each part of scripture something greater resounds: a God who shows us his countenance for the sake of our salvation and gives meaning to our lives in the here and now. The spiritual message of scripture in this exegetical, patristic, systematic, and historic matrix allows a fertile exchange with the great themes of every age.[15]

The weakness of some authors who write about Augustine is that they do not appreciate that for him Christian hermeneutics transforms the letter into the spirit of the gospel. The central Augustinian category "City of God" derives not from a nonbiblical, political, or philosophical theory but is inspired from the very midst of the Old Testament, particularly from the psalms. Ratzinger argues that one understands Augustine well only if one is already aware of Christian biblical hermeneutics. To the Christian mind, the whole of Jesus Christ, "*totus Christus*," head and body, that is, including the Church, is prefigured in the Old Testament. The Church is nothing short of the people of God. The Hebrews in the Old Covenant are a prolepsis of the mystical body of Christ. They are liberated as a community from the slavery of demons. One could not do any greater injustice to Augustine than to divorce his thinking from the great Christian ductus of his age: "Comprehending the one truth of Jesus Christ amid the vivacity of the lived [Eucharistic and ecclesial] presence."[16]

Ratzinger's study of Bonaventure confirmed these conclusions. The Old Testament is part of the history of dogma, and the drastic transition to the New Testament is a case of doctrinal development. Thus, Bonaventure sees a central weakness in Joachim of Fiore's theology of history because he overly stresses discontinuity. Bonaventure argues the Father, Son, and Spirit belong together. Thus, Christ becomes the center of history and remains so for all ages.[17] It is the grace of divine providence that allows every age, and every individual human being in human history since the Incarnation of the divine Logos, to behold anew the *forma Christi* (the form of Christ). Like St. Francis on Monte Alverno when he received the stigmata, every human being can be touched by Jesus Christ. The conjunction of God and humankind is a realizable possibility until the *Parousia* of the Lord.

The close proximity and interdependence of both testaments enables the reader to appreciate the Incarnation as *the* interpreting event: "The formula 'Jesus' is the 'Christ' entails that in the historic Jesus the Christ, the message of the Old Testament is fulfilled; the Old Testament understanding of who Jesus is, and what the Old Testament means, can be seen in light of the event of Christ."[18] In the event of Christ, the Old Testament as "scripture" receives its proper significance. The New Testament as scripture unlocks the Old Testament in light of the event of Christ. "It is, so to speak, the arrested process of the new exegesis of scripture from Christ."[19] Christ's ministry as it is fulfilled is exegesis, and it is here we find Christ's claim not to impart something radically novel but to attest to the proper interpretation of the Old Testament. As there is a difference between revelation and scripture, the latter must be interpreted in "the spirit of Christ," that is, from the spiritual authority of the Lord. Exegesis is bound to Christ.[20]

"And there has not arisen a prophet since in Israel like Moses, whom the Lord knew face to face" (Dt 34:10). This elegiac conclusion to the books of Moses is used by Ratzinger as a point of departure to demonstrate that no matter how well Israel might take hold of the Promised Land, deliverance could not be complete. This deliverance only comes about well over 1,250 years later in the *kerygma* (preaching) of Jesus Christ. "No one has ever seen God; it is the only Son, who is nearest to the Father's heart, who has made him known" (Jn 1:18). This arc from Moses to Jesus is the basis for the Christian claim of the intrinsic unity of the two testaments. The vague contours of Moses' outlines become concrete in Jesus Christ.

While there is no gainsaying that there was a genesis, that is, a historical becoming, that led up to the Christological creeds, this does not arrest the figure of Jesus Christ in historicity. Ratzinger points out that the fact that the First Vatican Council affirms dogmatic statements does not demonstrate the increasingly greater perfection of human efforts, but rather it is an expression of a divine deposit that the Church is called to guard and, on rare occasions, to define infallibly.[21] The fact that creedal statements and dogmas occur *in* history does not entail their reduction *to* history. Early on, Vincent of Lérins (died before 450) appreciated this in his famous *Commonitorium*: "*quod semper, ubique ab omnibus creditum*"[22] ("that which is believed always and everywhere by everyone"). The faith remains invariant as the Church grows in a deeper understanding of dogma. Faith in tradition thereby becomes the identifying instrument of the Church. Such a perspective overcomes von Harnack's famous hypothesis in his *Lehrbuch der Dogmengeschichte* regarding the Hellenization of Christianity in the first centuries.[23] Along with Heinrich Denzinger's work, the erudite studies of the Oratorian cardinal and librarian Cesare Baronio, Joseph Tixeront's contributions, and above all Newman's *An Essay on the Development of Christian Doctrine* must be mentioned.[24] The great challenge was to overcome nonhistorical theology—namely, neoscholasticism—without reducing theology to history.

Such a perspective enables beholding the earthly Jesus and the gloriously risen Christ as a single person. Referring back to the definitive Jesus enables one to await the risen Christ. "The incarnation, whereby humanity is assimilated to the Godhead, is begun in Jesus Christ but does not reach its final terminal in him."[25] A judicious study of dogmatics is impossible apart from the history of dogma, which in turn refers back to scripture and the faith of the apostles. Consonant with this insight and in reference to *Humani Generis*, Vatican II calls upon the study of the biblical foundation of doctrinal history. "The following order should be observed in the treatment of dogmatic theology: biblical themes should have first place; then students should be shown what the Fathers of the Church, both of the East and West, have contributed towards the faithful transmission and elucidation of each of the revealed truths; then the later history of dogma...."[26] All dogma, no matter how recent, is bound to the baptismal dialogue and thus is rooted in "the bond of existence in the way of Jesus Christ."[27] The language of dogma goes back to the creed. Like the creed, dogma forms a bond with Christ, provides access to supernatural life, and brings about the communion of believers. Beyond creating communitarian and liturgical realities, dogma relies on language. Terms such as *ousia* (nature), *hypostasis* (substance), *essentia* (essence), and *persona* (person) render divine revelation accessible. The formulas we have would have evolved according to different parameters had divine revelation first been given in India, rather than in Greece and Rome—but would have the same content.

No matter what area of theology Ratzinger addresses, liturgy, eschatology, or Mariology, all of his approaches and arguments are grounded in a Chalcedonian Christological center. Beholding Jesus, in the Christ, enables him to dare a synthesis of fidelity to the creed and scholarly exegesis that oftentimes offers surprising and new insights. This synthesis is not accidental as it draws from the spirit of patristic theology, faithful to the central intuition of *Nouvelle Théologie*. This is germane to theology as it is identical with the perspective the Second Vatican Council broadly developed in *Dei Verbum*. Beyond all human discussions and pondering, the text itself expresses something enduring and of central value:

> The text which was solemnly proclaimed by the Pope on this day, naturally is the result of many compromises. But the *fundamental* compromise

which pervades it is more than a compromise, it is a synthesis of great importance. The text combines fidelity to Church tradition with an affirmation of critical scholarship, thus opening up anew the path that faith may follow into the world today. It does not entirely abandon the position of Trent and Vatican I, but neither does it mummify what was held true at those Councils, because it realizes that fidelity in the sphere of the Spirit can be realized only through a constantly renewed appropriation.[28]

In *Jesus of Nazareth*, Pope Benedict welcomes the American spearheaded project of "canonical exegesis" that aims to read an individual text of scripture within the greater context of the biblical corpus. This is also the manner in which the Church reads texts, as *Dei Verbum* 12 reiterates. The message of a text becomes apparent within the greater context of the totality of scripture, as it is all inspired by the one Holy Spirit, giving it shape within the Old Covenant and the Church. Ratzinger beholds not autonomous authors at work in a haphazard fashion but authors at work as a collective subject. They are a part of and an expression of the "people of God." Amid the multitude of authors, scripture is indebted to one author. Scripture is born in this living body and attested to by the same. This ultimately leads to acknowledging the ecclesial locus of the text: the Church is its origin and therefore its indispensable interpretament.[29] This appreciation for the Bible's ecclesial origin allows Ratzinger to both affirm the historical-critical method as an indispensable tool and at the same time to remind the reader that the historical-critical method is complemented by the patristic teaching of the four senses of scripture. The latter are not disparate tools "but dimensions of the one word that reaches beyond the moment."[30] The assumptions of the modern scientific worldview may not be uncritically superimposed upon scripture. One must allow God to address a human being directly in scripture. Ratzinger writes:

> The connection with the subject we call "People of God" is vital for scripture. On the one hand, this book—scripture—is the measure that comes from God, the power directing the people. On the other hand, though, scripture lives precisely within this people, even as this people transcends itself in scripture. Through their self-transcendence (a fruit, at the deepest level, of the incarnate Word) they become the people of God. The People of God—the Church—is the living subject of scripture; it is in the Church that the words of the Bible are always in the present. This also means, of course, that the People has to receive its very self from God, ultimately from the incarnate Christ; it has to let itself be ordered, guided, and led by him.[31]

He thereby illustrates how untenable both biblicism (faith reduced to text) and magisterial positivism (whatever the teaching office holds) are. Likewise, also holding scripture as something disparate and discontinuous leads to a blind alley. The living *paradosis* (tradition) is the only credible option.

CHAPTER 13

The Biblical Basis of Christology

As a student, Ratzinger learned from Romano Guardini that liturgy is the proper context to understand the Bible: it is the product of the Church celebrating the Eucharist and proclaiming the gospel. Church, scripture, and liturgy form one hermeneutic unit.[1] A person cannot understand one without the two other elements. Famously, Kant had argued that the voice of being itself cannot be heard by human beings shackled to contingent, phenomenal reality. Only the postulates of practical reason access God. In contrast, John the Evangelist holds that the Spirit-inspired memory of the "we" of the Church brings about a remembering of the reality underlying scripture. Divine initiative is not constrained by a Kantian perspective. Only with the Easter Kerygma (preaching) does the integrity of scripture become apparent. All else evaporates into private musings or even ideologies. Good exegesis "is rooted in the living reality...of the Church of all ages."[2]

Two exegetes who as colleagues influenced Ratzinger were Heinrich Schlier (1900–1978) and Franz Mußner (b. 1916). Schlier had taught the New Testament in Bonn and converted to Catholicism in 1953 because he had reached the conclusion that the Catholic understanding of the relationship between revelation and scripture was the historically more accurate one. There cannot be a mutually excluding opposition between dogma and scripture as it is the Church celebrating liturgies that brings forth both. Both the creeds—Schlier refers to *praesymbola*—contained in the New Testament and central elements of the faith precede scripture both materially and chronologically. Most importantly for him, the Christological dogmas precede scripture. Schlier and Ratzinger offered summer courses together from 1970 until 1977.[3]

Franz Mußner shows in his research that the gospels served to justify and substantiate the already existing Christological *homologesis* (proclamation):[4] "Now Jesus did many other signs in the presence of the disciples, which are not written in this book; but these are written that you may believe that Jesus is the Christ, the Son of God and that believing you may have life in his name" (Jn 20:30f).

The "preferential option" for John's theology, which Ratzinger and numerous other theologians can be identified with, might seem one-sided from an isolated reading of the New Testament. However, John's Gospel is quite significant in many ways, not the least of which is that it reminds the reader that it stands in unbroken continuity with the Old Testament. The Jewish understanding of knowledge relies on experiential input rather than on philosophical hypotheses. In the final analysis it is grounded in the confidence that the relationship between humanity and God is the basis for true knowledge and existence. In Greek, and especially Platonic thought, in contrast, understanding is gained by contemplating the perfect forms and ideas of the *cosmos noetos* (inward meaning), while still arrested in the imperfect world of shadows, the *cosmos aisthetos* (outward beauty).[5] The Hellenistic Jewish philosopher Philo responded by conjoining the abstract Greek principles of *arche* (principle, beginning, primordial matter) and *logos* into the one reality of the dynamic and personal God of Israel.[6] Thus, John is able to state: "In the beginning (*arche*) was the Word (*logos*), and the Word was with God, and God was the Word. He was in the beginning with God.... And the Word became flesh and dwelt among us, full of grace and truth, we have beheld his glory, the glory as of the only Son from the Father" (Jn 1:1–2:14).

John is crucial because he provides a grand "Christological symphony": he synthesizes Greek philosophy and the Hebrew-Christian faith. Greek philosophical terminology is integrated into scripture, but under the conditions of a Jewish-Semitic understanding of God as personal and as engaging himself in the world of human beings. In fact, here an intensification of the divine-human occurs as inconceivable to both the Jewish faith and Greek philosophy: "I [Jesus] am in the Father, and you in me, and I in you" (Jn 17:21).[7] In John, the interaction between faith and knowledge reaches its unsurpassable culmination in the revelation of Jesus as the Christ. *Arche* (the ground or principle of being) and *logos* (as the key to understanding being, as Cleanthes [331–232 BC] stated in his *Hymn to Zeus* as the logos) collapse into one reality in Jesus of Nazareth. Jesus Christ—this is John's message—vouches for the unity of the Old and New Testaments *and* for the intelligibility of all of reality.[8]

An important theme for Christianity is "the Face of Christ." The Hebrew word for "face," *panim*, appears four hundred times in the Old Testament. In this Hebrew term, the people of the Old Covenant recognized God as being a person. God is concerned with his people. It is a term stressing that God accompanies the course of human history with concern and empathy. It expresses God's close relationship with the Israelites. Moses sought God's face and conversed with him (Ex 32:31f). A recurring topos is "seeking the face of God," especially within the psalms.[9]

For Ratzinger, Jesus' self-disclosure is the basis for all of the subsequent unfolding moments in Christology. Biblical titles such as Son and *Kyrios* (Lord) connect him with God's divine being. These titles are so closely linked to him that they became part of his name among people. Office, interpretation, and person blend into one reality. In this vein, Peter can state that Jesus is the Messiah, the Son of the living God. It is in light of this biblical background then, so Ratzinger informs us, that men standing in apostolic succession dared to continue to elaborate on the nature of Jesus. In AD 325, in the Anatolian town of Nicaea, they defined Jesus' relationship with

God the Father as "*homoousios*," that is, of one substance with his Father. This explains how exclusively[10] Jesus is able to state that he is the "Son of Man." In front of the most illustrious body of Jews—the Sanhedrin, Jesus states in a sovereign manner that he will be exalted and that they will see "the Son of Man seated at the right hand of the Power and coming with the clouds of heaven" (Mk 14:62). This title is a logical unfolding of the reality revealed by Jesus in the New Testament about himself. Yet, it is not an idiosyncratic allure of Jesus or an isolated New Testament charism. It has its preparatory basis in the book of Daniel (Dn 7:13f), where it is used to describe in prophetic language the coming kingdom of deliverance. Jesus' singularity is heightened by the fact that in his Incarnation on earth he possesses no property and no place to call home. In the humility of captivity, he is presented to the authorities and shares the fate of criminals. The paradox of Jesus Christ is revealed in his *kenosis* (condescending self-emptying). "The inner unity between Jesus' lived *kenosis* (cf. Phil 2:5–11) and his coming in glory is the constant motif of his words and actions; this is what is authentically new about Jesus, it is no invention—on the contrary, it is the epitome of his figure and words."[11] For Ratzinger this is the key for a proper anthropology: "This identity shows us the way, shows us the criterion according to which our lives will one day be judged."[12] The revealer of true humanity also becomes the instrument by which humankind can recover itself. Showing his divinity, Jesus is able to forgive sins (Mk 2:5). The unity of suffering and exaltation in Jesus' life shows proexistence as a central feature of his life in living for "the many" (Jn 11:52). By living in complete love and obedience to his heavenly Father, Jesus evidences that "He comes from God and hence establishes the true form of man's being...not just one individual, but rather he makes all of us 'one single person' (Gal 3:28) with himself, a new humanity."[13]

Another central figure for Ratzinger is the title Son. In Matthew 11:25–27 he discerns the key to understanding the filial relationship of Jesus with his Father: "no one knows the Son except the Father, and no one knows the Father except the Son and the one to whom the Son wills to reveal him" (cf. Jn 1:18). The author notes a unity of both knowledge and will between the Father and the Son. Thus God demonstrates his love for the world by giving "his only Son" (Jn 3:16). This interpretation is confirmed by the unique form of address the Son uses, "*Abba*," for God the Father. Here Ratzinger draws on research done by the Lutheran theologian Joachim Jeremias (1900–1979), a member of the anti-Nazi *Bekennende Kirche* (the minority wing within the German Protestant evangelical Church that opposed Hitler) over and against Adolf Jülicher's (1857–1938)[14] narrow understanding of the parables, Jeremias recovered the Hebrew roots of Jesus' *vox ipsissima* (that is, Jesus' very own voice) in the concrete living context of Jewish religiosity.[15] This perspective led him to appreciate the singularity of the Aramaic *Abba* predication. The singularity of Jesus naming his eternal Father *Abba* indicates the dawn of the kingdom of God and of salvation. Jesus reveals himself in this name as the Savior, bringing the good news to the poor. He rejects the oral Jewish tradition (*Halacha*). Charity is the life-principle of the kingdom of God. Determined by a sense of profound gratitude, the disciples are to communicate salvation. With Easter, Jesus' proclamation on earth is replaced by the faith witness of the Church.[16]

While written in history, scripture itself is not dependent on historic contingencies. While by its nature imbedded in a historical process, it expresses something of the transcendence of God's truth. Thus, the Church would betray the Lord if she exposed theological formulations exclusively to historical analysis and the historical-critical method. Mutable scientific methods and truths cannot be the yardstick for biblical and divine truth. Ratzinger argues three areas exist that cannot be submitted to historical judgment: Christology, revelation, and tradition. In all three fields, two seemingly incommensurate realities meet: the divine and human, the absolute and the contingent. In these instances, the interpretative norm lies outside the purview of human analysis. It is in faith that one learns that the earthly Jesus and the glorious, risen Christ, who will come again, are one identical person. Here past, present, and future are intertwined by faith. In linear history Christ, revelation, and tradition are explicated without dependence on history. "Textual analysis [alone] pushes Jesus back into the past; the Jesus of source criticism does not speak with us and says nothing to us."[17] The man or woman of faith bears in mind that an all too human history is the locale of divine sovereignty. By abasing himself in his kenotic movement toward humanity, God does not become definable within the categories of this world. In this ductus, in this vein, Ratzinger attests to the sacraments possessing a heuristic value: " 'Dogma,' that is, the self-engaging affirmation of faith, has its primary home in the event of baptism, and so in the liturgical sealing of a process of conversion wherein a man turns from belonging to himself alone and accepts in its place the bond of existence in the way of Jesus Christ."[18] This evidences truth as a gift and not as a possession, because this truth is one grounded in a relationship to a free Other. The fitting posture in such a situation is only one of humility, lest it lose the quality of a relationship "about which I may not boast, as though it were my own. If it is given to me, then that is a responsibility that puts me in the service of others as well."[19]

The theme of proving Jesus' divinity runs through the entire story of his life. Over and again, he is reproached for not proving himself sufficiently. However, were he "to prove" himself, he would disprove his divinity, his eternal Sonship. Physical proof or material satisfaction is not sufficient for humans. Ultimately, they want to have God enter their human hearts. A human being would never be satisfied by being offered convincing miracles, "the titillation of exciting stimuli, the thrill of which replaces religious awe and drives it away."[20]

The true message of Jesus Christ is for us to live and know his self-giving love as his disciples. This position of discipleship is of both salvific and heuristic relevance. The Israelites encountered this experience in the desert when they complained against God and Moses. Trust and faith cannot be reconciled with a controlling God. The ancient Israelites tried to compel God to prove his existence. Yet, requiring God to prove his existence not only denies divine sovereignty but also the human ability to live in trust and faith: true faith and knowledge is the certitude that when all else fails human beings will have a place in the arms of the Father. For this reason, he is not particularly enamored with Thomas Aquinas's *Quinque Viae* (five ways) of demonstrating God's existence.

While Ratzinger's book *Jesus of Nazareth, Vol. 1* is personal in tenor, it remains a scholarly reflection. Biographically it is a reflection of his labors as teacher of and researcher in fundamental theology and dogmatics. One senses throughout a line of demarcation between, but also a collaboration between, exegesis and systematic theology. He integrates the open-ended historical-critical method as a valid and necessary exegetical approach into his vision of Jesus Christ, insofar as it meets the dogmatic criteria as expressed by the Church councils of Nicaea and Chalcedon. He considers the historical-critical method indispensable for theology and the very structure of the faith. Nonetheless, he points out the limits of such a method. This method is, in his estimation, oftentimes much too interested in discovering a past, historic situation and context and too little interested in serving the very realities that brought scripture forth: divine initiative, faith, and the believing community. This method should be more interested in demonstrating its impressive theological achievements to the present. Exegetical results should assist pastoral theology, religious pedagogy, and homiletics in making the Christian faith fecund in the here and now. He sees no need to alter the mission and scope of biblical research. Rather, both scripture and the Christian faith community are normative for exegesis because the Bible and the Church reciprocally conditioned one another in their common genesis. In this sense alone is exegesis called to trust in a Spirit-guided tradition.

Both exegesis and Ratzinger in his book on Jesus intend to portray the Jesus of the gospels, the real and even historic Jesus. This Jesus is identical with God but emptied himself on the cross as Paul argues in Philippians 2:6–11. Thus, he alone merits universal adoration as foretold in Isaiah 45:23. Only through the eyes of faith joined to historical-critical exegesis does one apprehend a Jesus who is credible and, indeed, is provided with a fresh vivacity. This occurs for the individual believer in the liturgy. In this perspective, the achievements of the Enlightenment (that is, deism and its thesis of a clockmaker God) are put into relative terms. Such scholarship could only demonstrate that one encounters not a historic Jesus but the Christ of Christian faith. Ratzinger is mindful that the New Testament in its various writings offers a variety of Christologies not always easy to harmonize. To achieve this end, scripture must be seen as a canonical unit. The canonizing agent is the Church. Beyond all Christological fragments, in the Church celebrating the liturgy one encounters Jesus Christ. By implication Ratzinger seems to argue that only the Church in whose midst Christ is Eucharistically present can best present an obliging canon.

Ratzinger goes to great lengths to demonstrate that the New Testament's faith in Jesus' divinity is by no means something that developed later on. Along with Rudolf Schnackenburg, he argues that faith in the Incarnation is a feature of the New Testament from its very beginning. The noted German exegete Anton Vögtle had offered an alternative by stating that the proclaiming and the proclaimed Jesus are not identical. It is true there is a progressive component to revelation in the life of the earthly Christ.[21] This does not, however, signify a gap between "the historic Jesus" and "the Christ of the

Kerygma." The believing and Spirit-endowed community gradually came to understand who Jesus is.

The subject of faith is thus "redefined." Exegesis must acknowledge that ecclesial faith is a kind of "sym-pathy" (literally "suffering along with") without which there can be no access to the text. Faith must be recognized as a hermeneutics in understanding the text. Therefore, no "dogmatic" violence is being done to the biblical text. Rather, "it is the only viable manner to allow justice to be done to the biblical word."[22] The context of the New Testament coming about is that of faith, the Church, and the Holy Spirit. The very same tradition that became vivacious by virtue of Jesus as the foundation for the Christian faith provides the basis for trust in the biblical tradition. This invites far more trust than the attempt to distill "a chemically purified, historical Jesus, reconstructed by the retort of historical reason." In Ratzinger's estimation, only the hermeneutics of Chalcedon allows one to accept the whole of Jesus Christ.[23]

The provocative nature of Ratzinger's claim is that faith does not amount to a surrender to fideism. He rejects Karl Rahner's position of a bifurcation of exegesis and dogmatics. The biblical text remains the basis for all reflection. In Ratzinger's view, the other extreme is represented by Hans Küng, who claimed that historical exegesis is the sole basis for Christian thought. Ratzinger argues Küng sacrifices the faith of the ecclesial community as expressed in dogmas in favor of a Jesus understood as a Hegelian champion (*Sachwalter*) for humanity, a position Ratzinger maintains reminds one more of "the musty atmosphere of a lecture room in Tübingen than of the sunny expanses of Galilee." Faithful now to Harnack's thesis of Christianity being alienated from its own origins by Hellenization, "Jesuology" replaces Christology. The critical distance established between Jesus and the faith community allows Küng to succumb to a naïve trust in whatever the prevailing exegetical insights are. In nuanced contradistinction, the Second Vatican Council not only permitted the use of the historical-critical method, but promoted its use because the Logos truly entered into the human-historical condition. In this sense, it is a method that conforms aptly to the very structure and claim of Christianity. All of this forms a breathtaking, coherent symphony speaking powerfully afresh to each generation if only one is mindful of Pentecost.[24]

In his research on Bonaventure's understanding of revelation, Ratzinger discovered that revelation is a personal and dialogical event temporally preceding scripture; it is attested to by scripture but not identical with scripture. As such a living, dialogical event, revelation comes to completion when the addressee accepts it in faith. Ongoing revelation constitutively requires the Church as a believing subject generating tradition. The Church is the living organism handing down revelation. *Dei Verbum* 5 expresses this insight when stating that the Church's faith belongs to the nature of revelation. It is an essential prerequisite for tradition and scripture as the medium for the transmission of revelation. Not until Peter responds, "You are the Messiah, the Son of the living God" (Mt 16:17) is revelation complete, because the addressee appropriates God's self-communication. Mere literality does not make the Old or New Testaments, nor revelation. The New Testament is only there where the spirit of the scriptures is alive. The Christ-event is *the* spirit that interprets scripture. Objective revelation is not surrendered in favor of subjective actualism as this occurs within that special space that is Christ-filled: the Eucharist-celebrating Church. This faith is synthesized in the creed. The inner acceptance of the read text then becomes revelation. There is a flaw in Luther's reasoning when postulating the *sola scriptura*. Only in the hands of the living Church does scripture come to life. Against historic evidence and Bonaventure, the Thomistic language separating lived faith and objective revelation introduced an innovation Vatican II's dogmatic constitution on revelation, *Dei Verbum* (Ratzinger was granted a role drafting this document), corrected.

As living Word (1 Thes 2:13), revelation cannot be relegated to dead words or that which is merely historical. Preaching on the motto *vox temporis, vox Dei* of the former Munich archbishop Cardinal von Faulhaber, Ratzinger stated that far from abstractions, Faulhaber wanted to allow God's inexhaustible Word to speak to his age and time, as God is ever presentic. The Word is "never fathomed," "never suffered to the end," and "never thought fully through."[25]

The vivacious nature of revelation and scripture is connected to Christian dogma. Ratzinger's former colleague, exegete, and Bultmann student Heinrich Schlier (1900–1978), concluded in 1953 that the Catholic understanding of the relationship between scripture and tradition does the greatest justice to historic reality. He took the logical step and converted to Catholicism. Historical analysis demonstrated to him that creedal formulas serve as nutshells for the formation of scripture. They are crystallizing moments when early Christians "explosively" discovered their faith contained an explicit Christology. He called these very early statements *"praesymbola"* and thus coined a new term.[26] A *praesymbolum* is not the sum of a gospel narrative that came about later but its inner structure. It precedes canon formation and even the written form of many New Testament texts.

A fellow theologian in Regensburg, Franz Mußner, further expanded on Schlier's contributions. As John 20:30f establishes, the gospels are taken as confirmation of faith in Jesus the Christ as the Lord and Son of God, as practiced in proclamation and liturgy. The gospels further establish the already attested to and lived faith.

The exegesis operating from such a perspective was termed "canonical exegesis" by Brevard S. Childs. This means acknowledging that scripture is a product of the Church. Without the Church, scripture would be a collection of heterogeneous texts of varying antiquity. The Church does not enter the canonizing process as "the final Word." Rather, scripture is written, amended, and lived in the Church prior to its written form. The individual author is both transcended and sustained by a whole people. Until the final editing is done, the inspiring Spirit is effective. The Word leads to events and the events in turn lead to deeper verbalization. To express this process, Ratzinger uses the French term *"relecture"* (re-reading).[27] Because the historical-critical method is quite enthusiastically received, it is extremely difficult to convey the need to incorporate, equally, a hermeneutics fitting for revelation. The sad consequence is a plurality of confusing assumptions completely contrary to the heretofore lived Christian faith.

In a brief treatise titled "Zur Frage nach Grundlagen und Weg der Exegese heute" ("The Question of Foundations and Ways of Exegesis Today"), Ratzinger expresses much of his worry about some areas of biblical scholar-ship.[28] While as scholars they are in many ways outdated, Martin Dibelius and Rudolf Bultmann still set the tenor: "The word generates the scene." From this, Ratzinger concludes both men argue that any event must be secondary to, if not an altogether mythical manifestation of, the Word. Both Protestant theologians therefore assumed a disconnect between the pre-Easter Jesus and the Church. Another assumption he sees operative in these theologians, and in some contemporary exegesis as well, is this axiom: the more complex a statement, the further away it must be from its origin. All of this invariably leads some to conclude revelation does not count. As facts no longer seem rel-evant, a *"reductio historiae in philosophiam"* (reducing history into philosophy, in fact reducing history to private opinings) occurs. Every divine expres-sion is explained as mere myth. A docetist Christology is the outcome. The world is no longer creation but a meaningless reality. The exegete should not approach scripture with a sealed philosophy and may not preclude a pri-ori the possibility that God enters history. If exegesis is to have an edifying role in the Church, then it must be critical vis-à-vis its own philosophical presuppositions. It must be mindful of the unity of the two testaments and of canonical exegesis. In addition, one should realize that for a proper under-standing, the text requires faith with inner necessity. The teaching office is not over and above scripture or exegesis but an essential constituent of both. Ratzinger recalls for the reader Guardini's observation that even the apostolic witness cannot fully exhaust the original abundance of the event of Christ. The apostolic proclamation is a signpost leading to him. The reality of Christ always transcends the preached content.[29]

Faithful to the Second Vatican Council—"Sacred Scripture must be read and interpreted with its divine authorship in mind" (*Dei Verbum* 12)— Ratzinger reminds his audience to read scripture with the same spirit in which it has been written. The unifying, gravitational center is friendship with Jesus Christ. Echoing Rudolf Schnackenburg, this in turn may not sim-ply mean one chooses to like something at random, but rather that one can only fully understand life and one's self in God. Jesus spoke constantly of God and of entering God's kingdom, as he was profoundly one with God. "Jesus is only able to speak about the Father in the way he does because he is the Son, because of his filial communion with the Father."[30] Therefore, Ratzinger is in full agreement with Rabbi Neusner: the manner in which Jesus speaks during the Sermon on the Mount and elsewhere is only comprehensible if he speaks in the name of God. Yet, while Neusner rejects Jesus precisely for this reason in favor of the Old Testament,[31] Ratzinger agrees with Jesus and becomes his disciple. "The disciple who walks with Jesus is thus caught up with him into communion with God. And that is what Redemption means: this stepping beyond the limits of human nature, which had been there as a possibility and an expectation in man, God's image and likeness since the moment of creation."[32] Neusner also agrees with Ratzinger that

Jesus remains incomprehensible without the ecclesially grown dogmas. The Incarnational nature of Christian faith renders the historical-critical method indispensable.[33]

This sensibility to the biblical testimony comes as no wonder as he headed the Papal Biblical Commission—assembling the finest scripture scholars—for twenty-four years.

CHAPTER 14

A Twentieth-Century Classic:
Introduction to Christianity

But Christian faith really means precisely the acknowledgement that God is not the prisoner of eternity, not limited to the solely spiritual; that he is capable of operating here and now, in the midst of my world, and that he did operate in it through Jesus, the new Adam, who was born of the Virgin Mary through the creative power of God, whose spirit hovered over the waters at the very beginning, who created being out of nothing.[1]

How could the author arrive at this central statement in his classic *Introduction to Christianity*? He elaborates further on the paradox: "God is as he had expressed himself in Jesus Christ. God is not merely the infinite abyss or the infinite apex, sustaining everything, but never entering finitude. God is not merely infinite distance, but also infinite proximity. One can entrust oneself to him: He listens and sees and loves."[2] Is it not folly to declare one single figure is the gravitational center of the universe, to define someone of flesh as the meaning of all being? One who not only contains all of history but is its very *cardo* (that is, the pivotal linchpin)! God manifests himself to human beings through a human being in a definitive manner and this being is at the same time God. In a particularly heightened way after Kant's separation of the noumenal and phenomenal realms, this claim is nothing short of a scandal. The full truth of this (supposed) reality evades verification. How is one to find both Jesus and Christ in history?

"Because he has 'seen the Father,' Jesus Christ is the only one who knows him and can reveal him."[3] In Jesus Christ, human existence becomes oriented to the whole. Christian faith is an encounter with the living God. Baptism, as the symbolic death of Jesus Christ, links human beings to the renewal Jesus Christ achieved in his Resurrection. The humanists Plotinus and Goethe argued that the human eye could never recognize the sun were it not itself sunlike. One could say, likewise, that there is something in the human being that allows a *Christwerdung* (becoming Christlike) of the individual to come about. This is the great endeavor of history. God does not leave human beings indifferent or even uninvolved. Having breathed the air of great thirteenth-century theologians such as Thomas Aquinas and Bonaventure, the Italian poet Dante Alighieri (1265–1321) famously closed his *Paradiso* with the line that God himself is "the love that moves the sun and all the stars."[4]

How is contingent being to fathom divine charity? Likewise, however much one might try, a human being can never "think" God adequately without (prevenient) divine grace. In this sense revelation as a divine gift is preserved. No philosophical investigation into the *"Begriff"* (German for "term") of Christianity—as Karl Rahner attempted in 1976 in his classic *Foundations of Christian Faith*, eight years after Ratzinger's classic *Introduction to Christianity*—can yield such profundity and surety as faith effortlessly can, like Mozart, for instance, accomplished in music. The plausibility of faith is not unlocked via a "first philosophy," nor is it dependent on being understood by the investigating subject, such as Rahner's other classic *Hearer of the Word* (1941) might intimate.[5] Far removed from transcendental idealism, Ratzinger develops the inner coherence, akin to *perichoresis* (reciprocal interpenetration and indwelling), of the various aspects of faith. The gratuitous mystery of faith is thereby preserved. The organizing moments of *kerygma* (preaching) and *dogma* (teaching) grant a Christocentrism unreachable by autonomous reason. As an author, Ratzinger seeks to be transparent to Christ: *"Mea doctrina non est mea sed eius qui misit me"* ("My teaching is not my own but is from the one who sent me," cf. John 7:16).[6]

Significantly, Ratzinger begins his classic not with the elusive figure of a historical Jesus, but on the basis of the Church's faith: the Apostles' Creed.

Of fundamental importance for appreciating Ratzinger's *Introduction to Christianity* is the Catholic intuition of *"gratia praesupponit naturam"* ("grace presupposes nature"). Concerning this central area of theology—the relationship between grace and nature—Ratzinger did not devote a single line, but he relied on it implicitly. In addressing the habilitation of a priest member of the Integrated Community he did, however, write a few lines on the relationship between nature and grace. He observes that, even in Jesuit and Dominican theologies, grace was considered as restraining freedom. In the drama of humanity's seeking emancipation and greater freedom during the Enlightenment, and up to and including the present age, God's fatherly love is considered a leaden weight of heteronomy. God no longer enables one's own life but impedes it. The Enlightenment was glad to liberate humankind from this unwelcome burden. Little wonder then that in modern discussion, including that of liberation theology, grace is completely absent. Genuine freedom is defined as self-created freedom. It is relational only in the negative sense of the word. Modernity leads into the dead-end street that is the absurdity of autonomous freedom. Ratzinger believed it must be discovered anew that grace does not compete with freedom but enables it. Grace and freedom have a deep purpose, a purpose instilled in creation. Grace is the tool by which God establishes a kingdom of freedom and charity. In fact, each human being craves the realization of freedom so that charity might come about. Grace and freedom are interrelated. Freedom is thereby liberated from its "individualistic abstraction" and brought into the human community convoked by God, which is the Church. The Church enables genuine freedom through grace, and indeed the Church is the place of freedom par excellence.[7]

Introduction to Christianity was one of the first of a series of introductions to the creed written after the Second Vatican Council. Due to its stylistic brilliance and dialectical thinking, it quickly became a classic in its genre. First published in 1968,[8] it "arose out of lectures I gave in Tübingen in the summer term of 1967,"[9] and it aimed to provide some orientation during a time of cultural unrest in Western Europe, culminating in student riots and a radical redefinition of human self-awareness. His effort was much assisted by the fact that one of the consequences of the council was a more organic and holistic presentation of the faith, grounded in its founder, Jesus Christ. The *genius loci* also played a role. Karl Adam (1876–1966), a theologian-priest teaching at the same university, had written a much-read classic on the essentials of the Catholic faith some forty years earlier.[10]

Like Ratzinger, Adam had not been trained as a Thomist but as a patristic scholar in Munich. He was recognized as a noteworthy theologian early in the century with books on Tertullian's concept of the Church (1907) and Augustine's doctrine of the Eucharist (1908). The external occasion for Adam's book on the essentials of the Catholic faith had been twofold: (1) the presentations Friedrich Heiler delivered in Sweden in 1919 on the same topic, arguing from the perspective of a comparative study of religions,[11] and (2) the crisis Germany underwent following its defeat in World War I. In contrast to Heiler, Adam divines the essence of Catholicism in the Church from *within* the inner structures of its faith as the body of Christ, as the kingdom of God on earth. For Adam, the Church is the rule of God ineluctably leavening all of humanity, which is in need of redemption. The body of Christ finds its real expression as supra-personal unity in the Petrine ministry. From this follows the Church's features: catholicity, exclusivity, sanctity, and authority. Adam stresses God in Jesus Christ as the primary actor in the Church.[12]

Continuing broadly on this intellectual trajectory, it was Ratzinger's intention "to help understand faith afresh as something that makes possible true humanity in the world of today, to expound faith without changing it into the small coin of empty talk painfully laboring to hide a complete spiritual vacuum."[13] The circumstances surrounding the impetus of the book were compounded by the fact that some Christians subcutaneously assumed that revelation is at best something subjective, and faith is therefore something to be practiced in private. The solution to this tearing asunder of faith's connection with objective reality can only be the reaffirmation of the Incarnation of God in Jesus Christ, who is true God and true man, the second person of the Blessed Trinity. The "Jesus event," to use a term fashionable in the postconciliar years perhaps precisely by virtue of its inherent ambiguity, enables humankind to participate in divine life and to organize earthly existence in a manner commensurate with human dignity, which receives its basis from its future: its eternal destiny.[14]

Walter Kasper, now president of the Pontifical Council for Promoting Christian Unity, accused Ratzinger in 1970 of subscribing latently to idealism and sees the danger of secularism. God is even made "a correlate of man." He then discerned in Ratzinger's book an anthropological approach.[15]

It is quite telling that Thomas Aquinas is not once mentioned in this *Introduction to Christianity*, but nineteenth-century forerunners of Ressource-ment theology, namely, Johann Adam Möhler and Franz von Baader, are. The former rediscovered the Church as "the ongoing Incarnation of Jesus Christ," the latter coined the formula "*cogitor, ergo cogito, ergo sum*" ("I am being thought of [by another], therefore I think [possess consciousness], therefore I am"). It was the position of the Catholic Tübingen School of Theology in the first half of the nineteenth century that spirituality underlies all sound theology. Relationality and responsoriality are the recurring leitmotifs of von Baader's approach, thus attempting to overcome both impersonal neoscholasticism and solitary subjectivism. He does not put forth logical deductions but rather how the term "God" is part and parcel of human religious experience and tradition.

The German fairy tale of *Lucky Jack* (*Hans im Glück*), who squanders something precious and coveted, and Kierkegaard's portrait of a circus clown warning people in vain of an actual fire are used to illustrate the fact that man can be inattentive to life's essential things and to pressing issues. One needs to discover that Christianity preaches God's involvement in history. According to John's Gospel, Jesus is the Father's face. This thoughtlessness regarding the biblical testimony, that one understands God through Jesus, had been prepared by a long intellectual history. In his work, Ratzinger mentions, among others, Giambattista Vico (1668–1744), who held a thesis identifying *verum* with *factum*,[16] (the true and the made) and Karl Marx's immanentist, emancipatory pathos, to illustrate that anthropocentricism and the idea that humankind is but the product of chance à la Darwin coincided to trap humanity in a reality without a spiritual dimension. The notion of salvation history becomes an altogether foreign concept in such an outlook and consequently it is replaced by that of an immanentist perfection. The rough outlines of liberation theology are evident here.[17]

Christianity liberates humankind from a materialist reduction of reality by entrusting one's existence to a spiritual reality: entrusting oneself to that which has not been made by oneself and never could be made, and which, for that very reason, supports and renders possible all our making is a primordially religious gesture and finds in Jesus Christ its profoundest goal and expression. All other attempts suffer shipwreck as they are beholden to the Münchhausen syndrome (that is, "pulling oneself up by one's bootstraps").[18] Recognizing human reality as Logos-charged, that is, as reasonable and intelligible, establishes the consonance between human yearning for the infinite and Jesus as its fulfillment. It was the genius of the ancient Greek mind to spell this out in rational terms. The New Testament witness presents Our Lord as the fitting and culminating cornerstone of the world of reason. Thus, the encounter between the Christian narrative and the Hellenic culture must be described as kairotic, a unique moment of divine providence in history.[19]

The Apostles' Creed is the Church's formulation requiring the catechumen's and believer's assent be properly alive. In this sense, the Latin singular *credo*, "I believe," is preferable, while the original Greek plural *pisteuomen*, "we believe," emphasizes the need for creedal unity within the Church and the fact that faith is the outgrowth of the Church as a community of belief. In the tension between "I believe" and "we believe," Ratzinger notes something fecund is perceived: faith is never exclusively individual but also contains a corporate component. The "I-Thou structure" of faith automatically joins the "we." It was no accident that early Christians chose the word "*symbolon*" as the term for their profession of faith. It comes from antiquity where friends would recognize one another by each having, respectively, one-half of a corresponding shard, ring, staff, or tablet, called a *symbolon*. In the Church, unity among people is established by sharing the one Word, Jesus Christ.[20] In this vein, Ratzinger mentions Marius Victorinus, who in the fourth century discovered that in the Christian Church he encountered the Logos who vivifies the living: Christ is the center who brings about community in the Church.[21] The "we" of Christianity finds its hub in Jesus Christ. Ratzinger is indirectly reminiscent of de Lubac's magisterial *Catholicism* when he writes: "Christian belief is not an idea but life; it is not mind existing for itself, but incarnation, mind in the body of history and its 'We.'"[22] This explains why Ratzinger does not dwell on arguing in favor of the mere existence of a numinous reality. The Christian faith does not merely want to inform; it is an invitation to be fully human by encountering Jesus as the risen Christ.

In the year 2000, the seventh German language edition of *Introduction to Christianity* was printed with a new foreword. In the distance gained after thirty-two years, Ratzinger observes: "Man is becoming a technological object while vanishing to an ever greater degree as a human subject, and he has only himself to blame."[23] "What," he asks, "will be man's attitude toward man when he can no longer find anything of the divine mystery in the other, but only his own know-how?"[24] Ratzinger seems to argue here along the lines of Kant: human beings are no longer able to respect one another universally as *Zwecke an sich* (purposes unto themselves). Thus, they also stand to lose self-respect. He fears humankind will end in a state of inextricable, self-enamored solipsism. The individual human being will only be able to value others pragmatically, that is, insofar as they are of some utility for him or her. Ratzinger proposes only "the divine mystery in the other" can free humankind from such a prospect.[25]

The historic watershed inaugurated by Giambattista Vico still awaits being overcome. Vico stated, "All that we can truly know is what we have made for ourselves." Modernity is not interested in *verum est ens* (truth is being) but *verum quia faciendum* (truth because it is being made). The turn to the subjective is simultaneously a turn to functionalism. Thus, the individual loses his or her objective dignity. The yardstick for justice is functionality.

True to Bonaventure's thesis, Ratzinger maintains every age is one that enables an encounter with Jesus Christ, and he remains fundamentally optimistic. The point of departure is a basic question: "What is the meaning and significance of the Christian profession 'I believe' *today*, in the context of our present existence and our present attitude to reality as a whole?"[26] He divines in the present age a singular *kairos*, a privileged moment for a deeper appreciation of faith. "It is in fact the great opportunity of our historical moment that we can gain from it a completely new understanding of the position of faith between fact and *faciendum* (faith as a human construct); it is the task of theology to accept this challenge, to make use of this possibility, and to find and fill the blind spots of past periods."[27] The central redeeming concept is both a philosophical and theological category, that of relationality. Such a rapport between the divine and human comes about by embracing the proper understanding of belief as:

> A human way of taking up a stand in the totality of reality, a way that cannot be reduced to knowledge and is incommensurable with knowledge; it is the bestowal of meaning without which the totality of man would remain homeless, on which man's calculations and actions are based, and without which in the least resort he could not calculate and act, because he can only do this in the context of a meaning that bears him up.[28]

Faith is grounded in two motions: faith has to do with forgiveness and conversion. These two motions lead the human being out of self-centeredness and into the community established by the Word. The result is unity of mind. Such unity is rooted in God's dialogue with humans, yet paradoxically, "God's dialogue with men operates only through men's dialogue with each other." Such community is living Christian faith as it is one of both proclaiming and hearing God's Word. Merely human dialogue is intrinsically broken: human dialogue is incomplete, but it holds "one half of a broken *symbolon*" that can be matched by the entirely Other, God. In existential veracity, each human being ultimately seeks Someone: "'Are you really he?' Ultimately, all the reflections contained in this book are subordinate to this question and thus revolve around the basic form of the confession: 'I believe in you, Jesus of Nazareth, as the meaning (*Logos*) of the world and of my life.'"[29]

The *point d'appui* for him is the Old Testament, where God reveals his name to Moses (Ex 3:14): "I am who I am." It is no wonder the people submitted to a God who is, as "belief is wedded to ontology."[30] The divine self-disclosure states that God is the plenitude of being. Yet at this point Ratzinger makes a crucial distinction. God is not interested in simply sharing knowledge of his eternal ontology with Moses. Rather, he shares a central feature of his essence that is pivotal for Moses to continue leading God's people out of the inhospitable desert. He is a God sovereignly entering into a loyal relationship with people. God's "Being-for" is far more significant for Israel surviving the forbidding environment than is the actual manna he fed them. "When God names himself after the self-understanding of faith, he is not so much expressing his inner nature as making himself nameable; he is handing himself over to men in such a way that he can be called upon by them."[31] The Exodus, which occurred roughly 1,250 years before the Incarnation, is read by Ratzinger Christologically. Christ himself appears in the burning bush. The unconditional covenantal loyalty of God to humankind receives personhood in Jesus Christ and possesses a personal name. Thus, in Jesus Christ the name Yahweh receives an exposition.

"God as 'I' and 'Thou' in one. This new experience of God is followed finally by a third: the experience of the Spirit, the presence of God in us, in our innermost being... it is the manner in which God gives himself to us, in which he enters into us, so that he is *in* yet, in the midst of this 'indwelling,' is infinitely *above* him."[32] Belief in the biblical God expresses the conviction that the eternal mind produces a subjective mind that is called to apprehend itself as a declension of the former. Thus in a seemingly paradoxical mixture of awe and joy, human thinking finds itself "re-thinking" that which in reality had been divinely thought beforehand. With God, anthropology becomes complete. What then is freedom, if not acknowledged relationality? Indeed, "at the summit stands a freedom that thinks and, by thinking, creates freedoms, thus making freedom the structural form of all being."[33]

This brings up a question about the nature of creedal statements concerning the second person of the Blessed Trinity. Reaching the heights of personal faith, a human being comes into his or her own. Humankind becomes what it is! Therefore, Christian faith, Ratzinger asserts, "is not the acceptance of a system but the acceptance of this person who is his word; of the word as person and of the person as Word."[34] Human beings who dare such openness find themselves in God'sSonship as being at the service of something greater than themselves. Thus, in Christ human beings discover a recalibration of values: "He who surrenders himself completely to service for others to complete selflessness and self-emptying, literally *becomes* these things—that this very person is the true man, the man of the future, the coinciding of man and God"[35] Only in reaching beyond oneself does a human being come to his or her own, proper self. Just as Christ emptied himself, every human being is called to not cling to the self and never to stand on self-defined grounds. He or she is in union with the Other, in relation with the completely Other. Thus, faith is beyond a simple memorization of statements; it is an expression of love. In light of Christology, faith consequently is "entry into the universal openness of unconditional love."[36] This in turn is nothing formal or abstract but takes on concrete life in the liturgy. Christ's death, as Eucharist, "was in reality the one and only liturgy of the world, a cosmic liturgy, in which Jesus stepped... publicly, before the eyes of the world, through the curtain of death into the real temple... before the face of God himself, in order to offer... himself (Heb 9:11ff)."[37] In the liturgy, the participants emulate Christ's proexistence. If this indeed is true, Ratzinger concludes, then "the mode of our immortality will depend on our mode of loving."[38] The consummation of the world is then unlike a natural phenomenon because it is determined by a responsibility lived in freedom. The one awaiting humankind is not radically different from or alien to what human beings have come to know of life, but is the one who took upon himself suffering as sacrifice. Thus, a transformation of varying degrees occurs with human beings: it is a transformation in this world toward Jesus that establishes a certain congeniality between humankind and the one who awaits humankind, a transformation which becomes apparent in the final stage of the world.

"The all-encompassing 'complexification,' the unification infinitely embracing all, is at the same the final denial of all collectivism, the denial of fanaticism of the mere idea, even the so-called 'idea of Christianity.' Man, the person, always takes precedence over the mere idea."[39] This notion over-comes the neoscholastic approach to God that uses the false alternatives of either function or essence as the only proper ways to apprehend God. Ratzinger thereby proves his loyalty to the original personalist inspiration he was exposed to during his own formative theological studies. In an axiom-atic manner, he presents six *"Grundstrukturen"* ("foundational structures"). His premise is that the individual is posited a priori, however nebulously, in relationship to a divine whole or totality. This salient fact intensifies in history—it is at first a very vague relationship—when an individual becomes Christian and thereby ecclesially rooted as well. This, in turn, evidences being as essentially soteriological in nature. Being manifests itself as a loving "for," or as proexistence. This is demonstrated as an unacknowledged "incognito" (of Jesus) to the world. In his estimation, the reformer Martin Luther meant this when speaking of a *"sub contrario."* The German poet Friedrich Hölderlin (1770–1843) would later capture the same unfathomable givenness of human existence as *maximum in minimo* in the introductory aphorism to his work *Hyperion*.[40] Even in its disfigurement, the human minimum remains in refer-ence to the divine maximum in its overabundance, and "is located in the act of conversion, in the turn of one's being from worship of the visible and prac-ticable to trust in the invisible."[41] Thus in its deepest sense all of human hope is Christian by its very nature. It is ultimately grounded in God's salvific, definitive completion of this world. As God perfectly completes this world, history is ultimately a positive reality. Along with this insight, one must em-phasize Ratzinger's judgment concerning "the primacy of receiving" versus the primacy of making or performing, thereby offering the only real alterna-tive to becoming a real *Metropolis*.[42] In consequence, consciously perceiving human beings as spiritual creatures acknowledges the primacy of the in-visible. Faith entails taking a position regarding the unrecognizable totality of reality. Faith remains grounded in an incomprehensible mystery, which defies reckoning. Precisely such a constitution enables charity. He perceives faith as being essentially symbolic and thus social.[43] The ramifications for Christians are obvious: "All not-at-one-ness, all division, rests on a concealed lack of real Christliness, on a clinging to the individuality that hinders the coalescence into unity."[44] God can be reached through the God-man Jesus Christ. Christ brings about access to God while at the same time preserving and revealing God as mystery. Further, it is precisely this mystery that grants genuine community. Relationality (which for Aristotle is a category that describes contingent reality) is elevated in Jesus Christ's revelation of God as Trinity to "an equally primordial form of being" as substance.[45] This allows Christ and every Christian to say, "My teaching is not mine, but his who sent me" (Jn 7:17). This community keeps Christians from ending in a paradox or a blind alley, caught, as in the words of a popular song, in "a Lexus cage."[46] Inspired by Christ's words, Augustine concludes (and, every Christian may join him): "What is so much yours as yourself, and what is so little yours as yourself?"[47] The Logos liberates human beings into the magnanimity of the Blessed Trinity. The doctrine of the Trinity serves as a model for human unity. The Trinitarian pattern of the creed corresponds to a threefold renun-ciation of the world, flesh, and evil as is asked of every neophyte.

Personalism leads, in Ratzinger's estimation, to an Augustinian psychologism. If one accepts God as person, then a paradox follows: "Only what is hidden is accepted as the One who is near, only the inaccessible as the One who is accessible, the one as the One who exists for all men and for whom all exist."[48] Yet, the contingent human mind is able to fathom this objective reality. If this is truly the case, then it must follow that "our thinking is, indeed, only a rethinking of what in reality has already been thought out beforehand."[49] If human beings can freely assent to this reality, then it follows in turn that freedom is not an accidental feature of human existence but a constitutive element of being. "To this extent one could very well describe Christianity as a philosophy of freedom. For Christianity, the explanation of reality as a whole is not an all-embracing consciousness or one single materiality; on the contrary, at the summit stands a freedom that thinks and, by thinking, creates freedoms, thus making freedom the structural form of all being."[50] Thus, Christianity is a healthy corrective to, for example, an unruly democracy that runs the danger of losing the right to predicate itself "democratic."

Faith as lived, divinely beckoned freedom "is first of all a call to community, to unity of mind through the unity of the word...it aims at establishing unity of mind through the unity of the word."[51] Faith requires and entails historic concretion. Community comes about ever anew where proclamation and hearing are conjoined. This community may never be self-centered. Every believer holds "faith only as a *symbolon*, as a broken half, which signifies truth only in its endless reference to something beyond itself, to the entirely Other."[52] As it is proper to each person in the Blessed Trinity to be pure relation, it must be "the most absolute unity."[53] Painfully mindful of the incompleteness of life, human beings seek for something healing and completing and find it in a divine Thou: "Are you really he?"[54] The solution for our age is Christological. Ratzinger ponders the full meaning of the Greek word *Logos* to convey to the reader that the predication of Jesus as *the* Logos par excellence in John's Gospel is far richer than any dictionary entry may suggest.

Ratzinger argues the romantic German poet Joseph von Eichendorff (1788–1857) expressed this singularly well when writing on Christ's descent into hell: "Thou art he who gently breaks about our heads what we build, so that we can see the sky—therefore I have no complaint."[55] As Ratzinger writes in the preface to the new edition: "*Logos* signifies reason, meaning, or even 'word'—a meaning, therefore, that is Word, that is relationship, that is creative. The God, who is *Logos*, guarantees the intelligibility of the world, the intelligibility of our existence, the aptitude of reason to know God [*die Gottgemässheit der Vernunft*] and the reasonableness of God [*die Vernunftgemässheit Gottes*], even though his understanding infinitely surpasses ours and to us may so often appear to be darkness."[56] There is an implicit tendency in all human beings to seek a unity in truth, a unity in the absolute.

Christian faith is a certain piece of God's reality shared in common by the faithful. The faithful are defined as those in God's service, a God Ratzinger describes thereupon as Trinitarian and ergo relational by his very essence. God therefore proves to be most willing to enter into relationships. Yet, this

occurs in the most sovereign of manners. His divine "for" is by no means
a coerced one. This is expressed in biblical language in Exodus 3:14 where
God reveals his name to Moses not in his divine aseity but rather in his relation to humankind. Yet, this does not imply that the information humankind receives from God merely serves the cause of redemption. "God *is* as
he *shows* himself; God does not show himself in a way in which he is not.
On this assertion rests the Christian relation with God; in it is grounded the
doctrine of the Trinity; indeed, it *is* this doctrine."[57] Earlier on, Ratzinger
writes: "God's presence for Israel is emphasized; his Being is expounded,
not as Being in itself, but as Being-for."[58] Further on he elaborates: "When
God names himself after the self-understanding of faith, he is not so much
expressing his inner nature as making himself nameable; he is handing himself over to men in such a way that he can be called upon by them."[59] In history, this "for" is a personal presence that climaxes in the Incarnation of Jesus
Christ. This, however, does not suffice to describe God exhaustively. In a
dialectical manner, God's proximity and distance are related to one another.
God's closeness to humanity reveals his ineffable otherness. In a paradoxical
way, this also applies to God's might and his charity. He is caring without
losing his justice. Thus, the true intention of all biblical descriptions of an
anthropomorphic nature is to express divine unpredictability, as seen from
a human perspective, thereby describing the feature of divine sovereignty.
Faithful to Augustine, Ratzinger perceives the Blessed Trinity as essentially
pure relationality.

The acknowledgment of God as a unit, as one God, has significant ramifications. It transfers religion outside of the political realm and therefore
prevents religion from being politically instrumentalized by parties or gov-
ernments. At the same time, the dignity of matrimony is grounded and safeguarded by "belief in the unity and indivisibility of the love of God," as one
divine reality.[60]

On this broad canvas of a portrayal of God's nature, Ratzinger develops his
Christology. Jesus Christ is God's "*pro nobis*" ("for us"). In Johannine fash-
ion, Ratzinger transfers the Greek divine "*ego eimi*" ("I am") of YHWH in
Exodus 3:14 to Jesus:

> Christ himself, so to speak, appears as the burning bush from which
> the name of God issues to mankind. But since in the view of the fourth
> Gospel Jesus unites in himself, applies to himself the "I am" of Exodus
> 3 and Isaiah 43, it becomes clear at the same time that *he himself* is the
> name, that is the "invocability" of God. The name is no longer merely
> a word but a person: Jesus himself. Christology, or belief in Jesus, is
> raised to the level of an exposition of the name of God and of what it
> signifies.[61]

In Jesus Christ the faithful behold the complementarity of the Incarnation
and crucifixion. This in turn leads the faithful to appreciate the harmony of
protology (teaching on the world's beginning) and eschatology. From this
perspective Christ's death, descent into hell, and Resurrection are but stations of Christ's charity spanning all ages and including every human being.

Owing to Christ's passion, humanity can enter into God's absence, rendering the world mute.

This seeming paradox is the only viable response to life: "not to be coerced by the greatest, but to be contained by the smallest—that is divine." In Jesus Christ, the greatest possible being, God, takes on the form of human frailty.[62] In this scandal, a heuristic moment is found, for Christ grants existence, meaning, and relationship. This allows for creativity. The world's intelligibility is at the same time that which concerns every human being the most. Human reason's aptitude to know precisely this may serve as an indirect proof of God's existence.

The fact that God has become involved in this world through the covenant and the Incarnation of his Son has anthropological implications. It defines faith as much more than only having the dimension of a personal assent to abstract, propositional truth sentences à la neoscholasticism, or the abstract notion of a deist God uninvolved in his creation à la the Enlightenment. Only God defines fully who the human person is. He insists Christian faith is not the acceptance of a logical structure of truths but of a divine person as the fullness of being. He continues a few pages later that a Jesus defined as God-man must have anthropological implications: "He who surrenders himself completely to service for others, to complete selflessness and self-emptying, literally *becomes* these things—that this very person is the true man, the man of the future, the coinciding of man and God."[63] Previously, Ratzinger had already thematized the radical openness of Jesus as Christ when defining Jesus' personhood.[64] In facing the "alterity"—to use a term of the Jewish philosopher Levinas—of the Other human being, one becomes more one's authentic self.[65] This openness to unconditional charity forms the basis for liturgy and the believer's role therein. Christ's death on the cross "was in reality the one and only liturgy of the world, a cosmic liturgy, in which Jesus stepped...publicly, before the eyes of the world, through the curtain of death into the real temple...before the face of God himself, in order to offer...himself (Heb 9:11ff)."[66] The consequence is that human beings actualize themselves most when partaking in sacrifice and sacrificing themselves. Human eternity thus depends on a way of life here on earth that is *responsibly* conducted in freedom. The origin of both the English word "responsible" from "response," as well as the German term *"Verantwortung"* (responsibility) deriving from *"Wort"* (word) and *"Antwort"* (response), is significant. Human existence is called in charity to respond to the prevenient charity of God made manifest in Jesus Christ. The response will determine the quality of eschatological human existence: the manner by which we incorporate divine charity in a tangible form into our everyday lives will determine our eternity."[67] Jesus as the one who knows the human condition and suffered its fragility and brokenness will greet the human soul.[68]

It is not soaring thoughts that express the essence of history and humankind but rather a single individual: Jesus Christ. In Jesus Christ, God acquires a face. For Ratzinger, this is well expressed by Dante when he writes of God's mystery as "all-powerful love which, quiet and united, leads around in a circle the sun and all the stars."[69] The fact that in Jesus Christ we access God is an unheard of provocation. Harnack and Bultmann represent two alternative positions. While for the former everything hinges on history, the latter considers the actual significance to lie in the message. Either history becomes the decisive interpreter of Jesus and his message (Harnack), or one is content to merely state that Jesus had once lived, but the summoning to a decision is important (Bultmann).[70]

Harnack argued that what is necessary is not Christ but Jesus. Jesus is the source of charity whereas Christ is the expression of dogma causing strife. Everyone should unite under the one Father in charity. Yet still, in Harnack's day, the quest for the historical Jesus evaporated into nothing. In contrast, Bultmann was interested exclusively in the sole fact of Jesus having existed ("that" he had existed). What counts is only the fact of his existence, not the content of his sermons. This results in an emaciated Jesus, leading directly to the God-is-dead type of theology. The conclusion for Ratzinger is that one cannot have access to Jesus except when accepting Christ, and vice versa.[71] Such a figure is, for John the Evangelist, the Word. It is this Jesus Christ who grants meaning and purpose to humanity and the universe.

Ratzinger does not *in globo* reject these two extreme positions. He acknowledges the oscillation between "Jesus" and "Christ" as valuable because one cannot separate the historic Jesus from the exalted Christ. It illustrates the limits of the historical method, which cannot uncover the truth of the gospel. This insight yields the necessary humility to approach the image of Jesus Christ, as painted by the believing Church in its creed. Thus, one does not fall into the pit of archaeologism but encounters belief as a living reality. Via the Swiss Catholic theologian Hans Urs von Balthasar, Ratzinger argues along the lines of the Swiss Reformed theologian Karl Barth and, more importantly, in consonance with John's Gospel, in favor of the inseparable unity of Jesus' person and work.[72] Philosophical and theological truths coincide in the one, living divine person Jesus Christ, who is the self-expression of his Divine Father.

One hears here a conscious drawing away from neoscholasticism. Ratzinger takes pains to add that this close link of Jesus with Christ would remain inconsequential were he not the Son of God residing eternally in the Godhead. The early Christological definitions of the ecumenical councils of Nicaea and Chalcedon intended to establish the identity of being and service. For this reason, the council fathers were compelled to correlate Jesus' being with the Godhead. This requires constantly departing from where Christ is: from the Incarnation and finally to the cross. This leads Ratzinger to assess Anselm's theory of atonement in a more favorable light than other authors do.[73] (Anselm's theory of atonement holds that satisfaction was needed to restore universal harmony of a creation dislodged from paradise by sin.) A thorough exegetical *tour d'horizon* concludes that the cross is the ultimate revelation of Jesus as the Son:

> The open side of the new Adam repeats the mystery of the "open side" of man at creation: it is the beginning of a new definitive community of men with one another, a community symbolized here by blood and water, in which John points to the basic Christian sacraments of baptism

and Eucharist and, through them, to the Church as the sign of the new community of men. The fully opened Christ, who completes the transformation of being into reception and transmission, is thus visible as what at the deepest level he always was: as "Son."[74]

This insight allows Ratzinger to conclude that sacrifice is a constitutive element of human existence, flying in the face of a "cheerful romanticism of progress." Proexistence belongs to the very essence of Christianity, inseparably combining selfless glorification of God the Father with magnanimous service to humankind. The dogmas of Nicaea and Chalcedon bring together the two dimensions of Jesus Christ's existence as servant andSon (Phil 2:5–11) and the two dimensions of his ministry (as proexistence) and being. The human being strives to replicate this identity as the deepest of his or her desires. Christianity as a belief system and—for those churches in apostolic succession—as a sacramental system enables this to become reality. In Christ's folly of love à la Kierkegaard, the paradigm of fulfilled humanity shines forth. The loss of oneself affords access to genuine life. Contingent reality—including the dimension of human brokenness—is the only building material available to emulate and live Christ's magnanimity. In the cosmic liturgy, the Lamb is the pure existence for something else (Rv 5:1–14). Thus, Jesus is capable of addressing his Father as "*Abba.*"

In Ratzinger's mind, Jesus is fully understood as "being from and for." There is a total identity between Jesus' person, word, and mission. Positing an opposition between a Lord who serves and a glorified Lord does not do justice to Christology. John deeply understands the serving Lord in all his fullness. It is the self-sacrificing Lord on the cross who gathers all unto himself: "And I, when I am lifted up from the earth, will draw all men to myself" (Jn 12:32). The dispersed, indivisible human "monads"—each containing the whole of existence, according to the German philosopher Gottfried Wilhelm Leibniz (1646–1716)—are united in this Jesus Christ, and this is the purpose of human history. Jesus is opened morally and physically on the cross, "and at once there came out blood and water" (Jn 19:34)—when the spear pierces his side, and this event is of current relevance. The new Adam's side is opened.[75] In the image of the pierced Lord, all of history culminates. It is here that a new humanity takes shape. Jesus could only gradually lead a strictly monotheistic religion such as Judaism toward the wealth of a triune God.

Positivism—as taught, for instance, in Lessing's position of a separation between the contingent truth of fact and necessary intellectual truth—is an obstacle to understanding the call to true life.[76] Such positivism hinders people from living, as Mary did exemplarily throughout her life, but particularly during the annunciation, "the simplicity of acceptance, as the voluntary gift of the love that redeems the world."[77] This is the message of the Resurrection of Christ. He wrought in love the salvation of humankind by being murdered by a humankind denying love. As stated earlier, our Lord "will not advance to meet us as the entirely Other, but as one of us, who knows human existence from inside and has suffered."[78]

Ratzinger, as are all notable systematicians, is thoroughly Trinitarian. It is little wonder then that he adds a chapter on the Holy Spirit to his book

Behold The Pierced One. He states that the Apostle Creed's last part describes how the Holy Spirit works in history. Its members do not render the Church holy; rather, it is God who sanctifies her. God is not the aloof God of Greek philosophy. Instead, in the Church God deigns to involve himself with the soiled world of the Church. Ratzinger therefore warns his readers not to be overly confident regarding the possibility of ecclesial reform. It is not for Christians to enjoy a perfect ecclesial reality, nor is this the task of the Holy Spirit. Rather, this world offers us the opportunity to see and long for the real world: "'…be of good cheer, I have overcome the world' (Jn 16:33)."[79]

At the conclusion of his masterfully composed book *Introduction to Christianity*, Ratzinger observes that there is an intrinsic connection between matter and spirit, between body and soul. Therefore, in the eschaton there must be both an individual and a communal aspect, because one cannot conceive of eternal bliss without the fellowship of human beings with God and, therefore, with one another. "The goal of the Christian is not private bliss but the whole."[80]

While Bethlehem reveals the two persons of Father and Son in God, it immediately leads onward to the Holy Spirit. On the basis of the Johannine Jesus, Ratzinger writes of "God as 'I' and 'Thou' in one. This new experience of God is followed finally by a third: the experience of the Spirit, the presence of God in us, in our innermost being…it is the manner in which God gives himself to us, in which he enters into us, so that he is *in* man yet, in the midst of this 'indwelling,' is infinitely *above* him."[81]

The belief of the faithful in the Holy Spirit transforming them concretizes itself in the communion of saints. This comes about due to the divine remission of sins offered by the power of the Holy Spirit and exercised by the Church in the sacrament of reconciliation. In fact, the Church is fundamentally grounded in reconciliation: "The new being of forgiveness leads us into fellowship with those who live from forgiveness; forgiveness establishes communion; and communion with the Lord in the Eucharist leads necessarily to the communion of the converted, who all eat one and the same bread, to become in it 'one body' (1 Cor 10:17) and indeed, 'one single new man' (cf. Eph 2:15)."[82] The human link between sacrament and Church becomes apparent. Interestingly, at the same time the abiding presence of the Holy Spirit in the Church renders defining the Church as sacrament comprehensible. Dialectically, this Church is apprehended as both living from grace, that is, the individual seven sacraments, and as the sacramental reality administering them. This echoes a discussion that took place at the time of the composition of *Introduction to Christianity*.: the Church as primordial sacrament and the seven individual sacraments; all are rooted in Christ.[83] The ingredients that constitute the Church are the Eucharist, as divine initiative, and both the believers' faith and their receptivity to God's Word. The Church is most actualized when her members refrain from primarily defining themselves from their organizing, reforming, and governing, but simply and joyfully live the gift of faith. The sacraments of initiation most reflect the Church as the place of receptivity and faith: "Baptism, penance, and Eucharist are," in his estimation, "the framework of the Church, her real content and her true mode of existence." As noted previously, the Church is essentially a communion lived in forgiveness. One cannot divorce soteriology from metaphysics if one beholds Jesus Christ as the fulfillment of history and therefore knows history and being form one unit.

The bestowal of the gift of salvation in and through Jesus Christ grants the certitude of this unity of all beings. The sacramentality of the Church vouches for the sacramental nature of the individual sacraments. One cannot have one without the other. One understands the Church properly exclusively in the sacraments. All organization or structures within the Church are mere consequences of the invisible reality.

Ratzinger's closing reflection on the nature of the Church is significant as it addresses the critique of the late 1960s concerning the credibility of the Church as an institution. He responds to this: "The basic elements of the Church appear as forgiveness, conversion, penance, Eucharistic communion, and hence plurality and unity: plurality of the local Churches that yet remain 'the Church' only through incorporation in the unity of the one Church."[84] The episcopal constitution of the Church's structure is subservient to this sacramental and spiritual reality, and it is an expression thereof.[85] Hence, on the other hand, neither is the Church a purely spiritual reality à la the Protestant jurist Rudolph Sohm,[86] lest one not do justice to the mystery of the historic Incarnation and the drama of the ongoing Incarnation that is the Church.

On a different note, Ratzinger's nuanced distinction between biology and ontology in the introduction to his work as regards soteriology was pioneering. This means that Jesus' divine Sonship neither depends upon Our Lady's biological virginity nor on Joseph's not being the physical father of Jesus.[87] It *precedes* them and brings them about.

CHAPTER 15

Christ and the Pursuit of Happiness: Safeguarding the Nondisponibility of Christ*

In his foreword to the second edition of his *Habilitationsschrift* in 1992, Ratzinger explains his belief that liberation theology at its heart attempts a Christian utopia, uniting secular utopia and Christian eschatology—much like Joachim of Fiore tried to do. Not by chance were numerous idealistic Franciscans advocates of liberation theology. Like Bonaventure in the thirteenth century, Ratzinger had to address them. He warns one cannot separate Christ from the Holy Spirit, that is, a Christ-centered, institutional Church from a pneumatic-prophetic one.

During his stint as a helper in the German labor service digging antitank ditches in the futile attempt to prevent the advance of the Soviet army at the Austro-Hungarian border, young Ratzinger experienced how a state negating religion developed its own liturgical rituals: "The entire absurdity of the [Nazi] régime was demonstrated in the 'cult of the spade.' 'An intricate military drill taught us how to lay down the spade solemnly, how to pick it up and swing it over the shoulder; the cleaning of the spade, on which there should not be a single speck of dust, was an essential part of this pseudo-liturgy.' The whole scene was horribly punctuated by an image the spadeguards saw on the outskirts. This was 'the way of the Cross of the Hungarian Jews, who passed by us in long columns.' "[1] This sensitized the seventeen-year-old early on to the necessary tension between and relative autonomy of religion and politics. If this is not maintained, the attendant danger is twofold: that mockery is made of God and the state becomes inhumane.

During the time when Marxism exerted a fascination on many people in the West, Ratzinger gave a lecture at St. Ludwig's Church in Munich on June 10, 1980. He held the lecture in that church after he was forced by

---

*Jesus Christ as ineffable divine person cannot be defined, anticipated, or manipulated by human beings.

unruly communist students to leave Munich University's lecture hall. There, in the university church, he addressed the students and professors:

> Render unto God what is God's and unto Caesar what is Caesar's—these seemingly so simple words inaugurated a new phase in the history of the relationship between politics and religion. Until then it was commonly held that the political was also the sacred. Jesus cut apart this identification of the state's claim on man with the sacred claim of the divine will in the world. This placed into jeopardy the ancient idea of the state and it is understandable that the ancient state considered this negation of its totality as an attack on the very foundations of its existence, punishable on pain of death. If Jesus' word is valid, then indeed the Roman state could not continue in its previous construction. At the same time, it must be stated that this separation of state and sacred authority—and the new dualism inherent in it—represents the origin and abiding foundation of the Western idea of freedom.[2]

In *Jesus of Nazareth*, the Pope points out that only with caution did Augustus, the first Roman emperor to do so, proclaim himself "the Son of the Divine Caesar" and therefore the Son of God.[3] In contradistinction to the Roman rulers, Jesus Christ defines his divine kingship in altogether different terms. Authentic divine sonship rests on the unity of the Son with the Father and Spirit. In his understanding, therefore "the fundamentally apolitical Christian faith, which does not demand political power, but acknowledges the legitimate authorities (cf. Rom 13:1–7), inevitably collides with the total claim made by the imperial political power. Indeed, it will always come into conflict with totalitarian political regimes and will be driven into the situation of martyrdom, into communion with the Crucified, who reigns solely from the wood of the Cross."[4]

While Jesus Christ enters into the drama of human existence, he does not disavow his divine identity or redefine himself in so doing. Nothing "political or material" may replace Jesus' divine commission and eternal origin with the Father lest "the things of God fade into unreality, into a secondary world that no one really needs."[5] This is the importance of the temptation narratives, where the devil attempts to lure Jesus into the trap of seeking merely worldly power and sustenance. Jesus is not indifferent to human suffering. However, the proper priorities are called for if one is to truly satisfy human thirst. Genuine humanism hinges on listening to God and living with God. Then faith quite naturally leads to charity, "to the discovery of the other."[6] He insists that orthodoxy leads to orthopraxis. However altruistic it may be, a one-sided materialist approach to aiding developing countries in the Third World is hollow. "History cannot be detached from God and then run smoothly on purely material lines."[7] Taking up Gnilka's insight that the devil-tempter is arguing like a theologian,[8] Ratzinger reminds the reader that the Russian philosopher and convert to Catholicism Vladimir Soloviev also has the Antichrist appear on the stage of history in a center of Catholic learning, in Tübingen, as a scripture scholar. The Antichrist claims God cannot act in history. Instead, he advocates a new Bible, "The Open Way to

World Peace and Welfare." Rationally planned, the world on its own can become a place of perfect well-being. Not only did Barabbas and Jesus both entertain messianic claims, Ratzinger points out that the church father Origen mentioned that both Barabbas and Our Lord had in the gospels even the same first names: Jesus. For a common bystander the two must have appeared confusingly similar upon first sight. Thus, not only did Pontius Pilate offer the people the choice of freeing either Barabbas or Jesus Christ, there was a programmatic alternative between the two: the unruly crowd was asked to choose "between a Messiah who leads an armed struggle, promises freedom and a kingdom of one's own, and this mysterious Jesus who proclaims that losing oneself is the way of life."[9] The struggle of the Church for freedom from political embrace is a continuation of this theme. To Ratzinger's mind, "God is the issue: Is he real, reality itself, or isn't he? Is he the good, or do we have to invent the good ourselves?"[10]

In a way, it seems to Ratzinger that large parts of the intelligentsia are beholden to the Kantian distinction between phenomenon and noumenon. He finds this theologically best expressed in the thought of the Presbyterian John Hick (b. 1922). Identifying the historical Jesus with the divine Son of God, and therefore as the Christ, is regarded by Hick as a relapse into irrational, prescientific myth. Kant proved to him that the Absolute can neither be recognized nor appear in history. While Hick does believe Jesus to be one of the great religious leaders, sacraments, miracles, and mysteries, no matter of what religious origin, are superstitions.[11] This has supposedly been proven by an exegesis that is unable to apprehend Jesus as the Son of God and the incarnate divine Logos. For Hick and various others, ascribing to Jesus Christ and the Church a binding and always valid truth is the definition of fundamentalism. For the sake of a peace-loving humanism and following the Enlightenment's rallying call *écrasez l'infâme* (Voltaire's "Wipe out the infamous!"), Hick and others consider it imperative to divorce the historic Jesus from the divine Christ and to dissolve ecclesiology. Leaving all Christological dogmas in the dustbins of history supposedly frees humankind from fanaticism and particularism.[12] To many, Asian religions seem to hold the promise of a conflict-free practice. The absolute Logos as a personal reality dialoguing with people is sidestepped. "The relativism of Hick, Knitter, and related theorists is ultimately based on a rationalism which declares that reason—in the Kantian meaning—is incapable of metaphysical reasoning."[13] God then cannot be believed but merely experienced. What is significant in the New Age movements, which do not have a personal God, is that there is no longer orthodoxy but orthopraxis. The "sober inebriety" of the Christian liturgy cannot elevate its followers? In Ratzinger's judgment, such a pluralist theory is ineffective in the face of future threats to humanity.

In 1937 Paul Althaus (1888–1966), a Protestant systematic theologian at the Bavarian University of Erlangen, defended National Socialism in a book against the Barmen Declaration of the Confessing Church, made in 1934 by Karl Barth and other Protestant minority theologians.[14] In the Barmen Declaration, the declared revelation of the triune God in Jesus Christ, to be preached as God's free gift, is in no way subordinate to anything human. In contrast, Althaus advanced the theory of a primordial revelation, expressing itself in pre-Christian orders of creation.[15] This established primordially an inseparable link between the individual and the people, the *Volk*. The *Volk* is this divinely created order. The Nazi-ideology-driven monopolizing of the term "people" explains in no small degree Ratzinger's attraction to Origen and Augustine. In *Contra Celsum* and *De Principiis* Origen had refused to develop a theology of the nation. Augustine's *De Civitate Dei* is essentially an attack on political religion.[16] Religion, Ratzinger concludes, especially Christianity, may not be instrumentalized to sanction or canonize a body politic as Althaus and the National Socialists did. Ancient pagan religions succumbed naturally to this temptation. Yet, as Christ teaches, the world, and thus the *polis*, remain essentially transitional and therefore alien terrain for the Christian. However Christianized a society may be, the Church—as a sacramental-eschatological entity—points to the world yet to come, that is, to the "only Absolute, God, and the only mediator between God and man, Jesus Christ."[17]

One of the minds who shaped Ratzinger's was the convert to Catholicism Erik Peterson (1890–1960). In his seminal study *Der Monotheismus als politisches Problem* (*Monotheism as a Political Problem*), he argued that the European Enlightenment left only monotheism for believers.[18] Yet this form of belief is just as questionable as its political consequences. In contrast, Christians can participate in politics only under the premise of a triune God. Therefore, Christianity broke away from any form of political theology when it asserted itself in antiquity.[19] With the advent of Christianity, religion could no longer be used *nolens volens* (or willy-nillyto sanction a particular political reality. In the 1960s, political theology would evolve diametrically opposed to Peterson's thesis.

In Ratzinger's thought, the Church does not simply become an uncritical companion to the world. Rather, oriented to God as the *Bonum diffusivum sui* (the Good diffusing itself), "The Church lives in the Trinitarian mystery which has opened itself to her in Christ. The fact that there is a Church at all derives from the fact that God has opened himself."[20] God's own Word is to penetrate the world and transform people in divine charity. The Church lives in her ability to grant the world what the world can never generate on its own but longs for. All dialogue with the world serves this double charge of incarnating the Word and inspiring its inhabitants toward divine charity. Ratzinger points out that a significant difference exists between Socrates' dialogues and those of Jesus Christ. While in the Socratic dialogues both parties gain in knowledge, the Johannine presentation of Jesus' dialogues allows the reader to sense that two incommensurable planes exist between Jesus and his audience. In his words, Jesus Christ imparts something humanly unimaginable and unreckonable. Christianity proclaims this paradox because it communicates something for which there is an infinite longing and yet something that is also downright scandalous. Ratzinger insists with scripture that salvation has come to this world through only one man, Jesus Christ. The glory of the Church is grounded solely in representing Jesus Christ to the world. "Indeed, Ratzinger goes so far as to say, when we use the word 'Church' what we are naming is the *Unterwegssein*, the 'being-on-the-way,' of Jesus' message of the Kingdom to all the peoples."[21]

Salvation history is an area that interested Ratzinger early on. In 1969 he authored an article on *Heilsgeschichte* (salvation history).[22] He perceives modernity as informed by Martin Luther when seeing Christendom as a cause for discontinuity with previous history. Martin Luther had lost an appreciation for both the presence of the Holy Spirit in the Church and for the charism of apostolic succession. Thus, there is greater discontinuity than continuity between the time of Christ and the apostles and our own age. Our own age can no longer be perceived as part of an ongoing salvation history. At the same time, the community is no longer considered the basic reality but the individual; it becomes "subject-centered, pro me." The discontinuity between the Old and New Testaments is stressed. The accusation of the Hellenization of Christianity is raised, and finally in the 1960s the Protestant battle cry of salvation history supplants Catholic metaphysics, even within Catholicism itself. In 1982, Ratzinger defined the political theology advocated by Johann Baptist Metz as representing a naïvely optimistic option for history, while simultaneously rejecting "the past, a suspension of all reference to tradition in favor of a program of what is to be done."[23] Human beings are constantly laboring to make themselves, and they are fascinated by the postlapsarian temptation to be a *homo faber* (that is, "man, the maker"). While Ratzinger was intrigued by Rahner's concept of man as "hearer of the Word," he maintains salvation history as revelation history may not be collapsed into world history in a Hegelian sense of the progressive self-explication of humankind. Ratzinger considered this the danger of reading Rahner's *Grundkurs des Glaubens*.[24] In it, Ratzinger divines something of a (pseudo-) Hegelian reduction of God to a self-becoming of the Absolute Spirit in time and space. The concept of Karl Rahner's supernatural existential runs the risk of being misunderstood as the grace-free, self-becoming of humanity in history. This is latently and acutely accented in Johann Baptist Metz' political theology. It is as if Ratzinger were to hurl into this discussion a Barthian "*Deus semper maior!*" (God is always greater!). The point of history lies in Christification.[25] Humanity is redeemed by Jesus Christ *in* history but not *through* history. Human nature and grace, faith and reason, interact without becoming dialectic entities within a larger, faceless automatic process.[26] Reminding the reader of Martin Buber, Ratzinger in *Introduction to Christianity* argues that faith is always a leap or adventure requiring on the individual human being's part a volitional and existential effort.[27]

Not a believer's ideational consciousness but the historic self-revelation of God is crucial. The particular human being can identify his or her own being with that of Christ. Not a synthesis of a system is proper to human freedom, but lived commitment to the eternal Thou. Not "a term" but "tradition" bears witness to this.

The Jewish thinker Eric Voegelin (1901–1985), who had to flee Nazi persecution, demonstrated how Joachim of Fiore's (ca. 1135–1202) speculation led to modernity. While Augustine beheld the world as something transitory and only the *Civitas Dei* as worth defending, Joachim paved the way for an "immanentization of the eschaton." In Voegelin's estimation, this led to the notion of progress, a presumption numerous socialists and liberal capitalists subscribe to.[28]

Two tendencies continue to emerge in Ratzinger's thought. All attempts to create a perfect society devoid of a notion of transcendence are doomed to bring about an impersonal society beholden to economic or political perfectionism, disregarding the inalienable dignity of the individual human person and society as one of mutual respect and solidarity. This insight confirms the need for Christianity to play a foundational role in modern society as the latter strives to bring about a just and harmonious society. The understanding of a tension-filled relationship between the body politic and the Church is specific to the Catholic vision of the Church-state relation, but in the case of Ratzinger is indebted in a particular way to Augustine. In his doctoral dissertation, *The People of God and God's House in Augustine's Doctrine of the Church*, the tension between temporality and celestial permanence is not resolved but restated. The *De Civitate Dei* is his guide in relating to modern society. In essence, the thesis is that the City of Man and the City of God can never be conflated. This world necessarily remains incomplete and imperfect. To ignore this salient circumstance or to attempt to perfect it means doing violence to the created order. Sin colors the landscape of this world and no economic, technical, or political program can cancel out this fact. Indeed, precisely appreciating this world as imperfect and yearning for a perfection that is not self-produced allows the genius of the arts to arise and personal charity to triumph over injustice. It avoids the otherwise inevitable pitfall of disillusionment. Ratzinger is of the opinion that the aim to create an all-just society suggests the state can be the good moral agent, supplanting the individual's responsibility to labor for the good. Yet, invariably, political projects will succumb to some form of utilitarianism, rather than relying on moral norms that defy scientific verification. The remedies to such dangers can be found in Christianity. Society is called to acknowledge the transitory nature of this world and accept its imperfections. This honesty allows society to consciously live the supernatural virtue of a hope anchored in eternity. Human beings are then able to work to improve this world as a way to give expression to charity. In such acts, the Christian faith can provide society with the moral consensus it is in dire need of. This consensus can then become the source for moral norms that provide orientation for a society's politics and economics. A rigid grid of moral precepts is not imposed upon society. Rather, grounded in such a realism to an infinite Thou, it gains freedom. While never reaching divine justice, human justice is able to evaluate what is good and bad. For Ratzinger, moral truths are grounded in a transcendent source. Personal experience of the good is the basis for a healthy society.

There should remain a creative difference between the Christian faith and the political and economic arenas. This longstanding Catholic teaching is found in Pope Gelasius (492–496) in his twelfth letter to the Byzantine Emperor Anastasios I and completed in the fourth tractate on the teaching on the two powers (*utraque potestas* that is, both powers) Both kingship (*regnum*) and the priesthood (*sacerdotium*) are of divine origin. This was later coined the Doctrine of the Two Swords: both the state and the Church enjoy relative autonomy from each other.[29]

A nontheological reading of parts of the pastoral constitution on the Church in the modern world, *Gaudium et Spes*, especially of number 36, might to lead to a false optimism concerning the ability of the world to perfect its ways without grace. At long last, some argued after *Gaudium et Spes*, the Church has recognized the inherent goodness of modern culture. The sacraments can be considered mere customs. The world process on its own is good. To many in France in the 1960s, this meant the Church's final accommodation of the laicist constitution of France, and the French Revolution of 1789 that brought it forth, sanctioning the genocide of about 750,000 Catholics who had opposed it. In Germany, *Gaudium et Spes* had similar sociological ramifications: the nineteenth-century *Kulturkampf* was considered definitively over, with Catholic Germans becoming mainstream Germans. The utopia of a good world achieved without God was popularized in Germany in the 1960s by the Marxist philosopher Ernst Bloch in his book *The Principle of Hope*.[30] In it Ratzinger saw the looming danger of a deified society and self-perfecting history. Proponents of political theology, such as Johann Baptist Metz (b. 1925) and Juan Luis Segundo (1925–1996), supported a proletarian revolution. They thought *Gaudium et Spes* justified such a new view and inaugurated a definitive break with Pius IX's unqualified opposition to modernity. In contradistinction, in Ratzinger's mind *Gaudium et Spes* 22 insists that the remedy for all of humankind is Jesus Christ, and it is the responsibility of the Church to administer this medication. The human being yearns in the depths of his or her heart to be conformed to Christ—this includes suffering in the incongruencies of the *conditio humana* (human state) through the supernatural virtues of faith, hope and charity—and thereby giving witness to them.

One should note that Ratzinger never subscribed to a conservative, neo-conservative, liberal, or capitalist outlook. Before becoming prefect in Rome, he had stated that the "liberalism and capitalism fostered by Anglo Saxon powers had become an even more painful slavery" than the injustices of Spanish and Portuguese colonial rule in Latin America.[31] He is and has been far too much a part of a communitarian lifestyle as enunciated by Thomas Aquinas and Catholic social teaching—having lived in Bavaria—to become individualistic. Protestants know of no communal mediation of grace, but for Catholics and Eastern Christians the Church is a sacramental reality. Christ is the structural law and goal of history, and Christianity is the yardstick for measuring and the vehicle for reaching this goal.

On January 23, 1984, the Peruvian journal *Ogia* published an essay of Ratzinger's on liberation theology. At that time, the prominent founder of liberation theology, Gustavo Gutiérrez, was teaching at the University of Lima in Peru's capital. Ratzinger sent him a memorandum with ten critical inquiries regarding liberation theology. He perceived this theology posed a fundamental danger to the Church's faith. It was a novel current that defined itself as a new interpretation of Christianity: it considered itself a praxis of (material) liberation and thereby understood itself as the supplier of instructions for this transformation. In Ratzinger's eyes, this was a tall order. Also, for him, orthopraxis must not supplant orthodoxy. In Ratzinger's line of argument, the practice of charity may not be perceived as a replacement for "the proper way of adoring God."[32] In liberation theology, Ratzinger notes the subcutaneous influence of the Protestant theologian Rudolf Bultmann's concept of demarcating quite clearly between "the historical Jesus" and the "Christ of ecclesial tradition." Bultmann did this famously in *Die Geschichte der synoptischen Tradition* (*The History of the Synoptic Tradition*).[33]

Philosophically, Ratzinger is fully in accord with Plato. Politics does not produce truth. The attempt to comprehend the world merely by means of letters evokes his skepticism. Surrendering exclusively to a political method invariably occasions a loss of reality. As in philosophy, so also in morality good conduct must precede politics and form the basis for public welfare. Similar to Plato, he perceives tangible reality in confrontation with invisible substances, which are actually the more real entities. For the Christian-modified Platonist that Ratzinger is, this means tangible reality is approached by way of the faith. In 2002, he argued that according to the *Phaidrus*, the arrow of beauty strikes unexpectedly human beings, wounds, wings, and pulls them upward. And yet, beauty is not irrational but a higher form of insight. Here one detects influences of the philosopher, and expert on St. Thomas Aquinas, Josef Pieper (1904–1997), with whom Ratzinger maintained amiable contact over many years.[34] According to Plato, beauty is a form of a *"theia mania,"* of a divinely effected being besides oneself. In such an occurrence one cannot remain content or at home in the tangible, mundane reality surrounding one.

This is not too distant from Thomas Aquinas, who argued that beauty is a transcendental, a vehicle to discovering God.[35] On the twenty-fifth anniversary of John Paul II's pontificate, Ratzinger interpreted Beethoven's *"Freude schöner Götterfunken"* ("Ode to Joy") as a proof of God's existence; music supplies certitude. The mystery of the Incarnation of the Eternal Son receives further plausibility. The good Father is by no means merely a reality in the lofty heavens, but he is present among us in his divine Son. Ratzinger reiterates this when reflecting on Händel's *Hallelujah.* He perceives this piece of music as a light ray that enables the presence of Christ to continue to shine. He has made similar remarks on the *Cantata* of Johann Sebastian Bach. In each case the force of an essentially underlying reality (*anwesende Wirklichkeit*) is audible, which one can no longer arrive at via logical inference alone but by way of an immediate and irreversible *Erschütterung* (tremor) caused by the power of truth, which is rendered presentic by the composer's inspiration. Beauty is a manifestation of truth. Inspiration often implies nothing short of an encounter with a higher, divine power. It conveys a plenitude of insight that would otherwise remain unreachable.

Ratzinger's words must also be understood in the context of recent postwar German intellectual history. In a most pronounced way, the influential German philosopher Theodor Adorno (1903–1969) subscribed to anti-Platonism. The holocaust and the kitsch of National Socialist art discredited the appreciation of beauty. It likewise suggested the untenability of both German idealism and Platonism. The theory of a reality beyond an underlying palpable reality seemed obsolete. It is little wonder in 1948 Adorno postulated the provocative axiom that the inhumanity of art must excel that of the world, so that a remnant of humanity might survive.[36] Three years later, in 1951, he declared that everything contains negativity. One cannot see the blossoming of a tree without anguish, because the tree lies.[37] His *Aesthetic*

Theory was published posthumously in 1970. In it, he argues art is merely "the memory of accumulated suffering." To his mind, the only authentic form of music is that of Schönberg's twelve-tone technique. The tonality of Beethoven and Mozart is fraud. Ratzinger responds to such negative dialectics with the rhetorical question of whether all joy must be suppressed in order to exercise solidarity with the suffering. On the other hand, as regards the classical understanding of beauty, Ratzinger meets Adorno halfway: in Jesus Christ's passion, ugliness has become a part of art and beauty. The Greek understanding of aesthetics is not nullified by Jesus Christ's passion but transcended by it. Indeed, beauty has now received a new dimension of profundity and realism.[38]

With Johann Baptist Metz, the father of political theology, and the philosopher Jürgen Habermas (b. 1929) he assumes an inner connection exists between the Enlightenment and the terrible criminal aberrations in the twentieth century. In the final analysis, he suspects some liberation theologians of striving to create politically, or even by coercion, conditions in which human volition will be automatically good, just like they maintain human volition is necessarily bad in unjust, capitalist conditions. But as Ratzinger argues in *Deus Caritas Est* §28, politics does not seek to produce a technique to order the public square. Its true aim is justice and ethics. Everywhere, and at all times, each human being must face the challenge of an ethical effort on his or her own part. Genuine freedom requires this. It is not the result of exterior conditions. For this reason, prescribed justice does not liberate but imposes a dictatorship—it cannot suspend the human being as a moral agent. History is not the temple of God and the encounter with God is not identical with political efforts for a more equitable world. As charity is more than political love, Christ's Redemption is more than changing social conditions and political institutions—however much one is obligated to improve them.[39]

In 1996 Ratzinger cited Paul Knitter, who argued, "One cannot comprehend the absolute, but one can do it." Ratzinger responded to this apodictic statement with a rhetorical question: "Why not? Mere praxis is not light." The dominance of orthopraxis leads one into an aporia: there is no such thing as orthopraxis without the content of the profession of faith. In other words, an orthopraxis without reference to a creedal content leads to a tragic irony, namely, its own self-dissolution. Invariably, then, high-minded orthopraxis becomes the plaything of ulterior motives, with little regard for the gospel message. This could come about due to a rebellion of the human intellect against the faith. In his mind, this can only be explained by favoring utopia at the cost of Christian eschatology.[40] Nothing short of opting for self-Redemption versus grace occurs in such a theological current. It seems as if Ratzinger argues the Christian eschatological vision must be upheld for the sake of a realistic, humane, and Christian utopia.

As Prefect of the Congregation for the Doctrine of the Faith, in 1984 Ratzinger was responsible for the document *Instruction of the Congregation for the Doctrine of the Faith Concerning Some Aspects of Liberation Theology*. In 1985, at the Rheinisch-Westfälische Akademie der Wissenschaften, he presented a paper on the theological perils and philosophical miscalculations of some tendencies of liberation theology, using some theses from Gustavo

Gutiérrez's theology. Gutiérrez had coined the term "liberation theology." Ratzinger's reflections were published in 1986 as *Politik und Erlösung* (*Politics and Redemption*).[41] He considers the intimate connection between political and Christological issues crucial. In his introductory essay to *Introduction to Christianity* in 2000, he brings up some of the issues of lasting relevance that liberation theology addressed in the 1970s and 1980s. The questions raised then continue to be current and virulent beyond Latin America. In this perspective, he examines not so much the trends of liberation theology itself but rather the advancement of his own arguments and positions.

The essays in *Politics and Redemption* essentially center on Marxist thought and its attendant derivatives in Western society and in Christianity until the collapse of Soviet communism in 1989. A central issue is whether humans are able to heal and redeem themselves. According to Marxism, structures of injustice and impediments to freedom must be abolished, in faithfulness to the rallying cry "destroy whatever destroys you." This approach unleashed a remarkable transfusion of ideas and affected Christianity. The Christian urge to contribute to peace and justice was joined with secular political action. In Ratzinger's estimation, liberation theology was by no means a result of the admittedly unjust, and even inhumane, living conditions of numerous people in Latin America. Rather, it was first and foremost the articulation of an issue that arose in and concerned Western intellectual life. It was by no means an indigenous theology but the importation of ideas comingling the cultural life in North America and Western Europe:

> This new translation of ideas into practice, this new fusion of the Christian impulse with secular and political action, was like a lightning bolt; the real fires that set it, however, were in Latin America. The theology of liberation seemed for more than a decade to point the way by which faith might again shape the world, because it was making common cause with the findings and worldly wisdom of the hour.[42]

He apprehends in liberation theology something akin to "a liberation from theology" occurring. It suggests one must assume that a blatantly unredeemed condition is a social and economic phenomenon calling for political action. Therefore, Ratzinger argues, theology as the science of Redemption must in this line of thought adopt a political face.[43] As Gutiérrez described it, theology became "a critical theory."[44] Invariably for liberation theology, theology and the Church must analyze the biblical messages of Israel's liberation from bondage and Jesus' courageous disregard for oppressive social structures, which will enable them to lead modern society out of injustice. The Church and theology are called upon to alter the world. The essence of Christianity is discovered via a Marxist analysis of social conditions. Only by virtue of Marxist theory does Christianity now become fecund in the world. For liberation theology, Jesus Christ's liberation of the Jews is but one aspect of "a permanent and universal liberation." Hence, "history is [Hegelian] anthropophany" (the appearance and assertion of humankind).[45] This view is confident of creating a new, redeemed world brought about by human beings. Humanity is redeemed by historic, human activity. In this case, Ratzinger interjects, Redemption is no longer a theological category or religious term. Rather, it is a stage in history that is organized by human beings. Referring to the Brazilian philosopher and historian Ricardo Vélez Rodríguez, he demonstrates how Latin America, at its beginning as a collection of independent nations from 1760 until 1825, was influenced by the French philosopher and exponent of French socialism Saint-Simon. Claude Henri de Saint-Simon (1760–1825) was convinced religion always serves as the basis for politics and social life. However, in order for religion to become beneficial and able to promote fraternal charity, it must be rid of dogmas and priests. So that religion does not become independent and dehumanizing (that is, critical of political realities), a separation of spiritual and temporal powers must not exist for Saint-Simon. Thus, both Vélez and Ratzinger demonstrate that liberation theology is by no means indebted first and foremost to exemplary priests concerned with promoting social justice, such as Bartolomé de las Casas, OP (1474–1566) or Pedro Claver, SJ (1580–1654). Thought through to its final consequences, such a theology makes itself superfluous—and deceives well-intentioned people. Liberation theology liberates from theology. Tragically, *"teología de la liberación"* becomes simultaneously *"liberación de la teología."*

One might add it is deplorable that liberation theology advances theories on matters of society and economics with no reference to the social teaching of the Church. In a way, one can only consider such blindness to the human condition postlapsarian—by ignoring the deleterious consequences of original sin one enforces them. Liberation theology claims an automatism between revolutionary change, the improvement of living conditions, and Redemption. Yet, as Aristotle stated, there is a difference between having a good, fulfilled, and content life ($\varepsilon\upsilon\delta\alpha\iota\mu\omicron\nu\iota\alpha$; *eudaimonia*) and being simply lucky ($\varepsilon\upsilon\tau\grave{\upsilon}\chi\acute{\eta}$; *eutyche*), that is, being born into a normal family, being spared plagues, war or famine, finding loved ones, and being cherished. Particularly the latter example demonstrates that one cannot achieve a state of good fortune simply by technical or political means. Also, bliss is fairly independent of an economic or social state. It need be stated: a state of bliss might occur in an individual's life even if not all objective parameters are met. This entails the following insight: bliss cannot be constructed; it cannot be engineered.

In order to illustrate this, Ratzinger cites rather often the renowned German philosopher Robert Spaemann (b. 1927). Though fortune and good luck may be experienced in every day common life, the automatic translation of means into the fulfillment of a wished-for state does not exist, however many favorable prerequisites and circumstances may occur. In its original meaning, the Greek term *eudaimonia* (happiness, bliss) is good fortune that cannot be coerced. Its success does not depend on material human factors but on supernatural, religious forces. The exuberance of experiencing good fortune or good luck rests precisely on the very nature of good fortune: it is not something produced or achieved but rather something granted, donated, or given as a present. One cannot lay claim to *eudaimonia*. In this context, Spaemann speaks of "the mystical moment."[46] One's life-conduct and one's being led "from above" are interlocked in this perspective. While one is being led by supernatural *daimones* (spirits), one must prove oneself worthy of such benign guidance. Human existence, therefore, is not merely the existence of a puppet. One must struggle existentially to be worthy of such guidance so that one is, so to speak, "en-souled by a good spirit." To be "en-souled by a good spirit" means knowing by one's own spirit what is proper and fitting for a good life.

By way of Aristotle's understanding of *eudaimonia*, the core argument in Ratzinger's mind for opposing the general trajectory of liberation theology is its approach, which is absent theology and uses a technique for transforming reality that is a form of (Marxist) analysis alien to Christianity. Ratzinger, using Aristotle propaedeutically, illustrates that becoming fortunate in the sense of a *metabasis eis allo genos* (change by another kind) cannot be coerced, in fact, it cannot even be imagined by human beings on their own, however much they might yearn for it. Here is a case of false pretense. There can be no "casting of metaphysics into physics."[47] There can be no mechanical or organic transposing of the means of success into success. Even apart from the issue of liberation theology, the teaching office has often demonstrated that politics is unsuitable to achieve effective, that is, redeeming, Redemption. In this vein, the 1987 encyclical *Sollicitudo Rei Socialis* can be quoted: an exclusively economic development cannot truly liberate humankind. On the contrary, it just further enslaves it. Development without being mindful of "a cultural, transcendental and religious dimension" of humankind and society never offers the prospect for genuine liberation.[48] In the final analysis, Ratzinger observes that realistic hope for improvement only exists if one advocates evolution instead of revolution. Both terms are in his judgment "categories of deterministic thought."[49] Rather than being open toward a historic future and the "radically different," a revolution in particular establishes rules and criteria for the direction and quality of human development. Freedom is understood as that which develops in conformity with an inexorable historic process. Like Marxist analysis, liberation theology subscribes to an understanding of history as predetermined time. An immanentization of the *basileia tou Theou*, of the kingdom of God, occurs. Faithful to Ludwig Feuerbach (1804–1872), Marxism takes up the divinization of utopian thoughts of all possible and impossible variations of reality and inverts them into history. Without God, utopia becomes the actual creedal content. Indeed, history becomes the true deity. The consequence of such a hypertrophization of history is that the individual person as a *"rationalis naturae individua substantia"* (an individual substance of a rational nature), as defined by the Christian philosopher Boethius (ca. 480–524/6), evaporates into the anonymous collective whole. The spiritual dimension of humanity is lost, for one is no longer addressed by something numinous and supernatural.

This topic and struggle is according to Ratzinger not altogether novel. Early on, the Church fathers developed the distinction between the supernatural and natural realms, which finds its correspondence in the distinction between the Church and world. During the two world wars and particularly afterward in the 1950s, numerous theologians and philosophers argued one cannot speak of two levels of reality, one remaining unrelated to the other. The terms "supernatural" and "supernature" were judged artificial. In no time, the supernatural disappeared in favor of the concrete human being and

CHRIST AND THE PURSUIT OF HAPPINESS

horizontalized history. The obvious conclusion drawn was "the Christian must become worldly in order to be authentically Christian."[50] The remarkable consonance of the influences Ratzinger was exposed to come to the fore in his well-discussed introductory remarks to *Introduction to Christianity* that were first published in the Italian reprint: "The main thing affecting the status of Christianity in that period was the idea of a new relationship between the Church and the world. Although Romano Guardini in the 1930s had coined the expression *Unterscheidung des Christlichen* [distinguishing what is Christian]—something that was extremely necessary then—such distinctions now no longer seemed to be important; on the contrary, the spirit of the age called for crossing boundaries, reaching out to the world and becoming involved in it."[51] Instead of allowing the God of revelation to inform humanity regarding the meaning and purpose of an individual's life and the destiny of history, the world with its constantly shifting perspectives now sets the agenda for religion.

Along with some cardinals such as Frings and Döpfner, who during the last council had wished for a clearer separation of the natural and supernatural orders, in order to avoid a mingling of terrestrial progress and the theological concept of Redemption, Gutiérrez regrets the conflation of politics and religion. In Gutiérrez's judgment, a much needed clarification of the relationship between worldly progress and the growth of the kingdom of God has not occurred.[52] Generously, Ratzinger grants that for liberation theology the academic discipline of theology and politics are "extensionally not completely congruent" though intentionally they are. This de facto congruency is problematic.

Georg Friedrich Wilhelm Hegel (1770–1831) was the philosopher who inspired both Feuerbach and Marx. In Hegel's understanding of history, difference always implies opposition and, therefore, conflict. In most other bodies of thought, including Christianity, difference does not invariably entail opposition. Not every distinction produces opposition and dualism. Ratzinger points out that a duality of principles guarantees social unity. Thus, for instance, scholastic hylomorphism distinguishes between body and soul, but this tension actually safeguards the integrity of the human person.[53] He understands the danger of an excessive critique of dualism and two-tiered thinking. The dissolution of the metaphysical into history runs the risk of having theology serve an ideology (defined as a theory produced by human beings that claims an exhaustive understanding of the human being and of history's course and meaning). In fact, theology is at times even used to close rational gaps in economic or political logics. He writes, "All these plans for an epoch-making synthesis of Christianity and the world had to step aside, however, the moment that faith collapsed into politics as [the primary] salvific force." He continues, observing: "Man is, indeed, as Aristotle says, a 'political being,' but he cannot be reduced to politics and economics. I see the real and most profound problem with liberation theologies in their effective omission of the idea of God, which, of course, also changed the figure of Christ fundamentally.... Not as though God had been denied—not in your life! He simply was not needed in regard to the 'reality' that mankind had to deal with. God had nothing to do."[54]

By giving religion an excessive "relevance," one actually cancels out God and religion when at some point in history they no longer fill in the gaps. In spite of Bloch, Saint-Simon, and even Eusebius of Caesarea and the political Augustinianism of the Middle Ages advocating something akin to *Theopolitik*, Ratzinger pleads for the Aristotelian model providing for the relative autonomy of politics. He is in agreement here with Thomas Aquinas.[55] Along with Augustine's authentic position, Ratzinger insists on the two *civitates* as important in safeguarding the ineffable independence of God and the serene autonomy of theology vis-à-vis ideologies and politics.

Charles Dickens begins his novel *A Tale of Two Cities* with the famous line, "It was the best of times, it was the worst of times." There is detectable in this line a note of Augustine's teaching on the two cities. The evolution of two relatively autonomous spheres had been characteristic of the West: the tension between *sacerdotium* and *imperium* (Church and state)—thematized in an exemplary and normative fashion by Pope Gelasius I's letter to the Byzantine Emperor Anastasios[56]—manifested itself in the ongoing struggles concerning investiture, the development of different academic disciplines, the guilds, the arts, law, ethics, and so on. Yet, this world cannot be considered apart from *"sub specie aeternitatis"* ("under the aspect of eternity"), that is, apart from concepts such as the fullness of time, Before Christ and After Christ, and so forth. Thus, people in history do not perceive ultimate progress as an accomplishment of human labor. God is himself the *norma normans* (the ruling rule) of history. However, completely blending the two realms or radically separating them are both incorrect.[57] In contrast, Saint-Simon and his allies sought to negate the relative independence of the spiritual and worldly realms. It is precisely the independence of these realms that demonstrates the specific nature of faith and the inability of politics to substitute for it or altogether replace it as a source for values and orientation beyond pragmatic, penultimate human desires. According to Saint-Simon, dogma and religious practices can be suspended because religion serves exclusively to ameliorate the subjective perception of objectively unjust living conditions. But Saint-Simon elevates penultimate desires to the level of ultimate desires. In Ratzinger's judgment, this conflation is an unreasonable redefinition of hope and *eudaimonia* that will never convince the human being. In the final analysis for Ratzinger, "human life succeeds wherever man, living his empirical and moral reason [can fathom, or] is able to become ever again a human being."[58] Informed by the philosopher Robert Spaemann, Ratzinger realizes that, following Aristotle's early distinction, in the case of all higher creatures there is a difference between the tendency to live and the tendency to live well. Ethics is not merely concerned with preserving the species but contributing to "a good life."[59] Spaemann reminds one that the Greek expression ευ ζωή / *eu zoe*, the good life, is ambivalent: it may mean a morally good or pleasant life. In the same vein, Augustine argued in *De Civitate Dei* (book XIX, chapter 17) that both *civitates* consider terrestrial peace desirable, but human beings will never be content with simply achieving worldly nonbelligerence. Accordingly, in book XIX, chapter 20, Augustine concludes that beatitude cannot be a product of merely human efforts. Both realms, both *civitates*, are distinct but closely connected. Ratzinger concludes that a forced identification of the two would invariably lead to a disfigurement of the Redemption wrought by Christ.[60] This notwithstanding, the two are interrelated. In Ratzinger's vision, something like political or social liberation may legitimately exist. Yet, the theological concept of Christian Redemption is not congruous with worldly concepts of liberation.[61]

The peril of succumbing to the temptation of something akin to self-Redemption has always been latent in Christian history. This is the story of Pelagianism. Augustine's response to this correlation of theology and politics is his teaching on the two cities. In liberation theology, Ratzinger divines the danger of instrumentalizing theology for worldly ends. Such a view is totalitarian as it is nothing short of propagating a single, correct policy to inaugurate a cultural revolution, which in its final stage will produce "a factory of new human beings."[62] It is significant to note that such a Pelagian danger looms in every stage of history and must be rejected time and again. Liberation theology has been but one variant of this constant threat. At the beginning of the twenty-first century, such a peril was expressed in the attempt to generate an evolution controlled by human beings. This was expressed philosophically by the rather popular German philosopher Peter Sloterdijk, who recently pleaded the case for "rules for the human zoo."[63] Neither evolution nor revolution are terms adequate to capture human freedom. There has never been an age when human fortune could be achieved by canceling out freedom. On this point all diverging views agree.

As Plato illustrates, the response to poor schooling is not establishing a *tabula rasa* (a blank slate) but rather better education—*paideia*.[64] This is the case because human beings are bearers of culture. In Ratzinger's estimation, such *paideia*—the content of this Greek concept cannot be sufficiently conveyed in words such as "schooling" or "education"—is ultimately not a human product or accomplishment. This also implies that such a *paideia* is not the commensurate tool to achieve historic progress. As works alone do not justify one, so likewise they cannot redeem one. Quite apart from their good or bad convictions, neither Marx nor Hitler nor Peter Sloterdijk apprehended this.[65] If indeed works claim to redeem, they become but callous instruments of enslavement. In the final analysis, education in the Greek sense of *paideia* is, for the Church fathers, something that in its most sublime form only faith imparts. In this holistic sense, meditation on the triune God and participation in the sacraments educate. Christ redeems humanity from self-enamored self-preoccupation. Human beings are in dire need of Christ's Redemption as they are at no point in history able to create, reinvent, or redeem themselves. This leads to appreciating anew the foundational gratuity of human life and the relationship between faith and works.[66]

Unfortunately, one frequently applies terms such as "conservative" and "progressive" to demarcate theological positions. As the Church is not a political institution, but a divine-human work, such predications are unfitting and even harmful. The Christian discernment of spirits overcomes such generalizations. Such declarations fail to recognize differences and maintain tensions, and they polarize against God's call to communion. Acknowledging differences, polarities, opposites, and the multifaceted nature of reality keep one from becoming intolerant, that is, from subsuming one aspect under another. Such a nuanced appreciation enables the discovery of relatively autonomous spheres and the common ground within them.

In the final analysis, all thoughts concerning liberation theology and the attendant lack of sufficient differentiation highlight a Christological issue. The discussion is ultimately an intensive struggle regarding the two natures of Jesus Christ. Thus, "[w]hat remained was the figure of Jesus, who of course appeared now, no longer as the Christ, but rather as the embodiment of all the suffering and oppressed and as their spokesman, who calls us to rise up, to change society."[67] The discernment of the Christian—"*die Unterscheidung des Christlichen*," ("discerning the Christian proprium")—in the cases of both Augustine and Guardini is, whether verbalized or not, always virulent in history. It determines the proper understanding of Christology. Along with the disciples, human beings are called ever again to answer the question of who Jesus Christ is. "'Who do men say that I am?'...And he asked them, 'But who do you say that I am?'" (Mk 8:27, 29). The early, non-Christian thinkers Aristotle and Plotinus supplied theories and tools to distinguish reality: difference and identity, opposite and opposition, kind and genre, alterity and identity, actuality and possibility.[68] Such theories prevent simplifications and generalizations. It was precisely in light of this background that the councils of Nicaea and Chalcedon struggled to preserve the two natures of Christ.[69] Neither should Jesus Christ be dissolved into the exclusively divine nor, vice versa, reduced to the purely human. Thus, Christianity was spared the heresies of both monophysitism (Christ has only one, divine nature, fifth century) and monotheletism (professing only one will in the God-man, seventh century). Likewise, it safeguarded against the dissolution of the absolute God into a Hegelian kind of history. At the same time, it preserved the profession of the nontransferability of one nature into the other. Being Christian is synonymous with being constantly on the way to the truth that has taken hold of one. Faith can never be instrumentalized to sanction a particular human claim.

A reinterpretation of Christianity—along the lines of liberation theology—is unbiblical and defies the praxis of Christ. The Marxist position of class struggle clashes with Jesus Christ as the Lamb of God. It undermines the meaning of truth and presents the notion of class struggle as an objective, necessary law of history—evading the call to personal conversion. The spiritual quality of poverty as expounded by the prophets of the Old Testament and the spiritual masters of Christianity is ignored.[70] There is more to life than positive "facts" à la the positivism coined by Auguste Comte in the nineteenth century. The human spirit cannot be harnessed by a "biological evolutionism," as Ratzinger elaborated when receiving an honorary doctoral degree from Eichstätt Catholic University in 1987.[71] Being human is infinitely more than service to a function. Only the conviction that a God created human reason, somehow not completely dissimilar to himself (Augustine), can "The Abolition of Man" (C.S. Lewis) be avoided.

The adoration of the crucified Lord in the Eucharist and his presence in the tabernacle is the point of departure for all communion (1 Jn 1:3–7) and for genuine solidarity with the disenfranchised. Saints such as Martin de Porres and Mother Teresa made this abundantly clear in their witness. Communion with Jesus Christ is communion with God himself, who in turn urges Christians to practice solidarity. "I was hungry and you clothed me; I was sick and you visited me; I was in prison and you came to me" (Mt 25:35). Such selfless and disinterested concern for the other surpasses by far anything a Marxist or socialist model is able to evoke. In addition, a liberal system concerned primarily with the functioning of the overall picture—captured in statistics—is unable to do final justice to the individual. In this line of argument, one sees that Jesus Christ is the solution to social problems. The Eucharist is the sacrament of transformation to Jesus Christ and therefore to one another. It is there, on Golgotha, that suffering, violence, and death are transformed into an act of love.

PART III

The Church: The Christ-Filled Realm

CHAPTER 16

Communio: *Christian Brotherhood and the Church as One Reality*

The bracketing off from Christian piety the "we-reality" (that is, the communal nature) of the triune God in Augustine's theology has had long-term negative ramifications on Western ecclesiology. The attendant rich Christian understanding of the human person is lost sight of. The dimension of the "you" is forgotten. Due to Augustine's psychological teaching on the Blessed Trinity, the divine persons are beheld only in their inner-Trinitarian being.

Apostolic succession is bound to the church's participation in triune life. Only thereby is tradition plausible, securing faith against a high-handed interpretation à la gnosticism and other forms of unjustified presumptiveness. The categories of tradition, apostolic succession, liturgy, and scripture constitute one intertwined reality all conditioning one another. Thus, the individual believer and the sum total of all believers enter as church a greater, triune reality never of their own making.

As a consequence, Kant's transcendental philosophy cannot appreciate God as involved in this world. Feuerbach's theory of human projection onto a nonexistent God is the sad result. Thomas considered it legitimate to call God *una persona* (one person), though early Christianity had regarded it a heresy.[1]

Both Ratzinger and Karl Rahner considered the system of Thomistic and neo-Thomistic tractates on the Blessed Trinity wholly unsatisfactory. They considered them a system of abstract theories with no recognizable relevance for faith. They had the air of being doctrinaire and positivistic, closed unto themselves. In the course of a theology curriculum, one would first study *De Deo Uno*, discussing God's essence and properties and effects upon the outside world. Then one would study a tractate titled *De Deo Trino*, demonstrating how, according to the testimony of scripture, God is triune. While this is a broad generalization that does not do justice to some of the very fine expositions in the tractates, in general a lack of relevance of the Blessed Trinity for salvation history is noted in them. Following the neo-Thomistic axiom *"opera ad extra sunt una"* (the divine persons act together outside the Blessed Trinity), one could get the sense that a uni-personal God effects salvation. The Trinity as the subject of action in creation and salvation history becomes redundant.

God per se acts. The economic Trinity (the manner the Trinity acts toward the outside)—while still mirroring the inner Trinity—is now an imminent manifestation of the eternal and immutable God. Since the days of Cajetan, one assumed God acts necessarily in a manner that reflects the unison of being and act. Thus, both Rahner and Ratzinger bemoaned the occurrence of a *Trinitätsvergessenheit* (loss of awareness of the Blessed Trinity's spiritual relevance). The creeds profess a triune God, but catechetical instruction and homilies often fail to take this into account. The Blessed Trinity's relation to reality is often unacknowledged, and this is also often ignored as the most decisive factor separating Christianity from Islam and Judaism.

The modern tendency to reduce religion to the exercise of tolerant and benevolent behavior is in no small part indebted to a non-Trinitarian understanding of God. However, it is only in light of the Trinitarian background that Christian social ethics and Church life gain their full meaning. A disregard for creedal differences, however, has proven unhelpful as the basis for society to remain humane after the Enlightenment and after the technical-scientific era has set in. Only if God is charity—and this ultimately only a Trinitarian God can be—can human society, after the Enlightenment, remain humane, respecting human rights and not yielding to the temptation of reducing the human person to a mouse running in a treadmill. Only a Trinitarian God can liberate society from "the dictatorship of relativism," as Cardinal Ratzinger formulated it in his homily at the mass preparing for the conclave. Ultimately, only a tri-personal *communio personarum* (communion of persons) can seek us out in infinite, concrete closeness. Only a thus constituted God can become incarnate, die on the cross, resurrect, and nevertheless remain God. These Christological mysteries permit access to a God who created human beings in his image. With such a "Trinitarian we," the "we" of human society becomes comprehensible.

God did not create humankind out of a need for companionship. God is already (without considering his dialogue with human beings) a community and an inner vis-à-vis. Only upon this background can one understand history as a divine work of freedom and charity. "No one has ever seen God. The only Son, who is in the bosom of the Father, has made him known" (Jn 1:18). Along with other noted theologians such as Hans Urs von Balthasar and Gisbert Greshake, Ratzinger states: "The teaching on the Trinity did not arise out of speculation about God, out of an attempt by philosophical thinking to figure out what the fount of all being was like; it developed out of the effort to digest experiences."[2] The descent and *kenosis* of God (that is, the emptying of himself) to the human condition cannot be understood by human reason alone (*supra rationem*), but it is not therefore absurd or impossible. Likewise, it does not contradict human reason (*sed non contra rationem*). Ratzinger elaborates at another location that ecclesial teaching grasps God as mystery, as *the* mystery. Theology makes no claims to fully fathom God. Even the definition of the Blessed Trinity contains the element of a *mysterium stricte dictum* (that is, we cannot comprehend the Trinity). However, it is only in this mystery that one can think the notion of "God" in its noncontradictory, final conclusion. Without the Trinity, Christology—with the moments of Incarnation, Resurrection, and redemption—would be impossible. The teaching on the two natures of Christ would be unthink-able. Imagining the eternal perfection of the human person as participating in the triune life would be impossible. God remains God as he is not reduced to humanly comprehensible forms; God is not rationalistically downsized. However, as the human being is created in the image and likeness of God, there can be no absolute contradiction between cognition and faith. Fideism does not do justice to the dignity of the human person gifted with a rational soul. Rationalism, likewise, does not do justice to the concept of an ineffable God.[3] It is in the common denominator of personhood that the two meet. These two meet in the *communio* called Church.

A monotheistic God, who is not triune, could not possibly interact with the world because temporality and eternity would remain universes apart. Only Christ—as the second person in the Blessed Trinity—can "make sense" of God and of humankind to human rationality. This means that in the final analysis only a recovery of the soteriological, spiritual, and anthropological significance of the Blessed Trinity can provide a solid foundation for appre-ciating the reality of the Church and for establishing a future humane, global society. The Trinitarian "We" provides the basis for a humane "we."[4]

This is the gist of relational personalism as expounded in *Dogma and Preaching* and as advocated earlier by Martin Buber, Franz Rosenzweig, and Friedrich Ebner: "The I becomes itself in the Thou." The human being is essentially *desiderium naturale ad videndum Deum* (that is, has a natural desire to behold God). In this sense, Descartes' philosophically self-thinking (*cogito, ergo sum*—I think, therefore I am) subject is not madness, but God's qui-etly beckoning humanity to an inner-Trinitarian *communio*. In Ratzinger's approach, God is not an aloof, abstract reality. Ratzinger also very cautiously expressed his concern that Rahner, Schillebeeckx, and Vorgrimler dialecti-cally turned God into "an absolute subject" in such a way that God grows in the encounter with another, human thou. This is problematic as it levels the unique nature of God. It is thus little wonder that Rahner ends up sur-rendering the concept "person" in favor of "a distinct manner of subsistence" and "one single, real awareness."[5] Walter Kasper and Jürgen Moltmann agree with Ratzinger on this point.[6]

In his meditation *Behold the Pierced One*, Ratzinger explains the historic-ity and characteristics of the Jewish Passover Feast. For them, Passover was a community-constituting feast, a family celebration. Its spiritual significance lay in the fact that it was the annual event when Israel returned from threat-ening chaos to its sustaining origins. This was expressed first by smearing the blood of lambs on tents as a sign of protection against evil forces and also by journeying to Jerusalem until the night of Passover. According to Ratzinger, this feast receives a deeper meaning in the Christian context. Our Lord, as the true Passover Lamb, becomes the community-constituting reality through his passion and the Eucharist. As a people of faith, Christians "are Christ's *habhura*, his family, formed of his pilgrim company, of the friends who accompany him along the path of the gospel through the ter-rain of history."[7] The center of the human journey is no longer a geographic location, such as Jerusalem, but the sacramental Church. One sees a logical progression: while for the Pharisees *habhura* referred to the Passover assembly, in the Church it describes the cooperative gathering around the Eucharist. While in the Old Testament it was perceived as a sharing among human beings within a religious context, in the Church it connotes an assembly of human beings sharing with God. It is the paschal lamb Jesus Christ, the true Isaac, who was sacrificed for our sins, who links or brings into union God and creatures in heaven and earth; somehow allowing God and humans to be equals.[8]

The incarnate Son of God is *habhura* or communion (Jerome tellingly translated κοινωνια / *koinonia* as "communication" in the Vulgate) in the life of God. This is a tangible reality in the Eucharist where human beings consume the bread and wine of the liturgy, that is, the body and blood of Jesus Christ. It is not a physical but rather a metaphysical nourishment that occurs as one becomes part of the divine to which one is destined from the first moment of creation. The metaphysical relationship achieved then occasions a sociological "we" in this world, called Christian brotherhood, or the Church. "We are the bark [barque] of Peter, and thus we are those called by the Lord; we are partners of Peter, we are not the company of Peter, however, but the *communio* of the Lord himself, who bestows on us what we could never achieve."[9] It is the Christological dogma that allows this reality to be more profoundly fathomed. How are the human and divine elements in Christ to interact and yet remain free? The answer is found in the Council of Chalcedon's (AD 451) formulation that Jesus Christ is one person with two natures. This is adumbrated by the Third Council of Constantinople (AD 680–681) stating that Christ possessed two wills on the level of the acting person, but these two wills always worked in synchrony with each another (that is, significantly in κοινωνια). Being Christian is entering into and sharing in the mystery of the Incarnation. Jesus Christ enables the seemingly impossible: humans are assimilated into the divine without losing their human nature, much like Christ was human and divine while on earth. While the Eucharist is the basis for participation in the Easter mystery and forming the Church as the body of Christ, it also has significant ramifications for society: "The act whereby we participate in the Son's obedience, which involves man's genuine transformation, is also the only really effective contribution toward renewing and transforming society and the world as a whole."[10]

In this context, Ratzinger briefly touches the thorny issue of excommunication. Faithful to Bonaventure, he shows that such a statement never entails exclusion from all forms of communion. It is an invitation by way of fasting from the Eucharist to rediscover the dignity and meaning of the Eucharist and recover the manner in which it defines the Christian.

His understanding of freedom as the essential ingredient of faith is nuanced. For this reason he did not speak favorably of *Römische Schultheologie* (Rome-based theology); which he accusses of conformism. But loyalty to the Church and the episcopal office enables genuine freedom as commitment to Jesus Christ to come about. The Church is the realm of freedom because the Lamb is alive in the Church daily celebrating the Eucharist. The concretion of freedom is discipleship, fellowship, and participation in the Church, liberating people from anything that might separate them from Jesus Christ, who is the Way, the Truth, and the Life. Such freedom is not merely a lofty philosophical idea but is very real and personal. This Church frees Christians "from ultimate covetousness, free for one another."[11]

Genuine inter-human friendship and discipleship flow from the encounter and relationship with the triune God in the person of Jesus Christ, who is the Church as his mystical body. This is the central insight Ratzinger had when reading de Lubac and the vast oeuvre of Augustine in preparation for his dissertation. Cyprian of Carthage had already developed the concept of the Church as being the *mater ecclesia* (mother Church), referring to baptism, and *fraternitas Christianorum* (Christian brotherhood), relating to the Eucharistic assembly of believers. Optatus of Mileve spoke of "the importance of *communio* with the *cathedra Petri* at Rome." Christian brotherhood is grounded in the Eucharist and is the union between the *communio nostra* and the *communio vestra*, that is, between the universal church and the local Church.[12] In addition, Ratzinger's elder contemporary, Guardini, had thematized discipleship as a personal relationship with Jesus Christ in numerous writings and homilies: "Individuals come to him, too, men desiring to associate their lives exclusively with his.... Thus a community of disciples closely attached to the Master and to his destiny springs up around him...."[13] After the fateful "Kantian Turn" in the late eighteenth century, much like Newman's ingenious illative sense developed in *An Essay in Aid of a Grammar of Assent*,[14] Ratzinger proposed a lived encounter with Jesus Christ and Christian brotherhood as the hermeneutic keys to overcoming the split between the phenomenal and noumenal realms. As Benedict XVI writes in *Deus Caritas Est*: "Being Christian is not the result of an ethical choice or a lofty idea, but the encounter with an event, a person, which gives life a new horizon and a decisive direction.... Since God has first loved us (cf. 1 Jn 4:10), love is now no longer a mere 'command': it is the response to the gift of love with which God draws near to us."[15]

In his research on St. Augustine, the young Ratzinger discovered what was then an altogether new perspective for the theology of Augustine. All reviews of his dissertation agree unanimously on this. Augustine does not equate *Domus Dei* (the house of God) with the edifice of a temple but with the living parish, the people of God, and the universal Church. In agreement with the apostle Paul, Augustine prefers calling it the "body of Christ" (Rom 12:4f; 1 Cor 12:12–27). This Church manifests itself preeminently in the celebration of the Eucharist as lived *caritas* (charity) and *unitas* (unity). As the Church is charity and unity it thus lives Christian brotherhood.[16] Concerning the Church, St. Augustine preferred referring to the Church as the body of which the head is Christ: he spoke of it intimately as the "*totus Christus*." The head and body form one Christ loving himself *unus Christus amans seipsum*.[17] Fittingly, when he became archbishop of Munich in 1977, Ratzinger chose as his motto *cooperator veritatis* (cooperator with truth). This signifies his role as part of the organism of charity called the Church, living from the truth that is Jesus Christ. This is the deeper motivation behind the 1998 encyclical *Fides et Ratio*. Human reason must be capable of recognizing truth, lest it is unable to love. In the sweeping Augustinian ductus, the truth of faith quite naturally possesses the metaphysical moment of proclaiming and loving truth as two permanent dimensions. With his singular pregnancy,

Augustine summarized this triad in the words "*O aeterna veritas et vera caritas et cara aeternitas!*" ("Oh eternal truth and true love and beloved eternity").[18] Truth is a person, not a condition. It evokes a response. This is formulated in charity. Pope Benedict's coat of arms is adorned with a shell and a bear. This choice relates to St. Augustine. While the shell brings to mind the story of a boy trying to scoop the ocean into a ditch of sand and the inexhaustible mystery and greatness of God, the bear refers to Augustine's meditation on Psalm 73:23, "Even so, I stayed in our presence, you grasped me by the right hand." In this verse Augustine saw a metaphor for the burden of the episcopal office. It is charity—an attribute of the Blessed Trinity, which human beings can share in by virtue of creation and, consciously, through the sacraments— that enables one to bear it. Ratzinger is in this sense an "*Augustinus redivivus*" (a reappearing Augustine).This impels him to thematize brotherhood as so central to Christian and ecclesial existence that without it something constitutive is missing.

Christian brotherhood is an early theme in Ratzinger's writings as *Christian Brotherhood*, published in 1960, evidences.[19] He considers this topic germane to Christian existence and the Church. In this work, he discusses the people of the Old Testament as the first faith community. "Whereas [YHWH] was the father of all the peoples of the world through creation, he surpassed this as the father of Israel through election. However, this was so by the free disposition of God which could, therefore, be altered at any time."[20] But a question arises here: "[t]he great problem of brotherhood...is that all unions entail the separating off of those who are united from the rest whom they leave behind."[21] How can God have chosen a particular people among the nations, the elected few vis-à-vis the universality of the human race? The notion of brotherhood did not extend beyond the people of Israel. As Israel entered the Hellenistic orbit, some Jews felt uneasy with the fact that out of all the nations the Torah had been entrusted to only one people. Could God not have given the Torah to all peoples? Perhaps God had not been exclusive but only the Jews had accepted the Torah? Further, does not the Genesis narrative render all human beings brothers if they are descendents from Adam? Ratzinger immediately cautions that such a model is not viable because a brotherhood embracing everyone embraces no one. He calls to mind the egalitarian pathos exhibited during the French Revolution of 1789 where everyone was called to practice *fraternité*, resulting in one of the bloodiest civil wars ever witnessed. He continues by observing that Our Lord did not advocate indiscriminate brotherhood. For many the gospel will remain a scandal.

For Ratzinger, these considerations are important building stones for a theology of Christian brotherhood. Christian brotherhood must rest on a common belief. It is not based on common biological features, but on the common fatherhood that all are made conscious of by belief in the one, triune God. Such a group, enjoying the divine gift of brotherhood, must labor to remove all barriers to Christian brotherhood, lest it no longer merit being called Christian fraternity. An additional point is that such brotherhood must originate in Jesus. In the Eucharist, Christian brotherhood reaches its apex. This does not contain a rejection of the notion of universal brotherhood but is an essential part of Christian hope. Christian brotherhood evidences itself as genuine by a threefold practice of charity, mission, and suffering. This is supernatural brotherhood based on shared belief. While suffering is coredemptive, mission often requires holy discretion, yet charity can only be practiced if it has a sound doctrinal footing, otherwise mercy might become a hollow though jovial *bonhomie* (a mere pleasant and easy manner). Brotherhood requires discipleship. This mission is shared in a communion of persons who gain their identity from their life in Jesus Christ and thus share in his mission: "Christians...one in their calling by Jesus...are one in grace, they will also be one in their mission, which itself is grace."[22] The common bond is the Eucharist, which is *communio* and enables *missio*.

Something remarkable occurs within the ambience of Christian brother-hood: the idea of the whole of the *Catholica* takes precedence over the individual and precisely therein the individual fulfills his or her uniqueness to the highest possible degree. "When all other ways fail, there will always remain the royal way of vicarious suffering by the side of the Lord. It is in its defeat that the Church constantly achieves its highest victory, and stands nearest to Christ."[23]

For it is "Christ the Truth...[who] changes us from ignorant servants into friends inasmuch as he permits us to become sharers in his own divine self-knowledge."[24] Here one tangibly senses how the personal encounter with Jesus Christ breaks through the epistemological "Kantian barrier." Charity produces knowledge and brotherhood.

Thus, Christian brotherhood is neither merely a one-on-one friendship with Jesus Christ nor is it static. It is dynamic both in regard to that relation-ship and as a conscious participation in the grand drama of salvation history. It is the earnestness of partaking in the mystical body of Christ that is the Church. Who dares live a relationship with the divine, rather than probe a set of propositional truth sentences strung together? The latter may result in knowledge but the former in martyrdom. One may propose it is the will-ingness to accept martyrdom in the most extreme form possible in which Ratzinger divines the most profound basis for Christian brotherhood.

Discipleship and vocation are grounded in prayer events. They are anchored in the Son's intimacy with the Father in prayer. Thus all are enjoined to "pray therefore the Lord of the harvest to send out laborers into his har-vest" (Mt 9:38). Discipleship is essentially a question of choice on the part of the Lord, who in turn is in constant communion with God the Father and God the Holy Spirit. By Jesus' summoning the Twelve, Luke in his Gospel emphasizes that the whole of Israel, its integrity as it existed previously in the twelve tribes, has been restored. Thus, as Ratzinger does not tire of point-ing out: "Past, present, and future intermingle when viewed in terms of the Twelve."[25] This intricate interweaving is multiplied by the factor two: the mystery of the God-man can only be witnessed to if one lives in intimacy with Jesus Christ. This is also Mark's conviction. The task of the apostles is not merely to inform people of God's nature but also to impart something of God's goodness made manifest in Jesus: "to preach and have authority to cast out demons" (Mk 3:14f). The instructive-theoretical level must be left behind if one is to make Jesus Christ's salvation efficacious. Neoscholasticism is bid farewell. "But the preaching of God's kingdom is never just words, never just instruction. It is an event, just as Jesus himself is an event, God's Word in person. By announcing him, the Apostles lead their listeners to encounter him."[26] The demonic powers are exorcised not only from the ancient world but also from the present one. Rationally spoken, the world can only be healed when it is faith-filled, lest indeterminable forces take hold that are counter to divine providence and the good of the people. Thus, it is the apostle's task to exorcise the world also by employing merely human *ratio.* Taking on "the armor of God" equips one with the ability to penetrate the world rationally more profoundly, to appreciate humanity as a unity of body and soul. The point is not analysis but therapy, setting man in motion toward God. Over and again, Ratzinger invites his readers to an immediate encounter with the risen Lord. This is not a New Testament idiosyncrasy but one that emerged early on in the Old Testament when Exodus 1:5 relates that seventy, representing the whole world, accompanied Jacob to Egypt. Ratzinger detects in this a dynamic toward universality in the days of the Old Testament.

Adolf Jülicher interpreted the parables of Jesus as demonstrating "an apostle of progress." In contrast, Jeremias speaks of the eschaton breaking in as the kingdom of God. On this point, Jeremias was inspired by C. H. Dodd (1884–1973), who coined the expression "realized eschatology." This led Ratzinger to observe: "The deepest theme of Jesus' preaching was his own mystery, the mystery of the Son in whom God is among us and keeps his word; he announces the Kingdom of God as coming and as having come in his person."[27] This includes in a very defining way accepting the cross. The cross becomes the source for apostolic fecundity. "On Palm Sunday, the Lord summarized the manifold seed parables and unveiled their full meaning: 'Truly, truly, I say to you, unless a grain of wheat falls into the earth and dies, it remains alone; but if it dies, it bears much fruit' (Jn 12:24). He himself is the grain of wheat. His 'failure' on the Cross is exactly the way leading from the few to the many, to all: 'And I, when I am lifted up from the earth, will draw all men to myself' (Jn 12:32)."[28]

It is this passage from John's Gospel that had been pivotal for Romano Guardini's vocation many years earlier. Operating on the premise of an implicit Christology, the parables grant an understanding into the mystery of the cross, maintaining Jesus' divinity and the contradiction this entails. In the mystery of the cross, God is revealed as a person interacting with human history. This intervention is not done for the sake of simply saving his own creation but because he wills to be a part of every human person's history. By appreciating God's "translucence" to humanity, human beings understand themselves with and from God. The narrative of the Good Samaritan (Lk 10:25–37) is profoundly Christological. God does not turn to suffering humankind with a calculating "*do ut des*" ("I give so that you might give") but out of sheer charity. God stands to gain nothing from helping someone who fell among robbers. On a deeper level, consonant with the reading of the Church fathers on this pericope, Ratzinger understands Jesus as, through his divine charity, recovering everyone from alienation. "The 'yoke' of this arm is not a burden that we must carry, but a gift of love that carries us and makes us sons."[29] As the concretion of God's charity, Jesus is found at the very heart of the parable. This action must be obliging to the hearer of the Word: "We beseech you on behalf of Christ, be reconciled to God" (2 Cor 5:20). Jesus is the *cardo* (that is, the pivotal linchpin) to understanding God's will. In Jesus Christ, human freedom is liberated from a puerile understanding of freedom, which is actually slavery, and transformed into real sonship. The relationship is restored and facilitated through Jesus Christ. "God's sign for men is the Son of Man; it is Jesus himself. And at the deepest level, he is the sign in His Paschal Mystery, in the mystery of his death and Resurrection. He himself is the 'sign of Jonah.' He, the crucified and risen, is the true Lazarus. The parable of the rich man and Lazarus (Lk 16:19–31) is inviting us to believe and follow him, God's great sign. But it is more than a parable. It speaks of reality, of the most decisive reality in all of history."[30]

In both scripture and in Ratzinger's thought, Peter figures prominently in discipleship. The way of Jesus is the way to Jerusalem; discipleship entails sharing in this journey. To lose one's life is the indispensable prerequisite in order to follow Jesus (Mk 8:31–9:1; Mt 16:21–28; Lk 9:22–27). This also leads to the Transfiguration and Peter's confession. While there is albeit some knowledge of Jesus among the apostles, it remains inadequate. A more intimate knowledge depends on growth in discipleship. In this sense, the implication is that Christology as an academic discipline depends on partaking concretely in Jesus' unique way. The theologian called to minister as pope reminds the reader that, already in the Old Testament, Jeremiah is simultaneously the bearer of a promise and subject to suffering. The figure of a prophet is an "approximation" of who Jesus actually is. Placing Jesus on the same plane as the exemplary individuals of different cultures such as Buddha, Confucius, or Socrates—as the German philosopher Karl Jaspers did—does not provide access to Jesus.[31] "Every human subject can capture only a particular fragment of the reality that is there to be perceived, and this fragment then requires further interpretation."[32] In this perspective, one might admire or even emulate the human being Jesus but still not comprehend him, that is, behold his figure. For discipleship to come about, it is decisive to join oneself to Peter and conjoin one's existence with his simple words of confession: "'You are the Messiah [the Christ]' (Mk 8:29)." One then professes faith in Jesus as the Anointed One, the Christ (Lk 9:20), the "Son of the living God" (Mt 16:16), and "the Holy One of God" (Jn 6:69).[33] Ratzinger insists that these are verbal and substantive professions of faith. Without accepting that Jesus kenotically became incarnate, died on the cross, and rose from the dead, all predications, however lofty, ring hollow. Thus, it was consonant with his mission that Jesus told Peter, when Peter wanted to argue against his master's crucifixion, "Get behind me, Satan!" (Mk 8:33).

In the episode detailing the tangible, inexplicable phenomenon of an overflowing catch of fish, Peter no longer calls Jesus by the Greek title *epistata* (master, teacher, or rabbi) but rather by the title the Greek Septuagint had reserved exclusively for the Hebrew circumscription of God as "Yahweh," *Kyrios*, in English "Lord": "Depart from me, for I am a sinful man, O Lord" (Lk 5:8). This is paralleled by the words of the disciples when Jesus walks on the troubled waters: "Truly you are the Son of God" (Mt 14:22f). Jesus is acknowledged as nothing short of the epiphany of God (that is, a theophany) among humankind. Discipleship is grounded in recognizing Jesus as the Son of God. This in turn frees the disciples from defining hope in the categories of this world: categories such a material well-being. Nevertheless, the profession of faith does not give an answer to the riddle of inequity but affirms it. Thus, numerous potential disciples leave because they want a definition of God that matches their expectations. Representing the college of apostles, Peter answers Jesus' question about whether they too want to leave him: "Lord, to whom shall we go? You have the words of eternal life, and we have believed, and have come to know, that you are the Holy One of God" (Jn 6:68f). It is precisely Jesus' divine holiness that bars the apostles from categorizing Jesus in worldly terms. In this sense, Jesus is infinitely different from the numerous Old Testament prophets. Ratzinger finds this confirmed in the post-Easter faith. Exteriorly, nothing in the world had changed; yet for those who have the spiritual eyes of faith, everything had changed radically. The Messiah as the Anointed One and Son of God is *sui generis*, that is, revoltingly unique. Thus, the words the erstwhile doubting Thomas exclaims when touching the scars of the risen Christ are all human language is capable of: "My Lord and my God" (Jn 20:28).

In the Transfiguration narrative, Ratzinger interprets the white color of Jesus as anticipating the future of his disciples. This inspired the author of the Apocalypse of John to relate the white garments that will be worn by the saved in heaven (Rv 7:9, 13; 19:14). Participation in Jesus' baptism also entails entering into his passion.[34]

CHAPTER 17

Christ and the Church

In *Das neue Volk Gottes* Ratzinger writes:

> That there is only one legitimate form of the Church's openness to the world, and so must it certainly always be. That form is two-fold. It is: mission as the prolongation of the movement of the Word's procession, and the simple gesture of disinterested serving love in the actualizing of the divine love, a love which streams forth even when it remains without response.[1]

One of the more popular theologians in Germany is the priest and former occupant of the Guardini chair in Munich, Eugen Biser (b. 1918), considered by many to be "liberal"—a term that is infelicitous as it is borrowed from politics and ignores the one Eucharist all share in, canceling out all political considerations. In his judgment, Ratzinger had " 'set the course for overcoming the crisis of the Church...by giving life to the structures, in accordance with the principles of dialogue urged by the Second Vatican Council, which he implemented.' For him, Biser, Ratzinger had brought about something 'we had hardly expected at all: that is, the rediscovery of the Church.' He had succeeded in this, 'because he consistently referred the phenomenon of the Church and of Christianity back to the figure of Jesus....He is fundamentally a very modern man, and shares in modern man's existential poverty.' "[2]

Conciliar documents are the product of collaboration and compromise. The dogmatic constitution *Lumen Gentium* is no exception. In an effort to correct the strong emphasis on the Church's juridical nature, especially the Belgians Cardinal Leo Suenens (1904–1996) and Gérard Philips (1898–1972) contributed to the document's Christological and pneumatological language. In Ratzinger's view, the "Church grows from within and moves outwards, not vice-versa."[3] This dynamic perspective does not eliminate the juridical and hierarchical nature of the Church but explains how these necessary dimensions must be perceived as subservient to her Christological and spiritual dimensions. The Church has a juridical face as it is ontically grounded in communion with Jesus Christ. He had discovered this *communio* structure in his dissertation on Augustine (1954), discussed it with Rahner in 1962, and given it a more detailed description in the book he authored in 1969, *Das neue Volk Gottes: Entwürfe zur Ekklesiologie*.[4] As prefect, he wrote a definition of *communio*:

> As an invisible reality [the ecclesial communion] is the communion of each human being with the Father through Christ in the Holy Spirit, and with the others who are fellow sharers in the divine nature, in the passion of Christ, in the same faith and in the same spirit. In the Church on earth there is a relationship between the invisible communion and the visible communion in the teaching of the Apostles, in the sacraments and in the hierarchical order. By means of these divine gifts, which are very visible realities, Christ carries out in different ways his prophetical, priestly and kingly function[s] for the salvation of mankind. This link between the invisible and visible elements of ecclesial communion constitutes the Church as the Universal Sacrament of Salvation.[5]

Over a decade later, in his homily on the election of a new pope, Ratzinger tied this back to the Eucharistic ecclesiology of his hero during his days as a seminarian and student of theology, de Lubac: "Finally, there is the common participation in the growth of the body of Christ—of the transformation of the world into communion with the Lord.... Our ministry is a gift of Christ to humankind, to build up his body: the new world. We live out our ministry in this way, as a gift of Christ to humanity!"[6]

This demonstrates the foundational intuition of the pope's ecclesiology: it is a Eucharistic ecclesiology. "The main emphasis of the Eucharist here becomes apparent: the Eucharist is instrumental in the process by which Christ builds himself a Body, and makes us into one single Bread, one Body. The content of the Eucharist...is the uniting of Christians.... The Eucharist is thus understood in a dynamic ecclesiological perspective. It is the living process through which...the Church's activity of becoming Church takes place. The Church is Eucharistic fellowship."[7] This constantly vivacious reality is grounded in God's initiative; these are de Lubac's thoughts expressed by Ratzinger. He is highly indebted to de Lubac's groundbreaking work on the historical development of the concept of "the Body of Christ." He remains faithful to de Lubac's insight into the need to regain the sense of the Church as Eucharistic communion. Throughout Ratzinger's numerous writings one sees the echo of de Lubac's celebrated principle, "the Eucharist produces the Church and the Church produces the Eucharist."[8] In *Pilgrim Fellowship of Faith* Ratzinger observes: "The Eucharist effects our participation in the Paschal Mystery and thus constitutes the Church, the body of Christ: hence the necessity of the Eucharist for salvation. The Eucharist is necessary in exactly the sense that the Church is necessary...'Unless you eat the flesh of the Son of man and drink his blood, you have no life in you.' (John 6:53)."[9]

While de Lubac did much foundational "archaeological" work in this area, Ratzinger had the opportunity to explore the implications and bring them to a synthesis and conclusion. All of this, however, does not mitigate the fact that Ratzinger's dynamic insights into Eucharistic theology and its ramifications for liturgical renewal, ecclesial governance, and the everyday life of believers who are exposed to a world adrift amid a disorienting plurality of views, has produced a theology forged by the conflation of the Catholic faith and modern thought.

The term "People of God" is, of course, beyond any doubt biblical, patristic, and conciliar, but it is open to misunderstanding. The Church may not be interpreted externally as first and foremost democratic in nature. While there are democratic elements in the Church, which are warranted and indeed quite necessary to fulfill the participatory nature of the faith, this cannot lead to reducing Church life to a type of parliamentarian election in which different advocates represent a plethora of truths. This would fly in the face of the Incarnation of *the* Logos and *the* Truth par excellence. For this reason, movements such as *Wir sind Kirche* (We are Church) not only misrepresent the sacramental nature of the Church, but actually have contributed to a mass exodus from her in the last decades of the twentieth century. Some members of the people of God have been blind to the Eucharistic communion that is the essence of Church. In fact, the absurd situation is, they left a Church they had never understood.

The Church spans the local celebration of the Eucharist and the universality of the Eucharist. In Ratzinger's ecclesiology, the Church continues to make Jesus Christ's salvation effective in the world via the German concept of "*Stellvertretung*," which translates as "substitution" or "representation" into English. This never serves merely to expand Church membership like in a human society or club, but rather to incorporate all of humanity into the life-rhythm of the Trinitarian God. In the biblical concept of "the kingdom of God," Ratzinger apprehends an instrument to unlock this nature of the Church. The Church is preeminently Christological in nature. "Origen, basing himself on a reading of Jesus' words, called Jesus the *autobasileia* [that is, the kingdom itself, better: Jesus Himself is the kingdom itself], that is, the Kingdom in person. Jesus himself is the Kingdom; the Kingdom is not a thing, it is not a geographical dominion like worldly kingdoms. It is a person: It is he."[10] Thus, following along with the early patristic intuition, Ratzinger makes out the kingdom of God as "veiled Christology." This same thought led Origen to conclude that this kingdom is first and foremost an interior reality. As Ratzinger captures this reality, "It is located in man's inner being. It grows and radiates outward from that inner peace."[11] He acknowledges a tension exists between the kingdom of God and the actual Church. This should not, however, lead to the individualistic, moralistic conclusion of Adolf von Harnack, or Albert Schweitzer's early thesis, of Jesus proclaiming a not yet realized, but imminent, kingdom of God.

The Church is both visible and invisible. To explain this seeming paradox, Ratzinger employs the analogy of the Eucharist. While the Eucharist has interior and spiritual dimensions, it also possesses exterior and social dimensions. In the same way, as the Church is grounded in the Eucharist she has both visible and invisible components. He argues, "[T]he Church is the people of God by virtue of the body of Christ."[12] Thus, the Church has vertical and horizontal dimensions. The foundational reality holding all of it together is the Incarnation. Through Jesus, the Word of God among humanity, God embraced the world and became part of it. Thus, the Church becomes the principal agent of God's Word, "the prolongation of the movement of the Word's procession, and the simple gesture of disinterested serving love in the actualizing of the divine love, a love which streams forth even when it remains without response."[13] This entails dialogue with the world, not only with believers of other faiths, but even agnostics and atheists, beckoning all to an ever greater unity. The Church "only remains faithful to her own meaning, and only fulfills her task, inasmuch as she does not clutch the Gospel she has been given to herself, but carries it forth to the rest of mankind."[14]

The Church is in her essence a reality willed by God and in a mysterious way part of Our Lord. Thus, although numerous human elements do, and indeed do so by divine will, exist in the Church, she is not a human construction. Although countless ecclesial structures and organizations exist within her fold, no one member or collection of members owns her. She frees human beings to discover far more than simply their self-defined needs taken care of. She is Our Lord's constant invitation to bid farewell to one's petty self and share in the magnanimity of the second divine person, who became human, suffered, died, and victoriously rose from the dead. Transcending all sociological categories, the "People of God" is not a limiting definition, but one in continuity with the Old Testament past, inviting all and open to the second coming of the Lord. This Church is imaginable only in direct and vital relation to Christology: "The church, or, in other words, the Kingdom of Christ now present in mystery" (*LG* 3). This *communio sanctorum*, this communion of holy men and women, exists by the grace of the Good Shepherd, who gave his life for these. Thus, no sociological or political concept can capture her sacramental reality, which is derived exclusively from Jesus Christ.

This is not to make the case for a trite, self-immunization of the Church from criticism or reform. Rather, the conditions for genuine reform are spelled out. In the much noted *Ratzinger Report*, he observed in 1985 during an interview with Vittorio Messori:

> We must always bear in mind that the church is not ours but his. Hence, the "reform," the "renewals"—necessary as they be—cannot exhaust themselves in a zealous activity on our part to erect new, sophisticated structures. The most that can come from a work of this kind is a church that is "ours," to our measure, which might indeed be interesting but which, by itself, is nevertheless not the true church, that which sustains us with the faith and gives us life with the sacraments. I mean to say that what we can do is infinitely inferior to him who does. Hence, true "reform" does not mean to take great pains to erect new façades (contrary to what certain ecclesiologies think). Real "reform" is to strive to let what is ours disappear as much as possible so what belongs to Christ may become more visible. It is a truth well known to the saints. Saints, in fact reformed the church in depth, not by working up plans for new structures, but by reforming themselves. What the church needs in order to respond to the needs of man in every age is holiness, not management.[15]

Drawing on Peter Stuhlmacher, Ratzinger reminds the reader that the original Hebrew noun for kingdom, "*malkut*," is "an action word" referring to "the active lordship of the king."[16] The kingdom of God is thus a dynamic reality, affirming that God does indeed exist, even among his people. This leads him to conclude: "Its inner dynamism carries history beyond itself. And yet it is at the same time something belonging absolutely to the present." Its reality-transcending quality does not cancel out the immanence of the kingdom of God. While open toward the definitive future, it is not in any way Platonic. This is the reason the evangelists state: "The Kingdom of God is at hand" (Mk 1:15). "The reality that Jesus names the 'Kingdom of God, lordship of God' is extremely complex, and only by accepting it in its entirety can we gain access to, and let ourselves be guided by his message."[17]

While an undue emphasis on the hierarchical nature of the Church is unhealthy, one cannot consider it an accident. If it is divinely willed, then it is not caused by a primitive human craving for power. It is willed by Jesus Christ to give his body permanence amid the vicissitudes in history in order to allow every human being and every age to behold him. Ratzinger cautions against the concept "democracy." It would be "absurd" to entrust such a process to majority rule, giving the majority the task of determining what the content and nature of revelation is, what religious truth is, and what structures Christ has willed. Human reason has not discovered revelation. Otherwise, the divinity of Christ and God's sovereignty would be jeopardized to their cores. Yet, far be it for him to plead the case for institutional rigidity: "The universality of the Church involves, on the one hand, a most solid unity, and on the other hand, a plurality and a diversification, which do not obstruct unity, but rather confer upon it the character of 'communion.' This plurality refers both to the diversity of ministries, charisms and forms of life and apostolate within each particular Church and to the diversity of traditions in liturgy and culture among the various particular Churches."[18] Otherwise, one would do an injustice to the spiritual nature of the priesthood. It is never purely functional and bureaucratic but is most importantly charismatic.

Ratzinger's expectations for the outcome of the Second Vatican Council were not guided by a yearning for modernization or the implementation of progressive ideas, as an all too facile, popular misunderstanding of *aggiornamento*, coined by *Il Papa buono*, John XXIII, might suggest.[19] Rather, an individual's faith and the Church as a whole should live anew drawing from sacramental, biblical, patristic, and medieval sources. This was the spiritual concern of the great minds of Ressourcement, of de Lubac, Daniélou, Congar, and countless other theologians and philosophers. The Spirit that moved the Church fathers and saints—and also the council fathers—is the only viable, because it is trustworthy, spirit of renewal. Yves Congar well summarized both the council's and Ratzinger's concern in this regarding: "a 'return-to-sources' of Catholicism which is, by the same token, Catholicism wholly centered on Christ and also biblical, liturgical, paschal, community-minded, ecumenical and missionary...."[20] It is the Holy Spirit that safeguards the Church's selfsame identity through time and space, by allowing her to orient herself constantly afresh toward the one, risen, and coming Lord.

As a young *peritus*, Ratzinger regretted that both conservative participants in the council and ecumenical observers were concerned that the Church was succumbing to modernist allures; the *nota explicativa praevia*,[21] concerning the Church's governance, was perceived as a "primatialistic" countering overreaction. Ratzinger pointed out that numerous papal functions were actually performed by the officeholder as patriarch of the West and not as pontiff. Moreover, these points do not devalue the essence of the doctrine on episcopal collegiality, which is "the inner co-penetration of the plurality of sacramental communities and the papally preserved unity of service."[22]

On the occasion of his fellow Bavarian theologian Johann Baptist Metz's retirement in 1993, Ratzinger recalled Metz having lamented that nowadays the Church speaks more about herself than about God, as happened at the last council. In this same line, Ratzinger also recalled how the aged and highly esteemed theologian Bishop Michael Buchberger of Regensburg (1874–1961) had admonished his fellow bishops on the eve of the Second Vatican Council to reflect, not on the Church, but rather on God. As people of God, the Church references to and speaks of God.[23]

Whatever slight reservations Ratzinger may have harbored regarding *Lumen Gentium*, they were eclipsed by those he expressed concerning the text of *Gaudium et Spes*. He welcomed the council's intention to address the world head on, but he noted significant imbalances in its execution. He was glad that the document's style was "non-authoritarian" and personalist. Yet, he also noted a divorce between salvation and the description of the world in the mainly French-authored document. Scriptural references seem mere a posteriori ornaments. It uses the language of modernity, not that of the Bible or theology. In Nichols's translation of Ratzinger's report on the fourth session, one reads: "What is proper to theology, discourse about Christ and his work, was left behind in a conceptual deep-freeze, and so allowed to appear, in contrast with the understandable part, even more unintelligible and antiquated...."[24] The question concerning the nature of salvation was left unanswered. The document is far too naturalistic and unhistorical. It does not sufficiently note the phenomenon of sin and its consequences. As a result, the document is naïvely optimistic. Furthermore, religion appears almost as an accidental epiphenomenon.[25] Any attempt to describe humankind apart from faith cannot do justice to the greatness of the human spirit.

In addition, the document makes lofty demands and expresses a wish to entertain some connection with the world. It was the first conciliar pronouncement that expressed sympathy with the world of nonbelievers without arguing on the basis of the creed. It strikes an altogether unwarranted cheerful note, trusting in the modern notion of progress. It does not take note of the fact that material progress is ambivalent by its very nature: it may improve the human condition but also degrade humanity. Ratzinger counters: only sacrificing love can redeem the world. In the document, one detects something of a relentless motion toward unity, without marveling at the miracle of creation. Ratzinger declared the discussion on free will in article 17 was "downright Pelagian." In these factors, he detected a crude form of "Teilhardism." Technical improvements in progress and the human condition are allied too closely with Christian hope. Ultimately, neither apparatus nor technology can redeem the world. Only love can achieve this. During the council's last session, he also noted a crisis of the missionary spirit and a lack of biblical foundations. In addition, a general "climate of sensationalism" hindered a spiritual debate concerning serious issues, such as the ordination of *viri probati* (married laymen) to the priesthood. He was, however, grateful for the centrality Christ and the mystery of Easter enjoy in article 22 of the document and considered the treatment of atheism in articles 19–21 balanced and well founded, and he was glad Marxism was not expressly mentioned.

At the occasion of receiving an honorary doctoral degree from the University of Eichstätt, the only Catholic university in a German-speaking country, Ratzinger closed his presentation by reminding his audience of the faith of the *simplex et idiota,* that is, the simple of heart, such as Zechariah, Elizabeth, and Joseph were; which is a recurring theme in his writings. They turn for shelter to the Church with her ageless wisdom, which is not the cumulative insight of generations of believers but the way of the gospel. Ten years after the council, Ratzinger would remind one not to misuse *Gaudium et Spes* as *the* interpretation of, or as the hermeneutical key to, all of the other documents, but rather to appreciate it in its proper theological valence, that is, to read it in light of the preceding dogmatic constitutions.[26]

In the *Ratzinger Report* Ratzinger, who was then Prefect of the Congregation for the Doctrine of the Faith, argued that misinterpretations can be overcome by an authentic reception of the conciliar documents. "*Les extrêmes se touchent,*" as a French proverb maintains ("the extremes meet each other"). In Ratzinger's eyes, traditionalists and progressives commit the same error: they do not see the greater, underlying continuity as the indispensable basis for change. The Second Vatican Council stands in reference to, and in continuity with, tradition. The council fathers do not repudiate tradition but expand on it. They merely chose a different style and pastoral language. It must also be understood that *Gaudium et Spes* is subordinate to the two dogmatic constitutions on revelation and the Church (*Dei Verbum* and *Lumen Gentium*).[27]

Ratzinger's dissertation *On the People and House of God in Augustine's Teaching on the Church* is the point of departure for understanding his ecclesiology. The concept "house of God" is, in his consideration, of marginal significance for the council. However, the term "people of God" receives its proper valence "only and exclusively" in combination with the notion of the Church as the "body of Christ."[28] This is the pivotal claim of his dissertation. As he argues in the foreword to the reprint of his habilitation, liberation theology runs (unwittingly perhaps) the danger of jeopardizing the nature of the Church as the mystical body of Christ and, therefore, of surrendering the Church's sacramental-hierarchical constitution. Only if one tears asunder Christ and the Spirit in the Church, that is, its Christological-sacramental element from the pneumatological-prophetical element, can one arrive at an inner-worldly Christian utopia.[29] Ratzinger demonstrates that one cannot limit Christ's epiphany to the Joachimite second age. In a perspective that is neither linear nor circular, for Bonaventure there exists in every aspect of history the kairotic occasion to ascend to God in the form of a spiral. The divine economy exists for each individual soul personally. Bonaventure thereby preserves both the unique, unrepeatable event of Jesus Christ in history and his unique mediating role in the spiritual life of every individual believer until the day of last judgment. This implies the basal assumption of the noneternity of the world.

Amid the nonextricability from this noneternity of contingent existence there exists in the form of the Church a supra-temporal community of faith. De Lubac's epochal book *Catholicism* is a key to understanding Ratzinger's ecclesiology.[30] While still a seminarian in Freising, secluded from the world, Ratzinger read this book in the autumn of 1949.[31] It is within the Church that the truth of history becomes evident. De Lubac had also read Joachim of Fiore quite thoroughly. It is in human history that one can encounter the Christian God. This becomes tangible in the Church as community, that is, as the Eucharistic communion ever anew and constantly the same. While the Church may occasionally convene councils, she is essentially communion, not a chain of consultative meetings.[32] De Lubac considered "ill-fated individualism" a major stumbling block to Church reform and renewal. Such a renewal can occur by studying the Church fathers and living a lifestyle that takes the faith seriously as the early Christians did. Thus, the Christian is not a weak-willed object of a numinous power, but a conscious and free member of a body. The Christian is called to partake in ecclesial life and be of like mind with Christ. The Christian is called to move from being a private subject to unity with the body of Christ. This is facilitated in the Eucharist. While the individual is called to reconcile himself with God, he also experiences the Church on the path of purification. The Church is not the place of the all-pure, yet it is also not defiled as there is an indelible, holy, and pure core. Every member constantly endeavors to purify his or her own thoughts and intentions. The Church thereby becomes the fraternal/sororal community of the disciples of Christ. It was no accident that the first book Ratzinger penned as a professor was on Christian brotherhood. It is precisely the reminder of the constant need for purification that prevents the Church from becoming an instrument of suppression and alienation, enabling her to remain transparent to Jesus Christ. Ratzinger's is, therefore, a Church critique of an altogether different kind. At times he might suffer at the hands of the Church, yet more importantly the Church suffers his imperfections. These two dimensions are seen in union if Christians' struggle for a "communal way of life," where morality is not only discussed academically or intellectually but as the personal testimony to Christ risen, becomes an integral component of public and ecclesial life. Everyday life thus becomes festive, and this feast leads to a joyous liturgy. Ratzinger yearns for the holistic human being as thematized in the Romantic era of the first half of the nineteenth century.[33]

The Church as a sacramental reality cannot be apprehended either as an abstract Platonic idea or merely as an empirical entity. In Ratzinger's estimation, Augustine tended toward a double definition of the Church as *ecclesia sancta* and the concrete *ecclesia catholica*. While the concept of the *ecclesia sancta* refers to the untold number of saints, the *ecclesia catholica* relates to the Church spanning the globe. Though donatists and liberal Protestant theologians are therefore inclined to detect in Augustine's ecclesiology a bifurcated definition of the Church, Ratzinger maintains this cannot be the case.

Augustine, in Ratzinger's reading, sees Christ himself as aiding sinners to be transformed "into their true form of salvation."[34] The nature of the Church is not constituted primarily by the condition of her individual members but first and foremost by the mystery of the body of Christ. The people of God are *communio sanctorum* by virtue of their participation in the Eucharistic Lord. United with Christ, the Church becomes both the body of Christ and members of Christ's body. "The unification of man with Christ occurs not simply between the believer and Christ. The path to the spirit of Christ *never* occurs directly but always by entering the body of Christ in the Church. Hence, this is the actual nature of how man becomes one with Christ, by becoming one with the Church."[35] The Church is the enabling environment for Christian discipleship. In his judgment, this illustrates the central divergence between Augustinian and Lutheran ecclesiology. This is foundational for Ratzinger: the "I-Thou relationship," that is, of the believer with God, is possible and credible only by including and living out the "we of the Church." There exists an intimate connection between the believer and the Church. The relationship of the believer to God therein evidences itself as Christocentric because it is profoundly grounded in the sacramental reality of the Eucharist. In Ratzinger's view, this explains Augustine's position on the issues involving the baptism of heretics and the rigorist donatists. This insight into Augustine's ecclesiology is an abiding and often recurring theme and argument in Ratzinger's writings.[36]

There is a twofold reality to the Church: the Eucharist is an ecclesial celebration in which the body of Christ is truly present and in which the Church is this body of Christ. This reality is not one of mere mystical interiority. Rather, ontologically, the people of God are "incorporated" into the body of Christ. It is the real presence of the sacrament in the sense of the presence of that which is signified in the sign. For Augustine and Ratzinger, the Eucharist is the foundational experience of the people of God as the body of Christ. This is the leitmotif of Ratzinger's ecclesiology. One should keep in mind here the powerful experience of his youth in Bavaria where no liturgical or worldly event was celebrated with as much fervor and pageantry as the Solemnity of Corpus Christi. With passionate language, Ratzinger oftentimes stresses the connection between the Church and the Eucharist. Thus, like the monstrance containing the body of Christ, the Church as the people of God becomes the manner of God's being in the world. This in turn enables the Church to be the "real subject" of faith, tradition, and salvation in time and space.

Ratzinger takes care to point out that the opening paragraph of the Second Vatican Council's *Dogmatic Constitution on the Church* (*Lumen Gentium*) begins "*Lumen Gentium cum sit Christus*": "the Church is, so to speak, Christ." It is the eternal Son of God, Christ who is the Light of the peoples. The Church is effective only to the extent that she refers to Christ and reflects him. Thus, the image of the Church as the mystical body of Christ serves as a call to greater interiority and to live consciously from communion with Jesus Christ. In this sense, the Church must constantly grow toward Christ. *Lumen Gentium* liberates the Church from a moribund sterility, irrelevant to our age and time. Reminding one of Newman, Ratzinger states: "There is a real identity with the origin only where there is at the same time that living continuity which develops the origin, and in so developing it, guards it."[37] This can be communicated because God is not esoteric and his divine Son is not eccentric, but shares our *conditio humana*. The human being Jesus is not only the Son of God, he—as John reminds one with haunting clarity in the prologue to his gospel—is the Logos, that is, the key to understanding the whole of reality and life. Human reason is unable on its own to reach such heights. However, provided with the Logos' wisdom and grace, it is capable of knowing the very condition and ultimate goal of its existence. Precisely by not claiming to define the totality of reality on its own, that is, by self-limiting itself, it finds the deepest justification for all intellectual endeavors. Left to its own resources—that is, unaided by natural or supernatural revelation—human reason will attempt the absurd, namely, to justify the irrational.

To make his point, Ratzinger mentions the biologist and philosopher Jacques Monod (1910–1976). The French microbiologist Monod believed the origin of life is the result of extreme improbability, like winning a jackpot, and not divinely willed. As has already been noted, Ratzinger wrote his *Introduction to Christianity* amid the student revolts of the late 1960s. Recently, in 2007, the German philosopher and moderate advocate of the 1968 student-led revolution, Jürgen Habermas acknowledged in retrospect that without religion secular rationalism suffers from defeatism.[38] What was at that time a rather isolated critique of positivism eloquently voiced by Ratzinger has not only proven to be true, but it is a helpful remedy in the present age and time where positivism has subcutaneously asserted itself virtually everywhere. Simply put, positivism is the attempt to live apart from something numinous, ultimately to live apart from the Logos. Thus, it is condemned to constantly generate its own ephemeral truths derived from contingent reality alone.

The role of the Church, or her magisterium, is not simply to be the ultimate court of appeal for all matters, religious or civil, but to be the one indispensable component of a tension-filled dualism of Church and state. The Church is not the bearer of an ideology or of a party platform, because these are human constructs and therefore temporal. The Church does not construct truth but receives it as revelation. Thus, the Church is not humanly posited but posited by the Revealer, defining her in turn as the receiver. The Church is an ethical court of appeal *sui generis*.[39] On the other side of this tension-filled arc lies the state, which must acknowledge that it has no authority concerning either religious or ethical matters. It can but evidence secular truth as a constantly fluctuating consensus such as a parliament or the electorate may reach. In this sense, a healthy tension exists between Church and state. Both benefit from it. The individual and the state need to be aware of the intrinsic imperfection of the human condition per se. This insight need not be based on a theological claim, such as original sin. The insight of philosophers into the contingent nature of the human condition suffices. For the state's and the individual's well-being, religion must be granted its relative autonomy. As a case in point, Ratzinger mentions marriage. It is the nucleus of society. Nonetheless, the body politic on its own is unable to supply a justification for the institution of marriage. However, as it opts not to refer to religion to establish an ethical basis for marriage, it must countenance the dissolution of itself, that is, of marriage and therefore of society.[40] The Kafkaesque bureaucracy—welfare offices, counseling services, and so on-administrating such an undermined society is a sad reality. Another paradigm subcutaneously operative in modern society is Jean-Jacques Rousseau's (1712–1778) view in which he thought of citizens passing gradually from the condition of hetero-determination to one of auto-determination. He joined this to a Pelagian rejection of original sin and hell and a naïve affirmation of free will. As for him the gospel is always interpreted subjectively: morality too depends on one's preferences.[41]

In contradistinction, Ratzinger reminds the reader that the narrative of Israel's freedom began with two events: the exodus from the bondage of Egypt and receiving the commandments of God on Mount Sinai. Freedom has a point of origin and justification, namely God. Vis-à-vis God it actualizes its highest realization. For this reason, a healthy state will respect the Church's social teaching. Without God as the highest and nondisposable good, every value becomes totalitarian. God does not coerce but is as Trinity perfect freedom. In Christianity the nonidentity of God and earthly goods is preserved and maintained but in such a way that a tension is upheld. This mirrors *realiter* (in reality) the hypostatic union as the union of the divine and human natures in the one person of Jesus Christ. The reality of the Incarnation of Jesus Christ as true God and true man (Council of Chalcedon) and its relevance in defining human identity and freedom is not sufficiently borne in mind by contemporary thought.

In the alternating between the "I believe" and the "we believe" of the creed neither an individualistic understanding of faith nor a collectivistic understanding of faith is expressed: the Church herself becomes the subject of faith. It is this ecclesial constitution of faith—constantly preceding that of the individual—that is the enabling reality of an individual believer's recitation of the creed. In Ratzinger's estimation, this remains difficult to fathom as the Church is neither an empirical entity nor merely a lofty Platonic idea: she is a sacramental reality. The Church becomes the enabling principle of the *communio*-structure of the faithful, conditioning the "we-structure" of faith. Thus defined, one is able to apprehend the Church relating to the faithful as a body to her members or as a mother to her children.

As the Jesuit Otto Semmelroth (1912–1979), a fellow theological advisor during the Second Vatican Council, discovered concurrently with Ratzinger's research into the ecclesiologies of Augustine and Bonaventure, Jesus Christ as the root sacrament becomes the foundational reality for the Church, which is the primordial sacrament for the seven individual sacraments.[42] The Church receives the Eucharist as the sacrament of sacraments; it, rather she becomes his body. Further, this correlation wards off a peculiar danger. The Church can never self-constitute her particular subjectivity. On the contrary, she is ever mindful of Christ being her head and gratefully acknowledges herself as Christ's own gratuitous self-donation. Thus the unique nature of the Church, as that of Jesus as the Christ, can only be beheld in faith, and this recognition is itself an act of faith. Therefore, the Church is a reality *sui generis*; she is beyond any objectification apart from faith. This reality is comprehended, acknowledged, and lived out in the liturgy where Christians pray to Christ and with him to God the Father through the Holy Spirit. Apart from the liturgy, there is no avenue to appreciate the Church's essence.

According to St. Augustine, the true being and essence of the Church remains hidden. Nevertheless, as *corpus permixtum* (a mixed body) something of the Church is visible and tangible. As sacramental communion with Christ this Church becomes visible in the Eucharist. The concrete manifestation of the Church must be determined by this sacrament. Canon law is compelled to express this. The *Civitas Dei* is apart from any human *civitas terrena*, such as a pagan religious cult divinizing an emperor. It is only by virtue of the incarnational nature of faith that canon law forms a part of this Church. At this point, Ratzinger delineates Catholic ecclesiology as different from the Lutheran theologian Rudolph Sohm (1841–1917), who argued that law is by its very nature secular and hence contrary to the very essence of a Christian Church, which is essentially charismatic. Sohm thereby reintroduced a notorious distinction between the "church of love" and the "church of law."[43] In this perspective, Catholic canon law was considered contrary to early Christianity.[44]

In the Eucharist the structure of the Church as a "Christ corporation" is coconstituted: The *successio apostolica* (apostolic succession) guarantees Eucharistic unity. This insight is of relevance for ecumenical dialogue. For both Augustine and Ratzinger, the episcopal office has a Eucharistic constituent: "One ought to be mindful of the double-claim: the unity with the Roman bearer of succession and the Catholicity of the total community of communication."[45] While Augustine emphasizes "the unity with the total *Catholica*," the events surrounding the Pelagian controversies confirm Augustine's recognition of the value of hierarchical unity with Rome. The unity of the college of bishops and of the whole Church rests on their communion with the "*cathedra Petri*" in Rome. Otherwise, the reality of the one sacramental body of Christ would be lost.[46]

Therefore, one may summarize Ratzinger's position as follows: while the Church and state differ regarding their respective natures, the Church may not be deprived of her legal form proper to an institution. In other words, the Church's sacramentality does not occasion her spiritualization. For this reason, the solemnity of the Church as *Corpus Christi* does not deprive her of her worldliness and world-transforming nature. Yet, on the other hand, the Church likewise cannot be reduced to an exclusively juridical entity. The distinctions between sacramental and empirical and between ideal and pneumatic do not allow that one or the other component is completely absent. Only such a balanced perspective enables a judicious appreciation of Augustine's understanding of the *Civitas Dei*.[47]

Influenced by his collaboration in drafting *Lumen Gentium*, and also by the then novel and now nearly passé phenomenon of charismatic renewal, Ratzinger soon embarked on a new book reflecting on the ramifications of Church membership.[48] The donatist lay theologian Tyconius (d. 400) had perceived the Church as a purely pneumatological, and thus invisible, reality wholly divorced from structures and Christ. In response to this thesis, Augustine divined an indispensable ontic correlation between the structured and official Church and the spiritual Church. It is exclusively via the visible

Catholic Church that the true but invisible Church is accessed. Ratzinger discovered this when reading Augustine's *Soliloquia*. The dictum "God and the soul, nothing else" is concretized in the *Tractatus in Ioannem* as loyalty to Christ's Church: "Inasmuch as anyone loves Christ's Church, to that degree he possesses the Holy Spirit."[49] The affirmation of the Incarnation of Christ is part of professing loyalty to the mystical body of Christ. This entails loyalty to the Church as a yardstick for ascertaining possession of the authentic Spirit and genuine unity with God.[50] Augustine is careful to maintain a *via media*, that is, he avoids oscillating between either the exterior or interior aspects of the Church. The correlation of the two is necessary due to the Eucharist as the constant reconstitution of the Church as the body of Christ. In the recent past, great minds have explored this Eucharistic ecclesiology anew.[51] In this regard, Ratzinger was particularly influenced by de Lubac. Ratzinger hoped to overcome the dangers of both an exaggerated glorification of the Church or her overspiritualization. The world, and even more intensely the Church, receive unity from Christ's person and work. "The mystery of Christ is, for the Fathers, inherently and entirely a mystery of unity."[52]

Augustinian ecclesiology underwent a balanced specification in the fifteenth century through the Croatian Dominican John of Ragusa (Stoyković, ca. 1395–1443), who defined the Church as composed of three components: creedal confession, sacramental communion, and apostolic obedience. Before the Lutheran Augsburg Confession of 1530, which defined the Church as "the congregation of the holy people, in which the Gospel is taught purely and the sacraments administered rightly," John of Ragusa (Stoyković) had discovered that obedience to the apostolic ministry is central to determining what is "taught purely" and when "sacraments are administered rightly."[53]

A much contested expression introduced in the Second Vatican Council is the Latin phrase "*subsistit in.*" "This Church, constituted and organized as a society in the present world, subsists in the Catholic Church...." (*LG* 8). This term is sometimes used to advocate ecclesiological relativism, that is, to maintain there are a number of Christian denominations that merit being called "church." Ratzinger seems to argue that a fixation on a low Christology, that is, one that sees only the historical Jesus, leads to difficulties appreciating the Church as wrought by the Holy Spirit. The unicity of the Catholic Church is affirmed by the council. The term "*subsistit in*" is specified in *Dominus Jesus* to mean that in the Catholic Church the Church of Christ continues to exist fully. It declares, albeit in a footnote: "The interpretation of those who would derive from the formula *subsistit in* the thesis that the one Church of Christ could subsist also in non-Catholic Churches is contrary to the authentic meaning of *Lumen Gentium*."[54] The Church is not a confederation of churches such as is found in Protestant, congregationalist denominations. As early as the 1960s, Ratzinger wrote in this regard: "The Catholic is convinced that the visible existence of the Church is not merely an organizational cover for a real Church hidden behind it, but on the contrary that, for all its humanity and insufficiency, the visible Church is the actual dwelling place of God among men, that it *is* the Church itself."[55]

Currents in Catholic Systematic Theology

1800   1900   2000

MANUALISTS

NEO-SCHOLASTICISM (from 16th century onward)—Two-tier thinking: Separation of (pure) Nature and Grace; Strengths: Clarity, Faith's Intelligibility, Creedal Content; Weaknesses: Impersonal, Unhistorical, Intellectualistic

Cajetan (1480–1547), Suárez (1548–1617), Báñez (1528–1604), Molina (1536–1600), Joseph Pohle (1852–1922), Franz Diekamp (1864–1943), Martin Grabmann (1874–1969), Ludwig Ott (1906–1985)

NEO-THOMISM—Strengths: Recovery of original Thomas Aquinas, Intelligibility of Faith, Analogy of Being

1879 Leo XIII's encyclical *Aeterni Patris*, Etienne Gilson (1884–1978), R. Garrigou-Lagrange (1877–1964), Jacques Maritain (1882–1973), Marie-Dominique Chenu (1895–1990), Cornelio Fabro (1911–1995), Karol Wojtyla (1920–2005), Ralph McInerny (1922–), Jean-Pierre Torrell(1927–), Gilles Emery (1962–)

CHRISTIAN PERSONALISM—Strengths: Human Disponibility to God's call is Basis for Human Dignity

Martin Buber (Jewish, 1878–1965), Max Scheler (1874–1928), Gabriel Marcel (1889–1973), Romano Guardini (1885–1968), Emile Mersch (1890–1940): Christians "Sons and Daughters in the Son", Edith Stein (1891–1942), Luigi Giussani (1922–2005), Karol Wojtyla (1920–2005) Tadeusz Styczen (1931–), Joszef Tischner (1931–2000), Joseph Ratzinger (1927–)

LITURGICAL RENEWAL Prosper Guéranger (1805–75), Anselm Schott (1843–96), Pius X, 1909: "Active Participation"

PIUS XII: *Corpus Christi Mystici*, 1943

Romano Guardini (1885–1968), Joseph Ratzinger (1927–)

RESSOURCEMENT—Scripture & Patristics & Thomas Aquinas, Unity of Faith and Teaching: all of History is Salvation History, the Holy Spirit, grants Tradition, Presence of Holy Spirit and Eucharist in the Church

Henri de Lubac (1896–1991), Jean Daniélou (1905–1974), Yves Congar (1904–1995), Hans Urs von Balthasar (1905–1988), Hugo Rahner (1900–1968), Joseph Ratzinger (1927–) Aidan Nichols (1948–)

REDISCOVERY OF CHURCH FATHERS— Tübingen School of Theology; Roman School of Theology; Church is Continuous Incarnation of Jesus Christ, Organic Development of Dogma, Faith: Expression of the Trinity's Vivacity

Johann Adam Möhler (1796–1838), John Henry Newman (1801–90), Matthias Scheeben (1835–88)

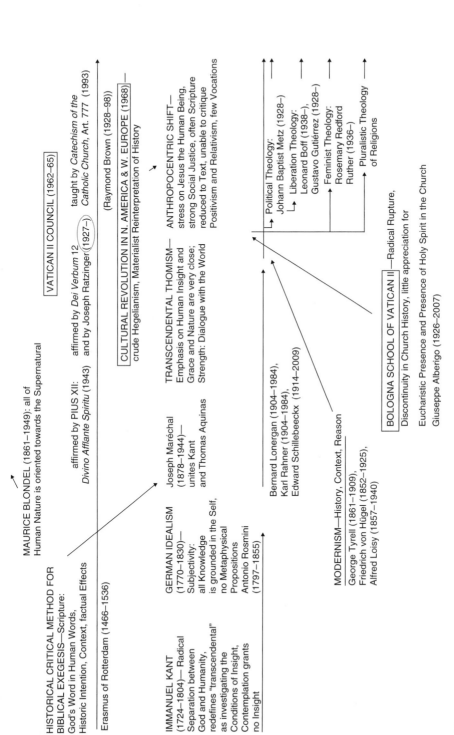

Plate 1 Currents in Catholic Systematic Theology

Plate 2 Pope Benedict XVI waves to a cheering crowd Tuesday, April 15, 2008, on his arrival at Andrews Air Force Base, Maryland, where he was greeted by President George W. Bush, Laura Bush, and their daughter Jenna. (White House photograph by Shealah Craighead.)

Plate 3 President George W. Bush and Laura Bush applaud as Pope Benedict XVI acknowledges being sung happy birthday by the thousands of guests Wednesday, April 16, 2008, at his welcoming ceremony on the South Lawn of the White House. (White House photograph by Eric Draper.)

CHAPTER 18

Christ and Ecumenical Dialogue

Ratzinger's ecumenical interests are genuine and based on personal acquaintance. Two of his more noted former doctoral students are the Greek Orthodox bishops Damaskinos Papandreou and Stylianos Harkianakis; both currently metropolitans of the Ecumenical Patriarchate of Constantinople.

After the publication of *Dominus Jesus*[1] in 2000, the Orthodox Church inquired whether Rome recognizes Orthodoxy as "Church" in the full sense of the word, or whether Rome reserves the full predication "Church" exclusively for the Roman Catholic Church. In response, Ratzinger, as Prefect of the Congregation for the Doctrine of the Faith, replied that the Roman Catholic Church feels herself "wounded" by the lack of unity between the two Churches.[2]

Seven years later the head of the Moscow patriarchate's section for external affairs, Metropolitan Cyril of Smolensk and Kaliningrad and presently the Patriarch of Russia, penned the foreword to the Russian edition of Ratzinger's classic *Introduction to Christianity* closing with the wish: "May it lead to a fruitful collaboration in the proclamation of Christian values. Precisely this spirit of fidelity to our common roots permeates Pope Benedict XVI's book."[3] After years of reciprocal alienation and suspicion, the last forty years have witnessed a remarkable rapprochement between these two largest Christian denominations. The fact that a significant official representative of the Orthodox world authored laudatory words about a Western theological classic, words that were intended for a predominantly Russian-Orthodox readership, is a noteworthy milestone.[4]

Also in 2007, the Ecumenical Patriarch Bartholomaios I from Constantinople wrote an introduction to *Jesus of Nazareth*. Fully in agreement with Ratzinger, the patriarch maintains knowledge of Jesus Christ grows most significantly through a personal relationship, sustained by a love for Christ that is not limited to mere sentiments and their corresponding expressions. Reason "entering" the heart prevents sentimentality from developing.

The solution can only be the recognition that, in and of itself, human efforts cannot give unity to a body that is neither political nor ethnic in nature but is the mystical body of Jesus Christ. Unity is a gift granted by Christ to his Church. The Church has a divine origin. Such "a unity from above" does not ignore existing theological or spiritual differences. Yet, by concentrating on the essence of faith, Jesus Christ, and therefore on the center of faith, one allows Christ to effect ecumenical unity so that he may bring about one Christendom anew. In a noted letter written in 1986 for the periodical *Theologische Quartalschrift*, Ratzinger argued Christianity cannot be defined merely by "activities," lest its contours become hazy. Such a definition cannot bring about lasting unity and the desired constancy of ecclesial life. It merely involves stumbling from one activity or platitude to another. The Church—and this includes all efforts toward ecumenical unity—is not the outgrowth of human pressure for success. To achieve ecumenical unity, what is required is to allow unengineered, unexpected events to become the stages of a foundation for unity. Ratzinger does not plead for passivity in ecumenical matters but rather for Christians of all denominations *to collaborate with God* and allow God to achieve such unity under his conditions.

In this sense, one should cherish reading God's Word together, the conciliar texts leading to the profession of faith in the triune God, in Jesus Christ as true God and true man, as well as reflecting on the nature of baptism and the remission of sins. The Decalogue (The Ten Commandments) can be read from a New Testament perspective. Thus, a basic image of God emerges that is common to many human beings. Such insights need to be lived, publicly acknowledged, and constantly deepened. This reaches a highpoint in joint prayer. In the process "a new wealth of listening and understanding develops" leaving behind misunderstandings and pointless polemics. Turning together to the Lord and praying the psalms are sources for hope. Such prayerful Trinitarian *koinonia* (communion) in the Father and his Son and in the Holy Spirit enables all participants to experience community as wrought by the third person of the Blessed Trinity. Such prayer in turn also leads to a deeper scholarly understanding of the Christian faith. Thus, ecumenical progress is achieved not by spectacular statements or events, but by listening to the subtle language of God and by appreciating that the human condition and human reason are God's gifts to humankind so that it might reach God within the contingent parameters of immanence.[5]

According to Ratzinger, the goal of all ecumenical efforts is the transformation of the separated confessional Christian denominations into authentic particular Churches, each embodying the one *Catholica*.[6] He rejects three hypotheses. It would be shortsighted to believe that merely a popular movement from below, ignoring theological research and the ordained ministry, could be successful. Likewise, he rejects the notion that unity among Church leaders alone—based on their ordination—could establish Church unity. In his judgment, this was the nature of the pioneering attempt made by Heinrich Fries and Karl Rahner in 1983.[7] This suggestion allots too much authority to bishops and the pope. It flies in the face of the concepts of the priesthood of the laity and the true nature of the Catholic ministerial priesthood; unity must be prayed for (*erbetet werden*). A third model he rejects is one that simply accepts every Christian practice in and of itself as a valid tradition without subjecting it to a theological analysis, thereby bypassing the testimonies of scripture and apostolic tradition. Genuine ecumenical progress, Ratzinger argues, can only be achieved if all three elements collaborate. The conscious and prayerful integration of scripture and tradition, the faith testimony of the faithful as people of God, and theology and doctrinal teachings yield the Christian hope for ecumenical progress.[8] This will allow all to appreciate the Church in her mystery as the subject, that is, the bearer, of the gospel.

Although it is a thorny issue, in his estimation it is also important in ecumenical matters to do justice to the papal office. In this context, he refers to the last Catholic archbishop of Canterbury,[9] Reginald Pole (1500–1558), who "saw in the papal power not a grotesque hyperinflation of ministerial authority, but its exact opposite. By identifying the confession of Peter with Peter himself, and the universal primatial office with the person of its officeholder, the Catholic Church—or so Pole thought—binds the Pope to the most complete obedience to Jesus Christ and his Cross."[10]

During the second session of the Second Vatican Council the decree on ecumenism, *Unitatis Redintegratio*, was composed. It intended not so much to address separated Christians but to heighten awareness among Catholics regarding the urgency of ecumenical efforts. Much like *Lumen Gentium*, it is not apologetically addressed to someone as much as it is an attempt to think through the believing community from her very spiritual foundations as the mystery of the Church. Emphasis is placed on the common ground for all Christians, that is, faith in Jesus Christ as the eternal Son of God and humanity's Savior, scripture, baptism, and in some cases other sacraments, and the numerous gifts of the Holy Spirit that are also operative in non-Catholic Christian denominations. Granting this, Ratzinger does not conclude, however, that the plurality of denominations need merely be organizationally coordinated. To perceive the Church Platonically is incorrect. There is the one Church that is concretized in a plurality of local churches (*Ortsgemeinden*) that do not require rigid absorption into the one church. This has remained a *cantus firmus* throughout Ratzinger's life. Church unity hinges on appropriating Jesus Christ in the Spirit. The Church can be lived only from its Christocentric and pneumatic origins.[11]

Ratzinger resolves the thorny issue of who should count as a member of the Church by suggesting everyone belonging to any Christian denomination should be considered as belonging to the *communio*, though he or she might be outside the *communio*'s unity.[12] The degree of being part of the Eucharistic Christ determines the progress ecumenical efforts can make. This requires an understanding of *who* Jesus Christ is and *what* the Eucharist is. The "Hinduization of Christianity" (à la Albert Görres) and other religions as has been propagated in Western Europe and North America by the New Age movement sidesteps these issues and is not quite honest. With the Eucharist as his background, Ratzinger insists being Church means more than belonging to a loose federation of like-minded people in the manner of the European Union or the British Commonwealth. In the Church, an ontological reality precedes baptism.[13] Ratzinger writes:

> Jesus did not found a Catholic party in a cosmopolitan debating society, but a Catholic Church to which he promised the fullness of truth.... A body which reduces its Catholics to a party within a religious parliament can hardly deserve to be called a branch of the Catholic Church,

but a national religion, dominated by and structured on the principles of liberal tolerance, in which the authority of revelation is subordinate to democracy and private opinion.[14]

As it is true that all salvation comes from Jesus Christ, and the Church is inseparably linked to him, the Church is a participant in Christ's universal mediation of salvation. She is the universal sacrament of salvation. This truth cannot be jeopardized in ecumenical dialogue. The principle of nondisponibility (which claims thatone cannot define or "make" church on one's own,and that the church is God's own foundation and property) must be adhered to. Prayer and penance must be integral to this process, as it is primarily a spiritual work achieved by the Holy Spirit and grounded in Jesus' prayer for the unity of his Church. Rather, this truth must be shared. As all Christians share in the sacrament of baptism, Ratzinger argues that Catholics are called upon to recognize in fellow Christians brothers and sisters in Christ. When the historic "Joint Declaration on the Doctrine of Justification" (1999) between the Roman Catholic Church and the Lutheran World Federation hit an impasse during its creation, it was Ratzinger "who untied the knots. Without him we might not have an agreement," admitted Bishop George Anderson, who at that time was head of the Evangelical Lutheran Church of America.[15]

As evidenced, Ratzinger's perspective on ecumenical dialogue is thoroughly Christological. In principle, he divines two fundamental types of Church schisms in Christendom and accordingly two types of Church unity/reunification. "We encounter the first type in the divisions in the ancient Church between Chalcedonian (dyophysite) and non-Chalcedonian (monophysite) churches; it is also typical of the split between East and West, although ecclesial differences of the hitherto unknown radicality played a role there. We encounter the second type in the divisions that have been formed in the wake of the reform movements of the sixteenth century."[16] The first case deals with a separation retaining some form of structural unity, while in the second case profound structural differences become apparent. Ratzinger delineated these distinctions in a paper he gave in 1976 in Graz, Austria, which was reprinted in 1982 in its entirety in his book *Principles of Catholic Theology*.

Ecumenism with the East

Once the necessary Christological reconsiderations and spiritual preparations were made in ecumenical dialogue, Ratzinger suggested the following revolutionary approach:

> Rome must not require more from the East with respect to the doctrine of primacy than had been formulated and was lived in the first millennium....Reunion could take place in this context if, on the one hand, the East would cease to oppose as heretical the developments that took place in the West in the second millennium and would accept

the Catholic Church as legitimate and orthodox in the form she had acquired in the course of that development, while, on the other hand, the West would recognize the Church of the East as orthodox and legitimate in the form she has always had.[17]

On the other hand, the East should not declare the developments of the West in the second millennium heretical. In his estimation Church unity with the East is theologically possible now, but spiritually it is not sufficiently prepared and therefore practically the circumstances have not yet matured.[18]

In his estimation, neither the separation into Chalcedonian and non-Chalcedonian churches after 451 nor the Great Schism of 1054 between Rome and Constantinople caused the destruction of faith or thorough ruptures in ecclesial structures. In his judgment, these were preserved due to the adherence of all these communities to the ecclesial structures as expressed and manifested during the Council of Nicaea in 325. He expresses this fact in the following words: "[i]t means unity not only with regard to a particular point but unity in the way in which the Church was formed from the word of Jesus and of the apostles, in the way in which Christianity was historically formed."[19] The retention of these structures guarantees ecclesial unity in spite of material differences. Ratzinger argues in favor of a coincidence of apostolic succession in both form and content by virtue of the sacramental ordination, and he therefore argues in favor of affirming a preserved apostolic tradition.

One crucial ecumenical issue is whether or not the plurality of bishops endangers the Church's unity. How must the Church be constituted so that its apostolicity cannot jeopardize its unity? Setting aside the gravity of the issues surrounding the question of the *filioque* (according to the Western tradition the Holy Spirit proceeds from both the Father and the Son) and the issue of papal primacy, the issue of unity and plurality is to this day the most relevant question for Orthodox Christians when dealing with Catholicism. Placing increasing emphasis on the synodal way, Orthodox ecclesiology surprisingly evolved into a model that is rather close to the Protestant consistorial model. "For, from the Orthodox point of view, at least according to one interpretation, the *monarchia papae* (papal primacy) means a destruction of the ecclesial structure as such, in consequence of which something different and new replaces the primitive Christian form."[20] Insisting that the Great Schism did not destroy the structure of ecclesial unity, Ratzinger stresses the West did not in a one-sided way subscribe to a legalistic understanding of apostolic succession and the sacramental nature of the Church; rather, it bears out the Christlike incarnational nature of the Church as the continued incarnation of Jesus Christ in the world. In his view, one cannot separate the sacramental and juridical forms of the Church. Yet, one must distinguish between the two. Judicial structures are based upon and justified only in virtue of the Church's sacramentality. This is a seemingly circular argument: the Church cannot exist without the Eucharist; yet, the Eucharist cannot come about without the Church. This dilemma is resolved by apprehending Jesus Christ, the root sacrament, as the foundational reality for both the Church as primordial sacrament and the Eucharist as Jesus Christ's real presence.

This approach permits Ratzinger to compare the strengths and weaknesses of the Orthodox and Roman Catholic models. Assumed contradictions to ecclesial unity are then uncovered as supposed alternatives. It is a misunderstanding to presume the teaching on papal infallibility and universal papal jurisdiction would elevate the papacy above the Church's sacramental order. Yet more erroneous is the assumption that the papal office could alter law or teaching at a whim. Only within the framework of episcopal collegiality, grounded in the local churches, can the Petrine ministry function properly. As Orthodoxy has not sufficiently developed distinctions between sacramental and legal structures, this Church has traditionally been less able to react theologically to heresies.

Ultimately, the distinction between *oikonomia* (merciful adjudication) and *acribeia* (the rigid upholding of principles) proves insufficient. In order to achieve ecumenical progress, some differentiations between the sacramental and legal ecclesial forms (the validity and liceity of sacraments) must be agreed upon. However, this may not lead to a real separation of the two:

> A closer approach to and awareness of one another can hardly ignore this fundamental unity, which, in the whole course of dispute, has never been impugned. The West may point to the absence of the office of Peter in the East—it must, nevertheless, admit that, in the Eastern Church, the form and content of the Church of the Fathers is present in unbroken continuity. The East may criticize the existence and function of the office of Peter in the West, but it must also be aware that, because of it, no other Church exists in Rome than that of the first millennium—of the time when a common Eucharist was celebrated and when but one Church existed.[21]

Ratzinger admits there is no denying that differences do indeed exist. They do not, however, go to the core of being Church. These differences never define principles. Ratzinger is intent on discussing such issues in an irenic tenor.

In 1967, the Ecumenical Patriarch Athenagoras I welcomed Pope Paul VI to the Phanar—the ecumenical patriarch's seat in Istanbul, Turkey—as successor of Peter, as the first in honor among us and as "president in charity." Ratzinger detects in these words the recognition that both sides have never lost being Orthodox and Catholic. As stated earlier, during an ecumenical gathering in Graz, Austria, in 1976, Ratzinger famously proposed that the Orthodox need not accept more in matters of primatial authority than had already been praxis in the first millennium. "Rome must not require more from the East with respect to the doctrine of primacy than had been formulated and was lived in the first millennium."[22] Both sides accede to the principle insight that the Church is formed by the will, the Word, and the deeds of Jesus Christ and continues through the mission of the apostles and their successors commissioned by the Lord. While not following the West in its definition of the Petrine office—especially that of the primacy of jurisdiction—both sides agree that both entities are the one and same Church as in the time of the Church fathers during the first millennium. The West should not expect a full recognition of papal jurisdiction. It should acknowledge the existing forms in the East as orthodox and juridically legitimate. However, neither should the East expect a redefinition, let alone the elimination, of the *filioque* or papal infallibility (and following from papal infallibility, the Marian dogmas of 1854 and 1950) from the obligatory magisterial canon. The East should not consider the last thousand years of the West as heretical, but as legitimate. The will and truth of Jesus should be beheld by all parties. Spiritual greatness, humility, a spirit of genuine brotherhood, and restraint in trying to pinpoint the causes and motivations for the historic separation are called for. Both sides essentially and solemnly affirmed this in Istanbul during Pope Benedict's visit to Patriarch Bartholomew in 2006.[23]

Ratzinger does not consider maximal claims helpful in finding the sought-after unity. The one thousand years held in common are the indispensable foundation for unity between the two sister Churches. He does not advocate the fusion of different concepts but uncovering elements that unite the two realities jointly in being Church.

His principle is that it is not ecclesial unity that needs to be justified but rather the separation of Churches that needs to be justified. Consequently, both sides are to refrain from stating maximum demands:

> On the part of the West, the maximum demand would be that the East recognize the primacy of the bishop of Rome in the full scope of the definition of 1870 and in so doing submit in practice, to a primacy such as had been accepted by the Uniate churches. On the part of the East, the maximum demand would be that the West declare the 1870 doctrine of primacy erroneous and in so doing submit, in practice, to a primacy such as had been accepted with the removal of the *Filioque* from the Creed and including the Marian dogmas of the nineteenth and twentieth centuries.[24]

Ecumenism with the West

Ratzinger developed something similar and yet qualitatively different regarding Protestantism:

> As regards Protestantism, the maximum demand of the Catholic Church would be that the Protestant ecclesiological ministries be regarded as totally invalid and that Protestants be converted to Catholicism; the maximum demand of Protestants, on the other hand, would be that the Catholic Church accept, along with the unconditional acknowledgement of all Protestant ministries, the Protestant concept of ministry and their understanding of the Church and thus, in practice, renounce the apostolic and sacramental structure of the Church, which would mean, in practice, the conversion of Catholics to Protestantism and their acceptance of a multiplicity of distinct community structures as the historical form of the Church. While the first three maximum demands are today rather unanimously rejected by Christian consciousness, the

fourth [indifference to revealed truth] exercises a kind of fascination for it—as it were, a certain conclusiveness that makes it appear to be the real solution to the problem.[25]

While the rejection of maximum demands both vis-à-vis Protestants and the Orthodox Church seem to run parallel, upon closer scrutiny a significant asymmetry appears. By rejecting the Protestant maximum demands, Catholics simultaneously implicitly reject the prevailing zeitgeist. In Ratzinger's understanding, the current zeitgeist and the main Protestant demands converge in the model of "reconciled differentness" (that is, in German, "*versöhnte Verschiedenheit*"). As Protestantism is indebted to the sixteenth century as its formative age, it is heavily influenced by a historically and systematically untenable reception of Augustine. This is manifested in a definition of the Church that confounds a search for commonality. "The concept of the Church was limited, on the one hand, to the local community; on the other hand, it embraced the community of the faithful throughout the ages who are known only to God. But the community of the whole Church as such is no longer the bearer of a positively meaningful content."[26] Ecclesial unity is deprived of its only foundation. In his estimation, the model of Church unity as sought by Protestant denominations is quite the opposite of what it purports to be. It is too much a blend of zeitgeist-conditioned models and too little expresses the mind of Christ. In fact such a model only results in the total renunciation of ecclesial unity and connatural with this—and more importantly—unity with Jesus. Ratzinger concludes that, "No real union would result from this, but that its very impossibility would become a single common dogma."[27] The particular reading of Augustine as differentiating strictly between a visible and spiritual Church results in Protestantism being something that no longer merits being called Church at all. This explains the basic asymmetry between Catholic, Oriental, and Orthodox *sister churches* (that is, celebrating all seven sacraments validly and standing in apostolic succession), on the one hand, and the Protestant *ecclesial communities* or *denominations* (having valid baptisms) on the other:

> Ecclesial organization is now borrowed from the political realm because it does not otherwise exist as a spiritually significant entity. Thus there does, it is true, exist an important community of belief with the ancient Church wherever the creedal texts are taken seriously, but its ecclesial anchor and, therefore, the binding authority that sustains its agreement or disagreements remains unclear although, in the ecclesiological development of the Protestant community, much has been restored as a matter of actual necessity that has in principle lost its raison d'être.[28]

Ratzinger does readily acknowledge the Augsburg Confession was written with the sincere intent of living evangelical Catholicity. As this document, however, is open to a variety of interpretations it would behoove the churches of the Reformation to spell out that the Augsburg Confession is to be read in line with and in the tradition of the early church's dogmas, thereby embedding it in the same ecclesial structure.[29] He questions what dogmatic value the Augsburg Confession has for Protestants. Is it just as significant as the Schmalcaldic Articles (statement of Lutheran faith, authored by Martin Luther in 1537)? This issue must be resolved by Protestant (Lutheran) theology first. Only thereupon can the Catholic Church consider recognizing the Augsburg Confession.[30] This notwithstanding, Ratzinger also values Protestantism's liberality, piety, and high spiritual claims.

On this occasion, Ratzinger only implies that to such an ecclesial structure both the episcopal *successio apostolica* and the Church as *Corpus Christi* belong. Both allow the Church to celebrate validly the Eucharist and to be the *Corpus Christi* renewed, as de Lubac famously rediscovered for modern Christianity in his seminal study *Corpus Mysticum*. These elements determine the Church as original and having a continuous self-identity. The Church as a Christological category has been altogether lost in the Protestant denominations after the Reformation but has been retained even after 1054 in Orthodoxy and the Catholic Church. In this context, it does not suffice if Lutherans concede that bishops standing in the apostolic succession belong to the *bene esse* (wellbeing) of Christendom. Apostolic succession must be acknowledged as ecclesiologically indispensable and thus professed.[31]

As early on as Ratzinger's appraisal of the first session of the Second Vatican Council, one detects a sobering caution regarding ecumenical enthusiasm. He welcomes the variety of gifts and charismas expressed in the Vatican II Council. However, he warns against assuming that the council itself can achieve ecumenical unity, however much this had been a heartfelt concern of the council fathers. Christian unity requires patient everyday labor sustained by trust in the Holy Spirit.[32] Unity is the result of spiritually living Christ's charity, not of an administrative approach.

CHAPTER 19

An Ecclesiological Dispute at the Turn of the Millennium

It is Ratzinger's claim that the universal Church (*ecclesia universalis*) is in its essence a mystery: it is a reality that takes precedence, both ontologically and temporally, over the individual local churches. Ratzinger describes the dispute between his thought and Walter Kasper's in the following terms: "The thesis of the ontological and temporal priority of the universal Church to the individual churches was now treated as a question 'not of church doctrine but of theological opinions and of the various related philosophies.' The statement by the Congregation for the Doctrine of the Faith was categorized as my personal theology and tied with my 'Platonism,' while Kasper traced his own view back to his more Aristotelian (Thomistic) approach."[1] But if one considers that the Church celebrates and lives the one body of Christ, the question is not one of choosing the appropriate philosophy, such as Platonism or Aristotelianism. Rather, the question becomes one of either ascribing a real, ontological valence to the Eucharist or of assuming something like a multitude of "bodies of Christ" existing within a loose federation or confederation of churches. Ratzinger summarizes this misunderstanding in his observation:

> Cardinal Kasper, invoking [the Catholic New Testament exegete] J. Gnilka observes that "in Paul the local community is the focus." But in [the Protestant exegete] Rudolf Bultmann we can read the exact opposite. According to Bultmann: "The church's organization grew primarily out of the awareness that the community as a whole takes precedence over the individual communities. A symptom of this is that the word *ekklesia* (church) is used to refer, in the first instance, by no means to the individual community but to the 'people of God.'...The notion of the priority of the church as a whole over the individual community is further seen in the equation of the *ekklesia* with the *soma Christou* (body of Christ), which embraces all believers.
>
> This conflict between Gnilka and Bultmann shows, first of all, the relativity of exegetical judgments. But for that very reason it is especially instructive in our case, because Bultmann, who vigorously defended the

thesis of the precedence of the universal church over the local church, could certainly never be accused of Platonism or of a bias in favor of bringing back Roman centralism. Perhaps it was simply because he stood outside these controversies that he was able to read and expound the texts with a more open mind."[2]

In his commentaries on the documents of the Second Vatican Council, Ratzinger enthusiastically welcomed the national bishops' conferences' responsibility in liturgical matters and acknowledged they had a certain authority of their own. He maintains that for the sake of the Church's vivacity, a certain degree of tension between the papacy and episcopacy is healthy. In communion with the bishop of Rome, the community of bishops as apostolic community enjoys full and highest authority in the Church.[3] However, later on, in reflecting on the heady two decades since the last council, Ratzinger would come to revise his opinion. He would also reflect upon the weakness of the collective body of German bishops in confronting Nazi ideology. (Some individual bishops and especially the pope did issue forceful statements condemning fascism.) In *The Ratzinger Report*, he argues that national bishops' conferences possess "no theological basis, they do not belong to the structure of the Church as willed by Christ...they only have a practical, concrete function.... 'The collective...does not substitute for the persons of the bishops.' No episcopal conference, as such, has a teaching mission; its documents have no weight of their own save that of the consent given to them by the individual bishops."[4] This issue was aggravated by a then common distortion of the Church as a sociological phenomenon. The notion "People of God" was considered an egalitarian category, leading the national bishops' conferences to be considered a type of parliamentarian agent. The result was that the universal Church was regarded as nothing more than the union of a multitude of episcopal conferences. In an article for *L'Osservatore Romano* in 2001, as prefect he wrote that baptism is a spiritual reality grounded in the Blessed Trinity and is not the social product of a local parish or particular nation. Likewise, the Eucharist is also not the product of a particular situation. Both sacraments are universal in scope and nature. In consequence, the Church "is not a local community that grows gradually [into a larger entity] but the leaven that is always destined to permeate the whole and, consequently, embodies universality from the first instant."[5] The church is first and foremost a spiritual, Christ-centered reality originating in the Godhead. As such, it defies a sociological description. This stance is not original to Ratzinger's thought but can be traced back to early Christianity. At the time of Ratzinger's seminary training, patristic insights on this theme were nicely summarized by the great Jesuit theologians Hugo Rahner in *The Church: Readings in Theology*[6] and de Lubac in *The Motherhood of the Church*: "The particular Church is always universalist and centripetal."[7] To fully understand this reality, one has to consider that the Church is nothing like, for example, the French state with a central government in Paris and a great number of departments or provinces. Rather, each particular Church is fully the Church and shares in Christ's magnanimity on the cross. Thus, the orientation toward Rome is both Christocentric and Petrine without yielding to an erroneous interpretation that refers to a parliamentarian or synodal model. The whole Catholic Church is already present in the twelve disciples. They are apostles not of a particular Church but of the whole. This notion of catholicity is found early on in the writings of Ignatius of Antioch, the Shepherd of Hermas, and Clement of Rome. The Catholic Church is not the product of numerous local churches but rather is their mother.

Sometimes one hears the term "ecclesiology of communities," implying a plurality of church communities or a federation of churches within the one Catholic Church. The term "communion" is at times even interpreted as presupposing a network of multiple ecclesial communities. The result is the perception that a multitude of forms of worship, doctrine, and discipline is foundational. Ratzinger points to scripture to resolve this virulent issue: "The chalice of blessing which we bless, is it not a participation in the blood of Christ? The bread which we break, is it not a participation in the body of Christ? Because there is but one bread, we who are many are one body, for we all partake of the one bread" (1 Cor 10:16ff). Ratzinger subscribes to a Eucharistic ecclesiology. The multitudes are transformed into the one Christ. Consonant with Henri de Lubac's thought in his book *Catholicism*, Ratzinger perceives the Church as a "universal social union."

Ratzinger's argument in favor of the ontological—not temporal—priority of the universal Church is grounded in four factors: (1) early on, the Church fathers were convinced of the underlying identity between ancient Israel and the Church; (2) as the body of Christ, the Church is Jesus Christ's enduring in the present; (3) for Paul and for the Jewish tradition, ancient Israel and the Church are the anticipation of the heavenly Jerusalem; and (4) around Mary the community is renewed. In early Christianity the priority of the universal Church was the objective case, notwithstanding the Lucan suggestion that several communities existed in the original community of Jerusalem. As it is intended to be brought to all cultures and peoples, the "People of God" is "not a local community that grows gradually but the leaven that is always destined to permeate the whole and, consequently, embodies universality from the first instant."[8] He argues against the ecclesiology in the form of congregationalism that was developed by the Russian émigré theologian Nicholas Afanasiev (1893–1966) in his book *The Lord's Supper*.[9] In his positions, Ratzinger is on firm footing with Vatican II: "In these communities, though they may often be small and poor, or existing in the diaspora, Christ is present through whose power and influence the One, Holy, Catholic and Apostolic Church is constituted" (*LG* 26). Or, as Ratzinger formulates it: "I can have the one Lord only in the unity that he himself is: In unity with the others who are also his body and who in the Eucharist must always become it anew."[10]

In contrast, the Reformer Martin Luther rendered the Greek term *ekklesia*, used in the New Testament to describe the "Church," into the German word for parish assembly: *Gemeinde*. This translation has indelibly formed and characterized all Protestant ecclesiologies to this very day. Luther almost completely eliminated the word "Church" from scripture. *Gemeinde*, or *congregatio* in Latin, means in Luther's usage the group of people gathered around word and sacrament. This understanding famously manifested itself in creedal form in the seventh article of the *Confessio Augustana*: *"congregatio sanctorum, in qua evangelium pure docetur et recte adminstrantur sacramenta."*[11] By choosing the Latin word *"congregatio"* instead of the Latin *"ecclesia,"* Luther favored interpreting "the faithful" in terms of "the (visibly) assembled" who receive instruction in the gospel and the sacraments. This sixteenth-century view poses the modern challenge par excellence for Catholic ecclesiology and ecumenical dialogue.

In Catholic theology, the definition of the church receives more specific contours: it is the *"ecclesia particularis, localis et universalis"* ("the particular, local, and universal Church) gathered around a bishop in a diocese. This was reaffirmed by the Second Vatican Council (*LG* 26; *SC* 42). It is not primarily the particular geographic gathering of a parish somewhere, but a territorially precisely circumscribed, permanent reality, localized within the greater horizon of the universal Church. It belongs to the very nature of every parochial, liturgical assembly to be part of the universal Church. By its very nature it is an institution grounded in the episcopal office. This dimension belongs inalienably to the Lord's community gathered to celebrate the Eucharist:

> Where the Eucharist is present—that is, in whatever place; in the congregation celebrating the Eucharist in one place—there the whole Lord and thus the whole Church are present with the whole mystery of the sacrament. A congregation celebrating the Eucharist needs nothing more. It has the whole Lord; in the sacrament, it thus has also the whole Church and *is* the whole Church. The Church is wholly present in the Eucharistic assembly, that is, in every local assembly; to this, the "universal Church" can add nothing more, for there *is* nothing "more" than the Eucharistic assembly. For such a view, the unity of the universal Church is a pleromatic enhancement but not a complement, not an augmentation of ecclesiality.[12]

In Ratzinger's Christocentric ecclesiology these are interdependent, reciprocally conditioning, and enabling elements. The Eucharistic community is, by standing in the *successio apostolica*, fully Church. "[I]t means that no group can constitute itself as church, but *becomes* a church only by being received as such by the universal Church. It means, too, that the Church cannot organize herself according to her own design but can become herself again and again only by the gift of the Holy Spirit requested in the name of Jesus Christ, that is, through the sacrament."[13] Thus, according to Ratzinger, due to the lack, prior to the sixteenth century, of a sufficient verbalization of the Eucharistic foundations of ecclesial life, Reformation ecclesiologies were (and are still today) unable to appreciate the universal Church as a spiritual entity worthy of being preserved. The provincial organization of the Church under a political lordship—as established in Protestant Germany until the demise of the Second Reich in 1918—is consonant with such a theology. The concrete ecclesial reality is favored vis-à-vis a more abstract and spiritual one.

In contrast, Ratzinger argues that the one body becoming an ever anew reality in a particular parish is the very same that becomes present everywhere.

This reality of being one in Christ does not occur in various locations independently from one another but only inasmuch as it traces itself back to the same origins and shares in the same Church-constituting elements. The Eucharistic particular reality is possible due to a preceding, a priori reality. As Ratzinger correctly points out, this is not disputed by the major Orthodox or Protestant denominations. However, it is complicated for Protestants due to Ratzinger's—and the Catholic Church's—claim that it is rooted also in the indispensable charism of apostolic succession. The Eucharist is bound to the bearer of apostolic succession. The parish's self-transcending toward the universal Church is nothing short of an expression of its oneness with the Lord. The desire for unity with Christ becomes a defining moment in being Church. Thus, the inner cause for the parochial or local church's participation in the universal Church is not a juridical or administrative consideration but a Eucharistic and, therefore, Christological one.[14] This comes about because of the one, eternal Holy Spirit effecting transubstantiation in the concrete and particular liturgical gatherings.[15] For this Christological and pneumatological reason, one is compelled as either an Eastern Christian and/or as a Catholic to assume the episcopal/apostolic nature as cogiven with every Eucharist and every particular gathering.

The local bishop vouches for the essence of the Eucharist as "*sacramentum unitatis*," celebrated at a particular location and time, as a sacrament of unity. One might ponder here in what way the individual participants and recipients of communion likewise contribute to the Eucharist as a sacrament of unity. Significantly, the bishop is not this unity but serves it. It is the one Lord who is this unity. The bishop serves the unity of the many and allows them in their diversity to be one in the Lord. Ratzinger readily admits that a one-sided legalistic understanding of the bishop's office in the past was a counterproductive disservice to the Church. In fact, even a bifurcation between the sacramental definition of the episcopal office during the liturgy and its jurisdictional function occurred in the past: "The separation of office as jurisdiction from office as rite was continued for reasons of prestige and financial benefits; the isolation of the Mass, its separation from the unity of the *memoria* and, therefore, its privatization were products of the amalgamation of Masses and stipends."[16] Ultimately, a separation between liturgy and office developed. Luther's protest against this must be considered well founded. However, by placing the apostolic ministry of the episcopacy at disposition, Luther jeopardized both the theological category of apostolic succession and the Catholicity and unity of the Church. For an episcopally formed reality, this principle of unity implies it must be oriented toward the totality of the mystical body of Christ and live from it in order to be and remain Church.

The *cardo* for all ecclesiology is the Eucharist, the presence of the victim and victor over death and sin, in the forms of bread and wine. The Church does not merely celebrate this extrinsically. She is actually essentially grounded in the Eucharist. It is the song of her being, the constant actualization of the covenant with God. In this regard, in 1987 Ratzinger highlighted the Eucharistic ecclesiology of the Russian Orthodox theologian Nicholas Afanasiev. Teaching at St. Sergius in Paris, this influential émigré priest-theologian held that because the Eucharist is of local relevance and the full Christ is present in every Eucharist, the universal Church cannot add anything ontologically to the local church.[17] Ratzinger understands Afanasiev as arguing effectively in favor of Protestant congregationalism. On the critical point regarding the universal Church, Ratzinger is in full agreement with the Greek Orthodox Bishop John Zizioulas. Ratzinger argues that as the Lord's body is one, Christians become one Eucharist celebrating body and Church again.[18] Every local church must existentially enter into a "structure of reception" with other local churches, lest it suffer ecclesial extinction. Thus, he amplifies *Lumen Gentium* 26: "The bishop, invested with the fullness of the sacrament of Orders is 'steward of the grace of the supreme priesthood,' above all in the Eucharist, which he himself offers, or ensures that it is offered, from which the Church ever derives its life and on which it thrives. This Church of Christ is really present in all legitimately organized local groups of the faithful, which, in so far as they are united to their pastors, are also quite appropriately called Churches in the New Testament." In all probability, this passage was drafted with full cognizance of Afanasiev's dissenting position.

Also of crucial importance in this context is the formula of the Second Vatican Council regarding the Church of Jesus Christ subsisting in the Catholic Church, led by the successor of Peter and the bishops in communion with him. "This Church, constituted and organized as a society in the present world, subsists in the Catholic Church, which is governed by the successor of Peter and by the bishops in communion with him" (*LG* 8). It is difficult to convey the subtle meaning of the Latin *subsistit* formula in English. It is the attendant feature of the Eucharistic community. The Jesuit *peritus* Sebastian Tromp (1889–1975) changed "*est in*" into "*subsistit in*" in order to reinforce the understanding of the unique character of the Roman Catholic Church as being, in her fullness, like no other Christian denomination. He held that in the full sense of the word "Church," there is an "exclusive" predication for the Catholic faithful; thus, "*subsistit in*" conveys the sense in which the Catholic Church has maintained, consistently throughout history, that which is unique to her. Or, as the Belgian theologian Gérard Philips (1898–1972) wrote, "...there [that is, in the Catholic Church] we find the Church of Christ in all its fullness and vigour...."[19] "No translation can fully capture the sublime nuance of the Latin text in which the unconditional equation of the first conciliar drafts—the full identity between the Church of Jesus Christ and the Roman Catholic Church—is clearly set forth: nothing of the concreteness of the conciliar concept of the Church is lost—the Church is there present where the successors of the Apostle Peter and of the other apostles visibly incorporate her continuity with her source." Yet, Ratzinger is careful to add, "This full concreteness of the Church does not mean that every other Church can only be a non-Church."[20] In this document, the full identity of the Church of Jesus Christ and the Roman Catholic Church and her continuity with the apostles is stressed in a way that is both theologically honest (that is, correct) and charitable to non-Catholic Christians. Therefore, no one may interpret the episcopal (or papal) office as an isolated, self-reliant entity. As a priest is not a presbyter on his own but by virtue of incorporation, that is, by way of ordination through an ordinary into the presbytery of his respective bishop, so likewise a bishop is not one in isolation, but derives his authority ontologically by being a member of the college of bishops. This unity of the college of bishops is expressed in their unity with the bishop of Rome. Outside such a unity, the theoretical legitimacy of an episcopal ordination into apostolic succession would be pointless. The imposition of hands occurs within the Church. Thus, no matter how "High Church" an episcopal ordination may be, it is rendered meaningless without being ordered toward this full ecclesial communion. Lacking full communion, such an ordination reduces the episcopal office to a liturgical and juridical formalism. Ratzinger divines in such a praxis something akin to a solipsistic, long passé, "*ex opere operato*" ("on the sole basis of the act performed") type of thinking at work. The imposition of hands and calling down of the Holy Spirit are not private actions, separate and distinct from the Church. Rather, they are expressions of the following elements: the ordinand, the ordained, and the present assembly living in conscious continuity with the Gospel of Christ and living in a Spirit-sustained tradition and, therefore, living in community with all the bishops.[21]

In the Catholic Church, Ratzinger—along with the Second Vatican Council in *Lumen Gentium* 8—sees the *notae ecclesiae* (features defining what is the nature Church: one, holy, Catholic, and apostolic) as expressed in the creed, realized: one, holy, Catholic, and apostolic (*una, sancta, catholica et apostolica*). This Church is led by the bishop of Rome and the rest of the bishops in communion with him. According to *Lumen Gentium* 23 (cf. LG 26; CD [Christus Dominus] 11), the one and unique Catholic Church is (*existit*) in and from individual local churches, presided over by individual bishops in communion with the college of bishops and the bishop of Rome. *Lumen Gentium* 26 adds that in all legitimate local communities (*in omnibus legitimis fidelium congregationibus localibus*) in which the unique Church of Jesus Christ subsists, the one and unique Catholic Church is truly present (*vere adest*). Thus, these local churches may predicate themselves as Church.

It is proper to every such Church to be related to the universal Church. In other words, the *ecclesia Catholica* is a *communio ecclesiarum* not in the sense of a simple summation of the individual churches collected into one whole. Nor is the universal Church a Platonic idea, floating on a lofty cloud set apart from, and unrelated to, the particular churches. The universal dimension belongs constitutively to every local church. Thus, conversely, the papal ministry cannot be conceived of apart from the college of bishops but only in collegial communion with it. All individual ecclesial elements and the whole ecclesial body are defined in the singular as "*communio.*"

Such an understanding seems to have been contradicted by the document the Congregation for the Doctrine of the Faith issued in 1992, *On Some Aspects of the Church Understood as Communion.*[22] It advances the thesis that the universal Church ontologically and temporally precedes the particular church.[23] It nonetheless does insist on the reciprocal interiority of the universal Church and particular Church, thus excluding that both might have their origins in something else. It affirms the priority of the universal Church. The particular Churches relate to the universal Church as daughters to their mother. By way of mediation, the particular Churches emerged faithful to the divine intention after Pentecost. To claim the ontological priority of the particular churches over and against the universal Church misinterprets the council.[24] Every bishop, as a bishop, is a member of the college of bishops and therefore not a monad. Directing a local church is only possible for bishops insofar as they serve the *communio* of the universal Church. The synod of bishops is not an executive or collegial organ but is merely advisory to the pope.[25]

This thesis was challenged even within Catholicism. In a *Festschrift** for the former bishop of Hildesheim, Josef Homeyer, Walter Kasper does not oppose the theory that the one Church exists in and from the particular churches. Nor does he object to the theory that the many particular churches exist from and of the universal Church. On this point, both Kasper and Ratzinger are much indebted to the organic ecclesiology developed by the Tübingen School of Theology. Johann Adam Möhler in particular had developed this. Kasper writes concerning his ecclesiology in succinct words: "According to Möhler's famous observation on the Church: 'neither can one [person] intend being all; only all can intend being all, and the unity of all [can] only [be] a whole.'"[26] Kasper merely critiques the temporal and ontological originality of the universal Church. According to divine will, in his understanding, the two are indissolubly united and brought forth simultaneously by the divine Spirit of Jesus Christ. Luke portrays both coming forth at Pentecost in the community of Jerusalem: "universal Church and local Church in one."[27] In Kasper's understanding, from the very beginning in Jerusalem there may have existed a plurality of communities. He assumes their co-originality and simultaneity. Therefore, he advocates supplementing the thesis "*Ecclesiae in et ex Ecclesia*" (churches in and from the Church) with the formula "*Ecclesia in et ex Ecclesiis*" (the Church in and from the churches) in order to emphasize the inner orientation of the first statement. He considers the first thesis not merely incomplete but even prone to misunderstanding. Ratzinger would concede that were one to identify unwittingly the universal Church exclusively with the archdiocese of Rome, the pope, and the curia, such a thesis in isolation, that is, without being supplemented as suggested previously, would contribute to the theological restoration of Roman centralism.[28]

In the feature section of the German daily *Frankfurter Allgemeine Zeitung* dated December 22, 2000, Ratzinger riposted with a lengthy article titled, "God's Big Idea of a 'Church' is Not a Fanciful Conjecture."[29] Therein he defends the notion of the ontological and temporal primacy of the universal Church. He affirms that one must speak of the Church manifesting itself in Pentecost as a universal reality prior to any particular church. In the Lucan narrative, the Church is born of the Holy Spirit. Ratzinger considers this a testimony to the temporal primacy of the universal Church able to speak in all languages. This historic perspective is supplemented by an ontological one. It is grounded in the preexisting mystery of the total Church chosen by God in Jesus Christ from eternity to reconcile and redeem humankind and the

---

*A collection of essays celebrating the academic achievements of a person.

world. This is the case no matter how the concrete church with her particular features and manifestations may have come about. While in Ratzinger's estimation Luke does convey the temporal primacy of the universal Church, it is in his judgment yet more significant to bear in mind that "the Church is born of the Twelve, in the Spirit, from the very beginning for all peoples and thus, from the very first moment, is oriented towards expression in all cultures and therefore to being the People of God: It is not a particular parish expanding slowly, but is leaven ordered to the whole and thereby contains universality from the very first moment"[30] At first, it was difficult for Ratzinger to comprehend the critique some raised against his position. Only now, under the false assumption of an identification of the universal Church with the Roman pontiff and curia does he appreciate the motivation behind such reservations. In no uncertain terms, the Congregation for the Doctrine of the Faith rejects such a simple identification. As primordial sacrament the Church does not define, let alone produce, itself. In its essence it is both sacramental and evangelical. Both sacrament and gospel are not self-fabricated but originate in Jesus Christ and are oriented toward him. It is its essential property never to be a hermetically closed, self-contained reality. In light of this background, it becomes evident that the universal Church's primacy is not congruent with the Roman primacy. Rather, the universal Church becomes the indispensable condition for the possibility of the Petrine ministry.

This insight allowed controversial positions to meet. It became evident that the statement concerning the ontological and temporal precedence of the universal Church does not entail an ontological and temporal precedence of the Roman Church vis-à-vis the local churches. Kasper is quite unequivocal about not arguing in favor of the "sociological reduction of the Church to individual parishes." By no means is he of the opinion that only individual parishes exist as "empirical realities."[31] In keeping with the Second Vatican Council, Kasper reminds the reader that the local church is not a mere department of the universal Church, nor is the local bishop merely a papal delegate. Consonant with the relevant ecclesiologies of the first patristic millennium, he emphasizes that neither a one-sided emphasis on the local churches nor an insistence on the universal Church is historically tenable.[32] This in turn is in harmony with the historic "Ratzinger-formula" the then theologian Ratzinger postulated at the Graz ecumenical gathering: as regards the teaching on the Roman primacy, Rome may not require the East to accept more than that which had been formulated in the first millennium.[33]

Thus Kasper acknowledged that he and Ratzinger share the same ecclesiological principles. The common roots can be traced back to the early nineteenth-century Tübingen School of Theology. He was therefore able to subtitle his contribution to the German Jesuit periodical on this issue, "Amicable Debate with the Critique of Joseph Cardinal Ratzinger." After sketching out the common ecclesiological principles, Kasper declares the dispute "a theological school debate." In his judgment, the teaching of the eternal preexistence of the Church is correct as it is grounded in the eternal salvific mystery of God. In fact, it is theologically "unsurrenderable" ("*unaufgebbar*"). However, he continues by asking if the universal Church is preexistent, does this not hold equally true for the local churches? Is not "the concrete Church 'in and of local' Churches" preexisting? Thus in his opinion the thesis of the church's preexistence yields nothing in the form of a supposed primacy of the universal Church. The thesis of the Church's preexistence is just as much an argument for the thesis of the simultaneity of universal and particular churches maintained by him and numerous others.[34]

In 2001, the friendly exchange between the two cardinals was concluded in English in the American Jesuit magazine *America*. Remarkably, Cardinal Ratzinger wrote an article conceding that it might have been better to start off the discussion stating not an ontological but a teleological primacy of the universal Church. As final causality, the universal Church preexists in God's will. Unambiguously he states: "The church of Rome is a local church and not the universal church—a local church with a peculiar, universal responsibility, but still a local church. And the assertion of the inner precedence of God's idea of the one church, the one bride, over all its empirical realizations in particular churches has nothing whatsoever to do with the problem of centralism."[35] Walter Kasper refers to this last statement in a letter to the editor of *America* when conceding that there is indeed an inner precedence of the unity of the Church prior to its essential diversity. For him, the "thesis of the priority of inner unity" is convincing both on philosophical and theological grounds because "unity as a transcendental determination of being makes variety and multiplicity possible to begin with."[36] In conclusion, Kasper affirms his ecclesiological thesis of a co-originality and simultaneity of the universal Church and local churches.

CHAPTER 20

Jesus Christ as the Unifying Ecclesial Reality

Ratzinger approaches issues of interdenominational interest with remarkable openness and freedom. Already in the summer semester of 1960 he organized in Bonn a seminar on "Church, Sacrament and Faith according to the Augsburg Confession." One year later he contributed to the most respected Protestant encyclopedia, *Religion in Geschichte und Gegenwart*.

In an Easter homily Ratzinger quotes a text ascribed to Epiphanius (ca. 315–403) where Jesus Christ says to Adam, "'I am your God, yet I have become your son. I am in you and you are in me. Together we are a single, indivisible person.' Thus it is clear that this Adam does not signify an individual in a dim and distant past: the Adam addressed by the victorious Christ is we ourselves—'I am in you, and you are in me.'"[1] Augustine's sad figure of the *homo incurvatus in se ipsum* (man closed in upon himself) is overcome. The dilemma of modernity where "hell is the other," according to Jean-Paul Sartre's famous play *No Exit*, is canceled out.

The Church as the kingdom of God on earth is the bearer of a saving message. This "*evangelium*, the Gospel, is not just informative speech, but performative speech—not just the imparting of information, but action, efficacious power that enters into the world to save and transform."[2] Thus, the Church is not merely a vessel containing instructions for a fulfilling and meaningful life but, in a very dynamic sense of the word, it is this reality. This is the novelty of the Second Vatican Council. It expresses a deeper understanding of the Church not as a mere library of divine information but as Christ's very own saving gesture in the world. The instructive-theoretical approach of respected theologians such as Joseph Pohle, Artur Landgraf, and Ludwig Ott is overcome. The disjunction between Christ and the Church that the Catholic theologian Alfred Loisy was famously thought to have discovered— "Jesus preached the Kingdom of God, and what came was the Church"—was overcome by the Second Vatican Council.

First and foremost, regarding the kingdom of God Ratzinger agrees with Origen, who called Jesus the *autobasileia*, that is, the kingdom of God is manifest in the person of Jesus. However, there are two additional dimensions,

Ratzinger quickly adds. Apart from the secular realms, "It is located in man's inner being. It grows and radiates outward from that inner space." Finally, he localizes the kingdom of God "more or less in close proximity" to the Church.[3] Disapproving of Adolf von Harnack's individualistic interpretation of Jesus' speech on the kingdom of God, Ratzinger emphasizes, in continuity with Judaism, the corporate nature of faith. The import of Jesus' testimony goes "beyond ethics." It does not suffice to invoke Jesus for the sake of "peace, justice, and the conservation of creation." In this "post-Christian" understanding of religion he sees something "disturbingly close to Jesus' third temptation" appear. He calls to mind the exegetical basis for a proper understanding of the Church. The Hebrew root of the word "kingdom" (*basileia*, in Greek) is *malkut*. It is an action word referring to "the regal function, the active lordship of the king."[4] In this sense, the kingdom of God is something that goes beyond history and yet it is part of the concrete present. "The reality that Jesus names the 'Kingdom of God, lordship of God' is extremely complex, and only by accepting it in its entirety can we gain access to and let ourselves be guided by his message."[5] The Church is open toward a future her members are never able to define. Likewise, the Church is part of the mystery of Jesus. In Jesus, God entered the history of humankind in a new way: in lowliness and hiddenness. Ratzinger quotes the exegete Jeremias stating, "To you [that is, to the circle of disciples] has God given the secret of the Kingdom of God: but to those who are without, everything is obscure, in order that they [as it is written] may 'see and yet not see, may hear and yet not understand, unless they turn and God will forgive them.'"[6] Ratzinger concludes, "When we say the word *our* [of the Our Father], we say Yes to the living Church in which the Lord wanted to gather his new family."[7] This is legitimate to the degree that Christians are Christ's disciples. Being Church and disciple means becoming translucent to God's Word.

Jesus Christ lives his sovereign, sinless holiness, not loftily set apart from the impure and those who despise the Torah, but in communion with the lost and sinners. He thereby attracted the curse of law upon himself and he, the sinless, became sin. God, however, awakened the crucified, and the cross of the resurrected became the tool of divine grace. It is the commission of the Church to attest, in word and sacrament, to God's grace in Jesus Christ for sinful humankind and lost creation in the power of the Holy Spirit. It is precisely the mystery of the Church that in "her paradoxical combination of holiness and unholiness the Church is in fact the shape of grace in this world."[8] In this vein the Church is able to refer to herself in the Second Vatican Council as both holy and sinful. Echoing with his own words the Swiss theologian Hans Urs von Balthasar,[9] Ratzinger observes: "Ultimately one can only acknowledge why one can still love this Church in faith, why one still dares to recognize in the distorted features the countenance of the holy Church."[10]

This insight into the paradoxical nature of grace within the Church has profound ramifications for the apostolic Church. The essential ecclesial attributes that make the Church comprehensible are the remission of sins, reconciliation, contrition, and Eucharistic communion. The content of the unity of the Catholic Church is primarily word and sacrament. The Church is unified in the "communion of the Eucharistic table" through "the one Word and the one bread."[11] The unity of the Church is grounded in and unlocked to the believer in the one Word and the one bread. By the personal integrity and unity of his divine and human being, and by virtue of the eternal communion of the Blessed Trinity, Jesus Christ vouches for the Church's essence as unity. This is the basis for the Church being able to manifest herself as a plural communion in unity.[12]

The constitutive commission of the episcopally constituted Church is to serve the unity of that plural community. This is not the obvious aspect of the Church but is the means by which such unity comes about. Bishops actuate the one unity in the unity of the local churches with the whole Church. The unity of the Church in a particular location and the unity of the multitude of churches reciprocally condition one another. It is the purpose of the existence of the bishops to minister to and enable the unity of the *ecclesia* as a *communio ecclesiarum*. By serving the ministry of the Bishop of Rome, bishops realize unity among the communion of all bishops.

It is certainly not the intention of the Church to place her episcopal constitution in the foreground. Rather, it is a subservient function. It is not a primary element of the Church. Bishops serve ecclesial unity but are not themselves this unity. The essential attributes of the Church are reconciliation, the remission of sins, contrition, and the Eucharist. The meaning of the Church is unlocked by way of these four realities. Therefore, the Roman primacy also serves this unity, which can best be captured in the word "Catholicity," and not vice versa. Consonant with this perspective, one apprehends that Roman Catholicism is a function of the Catholic Church. Inalienably, the papal ministry and episcopal ministries are but two moments of the one ministry belonging to the visible unity of the Church. This entails the following conclusion: the Church is not apprehended well when considered first and foremost as an ecclesial organization. Rather, one apprehends the ecclesial organization well only if first and primarily one bears in mind the nature of the Church as a Christocentric and Eucharistic reality brought about by the one and ever selfsame Holy Spirit.

It is this one reality in Christ that provided the early Church with the basic experience of *symphonia*, that is, a synthesis of unity and multiplicity. Very early on, this insight into the one, complex reality of the Catholic Church was central to the ecclesiologies of Clement of Alexandria (ca. 150–215), Methodius of Olympus (died ca. 311), and Eusebius, bishop of Doryleum (fifth century). The richness of tensions can be maintained while avoiding heresy. Horizontal symphony, that is, between God and man, brings about symphony between God and the faithful, that is, within the Church primarily, and secondarily within the world. Conversely, the believer shares the harmony he or she receives from God with others, thus contributing to the ecclesial symphony. While heretics may be intriguing to study, Ratzinger nonetheless prefers ecclesial theologians:

> When I consider the great theologians, from Möhler to Newman and Scheeben, from Rosmini to Guardini, or in our own epoch, de Lubac, Congar, Balthasar, how much richer and more truly contemporary is

their message than of those for whom the Church's fellowship has ceased to be....pluralism happens not because it is willed, but because each of them, equipped in his own time with his own powers, seeks for nothing other than the truth. Wanting the truth: that involves not making oneself its measure but, instead, welcoming as the voice and highway of truth the immense perspectives that the faith of the Church offers....Only that pluralism is great, which is directed towards unity.[13]

This is the subtle difference between fruitful and ruinous pluralism.

Someone thinking in terms of the categories "conservative/progressive" may ponder whether Pope Benedict XVI will remain faithful to these insights he expounded so well in his *Introduction to Christianity*, written amid the profound cultural crisis engulfing Western society in the 1960s. Yet, these positions were not ones he assumed by chance. They are the result of a careful and thorough reflection on the nature of the Church, as expressed by scripture, the Church fathers (especially Augustine and Bonaventure), the teaching office of the Church and—last but not least—the *sensus fidelium*(the believers' faith). They are in turn consonant with the Church's two-thousand-year-old profession of faith. To apprehend the complexity of the Church—so eloquently affirmed by the Second Vatican Council (*"una complexa realitas"*; "one complex reality which comes together from a human and divine element," *LG* 8)—ultimately means agreeing with the essence of Ratzinger's ecclesiology. It is nothing short of a conscious, theological consecration of the Chalcedonian creed. In retrospective, the greatness of a theologian is closely connected with his ability to spell out, in original words and concepts, the ever selfsame faith of the Church.

Such a premise permits the recognition of holiness in such diverse personalities as Pius IX, John XXIII, and John Paul II. However diverse and fraught with sin individual persons may be, it acknowledges that within this unity one cannot play one pope against another. Nor can one play one council against another, such as, for instance, the First Vatican Council against the Second Vatican Council. By the power of the Holy Spirit, the Church celebrates the one Word and one sacrament in the Eucharist in every age and pontificate. Denying this amounts to ignoring the very essence of the dynamic systematics internal to the Catholic faith.

Only upon such a basis can Christian brotherhood be built, as Optatus and Augustine have demonstrated.[14] Apostolic succession was instituted by Our Lord to further such a brotherhood. This was a historically unheard of challenge as Christianity burst forth from the constraints of a national religion—such as found in Israel, or a political religion as expressed, for example, by belief in the Roman deities—and acknowledged a universal redeemer-God calling his believers to form a universal, non-national community as the new people of God. As Ratzinger notes, in the Old Testament God was perceived as sovereign, which prepared the way to alter this unique, national relationship.[15] In fact, Hellenistic Judaism assumed Yahweh had offered the Torah to all the peoples but that only the people of Israel had accepted it. The election of the Hebrews does not eliminate the possibility of *goyim* (that is, the gentiles) joining the covenant, as the Old Testament anthropology sees all people as descendents of Adam. Having a common creator, all human beings are brothers and sisters.

If this is the basis for universal brotherhood, then it intrigues Ratzinger to discover in stoicism, the Enlightenment, and Marxism alike advocates of universal brotherhood, apart from the Hebrew faith and Christianity. Secularized forms of brotherhood, as expressed in the European Union's anthem *Ode an die Freude*, spell out a fraternity wrought by revolutionaries sharing a common cause. This was the background for Friedrich von Schiller's poem calling for "millions to be embraced," which was set to music by Ludwig van Beethoven. The utopia of a perfect circle of friends is advocated by numerous groups, such as the Masons, various liberals, and humanists. It is founded on shared political and social values. It experienced its tragic hypertrophy in Marxism, where doing harm to non-brothers was a feature of genuine brotherhood. Finally, Ratzinger arrives at scriptural evidence for brotherhood and acknowledges that Jesus' sayings seem to confirm what modern advocates of brotherhood have relentlessly promoted.[16] The differentiating feature, however, is belief in Jesus Christ. The universality of the concept is given credence by Jesus being the second Adam. Thus, potentially every human being can become one's brother or sister. Ratzinger draws here on the uneven testimony of the North African Church fathers with whom he is familiar.

Upon this basis, Ratzinger develops his own understanding of Christian brotherhood. Unlike secular variants of the theme, Christian brotherhood is not constructed on the hypothesis of a concept but on a person. All human beings have God as their ultimate Father. This fact of creation is made obvious by the mystery of the Incarnation: "Unlike the impersonal Stoic idea of God the Father and the vague paternal idea of Enlightenment, the Fatherhood of God is a Fatherhood mediated by the Son, and including brotherly union in the Son."[17] The union of grace enables human beings to live this reality. Christ allows human beings to pray the "Our" in the Our Father. This Ratzinger discovered when reading Cyprian of Carthage's commentary on the Our Father in *De Dominica Oratione* (ca. 252).[18] The medieval mystic Meister Eckhart confirms this.[19] Human beings share one body with Christ. Christ enables the individual to overcome the petty self and to remove all barriers to brotherhood. Among others this entails removing the barrier of nationalism. This outlook is not caused by a naïve enthusiasm but by the Chalcedonian formula that Jesus Christ is equally fully human and fully divine. In Jesus Christ's Incarnation, divine sonship is rendered available to all.[20]

However, Ratzinger cautions against an all too facile optimism. Genuine Christian brotherhood defines itself as service to the whole. It must always reach beyond the immediately personally known members and the already established ecclesial parameters. This includes missionary outreach to the yet unbaptized brother and sister. Ratzinger makes such statements partially influenced by the Reformed theologian Karl Barth.[21] Like Our Lord, the Christian must seek after, and hope and labor for, universal salvation. This will assuredly run the risk of failure, but precisely and exclusively therein will an authentic Christian victory be attained, namely, by sharing in Christ's passion.[22]

Ratzinger adds, as an afterthought, that this consequently leads to consciously addressing non-Catholic fellow Christians as brothers and sisters. The Eucharist Christ is the justification for this sweeping view of brotherhood and is the source for Christian brotherhood within the Church. The supernatural brings about brotherly community.

Being Christ to Others

CHAPTER 21

Christ and Freedom: Evangelization

Upon first reflection, it might seem rather unpromising to ponder Ratzinger's Christology under the consideration of evangelization as he has had—except for one year as parochial vicar—no experience in direct ministry. Yet, one recalls his books on the nature of liturgy and his significant role in putting forth a new catechism, the first following the Second Vatican Council. Last but not least, one remembers his careful, reflective words on the occasion of the fortieth anniversary of the conciliar document on the liturgy, *Sacrosanctum Concilium (SC)*, in 2004 at the Liturgisches Institut in Trier, Germany. The various theological disciplines are not unrelated to one another. Ratzinger has always been acutely aware of the interior orientation of all areas of theological disciplines to one another.[1] It is only from the very center of all theological endeavors that one can clarify issues that are quite practical in nature but seemingly unrelated to one another, ever mindful that faith is a reality pre-given (*vorgegeben*) by the ecclesial *communio*'s belief.[2] The whole of revelation is present in an undistorted manner in the Church's faith, but it requires constant fresh verbalization. Ratzinger does not tire of reminding his readers that the faith of the simple folk must be respected at all times. This concern brings him to a critical evaluation of the academic disciplines as a whole, as well as of practical or pastoral theology (that is, theological reflection) in particular. Not infrequently, the impression is conveyed that the humanities are the sole guiding star, the "*philosophia prima*," of practical theology. This may have given rise to excluding exegesis from theology and opting for theories borrowed, for example, from literary criticism.[3]

His own approach, which advocates localizing and mooring practical theology within the Christian faith, has oftentimes been considered rigidly doctrinaire. Often the accusation leveled against such a view can be summed up in the following words: here one senses a process of immunization at work against the profound changes occurring in the ways people think and feel in an age of rapid advances in the areas of science and technology. Such an attitude—thus the argument continues—risks making theology irrelevant to our age and time, marked as it is by a high degree of individualization. Is it correct to respond to the challenge of communicating the faith in our age and time simply with a nostalgic traditionalism and with unreflective, authoritarian sanctions? Such a simplistic portrayal of matters in crude black-and-white terms does little justice to both the Church's faith and Ratzinger's own position in this regard. Rather, this portrayal seems to arise from the quandary of having definitively left the era of a popular Church, that is, one deeply engrained in the culture of a people (*Volkskirche*) behind without having arrived yet at the stage of the Church thriving with individuals who have found the Catholic faith on their own (*Entscheidungschristentum*).

As a professor at the archdiocesan seminary in Freising in the winter semester of 1957–1958, while delivering his lectures on the Blessed Trinity, he made the following remark when commenting on Lamennais' (1782–1854)[4] traditionalism: "The Church condemns here the authoritarian system, which one wanted to give her."[5] At this point, one encounters a statement that would become foundational for Ratzinger's future theological outlook. The guideline of faith is not that of an ideology, devised by human beings, but of a prevenient reality beyond human control and manipulation. The occurrence of salvation once and for all times in the Church vouches for its vivacious reality. The believer partakes therein particularly during the liturgy. Christian faith is never merely an intellectual assent but has a particular "*Sitz im Leben*" ("place in life"). The primary locale for the faith is the liturgy.[6] Faith's authority is not achieved by way of power, coercion, and suppression but through truth's splendor and rational persuasion. The most basic and significant place for becoming aware of Christ's saving truth and presence is the liturgy. For this reason, Ratzinger's theology is preeminently practical in its orientation.

This insight was imparted to Ratzinger early on. First, while still a seminarian in Freising, he gained this perception via the abstract language of Henri de Lubac's *Catholicism*, where the French Jesuit relates dogma's relevance to the quality of social life. Subsequently, while residing in the Georgianum, the graduate seminary in Munich, he was exposed to the liturgical reflections of Romano Guardini and to the thoughts of the pastoral theologian and liturgist Joseph Pascher:

> Pascher...often struck our hearts directly with his lively spiritual conferences.... In his system of education everything rested on the daily celebration of Holy Mass. He opened up to us the nature and structure of the Mass in a series of lectures in the summer of 1948 which had already appeared in book form in 1947 under the title *Eucharistia*....Pascher's conferences, and the reverential manner in which he taught us to celebrate the liturgy in keeping with its deepest nature, made me a follower of the liturgical movement. Just as I learned to understand the New Testament as being the soul of all theology, so too I came to see the liturgy as being its living element without which it would necessarily shrivel up.[7]

Revelation is not merely a lofty, rational communication but a concrete, tangible "*Heilswirklichkeit*," an actual, saving reality that calls for a wholehearted appropriation. As tradition, revelation did not cease with the death of the last apostle but is a living reality, perduring ever fresh in the Church. It is heard constantly anew by the people of God in the particularizing categories of time and space. As Ratzinger memorably observed shortly after the Second Vatican Council: tradition is "the explication of the Christ event attested to in scripture in the history of the Church's faith."[8] One must consider this act of passive, but alert, "listening" as the pastoral *leitmotiv* of all Ratzinger's theological labors. This becomes apparent in his concern for evangelization and catechesis.

Human reason possesses a creative power that is encouraged by evangelization, overcoming both prerational myth and rationalistic ideology. It allows the human person to encounter God's being. It is the engagement with God as Logos that enables human beings to set the proper priorities in their lives. This encounter with God in a manner previously deemed impossible is earth shattering. Thus, there exists a primacy of contemplation, contemplation centered on the always-antecedent divine self-revelation, over and against the active life. Evangelization is an invitation to such a life that lives from the Logos and leads to ethos. Against the Faustian thesis "at the beginning was the deed" [Goethe], Christianity insists on the primacy of the Word. It is not activity, but contemplation, not morality but metaphysics, not effort but adoration that enjoys preference. Evangelization means: "Who has seen me, has seen the Father...nobody comes to the Father except through me" (Jn 14:9, 14:6). Christian existence is participation in Christ's salvation. Beyond Augustine's emphasis on justification—which, taken in isolation, is a rather petty, self-centered concern—God not only liberates humankind from sin but turns humans toward his grace and enables them to access the hidden nature of God, which remains inaccessible even to angels. This is achieved by way of a spiritual Christology: "You are Christ, the Son of the living God" (Mt 16:16). The Son, coessential with the Father, is the key.

It is imperative to understand that there is no mere dualism or parallelism but an intertwinedness of the divine and human natures in Jesus Christ. To Ratzinger this teaching of the Third Council of Constantinople (680–681) implies that there exists a proper dignity of Christ's human nature, which is being absorbed into the divine will; both blend into one will. The human and divine identities move into one subject as a pure affirmation of the Father's will.

In Jesus, human volition acquires a divine form and an "alchemy of being" occurs.[9] In evangelization the incarnational nature of Christianity should be explained. Our joy is in becoming the body of Christ and in his acceptance of us on a daily basis. Becoming Christian means offering earthly realities as the place of the Word. These are the implications of the Word's "*descendit de caelis*" (descended from heaven). This is the deep meaning of Vatican II: "In reality it is only in the mystery of the Word made flesh that the mystery of man truly becomes clear" (*GS* 22). This passage was drafted by Karol Wojtyla. Later, as John Paul II, he would state in his first encyclical, *Redemptoris Hominis* 14, "Without exception, Christ is connected somehow with every human being."[10]

In this sense, evangelization entails deliberately becoming communion; entry into Christ's body is the essential operating mode of the Holy Spirit. This means entry into the triune life and, simultaneously and inseparably, ecclesial existence. The supposed narrow Augustinian/Lutheran perspective on justification is burst open to deification as Christification.[11]

The Christian faith is not exhausted as a teaching but is an objective, ontic reality. All forms of terrestrial expression are "saved" in Christ's eternal being. Thus, Christ's childhood already reveals his celestial being. Human history is guided into eternity. All human matters can become eternal, in von Balthasar's diction. Evangelization means overcoming the dualism of God and creation that leads merely to the soul—and godless world of deism. God's continuous "making" of creation has been too little thematized in Christian literature. God's causality has been focused on too much, rather than the indwelling presence of God (Gn 2:2f). In addition, too often contemporary Christians live under the spell of Descartes' fateful bifurcation between *res cogitans* and *res extensa* (the realms of thought and matter). Ratzinger's spiritual Christology seeks to overcome this dichotomy that has confounded intellectual history ever since. Evangelization entails helping people have confidence in the Word God entrusted to his Church. Ratzinger stresses that the catechumen needs to learn to trust the infallible *auctoritas* (authority) of the Church, not in consideration of her power or canonical status, but because *she* is the Spirit-filled realm of Jesus Christ.

A well-presented evangelization gives an account to the world that reveals the nature of human beings because it discusses and lives Christ's revelation. It enters into Christ's reality: "Philip said to him, 'Master, show us the Father, and that will be enough for us.' Jesus said to him, 'Have I been with you for so long a time and you still do not know me, Philip? Whoever has seen me has seen the Father. How can you say, 'Show us the Father'? Do you not believe that I am in the Father and the Father is in me? The words that I speak to you I do not speak on my own. The Father who dwells in me is doing his works'" (Jn 14:9). Jesus' life is essentially mystery. Augustine states: "*Non est aliud Dei mysterium nisi Christus*"[12]—there is no other mystery of God but Christ. Christ is God's mystery and there is no greater mystery than he.

In every age, the faith is confronted with particular challenges. While in part this may be due to new ways of life and even the intellectual difficulties proper to a specific age, the faith is challenged to respell out its expressivity and livability anew. Also, certain quarters that formulate such exogenic contestations should be mindful that the inability to translate the faith easily into a new life-context, into an altogether novel and hitherto unknown awareness of life, does not discredit the faith. At this point, one must distinguish between faith per se and the bearer of the message, the witness and disciple. Faith can be "respelled" for a new age only if it is lived afresh and has a chance to find its proper idiom. Such a process is never easily achieved. It requires both time and, perhaps more importantly, an existential effort. Personal appropriation is indispensable. The famous expositions of the Catholic faith by Peter Canisius[13] and Jacques-Benigne Bossuet[14] are shining examples. They were able to speak in the idioms of their own ages on eternal matters.

The inherent danger of a catechism is that it may imply that faith is merely a communication-theoretical issue. The peril is to assume that by comprehending the logic of sentences one also "understands" the faith and even God. Such an approach may be called "intellectualistic." Thus, it is the challenge of every Christian catechism to intimate to the reader that faith is a living encounter with a living, personal God. A catechism objectifies such experience and gives it content. The *Catechism of the Catholic Church* is a fairly successful balance between a personally engaging narrative style and a compilation of succinct statements.[15]

Every translation process requires two elements in order to be successful: openness toward the new, in the sense of the biblical term "signs of the time" (Lk 12:54ff), and fidelity to definitive revelation. For the superficial commentator, the latter component might appear as a psychologically explicable, defensive (subconscious) reaction. This may indeed often be the case. That notwithstanding, however, Ratzinger argues Christian revelation is nothing short of God's own, definitive self-communication. Its selfsame identity throughout history is vouched for by the abiding presence of the Holy Spirit in the Church and the sacramental reality of apostolic succession inherent to her. Thereby, temporality in and of itself contains a salvific element. The material content of revelation does not change, and yet the cultural expressions it finds oftentimes do change. Thus, it would be inappropriate to concede to a particular age the right to decide what revelation is. Likewise, it would do violence to an age to impose upon it an expression of the faith from a different epoch containing its own distinctive flavor and context. In history, changes have often occurred over long time spans. For the first millennium of Christianity, the worldview did not alter, to which Romanesque architecture attests. More recently, however, such changes in the awareness of an age have occurred with accelerated rapidity. Thus, they are often painful and sometimes even violent. In gratitude for the Holy Spirit present in every epoch and for the efforts of previous generations of faithful believers, every age is called to acquire the faith and to live it. Faith, therefore, is nothing less than an organic continuity in time and space. Models borrowed from political life, while they perhaps correctly capture some elements, are ultimately not helpful in describing such a transforming process that is mindful of its indebtedness to God's self-revelation in Jesus Christ.[16] The tension between eternity and temporality must be upheld.

Faithful to the central inspiration of Bonaventure, Ratzinger, in his writings as a scholar on revelation and ecclesiology (1957–1977), expresses confidence in the abiding presence of the Savior through the centuries. This gives us the key to comprehending Ratzinger's catechetical efforts: his guiding thread is a Christocentric principle. The Church is the locale (1) where salvation in Christ is present, and (2) in which the Word of God is heard. Both ecclesial realities come about by the power of the Holy Spirit. The Church is in her essence the place where people can grow in faith. This means sensing, hearing, and partaking in the present Lord.

Upon this background, Ratzinger was sensitized early on to anthropological and pedagogical issues when faced with the tasks of catechesis and religious education. The question concerning the proper correlation of faith, revelation, scripture, tradition, and the Church became virulent. One central insight for him is that there is an inner tension that depends on the objective arch between dogma, scripture, the Church, and the present age. Each of these serves as a foundational column that may not be dismantled.[17]

In the significant study *Dogma und Verkündigung* he concludes one cannot simply leave dogma on the sidelines. In light of this background, around 1970 Ratzinger became concerned with the issue of correlating personal experience to the faith of the Church, which had become a major topic in the West. Indeed, by the present day it has become a fundamental question: how are faith and experience to be related to one another? Ratzinger's analysis at the time led him to insist on restoring the centrality of content over method. Yet, as Wollbold has stated, by that time the one-sided perception of Ratzinger as "*defensor fidei*" ("defender of the faith') was already dominant.[18] "It is certainly true that anyone who tries to preach the faith amid people involved in modern life and thought can really feel like a clown, or rather perhaps like someone who, rising from an ancient sarcophagus, walks into the midst of the world today dressed and thinking in the ancient fashion and can neither understand nor be understood by this world of ours."[19] One becomes painfully aware of the didactic challenges of inculcating the faith.

As archbishop of Munich and subsequently as Prefect of the Congregation for the Doctrine of the Faith, he applied his theoretical reflections in practice. His talk on the transmission of the faith in the French city of Lyon in 1983 produced a rather divided response.[20] The archbishops of Lyon and Paris had invited him, as the newly appointed prefect, to speak. Regarding experience-based and subject-oriented catechesis, in 1976 Bishop Elchinger from Strasbourg had observed, "A generation of children had been sacrificed."[21] The inductive method had brought about a pauperization of the faith among children. This occurred because such a method places experience first, faithful to the motto "seeing-judging-acting." One can perhaps detect here an overreaction to the intellectualism prevalent in theological and catechetical programs in the nineteenth and first half of the twentieth century. An exaggerated intellectualism invariably leads to yet another imbalance; namely, "to the fragmentation of faith claims and... a hypotrophy of method to the detriment of content."[22] Significantly, such an experiential approach was not originally intended in the area of religious instruction. Accordingly, an organic presentation of the faith is lacking in the French catechism *Pierres Vivantes* (*Living Stones*).[23] The result of these types of exaggerations is that both solidarity within the Church and dialogue between the Church's teaching office and catechetical praxis suffer, to the detriment of both. Frequently, Ratzinger's speech has been misinterpreted as favoring a merely intellectual catechetical restoration.

The anthropological or anthropocentric method favored "picking up young Christians where they are." Yet, faith is a gift; it is the participation in a mystery that is not of human making. Faith is the experience that, behind the *kenosis* of God's Word, amid the torrent of numerous human words, and even beyond the formulations of creedal statements, lies the encounter with God's charity, truth, and life. As Ferdinand Ebner formulated in 1946: "Praying the Our Father in the proper way means receiving the infinity of the divine Word in the finitude of my reason."[24] From his childhood, Ratzinger knew the lasting importance learning the catechism by heart and living it has for adult life and faith. The familiar sentences from the *Catechism* point to the Catholic faith's comprehensive wholeness and unity, thus enabling one to trust the ecclesial communion. This appreciation for the catechism likely led Ratzinger to edit a brief summary of the catechism.

The call for a reorientation in catechesis led to the presentation of the renewed *Catechism of the Catholic Church* on December 7, 1992, which had been requested by the Bishops' Synod and overseen by the Prefect of the Congregation for the Doctrine of the Faith. By and large, academic reaction to it has been lukewarm, if not decidedly critical.[25] Often the *Catechism* has been criticized on the grounds that it responds to the world with the means of a bygone era. Frequently a disconnect between identity and relevance, dogma and helping people live, teaching and experience, and catechesis and dialogue has been lamented. It has been seen as disregarding the subject of faith. The monological structure of past catechisms aimed at securing the identity and common narrative of the community of believers at the cost of dialogue. In fairness, one should note, however, that the level of schooling the average person enjoyed until after World War II was rather low. The accusation has even been leveled that the *Catechism* subcutaneously reinterprets such central concepts as "the faith," "the Church," and "the Second Vatican Council." Ironically, similar accusations were leveled against those who lamented the preconciliar informative-theoretical approach of books such as—to mention only the last—the manual by Ludwig Ott.[26]

In his programmatic homily at the opening mass of the conclave that was to elect him pope, Ratzinger noted a correlation between the phenomenon of relativism and the disappearance of Jesus Christ from the consciousness of numerous well-intentioned people. A multitude of ideologies and fashions not only produces the phenomenon of relativism but also is the basis for accusing any kind of truth claim as being, by its very nature, fundamentalist. This results in nothing less than "the dictatorship of relativism," acknowledging nothing as definitive. In contrast, Christianity recognizes Jesus Christ, rather than the petty self, as the yardstick to measure the conduct of the world and of the individual.[27]

In his judgment, only a clear and unambiguous orientation toward the Son of God and the true human being Jesus Christ is able to free humankind from being infatuated with its own needs and opinions. From this perspective, the cliché of Ratzinger as a *"Panzerkardinal"* (*Panzer* is German for a military tank), insisting on discipline and dogma, demonstrates a particular quality. This caricature associates him with the rigorous position of someone who considers human freedom and the individual's autonomy to be deleterious. The opposite is the case. Impressed by the hauntingly beautiful and profound homilies of Romano Guardini, Ratzinger had also read his essays on the religious figures in the Russian novelist Dostoyevsky's writings. As was mentioned earlier, one of the most impressive scenes in the novel *The Brothers Karamazov* is the dialogue between Jesus Christ and the Grand Inquisitor, called "The Legend of the Grand Inquisitor."[28] As a young professor, Ratzinger often had his retreatants read this excerpt. Upon first sight, one might assume Dostoyevsky argues against the Catholic Church. Actually, this is not the case. Rather, he shows that evil always tempts human beings to accommodate themselves to the comforts of this palpable world. The task of the Grand Inquisitor is to both assuage human fears and sublimate their ideals so they will become wholly materialistic and thus do justice to their bourgeois inclinations. The Grand Inquisitor argues in his monologue that Jesus Christ naïvely misunderstands human nature. Jesus Christ gouges a wound in humans by cruelly asking them for something they neither desire to possess nor can give. In Ratzinger's reading, the dark person found in the Grand Inquisitor can be replaced by other figures, such as the figure of "Big Brother" in George Orwell's *1984*. It is the challenge par excellence facing modernity: can this world not provide society with all the needs it has? Is not an "ism" sufficient? Will not the self-dynamics of the immanent, technical, scientific development of globalization satisfy all needs?

Certain theories posit that only the open-minded person, independent from the need to master the here and now and cling to ideologies and prejudices out of a psychological need for security, receives the inner sovereignty to arrive at a free, philosophical choice. Ratzinger maintains, however, that in fact only confronting the true God and the human being Jesus Christ brings about the unique opportunity, the *kairos* to become genuinely free. Ratzinger's anthropology is based on the assumption that human beings are inalienably Spirit-gifted, and therefore it is based on the undying confidence that human beings remain able to encounter truth and to live accordingly. "We have seen that the rationality of faith develops of necessity from the love that is intrinsic to it: the love that comes from faith must be a prudent love that is not content with providing the other with bread but also teaches him to see. A love that gives less, or that is unwilling on principle to extend itself to the other's need for truth, fails to attain a genuinely human level and is consequently not love in the full sense of the word."[29]

On this point Ratzinger is in agreement with a central concern of the Enlightenment. He trusts in humanity's ability to be educated. However, his vision is not confined to the notion that such an ability to be educated is to be welcomed and promoted simply for the sake of the moral edification of society. While human beings are interested in continued education and even formation, the evaluation of this process is not one they can design on their own. Neither do they produce the rule by which society, or an individual, can be judged. In Ratzinger's estimation, humans are the bearer of an indwelling entelechy to reach beyond themselves and to be formed by that which is infinitely beyond them: to encounter in Jesus Christ the Way, the Truth, and the Life. By inherently possessing this ability to encounter the second person of the Blessed Trinity, they are also capable of living by a measure not of their own design. This liberates human beings from justifying their own existence. "The confession of Jesus Christ as Logos [Word] means that in him God himself is revealed, the truth of all things. The Christian faith is thus at once more optimistic and more radical not only than the intellectual world of antiquity but precisely also than the intellectual world of the modern era, which regards the question of truth as something almost improper and, in any event, as highly unscientific and unintellectual. Only those systems that are 'right' in themselves, that are 'in tune,' can be affirmed, but truth—it remains hidden."[30]

What constitutes such an encounter with Christ? Does it merely rest on the authority or power of the Church? This leads to the question of what, according to Ratzinger, constitutes the Christian faith. Essentially, Jesus is the bearer of a message-seeking faith. It rests on responsoriality. This message does not contain a secret, gnostic teaching, counsel, or technique but rather attests to a historic event: "When Jesus says: 'The Kingdom of God is at hand,' then this means simply: God himself is near. You are in God's proximity; he is in your [proximity]. And God is an acting God...God is the practical and realistic theme for man—then and always."[31] Consequently, catechesis means proclaiming an event that concerns human beings to the utmost and against which all other issues pale in comparison. This has remained the case throughout the history of humankind. While scripture is not revelation, it accesses revelation. While not subscribing to the principle of *sola scriptura* (scripture alone), scripture remains indispensable for the Catholic faith. In his contribution to a publication he put out together with Karl Rahner in 1965 in light of the dogmatic constitution *Dei Verbum*, Ratzinger wrote: "Faith is entering the presence of Christ, in the 'presenting' reality of Christ, to which scripture bears witness, which, however, scripture is not already itself par excellence."[32] The proclaimed Word requires being heard, and it therefore exists only insofar as it is heard. This leads Ratzinger to conclude that scripture is selfsame only within the ecclesial community, which is the community of listeners of the Word. Only within the Church can scripture be read and understood as it is the Church's product. It was only within the sacramental reality of the Church and the seven individual sacraments that scripture came about, and it is only within this context that it can be lived and interpreted. Without the ecclesial community, neither scripture as text nor its interpretation is possible. An exegesis that attempts to abstract scripture from the Church and her witness would commit the mistake of trying to interpret scripture apart from the living Christ. Here again one detects subcutaneous echoes of the nineteenth-century Tübingen School of Theology. Johann Adam Möhler (1796–1838), its most recognized member, had famously defined the Church as the elongation of the Incarnation of Jesus Christ.[33] Apart from the objectivity the Church assures, the justification for revelation becomes a utilitarian one: "What relevance does scripture have for me?" In this, the divine sovereignty of Jesus Christ is missed. Revelation does not seek to confirm common human expectations but leads to the greater reality of and communion with God. Such a limited understanding of evangelization contains an altogether different understanding of truth. It reduces faith to something pragmatic, something used to master the here and now.

Christian revelation is bound to historicity and yet infinitely transcends the confines of a particular human person in time and space. In other words, faith is the means by which a human being leaves all constraints of his or her contingency behind. This includes leaving all relative and contingent ways of measuring behind. The ability to free oneself from cultural constraints and the "paradigms of an age" fundamentally hinges on a person's ability to encounter God in Christ in such a vivacious way that all else pales in comparison.[34] Thereby, in a thrilling way all things in this world receive their value and dignity. Faith is not a flight from the world but an affirmation of the world as a creation willed in divine goodness.

Human beings encounter revelation in its full truth and power within the realm of the Church. The Church is, so to speak, "the biotope" (author's choice) of living and ongoing revelation. This leads Ratzinger to conclude that the liturgy is the primary and ordinary place of revelation. In his farewell letter to the clergy of the Archdiocese of Munich in 1982, he calls upon them to engage the word of the liturgy in a meditative way. In his estimation, this is the key par excellence to hearing and proclaiming the Word. "[T]ranscending all kinds of information...The Word of revelation is able to become our 'form,' the formative force of our life, which is able to bring forth life again."[35] This notion of transcending oneself is a recurring theme in Ratzinger's writings. He does not tire of pointing out in his essay on the catechism that all of the collaborators did not seek to impose their own opinions but rather wanted to place themselves at the service of the Church "as the listening ear and speaking mouth of the ecclesial community. Such self-negation of thought, such a deprivation towards the totality [of God and the world] became a big and cheering experience. Everyone adopted this manner: My teaching is not my own teaching...."[36]

Evangelization is the foundational task of the Church. Evangelization means acquainting people with Jesus as attested to in the gospels. It implies introducing people to a long-term, living communion with him. In this sense, evangelization means an invitation to the companionship of disciples, who become the catechumen's new family.[37] It means being inducted into the "lifestyle of a Christian." Thus, catechesis serves a twofold mission: rational understanding and existential induction into the lifestyle of a Christian. As faith seeks understanding, the act of faith seeks its corresponding content. The *fides qua* (personal faith) dynamically strives to find its commensurate expression in the *fides quae* (faith of the Church). The trust one has expressed in the beginning of one's faith journey in the Church is now spelled out in sentences, teachings, and creedal statements. Christ as the Logos is the key to unlocking the true meaning of both the world and the individual person's existence. This struggle to ascertain the objectivity and exhaustiveness of truth in Christ Ratzinger sees as already virulent in Irenaeus of Lyon's debates with the gnostics during the second century.[38] In this regard, he insists on the indispensability of the four major elements of the faith: the creed, the Our Father, the Decalogue, and the sacraments. Thus it comes as no surprise that they also constitute the structuring elements of the *Catechism of the Catholic Church*.

With an appreciation for the historic roots of catechesis, he notes:

It must be remembered that from the earliest times of Christianity there appears a permanent and unrelinquishable "nucleus" of catechesis, hence of formation in the faith. Luther also employed this nucleus for his catechism, in the same matter-of-fact way as did the Roman catechism that had been decided upon at the Council of Trent. All that is said about faith, after all, is organized around four fundamental elements: the *Credo*, the *Our Father*, the *Decalogue*, the *sacraments*. These embrace the foundation of Christian life, the synthesis of the teaching of the Church based on scripture and tradition. Here the Christian finds all he must *believe* (the Symbol or Credo), *hope* (the Our Father), *do* (the Decalogue) as well as the *vital space* [*Lebensraum*] in which all this must be accomplished (the sacraments). Today this fundamental structure is neglected in extensive areas of present-day catechesis. The result, as we note, has been a disintegration of the *sensus fidei* in the new generations, who are often incapable of a comprehensive view of their religion.[39]

He states that there is the real chance the Church stands to lose an important element if one does not catechize: the *sensus fidelium* (sense of the faithful). There is no denying that on the point of the structural elements of catechesis, he is in full ecumenical agreement with the Reformer Martin Luther (1483–1546). Content is an indispensable part of the Christian faith and, therefore, also of catechesis. Christian faith does not evaporate into an impersonal, undifferentiated, divine One in the manner of the henology of the ancient, pagan philosopher Plotinus (ca. 205–270). The Christian God is a relational *who*; that is, the Christian God has a face and is a person, more precisely, is three persons in one.

Regrettably, Ratzinger's efforts have frequently been misunderstood as advocating the resurrection of an instructive-theoretical approach that was common through the early 1960s. This misunderstanding fails to appreciate the fact that, for him, revelation is precisely not merely the imparting of information but an encounter with the living Christ. The Church, as the enablement of such a revelation and encounter, does not ossify the experience of the apostles and first disciples but keeps it ever present as Christ's dwelling space. Revelation as God's self-communication is an objective reality within the life and faith of the Church, subjectively forming the whole human person. It follows that faith is acquired through an event of proximity to Jesus Christ. Any kind of reflection is secondary. "The real content of Christianity is not the discussion of its Christian content and of ways of realizing it: the content of Christianity is the community of word, sacrament and love of neighbor to which justice and truth bear a fundamental relationship."[40] Therefore, a significant interdependence exists among faith, proclamation, and theology. While theology is called to search for new ways to give a verbal, scholarly expression to the faith and does not stand above the faith, evangelization aims to assist people immediately in their concrete lives. On this level, it is important to spell out "what the Church believes and lives." Catechesis is what enables participation in the faith and life of the Church. While it should not cover up unresolved issues, catechesis does not have the task of problematizing the creed but of communicating it. This does not exclude theology from constantly informing catechesis. In fact, the latter is germane for a healthy catechesis. Good catechesis does not answer all human questions concerning the faith from the outset but allows them to be answered by the faith. It teaches that questions are often answered only by lived loyalty—by living out a commitment.[41] Catechesis and theology become great when they do not limit God within the range of their disciplines but readily admit that they live from something that in itself is more coherent and greater than human reason. Answers held in suspension are prayed for and answered in a life of sacramental loyalty more fully than imagined by the one posing the question. Ratzinger implies that all successful catechesis must be sustained by an expression of the joy of faith.

Going beyond all legitimate theological discussion, catechesis draws life from the living reality of faith and from the sacraments, particularly the Eucharist. Thus, it is related to "the totality of faith." It is not a cheap, ideological strategy of immunization against inconvenient questions but rather "the act of partaking in the whole of faith."[42] The basis for such a perspective is biblical. First John 2:20 speaks of baptized faith as anointing with the Holy Spirit. In baptism, the neophyte is touched by a reality. As a consequence, baptismal faith has primacy over theory.[43] This leads to the inevitable conclusion that any didactic passing on of the faith cannot supplant the content of faith. The method of evangelization remains a vehicle and does not become the measure of its content.[44] Pedagogy must not be disregarded but didactic methods must be commensurate with the content they are called to convey. It seems Ratzinger argues here against the aftereffects of nominalism. This medieval theory, associated especially with William of Ockham in the fourteenth century, held that universals exist only in the human mind. As a consequence, all reflection on faith disintegrates and reason cannot be applied to matters of faith. The realm of faith withdraws from reason as its ultimate court of appeal. Ratzinger also maintains it is not the concern of catechesis to present believers with a multitude of theologically unresolved issues, such as the quest for the historical Christ or the "Q" source. Rather, catechesis verbalizes that which has become a reality for the newly baptized.

A recurring theme in Ratzinger's works is the faith of the simple-hearted (1 Cor 1:21 and Mt 11:25). This obliges the teacher to communicate the simplicity of faith and to preserve accordingly the faith of the simple-hearted. Theology ministers to the comprehensibility and livability of such faith. This is the case because faith is the a priori of theology. He describes, "[T]he triangular relationship defined by the people of God, understood as the bearer of the *sensus fidei* [sense of faith] and the common locus of all faith, the Magisterium and theology. The development of dogma in the last 150 years is a clear index of how closely these three elements hang together: the dogmas of 1854, 1870 and 1950 became possible because the *sensus fidei* had discovered them, while the Magisterium and theology followed its lead and tried slowly to catch up with it."[45] In his foundational collection of essays *Principles of Catholic Theology*, he describes in great detail the relationship between the faith of the simple-hearted and the theological claim of faith's intelligibility.[46]

From this follows the need to present the faith in its entirety. The *sensus fidei* of believers must be kept from evaporating. This is the commission of the *Catechism of the Catholic Church*. If one rejects the structured presentation of the faith as expressed in the classical divisions of the creed, the sacraments, the Decalogue, and the Our Father, one invariably advocates the fragmentation of creedal statements. Such an approach opens the gates to arbitrariness. Faith appears as isolated and unrelated propositions that come about at random.[47] A clear, interrelated presentation of the faith as offered by the *Catechism* enables the faith to be presented as an organic whole with an inner, stringent logic and necessity. The instructor's task is not to provide answers to the innumerable possible issues and questions with which the student or society in general may be confronted; this would be an impossible mission. Rather, it is the mission of catechesis to impart a sense of confidence in the whole of the Church's faith in its entirety.

The time of familiarization with Christ and his Church found in undergoing catechesis includes the process of purification and conversion. During the Stations of the Cross at the Coliseum on Holy Friday in 2005, many took note of the future pope's unambiguous words regarding the sins of the Church.[48] This followed upon his past teaching in that in his first pastoral letter as archbishop of Munich he delineated in no uncertain terms the relationship between the Church and conversion. The proclamation of the kingdom of God is never mere preaching, never mere rhetoric. The proclamation of the kingdom of God essentially includes the gathering together and purification of people for this kingdom. For this reason, Ratzinger has reservations about identifying the Church with the perfect kingdom of God or the people of God.[49]

In his first pastoral letter as archbishop, relating to matters of first confession and first communion, he reminds his audience that awareness of the need for conversion is indispensable for the proper preparation and reception of communion, and indeed for salvation in general. Soon after, he authored a letter to everyone involved in religious education in grammar schools, in which he affirms his predecessor's, Cardinal Julius Döpfner's, insistence that the experience of reconciliation with God must precede first Holy Communion. He argues such indispensability (that is, that the confession of sin is the condition of entry into the Eucharist) to be intrinsic to the nature of the Eucharist. The penitential act precedes both the liturgy of the Word and the sacrament of the Eucharist and thereby becomes, so to speak, the gateway to the sanctuary of the liturgy. Only in the experience that the divine is not commonplace does something like "discernment of the body of Christ" occur (cf. 1 Cor 11:28).[50] There is the attendant danger of a "formalization of receiving communion" in which communion is experienced merely as a ritual, such as sitting, standing, or kneeling, with no existential involvement. Indicatively, during the enthronization of Pope Benedict XVI in St. Peter's Square a brief "*monitio*" ("admonition") to this effect was read just before communion. The central concern in this issue is not the concrete method to be employed but rather placing emphasis on the purity and sanctity of the Church. A catechesis attesting to the faith unambiguously allows its salutary and convincing luminosity to shine forth. Such a catechesis is then able to immerse the learning believer in Christian truth in such a way that it contributes to a deep and lasting renewal of faith.

These observations and exhortations are not expressions of Ratzinger's private, and perhaps even idiosyncratic, thoughts. They can be found in 1 Peter 3:15: "Always be prepared to make a defense to anyone who calls you to account for the hope that is in you." One should patiently receive inquiries regarding the faith and be willing to engage in dialogue. Every catechist, in offering answers, is called upon to be sensitive to the fact that answers involve an existential struggle on the part of the questioner, lest one fall back into a type of neoscholastic intellectualism. The catechist should be respectful, modest, and conscientious when giving witness to the hope that sustains him or her. This citation from Peter's first letter lays down the operating principles with Christians and nonbelievers alike. It is the *modus operandi* both in religious instruction in a school and in parochial catechesis. In both scenarios, one oftentimes encounters borderline cases where a person being instructed in the faith oscillates between faith and disbelief. Since around the 1950s there has been a collapse of confidence in faith on a broad scale. Until then faith was considered a self-evident fact of life—of the commonly accepted social fabric. The orthodoxy of the content figured prominently, with supposedly little regard for the translation of truth into everyday life. In many respects, Ratzinger's approach reminds one upon first sight of the material-kerygmatic method in use until roughly 1970.

An anthropocentric catechetical outlook stresses the need for children to realize that the Christian faith is helpful in understanding and mastering life. Ratzinger, however, warns that such a correlation between the content of the faith and concrete life experience runs the danger of shortchanging, or eliminating altogether, the kerygma of the faith. It is important to reflect more on the dimension of "inspiration" and, therefore, on the mediation of humankind and world by the Holy Spirit in the sacred realm of the Church, that is, on the fact that humankind encounters the fullness of being human in the Church. Specifically, more thought should be given to the fact that Christian faith is not a particular, individual variation of life but an inspiration with universal implications. Ratzinger does not simplistically plead the case for a long bygone material-kerygmatic model. Rather, he is mindful that all of Christian existence, as well as the Church, is based on a dynamic reality, namely, the constant conversion of its members. Its members must be willing to be transformed ever anew by Jesus Christ. Only thus can the believer apprehend the Church as the very reality that makes possible getting to know the faith and getting acquainted with the person of Jesus Christ. It is Jesus Christ inviting the individual, in the specific locality called the Church, to encounter him and his salvific truth. It is exclusively here that the individual surrenders to the mark of faith, the "standard of teaching" ("τύπος διδαχής," *"typos dadaches"* from Rom 6:17), which allows the individual to undergo experiences acquainting him or her with the relevance of faith. In an individual believer, faith and getting acquainted with the faith do not consist simply of learning central creedal tenets and understanding the coherence of the faith. Rather, what is important, and this is Ratzinger's overriding concern, is that catechumens, and believers in general, encounter in the Eucharistic Church the saving reality of Christ. A proper response to this call has yet to be developed by Catholic catechists in some quarters. Be that as it may, in the person and works of Joseph Ratzinger, one encounters, in an exemplary manner, harmony between theological science and the episcopal proclamation of the gospel.

CHAPTER 22

Christian Brotherhood: Entering into Jesus Christ's Earthly Ineffability

Christian brotherhood, unlike the purely secular brotherhood of Marxism, is, above all, brotherhood based on the common paternity of God. Unlike the impersonal Stoic idea of God the father and the vague paternal idea of the Enlightenment, the fatherhood of God is a fatherhood mediated by the Son and including brotherly union in the Son. If, therefore, Christian brotherhood is to be vitally realized, both a vital knowledge of the fatherhood of God and a vital joining with Jesus Christ in a unity of grace are necessary.[1]

While Ratzinger admits that Plato sees the concepts of Father and Lord in the eternal, transcendent idea of the *agathon*, of the good, it is doubtful whether Plato would combine that good with personhood. In the *Epictetus* an understanding of God's own Son ($\iota\delta\iota\varsigma$ $\upsilon\iota o\varsigma$ $\tau o\upsilon$ $\Theta\varepsilon o\upsilon$, *idios huios tou Theou*), a God with the caring, loving, and forgiving features of a person, are not seen. This God is but the climax of all the cosmic powers. In contradistinction to the Hellenic understanding of an "unmoved" god, the Christian—and Hebrew— notion of God is charged with personal features. In Christ Jesus, this God becomes personally addressable and a partner with humanity. Ratzinger shows how this evolves in ancient Israel until Jesus Christ becomes the epitome of the true Israel as the "son of God." "This accords with the fact that Jesus saw himself expressly as the founder of a new Israel already founded in his person—a conception that John expresses by having Jesus describe himself in two places in suggestive imagery as the new Jacob-Israel (Jn 1:51 [cf. Gn 28:12] and 4:6, 11–12)."[2] The divine Sonship of Jesus on earth and within the Blessed Trinity is the condition for the possibility of Christian brotherhood. In the Eucharist all become one "seed of Abraham." "You all are one in Christ Jesus" as Paul emphasizes in Galatians 3:28; thus, Christians gain true childhood in Christ Jesus (Gal 4:6; Rom 8:15f). Through the sacraments, Christians become the embodiment of Christ and transcend blood brotherhood. Christians enter the Sonship of Christ and simultaneously accept the Fatherhood of God. The vertical dimensions of Sonship and Fatherhood allow the horizontal, social dimension of the Christian faith to come about: Christian brotherhood. It is for this reason that Ratzinger refers to Cyprian of Carthage, who gave special attention to the word "our" in the Our Father. Christians live and pray as a community of brothers (and sisters).[3] It seems Harnack's understanding of God is more Greek than Judeo-Christian when he claims that the predication "son" is not part of the gospel proclaimed by Our Lord. Ratzinger argues on the contrary that the Christian God is

> the exact opposite of the Homeric "father of the gods and of men." That god was a domineering and unpredictable despot—not despite his fatherhood, but precisely because of it: there is a despotic quality in the Greek idea of fatherhood. And yet this despotic father was not himself the highest power, for above, or beside him stood *moira* (fate) and *themis* (the law of the cosmos), against which even he could do nothing. Against this background the biblical idea of fatherhood acquires its truest greatness. For this God is the ultimate power, power itself, *Pantocrator*, and at the same time, the most reliable, unfailing fidelity. Both these qualities are able to move man to an ultimate, unshakable trust that is love and worship in one.[4]

The Greek imagination could not allow human beings to be incorporated into the Son of God in the sense of us becoming "sons of the Son," merging into the unity of the body of Christ, which is the brotherhood of all Christians.

However, brotherhood is more than something simply grounded in being born as a human being as the stoic (Epictetus, Seneca, Musonius, Marc Aurel) and Enlightenment thinkers held. The notions of *fraternité* and *comrade* generated by the French revolutionaries of 1789 and Marxism have a hollow ring to them. They are based on a commonality of all people that remains undefined without the concept of the *imago Dei* (image of God). On the other hand, the "existing paradox" is that the Old Testament religion is based on a national God who is also a universal God. The chosen people are the platform for a singular historic process of interiorization. Belonging to the people is not determined by actual brotherhood but by loyalty to both tablets. This entails living in communion with YHWH and in solidarity with one's brethren. This is the import of Jesus' words: "Whoever does the will of God is my brother, and sister, and mother" (Mk 3:35). The concept of Israelite solidarity is expanded to include everyone who takes on the mind-set of Jesus Christ. Like Christ, one lives not for oneself but for others. For Ratzinger the consequence is not "to save souls" but to strengthen and expand the sacramental Church and thereby enter the greater magnanimity of Christ. Were it merely a question of being redeemed, all religions would be arrested in their particularities. The sacramental ministry entails reminding the ones receiving the sacraments that they are themselves a salvific sign for other brothers and sisters. *Communio* with Christ is never living for oneself but taking upon oneself the martyrdom of the Good. In a constant Pasch (Easter), one is sent for the other's sake. As Benedict XVI relates in *Deus Caritas Est*, the Roman emperor Julian would not become a Christian because his father Constantius had been murdered by supposed followers of

Christ. But he remained impressed by the system of charity that the Church members lived (§24).

Discipleship

In the Sermon on the Mount, Ratzinger discerns a key to understanding Christian discipleship. While the sermon is addressed to the whole world, it requires discipleship in order to be understood, and this in turn means following and accompanying Jesus. It was in dialogue with the Jewish scholar Jacob Neusner that Ratzinger became fully aware of the "greatness of Jesus' words."[5] Jesus was not just one more teaching rabbi in a long chain of rabbis. "Christ now stands on the mountain, he now takes the place of the Torah...lord of the Sabbath...God." This is to Neusner not only the novelty about Jesus but a blasphemy that sets the Nazarene apart.[6] This radical novelty indeed turns the community of Jesus' disciples into the new Israel. The all-dominant criterion now is belonging to the community of those sharing in Jesus' fate.

The primacy of Jesus' person thrusts aside the very foundations upon which Israel's religious and social order rests. Ratzinger writes, "In Jesus' case it is not the universally binding adherence to the Torah that forms the new family. Rather, it is adherence to Jesus himself, to his Torah." Therefore, he quotes Neusner, "I now realize, only God can demand of me what Jesus is asking."[7] This is the crucial issue. But Ratzinger immediately cautions against detecting in the Jew that acknowledging Jesus as the Son of God requires an anti-Jewish interpretation: "He has brought the God of Israel to the nations, so that all the nations now pray to him and recognize Israel's scriptures as his word, the word of the living God. He has brought the gift of universality, which was the one great definitive promise to Israel and the world."[8] In Jesus' sovereign words, Ratzinger refrains from countenancing an inflated "I." Jesus lives in complete subordination and obedience to God the Father. Taking "Whoever does the will of my Father in heaven is my brother, and sister, and mother" (Mk 3:34f) as his basis, Ratzinger demonstrates that Jesus always references his eternal Father. The new family is not a fan club surrounding a pompous guru by the name of Jesus but one united to the will of Jesus' divine Father. This freedom (Gal 5:13) found in Jesus is historically unheard of.

Discipleship means sharing Christ's fate. In bringing Christ to people, Paul is filled with an immense joy because he is connected to Jesus' cross and Resurrection. This voluntary abandonment to death allows Jesus to find expression in an individual human being's existence (2 Cor 4:11). Discipleship becomes an elongation of Christ's glory among men and women in both his suffering and victorious Resurrection. The Beatitudes are nothing short of an invitation to communion with Jesus and are included in the mystery of Christ: "But precisely because of their hidden Christological character, the Beatitudes are also a road map for the Church, which recognizes in them the model of what she herself should be."[9] In this context, poverty becomes that which allows God to grant people his gifts and permits them to live in harmony with God's will and the world. Such poverty never clings to divine gifts but generously shares all with all. In this sense, there cannot be a dissonance between Matthew talking of "the poor in spirit" and Luke's unqualified "poor." To read a social agenda into the Sermon on the Mount signifies blindness in not appreciating the spiritual dimension of poverty. The quality, for example, of Franciscan service to the poor does not depend on whether it brings about material change, though effecting a material improvement is a most welcome side effect.

A key term in Ratzinger's estimation is to render the Greek *praus* (*anawim*, in Hebrew) correctly in English as "meek" and not merely as "nonviolent." By being poor and meek one acquires the disposition proper to the kingdom of God. To underline this interpretation, Ratzinger quotes Psalm 37:11, "The meek shall possess the land." One's inner disposition and genuine goodness enable the believer to become the inheritor of the Promised Land. This goodness of heart is not something abstract or vague but something that imitates Christ as the new and true Moses: "Take my yoke upon you, and learn from me; for I am meek and lowly in heart" (Mt 11:29). This brings about a proper interpretation of Palm Sunday. When Our Lord asks his disciples to procure a donkey, he evidences himself as "your king... (meek) and mounted on an ass" (Mt 21:4f).[10] Such meekness is grounded in obedience to God the Father. Such obedience is the foundation for a proper interaction with nature. Only a heart purified by following Christ can do justice to both the first and second tablets of the Decalogue. In other words, Ratzinger argues, by fully conforming to Christ's mind frame, the disciple automatically becomes a blessing to his or her fellow human beings. As Paul declares emphatically: "It is no longer I who live, but Christ who lives in me" (Gal 2:20). Ratzinger continues, "The pure heart is the loving heart that enters into communion of service with Jesus Christ."[11]

Concerning the priesthood, Ratzinger observed during the ordinations of the *Integrierte Gemeinde* (Integrated Community):

> The messenger of Jesus Christ can never be a mere speaker, never merely a specialist of a special theory. For this reason, being the messenger of the sacramental ministry signifies a ministry to which word and being belong. And this, in turn, cannot simply come to pass in a heroic deed: being taken by the Lord, and dying unto him, and thus the Lord comes to human beings. We call this sacrament, this mystery of death occurring over and against all our own activities and all our own abilities and knowledge, self-surrender unto him, being accepted by him and through him, so that he might speak, live, and be present through us.... Being a priest means *diakonos Christou*, becoming Christ's servant; and this means not being at one's own locale, and the place of one's self that one had sought, but to be there where he is.[12]

Jesus Christ and the Homilist

On this topic, Ratzinger takes as his point of departure the acute eye of a convert, Erik Peterson (1890–1960). After overcoming Protestant theology's subjectivist understanding of the minister and homily, Peterson discovered that in the Catholic homily something more modest but also greater occurs: the transition from the eon of Adam to the eon of Christ.[13] Ratzinger succinctly summarizes this in the following words; for him, homily and theology are only possible within the brackets of the Church and dogma: "The inner tension of the sermon derives from the objective arc of the tension connecting dogma, scripture, the Church and the world of today. None of these pillars may be removed, except at the cost of the crumbling of the whole edifice."[14]

While the homilist is not the Word, he may become transparent to it. He can never bring this transparency about on his own. It can, however, come about if he knows himself as indebted, regarding his knowledge of Christ, to the Church's faith and sevenfold sacramental life and to the Church's preserving knowledge of Christ and rendering him ever present in the Eucharist. Like the homilist (a deacon, priest, or bishop), the Church also is mindful of the fact that she is not the Word but the place where the Word has taken up his abode. Thus, both the clerical homilist and the lay preacher allow the individual "I" to be spelled with a lowercase "i," so that the universal "we" of the creed may shine forth. This subjective "i" is aware that in the Greek original the creed began with "we believe." The lowercase "i" of the homilist or lay preacher finds its proper context, authority, and thus authenticity, in the lowercase "w" of the ecclesial "we." The lowercase "we" in turn draws its justification exclusively from the capital case "I" of the sovereign Lord of all history and redeemer, Jesus Christ. He is "the face of God, the Name of God, the possibility of invoking God as a Thou, as person, as heart. The proper name of Jesus unveils the mystery of the Name pronounced in the Burning Bush. It now appears that God had not pronounced definitively his own Name, that his discourse had been temporarily interrupted. The name of Jesus, in fact, contains the word YHWH in Hebrew form, and adds to it a further concept: 'God redeems,' 'I am who I am' signifies 'I am he who redeems you.' His being [alone] is redemption."[15]

This elongation of YHWH in Jesus Christ is only tenable if Jesus is continually, from all eternity, immersed in the Blessed Trinity and therefore in the closest possible communication with his divine Father. As it is constitutive for Jesus to be constantly the Son, so the homilist and preacher must live in the greater reality of the Church in order to be able to live from divine life. Otherwise, the crucial nexus between faith and reason will dissolve and cheap folklore will take over. The danger of Marcionism, divorcing Jesus from the God of the Old Testament, then draws near. One is then unable to apprehend in Jesus Christ God's definitive response to Job's reproaches in the Old Testament. The Incarnation of God in Jesus is central. Upon it one can proclaim the suffering God to humanity, the crucified and resurrected Son. One is able to proclaim that God does not eliminate suffering, but he is able to transform it. The homilist and preacher finds this existentially attested to by the saints. They have turned their hearts to the suffering brothers and sisters in the world. By sharing in God's passion for humanity, the homilist and preacher existentially acquire credibility amid cynicism and l'ennui (boredom).[16]

PART V

The Liturgy: Christ-Filled Worship

CHAPTER 23

The Transparency of Christ and Christians: The Liturgy

The Church is *communio*, she is God's communing with men in Christ, and hence the communing of men with one another—and, in consequence, sacrament, sign, instrument of salvation. The Church is the celebration of the Eucharist; the Eucharist is the Church; they do not simply stand by side; they are one and the same.[1]

The Eucharist and the Church are mutually enabling and conditioning one another. Ratzinger, brought up in a joyous culture where the intellectual, cultural, and aesthetic highlight of life was the Roman Catholic liturgy, cherishes early candlelit Advent masses (Rorate Masses, *Engelämter*), Lenten devotions, colorful Corpus Christi processions, Easter and Christmas celebrations, and beautiful Marian devotions (*Maiandachten*). The priest pronouncing "Christ is risen!" is to him the most impressive portrayal of the Lord's resurrection from the dead. He recalls his childhood in the lovely Upper Bavarian town of Aschau (1932–1937): "It was becoming more and more clear to me that here I was encountering a reality that no one had simply thought up, a reality that no official authority or great individual had created. This mysterious fabric of texts and actions had grown from the faith of the Church over the centuries."[2]

Such joy faces two hurdles today: (1) philosophy nowadays rejects a metaphysics assuming a creator God, and (2) the reduction of reality to physical causes and effects can no longer consider the possibility of divine intervention. Already Aristotle had considered it below the dignity of God to interact with the temporal realm. But, the triune God intervenes in history and establishes a relationship with humankind. This in turn allows people to pray and enter into worship. The *analogia fidei* allows for God's initiative: "The Eucharistic prayer is an entering into the prayer of Jesus Christ himself; hence it is the Church's entering into the Logos, the Father's Word, into the Logos' self-surrender to the Father, which in the Cross, has also become the surrender of mankind to him."[3]

During his trips back to Germany from Rome during the council he already noted with alarm that people considered everything in flux. Pastors began to develop liturgy according to their gusto. Placing Jesus' work at an individual's disposition renders the Church no longer salt of the earth and light to the world. He recorded these concerns in public on June 18, 1965.[4]

The liturgy is essentially God's mysterious work, mutable on the outside, but never fabricated. True, it has suffered at times from a life-inhibiting reduction to an abstract, neoscholastic sacramental theology. Yet, for Ratzinger, modernists and traditionalists alike have lost sight of the liturgy as a living whole far removed from the dictates of pastoral exigencies or liturgical archaeologisms. Since the thirteenth century, Ratzinger thinks the question of validity and the fixation on the words of institution (that read "that when spoken render bread and wine into the body and blood of Jesus Christ during the Eucharist") have come to obscure the nature of liturgy. A legalistic minimalism gradually set in, which in the second half of the twentieth century led to boundless creativity unimaginable in the Eastern rites. "*Les extrêmes se touchent*" ("the extremes touch each other", as the French say. He is much in agreement with the noted Benedictine liturgist Odo Casel (1886–1948), who bemoaned "an effectus-theology" and reminded all believers of the real re-enactment of the mysteries of Christ by his Church in the liturgy. A salvific encounter with the whole Christ-mystery occurs, not only with the Savior's death and Resurrection.

As the sovereign and free action of God, the Eucharist is woven into the ultimate destiny of humankind and the cosmos. The Church does not externally initiate the liturgy but dwells in it with the triune God. The early pagans and Christians saw in the Eucharist the decisive reality that defines Christianity. In the third century, the martyrs of Abitina replied to the Emperor Diocletian, "*sine dominico non possumus*" ("without the Sunday [Eucharist] we cannot [live]"). The worship of God is not an accidental accessory to Christianity but its very being. As Ratzinger elaborates in his *The Spirit of the Liturgy*, the Church's time in the Eucharist integrates the past, present, and future into one reality that "touches eternity." The Word of God becomes incarnate at the ambo as scripture and, at the altar, as sacrifice and meal. At every mass, the Annunciation and the "*Verbum caro factum est*" ("the Word was made flesh") reoccur. Far from being a mere liturgical game or ritual, it is "λογικὴ λατρεια, *logiké latreia*," Logos-filled worship that transforms human existence in the Logos, allowing the Christian's interior to become contemporaneous with Christ.

If all that gives meaning is beyond the world and history, then those seeking such meaning must part ways with the world. Interiorization and contemplation are possible in the world because of the mystery of the Incarnation. Divine charity can be experienced in the liturgy and therefore somehow lived by human beings. In this sense, Ratzinger agrees with Hans Urs von Balthasar, who captures this well in the book title *Glaubhaft ist nur die Liebe* (only love is credible).[5] The liturgy teaches that reality is more than what can be comprehended. This is what Ratzinger means when he introduces the difference between *verum quia faciendum* (that which is true is what seems feasible) and *verum quia factum* (that which is true is what is made preceding human fabrication). Nowadays—after Kant—one believes only in the *verum quia faciendum*. Truth is only that which the human subject can generate.

Truth is reduced to the range of what humankind can accomplish.[6] How can the divine Logos kenotically descend to the world and be recognized by human beings as the ground of all things and as something personal, as agape? How can marriage, the family, and especially the liturgy be apprehended as an expression and participation in such a divine agape? How can divine charity be appreciated, not as contradicting human love, but as its fulfillment? Ratzinger and Balthasar ask whether Jesus' words are accessible: "He who finds his life will lose it, and he who loses his life for my sake will find it" (Mt 10:39). Can baptism be seen as God's entry into our being, and vice versa, so that he becomes our measure and living space? Ratzinger asked this in a meditation given during Holy Week, "the Eucharist is a community with Christ that transforms us into him and leads us to one another, as we share in the same bread: The body of the Lord, which we, so to speak, do not incorporate into ourselves, but which, rather, takes us from ourselves and incorporates us into him, and thus truly intends to make us his Church."[7]

Indicatively, the first volume of the collected works of Ratzinger published is volume 11, a compilation of all his thoughts in the area of the liturgy.[8] In the introduction to this volume, he points out that the first constitution Second Vatican Council produced was the one on the liturgy, *Sacrosanctum Concilium*, approved solemnly on December 4, 1963. As Benedict XVI in his introduction expounds:

> By beginning with the theme "liturgy," the primacy of God, the priority of the "God" theme, was unequivocally brought to light. The first word of the first chapter in the constitution is "God." When the focus is not on God, everything else loses its orientation. The words of the Benedictine rule *"Ergo nihil Operi Dei praeponatur"* (43, 3; "So let nothing be put before the work of God") apply specifically to monasticism, but as a statement of priority they are also true for the life of the Church, and of each of its members, each in his own way. It is perhaps useful to recall that in the term "orthodoxy," the second half of the word, *"doxa,"* does not mean "opinion," but "splendor," "glorification": this is not a matter of a correct "opinion" about God, but of a proper way of glorifying him, of responding to him. Because this is the fundamental question of the man who begins to understand himself in the correct way: how should I encounter God? So learning the right way of adoration—of orthodoxy—is what is given to us above all by the faith.[9]

The liturgy was for young Ratzinger the way to experience the faith of his family and encounter God. The festive, luminous Baroque churches of Bavaria demonstrate the *doxa* of God, the splendor of truth as manifested liturgically. Ratzinger's temperament and personality found its fullest expression as a member of the liturgically convened Church. Later, the Munich theologians Söhngen, Schmaus, Pascher, and Guardini spelled out in scholarly language the central reality Ratzinger had already been a part of since baptism. He had chosen fundamental theology as his discipline of preference because he was preoccupied with the question about the fitting and proper response to God. What role does divine liturgy play in this response? In this sense Ratzinger was never interested in particular questions of rubrics or specific issues of liturgical studies but in the anchoring of the liturgy in the fundamental act of our faith, and therefore also its place in our entire human existence.

Joseph Maria Pascher (1893–1979) was a professor of religious pedagogy (1936–1940) and liturgy (1946–1960) in Munich. He served as a member of the preparatory commission to the Second Vatican Council and as *peritus* to Munich's archbishop Julius Cardinal Döpfner (1962–1963). In addition, he belonged to the committees translating the new Roman Missal and the Divine Office into German.[10]

In 2001, at the Benedictine monastery in Fontgombault, France, Ratzinger reminded his audience that the Second Vatican Council defined liturgy as "the work of Christ, the Priest and of His Body which is the Church." At another event, honoring the retirement of his brother, Monsignor Georg Ratzinger, he quoted the *Catechism*: "In Christian tradition (the word *liturgy*) means the participation of the people of God in 'the work of God' (*opus Dei*). Through the liturgy, Christ our Redeemer and High Priest continues the work of our redemption in, with, and through His Church."[11]

As the work of Christ, the liturgy refers primarily to the historical, redemptive actions of Jesus, his death and Resurrection. As it is God's action it is also beyond history. It becomes the expression of a divine will. As a consequence, one is reminded that the liturgy has Christ as its true subject and bearer. This insight reveals the Eucharist as both sacrifice and meal. It becomes a unique meal by being the gift of his body and blood in the form of a supper that is the celebration of a *communio*. In contrast to modernity's individualistic understanding of the human person, the Eucharistic assembly becomes one communion by sharing in Christ's self-sacrifice, and the communicants thereby do not become—so to speak—"self-consecrated." One also encounters this reality in scripture and its canon, bearing in mind that they are products of the living community, called the Church, celebrating the sacrament of the Eucharist. As sacrificial, paschal mystery it actuates the words of old: "This is the blood of the covenant which Yahweh makes with you in accordance with all these provisions" (Ex 24:8). The Old Testament sacrifices point to the sacrifice of Jesus Christ. In his talk to the monks of Fontgombault, Ratzinger cited Augustine: "All the divine prescriptions of scripture which concern the sacrifice of the tabernacle or the temple are figures which refer to the love of God and neighbor."[12] This initiates a second movement in the same direction: "The whole redeemed human community, that is to say the assembly and the community of the saints, is offered to God in sacrifice by the High Priest Who offered Himself."[13] This confirms the German philosopher Karl Jaspers's observation that Christianity is a religion of "self-transcendence," precisely in that it gives the individual's existence its deepest meaning. The believers join in the eternal Son's movement to the Father. The mediator no longer stands alone but draws the redeemed unto himself and thus fulfills the innermost hopes and completes the destiny of humankind (Jn 12:32). God no longer expects blood sacrifice from Christians but rather love. This allows Augustine to conclude: "Such is the sacrifice of Christians: the multitude is one single body in Christ. The Church celebrates this mystery by the sacrifice of the Altar, well known to believers, because in it, it is shown to her that in the things which she offers, it is she herself who is offered."[14] Over and against Martin Luther's aversion to the concept of sacrifice, Ratzinger does not tire of underlining that, according to John, it was in connection with the paschal lambs being immolated in the temple that Jesus Christ becomes the sacrificial Lamb. Upon this background, Peter Chrysologus enjoins all Christians: "It is a strange sacrifice, where the body offers itself without the body, the blood without the blood! I beg you—says the Apostle—by the mercy of God, to offer yourselves as a living victim."[15]

Thus, the term "congregation" has a unique meaning most difficult to capture by someone who has not entered deliberately into the Eucharist: "Neither the priest alone nor the [sociologically definable] congregation alone 'does' the liturgy. Rather, the divine liturgy is celebrated by the whole Christ, head and members: the priest, the [physically present] congregation, the individuals insofar as they are united with Christ and to the extent that they represent the total Christ in the communion of head and body. The whole Church, heaven and earth, God and man, takes part in every liturgical celebration, and that not just in theory but in actual fact. The meaning of liturgy is realized all the more concretely the more each celebration is nourished by this awareness and this experience."[16]

Ratzinger regrets that some readers and reviewers of *The Spirit of the Liturgy*, which appeared in the jubilee year 2000, focused so much on external forms, such as the position of the altar and the direction of liturgical prayer, that is, whether the priest and the people face the same direction, while disregarding his real interest, namely, Jesus Christ as the focal point of all liturgical activity. As he elaborates: "Priest and people certainly do not pray to each other, but to the same Lord." He welcomes the circumstance that increasingly the practice of placing a cross on the altar makes headway. Community is formed by a common interior orientation. Thus, the relationships between the Old Testament heritage and the New Testament, and between Christianity and the other world religions, becomes comprehensible. Following Maximus the Confessor (ca. 580–662) and Hans Urs von Balthasar, he emphasizes that the Christian liturgy perceives itself as cosmic: "The liturgy is celebrated within the vastness of the cosmos, it embraces creation and history at the same time." Liturgical orientation conveys the firm notion that the God who created the universe and human beings therein is also the one who redeems humanity. Ratzinger closes the introduction with a quote from Nehemiah 8:10: "The joy of the Lord is our strength." Affirming this Christological perspective, he writes in *Deus Caritas Est*:

> Jesus gave this act of oblation an enduring presence through his act of institution of the Eucharist at the Last Supper. He anticipated his death and resurrection by giving his disciples, in the bread and wine, his very self, his body and blood as the new manna (cf. Jn 6:31–33). The ancient world had dimly perceived that man's real food—what truly nourishes him as man—is ultimately the *Logos*, eternal wisdom: this same *Logos* now truly becomes food for us—as love. The Eucharist draws us into Jesus' act of self-oblation. More than just statically receiving the

incarnate *Logos*, we enter into the very dynamic of his self-giving. The imagery of marriage between God and Israel is now realized in a way previously inconceivable: it had meant standing in God's presence, but now it becomes union with God through sharing in Jesus' self-gift, sharing in his body and blood. The sacramental "mysticism," grounded in God's condescension towards us, operates at a radically different level and lifts us to far greater heights than anything that any human mystical elevation could ever accomplish.[17]

As the conciliar document *Sacrosanctum Concilium* reiterated, the Eucharist is the continuation of the Paschal Mystery. Renewing the Paschal Mystery, it anticipates the consummation of salvation history and the completion of the cosmos at the end of time. The Last Supper was thus quite unlike a commonplace meal. Its centrifugal point is the very words Jesus spoke. With these words, he transformed the meal into his self-giving as gift to the Father. As a *koinonia* or *communio* constituted by the Eucharist, the Church lives a profound reality in Jesus Christ.[18] Until the sixteenth century, the Eucharist was primarily referred to as a meal of saturation; a noted exception is 1 Corinthians 11 and discussions of it, as it emphasizes that no physical nourishment is signified. As the noted liturgist Josef Andreas Jungmann (1889–1975) discovered anew, the mass was always referred to as *Eucharistia*, that is, the prayer of thanksgiving.[19] The meal symbolism is not incorrect. It is merely emphasized too much in some quarters. The meal dimension, he insists, "is subordinated to a larger whole and integrated into it."[20] Ratzinger sharply distinguishes the Eucharist from the meals of fellowship Jesus initiated during his life. Ratzinger introduces a further nuance: the Last Supper is not the form for the Eucharist as liturgy but contains the foundation for the dogmatic content of the Christian Eucharist. Christ did not institute the Eucharist in sharp disjunction to the faith of Israel or diametrically opposed to the primordial religious intuitions of other cultures. It is the fulfillment of Israelite faith and that for which all human beings in the depths of their hearts long. "This new and all-encompassing form of worship could not be derived from a meal, but had to be defined through the interconnection of Temple and Synagogue, Word and Sacrament, Cosmos and Liturgy."[21]

Tradition itself bears out what is present *in nuce* in the Last Supper. The emergence of the mass as a rite was the spelling out of the Eucharist as the thanksgiving sacrifice to which Psalms 22, 40, 51, and 69 allude. Tradition is not a betrayal of the commandment of Jesus Christ, but the deliberate consecration and concretion of his will. Ratzinger seems to argue that to divine a rift between Jesus, the apostles, and the subsequent ecclesial reality would amount to a denial of Pentecost. The departure from an emphasis on the meal-character of the Eucharist would entail now changing the very architecture and organization of liturgical space: (1) reorientation to the risen Lord, symbolized by the rising sun in the east; (2) celebrating the presence of the Lord among the community, rather than the community celebrating itself, and; (3) by implication, a rediscovery of interiority. As early as the 1970s, he had postulated the need for a reemphasis on a Christ-centered community vis-à-vis the congregation.[22] The liturgy is not a gathering initiated by people, but a communion of those following Christ's invitation.

In *On the Way to Jesus Christ*, he writes: "Today in broad circles, even among believers, an image has prevailed of Jesus who demands nothing, never scolds, who accepts everyone and everything, who no longer does anything but affirms us." This, Ratzinger notes, is in marked contrast to the Jesus who oftentimes challenges and rebukes his listeners, the even scandalous Jesus portrayed in the Gospels, to whom the martyrs and saints bear witness, who is "demanding, bold... The Jesus of the Gospels is certainly not convenient for us." It is, however, this Jesus "that answers the deepest question of our existence, which—whether we want to or not—keeps us on the lookout for God, for a gratification that is limitless, for the infinite. We must again set out on the way to this real Jesus."[23] This issue is of vital importance, touching on every aspect of the faith. "The question of how we should read the Bible is inseparably bound up with the question about Christ. The topic of sacrament and liturgy deals with the presence of Jesus among us—with Christ not only yesterday but today."[24]

False images of Christ are, according to the author, comprised essentially of two components. The first is what might be called an absolutizing of the historical-critical method. "The one component is the analysis of the Gospel texts using the methods of historical criticism," which gives rise to "an increasingly complicated system of source-hypotheses and reconstructed redaction histories... which is impressive for its assiduous scholarship but also seems dubious because of its internal contradictions."[25] In its self-determination to be scientific, it has accepted "the postulate that nature is objective," which is the cornerstone of the scientific method. Such an approach keeps God from accessing the world and relegates the reality of God to the subjective experience of the recipient à la Kant and Schleiermacher. If the "objectivity principle" is indeed valid without restriction, then everything pertaining to God and his manifestations in history must be downgraded to unscientific, subjective experiences and feelings. He concludes, "subjectivity and perhaps the calculus of consequences, then, constitute the ultimate authority in matters of religion."[26] Any claim, then, regarding Jesus as the sole and universal source of salvation must be arrogantly presumptuous. The second component projects onto the historical figure of Jesus the values and aspirations of a particular time and place. Quite precariously close to Feuerbach's thesis of God as a mere projection, "Jesus is sought as a present-day figure... and therefore, in a second train of thought, the ideas and ideals of a given era are combined with this figure."[27] Together, these components construct a transformed Jesus, who is "a man who is nothing more than the advocate of all men."[28] Here the utter uniqueness of the God-man is surrendered for the sake of the supposed state-of-the-art techniques in scholarship. It is in this vein that Ratzinger appears to interpret the critical responses to *Dominus Jesus*. He writes, "Only [a Christ] who is both man and God can be the ontological bridge leading from the one to the other. And therefore he is this for everyone, not only for some."[29] To those who characterize assertions of the uniqueness and universality of Christ as mere presumptions, the author replies: "Is it not presumption to say that God cannot give us the truth as gift?" Here he returns to familiar themes: the priority of the truth and the nature of revelation as gift. "Truth cannot be a possession...I accept the knowledge as a gift, of which I become unworthy, about which I may not boast, as though it were my own." At issue here is the mystery of the gratuitousness of God's sovereign election. "God made a choice, established some for others and all for one another, and we can only acknowledge in humility that we are unworthy messengers who do not proclaim ourselves but rather speak with a holy fear about something that is not ours but that comes from God."[30]

At this point, Ratzinger argues against an unreflective understanding of pluralism that actually advocates, not genuine pluralism, but eclecticism. "Reason is critical of religion in its search for truth; yet at its very origins, Christianity sides with reason and considers this ally to be its principal forerunner." Indeed, he points out, the Church fathers found the seeds of the Word, not in pagan religions, but in philosophy, that is, "in the process of critical reason directed against the (pagan) religions, in the history of progressive reason, and not in the history of religion."[31] Striving together for truth, there is a dialectic of religion and reason. It is reason that challenges religion to live according to the claims of truth. To do otherwise, to argue that people should be allowed to live contentedly in the historical tradition into which they are born, "in fact, reduces religion to a mere habit and closes it off from the truth" separating people from one another.[32] And if, indeed, Christ is God's supreme gift and final Word to humanity, mediated through those he has chosen and are now present in his Church, then "this Church participates in (Christ's) universal mediation and...every relation to him somehow includes the Church."[33]

In describing how Christ, through the Spirit, transforms the world, Ratzinger describes five successive transformations the Eucharist effects. In the first transformation, Christ, in his vicarious passion, "transforms, from within, men's act of violence against him into an act of self-giving for these men—into an act of love....This is the fundamental transformation upon which all the rest is based." In this first transformation, "Death itself is transformed: love is stronger than death. It lasts. And so within this transformation is contained the further transformation of death into resurrection, of the dead body into the risen body."[34] This is the second transformation, which in turn leads to the third. The transformation of the mortal body into the resurrected body, "into 'life-giving spirit,'" makes the third transformation possible: "The gifts of bread and wine, which are gifts of creation and at the same time the product of human acceptance and 'transformation' of creation, are changed, so that in them the Lord who gives himself—his gift, he himself—becomes present, because he *is* self-giving." Fourth, the transformed bread and wine "are there to transform us men, so that we become one bread with him and then one body with him"[35]; "And so the goal is unity." Finally, the fifth transformation effects the transformation of all creation. "Through us, who have been transformed and have become one body, a life-giving spirit, all creation must be transformed. All of creation must become...the living dwelling place of God: 'that God may be everything to everyone' (1 Cor 15:28)." The point of departure is the Eucharist. In this sequence of transformations, Ratzinger provides a profound explication and meditation on the conciliar document *Sacrosanctum Concilium*'s characterization of the Eucharist as "the source and summit of the Christian life" (*SC* 47, *LG* 11).[36]

The remedy for the current distortions of Christ and his Church may be found in what Ratzinger calls "the new 'aesthetics' of faith" and "the arrow of beauty."[37] Quoting Nicholas Cabasilas, Ratzinger describes true knowledge as "being touched by reality, 'by the personal presence of Christ himself.'" Encountering the beauty of Christ is to encounter "a more real, more profound knowledge than mere rational deduction."[38] Reminiscent of von Balthasar, he states, "For faith to grow today, we must lead ourselves and the persons we meet to encounter the saints and to come in contact with the beautiful." This, however, imposes upon us the task of opposing "the cult of the ugly" and to "withstand the deceptive beauty that diminishes man instead of making him great and that, for that very reason, is false." Ultimately, the Church must present to the world the face of Christ crucified, a "face that is so disfigured [that] there appears the genuine, the ultimate beauty: the beauty of love that goes 'to the very end' and thus proves to be mightier than falsehood and violence."[39]

In order to avoid misinterpreting Ratzinger as a trite traditionalist, it is important to note the consonance between, first, his and de Lubac's understanding of the Church and the Eucharist and, second, his and Guardini's common concern for liturgical renewal. When speaking of "Catholicism," de Lubac means the same concept Pius XII identified in his encyclical *Mystici Corporis*: the Church is the mystical body of Christ. But de Lubac elaborates that this "supernatural unity supposes a previous natural unity, the unity of the human race."[40] All are "called" to join the Church. The purpose in creating the world was so that all might enter the Church one day.[41] *Qahal* in Hebrew and *ekklesia* in Greek bear out this meaning: *kletoi*—this people is "called"—prior to being actively *congregatio*, the Church is passively *convocatio*, "called by Christ." Much like Jesus Christ, the Church is fully divine and fully human; this Church is heavenly as regards its inner-Trinitarian origin but human as regards its composition. While standing in relation to us as a parent, it is as *Corpus Christi mixtum* composed of earthly and heavenly elements.[42] In the post-Reformation, scientific era, the popular, secularizing interpretation of the Church forgets that God is the originator of the Catholic Church, and he brings this reality about in and through the Eucharist.

In light of this background, the Eucharist is beheld as "the sacrament of the unity of the Church." The mystery of the real presence and the mystery of the Church are two sides of one coin. This identifying of the mystical body with both the Eucharist and the Church has roots going back to Origen, who referred to the "individual" body of Christ as "the typical body." Thus, the Church as "the real body" is the real presence of the eternal Logos Jesus Christ in the world.[43]

As already mentioned, as a student, Ratzinger also read de Lubac's *Corpus Mysticum*. In it the Jesuit lays out the threefold distinction reflecting a Trinitarian symbolism: (1) the body of Christ born of Mary and ascended into heaven, (2) the body of Christ consecrated on the altar, and (3) the body of Christ that Christians are and receive in the one reality bifurcated into two moments: Eucharist and Church.[44] At various episodes in history, the term *corpus mysticum* was applied to each of these three modes. These distinctions find their logical conclusion and climax in de Lubac's memorable statement in his later book *The Splendor of the Church*: "Thus everything points to a study of the relation between the Church and the Eucharist, which we may describe as standing as cause to each other. Each had been entrusted to the other, so to speak, by Christ; *the Church produces the Eucharist, but the Eucharist also produces the Church*."[45] Its ontic being is Christ. As he succinctly formulates:

> The Eucharist is the effective sign of the spiritual sacrifice offered by the whole Christ.... The Church thus really makes herself by the celebration of the mystery; the holy and sanctifying Church builds up the Church of the saints. The mystery of communication is rounded out in a mystery of communion—such is the meaning of the ancient and ever-fresh word 'communion' which is currently used to describe the sacrament. The Church of this world is embodied in the Church of heaven, and the ministerial hierarchy, thus preparing that kingdom of priests which Christ wishes to make of us all to the glory of His Father, is, in the exercise of its most sacred function, thus entirely at the service of the hierarchy of sanctity.[46]

Quite rightly the British priest and theologian Paul McPartlan constates the "mutual immanence" of Christians in such an ecclesiology.[47] Fifty-one years after *Catholicism*'s first publication, Ratzinger observed that a shift had occurred:

> If previously there was a narrowing of the Christian vision to an individualism, we are now in danger of a sociological leveling down. Sacraments are often seen merely as celebrations of community where there is no more room for the personal dialogue between God and the soul.... And so there has been a kind of reversal of the previous individualism that itself has fundamentally constructed the theological perspective and has also spread from the central theological themes to the most concrete personal applications.[48]

Nowadays one often encounters an inversion of the equation de Lubac had posited. An ecclesial egalitarianism based on psychological agendas and power relationships seems to have taken over. Like the apostles on the way to Jerusalem, or the disciples on the way to Emmaus, Catholics ignore the mystery of Christ and the Eucharist and are obsessed with who is the greatest or with concerns of short-term security.[49] Also, in order to bring de Lubac's understanding of ecclesiology into discussion again, Ratzinger penned *The Spirit of the Liturgy* and *God Is Near Us*. In his theology of the liturgy, he builds on the ecclesiological foundations laid by de Lubac, and he undertakes every effort to preserve the integrity of de Lubac's approach by supplying it with greater clarity through advancing into areas of deeper theological reflection.

In the introduction to his own *The Spirit of the Liturgy* Ratzinger writes:

I should like to suggest a comparison. Like all comparisons, it is in many ways inadequate, and yet it may aid understanding. We might say that in 1918, the year that Guardini published his book (*The Spirit of the Liturgy*), the liturgy was rather like a fresco. It had been preserved from damage, but it had been almost completely overlaid with whitewash by later generations. In the Missal from which the priest celebrated, the form of the liturgy that had grown from its earliest beginnings was still present, but, as far as the faithful were concerned, it was largely concealed beneath instructions for and forms of private prayer. The fresco was laid bare by the Liturgical Movement and, in a definitive way, by the Second Vatican Council. For a moment its colors and figures fascinated us. But since then the fresco has been endangered by climatic conditions as well as by various restorations and reconstructions. In fact, it is threatened with destruction, if the necessary steps are not taken to stop these damaging influences. Of course, there must be no question of its being covered with whitewash again, but what is imperative is a new reverence in the way we treat it, a new understanding of its message and its reality, so that rediscovery does not become the first stage of irreparable loss....My purpose in writing this little book, which I now lay before the public, is to assist this renewal of understanding. Its basic intentions coincide with what Guardini wanted to achieve in his own time with *The Spirit of the Liturgy*. That is why I deliberately chose a title that would be immediately reminiscent of that classic of liturgical theology.[50]

Ratzinger readily acknowledges that the Tridentine liturgy (the unification and harmonization into one form of various, already existing forms of the liturgy in the Latin part of the Catholic Church in 1570) had become rather elaborate and baroque, sometimes even theatrical and pompous, displaying a "ritual rigidity in need of defrosting." It is lamentable if the laity prefer to recite the rosary or private litanies rather than participate in the Eucharist. But the alternative to such a private understanding of the Eucharist cannot be believers who merely celebrate an event, or who celebrate themselves and each other in "togetherness." The greatest degree of humanism possible is reached in entering into the mystery of the God-man Jesus Christ in the Eucharist.[51]

Perhaps inspired by Hugo Rahner's clairvoyant, brief essay *Man at Play*,[52] Ratzinger, as well as Guardini, his mentor in liturgical matters, sees in the liturgy a purpose-free "play," where the human actors do not define the game's outcome or utility. Any schizophrenic separation into a utilitarian materialism and a deceitful spirituality should come to an end, as experienced in the early decades of the twentieth century. Both men do not wish to return to an idealized medieval past but to preserve its enduring message. Celebrating the liturgy signifies a Christian's true fulfillment and indeed the fulfillment of every human being. In his slim study, *Letter from Lake Como* (1923), Guardini warned against the technical abuse of the liturgy and—via extension—of all of human life. Immediate contact with life and nature have been lost in the modern lifestyle, and a technical-utilitarian, goal-oriented perspective seems to be relentlessly and inexorably replacing it. The inherent danger is that the liturgy will be misunderstood as serving extraneous purposes, such as providing mere moral formation or bringing about human collegiality. To both theologians these are simply secondary (albeit desirable) results. However many well-intended human activities enter into the liturgy, the primary actor always remains God. In the believers' awareness, the Logos must always take precedence over the ethos. Beyond required obedience in faith, only a symbolic-religious sense is able to celebrate genuine liturgy as Guardini famously and prophetically warned at a conference in Magonzo, Italy, in 1964.[53] An enlightened, goal-oriented understanding must not enter the liturgy. He warned against not sufficiently countenancing the possibility of such an outcome of liturgical renewal.[54]

Ratzinger's concerns with recent liturgical developments rotate around three areas: (1) the position of the presiding priest, (2) the interpretation of the notion of "active participation," and (3) the role of silence during the Eucharist. One of the Second Vatican Council's major debates revolved around the question of the liturgy. Ratzinger welcomed the priority the council fathers gave to the liturgy and particularly to the Eucharist. The Eucharist is the very center and heart of ecclesial life, allowing the Church to live constantly in the Lord. The Eucharistic sacrifice enables her to actualize her true mission, namely, to adore the Blessed Trinity. It was his hope that the Church would now consciously live from the true wellspring of her being, which is the liturgy. He continues in *Deus Caritas Est* by observing the ecclesia-building ramifications of the Eucharist:

> This sacramental mysticism is social in character, for in sacramental communion I become one with the Lord, like all other communicants. As Saint Paul says, "Because there is one bread, we who are many are one body, for we all partake of the one bread" (1 Cor 10:17). Union with Christ is also union with all those to whom he gives himself. I cannot possess Christ just for myself; I can belong to him only in union with those who have become, or who will become, his own. Communion draws me out of myself towards him, and thus also towards unity with all Christians. We become "one body," completely joined in a single existence. Love of God and love of neighbor are now truly united: God incarnate draws us all to himself. We can thus understand how *agape* also became a term for the Eucharist: there God's own *agape* comes to us bodily, in order to continue his work in us and through us.[55]

In *The Feast of Faith*, he writes about how the Eucharist formed the communal religion he had been a part of since his early childhood: "I can still smell those carpets of flowers and the freshness of the birch trees: I can see all the houses decorated, the banners, the singing; I can still hear the village band which, indeed, sometimes dared to do more, on this occasion, than it was able to! I remember the joie de vivre of the local lads, firing their gun salutes."[56]

For this reason, as *peritus* Ratzinger enthusiastically welcomed the dogmatic constitution *Sacrosanctum Concilium*. It returned the objective Sunday celebration of the Eucharist to its rightful position. It reemphasized the congregation's participation in the mystery of Christ's Redemption over and against the individual's private worship. He eagerly anticipated the new lectionary and communion under both species. He had expected particular churches to form an intermediary instance mediating between the See of Rome and the local bishop. In the same vein, he looked forward to the use of the vernacular in the liturgy as a way to overcome sterility in the liturgy and in theological scholarship. The wall of Latinity "had to be breached if the liturgy were again to function either as proclamation or as invitation to prayer."[57] The human personality as the agent who gives assent to God and is capable of living joyfully the mysteries of the Christian faith had been sidelined. Like Guardini, he had hoped the Church would awaken in the souls of believers in the postconciliar era. But, quite the contrary, he witnessed the breakdown of Eucharistic attendance and of Church unity.[58]

In his commentary on the the Vatican II Council's third session, he relates how at the council's opening liturgy he experienced something like the "last serene procession of the Counter-Reformation Church," expressing an "archeological liturgy."[59] Nonetheless, he had only expected a moderate use of the vernacular. The incessant commotion and verbosity of postconciliar liturgical praxis had not been anticipated by any of the council fathers. Nowhere had the council advocated the disappearance of traditional sacred music. The actual form of the liturgy had historically never been placed in the hands of individuals. It had always been strictly forbidden for the clergy and laity alike to alter the rubrics.[60]

His positions concerning the liturgy are consonant with both the letter and the spirit of the Second Vatican Council. The keynote address he gave at the renowned Liturgisches Institut in Trier, Germany, in 2003, during the fortieth anniversary of the promulgation of the *Constitution on the Sacred Liturgy* attests to this.[61] Nevertheless, he accentuates things differently than numerous liturgists have done since the council. Ratzinger emphasizes more the latreuic (worshipping) dimension of the Eucharist, without ignoring its fundamentally catabatic (descending from God to humankind) character. Within this slight shift of emphasis, he is fully mindful of the Eucharist as commemoration, thanksgiving, and as an event that forms a believing community. The council also holds this: "The sacred liturgy is principally the worship of the divine majesty" (*SC* 33). Liturgy is thanksgiving and adoration. In the immediate postconciliar era, oftentimes the dimension of cult enjoyed less attention. Ratzinger reminds us of the council stating: "Liturgy...is rightly seen as an exercise of the priestly office of Jesus Christ. It involves the presentation of man's sanctification under the guise of signs perceptible by the senses..." (*SC* 7). Along with the exalted Savior, the members of his body worship God the Father in gratitude.

If God and humankind meet in Jesus Christ's Incarnation and sacrifice, then, Ratzinger holds, one cannot discern a contradiction between history and the cosmos. Liturgy is both cosmic and historic, encompassing heaven and earth. Again, this aspect also is seconded by the council: "In the earthly liturgy we take part in a foretaste of that heavenly liturgy which is celebrated in the Holy City of Jerusalem.... With all the warriors of the heavenly army we sing a hymn of glory to the Lord..." (*SC* 8). The cross and Resurrection are "bridges, conjoining time and eternity." Utilizing the rich imagery of the sacrificial Lamb in the center of the heavenly liturgy in the book of revelation, heaven has been torn open by Christ's death and resurrection from the dead.[62] The liturgy is both celestial and terrestrial.[63]

It is therefore correct to define the liturgy as a part of creation coming to perfection in God. This stands to reason, as creation is the realm in which the encounter between God and humankind takes place, the Old Covenant was entered into, and the cult of Israel began. Therefore, the Christian cult also is historic, as Ratzinger states in *The Spirit of the Liturgy*.[64] Yet humans cannot produce or make a cult, lest it become idolatry. Thus, they must be commissioned by God for this task. It is in the word "sacrifice" that Ratzinger detects the crucial term. It may conjure up the notion of the destruction of a sacrificial entity. The essence of sacrifice, however, is gift. In this gift, one surrenders and hands oneself over to God almighty. The common goal of both the cult and of creation is the transfiguration of the world and humankind for the sake of unity with God. In this context, Ratzinger refers to Teilhard de Chardin, who held in *Hymn of the Universe* that the Eucharistic transubstantiation of the host is the anticipation of the perfection of the cosmos in Christ.[65]

Romano Guardini published the first edition of his epochal *Vom Geist der Liturgie* (*The Spirit of the Liturgy*)[66] in 1918 as the first volume of the liturgical series *Ecclesia Orans* (*Praying Church*). His aim was not to present a comprehensive theology of the liturgy. In fact, this little book exhibited no scholarly ambitions. Rather, his intention was to unlock for a large readership the concrete liturgical execution within an overarching anthropological, cultural, and philosophical (*kulturphilosophisch*) context. Almost overnight, it became the foundational text for the twentieth-century liturgical movement. Guardini argued that the Eucharist is the premier expression of the Church's essence.

Guardini's seven separate chapters deal with partial aspects of the whole.[67] The chapter on liturgical prayer demonstrates how the liturgy informs non-liturgical forms of prayer, without thereby making public worship superfluous. The discussion on liturgical community alerts the reader to the social context of the liturgy. It ought to be a concern for the liturgist to impose restrictions on the blossoming of one's own personality and to guide people cautiously toward the necessity of fitting into the greater ecclesial whole, that is, of limiting one's self-presentation in order to take one's place as a part of the whole, as willed by God. These terms describe well the sense of ecclesiality a Christian practices during the liturgy. He stresses that "Liturgy does not say 'I', but 'we.'"[68] Guardini succeeds in showing how the liturgy safeguards both the independence and interiority of individual prayer. He even discerns that what is, upon first sight, an impersonal and rather schematic stylization of religious forms of worship ultimately preserves the necessary unity of the tension between the individual and community. In a following step, he shows that the body and soul also form a tension-filled unity that impacts the liturgy. Building upon this insight, he is then able to address the issue of liturgical symbolics. A masterstroke is his treatment of the liturgy as play, comparing the liturgical act with the play of a child and the creative work of an artist. This discussion serves to convince the reader that the liturgy is not a purpose-oriented activity. Rather, its intention is to serve the realization, or better yet actuation, of "*Sinn*" ("meaning"). This central moment of the liturgy is grounded, in Guardini's judgment, in the transcendent reality of God's free being. Beginning with the fourth edition of 1919, the author added a chapter on liturgical sobriety (*liturgischer Ernst*). In this version of the text, he seeks to protect the book from the accusation of succumbing to aestheticism, that is, of subordinating truth to outward beauty. In the final chapter, Guardini stresses the preeminence of theoretical truth vis-à-vis ethical praxis. He captures this in the phrase "the primacy of the Logos over ethos" ("Primat des Logos über das Ethos"), an expression Ratzinger often repeats.[69] Precisely based on the liturgy's nature, Guardini is able to critique a modern tendency to yield to a reversal of this order.[70] This small gem of liturgical reflection was a major precursor and promoter of the notion of "active participation,"[71] particularly as expressed during the Second Vatican Council (*SC* 30) and the two decades immediately following it. It is no accident that Ratzinger put forth his own book on the liturgy under the same title as Guardini did decades earlier: the continuity of the one concern in both books should thereby be documented.

Ratzinger had devoured Guardini's classic soon after entering the seminary in 1946. It was a milestone in his intellectual and spiritual development. At the beginning of the second millennium, he wrote: "It helped us to discover the liturgy in all its hidden beauty, hidden wealth, and time-transcending grandeur, to see it as the animating center of the Church, the very center of Christian life. It led to a striving for a celebration of the liturgy that would be 'more substantial.' We were now willing to see the liturgy—in its inner demands and form—as the prayer of the Church, a prayer moved and guided by the Holy Spirit himself, in which Christ unceasingly becomes contemporary with us, enters our lives."[72] This explains how he could argue during the 1960s that the old mass was "archeological" and deplore how the participants in the old mass often appeared as if they were isolated individuals, drawing little spiritual sustenance from the liturgy and, frequently, immersed in a missal or a devotional book rather than engaged in the liturgy. This would explain why great Catholic mystics in the Baroque era, such as Saints John of the Cross and Teresa of Avila, make little mention of the spiritual benefits of the Eucharist.[73]

But instead of going back to the foundations, to rediscover the Lord and the liturgical sources of liturgy, the new liturgical praxis seemed to embrace modernity uncritically. Cultural fads were imitated, and the experimental was exalted at the cost of jettisoning Gregorian chant and polyphony from the liturgy. This development amounted to nothing short of a denial of one's own past, of a cultural revolution. Facing the congregation rather than the Lord became symptomatic of misunderstanding the liturgy: it signified spontaneously celebrating the community rather than worshipping the ever self-same God, emphasizing innovation rather than reverence. With a sort of youthful triumphalism, oblivious to the arduous task of rendering the past present, Guardini's "magnificent work" and other precursors of liturgical renewal were "thrown into the wastepaper basket."[74] To Ratzinger's dismay, the Church leadership was party to this by issuing an almost total prohibition of the old missal, an unheard of development in the whole of Church history. The new missal, while having many benefits, was no longer perceived as part of a living development. As a result, the liturgy now appeared self-made. Ratzinger makes out "the crisis in the Church" as essentially due to "the disintegration of the liturgy." He therefore calls for a new liturgical movement that reconciles the past and present and acknowledges "the unity of the history of the liturgy, and that understands Vatican II not as a break but as a stage of development."[75]

The motu proprio (papal letter) *Summorum Pontificum*, making the Tridentine Mass as the extraordinary form of the Roman rite more readily available within the Roman Rite, must be seen in this context. Only by celebrating the ordinary form with respect to its previous valid manifestation and the other approved rites within the Catholic Church can one celebrate the Eucharist with the proper inner disposition. No liturgy is "conservative" or "progressive." Every form of mass or rite is a particular expression of the whole. Pope Benedict XVI seems to argue: only by seeing the continuous presence of Jesus Christ in all validly celebrated forms and rites past and present, will Christians overcome politicizing Church life and be respiritualized. Opposition to this document is rather strong in some quarters, and thus unwittingly subscribes to the Bologna School's hypothesis of a "hermeneutics of discontinuity."[76]

Benedict XVI insists: an organic development of liturgy is called for, not a restoration of a past form. Such genuine development is only theologically convincing and spiritually edifying, if it evolves in grateful awareness of its past.

The future of the liturgy lies in affirming the self-giving God as the center of the Eucharist, as mediated by the Spirit-sustained tradition. Emphasis ought to be placed again on worshipping the Father in the Spirit and participating in the movement of the self-giving Son to the Father. Thus, the liturgy is not a human construct. Liturgical development was never meant to be starting fresh on a blank slate but rather a conscientious affirmation of past essential insights, refining and purifying the liturgy from unnecessary adornments. In this sense, the liturgy entails an entry into the *obsequium rationale*, the rational worship, of the incarnate Logos. The liturgy is not a human invention but a divine gift. Influenced by Klaus Gamber and his numerous encounters with Eastern Rite Catholics and the Orthodox, Ratzinger believes the term "divine liturgy" is helpful for the West to recovery its own identity.

He emphasizes that the Eucharistic prayer is, in a fundamental way, sacrifice. By praying over the bread and wine at the Last Supper, Jesus changes the Passover *Haggadah* (the Jewish Passover narrative). This prayer transforms the speaker's being into death and thanksgiving. The words "this is my body, this is my blood, given for you" blend the temple sacrifices and the sacrificial/vicarious suffering of the servant in second Isaiah into "the true sacrifice, the word of the Word: in it speaks the one who, as Word, is life."[77] More than simply the grace said before a sacred meal, the believers and the Church enter into the Father's Logos, by partaking in the self-surrender of the Son to the Father.

Ratzinger does not assume God requires a cult. The justification for a cult is profoundly anthropological. Human freedom is wounded and broken. While freedom is God's gift to humankind, it is often misunderstood as grounded exclusively in human nature. This misinterpretation indicates how awfully foiled human freedom has become due to the enigmatic power the Church terms *peccatum originale*, original sin. This evil reality attempts to thwart the goal of good creation, namely, the unity of God and humanity in charity.[78] "If 'sacrifice' in its essence is simply returning to love and therefore divinization, worship now has a new aspect: the healing of wounded freedom, atonement, purification, deliverance from estrangement. The essence of worship, of sacrifice... [is] thus the way into freedom."[79] "In the form of the cross" priest and sacrificial victim coincide in the one person of Jesus Christ. This divine self-sacrifice replaces the previous Israelite cult. Jesus' resurrection from the dead is God's affirmation of his charity to his Son "to the end" (εἰς τέλος: Jn 13:1), which simultaneously becomes a gift to humankind, both for freedom in the here and now and for the new and eternal life in the hereafter.

The key Eucharistic terms that make the liturgy present for each generation are "Christ's Passover" and "his passing from death to life (*transitus*)." Faithful to Thomas's principle of *gratia praesupponit naturam* (grace builds upon nature), the Christian Eucharist is seen as transforming the pagan religious customs into the memory of the life-sacrifice of Jesus Christ and the Church's sacrifice. More importantly, the new Christian cult is prefigured in the old cult as the New Covenant is prefigured in the Old Covenant. The sacrifice of Abraham (Gn 22) and the Passover sacrifice (Ex 12) are the bases for the Eucharist as cult. Rabbinical tradition held that Abraham sacrificing Isaac was vicariously presented by the Lamb. In the Jewish tradition, the sacrifice of Abraham is connected early on with its substitution by the paschal Lamb. This in turn means the paschal Lamb is the vicarious sacrifice assuring the survival of Israel's firstborn. Such understanding grounds the Hebrew and the subsequent Christian cult.[80] The actual firstborn is Jesus Christ (Lk 2:7). Paralleling but also transcending Isaac, Jesus places his spirit into his Father's hands (Lk 23:46). According to Revelation 5, the center of the celestial liturgy is Christ's sacrifice, the Lamb given as a gift from God, which once sacrificed lives on as sacrifice. It is this Christ who becomes truly present in the Christian Eucharist. Here Christ, the Paschal Lamb, establishes the real connection between Christians and the living God. Sacrifice is not an object, such as an animal, but rather truth, the second divine person of the Trinity (Jn 14:6). In Ratzinger's estimation, the notion of spiritual cult matured in ancient Israel during the exile. The response to the crisis of cult felt then throughout the ancient world is overcome by a Christian response that is captured in Paul's words, "λογικὴ λατρεία" and "θυσία" ("spiritual worship" and "sacrifice") (cf. Rom 12:1). By its very nature, the Christian liturgy is Logos-liturgy, adoration in truth and spirit, grounded in the incarnate

Logos, rendering the human prayer of Jesus part of the inner-Trinitarian divine life.[81]

While not officially recognizing the shell-silken rendering of Our Lord as authentic during his visit to Manopello (a place of pilgrimage in the Italian Abbruzzi Mountains, where an image of Our Lord is kept on the high altar) in 2006, Ratzinger took the opportunity to affirm that in Jesus' face we behold God's countenance. "The torn curtain of the Temple is the curtain torn between the world and the countenance of God. In the pierced heart of the Crucified, God's own heart is opened up—here we see who God is and what he is like. Heaven is no longer locked up. God has stepped out of divine concealment. That is why St. John sums up both the meaning of the Cross and the nature of the new worship of God in the mysterious promise made through the prophet Zechariah (cf. 12:10). 'They shall look on him whom they have pierced'" (Jn 19:37).[82] While the point of departure of the Christian liturgy is that of the synagogue, it is elevated to something the Hebrew cult could not envision. It has become universalized: "It is the worship of an open heaven."[83] This becomes manifested in "a liturgy fitting for the Logos": the Christian Eucharist.[84] This is the most appropriate expression of that in which Christians partake. All other terms, such as assembly or meal/supper, fall short of the Christological richness of the word "Eucharist." In the Eucharist, humankind experiences that, since his Ascension to the Father, Christ incorporates humanity into the celestial liturgy.

The Church's liturgy is intended for the interim between Christ's Ascension and his return. Were the Eucharist not Christ making himself present in scriptural readings and in visible and efficacious symbols, the liturgy would be an empty game. But for Ratzinger it is image and reality. The Eucharist is cosmic as it unites heaven and earth; it is grounded in both Jesus Christ's paschal sacrifice and his transition to heaven.[85]

The cosmic dimension of the Church's liturgy is explained by the fact that a human being suffered the passion and thereafter entered the mystery of the infinite God. Far from any kind of human busyness, the Church celebrates a liturgy in which the Son of God is with human beings. Christ becomes the actor in the Eucharistic cult. Human beings partake in the celestial liturgy of the Lamb. The addressee is God and the intention is that human, corporeal existence is united with Christ's sacrifice as a "living sacrifice" (Rom 12:1). "Christ himself offers worship as he stands before the Father. He becomes his members' worship as they come together with him and around him."[86]

Thus, Ratzinger's concerns regarding actual liturgical praxis are not those of a nostalgic antiquarian or cocksure rubricist. He is cognizant of the Christological center of the Christian liturgy and strives to safeguard it. It is in the liturgy that one experiences in the most intense form the risen Jesus Christ surrounding one and being one's gravitational center. The words of institution are essential: in them "the institution of the Eucharist is an anticipation of his death; it is the undergoing of a spiritual death."[87] It is Jesus Christ himself who is shared in the broken bread and the wine that is his blood, shared for the many.[88] These words of institution are decisive for determining the nature of the Eucharist. Taken in isolation, the suffering and death of Christ by themselves do not suffice to explain the Eucharist. The interrelation of the Last Supper, suffering, death, and Resurrection bring forth the full salvific richness of the Eucharist.[89] Along with current exegetes, Ratzinger favors the Johannine chronology of events, assuming Jesus died on the day before Passover, that is, before the lambs were being sacrificed (Jn 19:31). Also inspired by the writings of the Church fathers and Hugo Rahner's magisterial book on patristic ecclesiology,[90] Ratzinger understands that Jesus dies as the new Paschal Lamb and as the new Adam. "From the ultimate self-sacrifice of Jesus spring forth blood and water, Eucharist and baptism, as the source of a new community."[91] A proper understanding of the Eucharist can only be gained from the mystery of Easter, the words of institution, violent death, and sovereign resurrection. The death of Jesus is intrinsically a part of the Eucharist, and thus it is more than just a meal. In addition to this, it offers transformation. Without this last component, transforming death into life, it would be a mere commemoration of a past event. This self-sacrifice becomes present in the Eucharist but is based on God's initiative: "For God so loved the world that he gave his only begotten Son" (Jn 3:16). The Eucharist is not a human activity but God's sacrifice of his Son. This is borne out in the faithful's prayer: "*De tuis donis ac datis offerimus tibi*" (from your gifts and offerings we offer you).[92]

The Eucharistic communion is wholly relational: first, it is relational with God, and through God, in Christ with those present at the mass, especially those who share in the One Body. This is the consequence of self-giving: the Body given up for human beings is the "person existing for others." The partakers in the One Body are drawn into this dynamic by communion with Christ. Ratzinger calls this realm "the sphere of resurrection"—in a mysterious way akin to a "fourth dimension."[93] Human beings communicate through bodies and God has deigned to communicate with them on their level. This is twofold: "The resurrection simply means that the body ceases to be a limit and that its capacity for communion remains." Therefore, the fathers, as well as the Byzantine liturgy, call this sacrament the "medicine of immortality."[94]

In contrast, Cardinal Giacomo Lercaro (1891–1976), president of the *Consilium ad exsequendam constitutionem de sacra liturgia* preparing the new Roman Missal (1966–1968), subscribed to the view that the liturgy is practical. It is aimed at being something akin to a perennial reconstruction, as it must serve pastoral ends. This can be achieved only if the liturgy is in tune with the culture of the people it intends to serve.[95] Archbishop Annibale Bugnini (1912–1982), as secretary of the Consilium, was in full agreement with this perspective. This undifferentiated approach to culture granted it a hermeneutic role in defining the form of the liturgy; looking back with the benefit of hindsight, it appears naïve. The situation was exacerbated by the lack of a fully developed theology of worship, as Aidan Nichols would conclude when comparing *Mediator Dei* and *Sacrosanctum Concilium*. The result was a thoroughly pragmatic approach to the liturgy, ironically supported by a neoscholastic preoccupation with supplying definitions outside of concrete historical and cultural contexts.[96]

In the preface to liturgical scholar Alcuin Reid's book, Ratzinger writes concerning this approach:

> At this point Modernists and Traditionalists are in agreement. As long as the material gifts are there, and the words of institution are spoken, then everything else is freely disposable.... The Liturgical Movement had in fact been attempting to overcome this reductionism, the product of an abstract sacramental theology, and to teach us to understand the Liturgy as a living network of tradition which has taken concrete form, which cannot be torn apart into little pieces, but has to be seen and experienced as a living whole.[97]

Liturgy encompasses the whole Church, bridging time and space and all social stratifications. With respect to this organic nature of the Eucharist, all genuine liturgical renewal must be seen. This also applies to the pope, who "has the task of a gardener, not of a technician who builds new machines and throws the old ones on the junk-pile."[98] The garden is pre-given. The Liturgy is never fabricated. The Kantian fixation on the real and efficacious, and the Jansenist rejection of beauty, are willy-nilly collaborators in a project initiated by the Enlightenment in the eighteenth century introducing a pedagogical dimension. In contrast, genuine liturgical ritual is the goal—and purpose-free praise of God and entry into his divine life. All worldly concerns, however significant and justified they may be, are suspended after they are submitted to God's mercy by the faithful in the intercessions. Otherwise, the primary nature of the liturgy would change: it would no longer be divine worship that occurs but a solipsistic "we-centered" gathering. "The concern for atonement, sacrifice and the forgiveness of sin is replaced by the goal of securing community and escaping the isolation of modern existence—the point is to communicate experiences of liberation, joy, reconciliation, denounce what is harmful and provide impulses for action. For this reason the community has to create its own liturgy and not just receive it from conditions that have become unintelligible; it portrays itself and celebrates itself."[99]

He suggests remedies that are not novel but remind one of the practices of previous generations of believers and of practices in other Latin or Oriental rites. He invites the reader to find his or her place in the large choir of generations of the faithful and saints. While he agrees with Augustine and all of Christian tradition that Jesus Christ's redemptive works encompass all human beings, he believes the term $'υπερ\ πολλων$ (*hyper pollon*) if rendered lexically correct as *pro multis*, that is, "for many," not as "for all," would be helpful in discovering the unique nature of the sacrament of the Eucharist and being Christian as apart from the commonplace, but for others and in the world. This is consonant with both previous editions of the Roman Missal as well as with the various Oriental and Byzantine liturgies. Yet, more importantly, this is the authentic biblical text: "This is my blood of the (new) covenant, which is poured out for many" (Mk 14:24; cf. Mt 26:28; Lk 22:20 "for you"; and 1 Cor 11:25). Another means of rediscovering a liturgical disposition is kneeling. Numerous people fell to their knees before Jesus (Mt 17:14; Mk 1:40, 10:17). Peter knelt down when praying (Acts 21:5). It is the position assumed as normal when praying in the letter to the Philippians "at the name of Jesus every knee should bow (παν γόνυ κάμψη) in heaven and under the earth" (Phil 2:10).[100] The sign of peace is often a cause of distraction for many people as it is shared just before communion. Ratzinger suggests it is more logical to have this important gesture inserted before the presentation of the gifts.[101] He considers reciting the canon in silence at times part of the liturgical heritage that should be reimplemented. He proposes discovering the deeper meaning of the term "active participation." By this he does not mean busyness, managing, or producing the liturgy, but a kind of liturgical realism that places God in the center and allows God to speak to the believer and in turn allows the believer to enter into the mystery with undistracted sobriety. The efforts of the men entrusted with liturgical renewal in the late 1960s, Cardinal Lercaro and Archbishop Annibale Bugnini, to promote some external aspects have not proven conducive in this regard.

Liturgical music cannot be dictated by concerns for utility. The worshippers must join with the whole Church and the cosmos in glorifying the Creator, thus becoming as glorious as the saints. This finds expression in prayer and art. In fact, only the saints and Christian art produce genuine apologias for Christianity. In this sense, the liturgy is neither pedagogy nor psychotherapy but spiritualization by being active participation in the worship of, and life in, the triune God. As this worship is *sui generis*, one cannot uncritically incorporate non-Christian music, be it original to an indigenous culture or modern such as rock or techno music.[102] Here, no particular age, group, or fashion imposes itself. "In the solemnity of the worship, the Church expressed the glory of God, the joy of faith, the victory of truth and light over error and darkness. The richness of the liturgy is not the richness of some priestly caste: it is the wealth of all, including the poor, who in fact long for it and do not at all find it a stumbling block."[103] The whole communion of worshippers joins in being the one *praeclarus calix*, one illustrious and precious chalice "in which we are able to see and hear the glow of eternity."[104] The liturgy becomes a feast by virtue of transcending the human realms of that which is made, produced, or manipulated as "it introduces us to the realm of the given, living reality, which communicates itself to us."[105]

There is little information available concerning the actual form of the paschal meal or the Eucharist historically in the early Church. There is, however, no denying that the Christian Eucharist is modeled closely after the Jewish *berakah* ("blessing" or "prayer of thanksgiving to God"). In fact, *eucharistia* (thanksgiving) is the literal Greek translation of *berakah*. Both contain several elements: praise, thanksgiving, and blessing. The canon resembles Christ's own prayer. "The *berakah* was the essential and central element of the Last Supper of Jesus on the eve of his suffering and is the heart of the new spiritual sacrifice. That is why some of the Church Fathers described the Eucharist simply as 'prayer,' as the 'sacrifice' of praise, as a spiritual sacrifice, which, however, also becomes material and transforms matter; bread and wine become the Body and Blood of Christ, the new food that nourishes us until the resurrection, for eternal life."[106]

The Eucharistic canon is sacrifice in the manner of the Word, by having a priest act *in persona Christi*. In the priest's words "speaks the one who, as Word, is life."[107] As Judaism and Christianity parted ways, the two-part Eucharist with the liturgy of the word and liturgy of the bread evolved organically. As a consequence, the theses of the Christian Eucharist being simply a common meal or the continuation of a meal for reconciled sinners do not do justice to its Hebrew origins and the reality of Jesus Christ. On the other hand, the understanding of the Eucharist as both sacrifice and meal does not denigrate Christ's sacrifice on the cross:

> Christ's achievement consists precisely in his not remaining someone else, over and against us, who might thus relegate us once more to a merely passive role; he does not merely bear with us; rather, he bears us up; he identifies himself with us to such an extent that our sins belong to him and his being to us: *he truly accepts us and takes us up, so that we ourselves become active with his support and alongside him, so that we ourselves cooperate and join in the sacrifice with him, participating in the mystery ourselves.* Thus our own life and suffering, our own hoping and loving, can also be fruitful, in the new heart he has given us.[108]

The Eucharist is the most intense form of life imaginable. As verbal offering, the Eucharist becomes real by being combined with the substance of life, the eternal Word, who is the Logos. By putting Christ's words of institution into human mouths, his worship becomes the worship of humans and his sacrifice to the Father becomes our human sacrifice. In this, not only do heaven and earth meet but the Church, then and now, blend into one reality. This is the deeper meaning of including the pope, the local ordinary, and numerous saints in the canon. "*[T]he mass needs the person who does not speak in his own name, who does not come on his own authority, but who represents the whole Church, the Church of all places and all ages, which has passed on to him what was communicated to her.* The fact that the celebration of the Eucharist is tied to the ordination of a priest is not . . . something that the Church has invented. . . . It follows from the essential significance of these words, which no one has the right to pronounce on his own behalf."[109] Significantly, only "the sacrament of the Church as a whole" has the authority to pronounce these words. In this sense, priestly ordination entails an entry into the greater personality that is the Church. As it is not an open gathering, the Eucharist transcends all congregational categories and is the celebration of the people reconciled to God.

In this context, Ratzinger also addresses some recent questions regarding liturgical propriety since the reforms of the Second Vatican Council. But he is quite unambiguous when it comes to the question of liturgical orientation during the canon. With the destruction of the temple, Jews no longer had a reference point for their prayer, and for Christians this took new significance. There was no longer a temple to face toward in communal prayer, which grew out of the combination of temple and synagogal liturgies. The Resurrection cast new light on the identity of Jesus. He is the Lord, the Son of God. Christians now prayed facing east (*oriens*) and were thus oriented to Christ, the second person in the Blessed Trinity, who will come again in glory from the east. Both the altar and cross refer to the east and to Christ. The liturgy is first and foremost about God's relationship with human beings and their "wasting time" in his presence for the love and glory of God alone. Most naturally, love of neighbor will flow from there. The Lord is the point of reference and the rising sun of history. In the emphasis on the liturgy as a form of socializing ritual—very much dominant in the first thirty years after liturgical reform took root—he divines an overreaction to the almost "pietistic" and individualistic stress in the preceding decades. It is this that de Lubac attempted to overcome. An emphasis on the missionary element of liturgy in the 1950s led to an overly didactic method in liturgical praxis and style, as opposed to the Kievan Rus (early tenth-century Russia, centered in the city of Kiev), "which searched for the true faith and found in the Byzantine liturgy that 'God dwells there among people.' "[110] As Ratzinger reiterates, "the Eucharist is not aimed primarily at the individual. Eucharistic personalism is a drive towards union, the overcoming of barriers between God and man, between 'I' and 'thou' in the new 'we' of the communion of saints. People did not exactly forget this truth, but they were not so clearly aware of it as before."[111]

The beauty of the faith and Church is grounded in the *Verum Corpus*. The real presence of Christ is the guarantee of any unity at all. Eucharistic piety and theology did not suffer corruption or deformation in the Middle Ages, but registered in sum a gain; however, numerous private devotional practices crept into liturgical life. The Middle Ages did not lose sight of something central and germane to Christianity, but rather clarity came about, "through the experience of the saints, supported and illuminated by the reflection of the theologians," concerning the one reality, the Eucharistic presence of the Lord, everpresent throughout Christian history. "At the same time, this new development is in complete continuity with what had always been believed hitherto. Let me say again: this deepened awareness of faith is impelled by the knowledge that in the consecrated species he is there and remains there."[112] The presence of Christ in the Eucharist gets to the root source of the transformative power of the Eucharist and its transcendent meaning and reality in relation to the cross of Christ. The Old Testament in its totality of worship and atonement is not only surpassed by Christ, it anticipates and prefigures him. The Eucharist's power to transcend the time and space of the cosmos finds it basis in the fact that the Eucharist is more than transforming; it is transcendent.[113] This theology of the Eucharist as the transcendent sacrament of the Paschal Mystery is intimately linked with the theology of martyrdom and preaching. Thus a Eucharistic gathering becomes Eucharistic to the degree it acquires the self-immolating mind of Christ Jesus. It may never be limited to the exterior fact of a sociological meeting. The Eucharistic presence of Christ automatically bestows grace that brings about a more profound sense of togetherness. This requires a *rationale obsequium* (intellectual obedience) to set into our very personhood and bodiliness, continuing the drama of the Incarnation of the Logos. "Thus adoration is not opposed to Communion, nor is it merely added to it. No, Communion only reaches its true depth when it is supported and surrounded by adoration."[114]

Likewise, he rejects the notion of naïve realism, equating the Eucharistic species with the body of the crucified Lord. The Eucharistic change of substance does not relate to accidentals. The species does not change, either in consistency, or in atoms; the accidental bread remains, but its substance undergoes change. The matter remains the same. While not undergoing a physical alteration, the substance of the host and wine is changed, completely becoming the body and blood of Christ. He notes that Christ's body cannot be simply added unto the physical realities of the bread and wine. This would imply Lutheran consubstantiality. Rather, an actual transmutation occurs, which he at times refers to as *Umsubstantiierung* (resubstantiation). The risen Lord makes the two species his own; they are symbols of his presence in the bread and wine. Ratzinger is careful to point out that the species do not only receive a new meaning, as the term "transignification" might suggest, or a new function, as the term "transfinalization" might suggest—concepts proposed in the 1970s. For this reason, the Lord remains present beyond the Eucharistic celebration. Eucharistic adoration is an expression of this belief among the faithful.[115]

Imitating Jesus, every Christian must have the center of his or her life in "prayerful communion with the Father."[116] This occurs because we are integrated into Jesus' filial relationship with his Father. The climax of Eucharistic prayer is community with Christ and his prayer. As both the acclamation "mystery of faith" and "the Lamb of God" bear out, the Son also is addressed. Genuflecting after the consecration and before communion emphasizes this adoration of the Son. In the words of Augustine: genuine communion is preceded by adoration. To speak of a mere meal is an untenable simplification that invariably leads to a fateful separation between dogma and liturgy. The central component is Christ's prayer as thanksgiving over the gifts. By partaking in this prayer, Christians are transformed, becoming what God the Creator had always intended them to be.[117] The Eucharistic tabernacle as the new *Shekinah* of glories (while not attested to in the Old Testament, this term is used by Jews to signify "the dwelling" place of God among men, while avoiding anthropomorphism; it is often translated as *doxa* in Greek and *gloria* in Latin) does not therefore compete with the Eucharistic celebration but signifies the latter's fulfillment and that our churches are more than empty spaces; they are places of the celebration of life. This is the very essence of *communio*-ecclesiology: union with God the Father is mediated through Jesus Christ, by the power of the Holy Spirit, in the Church via the Eucharist. De Lubac's book *Corpus Mysticum* did much to establish this ecclesiological outlook.

As one sees, the liturgy is not of marginal interest to Ratzinger but is a profoundly Christological and therefore central concern. In a post-Darwinian world of "chance and necessity," the constitutive elements of the human person remain unexplained and run the danger of being ignored.[118] All biblical prayer, in contrast, is essentially one between free persons, divine and human. Thus the Christian liturgy—as the individual meeting with "the Other," the numinous—is a most human affirmation of personhood. This may be disturbing to some, as they have been conditioned by the contemporary mass culture to be content performing and consuming within the confines of an a priori established economic process. Such a human being would have difficulties being a mature liturgical agent. Is any participant in the liturgy able to appreciate God as speaking and the Son and Spirit at first as passive "hearing," as Johannine theology thematizes? Does not this alone allow modern humankind to countenance the divine Logos as the ontological ground for prayer and liturgy?[119] Through the mystery of the Incarnation, Jesus Christ is shown to be in relationship with his eternal Father. This brings Ratzinger to interpret the prologue to John's Gospel as stating a constant "communication" between the Word and God.[120] Through the salvific economies of the Son and the Spirit, human beings can enter into a prayerful dialogue with God within the locale of Christ and the Spirit, namely, the Church. The basis for such language is the fact that the Church is the Lord's body and—since the Annunciation, the Crucifixion, and especially Pentecost—the Spirit's work. This enables the Christian to pray to God as Our Lord did: in the same intimate manner Jesus did using the Aramaic familiar form of *Abba*. Such prayer permits the deepest form of an "I-Thou" relationship to occur in contingent reality. By way of identifying with the Church, the individual finds the profoundest recesses of prayer and his or her own true self. This is what constitutes freedom fully realized.[121]

Acquiring an *anima ecclesiastica* (an ecclesial mind trusting the greater wisdom of the Church and serving it) thus does not serve as a buttress for an institution, defending it with uncritical and unquestioned loyalty à la "my country right or wrong," but as a vehicle for purifying oneself and acquiring the proper disposition, which imitates the same magnanimity Our Lord had. As a member of the faithful, one is able to address the transcendent object, God. Thus in the Christian liturgy, the believer and God become subjects of *opus Dei*, of the one work of God. In Ratzinger's estimation, this is precisely what Romano Guardini wished to convey when he stated that, in the Church's liturgy, God in Jesus Christ shares human time.[122] In this sense the Eucharist is the real presence of God, that is, it is human partaking in the eternal, triune communication of Father, Son, and Holy Spirit. Both Guardini and Ratzinger understand the liturgy as living from three ontological dimensions: cosmic, historic, and mysterious. Every attempt to depart from the Spirit-inspired past deprives the contemporary liturgy of its inherent quality as *opus Dei* and leads it to degenerate into human self-celebration. Thus, care must be taken that liturgical signs, language, and music reference the death-overcoming Lord. The Incarnation occurs anew when body and voice praise God in Jesus Christ. Thus, language, gesture, and music are not vehicles for escapism but for a holy sobriety, for a spiritual composure that aims to acquire the mind of Christ. Rather than borrowing uncritically from a mass culture that wreaks havoc on the individual, Christianity can baptize the current culture by inviting it to join its ranks in praising God and living in his presence. This will assist the present culture in gaining an appreciation for interiority and living in the silence of God. Not without good reason does Ratzinger rather often quote William of St. Thierry (1075/80–1148) in his *Golden Epistle*: "Whoever is with God is never less alone than when he is alone."[123]

Gestures allow Christians to acquire the mind of Jesus. In *The Feast of Faith* Ratzinger reminds the reader that Jesus himself knelt when praying, as did the apostles and martyrs.[124] The Christ-hymn in Philippians 2:6–11 calls upon all to bend their knees before the kenotic Lord. Praying the Eucharist predominantly facing east expresses Christians' celebration of the Lord's Resurrection and longing for the eschatological coming of the Lord on the Day of Judgment, while the priest's occasional facing toward the people stresses the dialogical structure of some prayers. However, were the celebrant always to face the congregation, the "explosive Trinitarian dynamism which gives the Eucharist its greatness" would be lost.[125] In this regard, Ratzinger does not assume an esoteric position. For the first millennium, the orientation of all Christian churches was eastward, and this continues to be the case for all Eastern Rite churches. In Christian antiquity, worshippers faced each other at a convex or C-shaped table or altar in an open space. Quite deliberately, the opposite side was left empty because it was understood to be filled by the invisible, but present, Lord Jesus Christ. Moreover, quite a number of schol- ars (Josef Andreas Jungmann, the author of the *Missarum Sollemnia*,[126] Louis Bouyer, Everett Diederich, Erik Peterson, Aidan Nichols, Klaus Gamber, and Uwe Michael Lang)[127] agree that when facing the east together, the clergy and congregation form a community looking to the Blessed Trinity. This was implemented by celebrating toward the cross, nota bene, not toward the tabernacle or altar. Ratzinger suggests reintroducing this central dimension of the Eucharist, not necessarily by changing the direction of prayer, but by adding an altar crucifix. Thus, the congregation and priest would both face "the Pierced Savior."[128]

This focus unlocks the true meaning of the term "full, conscious and active participation" as stressed in *Sacrosanctum Concilium* 14: "Mother Church earnestly desires that all the faithful should be led to that full, conscious and active participation in liturgical celebrations which is demanded by the very nature of the liturgy, and to which the Christian people...have a right and obligation by reason of their baptism." *Participatio actuosa* means "to quiet our chatter in favour of attention to the Word of God, in reflection on scripture, in which God too is present, and in our sacramental encounter, in adoration and communion, with the great self-gift of the Word incarnate in the Blessed Sacrament."[129] Such participation frees human beings from the constant bar- rage of human activities to enter into the eternal ground of all being. It is not human gestures and voices that sustain the liturgy but the divine, never self- referencing, goodness of Christ's self-giving on the cross. Appropriate bodily gestures and recollected silence allow Jesus Christ to enter human hearts. Such a view explains why, for Ratzinger, celebrating the Eucharist *versus populum* (toward the people) not only reduces it to the dimension of a meal alone but invites activism. Such a position cannot invoke the Second Vatican Council, or a healthy anthropology, let alone sound theological research. Orienting Eucharistic prayer toward the Risen Christ symbolizes the people of God's openness toward the eternity that only God can grant as a personal gift.[130]

As a result of the new, exterior manifestations of the Church (in clerical and religious attire, in the Eucharist, and in language, thought, etc.) follow- ing the council, the overwhelming majority were convinced that a rupture had thus developed under Pope Paul VI between the renewed liturgy and tradition and that a disjuncture had occurred in Church history. In ancient Greece, one strove to keep joy and temperance in balance, expressed by the two gods Dionysius and Apollo. In modern culture, the Dionysian element of chaos, as expressed in some forms of music (rock and roll, techno, etc.) has thus eliminated the Apollonian element of harmony, symbolizing Jesus Christ. Expressing elemental passions and verging on the cultic, pop, rock, and techno music unwittingly diametrically oppose Christian worship. They cultivate an obsessive concentration on the self. They are not integrative to the human person and deny the cosmic harmony intended by God. The German philosopher Hegel defined music as just an expression of the subject and of subjectivity. Perhaps, this has led to an anarchistic "deconstruction" of the subject and to mass depersonalization.

Such an understanding of music is in sharp contrast to both Pythagoras' and Augustine's perception of music as something corresponding to a pre-given order. In the Holy Spirit, Christian music joyfully celebrates Jesus Christ and anticipates the Resurrection. It is prayer sung to God. Sacred music decreases irrationality and immoderation and is a conscious entry into the sobriety of God and the deep rationality of the cosmos (which, nota bene, means "order") and God. Sacred music is part of Logos-filled worship. It brings about and expresses *sursum corda*, hearts lifted up to the Lord.

The congregation as *synagogē/ekklesia/convocatio* (that is, the passive voice of "to be called together," in the Greek and Latin roots) is the assembly of the people called together by God. In the synagogue, the rabbi would look, together with everyone else, toward "the ark of the covenant" or the shrine of the Torah. During the liturgy of the Word, the Christian assembly would stand around the bishop, and following the call *Conversi ad Dominum* ("Turn to the Lord!") they would walk with the bishop and face the altar together. Nothing superhuman or foreign to the Christian liturgy is required to bring about this return of Christ to the center of the liturgical assembly. Ratzinger hopes the present-day Roman Rite liturgy will become more in tune with the remaining other twenty-some rites within the Catholic Church. His understanding of liturgy is eminently Christocentric:

> Jesus gave this act of oblation an enduring presence through his act of institution of the Eucharist at the Last Supper. He anticipated his death and resurrection by giving his disciples the bread and wine, his very self, his body and blood as the new manna (cf. Jn 6:31–33). The ancient world had dimly perceived that man's real food—what truly nourishes him as man—is ultimately the *Logos*, eternal wisdom: this same *Logos* now truly becomes food for us—as love. The Eucharist draws us into Jesus' act of self-oblation. More than just statically receiving the incarnate *Logos*, we enter into the very dynamic of his self-giving. The imagery of marriage between God and Israel is now realized in a way previously inconceivable: it had meant standing in God's presence, but now it becomes union with God through sharing in Jesus' self-gift, sharing in his body and blood. The sacramental "mysticism," grounded in God's condescension towards us, operates at a radically different level and lifts us to far greater heights than anything that any human mystical elevation could ever accomplish.[131]

He continues in the same encyclical *Deus Caritas Est*:

> As Saint Paul says, "Because there is one bread, we who are many are one body, for we all partake of the one bread' (1 Cor 10:17). Union with Christ is also union with all those to whom he gives himself. I cannot possess Christ just for myself; I can belong to him only in union with all those who have become, or who will become, his own. Communion draws me out of myself towards him, and thus also towards unity with all Christians. We become "one body," completely joined in a single existence. Love of God and love of neighbor are now truly united: God incarnate draws us all to himself. We can thus understand how *agape* also became a term for the Eucharist: there God's own *agape* comes to us bodily, in order to continue his work in us and through us.[132]

In sum, the concrete form the Eucharist takes—when using the term "liturgy," Ratzinger almost always means the Eucharist—is significant. The notion of the priest and the people viewing one another during prayer had been completely alien within Christianity at all times in its history. The clergy and people do not pray toward one another but jointly to the Lord. Thus they usually pray together: (1) to the east as the cosmic symbol for the coming Lord, or (2) to a rendition of Christ in the apse, or (3) simply upward to heaven. This appreciation requires knowledge of the cultic celebration as not being a creative invention by human beings but as an activity both authorized and brought about by God. For this reason, the Eucharistic assembly is not a random event, however the outside, accidental features may have human elements and chance such as time, place, and a Church's design. In light of Romans 12:1, "I appeal to you...to present your bodies as a living sacrifice, holy and acceptable to God, which is your spiritual worship," one appreciates the Christian liturgy as based on the sacrificial cult of the Old Testament. In the Christian Eucharist, the sacrificial practices of ancient religions and of the Old Testament converge in the reality of the Incarnation of the eternal Logos. While terms such as "meal" and "assembly" capture quite correctly important moments of the Eucharist, the foundational reality is that of the paschal death and Resurrection of Jesus Christ.

Ratzinger opposes in no uncertain terms a devaluation of Eucharistic adoration and piety in general. Significant and convincing Eucharistic principles wait to be discovered anew by architects and artists designing sacred spaces. In the Eucharist, Jesus Christ surrenders and sacrifices himself to the Father on behalf of humankind. Ratzinger fears that underlying the interior rejection of the Tridentine Mass form of 1962 is the implicit, de facto rejection of the Tridentine Council's affirmation of the sacrificial nature of the Eucharist. In order to affirm the unchanging identity of the Church brought about over two millennia by the daily celebration of the Eucharist, recognition of the extraordinary form is pivotal: only upon this background can the ordinary form of 1970 be properly celebrated by priests and assemblies alike. For this reason, early on Ratzinger was a rather vocal supporter of retaining the celebration of the 1962 Missal as an option. It documents the rupture-free continuity of the *corpus mysticum*, of the one church continuously celebrating the one sacrifice of Jesus Christ. Eucharistic sacrifice, on the part of every participant, means the transformation of human existence into the one Logos, becoming one with Jesus Christ. The notion of the Eucharist being organized or managed by however well intentioned human beings is theologically unsound and is a misunderstanding of its essence. Were the Eucharist merely "the reflex of the religious feelings or experience of a congregation," this would amount to the destruction of the liturgy as the presence of mystery. At the center of an authentic theology of the Eucharist is the knowledge of God acting through Christ in the liturgy, and of human beings as acting only in and through him. It is detrimental for the liturgy when it degenerates into a laboratory for experiments of theological hypotheses fashionable at one point or another in history. This would supplant the authority of the mystical body with individual, human, and therefore contingent, that is, fallible, experts. Alas, the Liturgical Movement did not anticipate this looming danger in preconciliar days. It became a major temptation in the subsequent decades. In this sense, Ratzinger is neither a radical renewer of the liturgy nor a radical rejecter of liturgical renewal. He pleads for a liturgical renewal that is mindful of the liturgical principles underpinning the ever selfsame Eucharist in the (therefore) ever selfsame Church. Only a faith that seeks to become incarnate again can have the courage to give the liturgy and liturgical space new forms. Precisely by doing this, fidelity to Christ is not an abstraction but credible. Genuine growth occurs by living the same identity. It requires attentiveness to the interior building stones of the one organism.

At the beginning of his ministry as a theologian, Ratzinger wrote a doctoral thesis. The epigraph to his dissertation on the people and house of God read *"unus panis, unum corpus, sumus multi"* ("One bread, one body, we are many"). Ratzinger encapsulates well his ecclesial-liturgical synthesis in *God Is Near Us* in a homily he delivered on Acts 2:42:

> We can see in this a sketch of the primitive Christian service of worship...it reaches a climax in the eucharistic encounter with the Lord...and resounds in songs of praise. *The Church is adoration.* The passage is telling us that the Church subsists as *Liturgy* and in Liturgy. She is the living temple that even within the stone Temple in Jerusalem, dedicated to destruction, is growing up on the foundation stone of Christ....Nonetheless, this does not represent any kind of transfiguring or narrowing down, in an aesthetic or liturgical direction, of the situation or the nature of the Church. For the shape of Christian worship reproduces, at the same time, *both the way to go and the manner of going in human life.* Human life is, in the first place, a search for *meaning*, the search for some message that can show me the path and give me direction. Because of its whole direction, life is a search for a supportive *community*, since man is created for community. It is a search for a love that shares, that teaches us to trust, and that can be trusted right to the end of mutual giving. And thus it is a demand that the world should be transformed by love into *praise*: prayer embraces the whole world, and the world is comprehended within prayer.[133]

CHAPTER 24

Regensburg: Provocation or Jesus Christ as the Basis for Civilized Discourse? Jesus Christ as the Reconciler of Faith and Reason

The introduction to *The Spirit of Liturgy* contains a mystagogy, leading one to the Church's tradition: living as the body of Christ. Liturgy's dignity is being God's icon to the world. This in turn grants dignity to the human person.

Ratzinger's basic assumption is that Jesus is reason par excellence. This is the key definition of John's Gospel, "*ho Logos sarx egeneto*" (The Word became flesh, Jn 1:14). Logos means "reason," "meaning," and also "word," as Ratzinger elaborated in the year 2000 in the foreword to his *Introduction to Christianity*. God the Creator, as reason, vouches for the reasonableness of the world and our own being. Yet, this does not make Ratzinger a disciple of the German philosopher Georg Wilhelm Friedrich Hegel. He is all too mindful of the darkness that oftentimes confounds human reason. Nonetheless, this world is fundamentally "positive." The fact is that humanity is grounded in God's reason, and the Logos forms the basis for "an ethos of re-sponsibility, as response to the Word." This has inestimable relevance for interreligious and intercultural dialogue. Not only can one now discern a convergence between the major monotheistic religions, but also among other forms of religiosity such as Taoism and Confucianism: all communicate a yearning for something ennobling the human person, that cannot be simply generated by human efforts. In 1999 Ratzinger shared these positions with the general public during his lecture in Paris at the Sorbonne University. They were reaffirmed at his famous Regensburg lecture. Yet, as early as his inaugural lecture as professor at the University of Bonn on June 24, 1959, he had spoken on this germane topic.[1] There he reminded the students that Christianity had connected with Greek thought, but not with the polytheistic and mythical approaches of the poets and priests, nor with a politically expedient theology of the state. There is a kairotic moment in the Incarnation within a Jewish-Hellenistic milieu, allowing the world to come into its own, its own which was given to it in its outlines from the very beginnings of creation. It is certainly not by chance that God revealed himself to the Jews in Palestine, close as they were to the refined philosophy developed in nearby ancient Greece. Three hundred years before Christ, the Holy Land had been exposed to the Hellenic culture, when Alexander the Great conquered it. Moreover, in the subsequent Hellenistically formed Diaspora Judaism, the biblically affirmed unity of faith and reason, of faith's universal rationality, was lived in vague outlines. When the scholar Faust in the drama by the same name ponders the question whether Word (Logos) or deed (*Wort oder Tat*) were first at creation, the German poet Goethe attests to the enduring legacy of this relationship throughout history. He finally decides in favor of the primacy of the Logos, which is Christianity's very own message. Thus, Ratzinger dares posit a provocative conclusion: "In Christianity enlightenment became religion...enlightenment can become religion as God himself entered religion" in Jesus Christ.[2] No particularity does violence unto the rest. Every individual feature may serve the symphony of the whole. The human spirit is confronted with the most meaningful justification for its quest for purpose and meaning in the Logos that is Jesus Christ. In charity the Christian religion becomes universally valid.

This synthesis of philosophical reason and content-filled faith was further developed as faith in Jesus Christ was deepened and safeguarded against simplifications by way of theological discussions leading to definitive, binding, reasonable statements called dogmas. The European Enlightenment, however, much sustained by a shortsighted emancipatory pathos against the "myth" of religion in the eighteenth century, was based on a confidence in human reason's capacity that is in fact grounded in Christianity. Without Jesus Christ, modernity's trust in the reasonableness of human endeavors, such as providing justice for all, or achieving technical mastery and economic progress, must suffer shipwreck, as postmodernity's underlying melancholy so eloquently demonstrates. Thus much of contemporary philosophy adroitly sidesteps the great metaphysical questions that have preoccupied major thinkers throughout history. In this sense, Ratzinger inveighs against a theology that shies away from the semantic breadth and wealth of the term and the person called *Ho Logos*. In "Jesus of Nazareth" he wants to free theology from the stranglehold of pedantically believing only what the historical-critical method supposedly deems viable. Such a critically unreflecting hermeneutics deceives one into assuming the exclusion of God acting in the world. The invariable consequence is a denial of the realism of the biblical creed (1 Cor 15:3–5); the handed-down narratives of miracles, such as healings and the Resurrection; and finally the dogmatic definitions concerning the Blessed Trinity, Jesus Christ, and Our Lady. He asks whether an anti-Incarnational docetism of a dualistic kind is the inevitable outcome. He remains open to reinterpretations, sometimes freeing texts from touches of the mythical. But the measure of a legitimate demythologization is not an, at any one particular time, contemporary worldview but ecclesial faith itself. One may not "dogmatize" the natural sciences à la Bultmann, lest one is blind to the power of God over being and history. In this vein, Ratzinger defends the unity of word and deed as expressed in the Second Vatican Council's *Dei Verbum* 2. The pope spells this out in some length in his book *Jesus of Nazareth*: "This is the point around which I will construct my own book. It sees Jesus in light of his communion with the Father, which is the true center of his personality; without it, we cannot understand him at all, and it is from this center that he makes himself present to us still today... *et incarnatus est*—when we say these words, we acknowledge God's actual entry into real history."* Theology ought to be reasonable in consideration of this.

Fides et ratio (faith and reason) do not collapse in Ratzinger's system into one reality. Like the Christological definition at Chalcedon in AD 451, which defines Jesus Christ as possessing possessing both a divine and a human nature on earth and sharing our condition. Nevertheless, the divine and human natures in Christ remain separate and distinct. The two have their respective autonomous areas. Increasingly, analytical philosophers agree with Ratzinger's basic assumption that philosophy on its own cannot supply universally valid insights that can provide life-sustaining meaning to ultimate questions.[4] The Reformed theologian Markus Mühling is in agreement with the general direction of the Regensburg lecture, because postlapsarian reason is truly in need of the outside illumination supplied by the Logos.[5] The concept of God as the unmoved mover and of pure human reason, uninformed by faith and grace, as developed, for instance, by Aristotle, remains deficient vis-à-vis that of the self-revealing God in Jesus Christ. The prime mover could never be imagined as moving toward humankind as the God of Israel has. Benedict XVI expounds on this in *Deus Caritas Est* 9. Such a nuanced "de-Hellinization" of Christianity does not lead to the separation of Jerusalem and Athens, but to an artificial divorce between the goal of human thought and yearning and its true fulfillment. Confronted with grace, human reason experiences purification and transformation. Only faith can provide such sufficient reasonableness for Christianity that can legitimize it in the court of rationality. Only faith can supply the basis for understanding the faith. Admittedly, in logic this is called *petitio principii* or a circular argument. However, this must be the case as human beings are not residing in heaven, that is, they are contingent, and they live after the fall. There is no such thing in Ratzinger's estimation as a radically autonomous reason; there is only a relatively autonomous reason. External aids, such as faith, are indispensable to reach the goal that human reason, by virtue of its creatureliness, aims for.[6] On the other hand, human reason remains essentially bound to history and language. This was in his judgment the reason for neoscholasticism's failure. One cannot reconstruct the preamble of faith with rationalistic certitude. Interestingly, for him this is also the central issue and a cause for disagreement with representatives of a pluralistic theology of religions, as advocated by John Hick, Paul Knitter, and Perry Schmidt-Leukel. In subtle ways, Ratzinger avoids the temptations of both fideism and rationalism. Faith needs reason to acknowledge the fullness of Jesus Christ. Reason needs faith to become a personal "responsibility." Faith reveals independent thinking as stale. Thus, Ratzinger does not develop apodictic, stringent arguments proving the existence of God beyond any doubt.[7] At the Sorbonne in 1999, Ratzinger readily and quite

---

*Ratzinger, *Jesus of Nazareth*, 4.

cheerfully admitted no ultimate proof exists of God's existence. Far from being a negative fact, it is the chance to develop a personal faith.

More precisely, following Kant's destruction of rational metaphysics there no longer exists a rationalistic proof of "the Christian fundamental option." Ratzinger implies that however historically shattering this may have been, it must ultimately be welcomed as it allows the true face of religion to emerge. He therefore does not in principle deny the need for ontology and metaphysics in theology. This "modesty" of Christianity as he perceives it is certainly due in no small way to the Franciscan school of theology, which preferred emphasizing the correlation of philosophical reason and faith as well as its dependence on faith. Bonaventure subsumes everything under the *"auctoritas fidei"*(authority of faith). This thesis corresponds seamlessly to the notion of human reason's need for purification and transformation through faith. Such insight fills the human being with confidence in a personal and dialoguing God as delineated by Martin Buber and Ferdinand Ebner. God's creative thinking of me precedes my becoming aware of and thinking of myself.[8] This is paralleled in the writings of Hans Urs von Balthasar.

Within the framework of a universe perceived as creation, a dialogical understanding of personhood makes sense and is, perhaps, the only justification for the dignity of the human person. It has a Christological basis and ethical ramifications. This is also the key for accessing his concept of human reason. The complete human person, including his or her reason, grows and finds its proper realization in engaging with another person. This finds its culmination and fulfillment when a human being goes beyond himself or herself. This anthropology demonstrates Jesus Christ as the exemplary human being. By going completely beyond himself, the God-man arrived truly at himself.[9] This occurs constantly within the Blessed Trinity and occurred during his life on earth. It also has implications for human reason because it prepares human reason to receive something from other beings who are likewise gifted with reason. The critical issue is how can human reason know that it must receive something from an external source in order to be its authentic self and not be deceived? Must the criterion for reasonableness come from outside of human reason? Perhaps, but this is only partially so because the human person is already oriented to the divine. Yet, there is no denying that one cannot prove the reasonableness of reason. It would require an outside agent other than reason. To demonstrate this salient feature of human cognition, Ratzinger turns to Socrates' and John the Evangelist's understanding of *anamnesis*. The external impulse serves to bring to the fore that which is somehow yearned for by the human spirit. In knowing, something like a remembering or recollection of something that is already present occurs. The human being is bearer of more than what is present to himself or herself. This applies also to the realm of the true and good and therefore to ethics. Faith fulfills the task of liberating reason from false autonomy by reminding it of its creatureliness. The "I" of the person becomes the place of greatest self-transcendence when it is "touched" by one's origin and destination.[10] In this dynamic encounter, the "I" is not reduced to inertia, but on the contrary is honored as understanding, reasonable, and endowed with unconditional dignity. On the part of each person, this requires the "I" to recognize itself as addressed, as not belonging to itself, and it requires itself to will self-transcendence. In what manner does created reason become mindful of these "facts"? Ratzinger shies away from simply stating that the transcendental "I" is an implication of the abstract notion of "God." In contrast, he offers a multitude of observations.[11]

Creaturely human reason corresponds to its cultural and linguistic self-communication. Within the culture of ancient Greece, a philosophy of universal insight regarding God developed, proving in turn the universality and wealth of human reason. Thus language and culture are not, in principle, a priori impediments to reason—such a position would serve as an argument in favor of relativism—but are the very conditions for the possibility of its realization. Terms such as freedom, reason, purpose, "I," consciousness, subject, and so on can be universalized. The principles of logic and deduction are universal, though perhaps developed best in Greece. The cultural "we" enables the individual to become veracious as it permits access to the wide horizon of truth. Speaking to humankind thus constituted, Christianity's reasonableness invites *metanoia* (conversion) and transformation. As human beings seek a "total" (comprehensive) answer, the other answers to this search for meaning that absolutize humankind, technology, and so forth recede. They lead to an overestimation of human reason and of contingent reality. Even a supposedly humble epistemology regarding what the human mind can access can lead to such hubris. Using reason alone, one ultimately must acknowledge polytheism, a reduction of salvation to history (see Joachim of Fiore), or instrumentalizing God for human political or ideological goals as all equally unreasonable. All these goals remain penultimate and supply no final or ultimate justification. Hegel challenged his age to discover a point of departure that was self-evident, with no prerequisites. However, all known entities are finite. Only the absolute satisfies these criteria. Whoever is dissatisfied with such a position because of the finite nature of human insight will oscillate around penultimate entities.[12]

CHAPTER 25

Jesus Christ, the Definer and Personification of the Eschaton

All philosophical inquiries into the origin and purpose of history can be traced back to prephilosophical interpretations of reality, insofar as there is contained in the philosophical query something that is not generated by philosophy on its own, but is, nevertheless, original to that discipline. There exists something like an inchoate revelation of God in the primordial creative forces that predates God's explicit self-disclosure in scripture and Jesus Christ. Jesus Christ is experienced as "the end of history," inasmuch as history has been confronted with its terminal point. History is unveiled as a single Theo-human drama, as God's offer to humanity of dialogue with him. All secularized, often ideology-driven, attempts to find meaning without God—be they religious or areligious—are unmasked as sublimated efforts to redirect human hope toward an inner-worldly perfection. Giordano Bruno's (1545–1600) humanist attempt to divinize the cosmos was later reinforced by Georg Friedrich Wilhelm Hegel (1770–1831). Hegel tried to overcome dualism by reducing God to an entity *within* the world process. To the believer, in contrast, in the God-man Jesus Christ the meaning of history is definitively revealed. "The beginning and end of this new history is the Person of Jesus of Nazareth, who is recognized as the last man (the second Adam), that is, as the long-awaited manifestation of what is truly human and the definitive revelation to man of his hidden nature; for this very reason, it is oriented toward the whole human race and presumes the abrogation of all partial histories, whose partial salvation is looked upon as essentially an absence of salvation."[1]

Also, the endeavors of Christian thinkers such as Adolf von Harnack or Hans Küng, however laudable their efforts in themselves may be, do not go beyond the common trajectory of the eighteenth-century Enlightenment position of instrumentalizing religion for the purpose of moralizing society for the betterment of the human race. However, the point of morality is not moralism. Morality (nota bene, not moralism) as a global phenomenon, found in all pre-Christian cultures, is the consequence of an encounter with the divine. Thrilled by the numinous' existence and perhaps revelation, the human being longs to be good. Morality is a response to some kind of divine self-disclosure. When reflecting on the nature of a new Europe, Ratzinger observes that the Christian religion is not a mere stone quarry for humanist values. It must strive to convince people of its inherent truth concerning God—and thus coherent truth about humankind. The point of history, of human beings' existence, is to become participants in the worship of the one and triune God. Christianity must evangelize peoples so that they will be prepared to meet Jesus Christ at the end of history. "The political moralism that we had lived through, and are living through still, not only does not open the way to regeneration, it actually blocks it. The same also holds therefore for a Christianity and a theology that reduce the core of Jesus' message, the 'kingdom of God,' to the 'values of the kingdom' while identifying these values with the main watchwords of political moralism, and proclaiming them, at the same time, to be the synthesis of all religions—all the while forgetting about God, despite the fact that it is precisely He who is the subject and the cause of the kingdom of God."[2]

As one would expect of a Christian, Ratzinger's eschatology is eminently Christological, and it contains a rarely reached intensification toward Christ: eschatology can only be made sensible in light of Jesus Christ awaiting each individual believer on Judgment Day. It is helpful to call to mind the debate that was raging in the area of Christian eschatology at the time of Ratzinger's composition of his frequently revised book on eschatology. Famously, in *The Critique of Pure Reason* Immanuel Kant argued that due to the structure of human cognition, one cannot step outside of spatial and temporal categories.[3]

The Protestant theologian Jürgen Moltmann, who taught in Tübingen, prefers to speak of the "resurrection of the dead," rather than of "the soul's immortality."[4] Christian hope in the resurrection of the flesh prohibits disparaging corporeal life. Consonant with Isaiah 43:1, Moltmann holds that the human soul is embodied and this in turn defines the human being's personhood. In this context, he refers to the terms "transformation" and "transfiguration" while maintaining that life after death does not herald a radically new reality. "At the end nothing new replaces the old, but rather this old is being newly created."[5] There is no actual lifeless intervening period between physical death and resurrection. This intervening period is already one "in Christ." As Moltmann firmly maintains, the deceased are not yet resurrected but are grasped by the resurrected Christ and enjoy community with him. In keeping with Philippians 1:23, this awakened existence is not yet resurrection, but one of security (*Geborgenheit*) in Christ—without any purifying fire and penance.[6]

In 1969, the Catholic theologian Gisbert Greshake (b. 1933) contributed to the breakthrough of the thesis of "a resurrection in death." He claimed there is no such thing as an *anima separata* (a soul separated) from the body; otherwise, the integrity of the human person would suffer annihilation.[7] Because a human being is not an unrelated monad, the whole, undivided, and historically evolved human person is "secure." Actually, not merely the human body, but all of one's interhuman relationships, including one's spiritualized and interiorized corporeality, are transfigured. Thus, Greshake maintains a *diastasis* (separation) between mere corporeality as matter per se and bodiliness.

While Greshake and Moltmann assume a particular form of temporality in the *eschaton*, the former Tübingen New Testament scholar Gerhard Lohfink—and now member of the Katholische Integrierte Gemeinde (Catholic Integrated Community)—rejects the notion of limbo and emphasizes a postmortal existence beyond time. He situates the *eschata* in death. This is also Ratzinger's position. He maintains that one should bid farewell to an understanding of the coming of the Lord at the end of a linear timeline. The *Parousia* of Christ occurs at the death of every individual. The personal and universal judgments and resurrections coincide. Thus, the kingdom of God becomes a reality simultaneously for both the individual and the world.[8] His book *Eschatology, Death and Eternal Life* is by far the most revised and also most systematic of his writings. Due to his appointment as Archbishop of Munich and Freising in 1977, he had been prevented from writing the other volumes in the series *Dogmatic Theology*, which he had intended to co-author with fellow dogmatician Johann Auer (1910–1989).[9] Already in the late 1950s Alois Grillmeier, SJ, and he had planned writing jointly a multivolume presentation of Catholic dogmatics. Then the approaching Vatican II Council had derailed their plans.

It was his intention to contribute to the series incorporating the theological vision of the most recent council. Nevertheless, this book is no accident. There is no denying that the eschatological arena intrigued him so much that he dedicated twenty-five titles to this area alone. In his inaugural lecture at Tübingen University, he addressed the issue of "Salvation History and Eschatology."[10] This inaugural lecture delineated his overarching concern. It is a double delimitation against: (1) a radically existentialist and dehistorizing tendency, and (2) a historizing, utopian, and political interpretation.

The (1) existentialist variant strove to free the New Testament teaching on last things from time-conditioned mythological concepts. What actually counts, in Ratzinger's view, is relating one's own existence not to "things" but to the encounter with the kerygma of Jesus Christ. For Bultmann, only the encounter with the disembodied, pneumatic Christ matters. Placing Christianity outside reality, it rests solely on a single moment. By removing faith from common, everyday experience, Ratzinger argues, faith actually becomes quite irrelevant to human life—if one remains arrested to an extrinsic body-soul dilemma. This enabled an immanentist inversion of eschatological hope to come about: Marxism.[11]

This leads to (2) the utopia and political variant. Indebted to Bonaventure, Ratzinger is able to illustrate how very unchristian the effort to establish immanent, inner-worldly perfection à la Joachim of Fiore is. This issue, so virulent in the thirteenth century, influenced in different ways such noted thinkers as Georg Wilhelm Friedrich Hegel, Karl Marx, and Jürgen Moltmann, as well as Johann Baptist Metz's political theology, liberation theology, and other emancipatory movements. Such chiliastic attempts temporalize and politicize the incontrovertible fact of human hope for an eternal future. In addition, Christian hope is no longer countenanced as a supernatural virtue. Christians are then no longer intrigued by such a theological understanding of hope and no longer reach out to do justice to the biblical concept of "the kingdom of God." However, human freedom is always prone to sin and failure. History is not a mechanism one can plan. It becomes itself "an irrational promise"[12] and "a primitive myth"[13] with incalculable, dehumanizing consequences.

Neoscholastic treatments were preoccupied with dwelling on the future nature of completion and perfection, following the patristic penchant for the literal meaning of prophetic statements in scripture. Death and resurrection, personal and universal judgment, heaven, purgatory, and eternal damnation receive distinguishing Christian contours in the books on eschatology of the first half of the twentieth century. Now, eschatological reflections allow one to give a deeper meaning to the present situation, defined *from* the eschaton. There is something like a genuine and healthy anthropological concern in the air: the *pro nobis* of Redemption. Drawing on exegesis and tradition, modern-day questions have to be taken seriously without allowing them to become the measure of truth. "The center of the Christian faith" must integrate the human into one systematic whole, thereby enabling a deeper understanding of that faith. The eschatological question relates to the question of the historical Jesus and to the Christ of faith. In the final analysis, a Catholic theologian is acutely aware that he is unable to retrieve something behind or prior to the living interpretation of the ecclesial community. The Word of Jesus exists only as a heard and ecclesially mediated and received word.[14] The historic subject of the Christian faith is the Church. Here one senses how much his ecclesiology and exegesis come to bear in the area of eschatology.

The most prominent critic of this model of "resurrection in death" is Joseph Ratzinger. His scholarly study *Eschatologie. Tod und ewiges Leben* (*Eschatology, Death and Eternal Life*), first published in 1977, triggered a lively debate.[15] This erudite volume was the last book he authored while he still had the leisure of an academic teacher.[16]

In a genuinely unpolemical manner, Ratzinger raises three major objections. He critiques Greshake's underlying understanding of matter (*Leiblichkeit and Körperlichkeit*) as spiritualizing human interiority by assuming it capable of eternity but ignoring the nonhuman components of creation. The thesis of "resurrection in death" dematerializes resurrection.[17] The second inquiry is directed at Lohfink's model of determining the relationship between time and eternity as a radical opposition between terrestrial temporality and postmortal eternity.[18] Ratzinger argues that time is not primarily a physical reality but an anthropological category, formed by human relationships.[19] Closely allied with this notion is the objection of devaluing history. This is the consequence of stating an incommensurability between terrestrial time and eternity. Does not the thesis of a resurrection in death denigrate history, if one assumes all of history has come to an end? This leads Ratzinger to plead the case in favor of a limbo. Remarkable agreement exists on this point among Ratzinger, Moltmann, and Greshake. Ratzinger introduces the vision originally expressed by Origen in his seventh homily on the book of Leviticus of all the dead waiting in solidarity together with the risen Christ. This serves as proof for his theory of the individual's relationship in solidarity with his fellow human beings well beyond this life. This is enlarged then to include solidarity with all of history, that is, with people of all ages.[20]

This study is guided by the insight "that Jesus' preaching was soaked thoroughly with eschatology."[21] It becomes a part of Christian awareness of the tension between the "already" and the "not yet." "As such, it must be understood in terms of the mode of prayer proper to that celebration which always carries a reference to both present and future. The Eucharist is at once the joyful proclamation of the Lord's presence and a supplication to the already present Lord that he may come, since, paradoxically, even as the One who is present he remains the One who is to come."[22] Defying the reduction of Christianity to individualism and otherworldliness, the communal prayer of the believing community, through the ebb and tide of Church history, has never lost this dimension of eschatological hope. It is not the *Dies Irae* (*Day of Wrath*) but the litany of saints that expresses this hope. "The Christian lives in the presence of the saints as his own proper ambience, and so lives 'eschatologically.' "[23] The communion of saints redeems the person from a self-centered hope. It "marries" person and community in such a way that both elements gain a deeper understanding of the real promise of faith.

With perhaps too little reference to specific Bible passages, Ratzinger correlates eschatology with scriptural witness.[24] In particular, he is interested in the degree to which the historical Jesus included in his preaching an expectation of an end to the world. What relevance do Jesus Christ and his message have if he recedes into a faraway, undeterminable future? He notes that the concepts "kingdom of God" and "kingdom of heaven" are central themes for Jesus; so much so that they are the true *leitmotivs* of his preaching. " 'The time is fulfilled and the Kingdom of God is at hand: repent, *metanoeite*, and believe in the Gospel.' "[25] Indeed, Jesus did not explicitly teach a Christology in a self-referencing manner but rather he taught about the kingdom "among you." Therefore, Ratzinger is in full agreement with Origen, who held that Our Lord is the personification par excellence of that kingdom. "In a splendid coinage of Origen's, Jesus is *the autobasileia*, 'the Kingdom in person.' "[26] In the person of Jesus Christ a congruence occurs between the here and now and the *Parousia*. In this perspective, Ratzinger perceives many valuable aspects in political theology and in liberation theology, but he warns of wedding eschatological hope to the many hopes the world offers, lest deceptive surrogate hopes define Christian hope.

Eschatological perfection is centered on Christ. The Lutheran New Testament scholar Oscar Cullmann (1902–1999), an observer during Vatican II and an acquaintance of Ratzinger, maintained an abiding *"diastasis"* (space or separation) between the "already" and the "not yet." With its end in Jesus Christ, the end of the world has definitively begun; however, he also cautions against the naïve assumption that this would occur *in* history. Christ alone is the point that draws together both the definitive, once and for all effected Redemption, and the yet to be expected completion.[27] Inevitably, partaking in Jesus' fate leads to the cross, enabling "his body to become our souls' bridge."[28] History's omega is also its alpha and explains everything in-between.

Perfection means transformation into a thou: as creature, the human being is intended for perfection in Christ. Deification of humankind entails a path of self-humiliation rather than self-exaltation. It is not Prometheus but Christ who grants eternal meaning. In the encounter with Christ, the eschaton becomes already tangible. The eschaton is not a human achievement but divine work; namely, it is the *Parousia* (arrival) of the sovereign Lord of all time. This is politically relevant as it prevents politics from defining the purpose of history. Jesus Christ is the formative truth in this life and the ultimate dispenser of justice in the next. Therefore, he is also the ultimate measure of all human activities. The naïve Platonic model of the ideal state finds its commensurate goal here in human freedom as openness to the ontic ground of existence: Jesus Christ. The Platonic understanding of order and the Christian Logos converge in this regard.

In more recent history, an antithesis between biblical faith and the Greek culture has been stated, perhaps most notably by the Protestant theologian Adolf von Harnack. In Greek thought, the soul represents an essential, eternal constituent of the human person that leaves behind mortal materiality. This notion of the soul's moral superiority had been thematized by Plato and radicalized by Plotinus. Ratzinger readily admits he had at one time belonged to the camp of "de-Platonizers."[29] Upon further consideration, he discovered "the inner logic of ecclesial tradition." Until around 1970, he saw opposing alternatives: the immortal soul is not so much a "Catholic" biblical, but a Greek ontological, category, the *aporia* (a mental blind alley) of either "immortality of the soul" or "awakening of the dead." In his book *Eschatology* he apprehends the fear of being accused of "a dualism" in recent theology. He regrets that it found formal entry into the Missal of Paul VI. He sees biblical evidence favoring the concept of the "immortality of the soul" and that of "the awakening of the dead." In 1972 he considered the notion "soul" the "hermeneutic" nexus preserving the identity of the terrestrial person with the one entering the beatific vision.[30] In 1977 he argued that the Christian faith and the Greek search for the Logos join together in the search for "*die Vernunft der Dinge*" (the reason of all being).[31] As he stated in 1972, the terms "immortality" and "soul" are no longer taboo.[32]

One discovers two major concerns in Ratzinger's *Eschatology*. Apart from foreign, Greek influences, the Old Testament gives testimony to a genuine, theological understanding of human immortality after physical death. While not identical with resurrection, it calls for the term "soul." YHWH himself becomes the life of the deceased in Job and Ecclesiastes. For the just, suffering becomes the path to YHWH. The prospect of communion with God provides strength and consolation in the time of exile. This faith becomes most tangible in Jesus Christ, who as God has entered into the realm of death. At Christ's cross, death becomes entry into something more in life. Christians entrust themselves to the truth of God, just as Jesus did. In the New Testament, Old Testament eschatology is concretized in Jesus Christ: Christians will abide in Christ. Immortality arises from communion with the divine-human Thou of Jesus Christ. Believing in God and belief in resurrection become synonymous. The dialogical relationship with Jesus Christ vouches for each soul's immortality. Ratzinger's second concern is the notion of "limbo," which severs the individual from the general resurrection. The concept of "soul" does not allow for upholding the notion of "resurrection in death."

Indebted in part to Josef Pieper, Ratzinger points out that the present Western civilization both celebrates and trivializes death, almost consciously laboring for an intoxication that allows society to evade the sobering earnestness of death. Drawing on Plato's understanding of human society, he illustrates how living for the cause of truth, and risking self-abandonment in the process, can only be sustained if there is immortality.[33] By meditating ever anew on Christ, the Church must necessarily oppose the modern attempt to suppress death. For every attempt to sublimate death grants death a chance to carry off the victory. But the risen Christ, as "the very *arbor vitae* [tree of life]," is the beacon of eternal life and communion with God.[34] The eschaton is properly understood only from the perspective of the paschal kerygma. After reference to the *Fides Damasi*[35] and the Council of Toledo in 675,[36] Ratzinger considers the issue settled by Pope Benedict XII in 1336 in promulgating *Benedictus Deus*[37]: "In this bull the Pope taught that, in the time after Christ's passion, death and ascension into heaven, the souls of those departed persons who stand in no further need of purification do not have to linger in an intermediate state . . . [but are] replaced by a definitive Trinitarian condition."[38] Life in Christ is more powerful than death and this energy resurrects the otherwise mortal flesh.

Ratzinger maintains the nonidentity of resurrection and *Parousia*. Resurrection occurs not merely to the body but as living flesh. Ratzinger distills this from both 1 Corinthians 15:35 and a treatise titled *De Resurrectione*, likely authored by Justin Martyr. The latter states emphatically: "If the gospel of salvation is proclaimed to humanity, then salvation is also proclaimed to the flesh."[39] He sees this line in direct response to the Egyptian gnostic Valentinus, who, stressing the resurrection of the flesh, had nonetheless completely spiritualized Christian eschatology. Ratzinger appreciates in Thomas's formula of *anima forma corporis* (the body is the soul's form) how both body and soul condition one another. Together they constitute the human person. The correlation of the two is reminiscent of Teilhard de Chardin.[40] Nevertheless, Christ's coming is not the product of an inner-worldly evolution or a dialectical process.

It is not substance-ontology that is the guiding star, as is the case with Thomas and neoscholasticism, but the personal-dialogical category. The independence of the soul is not determinative but the soul's entry into the greater Thou of God. This means the human body becomes the place where salvation occurs. There is no longer a body-soul opposition; rather, the vis-à-vis of creature and Creator is the orientation for Christian eschatology. In this sense, the biblical testimony is holistic without yielding to a dualism of body and soul.[41]

In scholastic theology the soul was separated from its body. The *visio beatifica* (beholding God face to face) was considered the highest form of bliss, but without a corporeal component. In the twentieth century this view had become increasingly difficult to maintain. In particular, the dogma of 1950, stating Our Lady's Assumption into heaven with her body and soul, problematized the scholastic position of the *anima separata* (separated soul).

In order to resolve this dilemma Gisbert Greshake postulated, in his dissertation published in 1969 and further elaborated in 1974 in the *Quaestiones*

Disputatae series, his theory of "resurrection in death." The human being is not separated from his or her body in death. In eternal perfection, the immortal soul and mortal body are one (body in soul). He does not mean here the actual physical body but human communicability and relationality. In 1977, in his book *Eschatology*, Ratzinger expressed sympathy but also reservations regarding Greshake's proposal. He believes Greshake's hypothesis favors a spiritualization of resurrection: matter is being perfected in perfected history. Very much in the vein of Idealism, the claim is made that matter is interiorized, in spirit (cf. Karl Rahner, Johannes B. Lotz). One cannot dissolve the soul's orientation to a particular body. Also, he rejects an Idealist solution as conscious, definitive self-execution, as postulated by Karl Rahner. The body need be transformed concretely into the soul's realm. The human being as *ens compositum* (a being consisting of a multitude of elements) remains such. Matter is perfected not in the soul, but by the soul. This new constitution of matter cannot be grasped by a mind not yet resurrected. But, in a rather modern way, Ratzinger insists that the soul is the "*Ort*" (location) of such a body-soul resurrection.

Another point he advances is that "resurrection in death" seems to assume a running parallel of temporality and eternity. The old scholastic understanding of limbo was able to emphasize the preliminary and unsatisfactory nature of individual existence vis-à-vis the resurrection of the whole cosmos. He calls the position "resurrection in death" one that in the final analysis negates resurrection.[42]

In agreement with Jean Daniélou, Ratzinger states that "Christ is at once the *telos*, the 'end' or 'goal' of history, and its *peras*, its 'boundary' or 'limit.' Daniélou means that Christ is the fulfillment, *telos*, of all reality, and so cannot be measured against the continuous time of this world and of history...."[43] The transformation occurs not according to the parameters of worldly expectations but is a transformation for the sake of this world. This is not merely an occurrence at the end of time. In anticipatory fashion, the *Parousia* occurs in every Eucharist, as the Lord's coming.

Christ, in his redemptive works of suffering, death, and descent into hell, takes humans seriously in their freedom. This includes responsibility for their ultimate destiny. Thus, Ratzinger rejects Origen's notion of an *apokatastasis ton panton*, of a universal reconciliation at the end of times. He prefers allying his position with John of the Cross and Thérèse of Lisieux[44] rather than with Hegel or Balthasar.[45] With these saints, one realizes that hell "is not so much a threat to be hurled at other people but a challenge to oneself." It is the invitation to suffer in solidarity with the eternal Word of God in his dark solitude. "In such piety, nothing of the dreadful reality of Hell is denied."[46] He pleads for a "resurrection (at the day of final judgment)" consonant with tradition but one that is anthropologically sensitive.

Inspired by Augustine's understanding of the various forms of temporality in his famous book XI in his *Confessions*, Ratzinger introduces an anthropological element into the term "time." The human "*memoria*" is different from objective, physical time. Time as experienced by human beings is personal and binds people together.

While leaving the arena of physical time at the moment of death, the human being does not enter eternity: it is the dynamic space of human relationships.[47] Greshake is not mindful of this relational dimension, to which God has been a partner to. One senses at this point the strong influence of personalism. In Jesus Christ, God entered human history and dignifies it with a very intense relationship. History is completed only when the individual finds his or her place in the whole. The communal fullness becomes a full reality on the day of last judgment. As God entered history, history in turn opens toward eternity; it is not closed, as in Greshake's case. For both Ratzinger and von Balthasar, God is not ahistorical. All alienation between God and matter, world and spirit, cosmos and history, will be overcome. All these dimensions will interpenetrate. In a general way, the reader is reminded at this point of Teilhard de Chardin (1881–1955). However, Ratzinger has always maintained some distance from Teilhard's project.[48]

To Ratzinger's mind, the soul in limbo is not detached from matter. The soul retains in the body of the glorified Lord a connection with all those redeemed. This is the significance of the Christian concepts of the mystical body and *communio sanctorum* (communion of saints in heaven and all members of the Church). No matter what the course, or lack thereof, of history may be, the individual human soul retains a specific relationship to God and the world even before the day of last judgment.[49] God's universal and individual salvific will is one reality. Assuming the course of history to continue unaffected after the individual had been perfected amounts to tearing salvation history apart. Having entered the body of Christ, his Church, then this reality called Church is not annulled at death. There is no such thing as a private, unsocial repose of the soul. Based on Augustine's understanding of time as *memoria*, the deceased remain related to time and history. Without such a view one cannot do justice to the notion of the body of Christ, as a people partaking in one organ and fate. Otherwise, invariably, docetism would be the consequence and history would hold no promise. The Eucharist is lived charity and solidarity of all in Christ.

The riddle of death is resolved via Christology. All eschatological claims make sense as long as the integrity of Christology is safeguarded. The mystery of the Incarnation is God's entry into dialogue with human beings. Thus, Jesus Christ becomes resurrection and life to all who believe in him. Here one hears an echo of Augustine's *Christus totus* teaching, Christ, head and members. The Eucharistic mystical body never ceases to exist.

In a masterful way, Ratzinger synchronously unfolds Christian anthropology, Christology, and eschatology. Death does not terminate one's trust in Christ and the Church, for Christ himself becomes the purifying fire in purgatory. If purgatory takes on such a Christological quality, this must apply to heaven yet more intensely. It must be that in heaven human beings become fully what they are, not in the sense of a perfect extrapolation of earthly realities, but that human beings are granted a place in heaven. Heaven means existing in God with Christ. "For this reason, heaven, as our becoming one with Christ, takes on the nature of adoration.... Christ is the temple of the final age; he is heaven, the New Jerusalem...."[50] The paschal mystery is not a once-for-all-time bygone event, but abides in heaven. Reminiscent of Augustine, Ratzinger formulates the position that the whole Christ, head and members, are in heaven. Heaven is a stranger to isolation and particularity.

Thus, he dares state: "The Lord's exaltation gives rise to the new unity of God with man, and hence to heaven. The perfecting of the Lord's body in the *pleroma* [fullness] of the 'whole Christ' brings heaven to its true cosmic completion...the individual's salvation is whole and entire only when the salvation of the cosmos and all the elect has come to full fruition. For the redeemed are not simply adjacent to each other in heaven. Rather, in their being together as the one Christ, they *are* in heaven."[51]

At the beginning of the twenty-first century, humankind seems to face three major challenges that perhaps even endanger its very survival: (1) the loss of personhood amid a globalized mass culture, (2) the loss of an environment capable of sustaining humankind, and (3) a nuclear war. While all three are to be taken seriously independently from one another, they all can be traced back to the disappearance of God from human consciousness.

During his homily on the Islinger Field outside Regensburg on September 12, 2006, after having delivered the memorable Regensburg lecture, Pope Benedict XVI reiterated that Christian faith is "simple."[52] Christian faith means believing in a God with a human face. In an age when life-threatening pathologies of faith and reason, hatred and fanaticism destroying the image of God manifest themselves, the definition of the truest human yearning as seeking God's face reminds us of our true identity. By living life with Jesus Christ we become illumined and capable of living truth and goodness, that is, by allowing Christ's truth and goodness to shine forth in ourselves, we are no longer beholden to darkness. Speaking during Easter 2006 on baptism, Ratzinger compressed this insight to the brief formula: "I but no longer I." Christians are transformed and the degree to which this transformation takes roots in us is measured by the degree to which we become translucent to God's goodness, truth, and charity. Discipleship means seeking God's face. Beholding God's divine countenance in this world takes the form of following Jesus Christ; seeing is walking. Suddenly, baptism also takes on social and political dimensions. In Ratzinger's view, spirituality may not discount the possibility of political testimony. Whoever immerses himself or herself into the life and passion of Jesus invariably is mindful of the nonnegotiable principles of humane social life. Human dignity is not grounded in positive statutes of laws but in the fact that every human being is called to behold God's face. This is the basis for Christian commitment to the causes of justice, liberty, and the defense of human life.

In 2004, both then Cardinal Ratzinger and the German philosopher Jürgen Habermas agreed on a necessary corelationality between faith and reason. This inter-relationality between the two is necessary for the sake of mutual purification and healing. In the center of the discussion stood the so-called Böckenförde paradox: the liberal, secularized state lives from prerequisites it cannot guarantee. In 2007, Habermas further elaborated that autonomous secular reason produces a sense of loss, melancholy, and "defeatism."[53] These ruptures are not found in the hypotrophy of secular reason by accident. They are not caused exclusively by exogenic factors, but arise *intra muros*, from within Christianity. Reacting to a faith defined by, and hermetically enclosed within, a rigid philosophical system, the Reformation stipulated the principle of *sola scriptura* (scripture alone). It thereby reduced faith to text, losing sight of the faith vouched for by a living organism called the Church and actuated and celebrated continuously in the liturgy. In the nineteenth and twentieth centuries, this in turn led to liberalism claiming truth is generated by concrete reality alone. Adolf von Harnack, in his epochal *What Is Christianity?* published in 1900, is perhaps the single most important representative of this group of demythologizers of the Christian gospel.[54] The dogma of the God-man Jesus Christ dissolves into the exemplary ethical personality of a human being called Jesus. In this, Ratzinger perceives religion falling victim to the pathology of reason. Though the Christian dogma of Jesus Christ being fully human and fully God is a provocation to Jews, the Jewish scholar and rabbi Leo Baeck (1873–1956) accused Harnack, in his great apologetic repost *Das Wesen des Judentums* (*The Essence of Judaism*) (1905),[55] of ridding Jesus of all Jewish elements by imposing Harnack's private interpretations onto him. Without tradition and culture no being exists. Baeck insists Jewish faith is based on tradition and rooted in history. Every conviction requires tradition. Vice versa, without tradition, firm convictions cannot develop. For Pope Benedict XVI, Christianity is grounded in Jewish belief, which is the living and valid matrix for Christianity.

The triad of profound Christian interiority, increased empathy with the world, and renewed Christian brotherhood are essential contributions to peace and saving the world from its loss of purpose—the consequence of relentless economic pragmatism and fanaticism—which is ultimately the expression of a loss of justification for religion in the modern world. From the eschaton in Christ all questions of human existence and seeming contradictions are resolved.

CHAPTER 26

Mary: In Christ, the First Free Human Being

In the homily at the funeral mass for John Paul II on April 8, 2005, Cardinal Ratzinger said: "He [Pope John Paul II] heard the words of the crucified Lord as addressed personally to him: 'Behold your Mother.' And so he did as the beloved disciple did: 'He took her into his own home.' (Jn 19:27)— '*Totus Tuus.*' And from the Mother he learned to conform himself to Christ."[1] What is the correlation between Christian existence and Marian devotion? On what basis can one claim Mary is pivotal for a balanced spirituality? Is it theologically viable, or merely a sentiment?

Joseph Ratzinger was born in hiking distance from the popular Marian shrine Altötting. Its black Madonna is carved of linden wood and has since 1385 been located in an old Carolingian chapel. It is black because it miraculously survived a fire in the chapel. In 1489, Our Lady of Altötting heard the pleas of a mother whose boy had been presumed dead. In this chapel, the hearts of the deceased members of the ducal (later royal) family of Bavaria (Wittelsbach) are kept, representing the whole of the Bavarian population. Over a million pilgrims come each year, thousands of whom actually walk and hike there, sometimes over 100 miles, to visit this inconspicuous chapel housing the richly dressed black Madonna.

Ratzinger has described the *Gnadenkapelle* of Altötting as: "[T]he Chapel of Grace with its mysterious darkness, the sumptuous raiment of the black Madonna surrounded by votive gifts, so many people silently praying...all that moves my heart just as much today as in those lost years. The presence of something good, something saintly and healing, the Mother's goodness, through which the goodness of God himself is shared with us."[2]

No matter where they lived, the Ratzinger family regularly sojourned to Our Lady of Altötting. In 1934 young Joseph Ratzinger visited the place to celebrate the canonization of the Capuchin brother Konrad of Parzham (1818–1894), who had been a great admirer of Our Lady of Altötting. While born nearby in Lower Bavaria, Brother Konrad served as *Pförtner* (gatekeeper) in the Capuchin monastery of Altötting, distributing soup to the poor and spending his life immersed in prayer. Needles to say, for Ratzinger, Altötting was the highlight of his visit to Germany in 2006. There he described in the following words Mary's example as:

> ...not seeking to assert before God our own will and our own desires, however important they may be, however, reasonable they might appear to us, but rather to bring them before Him and to let Him decide what He intends to do. From Mary we learn graciousness and readiness to help, but we also learn humility and generosity in accepting God's will, in the confident conviction that whatever it may be, it will be our and my own, true good.[3]

A rather unusual dichotomy appears when looking at Marian devotion and belief today. On the one hand, Mariology seems to be something like a reduced form of Christology, integrating and securing the whole of faith. On the other hand, there is little evidence of Mary in the New Testament. Not a few theologians would even argue that Marian devotion arises on irrational grounds. The roots are not theological or biblical but pagan. It is often held that Marian spirituality is the result of Egyptian myths or is a derivative of veneration to the great Diana of Ephesus. At first glance, this might even sound plausible, as she is not mentioned in the creed of the New Testament. In order to address this accusation of Marian veneration as an idolatrous custom contrary to Christian truth, the figure of Mary was integrated into the faith as the *Theotokos* (Mother of God) at the Council of Ephesus in 431. Ratzinger considers Hans Küng's observations representative for the prevailing views generally held in this regard in academia and the Catholic intelligentsia. Küng claims Mary played no role in early Christian witnesses. She is but a "postbiblical" "poetic statement." Allegedly, Cyril of Alexandria single-handedly manipulated the whole Council of Ephesus prior to the arrival of the party from Antioch. A simple transference from the goddesses Artemis and Diana to Mary occurred.[4]

In reaction to this quite prevalent view, Ratzinger argues from within the biblical testimony that the unity of both Testaments must always be borne in mind. The image of Mary in the New Testament is woven entirely of Old Testament threads. Mary can be seen mirrored in Sarah and Hannah. She represents to Christians the concrete daughter of Zion. In this daughter, the covenantal love of God for Israel is concentrated. The figure of Eve finds its fitting, positive counternarrative in Mary. The figures of women in the history of ancient Israel serve as anticipations of the promises fulfilled in Mary. Too much emphasis is sometimes placed by some contemporary exegetes on the Old Testament prophets who argue against the danger of seeing a fertility goddess in heaven. Ratzinger reminds the reader that it was the achievement of the French convert and theologian Louis Bouyer to demonstrate the central role played by women in the cultic and religious life of the Old Covenant.[5] Quite deliberately did the council fathers of Ephesus in AD 431 reject the pagan notion of a woman as "the Great Mother." The term *Theotokos* defends Christianity against becoming a heathen gathering on that point and preserves the mystery of the Incarnation of Jesus Christ. The old adage "either Marian or Arian" Arius held Jesus was not the eternal, divine son of God holds true. Mariology is not the illegitimate intrusion of alien concepts into Christianity.

While rejecting the model of deities or "syzygies," the Old Testament gives women an indispensable place in the covenant. It is a woman who frees man to a relationality in which both together become a living parable of God's covenant with the human race. Despite some compromises in the Old Testament, in the Old Covenant it is only through matrimony that one lives out God-given covenantal creatureliness in a way pleasing to YHWH.[6] In this sense, Mark 10:1–12 and Ephesians 5 lead to further development of the charism of virginity, not in opposition to marriage, but as its spiritual continuation and its deepest confirmation.

The mutual reference of men and women is expressed in the "legend" or "myth" of Eve's coming from Adam's rib and not from the earth. Together both genders "cryptically" link humankind to its resemblance to God. Significantly for Ratzinger, the dignity of womanhood is underlined by the fact that only after the fall and after God's verdict is Eve given her name (Gn 3:20). Called "life" and "the living one," Eve becomes "the keeper of the seal of life and the antithesis of death." Mary's *Magnificat* (Lk 1:46–55) places her in direct continuity with the women of the Old Covenant: Sarah–Hagar, Rachel–Leah, and Hannah–Peninnah (1 Sm 2:7f). The paradigm of the unblessed–blessed women finds its terminal point in Mary. The uncovering of human hubris occurs in Mary's election, where powerlessness becomes fertility. Likewise, the salvific women Judith and Esther find their culmination in Mary as the mother of life par excellence.

It is in the figure of a woman that Israel faces God. Ratzinger argues that a grand arc spans from Israel to Mary, from the synagogue to the Church:

> "How could I betray you Ephraim, or hand you over, Israel…? My heart turns against me, my mercy catches fire all at once. I do not act according to the fire of my anger, I no longer annihilate Ephraim, for I am God and not man, the Holy One in your midst. I do not come to destroy all in flames" (Hos 11:8ff). God's divinity is no longer revealed in his ability to punish but in the indestructibility and constancy of his love. This means that the relationship between God and Israel includes not only God but also Israel as woman, who, in this relationship with God, is at once virgin and mother.[7]

As the Daughter (CAPITAL AS A TITLE) of Zion represents Israel, so in Mary the *ecclesia*, the Church, is represented. Along with von Balthasar, Ratzinger insists on personalization as constitutive for both the Old Testament and Christianity.[8] The personal concreteness in Mary is of foundational importance for the Church. Though probably secular in origin and nature, the Canticle of Canticles has entered the canon on these grounds, as the canticles are an allegorical expression of God's dialogue with Israel. To these Marian prefigurations in Esther, Judith, Eve, and so on one must add the abstract term "wisdom." While liturgists today may emphasize the Christocentric nature of the liturgy, there is in Ratzinger's judgment no gainsaying that the Wisdom texts do not allow for only a Christological interpretation. Wisdom is feminine, both in Hebrew and in Greek. This also applies to "spirit," "*ruah*" in Hebrew. In the Mary of the Annunciation scene, the Greek word *Sophia* (meaning wisdom) becomes the feminine pendant to the masculine Logos: *Fiat mihi secundum verbum tuum,* (do unto me according to your word) Lk 1: 38. All this leads Ratzinger to conclude that the figure of the woman belongs indispensably to "the structure of biblical faith." In Mary, the typological portrait receives a concrete reality. Building upon the hardly noticed pioneering work of the Jesuit Erich Przywara on the nature of the *analogia entis* (analogy of being) as coming to its full form in the cross,[9] Ratzinger observes with inimitable analytical precision:

> She [Mary] emerges as the personal epitome of the feminine principle in such a way that the principle is true only in the person, but the person as an individual always points beyond herself to the all-embracing reality that she bears and represents. To deny or reject the feminine aspect in belief, or more concretely, the Marian aspect, leads finally to the negation of Creation and the invalidation of grace. It leads to a picture of God's omnipotence that reduces the creature to a mere masquerade and that also completely fails to understand the God of the Bible, who is characterized as being the creator and the God of the covenant—the God for whom the beloved's punishment and rejection themselves become the passion of love, the cross. Not without reason did the church fathers interpret the Passion and cross as marriage, as that suffering in which God takes upon himself the pain of the faithless wife in order to draw her to himself irrevocably in eternal love.[10]

In the introductory essay to the encyclical *Redemptoris Mater,* Ratzinger expresses disappointment that the Marian year had met little enthusiasm in German-speaking Catholicism. People often feel a consideration of Mary in salvation history would strain the ecumenical climate, where one is dialoguing with a Protestant majority. An additional obstacle is the rise of feminism. Marian statements are frequently understood as signifying a sanctioning of women's dependent status and even a glorification of their oppression. The feminist reading of scripture attempts to discover a free and self-confident woman in the person of Mary. This novel interpretation then aims to contribute to the general emancipation of women. While not trivializing the oppression of women, Ratzinger sees the danger of radical feminism ignoring the biblical witness and succumbing unwittingly to a neo-gnostic temptation. For the rejection of God as Father and Son is then inevitable. This strikes at the very heart of the biblical message. Such a radically novel interpretation of Mary thereby leads to an evaporation of God and Christology.

First and foremost, it is important to appreciate biblical testimony. In the person of Jesus Christ, Mary occupies a special place in the economy of salvation (Eph 1:4–7). Thus, the crucial nexus between Mariology and Christology is established. As Christ is the Father's eternal Son and yet was received by a human mother, Jesus is both our brother and the enablement of our sharing his divine sonship with the Father. Thus, St. Paul is capable of stating God "chose us before the world began; he predestined us, in love; to be his adopted sons through Christ Jesus in whom the world began; he predestined us, in love, to be his adopted sons through Christ Jesus in whom we have forgiveness of sins…" (Eph 1:4–5). Through Mary, we share in the redemptive mission of her son. All these dimensions of faith are possible only due to Mary's cooperation in the mystery of Christ's life on earth.

As the integrated and integrating member of the Church, she is like us and yet her role is most singular. As the mother of Our Lord whose mission was ever present in the Father's eternal will, Mary becomes ever present to our spiritual eyes as Church in its fullest sense. In this capacity, she accompanies us on our journey to meet the Father and his Son in the heavenly kingdom. The Holy Spirit overshadowed her and at the cross Our Lord entrusted her to St. John. Thus, her memory is entrusted to the Church, which renders her the mother of all of humanity, as Jesus died for the sake of redeeming humanity on the cross.

Her assumption into heaven—body and soul—crowns Our Lady with a glory that manifests her participation in that kingdom. There she has the capacity to listen to and "mediate" our petitions. Three elements are foundational in this regard: (1) Mary's faith, (2) Mary as preceding Christ's founding the Church, and (3) Mary as virgin and mother.[11] Prior to receiving physically, "she received in her spirit" as Augustine put it. In this sense, she assists humankind in realizing God's plan for us. This disponibility, which reaches its climax in Mary, stretches back to the days of Abraham and forward to the day of final consummation. As Luke 1:45 expresses it, "Blest is she who trusted that the Lord's words to her would be fulfilled," because by virtue of her faith she was able to entrust herself fully, in intellect and will, to God. Precisely due to her great humility beyond measure, she is the bearer of a great mission. The angel promises her a son who, though inheriting a great kingship, will cause great pain to her and she even will bear glorious suffering because a sword will pierce her heart. All these weighty words caused amazement on her part but she "kept and pondered everything in her heart" (Lk 2:19).

The prophecy of Christ being the Son of the most high, the unexpected threats leading to the escape into Egypt, and the answer of Jesus to his parents when they find him in the temple, all point to Mary's suffering at the foot of the cross. Taking all these things into her heart—without knowing about the Resurrection and Easter—illustrate how strong and yet how humble Our Lady was. To persevere in faith, as Mary did, in spite of all seemingly legitimate reasons for doubt, is the great challenge of all times. Today, it seems to be all too reasonable to doubt Our Lord. As Abraham felt a big lump in his chest when told by the angel to sacrifice his son Isaac, Mary must have suffered great pain seeing Our Lord suffer disgrace and pain as he died on the cross. The spectrum of biblical events demonstrate Mary's role in the fulfillment of the Old Testament. God's economy of salvation takes on visible form in Mary's faith and she thereby becomes the example worthy to imitate. "Faith as lived by Mary is total, trusting, self-surrender of mind and body to God…it is self-effacing, living humility; but it is also acceptance of the responsibility to God's biddings."[12]

This establishes another dimension: Mary as the prototype of the Church. As Ratzinger asserts, her faith at every stage—the Annunciation, life, ministry, suffering, death, and Resurrection of Our Lord—is the manner in which the Church is to believe. Mary is the centerpiece of salvation history. Her life is the unfolding of the Church's mission and of the Holy Spirit. She is prayerfully present at Pentecost. In Mary the Church arrives at her victorious end, prepared and anticipated by Our Lord and Mary. She is the original witness of God's plan. By following her heroic persistence in faith and commitment to the mysteries of faith, the "Church is rightly seen as bringing forth, in the mystery of the sacraments, new spiritual life."[13] Through her everlasting motherhood, Mary participates and cooperates in "the development of the sons and daughters of the Mother Church." Mary becomes the symbol of personal, inward sanctity and of the Church as the visible authority through the apostles. The two are intimately intertwined to such a degree inasmuch as the Church must reach out continuously to live that Marian interior disposition, lest she jeopardize her mission. In Mary's virginity, God's Word in purity and sanctity is preserved. Her *Magnificat* expresses her interest in the disadvantaged and points to the Church's obligation to care for the humble and poor. Through Mary, we are reminded of this time and again. This in turn requires spiritual poverty. Mary "is poor in a material sense, yet she rejoices not over material gifts...but over the gift without price, over being mother of the Messiah."[14] As occurred during the wedding at Cana, where she interceded on behalf of the guests' need for wine, so she continues to intercede with her Son in heaven on behalf of humankind. This mediation is intimately linked to her divine motherhood.

Scripture reveals Mary as a believer. Elizabeth exclaims when greeting Mary: "Blessed is she who believed" (Lk 1:45). This is a key word for Mariology. Mary contains the paradigm of the pious believer. In this way, she stands in the tradition of Abraham. For both Abraham and Mary, faith is trust in and obedience to God's Word; this is of paramount import. As Abraham's faith stood at the beginning of the Old Covenant, so Mary's stands at the beginning of the New Covenant. This belief prepared the scene for the mystery of all mysteries. Ratzinger writes that if one begins listening to the creed's statement "*et incarnatus est de Spiritu Sancto ex Mariae Virgine*" (by the power of the Holy Spirit, he was born of the Virgin Mary), then it must become apparent that there are actually four subjects in this sentence: the Holy Spirit, Mary, "he [Jesus Christ], and God. Christ is the only begotten Son of God...true God from true God...consubstantial with the Father, with whom he is one in essence and so can be called God from God." This means the primary and proper subject of this sentence is God in the Blessed Trinity, while the "*ex Mariae virgine*" belongs to the statement concerning action, in which the "three Divine persons are involved each in his own way." Without Mary, God's entrance into history would not achieve its intended purpose. Mary called herself lowly (Lk 1:48), that is, namelessness, which stands at the core of the profession of faith in the living God, and it is impossible to imagine it without her.[15]

Mary as Daughter Zion

The economy of salvation unfolds fully in Mary. Therefore, Mariology cannot be a dispensable adiaphoron to theology. While Ratzinger is mindful that Mary as a topic in theology continues to be contested and much sidelined, Mariology is a worthwhile endeavor in his judgment on two grounds. Mary merits attention due to her supreme role in salvation history and because she thereby serves as a guard for both Jesus Christ's humanity and divinity. It is incorrect to treat Mariology as "a scaled-down duplicate of Christology that somehow arose on irrational grounds;...but [is rather] the echo of ancient models found in the history of religions."[16] This would reduce the figure of Mary to the object of an overly emotional devotion. Such an assumption fails to countenance the Marian truths and tears asunder the correlation between truth and life.

As previously stated, Mary stands in covenantal continuity with the women of the Old Testament dating back to Eve. The circumstance that women there often occur in pairs, such as Sarah–Hagar, Rachel–Leah, and Hannah–Penninah, contains a message: the infertile ones become blessed. Therein Ratzinger detects a hidden praise of virginity. All women remain "mothers of life." One cannot divorce these women from the history of the Old Testament. Marriage is an expression of God's covenant. This narrative is completed in the New Testament in the woman who is the true, holy remnant and the authentic Daughter of Zion and "who is thereby the mother of the savior, yes, the mother of God."[17] Also in Mary, the two testaments are unified. On the other hand, it is only the unity of both that allows Mary to be part of the integrity of the doctrines of creation and grace.

This background enables Ratzinger to see in Mary the Virgin and Mother of God. One of the daring Christological statements is found in Galatians 4:4: "born of a woman." This, along with the gospel genealogies demonstrates that "Jesus can be the maturing fruit of history only because in him a new power has entered into the withered tree from history," as he is both from above and from below.[18] The parallel to Zephaniah 3:14–17 evidences her as the true Zion, the spouse of Yahweh, the true Israel, and the mother of the people of God. The announcement of the Holy Spirit coming upon her references Genesis 1:2 and thus defines the event as new creation. The term "the power of the Most High will overshadow you" is clearly taken from the Jewish cult indicating the presence of God, the *Shekinah*, in Mary. She becomes a sacred tent, the new Ark of the Covenant. In her as fulcrum the Old Testament is revealed as fulfilled in the New Covenant. It is significant for Ratzinger that John transforms Paul's expression "born of a woman" (Gal 4:4), which he insists is historical and unique, to a spiritual and universal plane: all of humanity is invited to participate in Christ's birth through rebirth (Jn 1:13).[19]

Here God conveys a message: in Mary, Christ can begin a new beginning "in the midst of a barren and hopeless humanity."[20] She corresponds to Christ's mission. What God initiated in Christ as the true prophet, namely, salvation, meets a response in Mary. "In this way Mary, the barren, blessed one, becomes a sign of grace, the sign of what is truly fruitful and salvific: the ready openness which submits itself to God's will."[21] In Mary, Christian virginity receives its profound meaning.

The miracle of Christ's birth defies Cartesianism (in the sense of an exact mathematical comprehension) and the criterion of plausibility. It challenges both Christology and Mariology. After Kant one tacitly accepts that God could not be involved with *bios*, the natural realm. Ratzinger reminds the reader that the presupposition that God does not "reach into earthly history" is ultimately operative in those positions that reject the Marian dogmas. Jesus' supernatural birth from a Virgin "intends to affirm these two truths: (1) God really acts—*realiter*, not just *interpretative*, and (2) the earth produces its fruit—precisely because he acts."[22]

Ratzinger's argument in favor of the dogma of the Immaculate Conception is similar. It seems to defy the boundaries of speculation and jeopardizes the universality of grace. In contradiction to Barth, who advocated in favor of a dialectical approach, vis-à-vis an analogical one, in order to uphold the unmerited nature of grace, Ratzinger argues that the biblical notion of holy remnant (that is, in trying times, only this small part of Israel or Christianity would remain loyal to God [Gn 7:23; Rom 9:27, 11:5]) supports the dogma of 1854. With the fathers of the Church, Ratzinger considers the analogical/typological interpretation legitimate. It is this that allows women "to be the complement that exists entirely in its derivation from the other, and nevertheless remains its complement," reaching its perfection in Mary, who is the "pure derivation from God and at the same time the most complete creaturely complement—a creature that becomes response."[23] As original sin could only be known via typology, it follows in his perspective that Mary's freedom from original sin can only be known via typology also. As the abstract reality of the Church is free of sin, the possibility follows that a person is likewise free from original sin. Significantly, Ratzinger believes this can only be appreciated if one does not subscribe to an individualistic understanding but apprehends the human being as essentially relational. He divines in Mary what is intended for every human being: "[p]recisely in the total dispossession of self, in giving herself to God, she comes to the true possession of self. Grace as dispossession becomes response as appropriation."[24]

The dogma of the bodily assumption of Our Lady is the highest form of canonization possible, implying that in Mary eschatological fulfillment is fully realized. By giving birth to Jesus the Christ, the eternal Son of the Father, she gave birth to the fullness of life. As virgin and Mother of God she has no stain of death on her. The consequence is that "[s]he who is wholly baptized, as the personal reality of the true Church, is at the same time not merely the Church's *promised* certitude of salvation but its *bodily* certitude as well."[25]

Mary and the Church

The figure of Mary can deepen the understanding of the Church in two significant ways. First, the *populus Dei* is feminine as *ecclesia* in both its original

Greek and Latin forms. The Church, he argues, is not fully comprehended unless one beholds her spiritual reality: "[She] is more than structure and action: in her lives the mystery of motherhood and that of spousal love which makes motherhood possible."[26] Beyond sociological comprehension, the Church is thus perceived as the mystery that unifies all peoples. Eclipsing mere structures and activities, the Church is maternal. Maternity accesses an additional ecclesial dimension: bridal love.[27] This is borne out in both the biblical and patristic testimony. Second, Mary as Mother of the Church allows one to appreciate better the Church as the mystical body of Christ. The Church is not an abstract, impersonal organization, but a living organism. The Old Testament notion of "the pilgrim people of God" is transposed to the notion of "the Body of Christ." Continuously anew in the Eucharist the people become Jesus Christ. Using a thought from von Balthasar, Ratzinger shows that the spiritual tension of love in Adam and Eve (Gn 2:24) receives proper dialogical reciprocity in (standing vis-à-vis:) Paul's words (1 Cor 6:17: "However, he who binds himself to the Lord is of one mind with him"). By being a listening handmaid, the Church as Mary becomes bride and thus body. Ratzinger avers that Mary is the believing vis-à-vis whom God calls. As such, she represents creation, which is called to respond to God, and the freedom of the creature, which does not lose its creatureliness, but attains completion therein.[28] The proper disposition of the believer is that of Mary, who possesses advental piety.

In this vein, then, it was consonant to treat Mary not in a separate con-ciliar document during Vatican II but in the constitution on the Church, *Lumen Gentium* 54–69. This is based in no small way on the research con-ducted by men such as Hugo Rahner, A. Muller, René Laurentin, and Karl Delhaye. Like Mary, the Church is virgin and mother at the same time. Like Mary, Christians in the Church are not individualists but generous mem-bers of a supra-society. In addition, they are not members of an impersonal entity. Far beyond any mere institution, the Church herself is the bearer of personhood. This understanding of the first Christian millennium ought to be recovered.

In the speech he prepared for Cardinal Frings in 1961 in preparation for the Second Vatican Council, Ratzinger wrote:

> With ever increasing clarity one must acknowledge that Mary does not stand in isolation, but is rather the primordial form and image of the *mater ecclesia* par excellence. She is the living sign of the fact that Christian piety does not stand in isolation before God; Christianity is never concerned with a mere "Christ and me." Christian existence is also entry into the Marian mystery; I am posited in the communion of saints, the center of which is Mary, the Mother of the Lord. She is the sign that Christ does not intend to remain alone, but rather that redeemed, believing human-kind has become one body with him, one single Christ, "the whole Christ, head and members," as St. Augustine said with unsurpassable beauty. Thus, Mary refers to the Church, to the communion of saints, assembled for prayer in liturgy. It will likely be the task of the follow-ing decades to incorporate such thoughts from the Marian movement

into the liturgy, to fit Mary into the great theological themes.... [The Marian movement] should give liturgical people a share in [Mary's] heart-warmth, her personal interiority, and emotion ["touchedness," *Ergriffenheit*, her being taken hold of by God], her profound willingness to do penance and repentance and vice-versa... [the Marian movement] could receive something of the holy sobriety and clarity, the luminosity and the strict earnestness, of the great old laws of Christian piety and thinking, which give limit to an overly enthusiastic "winged" fantasy of a loving heart, granting it its fitting place.[29]

Epilogue: Jesus Christ Offering the World Identity and Meaning

At the mass prior to the conclave convened to elect the bishop of Rome, the then dean of cardinals stated in his homily on April 18, 2005:

> Christ's mercy is not a grace that comes cheap, nor does it imply the trivialization of evil. Christ carries the full weight of evil and all its destructive force in his body and in his soul. He burns and transforms evil in suffering, in the fire of his suffering love.... How many winds of doctrine have we known in recent decades, how many ideological currents, how many ways of thinking. The small boat of the thought of many Christians has often been tossed about by the waves—flung from one extreme to another: from Marxism to liberalism; from collectivism to radical individualism; from atheism to a vague religious mysticism; from agnosticism to syncretism and so forth. Every day new sects spring up, and what St. Paul says about human deception and the trickery that strives to entice people into error (cf. Eph 4:14) comes true.
>
> Today, having a clear faith based on the Creed of the Church is often labeled as fundamentalism. Whereas relativism, that is, letting oneself be "tossed here and there, carried about by every wind of doctrine," seems the only attitude that can cope with modern times. We are building a dictatorship of relativism that does not recognize anything as definitive and whose ultimate goal consists solely of one's own ego and desires.
>
> We, however, have a different goal: the Son of God, the true man. He is the measure of true humanism. An "adult" faith is not a faith that follows the trends of fashion and the latest novelty; a mature adult faith is deeply rooted in friendship with Christ. It is this friendship that opens us up to all that is good and gives us a criterion by which to distinguish the true from the false, and deceit from truth.[1]

This homily was greeted with spontaneous applause by those assembled in St. Peter's Square. No explicit or unwitting subscription to an ideology, such as Marxism, liberalism, neoliberalism, collectivism, relativism, or communism, can satisfy the human heart. It is created by God for eternity. It is the beautiful charge of pastors to sow in the hearts of people the Word of God, Jesus Christ.

Thus, the expectations Ratzinger has for the new pontiff are abundantly clear: "Most especially in this hour, we ask the Lord, following his great gift of John Paul II, to grant us another shepherd in accordance with his will, a shepherd who will lead us to the knowledge of Christ, to his love, and true joy."[2]

In his first message as newly elected pope after the conclave he promised, in accordance with the teachings of the Vatican II Council, "to proclaim the living presence of Christ to the whole world.... The Church of today must revive her awareness of the duty to re-propose to the world the voice of the One who said: 'I am the light of the world. No follower of mine shall ever walk in darkness; no, he shall possess the light of life' (Jn 8:12). In carrying out his ministry, the new Pope knows that his task is to make Christ's light shine out before the men and women of today: not his own light, but Christ's. If we let Christ into our lives, we lose nothing, absolutely nothing of what makes life free, beautiful, and great. No! Only in this friendship are the doors of life opened wide. Only in this friendship is the great potential of human existence truly revealed. Only in this friendship do we experience beauty and liberation.... Yes, open wide the doors to Christ—and you will find true life."[3]

There is significance in Benedict XVI no longer using the tiara, the papal crown, but rather the episcopal miter, in his coat of arms. Not a shedding of religious or political authority is signified by this. Quite the contrary, it accentuates the fact that the glory of the Church rests on her orientation toward Jesus Christ. As is faith, spiritual authority—*sacra potestas*—is a free and unmerited gift and not an entitlement and as such obliges the one it is so generously bestowed upon. Beholding this spiritual dimension of the Church is important. It illustrates that the Church is nothing short of "Christ's very own inviting gesture to all of humankind." Ratzinger sends forth this signal quite deliberately in an era in which there is no longer any social corporation or philosophy that offers a revolutionary idea holding the promise of the renewal of humanity. Nowadays no worldview captures the imagination of the people. Sheltered in the liturgical ritual of the Church, the human being encounters Christ in the readings and the gospel and in the most personal form in the real presence of the Eucharist. In this each person understands in the deepest sense possible his or her own identity and purpose. In worship, an encounter with Christ occurs that enables the individual to find or recover his or her location in the world. As people appreciate liturgical ritual anew, they might also discover the value of manners in private and public life. In the long term, this might have social and political ramifications, something that until very recently has been considered unrealistic. A heightened sense of awe and reverence in the liturgy may lead to more civilized discourse, perhaps restoring a democracy now imperiled by the superficial media age. It could free contemporary forms of democracy from the prospect of degenerating into a tenuous balance of egoisms and pay again the common good the respects it deserves. By fixing one's gaze firmly on the liberating cross of Jesus, one experiences how the splendor of Christ's Resurrection from the dead outshines secularism's inane and humorless rationality.

As Ratzinger demonstrated in his inaugural lecture in Bonn in 1959, "The God of Faith and the God of Philosophers: A Contribution to the Problem of Natural Theology,"[4] in Jesus Christ the mute and inexpressible God of the philosophers becomes a speaking and listening God. In this sense, the interior claims of biblical faith are being fulfilled. The Truth of the Logos becomes man; this Logos, uniting the God of faith with the God of the philosophers, is Jesus the Christ. This one divine person, with divine and human natures, is the fulfilling center of human existence. At the close of his lecture, the future Pope Benedict XVI quoted a theological precursor to Bonaventure, Richard of St. Victor (d. 1173): *"Quaerite faciem eius semper"* ("seek his face incessantly").[5] This line comprises the whole program of the theologian and pope: personally beholding the Lord brings us to the faith. The task of theology is to reflect on this search for, and the promise of, his countenance.

It is quite impossible to assume an autonomous reflection on the conditions for the possibility of insight (Kant), as conducted by the anthropocentric shift (theology especially en vogue in the 1970s), is a viable option. The initiative is God's. First God speaks, shattering all human assumptions. The Roman adage *primum vivere, deinde philosophare* (live first, then reflect on life) holds true. First, we experience life, and life in its overwhelming vivacity speaks to us. Only subsequently do we reflect upon this experience. This circumstance has significant implications: neither Jesus Christ nor divine revelation can be generated by the human mind a priori, that is, without a prior encounter with the Son of God and revelation. The range of human reason without an encounter with the divine is smaller than that after the experience of the divine. The cognitional conditions for both can be spelled out as both cover some common, overlapping areas. The greater range of faith-filled intelligence is granted in grace. The intelligibility of faith is obvious, as the Logos is its origin, but it does not fall under the control of rationalism. Thus, the *cooperator veritatis* (the coworker of truth) never becomes the *operator veritatis* (the one controlling truth). As the patristic notion of the $\lambda o \gamma o \iota \ \sigma \pi \acute{\epsilon} \rho \eta \alpha \tau \iota \kappa o \iota$ (in Latin, the *rationes seminales*—seedlike words) intimates, the potential growth of meaning is assumed. In this vein, scripture, as attestation to the Christ event, is closed, yet open for appropriation. This allows salvation to have an encounter with Christ in history. In time, the fullness of time in Christ comes about. For the Bonaventurean Ratzinger, a relative autonomy of judgment on divine matters without God does not exist.[6] As the eternal Christ is its fulfillment, history is not eternal, but the whole of history, and every individual human being's existence, receives its most profound meaning. Human reason is relatively autonomous but fully actuates itself only in Jesus Christ. It stands "to reason" that there does not exist an external court of appeal for Christocentric rationality, as this would mean judging from the perspective of the triune God. Rather, created human reason comes to its true and fullest realization as graced reason, in the human being who lives the sacramental life of the Church, which is the elongation of the Logos' Incarnation.

This explains Ratzinger's qualified support for the historical-critical method. Because revelation is historical, this method is fundamental to theology but not fully satisfactory. It does not necessarily lead to the Jesus Christ of faith. It does not force one to behold the form (*Schau der Gestalt*), the divine essence, of Jesus as the Christ. Faith is knowledge of God's love. Critical rationality alone cannot lead to such a God. Rejecting both the rationality of neoscholasticism and the reductionism of the anthropocentric shift, Ratzinger welcomes this, because only a God that cannot be proven can be the God of charity. God must reveal himself because otherwise God would be known without being loved. Only one who loves Jesus knows Jesus, *Deus Caritas Est.*

This leads to a seeming paradox: one cannot know Jesus without Jesus! As there is a difference between grace and nature and between faith and reason, there is also a difference between belief in Christ and the historical-critical method. The historical-critical method is an outgrowth of the ascendance of the scientific-technical age. But were this method to be absolutized, it would be a case of reducing the range of faith to that of reason unaided by grace, which is hubris. One would reduce faith to verifiable things. On the other hand, were one to negate this method, then one would be denying historicity—and thus Incarnation. The tension between the two must be maintained because revelation is historical, as *Dei Verbum* teaches. Only by maintaining this difference can God be known in his ineffable love.

With the patristic concept of "the reason-gifted liturgy" ($λογική λατρεια$) both God and human beings do justice to the inner entelechy of human reason and nature, without reducing God to what human reason can fathom. This is the inextricable and irreducible fact: we know of Jesus Christ only through the post-Easter eyes of Christians. Josephus Flavius and others suffer a paucity of evidence that leaves faith its chance to know Jesus Christ, better than any historic record could ever convey, as charity. This is the import of Cornelius after Jesus died on the cross: seeing God face to face (Mk 15:39; Mt 27:54).

Well before the Second Vatican Council and the development of the anthropocentric shift, Ratzinger argues that a *theologia naturalis* not embraced and sustained by the Christian hermeneutics of salvation history is unimaginable. A Cartesian egocentric view is denied credibility because meaning is not a dependent corollary of human knowledge.[7] Delimiting the Catholic faith from both neoscholasticism and the anthropocentric shift, Ratzinger treads in good conscience the path of a *reductio in mysterio* because it is a reduction to Jesus Christ who is *the* Logos, the supreme reason. Therefore, faith is not an alogical or irrational attempt. The intelligibility of faith is not only preserved but precisely therein the full intelligence of human existence is revealed. From a different angle, the famous Protestant philosopher Hans-Georg Gadamer (1900–2002) demonstrated this in his epochal study *Truth and Method.*[8] Truth is unlocked in the process of *Verstehen*, of understanding. Ratzinger demonstrates how faith is preserved in its autonomy as a supernatural virtue without yielding to either fideism or rationalism. Thus, one can assert the dogma of Christ's Incarnation. The creeds of the Church are based on a collective, common faith experience of Christ. As the Ephata Rite (that part of refers to the part of baptism, when the child is invited to "open" its eyes, mouth and eyes to the Lord) during baptism reminds us (Mk 7:31–37): it is the Church in Christ who (!) opens communal understanding.

Life in its varied overabundance is far too powerful to be grasped or harnessed by a system. This is the Christocentric shift. In this sense one would do a great injustice to Ratzinger's theology were one to press it into a self-contained, closed box containing timeless truths. He has always avoided such a temptation in his own theology. He is an advocate of a legitimate plurality of approaches to the one truth that is Jesus Christ. Such cognitional pluralism is grounded in the weakness of every human word and the sublime nature of the Word. But amid human frailties, the Word did indeed become incarnate. This is the incontrovertible reality and the truth. In his book *Jesus of Nazareth*, Ratzinger reminds his readers worldwide that Christ's presence in the Church is real and not ambivalent. One cannot doubt it and still call oneself a Christian. All scholarly efforts are but humanly expressed signposts, references to this ineffable mystery—to the *mysterium fascinosum et tremendum* (the awesome and formidable mystery). As is the case for every Christian, every theology, and every theologian, bishop, or pope as well, they receive their true greatness by becoming similes or parables for God, by participating in the natural-supernatural life of Jesus Christ, who is the *Logos* and thus permitting the Incarnation of God in Jesus to continue to the end of time. "The courage to engage the whole breadth of reason [*Logos*], and not the denial of its grandeur—this is the program with which a theology grounded in biblical faith enters into the debates of our time. 'Not to act reasonably, not to act with *logos*, is contrary to the nature of God.'... It is to this great *logos*, to this breadth of reason, that we invite our partners in the dialogue of cultures."[9]

NOTES

Prelims

1. Benedict XVI, *Easter Sunday Homily*, March 23, 2008, http://chiesa.espresso.repubblica.it (accessed March 25, 2008). For purposes of clarity, in general he will be referred to as (Joseph) Ratzinger when discussing his life and work prior to becoming pope. For references to him after his election to the papal office, he will be referred to as *Pope Benedict XVI*.

2. John F. Thornton and Susan B. Varenne, *The Essential Pope Benedict XVI: His Central Writings and Speeches* (San Francisco: Harper, 2007), 35. A foundation dedicated to the research and dissemination of Benedict XVI's thought was established in November 2008 in Munich. Benedict XVI supplied the initial funds for this intellectual enterprise. The archbishop of Vienna, Cardinal Schönborn, a doctoral student of Ratzinger, serves as the head of its board of trustees: Joseph Ratzinger/Benedikt XVI. Stiftung. It also supports up-and-coming theologians and plans to endow a chair for a visiting professor. Not to be confused with this foundation, the Institut Papst Benedikt XVI operates from the Regensburg seminary. It was founded by the bishop of Regensburg, a noted theologian in his own right, Gerhard Ludwig Müller. The Trier dogmatician Rudolf Voderholzer serves as its editor. Under "Joseph Ratzinger" as the author's name, it aims to publish the collected works of *Pope Benedict XVI* in a critical, annotated sixteen-volume series. This institute is approved by Benedict XVI. He intends to read every volume prior to its publication. The first published volume is: Joseph Ratzinger, *Theologie der Liturgie. Die sakramentale Begründung christlicher Existenz*, vol. 11, in *Joseph Ratzinger: Gesammelte Schriften* (Freiburg i. Br.: Herder, 2008), 752 pp.; the second: Joseph Ratzinger, *Offenbarungsverständnis und Geschichtstheologie Bonaventuras*, vol. 2, in *Joseph Ratzinger: Gesammelte Schriften* (Freiburg i. Br.: Herder, 2009), 672 pp. For an exhaustive bibliography on Joseph Ratzinger's authorship cf. Vinzenz Pfnür, ed., *Joseph Ratzinger/Papst Benedikt XVI, Das Werk, Veröffentlichungen bis zur Papstwahl* (Augsburg:, 2009). The former doctoral students of Ratzinger compiled a list of not less than 1,510 entries.

3. Cf. Friedrich Nietzsche, *The Gay Science: With a Prelude in Rhymes and an Appendix of Songs* (New York: Cambridge University Press, 2001).

4. If one is to regret something in Ratzinger's vast theological oeuvre, it is the comparative paucity of references to the Holy Spirit.

5. Yves Congar, *I Believe in the Holy Spirit* (New York: Crossroad, 2001). Heribert Mühlen, *Der Heilige Geist als Person: Beitrag zur Frage nach dem Heiligen Geiste eigentümlichen Funktion in der Trinität, bei der Inkarnation und im Gnadenbund* (Münster: Aschendorff, 1963).

6. Romano Guardini was a priest, philosopher of religion, pioneer of the liturgical movement, and a leader of Catholic renewal who anticipated much of the teachings of Vatican II. The Nazis "retired" him from his teaching position at the University of Berlin.

7. Romano Guardini, *Religiöse Gestalten in Dostojewskis Werk* (Mainz/Paderborn: Matthias Grünewald/Schöningh, 1989), 129–79, first published 1933.

8. Cf. Jonathan Sutton, *The Religious Philosophy of Vladimir Solovyov* (New York: St. Martin's Press, 1988).

9. Among other institutions, he is also a member of the *Rheinland-Westfälische Akademie der Wissenschaften* and the *European Academy of Sciences and Arts*.

Introduction: The Christocentric Shift

1. Joseph Ratzinger, *Introduction to Christianity* (San Francisco: Ignatius, 2004), 157. Admittedly "charity" sounds a bit antiquated, but cf. Benedict XVI's encyclical *Deus Caritas Est*.
2. Aidan Nichols, *The Thought of Benedict XVI: An Introduction to the Theology of Joseph Ratzinger* (New York: Burns & Oates, 2005), 1.
3. Arguably Karl Rahner was the most influential Catholic systematician during the last forty years of the twentieth century. Some consider that Rahner's Christology treats Jesus Christ as a special case of human self-transcendence to the Absolute. In the vein of George Lindbeck, Bruce Marshall makes this case in: ibid., *Christology in Conflict: The Identity of a Saviour in Rahner and Barth* (Oxford: Blackwell, 1987). This perspective that Rahner espoused an anthropocentric view is shared a fortiori by Patrick Burke in: ibid., *Reinterpreting Rahner: A Critical Study of His Major Themes* (New York: Fordham University Press, 2002).
4. Joseph Ratzinger, *On the Way to Jesus Christ* (San Francisco: Ignatius, 2005), 7f.
5. Ratzinger, *The Yes of Jesus Christ* (New York: Crossroad, 2005), 48.
6. Ibid., 68.
7. Ibid., 110.
8. Ibid., 68.
9. Joseph Ratzinger, "Die Gabe der Weisheit," in *Die Gaben des Geistes*, ed. W. Sandfuchs (Würzburg: Echter, 1977).
10. Joseph Ratzinger, "Ich glaube an Gott, den allmächtigen Vater," *Communio* 4 (German, 1975): 10–18. Joseph Ratzinger, "Meditation and Progress," *Communio* 25 (1998): 325–39 (original 1974).
11. Joseph Ratzinger, *Behold the Pierced One* (San Francisco: Ignatius Press, 1986 [1984]), 35.
12. Joseph Ratzinger, *The Nature and Mission of Theology* (San Francisco: Ignatius), 51.
13. Joseph Ratzinger, *Der Gott Jesu Christi, Betrachtungen über den Dreieinigen Gott* (Munich: Kösel, 1976), 55.
14. Ibid., 55.
15. Cabasilas argued that through the mysteries of baptism, confirmation, and the Eucharist spiritual union with Christ can be achieved. Nicholas Cabasilas, *The Life in Christ* (New York: St. Vladimir, 1974).
16. Ratzinger, *On the Way to Jesus Christ*, 32, 36.
17. Ibid., 40.
18. Ibid., 39.

1   Highlights of a Lifelong Ministry

1. Norbert Trippen, *Josef Kardinal Frings (1887–1978)*, vol. II (Paderborn: Schöningh, 2005), 292–96, at 296.
2. This is indeed how numerous Catholics in "Altbayern" ("Old Bavaria," which is more or less identical with southern Bavaria) termed the installation of Munich's new archbishop.
3. As Utrecht was part of the Holy Roman Empire at the time, sometimes the tragic Reformation era pope Hadrian VI (1522–1523) is counted among them.
4. Eberhard Jüngel, "Sie haben einen Papst," in *Neue Zürcher Zeitung*, April 21, 2005, http://www.nzz.ch (accessed April 22, 2005).
5. Joseph Ratzinger, *Milestones: Memoirs 1927–1977* (San Francisco: Ignatius, 1998), pp. 153–56.

2   Personality and Temperament

1. For a superb description of the rich historic and cultural tapestry of Bavaria, see Aidan Nichols, OP, *The Thought of Benedict XVI: An Introduction to the Theology of Joseph Ratzinger* (New York: Burns & Oates, 2005), pp. 5–26.
2. Peter Seewald, *Benedict XVI: An Intimate Portrait* (San Francisco: Ignatius, 2008), 138.
3. Joseph Ratzinger, *Salt of the Earth: The Church at the End of the Millennium: An Interview with Peter Seewald* (San Francisco: Ignatius, 1997 [1996]), 27.

4. Joseph Ratzinger, *On the Way to Jesus Christ* (San Francisco: Ignatius, 2005), 38. Following the trajectory established by Plato, Plotinus, Augustine, and Albert the Great, Thomas Aquinas argues that beauty is, along with truth, a transcendental. See Cf. *De Veritate*, q. 22 a. 1 ad 12.

5. Joseph Ratzinger, *Milestones: Memoirs 1927–1977* (San Francisco: Ignatius, 1998), 8.

6. In his inaugural lecture in 1959, Ratzinger argued that the analogy of being is a necessary dimension of Christian faith. Otherwise, Christ as the Logos would become incommunicable. However, with Augustine he insists on a *ratio purificata* (purified reason), as pure reason can be turned "in many directions." See Cf. Joseph Ratzinger, *Der Gott des Glaubens und der Gott der Philosophen, Ein Beitrag zum Problem der theologia naturalis* (Munich: Schnell & Steiner, 1960), 23–35; Joseph Ratzinger, *Introduction to Christianity* (San Francisco: Ignatius, 2004), 98–100.

7. Ratzinger, *Introduction*, 52–57.

8. *Frankfurter Allgemeine Zeitung*, April 14, 2005, no. 86.

9. Susanne Kornacker, "Der junge Joseph Ratzinger und sein Bischof Michael Kardinal von Faulhaber," in *Joseph Ratzinger und das Erzbistum München und Freising, Dokumente und Bilder aus kirchlichen Archiven, Beiträge und Erinnerungen*, ed. Peter Pfister, 53–83, at 67f. (Regensburg: Schnell und Steiner, 2006).

10. Ratzinger, *Milestones*, 100. This is the actual point of departure for Ratzinger favoring celebrating the Eucharist *ad orientem*—to the east. This consideration is perhaps yet more important than incontrovertible archaeological evidence, the liturgical praxis of the Eastern rites, or liturgical considerations. It is not the priest but Jesus Christ—fully a human being and fully God's eternal Son—who stands in the center.

11. Brennan Pursell, *Benedict of Bavaria: An Intimate Portrait of the Pope and His Homeland* (N.p.: Circle Press, 2008), 57.

12. Marco Bardazzi, *In the Vineyard of the Lord: The Life, Faith, and Teachings of Joseph Ratzinger, Pope Benedict XVI* (New York: Rizzoli, 2005), 88.

13. Ratzinger, *Milestones*, 27.

14. Seewald, *Benedict*, 55.

15. Ibid., 76.

16. Ibid., 23. For a nuanced appraisal: M. F. Feldkamp, *Mitläufer, Feiglinge, Antisemitismus? Katholische Kirche und Nationalsozialismus* (Augsburg: Sankt Ulrich, 2009).

17. J. Kirchinger and E. Schütz, eds., *Georg Ratzinger (1844–1899). Ein Leben zwischen Politik, Geschichte und Seelsorge* (Regensburg: Schnell & Steiner, 2008). It is likely he was born on the Ratzinger-Hof (Ratzinger Farm), located in the town of Rickering, a part of Winzer, in the county of Deggendorf. The Ratzinger family often visited there; Joseph Ratzinger has done so until recently. Mr. and Mrs. Anton Messerer, relatives of Pope Benedict, run a farm there specializing in poultry. http://www.br-online.de (accessed August 27, 2006).

18. Seewald, *Benedict*, 132f.

19. Ibid., 246.

20. Karl H. Neufeld, *Die Brüder Rahner, Eine Biographie*, 2nd ed. (Freiburg i. Br.: Herder, 2004), 2nd ed., pp. 30–59.

21. Ratzinger, *Milestones*, 23.

22. The educational reforms of secondary schools in the 1970s and again during the European Bologna Process (1998–2010) have had the unfortunate tendency of eliminating the study of classical languages from the curricula. The thirteen-year school curriculum is being reduced to twelve, and the time spent in the *Gymnasium* from nine to six. Thus, students no longer acquire a thorough knowledge of classical languages. In addition, as now on the university level modules provide focused curricula and goals have to be defined before embarking on research, purpose-free studies become impossible. As a consequence, originality and serendipity suffer.

23. Ratzinger, *Milestones*, 50.

24. Seewald, *Benedict,* 185.

25. Pursell, *Benedict of Bavaria*, 75ff.

26. Ratzinger, *Milestones*, 63 and 99.

27. Ibid., 99. The designation *Dom* is a nostalgic remnant from the time when it had served as the cathedral of the archdiocese of Munich-Freising. Since the early nineteenth century the cathedral has been located in the city of Munich.

28. Beginning in 1939, the rector of the high school seminary automatically registered all seminarians with the Hitlerjugend. See. Volker Laube, "Das Erzbischöfliche Studienseminar St. Michael in Traunstein 1933 bis 1945 und der junge Joseph Ratzinger," in Pfister, *Joseph Ratzinger*, 24–52, at 34–38.

29. Alfred Delp, SJ, *Der Mensch und die Geschichte* (Nuremberg: Glock und Lutz, 1974).

30. "Seelsorge heißt für mich helfen durch die Wahrheit" is the inscription on the memorial plaque in Munich's *Ludwigskirche*. Guardini had been university homilist there, and in this church his earthly remains were laid to rest in a side chapel.

31. Ratzinger, *Milestones*, 100f.

32. Alfred Läpple, *Benedikt XVI und seine Wurzeln, Was sein Leben und seinen Glauben prägte* (Augsburg: Sankt Ulrich, 2006), 98f.

33. See. Joseph Ratzinger/Pope Benedict XVI, *Jesus of Nazareth: From the Baptism in the Jordan to the Transfiguration*, trans. Adrian Walker, 33 (New York: Doubleday, 2007).

34. Läpple, 100f. A selection of Delp's thoughts can be found in: Alfred Delp, SJ, *Advent of the Heart: Seasonal Sermons and Prison Writings, 1941–1944*, transl. Abtei St. Walburg, Eichstätt, Germany (San Francisco: Ignatius, 2006).

35. "Wie auch die Winde wehen: / sollt ihnen zum Trotze stehen; / Wenn auch die Welt zerbricht— Dein tapferes Herz verzaget nicht. Ohne die Tapferkeit des Herzens, die den Mut / hat, uner- schütterlich den Geistern der Zeit und / der Masse zu trotzen, können wir den Weg zu Gott und den wahren Weg unseres Herrn nicht finden." Pursell, *Benedict of Bavaria*, 80.

3   Formative Early Encounters as a Seminarian: Personal Existentialism Grounded in Jesus Christ

1. John Paul II, *Encyclical Letter, Fides et Ratio: On the Relationship Between Faith and Reason* (September 14, 1998), §§ 57ff.

2. One of the less charitable observations is: "The God of the Bible and the Gospel has been reduced to a *caput mortuum* (a head of the dead) of frozen abstractions…overwhelmingly bor- ing…nothing but a gigantic and futile exercise in tautology." Louis Bouyer, *The Invisible Father: Approaches to the Mystery of the Divinity* (Edinburgh: T & T Clark, 1999), 248.

3. Richard Peddicord, *The Sacred Monster of Thomism: An Introduction to the Life and Legacy of Reginald Garrigou-Lagrange OP* (South Bend, IN: St. Augustine's Press, 2005), 2. Cf. Aidan Nichols, *Reason with Piety, Garrigou-Lagrange in the Service of Catholic Thought* (Naples, FL: Sapientia Press, 2008). Especially Nichols demonstrates that such bifurcation between spiritu- ality and theology does not do full justice to Garrigou-Lagrange.

4. Using Aristotelian, stoic, and scholastic thought, Christian Wolff (1679–1754) was the domi- nant philosopher in eighteenth-century Germany. His supreme confidence in human reason influenced Immanuel Kant and was cause for much irritation.

5. Thomas F. O'Meara, OP, *Thomas Aquinas Theologian* (Notre Dame, IN and London: University of Notre Dame Press, 1999), 182.

6. Joseph Ratzinger, *The Nature and the Mission of Theology: Approaches to Understanding Its Role in the Light of Present Controversy* (San Francisco: Ignatius, 1993), 16f.

7. Joseph Ratzinger, *Principles of Catholic Theology: Building Stones for a Fundamental Theology* (San Francisco: Ignatius, 1987 [1982]), 160.

8. For a critical summary assessment of transcendental Thomism cf. Aidan Nichols, "Anonymous Christianity," in *Beyond the Blue Glass: Catholic Essays on Faith and Culture*, vol. I (London: St. Austin Press, 2002), 107–28.

9. Henri de Lubac, "Nature and Grace," in *The Word in History: The St. Xavier Symposium*, ed. T. Patrick Burke, 33 (London: Collins, 1966).

10. Tracey Rowland, *Ratzinger's Faith: The Theology of Pope Benedict XVI* (Oxford: Oxford University Press, 2008), 7f.

11. See in particular George Tyrrell, *Medievalism: A Reply to Cardinal Mercier* (Tunbridge Wells: Burns & Oates, 1994), reprint of the third revised and enlarged edition of 1909. Cf. also Ellen M. Leonard, *George Tyrell and the Catholic Tradition* (London: Darton, Longman and Todd, 1982); Nicholas Sagovsky, *"On God's Side": A Life of George Tyrrell* (Oxford: Clarendon, 1990). Tyrrell's ghost haunted some during Vatican II. Probably due to a prompting from the American theologian Joseph Fenton, Cardinal Ernesto Ruffini from Palermo complained in an intervention that the first chapter of *Lumen Gentium* emphasized, much like Tyrell, the Church as sacrament and mystery. Cf. Giuseppe Alberigo and J. A. Komonchak, eds., *History of Vatican II*, vol. III (Maryknoll, NY: Orbis / Leuven: Peeters, 2000), 30 and 50.

12. Thomas Aquinas *Summa Theologiae* 1 a. 1, 8 ad 2m.

13. Hans Urs von Balthasar, *The Glory of the Lord: A Theological Aesthetics V: The Realm of Metaphysics in the Modern Age* (Edinburgh: T & T Clark, 1991), 21–29.

14. Walter Kasper, *Theology and Church* (London: SCM, 1989), 1.

15. Freising had been from the very beginning, under the Irish missionary Bishop Corbinian, the residence of the (arch)bishop of Freising-Munich. The switch occurred under King Ludwig I in the first half of the nineteenth century.

16. He taught in the seminary as docent from 1948 until 1952. Ratzinger became his successor. Alfred Läpple, *Benedikt XVI und seine Wurzeln, Was sein Leben und seinen Glauben prägte* (Augsburg: St. Ulrich, 2006), 41.

17. Along with Romano Guardini, Steinbüchel prepared the way for a more Christ-centered theology in Germany. His philosophical dissertation, *Der Zweckgedanke in der Philosophie des Thomas von Aquin* (Münster, 1921), and his theological dissertation, *Der Sozialismus als sittliche Idee, ein Beitrag zur christlichen Sozialethik* (Düsseldorf, 1921), were much noted. His major work was *Eine philosophische Grundlegung der katholischen Sittenlehre* (Düsseldorf, 1951). In it he tried to supplement Thomas's "Wesensethik" (ethics of essence) with a "Situationsethik" (situations ethics), bringing Kant's and Hegel's thought to bear. A member of the *Beuroner Arbeitskreis*, he promoted dialogue between Christians and Marxists. He is one of the contributors to an "anthropological turn" in theology. The noted German moral theologians Alfons Auer and Bernhard Häring were his students.

18. Joseph Ratzinger, *Milestones: Memoirs 1927–1977* (San Francisco: Ignatius, 1998), 43f.

19. Joseph Ratzinger, "Homily for Luigi Giussani," *Communio* 31 (2004), 685–7, at 685.

20. Cf. As representative of this perspective: Hans Urs von Balthasar, *Love Alone Is Credible* (San Francisco: Ignatius, 2005).

21. Joseph Ratzinger, *Values in a Time of Upheaval* (San Francisco: Ignatius, 2006), 85.

22. Rowland, *Ratzinger's Faith*, 76.

23. Joseph Ratzinger, "Cardinal Frings's Speeches during the Second Vatican Council: Apropos A. Muggeridge's *The Desolate City*," *Communio* 15 (1988): 130–47, at 147.

24. Theodor Steinbüchel, "Die personalistische Grundhaltung des christlichen Ethos," *Theologie und Glaube* 31 (1939): 392–407.

25. Martin Buber, *Ich und Du* (Leipzig: Insel, 1923).

26. Cf. Martin Buber, *Das Problem des Menschen* (Heidelberg: Lambert Schneider, 1948), 168f.

27. For a general overview, see P. A. Schlipp and M. Friedman, eds., *Martin Buber* (Frankfurt am Main: Suhrkamp, 1963). Hermann L. Goldschmidt, *Dialogik: Das Problem der Neuzeit* (Frankfurt am Main: Europäische Verlagsanstalt, 1964). Michael Theunissen, *Der Andere. Studien zur Sozialontologie der Gegenwart* (Berlin: de Gruyter, 1965). Werner Grünfeld, *Der Begegnungscharakter der Wirklichkeit in Philosophie und Wirklichkeit Martin Bubers* (Ratingen: Henn, 1965). Schalom ben Chorin, *Zwiesprache mit Buber, ein Erinnerungsbuch* (Munich,1966). Heinz. H. Schrey, *Dialogisches Denken* (Darmstadt: Wissenschaftliche Buchgesellschaft, 1970).

28. One detects here a broad-based current as opposed to a narrow rationalistic or neoscholastic intellectualism.

29. In this regard cf. Bernhard Casper, "Rosenzweig's Criticism of Buber's 'I and Thou,'" in *Martin Buber: A Centenary Volume*, ed. Haim Gordon and Jochanan Bloch, 139–62 (New York: Ktav, 1984).

30. Fergus Kerr, *Twentieth Century Catholic Theologians: From Neo-scholasticism to Nuptial Mysticism* (Malden, MA: Blackwell, 2007), 184.

31. Casper, "Rosenzweig's Criticism," 44.

32. Francis Schüssler Fiorenza, "From Theologian to Pope: A Personal View Back, Past the Public Portrayals," *Harvard Divinity Bulletin* 33 (2005): 56–62, at 56. Joseph A. Komonchak, "The Church in Crisis: Pope Benedict's Theological Vision," *Commonweal* (June 3, 2005): 11–14, at 13.

33. Benedict XVI, "Christmas Message," *L'Osservatore Romano*, January 4, 2007, 7.

34. August Adam, *The Primacy of Love* (Westminster, MD: Newman, 1958 [original 1933]). August Adam (1888–1965) was the younger brother of Karl Adam. He studied in Regensburg, Tübingen, and Freiburg, in 1924 earning a doctoral degree with the dissertation *Arbeit und Besitz nach Ratherius von Verona* under the direction of Otto Schilling. Unlike his brother, he always maintained a critical distance from National Socialism. Due to his rather innovative position, he was prevented from assuming a teaching position at Passau University in 1929

and again in 1932. From 1924 onward, he taught in the Bavarian town of Straubing, first at a secondary school and then, from 1928 until 1953, at the *Humanistisches* (today it is the *Turmair*) *Gymnasium* (advanced secondary school). Cf. http://www.die-tagespost.de, March 2, 2006 (accessed March 14, 2006). This is similar to an approach taken by the convert Dietrich von Hildebrand, who was his contemporary. Both contributed to what later would be termed a "Theology of the Body." While John Paul II had read von Hildebrand, it cannot be ascertained that he had direct knowledge of Adam.

35. Cf. *Deus Caritas Est*, no. 11.
36. Läpple, *Benedikt XVI*, 16f.
37. Ibid., 19.
38. Søren Kierkegaard, *Practice in Christianity* (Princeton, NJ: Princeton University Press, 1991).
39. Heinrich Denzinger, *Kompendium der Glaubensbekenntnisse und kirchlichen Lehrentscheidungen*, improved and edited by Peter Hünermann, 4th ed. (Freiburg i. Br.: Herder, 2005).
40. Kierkegaard, *Practice*, 45.
41. "Zu diesem Gott kann der Mensch weder beten, noch kann er ihm opfern. Vor der Causa sui kann der Mensch weder aus Scheu ins Knie fallen, noch kann er vor diesem Gott musizieren und tanzen." Martin Heidegger, *Identity and Difference* (Chicago: University of Chicago, 2002), 54.
42. Alfred Delp, SJ, *Facing Death* (London: Bloomsbury, 1962), 117.
43. "Die Person gewinnt sich, indem sie sich in Gott verliert." Läpple, *Benedikt XVI*, 36.
44. At this point one might argue Ratzinger's theology lacks an appreciation for the heuristic value of doubt. In the Augustinian psychological perspective, doubt in central matters of faith, while having epistemological relevance, is a sign of distance, of alienation, from God.
45. Joseph Cardinal Ratzinger, in *John Henry Newman: Lover of Truth*, ed. Margarete Strolz and Maria Binder, 141–6 (Rome: Pontificia Universitas Urbaniana, 1991).

4   Graduate Studies in Munich

1. Joseph Ratzinger, *Milestones: Memoirs 1927–1977* (San Francisco: Ignatius, 1998), 50f.
2. However, cf. Ratzinger, *Milestones*, 55. There he mentions Söhngen and Pascher alongside one another.
3. A helpful synopsis of his theology can be found in his quite original article, Gottlieb Söhngen, "Die Weisheit der Theologie durch den Weg der Wissenschaft," in *Mysterium Salutis*, vol. I, ed. Johannes Feiner and Magnus Löhrer, 905–80 (Einsiedeln: Benzinger, 1965). Transcending the common clichés of neoscholasticism, the liberal vision of this theologian spans a vast area: "Anselm's Proslogion" (1938), "Newman as Philosopher of Religion; Analogy of Being" (1934), "Symbol and Reality in the Cultic Mystery" (1937), "The Sacramental Essence of the Mass as Sacrifice" (1946), "Analogy and Metaphor" (1962), and "Christ's Presence in Faith and Sacrament" (1967).
4. "Das ist der Schüler, der meine Gedanken aufnimmt, der sie weiterführt. Mein Schüler wird mehr finden als ich." Söhngen as quoted by Läpple in Thomas Forstner, "Zeitzeugenberichte über die Freisinger und frühen Münchener Jahre Joseph Ratzingers (1945–1959)," in *Joseph Ratzinger und das Erzbistum München und Freising*, no. 10, ed. Peter Pfister, 120. Dokumente und Bilder aus kirchlichen Archiven, Beiträge und Erinnerungen, Schriften des Archivs des Erzbistums München und Freising. (Regensburg: Schnell & Steiner, 2006).
5. Alfred Läpple, *Benedikt XVI und seine Wurzeln, Was sein Leben und seinen Glauben prägte* (Augsburg: St. Ulrich, 2006), 80.
6. Gottlieb Söhngen, *Die Einheit der Theologie, Gesammelte Abhandlungen, Aufsätze, Vorträge* (Munich: Karl Zink, 1952). This book is worth reading to this date and must be considered a little-noted twentieth-century classic.
7. Söhngen, "Weisheit," 961.
8. For a thorough presentation and discussion of Söhngen's theology, see J. Graf, *Gottlieb Söhngens (1891–1971) Suche nach der "Einheit der Theologie." Ein Beitrag zum Durchbruch heilsgeschichtlichen Denkens* (Frankfurt am Main: Peter Lang, 1991).
9. Laurence Paul Hemming, *Benedict XVI: Fellow Worker for the Truth* (London: Burns & Oates, 2005), 16.

10. Ratzinger, in *Deutsche Tagespost*, December 23, 1971.

11. Ratzinger, *Milestones*, 98.

12. Henri de Lubac, *Catholicism: Christ and the Common Destiny of Man* (San Francisco: Ignatius, 1988), 360.

13. Fergus Kerr, *Twentieth-Century Catholic Theologians: From Neo-scholasticism to Nuptial Mysticism* (London and Malden, MA: Blackwell, 2007), 71.

14. A most telling line reads: "In these conditions, all infidelity to the divine image that man bears, every breach with God, is at the same time a disruption of human unity. It cannot eliminate the natural unity of the human race—the image of God, though it may be, is indestructible—but it ruins that spiritual unity which, according to the Creator's plan, should be so much the closer in proportion as the supernatural union of man with God is more completely effected." De Lubac, *Catholicism*, 33. Whether such a sweeping predication as "individualistic" is justified is open for debate.

15. Cf. "In the fullest meaning of the word she brings into existence and gathers them together into one Whole. Humanity is one, organically one by its divine structure; it is the Church's mission to reveal to men that pristine unity that they have lost, to restore and complete it." De Lubac, *Catholicism*, 53.

16. De Lubac, *Catholicism*, 141. See also: "But the Church, the only real Church which is the Body of Christ, is not merely that strongly hierarchical and disciplined society whose divine origin has to be maintained. . . . If Christ is the sacrament of God, the Church is for us the sacrament of Christ; she represents him in the full and ancient meaning of the term; she really makes him present. She not only carries on his work, but she is his very continuation. . . ." Ibid., 76.

17. Eugen Maier, *Einigung in der Welt in Gott. Das Katholische bei Henri de Lubac* (Einsiedeln: Johannes, 1983). Hans Urs von Balthasar, *The Theology of Henri de Lubac* (San Francisco: Ignatius, 1991), 35–43. Henri de Lubac, *Meine Schriften im Rückblick* (Einsiedeln: Johannes, 1996).

18. De Lubac, *Catholicism*, 73.

19. Ibid., 339.

20. For details regarding this critical phase in Balthasar's life, cf. Hans Urs von Balthasar, *Unser Auftrag, Bericht und Entwurf* (Einsiedeln: Johannes, 1984), 66f and 402–8 for his farewell letter to the Jesuit order. Elio Guerriero, *Hans Urs von Balthasar, Eine Monographie* (Einsiedeln: Johannes, 1993), 161f. A good summary of this painful process is found in: Michael Schulz, *Hans Urs von Balthasar begegnen* (Augsburg: St. Ulrich, 2002), 58–61. After leaving the Jesuit order, he not only founded both a publishing house, Johannes Verlag, and the *Johnnesgemeinschaft* (community of St. John), but also pursued a career as a theological and spiritual author while continuing to serve as a priest incardinated into the diocese of Basle.

21. Cf. Guerriero, *Hans Urs von Balthasar*, 379ff, and Schulz, *Hans Urs von Balthasar begegnen*, 61–65.

22. As recorded in Läpple, *Benedikt XVI*, 85.

23. Guardini is mentioned briefly in Ratzinger, *Milestones*, 43.

24. Joseph Ratzinger, *Introduction to Christianity* (San Francisco: Ignatius, 2004), 309.

25. Cf. Robert A. Krieg, ed., *Romano Guardini: A Precursor of Vatican II* (Notre Dame, IN and London: Notre Dame Press, 1997).

26. Joseph Ratzinger, *The Spirit of the Liturgy* (San Francisco: Ignatius, 2000), 7.

27. Romano Guardini, *The Lord* (Washington, DC: Regnery, 2002), with an introduction by Joseph Cardinal Ratzinger, xi–xiv.

28. Cf. Romano Guardini, *Das Wesen des Christentums* (Würzburg: Echter, 1949).

29. Guardini, *The Lord*, 139.

30. Ibid., 319.

31. Verbatim: "Die Mystik erwachte in den Seelen und mit ihr uralte Elemente der Kunst." Franz Marc, "Die 'Wilden' Deutschlands," in *Der Blaue Reiter. Dokumentarische Neuausgabe von K. Lankheit*, ed. Wassily Kandinsky and Franz Marc, 28–32, at 30 (Munich: Piper, 1965).

32. "Es müsse noch eine andere Mystik geben, in welcher die Innigkeit des Geheimnisses mit der Größe der objektiven Gestalten verbunden sei." Romano Guardini, *Berichte über mein Leben*. (Düsseldorf: Patmos, 1984), 88.

33. Augustine *Soliloquium* I, 2, 7. Cf. Romano Guardini, *Unterscheidung des Christlichen*, (Mainz: Grünewald, 1963), 350–8, at 356. Ibid., *The Conversion of Augustine* (Westminster, MD: Newman Press, 1960), 28f. Ibid., *Die Bekehrung des Aurelius Augustinus*, 4th ed. (Mainz: Grünewald, 1989), 31.

34. Romano Guardini, *Sinn der Kirche: fünf Vorträge* (Mainz: Grünewald, 1922).

35. While describing Koch's thinking "wie reine Luft und klaren Raum" (as pure air and clear space), Guardini admits Koch's theology was "für sich allein…einfach zu wenig" (by itself…simply too little). Koch's approach relied too much on a historic-positive method. Guardini, *Berichte*, 85.

36. Ibid., 86.

37. Alfons Knoll, "'Die Seele wieder finden'—Romano Guardini auf der Suche nach einer 'anderen' Theologie," in *Konservativ mit Blick nach vorn, Versuche zu Romano Guardini*, ed. Arno Schilson, 11–31, at 19 (Würzburg: Echter, 1994).

38. Romano Guardini, *Christentum und Kultur* (Mainz: Grünewald, 1926), 154f. Ibid., *Das Wesen des Christentums—Die menschliche Wirklichkeit des Herrn. Beiträge zu einer Psychologie Jesu*, 7th ed. (Mainz-Paderborn: Matthias Grünewald, 1991), 68.

39. Romano Guardini, *Die religiöse Offenheit der Gegenwart* (Mainz: Grünewald, 1934), 92. This by no means relativizes the Church's significance. Rather, he makes out "a new intensification and legitimation." Ibid., 91.

40. "Die Kirche alleine erkennt Gott, soweit Endliches den Unendlichen erkennen kann.…Was auf den ersten Blick wie Vergewaltigung des wissenschaftlichen Denkens erschien, ist für eine tiefere Betrachtung die einzige mögliche Grundlage theologischer Wissenschaft: Eigentliches Subjekt der Theologie ist die Denkgemeinschaft der Kirche." Romano Guardini, *Auf dem Wege* (Mainz: Grünewald, 1923), 58.

41. Joseph Ratzinger, "Von der Liturgie zur Christologie, Romano Guardinis theologischer Grundansatz und seine Aussagekraft," in *Wege zur Wahrheit, Die bleibende Bedeutung von Romano Guardini*, ed., Eugen Biser 132 (Düsseldorf: Patmos, 1985).

42. "Einmal macht es [= das Dogma] ganz klar, daß Träger und Norm des Glaubensinhalts nicht die Schrift ist, sondern die Kirche. Und die Schrift in der Hand der Kirche. Ich habe nie anders gedacht. Die Kirche ist Prophet. Sie lehrt und verbürgt. Ihr muß man vertrauen. Alles andere ist halb und macht die Position unecht." Hanna-Barbara Gerl-Falkovitz, *Romano Guardini, 1885–1968. Leben und Werk* (Mainz: Matthias Grünewald, 1985), 57f.

43. Guardini, *The Lord*, xiv.

44. Gerl-Falkovitz, *Romano Guardini*, 93.

45. Guardini, *The Lord*, xv–xvii.

46. Ibid., xvi.

47. Ibid., xvii.

48. Guardini, *Auf dem Wege*, 165.

49. Ratzinger, "Von Liturgie zur Christologie," 141f.

50. Ibid., 142.

51. Guardini, *The Lord*, 222.

52. Ibid., 151.

53. Ibid., 433.

54. Concerning this Ratzinger writes: "We can only speak rightly about him if we renounce the attempt to comprehend and let him be the uncomprehended." Ratzinger, *Introduction to Christianity*, 171.

55. Guardini, *The Lord*, 78.

56. Aidan Nichols, *Catholic Thought Since the Enlightenment* (London: Gracewing, 1998), 84.

5   His Language and Style

1. Thomas Forstner, "Zeitzeugenberichte über die Freisinger und frühen Münchener Jahre Joseph Ratzingers (1945–1959)," in *Joseph Ratzinger und das Erzbistum München und Freising*, no. 10, ed. Peter Pfister, 132. *Dokumente und Bilder aus kirchlichen Archiven, Beiträge und Erinnerungen, Schriften des Archivs des Erzbistums München und Freising* (Regensburg: Schnell & Steiner, 2006).

2. Hans Meier, "Bayer und Weltbürger," in *Eine Theologie in der Nachfolge Petri: Papst Benedikt XVI*, special issue of *Münchener Theologische Zeitschrift* 5 (2005): 498–504, at 500.

3. Joseph Ratzinger, *Milestones: Memoirs 1927–1977* (San Francisco: Ignatius, 1998), 29.

4. Cf. Marion Stojetz, *"Aus tiefem Abend glänzt ein heller Stern," Welt- und Natursicht in der Lyrik Hans Carossas* (Berlin: Lit Verlag, 2005). E. Kamphausen-Carossa, ed., *Hans Carossa, Leben und Werk in Bildern und Texten* (Frankfurt am Main: Insel, 1993).

5. Alexander Kissler, *Der Deutsche Papst, Benedikt XVI und seine schwierige Heimat* (Freiburg i. Br.: Herder, 2005), 28.

6 Academic Teacher: Truth as Person

1. Maximilian Graf von Dürckheim and Esther von Krosigk, *Worüber der Papst lacht* (Saarbrücken: VDM, 2005), 35. From 1954 until 1959 in Freising he taught courses and seminars in the following areas: The Trinity, Creation, Augustine's *Confessions*, Salvation in Christ Jesus, Fundamental Theology I (the truth and essence of religion), Modern Christological and Mariological Literature, Grace, Fundamental Theology II (religion and revelation), Grace in Thomas Aquinas, Sacramental Theology, Ecclesiology, Eschatology, Mariology, Theological Epistemology, The Natural and Supernatural, Soteriology, and on the Augsburg Confession. Thomas Forstner, "Zeitzeugenberichte über die Freisinger und frühen Münchener Jahre Joseph Ratzingers (1945–1959)," in *Joseph Ratzinger und das Erzbistum München und Freising*, no. 10, ed. Peter Pfister, 84–127, at 90, fn19. *Dokumente und Bilder aus kirchlichen Archiven, Beiträge und Erinnerungen, Schriften des Archivs des Erzbistums Münchens und Freising* (Regensburg: Schnell & Steiner, 2006).
2. Stefan von Kempis, *Benedetto: die Biografie* (Leipzig: St. Benno, 2006), 169–72.
3. Cf. Herbert Vorgrimler, gen. ed., *Commentary on the Documents of Vatican II* (New York: Herder and Herder, 1969); by Ratzinger: vol. I, *Lumen Gentium*, Nota Praevia, 297–305; vol. III, *Dei Verbum*, 155–98 and 262–72; vol. V, *Dignitatis Humanae*, 115–63.
4. Joseph Ratzinger, *Introduction to Christianity* (San Francisco: Ignatius). Published with a new preface 2000 (German) and 2004 (English). First published in German as *Einführung in das Christentum* in 1968.
5. Joseph Ratzinger, "Der Katholizismus nach dem Konzil," *Auf Dein Wort hin*. 81. Deutscher Katholikentag [German Catholic Diet], July 13–17, 1966, in Bamberg (Paderborn, 1966), 245–64, at 263 and 259, respectively. The American biographer of Ratzinger, John Allen, *Cardinal Ratzinger: The Vatican's Enforcer of the Faith* (New York: Continuum, 2000), claims his "coming out" as conservative dates back to 1971. A closer examination of Ratzinger's theological studies reveals a remarkable consistency in his views in matters of the faith since the 1950s.
6. Peter Seewald, *Benedict XVI: An Intimate Portrait* (San Francisco: Ignatius, 2008), 86–90.
7. Gianni Valente, "The Difficult Years," *Thirty Days* 5 (2006): 42.
8. Gianni Valente, *Student, Professor, Papst. Joseph Ratzinger an der Universität* (AU: Augsburg: St. Ulrich, 2009), 106f.
9. Romano Guardini, *Unterscheidung des Christlichen* (Mainz: Grünewald, 1963).
10. Marco Bardazzi, *In the Vineyard of the Lord: The Life, Faith, and Teachings of Joseph Ratzinger, Pope Benedict XVI* (New York: Rizzoli, 2005), 43 and 45f.
11. Presently this journal is published in seventeen language editions internationally. Worldwide recognized scholars such as Rémi Brague, Walter Kasper, and Christoph Schönborn belong to its editorial board.
12. It should be noted that this group defined itself as part of a movement or current. The exponents were thus dubbed by their opponents (such as Réginald Garrigou-Lagrange, OP), John Milbank, *"The Suspended Middle," Henri de Lubac and the Debate Concerning the Supernatural* (Grand Rapids, MI: Eerdmans, 2005), 7.

7 Pastor to "Radical Christians": The Catholic Integrated Community

1. Pope Paul VI, *Decree on the Apostolate of the Laity, Apostolicam Actuositatem [AA]* (November 18, 1965). A group apostolate "offers a sign of the Communion and unity of the Church in Christ, who said: 'Where two or three are gathered together in my name, I am there in their midst' (Mt 18:20)" (*AA* 18). They "promote a more intimate unity between the faith of the members and their everyday life. Associations are not ends in themselves; they are meant to be of service to the Church's mission to the world. Their apostolic value depends on their conformity with

the Church's aims, as well as on the Christian witness and evangelical spirit of each of their members and of the association as a whole" (*AA* 19).

2. Traudl Wallbrecher, Ludwig Weimer, and Arnold Stöltzl, eds., *30 Jahre Wegbegleitung, Joseph Ratzinger, Papst Benedikt XVI und die Katholische Integrierte Gemeinde* (Bad Tölz: Urfeld, 2006), 29.

3. Michael Winter, "In der Mitte der Kirche, Warum die Integrierte Gemeinde neu ins Blickfeld gerückt ist," in *Herderkorrespondenz* 1, No.62 (2008): 38–44. For a less flattering evaluation of this movement see Peter Seewald, *Benedict XVI: An Intimate Portrait* (San Francisco: Ignatius, 2008), 196–8.

4. "Glaubenskraft der frühen Gemeinde," cf. Alexander Kissler, *Der Deutsche Papst, Benedikt XVI und seine schwierige Heimat* (Freiburg i. Br.: Herder, 2005), 85.

5. Norbert Lohfink, *Church Dreams: Talking against the Trend* (North Richland Hills, TX: Bibal, 2000). Gerhard Lohfink, *Jesus and Community: The Social Dimensions of Faith* (New York: Paulist, 1984).

6. Gerhard Szczesny, *Das Elend des Christentums oder Plädoyer für einen Humanismus ohne Gott* (Reinbek: Rohwolt, 1968). Cf. ibid., *Die Zukunft des Unglaubens, Zeitgemäße Betrachtungen eines Nichtchristen* (Munich: List, 1972).

7. Kissler, *Der Deutsche Papst*, 88.

8. Joseph Ratzinger, *The Theology of History in St. Bonaventure*, trans. Zachary Hayes (Chicago: Franciscan Herald, 1971), 157.

9. Kissler, *Der Deutsche Papst*, 132. Joseph Ratzinger/Benedikt XVI, *Gottes Projekt. Nachdenken über Schöpfung und Kirche* (Regensburg: Pustet, 2009).

10. Adolf von Harnack, *What Is Christianity? Lectures Delivered at the University of Berlin during the Winter Term 1899–1900*, trans. T. Bailey Saunders (London: SPCK, 1901).

11. Kissler, *Der Deutsche Papst*, 99.

12. Ibid., 103.

13. See http://www.ltvg.org.

14. Kissler, *Der Deutsche Papst*, 87.

15. Gerhard Lohfink, *Braucht Gott die Kirche?* 4th ed. (Freiburg i. Br.: Herder, 1999).

16. Kissler, *Der Deutsche Papst*, 100.

17. Ibid., 95.

8   The Beginnings of His Theology

1. Traudl Wallbrecher, Ludwig Weimer, and Arnold Stötzl, eds., *30 Jahre Wegbegleitung, Joseph Ratzinger, Papst Benedikt XVI und die Katholische Integrierte Gemeinde* (Bad Tölz: Urfeld, 2006), 155–7.

2. Joseph Ratzinger, *Volk und Haus Gottes in Augustins Lehre von der Kirche, Münchener Theologische Studien* II, 7 (Munich: Karl Zink, 1954; repr., St. Ottilien: EOS, 1992).

3. Hermann Reuter, *Augustinische Studien*, 2nd ed. (Gotha: Perthes, 1887).

4. Fritz Hofmann, *Der Kirchenbegriff des hl. Augustinus in seinen Grundlagen und seiner Entwicklung* (Munich: Hueber, 1933).

5. Erich Przywara, *Augustinus, die Gestalt als Gefüge* (Leipzig: Hegner, 1934); English: ibid., *An Augustine Synthesi*s (New York: Harper, 1958).

6. Joseph Ratzinger, *Milestones: Memoirs 1927–1977* (San Francisco: Ignatius, 1998), 44. Augustine *Confessions* 4, 30.

7. Augustine *Letters* 120, 13.

8. Augustine *On Christian Science* 4, 27.

9. Aiden Nichols, *The Thought of Benedict XVI: An Introduction to the Theology of Joseph Ratzinger* (New York: Burns & Oates, 2005), 43.

10. Ratzinger, *Volk*, 8.

11. "Gott: dem letzten Ziel seines Ringens begegnet, währt nur einen kurzen Augenblick. Er kann das Verständnis nicht fortwährend gegenwärtig halten.... Darin erfährt Augustin eine 'infir-mitas,' gegen die ihn die Philosophie nicht schützt. Ein anderes Mittel muß kommen, ihm zu helfen. Er greift wieder zur Schrift... Die 'Speise' Gott in ihrer reinen Gestalt kann Augustin in seiner Schwachheit nicht ertragen... Hier liegt—nach der Darstellung der Confessiones—der

Kirchenbegriff des Augustin der Bekehrungszeit: In sichtbaren Gestalten gibt uns Gott in der Kirche das Unsichtbare zu essen und führt uns so immer mehr auf das Unsichtbare hin...." Ratzinger, *Volk*, 9.

12. Ratzinger, *Volk*, 11 with fn33.

13. Ibid., 36. Augustine *De Magistro* 1, 2.

14. Ratzinger, *Volk*, 44–47.

15. Nichols, *Benedict*, 36.

16. Ratzinger, *Volk*, 65.

17. Lk 24:44–47. Ratzinger, *Volk*, 133.

18. "Wenn aber die *Communio* des Katholiken caritas ist und anderseits Kirche wesentlich *Communio* ist, so rücken catholica und caritas in eine Nähe, die es schließlich zu erlauben scheint, die catholica als die objektive caritas anzusprechen, an der man durch Teilnahme der diese caritas darstellenden *Communio* Anteil gewinnt. Caritas und ecclesia rücken hier so eng zusammen, dass man sie in einem gewissen Sinn als identisch hinstellen darf." Ratzinger, *Volk*, 138.

19. Ratzinger, *Volk*, 146.

20. Nichols, *Benedict*, 44.

21. Ratzinger, *Salt of the Earth: The Church at the End of the Millennium: An Interview with Peter Seewald* (San Francisco: Ignatius, 1997 [1996]), 41.

22. Ibid., 61.

23. Laurence Paul Hemming, *Benedict XVI: Fellow Worker for the Truth* (London: Burns & Oates, 2005), 41. Cf. Nichols, *Benedict*, 47.

24. Ratzinger, *Volk*, 56.

25. De Lubac, *Catholicism: Christ and the Common Destiny of Man* (San Francisco: Ignatius, 1988), 376, 393, 440f.

26. For an interesting discussion on de Lubac's ecclesiology cf. Hubert Schnackers, *Kirche als Sakrament und Mutter: zur Ekklesiologie von Henri de Lubac* (Frankfurt am Main: Peter Lang, 1979).

27. Paul McPartlan, *The Eucharist Makes the Church: Henri de Lubac and John Zizioulas in Dialogue* (Edinburgh: T & T Clark, 1993).

28. Joseph Ratzinger, *Die Geschichtstheologie des heiligen Bonaventura* (Munich: Schnell and Steiner, 1959; repr., St. Ottilien: EOS, 1992). English: *The Theology of History in Saint Bonaventure*, trans. Zachary Hayes (Chicago, IL: Franciscan Herald, 1971).

29. Ratzinger, *Milestones*, 106–14.

30. Thomas Forstner, "Zeitzeugenberichte über die Freisinger und frühen Münchener Jahre Joseph Ratzingers (1945–1959)," in *Joseph Ratzinger und das Erzbistum München und Freising*, no. 10, ed. Peter Pfister, *Dokumente und Bilder aus kirchlichen Archiven, Beiträge und Erinnerungen, Schriften des Archivs des Erzbistums München und Freising* (Regensburg: Schnell & Steiner, 2006), 136. Having failed to prevent Ratzinger from earning a habilitation, Schmaus (1) attempted to thwart Ratzinger from becoming professor of fundamental and dogmatic theology in Freising, then having failed this he (2) wanted to sideline him to an insignificant pedagogical college located in Munich-Pasing—just to be informed by the victim that he had been appointed professor to the University of Bonn. As numerous of Schmaus's students were placed in different institutions throughout Germany and worldwide, he nevertheless succeeded in isolating Ratzinger in the academia.

31. Bonaventure, *The Mind's Road to God* (Englewood Cliffs, NJ: Prentice Hall, 1953), 45.

32. Ratzinger, *Bonaventure*, 14.

33. Marco Bardazzi, *In the Vineyard of the Lord: The Life, Faith, and Teachings of Joseph Ratzinger, Pope Benedict XVI* (New York: Rizzoli, 2005), 29.

34. Ratzinger, *Bonaventure*, 54f.

35. Ibid., 161f. The Russian novelist Nikolai Leskov argued the same position from a different angle. Cf. ibid., *The Cathedral Folk* (Westport, CT: Greenwood, 1971).

36. Ratzinger, *Bonaventure*, 157f.

37. He made abundant use of Aimé Forest, Ferdinand van Steenberghen, and Maurice de Gandillac, *Le Mouvement Doctrinal du IXe au XIVe siècle* (Paris: Bloud & Gay, 1951) and Ferdinand van Steenberghen, *Aristotle in the West: The Origins of Latin Aristotelianism* (Louvain: Institut Supérieur de Philosophie, 1955). Cf. also Joseph Ratzinger, "'Consecrate Them in the Truth': A Homily for St. Thomas' Day," *New Blackfriars* 68, 803 (March 1987), 112–5. Cf. Nichols, *Benedict,* 62.

38. Nichols, *Benedict*, 63.
39. While Ratzinger considers this dynamic understanding of time singular to Bonaventure and diametrically opposed to the dominant idea of time as unchangeable and immutable, Colt Anderson in *A Call to Piety: Saint Bonaventure's Collations on the Six Days* (Quincy, IL: Franciscan Press, 2002) on p. XII observes that other medieval minds, such as Gregory the Great, Rupert of Deutz, and Hugh of St. Victor, also shared Bonaventure's progressive view of history.
40. Ratzinger, *Milestones*, 110f.
41. Alexander Kissler, *Der Deutsche Papst, Benedikt XVI und seine schwierige Heimat* (Freiburg i. Br.: Herder, 2005), 48.
42. Ibid., 73.
43. It seems that the Rahnerian notion of "the supernatural existential" has been tragically misunderstood in this vein. Remarkably, this term was added to the second edition of *Hearer of the Word* by his doctoral student Johann Baptist Metz.

9   The Inaugural Lecture in 1959

1. Joseph Ratzinger, *Der Gott des Glaubens und der Gott der Philosophen. Ein Beitrag zum Problem der theologia naturalis*, ed. Heino Sonnemans (Trier: Paulinus, 2006). Probably (?) trusting his mentor Söhngen, he had declined professorship at the Katholisch-Theologische Fakultät in Mainz (1956) and at the Pädagogische Hochschule in Munich-Pasing (1958).
2. Joseph Ratzinger, *Truth and Tolerance: Christian Belief and World Religions* (San Francisco: Ignatius, 2004).
3. Joseph Ratzinger, *Introduction to Christianity* (San Francisco: Ignatius, 2004), 190. Cf. Augustine *In Ioannis Evangelium tractatus* 29, 3 in *Corpus Christianorum* 36, 285.
4. John Paul II, *Fides et Ratio* (Vatican City: Libreria Editrice Vaticana, 1998), prooemium, 3.
5. Ratzinger, *Truth and Tolerance*, 127.
6. Martin Heidegger, *Identität und Differenz* (Pfullingen: Neske, 1957), 70.
7. "Joseph Ratzinger Stellungnahme," *Zur Debatte* 34, no. 1 (2004): 5–7.
8. "Im Gegensatz zur metaphysischen Gotteslehre der Zeit mit ihrem rein theoretischen Gott versuchen sie von der Wirklichkeit des konkreten Menschseins mit seinem unlösbaren Ineinander von Größe und Erbärmlichkeit unmittelbar in die Begegnung mit dem Gott zu führen, der die lebendige Antwort auf die offene Frage des Menschseins ist—und das ist kein anderer als der in Jesus Christus gnädige Gott, der Gott Abrahams, Isaaks und Jakobs." Joseph Ratzinger, *Der Gott des Glaubens und der Gott der Philosophen. Ein Beitrag zum Problem der theologia naturalis* (Munich: Schnell & Steiner, 1960), 12.
9. Friedrich Schleiermacher, *The Christian Faith* (Edinburgh: T & T Clark, 1928), 32.
10. Ibid., 13.
11. Thomas Aquinas *Summa Theologiae*, q. 2 a. 2 ad 1.
12. "Der Gott des Aristoteles und der Gott Jesu Christi ist ein und derselbe, Aristoteles hat den wahren Gott erkannt, den wir im Glauben tiefer und reiner erfassen dürfen, so wie wir in der jenseitigen Gottesschau abermals inniger und näher Gottes Wesen erfassen werden." Ratzinger, *Der Gott des Glaubens*, 16.
13. Ratzinger, *Der Gott des Glaubens*, 16ff. Ratzinger refers here especially to Emil Brunner, *Die Christliche Lehre von Gott, Dogmatik*, vol. I, 3rd ed. (Zurich: Zwingli Verlag, 1953), 121–40. Cf. also Emil Brunner, *Wahrheit als Begegnung. Sechs Vorlesungen über das christliche Wahrheitsverständnis* (Zurich: Zwingli Verlag, 1938).
14. His own dissertation director, Gottlieb Söhngen, had discussed this contentious issue in Gottlieb Söhngen, *Die Einheit der Theologie, Gesammelte Abhandlungen, Aufsätze, Vorträge* (Munich: Karl Zink, 1952), 235–64.
15. M. Terentius Varro *Antiquitates rerum humanarum et divinarum*. Only fragments have survived: F. Semi, *Terentius Varro: quae extant*, 1965–1966.
16. Cf. Tertullian *Ad Nationes* II, 1–8 and Augustine *De Civitate Dei* VI, 5ff. Ratzinger discusses this area already in Joseph Ratzinger, *Volk und Haus Gottes in Augustins Lehre von der Kirche* (Munich: Karl Zink, 1954), 265–76.
17. Ratzinger, *Volk*, 32.

18. Richard of St. Victor *De Trinitate* III, 1. Cf. *PL* 196, 916. For Augustine cf.: *Enn in Ps* 104:3, *Corpus Christianorum* 40, 1537.
19. Ratzinger, *Der Gott des Glaubens*, 35.

10 Jesus Christ, the Sovereign, Unsurpassable Revealer of Revelation

1. John F. Thornton and Susan B. Varenne, *The Essential Pope Benedict XVI: His Central Writings and Speeches* (San Francisco: Harper, 2007), 23.
2. Joseph Ratzinger, *Jesus of Nazareth: From the Baptism in the Jordan to the Transfiguration*, trans. Adrian Walker (New York: Doubleday, 2007), xxii.
3. Joseph Ratzinger, *Theological Principles* (San Francisco: Ignatius, 1987), 23.
4. Rudolf Schnackenburg, *Jesus in the Gospels: A Biblical Christology*, trans. O. C. Dean, Jr. (Louisville, KY: Westminster John Knox Press, 1995). Thomas Söding, "Die Lebendigkeit des Wortes Gottes. Das Verständnis der Offenbarung bei Joseph Ratzinger," ed. Frank Meier-Hamidi and Ferdinand Schumacher, *Der Theologe Joseph Ratzinger, Quaestiones Disputatae* 222 (Freiburg i. Br.: Herder, 2007): 12–55.
5. Joseph Ratzinger, *The Spirit of the Liturgy* (San Francisco: Ignatius, 2000), 20.
6. Joseph Ratzinger, *Salt of the Earth: The Church at the End of the Millennium: An Interview with Peter Seewald* (San Francisco: Ignatius, 1997 [1996]), 282.
7. Robert A. Krieg, ed., *Romano Guardini: A Precursor of Vatican II* (Notre Dame, IN and London: University of Notre Dame Press, 1997), 67.
8. Paul Evdokimov, *The Art of the Icon: A Theology of Beauty* (Redondo Beach, CA: Oakwood, 1990).
9. Ratzinger, *Jesus of Nazareth*, 20.
10. Romano Guardini, *Das Wesen des Christentums—Die menschliche Wirklichkeit des Herrn. Beiträge zu einer Psychologie Jesu* (Mainz-Paderborn: Matthias Grünewald, 1991).
11. Augustine *Confessions*, III, 6, 11.
12. Vladimir Soloviev, *The Antichrist*, trans. W. J. Barnes and H. H. Haynes (Edinburgh: Floris Classics, 1982).
13. Ratzinger, *Jesus of Nazareth*, 39.
14. Ibid., 44. There is perhaps too little emphasis on becoming Christoformic and participation in the divine life as the purpose of earthly human existence.
15. Ibid., 138.
16. Ibid., 131 and 137.
17. Ibid., 149.
18. Jean Daniélou, *The Bible and the Liturgy* (University of Notre Dame, IN: Notre Dame, 1956).
19. Ratzinger, *Jesus of Nazareth*, 306 and 310.
20. Ibid., 317.
21. Ibid., 321.
22. Ibid., 330.
23. Ibid., 334.
24. Ibid., 353. Cf. C. K. Barrett, *The Gospel According to St. John*, 2nd ed. (London: SPCK, 1978), 88.
25. Ratzinger, *Jesus of Nazareth*, 355.
26. Rudolf Bultmann, *The Gospel of John: A Commentary* (Oxford: Blackwell, 1971), 26. Cf. Ratzinger, *Jesus of Nazareth*, 220.
27. Martin Hengel, *The Son of God: The Origin of Christology and the History of Jewish-Hellenistic Religion* (Philadelphia, PA: Fortress, 1976), 33.
28. Ulrich Wilkens, *Theologie des Neuen Testaments*, vol. 2, pt. 4 (Neukirchen-Vluyn: Neukirchener Verlag, 2005), 155–58.
29. Peter Stuhlmacher, *Biblische Theologie des Neuen Testaments*, vol. II (Göttingen: Vandenhoeck & Rupprecht, 1999), 206f.
30. Ratzinger, *Jesus of Nazareth*, 235.
31. Ibid., 245f.

32. Ibid., 248. Cf. Barrett, *The Gospel*.
33. Ratzinger, *Jesus of Nazareth*, 254. Barrett, *The Gospel*, 188.
34. Ratzinger, *Jesus of Nazareth*, 260.
35. Ibid., 284.
36. Joseph Ratzinger, *Introduction to Christianity* (San Francisco: Ignatius, 2004), 28.
37. Cf. Plato *Phaedrus* and Augustine *De pulchro et apto*. This reaches one of its most profound expressions in the classic of Christian spirituality: Nicholas Cabasilas, *The Life in Christ*, Book II, 15. "When men have a longing so great that it surpasses human nature, and eagerly desire and are able to accomplish things beyond human thought, it is the Bridegroom who has smitten them with this longing. It is he who has sent a ray of his beauty into their eyes. The greatness of the wound already shows the arrow which has struck home, the longing indicates who has inflicted the wound." As quoted in Thornton and Varenne, *Pope Benedict XVI*, 49.
38. Thornton and Varenne, *Pope Benedict XVI*, 47f.
39. Ratzinger, *Introduction to Christianity*, 141ff. Friedrich Hölderlin, *Werke*, vol. 3 (Darmstadt: Wissenschaftliche Buchgesellschaft, 1965), 346f.
40. Joseph Ratzinger, *Behold the Pierced One: An Approach to a Spiritual Christology* (San Francisco: Ignatius, 1986 [1984]).
41. Alois Grillmeier, *Christ in Christian Tradition* (Louisville, KY: John Knox, 1975).
42. Ratzinger, *Behold the Pierced One*, 46.
43. Ibid., 90.
44. Ratzinger, *Principles of Catholic Theology: Building Stones for a Fundamental Theology* (San Francisco: Ignatius, 1987 [1982]), 32.
45. Joseph Ratzinger, *Volk und Haus Gottes in Augustins Lehre von der Kirche*, Münchener Theologische Studien II, 7 (1954; rpr., St. Ottilien: EOS, 1992), XIV.
46. Ratzinger, *Behold the Pierced One*, 18.
47. Ratzinger, *Principles*, 41.
48. Ibid., 36.
49. Ibid., 45f. Cf. Benedikt XVI, *Glaube, Vernunft. Die Regensburger Vorlesung*. Complete edition, commentary by Vollständige Ausgabe. Kommentiert von Gesine Schwan, Adel Theodor Khoury, Karl Lehmann (Freiburg i. Br.: Herder, 2006).
50. Ratzinger, *Behold the Pierced One*, 22.
51. "Alles in Worten Festzuhaltende, also auch die Schrift, ist dann Zeugnis von Offenbarung selbst ist auch im eigentlichen Sinn 'Quelle,' die Quelle, aus der die Schrift sich speist. Wird sie von diesem Lebenszusammenhang der Zuwendung Gottes in Wir der Glaubenden abgelöst, dann ist sie aus ihrem Lebensgrund herausgerissen und nur durch, Buchstabe, nur noch,'Fleisch.'" Joseph Ratzinger, *Vom Wiederauffinden der Mitte* (Freiburg i. Br.: Herder, 1997), 94.
52. Ratzinger, *Wiederauffinden*, 83f.
53. Joseph Ratzinger, *Milestones: Memoirs 1927–1977* (San Francisco: Ignatius, 1998), 120–31. Josef Frings, *Für die Menschen bestellt. Erinnerungen des Alterzbischofs von Köln* (Cologne: Bachem, 1973), 248f.
54. Frings, *Für die Menschen bestellt*, 249.
55. *Deutsche Tagespost*, July 24, 2008, 7.
56. Guido Treffler, "Der Konzilstheologe Joseph Ratzinger im Spiegel der Konzilsakten des Münchener Erzbischofs Julius Kardinal Döpfner," in *Joseph Ratzinger und das Erzbistum München und Freising*, ed. Peter Pfister, 151–83, at 159 (Regensburg: Schnell and Steiner, 2006).
57. Treffler, "Der Konzilstheologe Joseph Ratzinger," 165.
58. Ibid., 166f.
59. Joseph Ratzinger, *Die erste Sitzungsperiode des Zweiten Vatikanischen Konzils, Ein Rückblick* (Cologne: Bachem, 1963), 11–17. John XXIII stressed in his solemn opening allocution the need to investigate and interpret "the certain and consistent" Christian teaching: "L'Allucuzione Gaudet mater Ecclesia di Giovanni XXIII (11 ottobre 1962)," in *Fede, Tradizione, Profezia. Studi su Giovanni XXIII e sul Vaticano II*, ed. G. Alberigo and A. Melloni, (Brescia: Paideia, 1984), 185–283.
60. Yves Congar, *Mon Journal du Concile*, vol. I (Paris: Cerf, 2002), 490.
61. Ibid., vol. II, 355f.
62. "Prima doctrina est de duobus fontibus revelationis…Hic modus loquendi de duobus fontibus revelationis non est antiquus. Alienus erat a Sanctis Patribus, alienus a scholasticis et etiam a S. Thoma, alienus ab omnibus Conciliis Oecumenicis. Introductus videtur esse saeculo elapso,

temporibus historicismi. Nec profunda est haec locutio de duobus fontibus revelationis. Potest quidem verificari in ordine cognoscendi pro nobis hominibus; sed in ordine essendi *unus et unicas fons* [italics added by author], scilicet ipsa revelatio, verbum Dei. Et valde dolendum est, de hac re nihil, fere nihil dici in schemate." *ASCOV (Acta Synodalia Sacrosancti concilii oecumenici Vaticani Secundi)*, I/3, 35. Vatican: Libreria Vaticana Editrice, 1970–1978.

63. Henri de Lubac, *Die göttliche Offenbarung, Kommentar zum Vorwort und zum ersten Kapitel der dogmatischen Konstitution Dei Verbum des zweiten Vatikanischen Konzils* (Freiburg i. Br.: Herder, 2001), 42.

64. Treffler, "Der Konzilstheologe Joseph Ratzinger," 153.

65. Yves Congar, "Erinnerungen an eine Episode auf dem II. Vatikanischen Konzil," in *Glaube im Prozeß. Christsein nach dem II. Vatikanum. Für Karl Rahner*, ed. Elmar Klinger and Klaus Wittstadt (Freiburg i. Br.:Herder, 1984), 22–64.

66. Norbert Trippen, *Josef Kardinal Frings (1887–1978)*, vol. 2: *Sein Wirken für die Weltkirche und seine letzten Bischofsjahre* (Paderborn: Schöningh, 2005), especially 210–511. For a summary see Norbert Trippen, "Joseph Ratzinger als Mitgestalter des II. Vatikanischen Konzils," in *Communio* (German) 35 (2006), 541–44.

67. Trippen, *Frings*, 314.

68. Joseph Ratzinger, "Offenbarung—Schrift—Überlieferung, Ein Text des hl. Bonaventura und seine Bedeutung für die gegenwärtige Theologie," in *Trierer Theologische Zeitschrift* 67 (1958): 13–27, at 27. Romano Guardini had argued in the same vein: religiously inclined people did not generate Jesus' divine nature after his life ended. Rather, vice versa, the apostolic charism can never exhaust the original plenitude of the divine Logos' Incarnation.

69. Romano Guardini, *Die menschliche Wirklichkeit des Herrn. Beiträge zu einer Psychologie Jesu* (Mainz: Grünewald, 1958), 85.

70. Joseph Ratzinger, "Dogmatic Constitution on Divine Revelation," in *Commentary on the Documents of Vatican II*, vol. III, ed. Herbert Vorgrimler (New York: Herder and Herder, 1969), 155–98.

71. Ratzinger, *Milestones*, 50–53. Joseph Ratzinger, "Die Beziehung zwischen Lehramt der Kirche und Exegese im Licht des 100 jährigen Bestehen der päpstlichen Bibelkommission," in *L'Osservatore Romano*, German ed., no. 21, May 23, 2003, 9f.

72. Ratzinger, *Commentary on the Documents of Vatican II*, vol. IV, 167.

73. Ratzinger, *Theological Highlights of Vatican II* (New York: Paulist, 1966), 98f and 149.

74. Ratzinger, "Dogmatic Constitution on Divine Revelation," 170.

75. Tracey Rowland, *Ratzinger's Faith: The Theology of Pope Benedict XVI* (Oxford: Oxford University Press, 2008), 48.

76. Joseph Ratzinger, *On the Way to Jesus Christ* (San Francisco: Ignatius, 2005), 79ff.

77. Thomas Söding, "Die Seele der Theologie," *Communio* 35 (2006), 545–57, at 548.

78. Ratzinger, "Revelation Itself," in *Commentary on the Documents of Vatican II*, vol. III, 171.

79. Augustine *De Civitate Dei*, XVII, 6, 2.

80. Ratzinger, *Commentary*, vol. II, 181.

81. Ibid., 187–92.

82. Ibid., 192f.

83. Joseph Ratzinger, "Ein Versuch zur Frage des Traditionsbegriffs," ed. Joseph Ratzinger and Karl Rahner, *Offenbarung und Überlieferung, Quaestiones Disputatae* 25 (Freiburg i. Br.: Herder, 1965): 25–69. Cf. Joseph Ratzinger, *Wort Gottes. Schrift—Tradition—Amt* (Freiburg: Basel, Wien, 2005), 37–81, at 53.

84. Ratzinger, "The Transmission of Divine Revelation," in *Commentary on the Documents of Vatican II*, vol. III, 181.

85. Rowland, *Ratzinger's Faith*, 53.

86. Ratzinger, *Principles*, 100f.

87. Rowland, *Ratzinger's Faith*, 60.

88. Ratzinger, *Principles*, 87.

89. Ratzinger, *Gottes Wort*, 56–61.

90. Ibid., 83–116.

91. Söding, "Die Seele der Theologie," 554.

92. Ratzinger, *Vom Wiederauffinden der Mitte*, 158–73.

93. Ratzinger, *Gottes Wort*, 116.

94. Ratzinger, *Commentary*, vol. IV, 174.

95. Ibid., 263.

96. Ibid., 184.

97. Cf. Joseph Ratzinger, "Buchstabe und Geist des Zweiten Vatikanischen Konzils in den Konzilsreden von Kardinal Frings," *Communio* (German) 16 (1987), 251–65. Ibid., "Stimme des Vertrauens. Kardinal Josef Frings auf dem Zweiten Vaticanum," in *Ortskirche im Dienst der Weltkirche. FS für die Kölner Kardinäle Erzbischof Joseph Höffner und Alt-Erzbischof Josef Frings*, eds. Norbert Trippen and W. Mogge (Cologne: Bachem, 1976), 183–90. Cf. also Dorothee Kaes, *Theologie im Anspruch von Geschichte und Wahrheit. Zur Hermeneutik Joseph Ratzingers* (St. Ottilien: EOS 1997).

98. Ratzinger, "Offenbarung—Schrift—Überlieferung," 13–27. Now published in its entirety as: Joseph Ratzinger, *Gesammelte Schriften*, vol. 2, *Offenbarungsverständnis und Geschichtstheologie Bonaventuras* (Freiburg i. Br.: Herder, 2009).

99. Thornton and Varenne, *Pope Benedict XVI*, 49.

100. Ibid., 55.

101. Alexander Kissler, *Der Deutsche Papst, Benedikt XVI und seine schwierige Heimat* (Freiburg i. Br.: Herder, 2005), 49.

102. Aiden Nichols, *The Thought of Benedict XVI: An Introduction to the Theology of Joseph Ratzinger* (New York: Burns & Oates, 2005), 88. Cf. Joseph Ratzinger, *Das Konzil auf dem Weg. Rückblick auf die zweite Sitzungsperiode* (Cologne: Bachem, 1964), 19.

103. Nichols, *Benedict*, 78.

104. Ratzinger, *Das Konzil*, 36.

105. Ibid., 48.

106. Joseph Ratzinger and Vittorio Messori, *The Ratzinger Report: An Exclusive Interview on the State of the Church* (San Francisco: Ignatius, 1985), 104–6.

107. Nichols, *Benedict*, 93.

108. Joseph Ratzinger, *Pilgrim Fellowship of Faith: The Church as Communion* (San Francisco: Ignatius, 2005), 144–9.

109. Ratzinger, *Milestones*,108f.

110. Ratzinger, "Ein Versuch zur Frage des Traditionsbegriffs," 25–69.

111. Ibid., 32.

112. Ibid., 34–36.

113. Hermann Häring, *Theologie und Ideologie bei Joseph Ratzinger* (Düsseldorf: Patmos, 2001). See also Hermann Häring, *Im Namen des Herrn: Wohin der Papst die Kirche führt* (Gütersloh: Gütersloher Verlag, 2009). With almost no attention to Ratzinger's theology or the nature of the spiritual nature of the Church, the author assumes a political process involved. With no appreciation for the Eucharistic nature of the Church community, Häring subscribes to a hermeneutics of a radical discontinuity. Thomas Rausch is far more judicious, balanced, and erudite in his analysis of Ratzinger's theology: Thomas P. Rausch, *Pope Benedict XVI, An Introduction to His Theological Vision* (Mahwah, NJ: Paulist, 2009). Unfortunately, he surveys Ratzinger's writing through an either-Plato/Augustine-or-Aristotle/Thomas lens and uses many secondary sources.

114. Häring, *Theologie*, 83.

115. *Catechism of the Catholic Church*, no. 18 (Washington, DC: USCCB, 2006).

116. Interview with Gianni Cardinale in *30 Tage*, no. 4, 2003, 12–15, at 14.

117. Ratzinger, *Milestones*, 127.

118. Ratzinger, "Offenbarung—Schrift—Überlieferung," 26. Ratzinger had been influenced by his New Testament teacher Friedrich Wilhelm Maier at the University of Munich. Due to his bias toward the historical-critical method, Maier had to leave his teaching position in Strasbourg. Cardinal Bertram rehabilitated him. One of Ratzinger's central concerns has been to pursue a theology that is inspired by exegesis. See also Ratzinger, "Die Beziehung zwischen Lehramt der Kirche und Exegese," 9f.

119. "[D]ie den Literalsinn erforscht und so aller Gnosis entgegen die Bindung an die Sarx des Logos hütet." Joseph Ratzinger, "Versuch zur Frage des Traditionsbegriffs," 47.

120. John Henry Newman, *An Essay in Aid of a Grammar of Assent* (Notre Dame, IN: University of Notre Dame, 2001). Cf. M. M. Jaime Ferreira, *Doubt and Religious Commitment: The Role of the Will in Newman's Thought* (Oxford: Oxford University Press,1980).

121. Lothar Kuld, *Lerntheorie des Glaubens: religiöse Lehren und Lernen nach J. H. Newmans Phänomenologie des Glaubensaktes* (Sigmaringendorf: Regio-Verlag Glock und Lutz , 1989).

Roman Siebenrock, *Wahrheit, Gewissen und Geschichte* (Sigmaringendorf: Regio-Verlag Glock und Lutz, 1996).

122. Albert Schweitzer, *Die Geschichte der Leben-Jesu-Forschung* (Tübingen: Mohr, 1913). English: ibid., *The Quest for the Historical Jesus: A Critical Study of its Progress from Reimarus to Wrede* (New York: Schirmer, 1968). Cf. Henning Pleitner, *Das Ende der liberalen Hermeneutik am Beispiel Albert Schweitzers* (Tübingen: Francke, 1992).

123. Gerhard Ludwig Müller, "Exegese V. Exegese und Systematische Theologie," *Lexikon für Theologie und Kirche*, vol. III, 3rd ed. (Freiburg i. Br.: Herder, 1995), 1101–3.

124. Joseph Ratzinger, "Dogmatic Constitution on Divine Revelation," 155–98, at 168.

125. Ibid., 169.

126. Joseph Ratzinger, "Die Christologie im Spannungsfeld von altchristlicher Exegese und moderner Bibelauslegung," in *Urbild und Abbild. FS Herbert Doms*, ed. Johannes Tenzler, 359–67 (Regensburg: Pattloch, 1972).

127. "Die Antithese zur Ontologie ist kein *Produkt* der Exegese, sondern ihr modernes Apriori; das Neue Testament kennt keinen Antihellenismus, es versteht sich vielmehr als die Bewegung des Übergangs der Botschaft von den Juden zu den Hellenen, ein Gedanke, der in der Apostelgeschichte rückschauend thematisiert und reflektiert wird." Ibid., 362f.

128. The exegete "darf nicht a priori ausschließen, dass Gott in Menschenwort als er selbst in der Welt sprechen könne; er darf nicht ausschließen, dass Gott als er selbst in der Geschichte wirken und in sie eintreten könne, so unwahrscheinlich ihm dies auch erscheinen mag." Joseph Ratzinger, "Zur Frage nach Grundlagen und Weg der Exegese heute," ed. Albert Gelin and Anton Vögtle, *Schriftauslegung im Widerstreit*, Quaestiones Disputatae 117 (Freiburg i. Br.: Herder, 1989), 10.

129. Immanuel Kant, *Critique of Pure Reason*, 2nd ed. (1787), A 236/B 295–A 260/B 315. Cf. Plato *The Republic*, book 6.

130. Ratzinger, *On the Way to Jesus Christ*, 62.

11   The Question of Faith in the World

1. Joseph Ratzinger, *Theological Highlights of Vatican II* (New York: Paulist, 1966), 40.

2. Ratzinger, *Highlights*, 2.

3. Ratzinger, "The Dignity of the Human Person," in *Commentary on the Documents of Vatican II*, vol. V, ed. Herbert Vorgrimler, 118 (New York: Herder and Herder, 1969).

4. Ratzinger, "Dignity," 119.

5. Thomas Aquinas *Summa Theologiae*, q. 85.

6. Augustine *De Trinitate*, VI, 12.

7. Ratzinger, "Dignity," 136.

8. Avery Dulles, "Benedict XVI: Interpreter of Vatican II," Laurence J. McGinley Lecture (New York: Fordham University, 2005), 19.

9. Karl Barth, *Ad Limina Apostolorum* (Edinburgh: St. Andrew's Press, 1969), 20.

10. Joseph Ratzinger, *Das neue Volk Gottes. Entwürfe zur Ekklesiologie* (Düsseldorf: Patmos, 1969), 146.

12   The Unity of the Old and New Testaments

1. Joseph Ratzinger, "Biblical Interpretation in Crisis: On the Question of the Foundations and Approaches of Exegesis Today," delivered at St. Peter's Church, New York City, January 27, 1988. Cf. John F. Thornton and Susan B. Varenne, *The Essential Pope Benedict XVI: His Central Writings and Speeches* (San Francisco: Harper, 2007), 243–58, at 243.

2. Werner Heisenberg, *Das Naturbild der heutigen Physik* (Hamburg: Rowohlt, 1955), 15–23.

3. Paul Ricoeur, *Hermeneutik und Strukturalismus 1* (Munich: Kösel, 1973); *Hermeneutik und Psychoanalyse* (Munich: Kösel, 1974). Peter Stuhlmacher, *Von Verstehen des Neuen Testaments: Eine Hermeneutik* (Göttingen: Vandenhoeck & Ruprecht, 1986). Ignace de la Potterie, in the

introduction to P. Toinet, *Pour une Théologie de l'Exégèse* (Paris: Cerf, 1983). René Laurentin, *Comment Réconcilier l'Exégèse et la Foi* (Paris: O.E.I.L., 1984).

4. Rudolf Bultmann, *Urchristentum* (Zurich: Artemis, 1954), 110ff.

5. Gregory of Nyssa, *Contra Eunomium* 10, *PG* 45, 828C.

6. Gregory of Nyssa, Hom. 10 in cant., *PG* 44, 980BC. As quoted in Thornton and Varenne, *Pope Benedict XVI*, 254.

7. Thomas Aquinas *In Matthaeum* 27, no. 2321: "Officium est enim boni interpretis non considerare verba sed sensum."

8. Simone Weil, *Gravity and Grace* (London: Routledge and Kegan Paul, 1952), 64.

9. Thornton and Varenne, *Pope Benedict XVI*, 266f.

10. Wallbrecher, Traudl, Ludwig Weimer, and Arnold Stöltzl, eds. *30 Jahre Wegbegleitung, Joseph Ratzinger, Papst Benedikt XVI und die Katholische Integrierte Gemeinde* (Bad Tölz: Urfeld, 2006), 90.

11. Ibid., 93.

12. Augustine *Quaest. in Hept.* 2, 73; *PL* 34, 623.

13. "Der entscheidende Schritt war...für mich, den Zusammenhang von Altem und Neuem Testament verstehen zu lernen, auf dem die ganze Vätertheologie beruht. Diese Theologie hängt an der Auslegung der Schrift; der Kern der Väterexegese ist die von Christus im Heiligen Geist vermittelte Concordia testamentorum. Auf dem Weg zu dieser Erkenntnis hatte mich entscheidend Lubacs Werk ‚Corpus Mysticum' geholfen." Cf. Joseph Ratzinger, introduction to the reprint of his dissertation, *Volk und Haus Gottes in Augustins Lehre von der Kirche, Münchener Theologische Studien II*, 7 (1954; repr., St. Ottilien: EOS, 1992), XV.

14. Joseph Ratzinger, *Milestones: Memoirs 1927–1977* (San Francisco: Ignatius, 1998), 93.

15. Joseph Ratzinger, *Jesus of Nazareth: From the Baptism in the Jordan to the Transfiguration*, trans. Adrian Walker, 112–15 (New York: Doubleday, 2007).

16. "Man könnte Augustin kein größeres Unrecht tun als ihn zu lösen aus dem lebendigen Gang seiner Zeit, um ihn zum zweitlosen Denker zu stempeln. Bei ihm ist etwas ganz anderes Ereignis geworden: Das Begreifen der einen Wahrheit Jesu Christi mitten aus der Lebendigkeit der eben gelebten Gegenwart heraus." Ratzinger, *Volk und Haus Gottes*, 307.

17. Joseph Ratzinger, *Die Geschichtstheologie des heiligen Bonaventura*, 2nd ed. (1959; repr., St. Ottilien: EOS, 1992), 120.

18. Joseph Ratzinger, "Ein Versuch zur Frage des Traditionsbegriffs," ed. Karl Rahner and Joseph Ratzinger. *Offenbarung und Überlieferung, Quaestiones Disputatae* 25 (Freiburg i. Br.: Herder, 1965): 36f.

19. Ibid., 38.

20. Ibid., 47.

21. DH 3020.

22. R. Demenlenaere, ed., *Corpus Christianorum seu nova Patrtum collection, series Latina,* (Turnhout/ Paris: Cerf , 1985), 125–231.

23. Adolf von Harnack, *Lehrbuch der Dogmengeschichte*, vol. I, 5th ed. (Tübingen: Mohr, 1931), 340ff.

24. Cesare Baronio, *Scritti vari* :Rome: Athenaeum società romana, 1911). Joseph Tixeront, *History of Dogmas* (Westminster, MD: Christian Classics, 1984 [1910]). John Henry Newman, *An Essay on the Development of Christian Doctrine* (Notre Dame, IN: University of Notre Dame Press, 1989).

25. Aidan Nichols, *The Thought of Benedict XVI: An Introduction to the Theology of Joseph Ratzinger* (New York: Burns & Oates, 2005), 229.

26. Paul VI, *Decree on Priestly Training, Optatam Totius* (October 28, 1965), 16.

27. Joseph Ratzinger, *Storia e Dogma* (Milan: Jaca Books, 1971). As quoted in Nichols, *Benedict*, 232.

28. Joseph Ratzinger, "Dogmatic Constitution on Divine Revelation," in *Commentary on the Documents of Vatican II*, vol. III, ed. Herbert Vorgrimler, 164f (New York: Herder and Herder, 1969).

29. Ratzinger, *Jesus of Nazareth*, xviii.

30. Ibid., xx. Cf. Henri de Lubac, *The Four Senses of Scripture*, vols. 1 and 2 (Grand Rapids, MI: Eerdmans, 1998, 2000).

31. Ratzinger, *Jesus of Nazareth*, xxi.

13   The Biblical Basis of Christology

1. Joseph Ratzinger, "Guardini on Christ in Our Century," *Crisis* (June 1996): 14.

2. Joseph Ratzinger, "Assessment and Future Perspectives," in *Proceedings of the July 2001 Fontgombault Liturgical Conference*, ed. Alcuin Reid (Farnborough: St. Michael's Abbey Press, 2003), 148.

3. Joseph Ratzinger, *Milestones: Memoirs 1927–1977* (San Francisco: Ignatius, 1998), 145f. Heinrich Schlier, *Die Zeit der Kirche* (Freiburg i. Br.: Herder, 1955). Cf. Ratzinger's foreword to Heinrich Schlier, *Der Geist und die Kirche, Exegetische Aufsätze und Vorträge* (Freiburg i. Br.: Herder, 1980).

4. Franz Mußner, *Die johanneische Sehweise, Quaestiones Disputatae* 28 (Freiburg i. Br.: Herder, 1965).

5. Plato *Timaeus*, 51d; cf. *Theaetetus*, 208b–d.

6. Philo *De Opificio Mundi*, book I, i.

7. Cf. Paul VI, *Decree Concerning the Pastoral Office of Bishops in the Church, Christus Dominus* (October 28, 1965), §6, §23.

8. Cf. Martin Hengel, *Judaism and Hellenism: Studies in Their Encounter in Palestine during the Early Hellenistic Period* (Philadelphia, PA: Fortress Press, 1974).

9. Joseph Ratzinger, *On the Way to Jesus Christ* (San Francisco: Ignatius, 2005), 13–27.

10. Exception: the dying deacon Stephen uttered, not long after Jesus' ascension into heaven, "Behold, I see the heavens opened, and the Son of Man seated at the right hand of God" (Acts 7:56).

11. Joseph Ratzinger, *Jesus of Nazareth: From the Baptism in the Jordan to the Transfiguration*, trans. Adrian Walker (New York: Doubleday, 2007), 330.

12. Ibid., 328.

13. Ibid., 334.

14. Adolf Jülicher, *Die Gleichnisreden Jesu*, vols. 1 and 2 (Tübingen: Mohr, 1886, 1899).

15. Joachim Jeremias, *Die Gleichnisse Jesu* (Zurich: Zwingli Verlag, 1947).

16. Joachim Jeremias, *Neutestamentliche Theologie, Erster Teil: Die Verkündigung Jesu* (Gütersloh: Mohr, 1971).

17. Ratzinger, *On the Way to Jesus Christ*, 62.

18. Joseph Ratzinger, *Introduction to Christianity* (San Francisco: Ignatius, 2004), 232.

19. Ibid., 69.

20. Ibid., 93.

21. Anton Vögtle, *Das Evangelium und die Evangelien* (Düsseldorf: Patmos, 1971), 26–30.

22. Joseph Ratzinger, "Zur Frage nach Grundlagen und Weg der Exegese heute," ed. Albert Gelin and Anton Vögtle, *Schriftauslegung im Widerstreit, Quaestiones Disputatae* 117 (Freiburg i. Br.: Herder, 1989): 15–44, at 43f.

23. Joseph Ratzinger, "Antwort," in *Wer ist Jesus von Nazaret—für mich? 100 zeitgenössische Antworten*, ed. Heinrich Spaemann, 23–26 (Munich: Kösel, 1973).

24. Karl Rahner, *Grundkurs des Glaubens* (Freiburg i. Br.: Herder, 1976), 25. Hans Küng, *Menschwerdung Gottes. Eine Einführung in Hegels theologisches Denken als Prolegomena zu einer künftigen Christologie* (Munich and Zurich: Piper, 1970. Ibid., *Christsein* (Munich and Zurich: Piper, 1974). Cf. Alois Grillmeier, "Jesus von Nazaret—im Schatten des Gottessohnes?" in *Diskussion über Hans Küngs "Christsein,"* by Hans Urs von Balthasar (Mainz: Grünewald, 1976), 60–82. Joseph Ratzinger, "Wer verantwortet die Aussagen der Theologie?" ibid., 7–18. Congar relates Paul VI observing Küng to be "young....But he is without love. He will not be" a leading theologian. Yves Congar, *Mon Journal du Concile*, vol. II (Paris: Cerf, 2002), 336.

25. Joseph Ratzinger, "Die Stimme der Zeit–die Stimme Gottes. Michael Kardinal Faulhaber," in ibid., *Christlicher Glaube und Europa. 12 Predigten* (Munich, 1981): 128f.

26. Heinrich Schlier, "Kerygma und Sophia," in *Die Zeit der Kirche*, 206–32, at 216, fn17. Ratzinger offered one-week summer seminars from 1970 until 1977 with Schlier. Ratzinger, *Milestones*, 146.

27. Cf. Albert Gelin, "La Question des 'Relectures' Bibliques à l'Intérieur d'une Tradition Vivante," *Sacra Pagina: Miscellanea Biblica I, Bibliotheca Ephemeridum Theologicarum Lovaniensium* XII (Gembloux: Duculot, 1958): 303–5.

28. Ratzinger, "Zur Frage nach Grundlagen und Weg der Exegese heute," 15–44.

29. Romano Guardini, *Die menschliche Wirklichkeit des Herrn. Beiträge zu einer Psychologie Jesu* (Mainz: Grünewald, 1999), 85. See also Rudolf Voderholzer, "Schriftauslegung im Widerstreit, Joseph Ratzinger und die Exegese," in *Der Glaube ist einfach, Aspekte der Theologie Papst Benedikts XVI*, ed. Gerhard Ludwig Müller, 54–84 (Regensburg: Patmos, 2007).
30. Ratzinger, *Jesus of Nazareth*, 7.
31. Jacob Neusner, *A Rabbi Talks with Jesus: An Intermillennial, Interfaith Exchange* (New York: Doubleday, 1993).
32. Ratzinger, *Jesus of Nazareth*, 8.
33. Ibid., 12.

14 A Twentieth-Century Classic:
Introduction to Christianity

1. Joseph Ratzinger, *Introduction to Christianity* (San Francisco: Ignatius, 2004), 279.
2. Joseph Ratzinger, "Was bedeutet Jesus Christus für mich?" in *Wer ist Jesus von Nazaret—für mich? 100 zeitgenössische Zeugnisse*, ed. Heinrich Spaemann, 23–26, at 23 (Munich: Kösel, 1973).
3. *Catechism of the Catholic Church*, no. 151 (Washington, DC: USCCB, 2006).
4. Dante, *Paradiso*, 33:145.
5. Karl Rahner, *Hearer of the Word: Laying the Foundation for a Philosophy of Religion* (New York: Continuum, 1994).
6. Augustine *De Trinitate*, XV, 27, 48.
7. Cf. Joseph Ratzinger, foreword to: *Ludwig Weimer, Die Lust an Gott und seiner Sache—oder: Lassen sich Gnade und Freiheit, Glaube und Vernunft, Erlösung und Befreiung vereinbaren?* 2nd ed. (Freiburg i. Br.: Herder, 1982).
8. Joseph Ratzinger, *Einführung in das Christentum* (Munich: Kösel, 2000).
9. Ratzinger, *Introduction to Christianity*, 32.
10. Karl Adam, *Das Wesen des Katholizismus* (Düsseldorf: Patmos, 1928; English: *The Spirit of Catholicism*, London: Sheed and Ward, 1934). This is a collection of lectures he delivered during the winter semester of 1923–1924. Cf. Robert A. Krieg, *Karl Adam: Catholicism in German Culture* (Notre Dame, IN: University of Notre Dame Press, 1992).
11. Friedrich Heiler, *Der Katholizismus: seine Idee und Erscheinung* (Munich: Reinhardt, 1923).
12. Hans Kreidler, *Eine Theologie des Lebens. Grundzüge im theologischen Denkens Karl Adams, Tübinger Theologische Studien* 29 (Mainz: Grünewald:, 1988).
13. Ratzinger, *Introduction to Christianity*, 32.
14. Ibid., 16.
15. Walter Kasper, "Theorie und Praxis innerhalb einer theologia crucis," *Hochland* 62 (1970): 152–9.
16. "Verum quia factum seu faciendum," see Giambattista Vico, *The New Science (1725)* (Ithaca, NY: Cornell University Press, 1984). Cf. Leon Pompa, *Vico* (Cambridge: Cambridge University Press, 1975).
17. Ratzinger, *Introduction to Christianity*, 59ff.
18. Ibid., 40.
19. Ibid., 118f and 137–43.
20. Ibid., 84–100.
21. Ibid., 99. Cf. Augustine *Confessions*, VIII. 2, 3–5. Cf. Anton Ziegenaus, *Die trinitarische Ausprägung der göttlichen Seinsfülle nach Marius Victorinus* (St. Ottilien: EOS, 1972).
22. Ratzinger, *Introduction to Christianity*, 100.
23. Ibid., 17. Cf. Guardini's critique of technology, ibid., *Letters from Lake Como: Explorations in Technology and the Human Race* (Grand Rapids, MI: Eerdmans, 1994).
24. Ratzinger, *Introduction to Christianity*, 18.
25. Ibid.
26. Ibid., 47.
27. Ibid., 68.
28. Ibid., 72.
29. Ibid., 80f.

30. Ibid., 119.
31. Ibid., 134.
32. Ibid., 164.
33. Ibid., 158.
34. Ibid., 205.
35. Ibid., 226.
36. Ibid., 208.
37. Ibid., 286.
38. Ibid., 306.
39. Ibid., 322.
40. "'Non coerceri maximo, contineri tamen a minimo, divinum est.' (Not to be compassed by the greatest, but to let oneself be encompassed by the smallest—that is divine)." Ibid., 146f. Ratzinger admits that he is indebted for this profound saying to Hugo Rahner, "Die Grabschrift des Loyola," *Stimmen der Zeit* 72, vol. 139 (February 1947): 321–37, echoing late Jewish literature. There is in every human being an insatiable yearning for the divine. By discovering divine beauty, one is liberated from the constraints of the contingent order and discovers a unity between simplicity and education, a harmony between God and nature, and is thus able to do justice to the seemingly insignificant in this world, while not being arrested in worldliness.
41. Ratzinger, *Introduction to Christianity*, 88.
42. "[T]he salvation of the world does not come from man and from his own power; man must let it be bestowed upon him, and he can only receive it as a pure gift." Ibid., 277. *Metropolis* is a science fiction film by Fritz Lang produced in 1926 warning of a future where individuals are degraded into huge, depersonalized working masses, subservient to the interests of large corporations.
43. One detects here an echo of Ratzinger's early, formative lecture on de Lubac's epochal *Catholicism*.
44. Ratzinger, *Introduction to Christianity*, 187.
45. Ibid., 183.
46. Cf. song "Gone" by the artist Switchfoot in the album *The Beautiful Letdown*, particularly the line "But do we know what life is, outside of our convenient Lexus cages?"
47. Ratzinger, *Introduction to Christianity*, 189f.
48. Ibid., 136.
49. Ibid., 153.
50. Ibid., 158.
51. Ibid., 93.
52. Ibid., 98.
53. Ibid., 187.
54. Ibid., 80.
55. Ibid., 296. "Du bist's, der, was wir bauen, / Mild über uns zerbricht, / Daß wir den Himmel schauen / Darum so klag ich nicht." Ratzinger, *Einführung*, 216.
56. Ratzinger, *Introduction to Christianity*, 26.
57. Ibid., 165.
58. Ibid., 129.
59. Ibid., 134.
60. Ibid., 75f.
61. Ibid., 133.
62. Ibid., 146f.
63. Ibid., 226.
64. Ibid., 186f.
65. It would be intriguing to further develop parallels between Ratzinger's Christology and Levinas's notion of alterity.
66. Ibid., 286.
67. Ibid., 306.
68. "The judge will not advance to meet us as the entirely Other, but as one of us, who knows human existence from the inside and has suffered." Ibid., 327.
69. Ibid., 194. Dante, *Divina Commedia: Paradiso*, XXXIII, 127 in conjunction with V, 130f.
70. Adolf von Harnack, *What Is Christianity?* (New York: Harper, 1957). Rudolf Bultmann, *The Relationship of the Primitive Christian Gospel of Christ to the Historical Jesus*, typescript, 1960.

71. Joseph Ratzinger, *Jesus of Nazareth: From the Baptism in the Jordan to the Transfiguration*, trans. Adrian Walker, 19ff (New York: Doubleday, 2007). Josef Kreiml, "Gott ist unendliche Nähe," in *Der Glaube ist einfach, Aspekte der Theologie Papst Benedikts XVI*, ed. Gerhard Ludwig Müller, 85–100 (Regensburg: Pustet, 2007).

72. Ratzinger, *Introduction to Christianity*, 204. Cf. Hans Urs von Balthasar, *Explorations in Faith*, vol. III (San Francisco: Ignatius, 1993), 85–102, quoting p. 100. Karl Barth, *Kirchliche Dogmatik*, vol. III, no. 2 (Zurich: Theologischer Verlag, 1948), 66–69.

73. Ibid., 231–34 and 281.

74. Ibid., 241. See also Joseph Ratzinger, *Behold the Pierced One: An Approach to a Spiritual Christology* (San Francisco: Ignatius, 1986), where the author elaborates on this theme.

75. "Pleura" means "side," not "rib" in Greek, cf. Gen 2:21f.

76. Ratzinger, *Behold the Pierced One*, 269.

77. Ibid., 278.

78. Ibid., 327.

79. Ibid., 359.

80. Ibid., 358.

81. Ratzinger, *Introduction*, 164.

82. Ratzinger, *Behold the Pierced One*, 336.

83. Cf. Thaddaeus Soiron, *Der Sakramentale Mensch* (Freiburg i. Br.: Herder, 1949); Karl Rahner, *Kirche und Sakramente* (Freiburg i. Br.: Herder, 1960); Eduard Schillebeeckx, *Christus, Sakrament der Gottesbegegnung* (Mainz: Grünewald, 1960); Otto Semmelroth, *Die Kirche als Ursakrament*, 3rd ed. (Frankfurt am Main: Knecht, 1963).

84. Ratzinger, *Introduction to Christianity*, 345f.

85. As he phrases it: "The Church is not to be deduced from her organization; the organization is to be understood from the Church." Ibid.

86. Cf. Rudolph Sohm, *Institutionen des römischen Rechts* (Hannover: Duncker & Humblot, 1883).

87. Ratzinger, *Introduction to Christianity*, 271–80. This view gradually evolved, cf. Ratzinger, *Daughter Zion* (San Francisco: Ignatius, 1983).

15   Christ and the Pursuit of Happiness: Safeguarding the Nondisponibility of Christ

1. Peter Seewald, *Benedict XVI: An Intimate Portrait* (San Francisco: Ignatius, 2008), 177.

2. Traudl Wallbrecher, Ludwig Weimer, and Arnold Stötzl, eds., *30 Jahre Wegbegleitung, Joseph Ratzinger, Papst Benedikt XVI und die Katholische Integrierte Gemeinde* (Bad Tölz: Urfeld, 2006), 43.

3. Cf. P.W. von Martitz, *TDNT* (Theological Dictionary for the New Testament, vol. VIII, (Grand Rapids, MI: Zondervan, 2000), 334–40.

4. Joseph Ratzinger, *Jesus of Nazareth: From the Baptism in the Jordan to the Transfiguration*, trans. Adrian Walker (New York: Doubleday, 2007), 338f, at 339.

5. Ibid., 28f.

6. Ibid., 32.

7. Ibid., 34.

8. Joachim Gnilka, *Das Matthäusevangelium*, I, (Freiburg i. Br.: Herder, 1986), 88.

9. Ratzinger, *Jesus of Nazareth*, 41.

10. Ibid., 29.

11. See Immanuel Kant, *Religion within the Limits of Reason Alone*, B 302.

12. See John Hick, *An Interpretation of Religion: Human Responses to the Transcendent* (New Haven, CT: Yale University Press, 1989).

13. Cf. the paper Ratzinger delivered to the presidents of the doctrinal commissions of the bishops' conferences of Latin America in May 1996 in Guadalajara, Mexico, "Relativism: The Central Problem for Faith Today." John Thornton and Susan B. Varenne, *The Essential Pope Benedict XVI: His Central Writings and Speeches* (San Francisco: Harper, 2007), 227–40, at 234.

14. Text in Kurt D. Schmidt, ed., *Die Bekenntnisse und grundsätzlichen Äußerungen zur Kirchenfrage*, vol. 2 (Göttingen: Vandenhoeck & Ruprecht, 1935), section 42, 91–98.

15. Paul Althaus, *Völker vor und nach Christus* (Leipzig: Deichert,1937). Cf. Robert P. Ericksen, *Theologians under Hitler, Gerhard Kittel, Paul Althaus, and Emanuel Hirsch* (New Haven, CT and London: Yale University Press, 1985), 79–119.

16. Aidan Nichols, *The Thought of Benedict XVI: An Introduction to the Theology of Joseph Ratzinger* (New York: Burns & Oates, 2005), 148.

17. Joseph Ratzinger, *Die Einheit der Nationen: Eine Vision der Kirchenväter* (Salzburg-Munich: Müller, 1971; repr., 2005), 102–6, at 106.

18. Erik Peterson, *Der Monotheismus als politisches Problem, Beiträge zur Geschichte der politischen Theologie im Imperium Romanum* (Leipzig: Hegner, 1935).

19. Erik Peterson, *Frühkirche, Judentum und Gnosis, Studien und Untersuchungen* (Freiburg: Herder, 1959; repr.: Darmstadt: Wissenschaftliche Buchgesellschaft, 1982).

20. Joseph Ratzinger, *Das neue Volk Gottes. Entwürfe zur Ekklesiologie* (Düsseldorf: Patmos, 1977), 283.

21. Nichols, *Benedict*, 154. Cf. Ratzinger, *Das neue Volk Gottes*, 273.

22. Joseph Ratzinger, "Heil und Geschichte. Gesichtspunkte zur gegenwärtigen theologischen Diskussion des Problems der 'Heilsgeschichte,'" *Regensburger Universitätszeitung* 5 (1969): Heft 11, 2–7. Please note, all German citizens were forced to greet one another with "Heil Hitler" during the Third Reich. "Heil" (salvation) is the root word for "salvation history" (*Heilsgeschichte*) in German. Hitler perceived himself as the eschatological ruler, the true messiah. This explains to no small degree Ratzinger's care for a proper Christian understanding of salvation history, setting it apart from political forms of salvation.

23. Joseph Ratzinger, *Principles of Catholic Theology: Building Stones for a Fundamental Theology* (San Francisco: Ignatius, 1987 [1982]), 157.

24. In English: Karl Rahner, *Foundations of Christian Faith: An Introduction to the Idea of Christianity* (London: Darton, Longman and Todd, 1978). German edition published in 1976.

25. This is a notion Ratzinger does not emphasize, but it is important to augment the Western fixation on justification.

26. Ratzinger, *Principles*, 166.

27. Joseph Ratzinger, *Introduction to Christianity* (San Francisco: Ignatius, 2004), 25.

28. Eric Voegelin, *The New Science of Politics: An Introduction* (Chicago: University of Chicago Press, 1952), 111–27. There is nothing to suggest Ratzinger was influenced by Voegelin, though there do exist occasional references to him. Cf. Ratzinger, *Die Einheit der Nationen*, 25; as well as Joseph Ratzinger, *Der Gott Jesu Christi: Betrachtungen über den Dreieinigen Gott* (Munich: Kösel, 1976), 36.

29. A. K. Ziegler, "Pope Gelasius I and His Teaching on the Relation of Church and State," *Catholic Historical Review* 27 (1942): 412–37.

30. Ernst Bloch, *The Principle of Hope* (Cambridge, MA: MIT, 1986).

31. Ratzinger, *Principles of Catholic Theology*, 385.

32. Alexander Kissler, *Der Deutsche Papst, Benedikt XVI und seine schwierige Heimat* (Freiburg i. Br.: Herder, 2005), 160.

33. Rudolf Bultmann, *The History of the Synoptic Tradition* (New York: Harper and Row, 1963).

34. See Josef Pieper, *Begeisterung und göttlicher Wahnsinn: über den platonischen Dialog "Phaidros"* (Munich: Kösel , 1962.

35. *De Veritate*, q. 22 a. 1 ad 12.

36. "...die Unmenschlichkeit der Kunst muß die der Welt überbieten, um des Menschlichen willen."

37. "...es gibt nichts Harmloses mehr. Noch der Baum, der blüht, lügt in dem Augenblick, in welchem man sein Blühen ohne den Schatten des Entsetzens wahrnimmt. Es ist keine Schönheit und kein Trost mehr außer in dem Blick, der aufs Grauen geht, ihm standhält und im ungemilderten Bewusstsein der Negativität die Möglichkeit des Besseren standhält." Theodor Adorno, *Minima Moralia: Reflexionen aus einem beschädigten Leben* (Berlin: de Gruyter, 1951), 21.

38. Kissler, *Der Deutsche Papst*, 176ff.

39. Tiemo Rainer Peters and Claus Urban, eds., *The End of Time? The Provocation of Talking about God: Proceedings of a Meeting of Joseph Cardinal Ratzinger, Johann Baptist Metz, Jürgen Moltmann, and Eveline Goodman-Thau in Ahaus* (Mainz: , 1999). Jürgen Habermas and Joseph Ratzinger, *Dialektik der Säkularisierung. Über Vernunft und Religion* (Freiburg i. Br.: Herder, 2005).

40. Kissler, *Der Deutsche Papst*, 162.

41. Joseph Ratzinger, *Politik und Erlösung: zum Verhältnis von Glaube, Rationalität und Irrationalem in der sogenannten Theologie der Befreiung,* Rheinisch-Westfälischen Akademie der Wissenschaften, G 279 (Opladen: Bachem, 1986).

42. Ratzinger, *Introduction to Christianity,* 14.

43. Ratzinger, *Politik und Erlösung,* 7.

44. Though liberation theology is a multifarious phenomenon, the instruction discusses Gutiérrez's theories as he coined the term "liberation theology" in 1969. The term is used here simply to distill the essence from this theology.

45. Ratzinger, *Politik und Erlösung,* 14.

46. Robert Spaemann, "Philosophie als Lehre vom glücklichen Leben," in *Die Frage nach dem Glück,* ed. Günther Bien, 1–19, at 17–19 (Stuttgart: Klett-Cotta, 1978).

47. Ratzinger, *Politik und Erlösung,* 20f. Cf. Christian Schäfer, "Politik und Erlösung im Spiegel der zwei civitates," in *Eine Theologie in der Nachfolge Petri: Papst Benedikt XVI,* special issue of *Münchener Theologische Zeitschrift* 56, vol. 5 (2005): 415–34, at 421.

48. John Paul II, *Encyclical Letter, Sollicitudo Rei Socialis,* VII (December 30, 1987), 46.

49. Ratzinger, *Politik und Erlösung,* 23.

50. Ibid., 12f.

51. Ratzinger, *Introduction to Christianity,* 13. The German word "*Unterscheidung*" may also be rendered "discernment" in English.

52. Ratzinger, *Introduction to Christianity,* 13.

53. Ibid., 26.

54. Ibid., 16.

55. Ibid., 21f.

56. Cf. "Epistola ad Imperatorem Anastasium," in P. Jaffé, *Regesta Pontificium Romanorum ab Condita Ecclesia ad Annum post Christum Natum MCXCVIII,* 2nd ed., 2 vols., ed. G. Wattenbach, 83–95 (Leipzig: Hegner, 1885–1888).

57. Ratzinger, *Introduction to Christianity,* 35f.

58. Ibid., 22.

59. Robert Spaemann, *Glück und Wohlwollen. Versuch über Ethik* (Stuttgart: Klett-Cotta, 1989), 40f and 65.

60. Ratzinger, *Politik und Erlösung,* 24.

61. "Denn der Mensch ist nicht Gott und die Geschichte ist es nicht; wo man aber das eine oder das andere voraussetzt, kann solche Unwahrheit nur zur Zerstörung des Menschen, zum Zerrbild der Erlösung geraten." Ratzinger, *Politik und Erlösung,* 24.

62. Ibid., 20.

63. Peter Sloterdijk, *Regeln für den Menschenpark. Ein Antwortschreiben zum Brief über den Humanismus* (Frankfurt am Main: Suhrkamp, 1999).

64. Plato *Politeia,* 375d–378b and *Phaidon,* 89de.

65. Sloterdijk claims humanity lives in a posthumanistic age. The new "anthropotechniques" render religion as a civilizing tool irrelevant. Genetic technology and others have taken its place in the grand project called the "self-taming" of humanity. Sloterdijk, *Regeln für den Menschenpark,* 34f.

66. Ratzinger, *Politik und Erlösung,* 24.

67. Ratzinger, *Introduction to Christianity,* 15.

68. Aristotle *Categories,* 14a. Plotinus *Enneads* V.2.17ff.

69. "[O]ur Lord Jesus Christ, the same perfect in divinity and perfect in humanity, the same truly God and truly man, composed of rational soul and body; consubstantial with the Father as to his divinity and consubstantial with us as to his humanity; like unto us in all things but sin." ND 614. Cf. DH 301.

70. Cf. *Libertatis Nuntius,* nos. 8 and 10.

71. Joseph Ratzinger, *Abbruch und Aufbruch. Die Antwort des Glaubens auf die Krise der Werte,* Eichstätter Hochschulreden 61 (Munich: Kösel, 1987).

16 *Communio*: Christian Brotherhood and the Church as One Reality

1. This is the general English rendering of a passage in Joseph Ratzinger, *Dogma und Verkündigung* (Munich: Wewel, 1977), 219. This portion of the book has not been translated into English.

For his ecclesiology and views on ecumenism cf. Joseph Ratzinger, *Gesammelte Schriften,* vol. 5 *Zeichen unter den Völkern: Schriften zur Ekklesiologie und Ökumene* (Freiburg i. Br.: Herder, 2009).

2. Joseph Ratzinger, *Introduction to Christianity* (San Francisco: Ignatius, 2004), 163.

3. For the point of departure of Ratzinger's understanding, see Augustine *De Academicis* III, 20; 43 and *Epistulae* 120, 3.

4. Ratzinger, *Dogma und Verkündigung,* 218.

5. Karl Rahner, *Mysterium Salutis,* vol. 2 (Einsiedeln: Benzinger, 1967), 388. Cf. Hans Christian Schmidbaur, *Personarum Trinitatis. Die trinitarische Gotteslehre des hl. Thomas von Aquin* (St. Ottilien: EOS,1993), 537–44.

6. Walter Kasper, *Der Gott Jesu Christi* (Mainz: Grünewald, 1982), 351ff. Jürgen Moltmann, *Trinität und Reich Gottes. Zur Gotteslehre* (Munich: Kaiser, 1980), 154–66.

7. Joseph Ratzinger, *Behold the Pierced One: An Approach to a Spiritual Christology* (San Francisco: Ignatius Press, 1986 [1984]), 105.

8. Ratzinger, *Behold the Pierced One,* 71–100.

9. Ibid., 83.

10. Ibid., 93.

11. Ibid., 108.

12. Aidan Nichols, *The Thought of Benedict XVI: An Introduction to the Theology of Joseph Ratzinger* (New York: Burns & Oates, 2005), 40.

13. Romano Guardini, *The Lord* (Washington, DC: Regnery, 2002), 40. Cf. Ratzinger, *Introduction to Christianity,* 188: "It seems to me that this is the reason for what to other world religions and to the man of today is always completely incomprehensible, namely, that in Christianity everything hangs in the last resort on one individual, on the man Jesus of Nazareth."

14. John Henry Newman, *An Essay in Aid of a Grammar of Assent,* chap. 9 (Notre Dame, IN: University of Notre Dame, 2001), 270–99.

15. Benedict XVI, *Encyclical Letter, Deus Caritas Est,* Introduction (December 25, 2005), 1.

16. Nichols, *The Thought of Benedict XVI,* 66.

17. Cf. Augustine *Commentary on 1 John 10:3.*

18. Augustine *Confessions,* 7,16.

19. Joseph Ratzinger, *Christian Brotherhood* (London, Burns & Oates: ,2005).

20. Ratzinger, *Christian Brotherhood,* 8.

21. Nichols, *Benedict XVI,* 66.

22. Ratzinger, *Behold the Pierced One,* 83.

23. Ratzinger, *Christian Brotherhood,* 84f.

24. Joseph Ratzinger, *Jesus Christ: Today, Yesterday and Forever* (Washington DC, John Paul II Institute, 1990), 13.

25. Joseph Ratzinger, *Jesus of Nazareth: From the Baptism in the Jordan to the Transfiguration,* trans. Adrian Walker (New York: Doubleday, 2007), 171.

26. Ratzinger, *Jesus of Nazareth,* 173.

27. Ibid., 188.

28. Ibid., 190.

29. Ibid., 207.

30. Ibid., 217.

31. Cf. Karl Jaspers, *The Great Philosophers,* vol. 1 (New York: Harcourt, Brace and World, 1962).

32. Ratzinger, *Jesus of Nazareth,* 293.

33. Ibid., 293f.

34. Ibid., 310–16.

17   Christ and the Church

1. Joseph Ratzinger, *Das neue Volk Gottes* (Düsseldorf: Patmos, 1977) as quoted in Aidan Nichols, *The Thought of Benedict XVI: An Introduction to the Theology of Joseph Ratzinger* (New York: Burns & Oates, 2005), 107.

2. Peter Seewald, *Benedict XVI: An Intimate Portrait* (San Francisco: Ignatius, 2008), 54.

3. Joseph Ratzinger, "The Ecclesiology of Vatican II," Aversa Congress, September 15, 2001, as quoted in Tracey Rowland, *Ratzinger's Faith: The Theology of Pope Benedict XVI* (Oxford: Oxford University Press, 2008), 84.

4. Joseph Ratzinger and Karl Rahner, *The Episcopate and the Primacy* (New York: Herder and Herder, 1962), 45.

5. "Letter to the Bishops of the Catholic Church on some Aspects of the Church Understood as Communion," Document of the Congregation for the Doctrine of the Faith, May 28, 1992, art. 4.

6. Homily on the election of a new pope, April 18, 2005. In John F. Thornton and Susan B. Varenne, *The Essential Pope Benedict XVI: His Central Writings and Speeches* (San Francisco: Harper, 2007), 22–24.

7. Joseph Ratzinger, *God Is Near Us: The Eucharist, the Heart of Life* (San Francisco: Ignatius, 2003), 114f.

8. Henri de Lubac, *The Splendor of the Church* (San Francisco: Ignatius, 1999), 134.

9. Joseph Ratzinger, *Pilgrim Fellowship of Faith: The Church as Communion* (San Francisco: Ignatius, 2005), 82f.

10. Joseph Ratzinger, *Jesus of Nazareth: From the Baptism in the Jordan to the Transfiguration*, trans. Adrian Walker (New York: Doubleday, 2007), 49.

11. Ibid., 50.

12. Nichols, *Benedict*, 138.

13. Ibid., 151.

14. Ibid., 154.

15. Joseph Ratzinger and Vittorio Messori, *The Ratzinger Report: An Exclusive Interview on the State of the Church* (San Francisco: Ignatius, 1985), 53.

16. Ibid., 55. Cf. Peter Stuhlmacher, *Biblische Theologie des Neuen Testaments*, vol. I (Göttingen: Vandenhoeck & Ruprecht, 1992), 67.

17. Ratzinger, *Jesus of Nazareth*, 59.

18. Ratzinger, "Letter to the Bishops of the Catholic Church," art. 15.

19. The Italian abstract noun "*aggiornamento*" is a derivative of the word "*il giorno*," meaning "day." Therefore "*aggiornamento*" may convey the meaning "updating" or "making present, current, or relevant for today."

20. Yves Congar, *Report from Rome II* (London: G. Chapman, 1964), 82. Cf. Nichols, *Benedict*, 97f.

21. Called *nota explicativa praevia*, at four points Paul VI had added clarifying endnotes, especially in article 22 of *Lumen Gentium* regarding episcopal collegiality. His views on the papal office and on the distinction between pope and patriarch of the West would evolve gradually. Giacomo Lercaro, Cardinal of Bologna, sent his collaborator, Giuseppe Alberigo, to Ratzinger asking for his counsel and suggesting he advise Frings to intervene in the conciliar aula against the *nota praevia*. This request Ratzinger rejects as unacceptable. Giuseppe Alberigo, *Breve Storia del Concilio Vaticano II* (Bologna: Il Mulino, 2005), 108.

22. Joseph Ratzinger, *Die letzte Sitzungsperiode des Konzils* (Cologne: Bachem, 1966), 12.

23. Thornton and Varenne, *Pope Benedict XVI*, 86.

24. Ibid., 41, Cf. Nichols, *Benedict*, 100.

25. Yves Congar, *Mon Journal du Concile*, vol. 2 (Paris: Cerf, 2002), 395.

26. Joseph Ratzinger, "Der Weltdienst der Kirche. Auswirkungen von *Gaudium et Spes* im letzten Jahrzehnt," *Zehn Jahre Vaticanum II*, ed. Michael Seybold (Regensburg, 1976): 36. For a detailed discussion of the canonical status of the conciliar documents, see Josef Gehr, *Die rechtliche Qualifikation der Beschlüsse des Zweiten Vatikanischen Konzils* (St. Ottilien: EOS, 1997).

27. Ratzinger and Messori, *Ratzinger Report*, 40f.

28. Joseph Ratzinger, *Volk und Haus Gottes in Augustins Lehre von der Kirche*, *Münchener Theologische Studien II*, 2nd ed. (1954; repr., St. Ottilien: EOS, 1992), xiv: "nur im und durch den Leib Christi." In the new introduction.

29. Bonaventura "war freilich unerbittlich in der Ablehnung von Bestrebungen, die Christus und Geist, christologisch-sakramental geordnete Kirche und pneumatologisch-prophetische Kirche der neuen Armen zu teilen versuchten und dabei in Anspruch nahmen, Utopie durch ihre Lebensform selbst vergegenwärtigen zu können." Joseph Ratzinger, *Die Geschichtstheologie des Heiligen Bonaventura* (1959; repr., St. Ottilien: EOS, 1992), Introduction.

30. This book is a key to understanding much of the thought that led up to the Second Vatican Council. It was first published in French in 1938. The German edition was translated by de Lubac's student Hans Urs von Balthasar and printed in 1943.

31. Joseph Ratzinger, *Milestones: Memoirs 1927–1977* (San Francisco: Ignatius, 1998), 98.

32. Upon this background von Balthasar, de Lubac, Lehmann, and Ratzinger founded the periodical *Communio* in 1972, as a counterpiece to the magazine *Concilium*.

33. Alexander Kissler, *Der Deutsche Papst, Benedikt XVI und seine schwierige Heimat* (Freiburg i. Br.: Herder, 2005), 97.

34. Ratzinger, *Volk und Haus Gottes in Augustins Lehre von der Kirche*, 146.

35. Ibid., 210.

36. Ibid., 157f, fn78.

37. Joseph Ratzinger, *Kirche, Ökumene und Politik* (Einsiedeln: Johannes, 1987), 16. As translated in Nichols, *Benedict*, 245.

38. Jürgen Habermas, "Ein Bewusstsein von dem, was fehlt. Über Glauben und Wissen und den Defaitismus der modernen Vernunft," *Neue Zürcher Zeitung*, February 10, 2007 (accessed February 11, 2007). This admission is most remarkable. With recourse to Kant, Hegel, and Marx and as a second-generation representative of the Frankfurt school of philosophy, he had previously negated the possibility of objective insight in "Erkenntnis und Interesse" (1968, translated as *Knowledge and Human Interests* [London: Oates, 1972]). Thereafter his monumental study "Theorie des kommunikativen Handelns" (1981, translated as *Theory of Communicative Actions*, 2 vols. [Boston: Beacon Press, 1984 and 1989]) supposedly supplies the proof that the normative bases for social processes lies in language. This aims to further establish that truth is the product of a social consensus (1973).

39. Ratzinger, *Kirche*, 150f.

40. Ibid., 195ff.

41. Nicholas J. H. Dent, *Rousseau: An Introduction to His Psychological, Social, and Political Theory* (Oxford: Oxford University Press, 1988). *The Cambridge Companion to Rousseau*, ed. Patrick Riley (Cambridge: Cambridge University Press, 2001).

42. Otto Semmelroth, *Church and Sacrament* (Notre Dame, IN: Fides, 1965; original 1953).

43. Ratzinger, *Volk und Haus Gottes*, 318–22.

44. Rudolph Sohm, *Verhältnis von Staat und Kirche, aus dem Begriff von Staat und Kirche entwickelt* (Darmstadt: Wissenschaftliche Buchgesellschaft, 1965 [1873]); Ibid., *Kirchenrecht*, 2 vols. ed. E. Jacobi and O. Mayer (Munich:Duncker & Humblot, 1923 [1892]); and ibid., *Wesen und Ursprung des Katholizismus* (Darmstadt: Wissenschaftliche Buchgesellschaft, 1967 [1909]).

45. "…wobei eine Doppelforderung zu beachten ist: Die der Einheit mit dem römischen Sukzessionsträger und die der Katholizität der Gesamtkommunikationsgemeinschaft." Ratzinger, *Volk und Haus Gottes*, 319.

46. Ibid., fn20.

47. "Als Gemeinschaft vom Sakrament her ist sie konkret, aber ihre Konkretheit ist nicht bloß die des Empirischen, sondern eben die des Sakramentalen, das als Zeichen des Bundes stets mehr als bloßes Faktum, als bloßes Ding ist. Als Sakrament ist die Kirche nie ohne institutionelle Form, aber sie geht auch nie in der fassbaren juridischen Struktur auf. Um das Wesen der augustinischen Konzeption von Civitas Dei zu begreifen, muß man den Unterschied von idealistisch und pneumatologisch, von sakramental und empirisch verstehen. Nur dann nähert man sich der besonderen Art von Wirklichkeit, die hier beschrieben werden will." Ibid., xvii.

48. Joseph Ratzinger, *Das neue Volk Gottes. Entwürfe zur Ekklesiologie* (Düsseldorf: Patmos, 1977).

49. Cf. *Soliloquia* I, 2, 7 and *Tractatus in Ioannem* XXXII, 8.

50. Ratzinger, *Das neue Volk Gottes*, 46.

51. Emil Mersch, *Le Corps Mystique du Christ. Etudes de Théologie Historique* (Louvain: Museum Lessianum, 1936).

52. Joseph Ratzinger, *Die Einheit der Nationen: Eine Vision der Kirchenväter* (Salzburg-Munich: Pustet, 1971), 31. Cf. Nichols, *Benedict*, 145.

53. Ratzinger, *Das neue Volk Gottes*, 105f. John of Ragusa, *Tractatus de Ecclesia* (Zagreb: Krkve, 1983). Cf. J. Santiago Madrigal Terrazas, *La Ecclesiologia de Juan de Ragusa OP (1390/95–1443), estudio e interpretación de su Tractatus de Ecclesia* (Madrid: Universitad de Madrid, 1994).

54. Joseph Cardinal Ratzinger, *Dominus Jesus: Declaration on the Unicity and Salvific Universality of Jesus Christ and the Church* (issued by the Congregation for the Doctrine of Faith, August 6, 2000), 17.

55. Joseph Ratzinger, *Theological Highlights of Vatican II* (New York: Paulist, 1966), 71.

18 Christ and Ecumenical Dialogue

1. Joseph Cardinal Ratzinger, *Dominus Jesus: Declaration on the Unicity and Salvific Universality of Jesus Christ and the Church* (issued by the Congregation for the Doctrine of Faith, August 6, 2000).

2. Joseph Ratzinger, *Pilgrim Fellowship of Faith: The Church as Communion* (San Francisco: Ignatius, 2002), 217–41. Cf. Fergus Kerr, *Twentieth-Century Catholic Theologians: From Neo-scholasticism to Nuptial Mysticism* (London and Malden, MA: Blackwell, 2007), 183.

3. *KNA-Ökumenische Information* 19, May 8, 2007, 9.

4. Numerous measures have led to such an atmosphere: the joint declaration of Pope Paul VI and Patriarch Athenagoras I on December 7, 1965; the Vatican II decree on Ecumenism, *Unitatis Redintegratio*, numbers 14–18; and, to a lesser degree, the decree on Catholic Eastern Rite Churches, *Orientalium Ecclesiarum*.

5. Joseph Ratzinger, "Zum Fortgang der Ökumene. Brief an den Moderator dieses Heftes," *Theologische Quartalschrift* 166 (1986): 243–8.

6. Joseph Ratzinger, *Kirche, Ökumene und Politik* (Einsiedeln: Johannes, 1987), section II.

7. Heinrich Fries and Karl Rahner, *Einigung der Kirchen—reale Möglichkeit*, Quaestiones Disputatae 100 (Freiburg i. Br.: Herder, 1983). English: ibid., *Unity of the Churches: An Actual Possibility* (New York: Continuum, 1985).

8. As Nichols points out, this reminds one of the church Newman described in John Henry Newman, *The Via Media of the Anglican Church* (London: B.M Pickering, 1877), XV–XCI.

9. Ratzinger, *Kirche, Ökumene und Politik*, 41ff.

10. Aidan Nichols, *The Thought of Benedict XVI: An Introduction to the Theology of Joseph Ratzinger* (New York: Burns & Oates, 2005), 278.

11. Joseph Ratzinger, *Das Konzil auf dem Weg. Rückblick auf die zweite Sitzungsperiode* (Cologne: Bachem, 1964), 53–63.

12. Joseph Ratzinger, *Das neue Volk Gottes. Entwürfe zur Ekklesiologie* (Düsseldorf: Patmos, 1977), 102.

13. Joseph Ratzinger, *Truth and Tolerance: Christian Belief and World Religions* (San Francisco: Ignatius, 2004), 45.

14. Joseph Ratzinger, *Church, Ecumenism and Politics* (New York: Crossroad, 1988), 91.

15. John Allen, "Ratzinger Credited with Saving Lutheran Pact," *National Catholic Reporter*, September 10, 1999.

16. Joseph Ratzinger, *Principles of Catholic Theology: Building Stones for a Fundamental Theology* (San Francisco: Ignatius, 1987 [1982]), 193.

17. Ratzinger, *Principles*, 199.

18. Joseph Ratzinger, "Zum Fortgang der Ökumene. Ein Brief an die Theologische Quartalschrift–Tübingen," in *Kirche, Ökumene und Politik*, 128–34, at 130.

19. Ratzinger, *Principles*, 193f.

20. Ibid., 194.

21. Ibid., 195f.

22. Ibid., 199. For a survey of the aftereffects of this lecture see (Bishop) Damaskinos Papandreou, "Die Beziehungen zwischen der römisch-katholischen und der orthodoxen Kirche. Hoffnungsvolle Gedanken des Papstes," *Communio* (German edition) 35 (2006): 537–40.

23. "Joint Declaration of Pope Benedict XVI and Patriarch Bartholomaios," November 30, 2006, http://www.vatican.va/holy_father/benedict_xvi/speeches/2006/november/documents/hf_ben-xvi_spe_20061130_dichiarazione-comune_en.html.

24. Ratzinger, *Principles*, 197.

25. Ibid., 197.

26. Ibid., 196f. As an a posteriori confirmation of this diagnosis, cf. Robert Neelly Bellah, *Habits of the Heart: Individualism and Commitment in American Life* (Berkeley: University of California Press, 1985) and the therefrom derived notion of "Sheilaism." In this vein, in the year 2000, U.S. Methodists devised the concept of "blessed worship." As content can no longer be defined and communicated, it is substituted by notions such as the "purpose-driven church" à la Rick Warren, cf. Richard Warren, *The Purpose-Driven Church: What on Earth Am I Here For?* (Grand Rapids, MI: Zondervan, 2002).

27. Ratzinger, *Principles*, 197f.

28. Ibid., 197.

29. Ibid., 201ff.

30. Ratzinger, *Church, Ecumenism and Politics*, 223.

31. Cf. Gunther Wenz, "Die große Gottesidee 'Kirche,'" *Münchener Theologische Zeitschrift* 5 (2005): 449–71, at 459.

32. Joseph Ratzinger, *Die erste Sitzungsperiode des Zweiten Vatikanischen Konzils, Ein Rückblick* (Cologne: Bachem, 1963), 56ff.

19   An Ecclesiological Dispute at the Turn of the Millennium

1. John F. Thornton and Susan B. Varenne, *The Essential Pope Benedict XVI: His Central Writings and Speeches* (San Francisco: Harper, 2007), 105.

2. Ibid., 108f. Cf. *America* (Magazine), April 23, 2001. Ratzinger quotes Rudolf Bultmann, *Theoolgie des Neuen Testaments*, 3rd ed. (Tübingen: Mohr, 1958), 96.

3. Joseph Ratzinger, *Theological Highlights of Vatican II* (New York: Paulist, 1966), 112f.

4. Joseph Ratzinger and Vittorio Messori, *The Ratzinger Report: An Exclusive Interview on the State of the Church* (San Francisco: Ignatius, 1985), 59f.

5. Joseph Ratzinger, "The Ecclesiology of the Constitution on the Church, Vatican II," *L'Osservatore Romano*, September 19, 2001, 5.

6. Hugo Rahner, *The Church: Readings in Theology* (New York: Kenedy, 1963).

7. Henri de Lubac, *The Motherhood of the Church* (San Francisco: Ignatius, 1982), 199.

8. Thornton and Varenne, *Pope Benedict XVI*, 94. JOSEPH RATZINGER, THEOLGICAL HIGHLIGHTS OF VATICAN II (NEW YORK: PAULIST, 1966), 122F.

9. Nicholas Afanasiev, *Trapeza Gospodnia* (*The Lord's Supper*) (Paris: YMCA Press, 1952).

10. Joseph Ratzinger, *Kirche, Ökumene und Politik* (Einsiedeln: Johannes, 1987), 19.

11. *CA* VII, 2.

12. Joseph Ratzinger, *Principles of Catholic Theology: Building Stones for a Fundamental Theology* (San Francisco: Ignatius, 1987 [1982]), 292.

13. Ibid., 293.

14. As Ratzinger, ibid., 292, points out, despite his erroneous ecclesiology, the Russian theologian Nicholas Afanasiev in his essay *La Primauté de Pierre dans l'Église Orthodoxe* (Neuchâtel: Delachaux et Nestlé, 1960) contributed to a rediscovery of the church not as a juridical entity but a Eucharistic reality.

15. Ratzinger, *Principles*, 293.

16. Ibid., 254–57, at 256.

17. Afanasiev, *The Lord's Supper*.

18. Ratzinger, *Kirche, Ökumene und Politik*, 19. As translated in Aidan Nichols, *The Thought of Benedict XVI: An Introduction to the Theology of Joseph Ratzinger* (New York: Burns & Oates, 2005), 246. Cf. Jean Zizioulas, *Being as Communion: Studies in Personhood and the Church* (London: Darton, Longman and Todd, 2004).

19. Karl Josef Becker, SJ, "An Examination of '*subsistit in*': A profound theological perspective," *L'Osservatore Romano* (English) 50 (December 14, 2005): 11–14, at 12.

20. Ratzinger, *Kirche, Ökumene und Politik* 230f.

21. Ibid., 245–7.

22. "In order to grasp the true meaning of the analogical application of the term Communion to the particular Churches taken as a whole, one must bear in mind above all that the particular Churches, insofar as they are '*part of the one Church of Christ*,' (*Christus Dominus* 6) have a special relationship of '*mutual interiority*' with the whole, that is, with the universal Church, because in every particular Church '*the one, holy, catholic and apostolic Church of Christ is truly present and active*' (*Christus Dominus* 11). For this reason, '*the universal Church cannot be conceived as the sum of the particular Churches, or as a federation of particular Churches*.' It is not the result of the Communion of the Churches, but, in its essential mystery, it is a reality *ontologically and temporally* prior to every *individual* particular Church." Congregation for the Doctrine of Faith, "Letter to the Bishops of the Catholic Church on Some Aspects of the Church Understood as Communion," May 28, 1992 (accessed April 17, 2006 at http://www.vatican.va/roman_curia/congregations/cxfaith/documents/rc_con_cfaith_doc_28).

23. See also Walter Kasper, "On the Church," *America* (April 23–30, 2001): 8–14. Joseph Ratzinger, "The Local Church and the Universal Church: A Response to Walter Kasper," *America* (November 19, 2001): 7–11. For a survey of this discussion see Kilian McDonnell, OSB, "The Ratzinger/Kasper Debate: The Universal Church and Local Churches," *Theological Studies* 63 (2002): 227–50. Medard Kehl, SJ, in *Stimmen der Zeit* 128 (2003): 219–32. Much expanded: "Zum jüngsten Disput um das Verhältnis von Universalkirche und Ortskirche," in *Kirche in ökumenischer Perspektive*, FS Walter Kasper, ed. P. Walter, K. Krämer, and G. Augustin, 81–113 (Freiburg i. Br.: Herder, 2003).

24. Joseph Ratzinger, *Pilgrim Fellowship of Faith: The Church as Communion* (San Francisco: Ignatius, 2005), 133–44.

25. Joseph Ratzinger, *Church, Ecumenism, and Politics* (New York: Crossroad, 1988), 42–62.

26. Walter Kasper, preface to Harald Wagner, ed., *Johann Adam Möhler (1796–1838)—Kirchenvater der Moderne* (Paderborn: Bonifatius, 1996), 7–9, at 9.

27. " 'Universal- und Ortskirche in einem.' Walter Kasper, Zur Theologie und Praxis des bischöflichen Amtes," in *Auf neue Art Kirche sein. Wirklichkeiten—Herausforderung—Wendungen*, FS Josef Homeyer, ed. Werner Schreer and Georg Steins, 32–48, at 44 (Munich: Bernward bei Don Bosco, 1999).

28. On a more unambiguous note, "wenn die eine universale Kirche unter der Hand mit der römischen Kirche, *de facto* mit Papst und Kurie, identifiziert wird. Geschieht dies, dann kann man das Schreiben der Glaubenskongregation nicht als Hilfe zur Klärung der *Communio*-Ekklesiologie, sondern muß es als deren Verabschiedung und als Versuch einer theologischen Restauration des römischen Zentralismus verstehen. Dieser Prozess scheint in der Tat im Gange zu sein." Ibid., 44.

29. Joseph Ratzinger, "Die große Gottesidee 'Kirche' ist keine Schwärmerei," *Frankfurter Allgemeine Zeitung, Feuilleton*, no. 298, December 22, 2000.

30. "Vielleicht braucht man die Frage nach der temporalen Präzedenz der Universalkirche, die Lukas in seinem Bericht eindeutig darstellt, nicht überzubewerten. Wichtig bleibt doch, dass die Kirche in den Zwölfen vom einen Geist von Anfang an für alle Völker geboren wird und daher auch vom ersten Augenblick an darauf ausgerichtet ist, sich in allen Kulturen auszudrücken und eben so das eine Volk Gottes zu sein: Nicht eine Ortsgemeinde erweitert sich langsam, sondern der Sauerteig ist immer dem Ganzen zugeordnet und trägt daher Universalität vom ersten Augenblick an in sich." Ibid.

31. Walter Kasper, "Das Verhältnis von Universalkirche und Ortskirche. Freundschaftliche Auseinandersetzung mit der Kritik von Joseph Kardinal Ratzinger," *Stimmen der Zeit* 218 (2000): 795–804, at 797.

32. Ibid., 798.

33. Ibid. This statement illuminates a certain papalism present in the second millennium, in which all ecclesiastical authority is derived from the pope, as manifested in the papal primacy of jurisdiction and the promulgation of the *Codex Iuris Canonici* in 1916. This was the case until the Second Vatican Council attempted to bring the First Vatican Council's teaching in harmony with the old Christian concept. Ibid., 799.

34. "Es fragt sich aber, wie sie für unsere Frage nach dem ontologischen Primat der universalen Kirche konkret austrägt. Denn wer sagt, dass die Präexistenz nur von der universalen Kirche und nicht von der konkreten Kirche 'in und aus' Ortskirchen verstanden werden kann? Warum soll die eine Kirche nicht als Kirche 'in und aus' Ortskirchen existieren? Die These von der Präexistenz der Kirche beweist deshalb nichts für die These vom Primat der universalen Kirche. Die Präexistenz der Kirche kann genauso gut die von mir und von vielen anderen vertretene These von der Simultaneität universaler und partikularer Kirchen begründen." Ibid., 801f.

35. Joseph Cardinal Ratzinger, "The Local Churches and the Universal Church," *America* 185 (2001): 7–11, at 10.

36. Walter Cardinal Kasper, *America* 185 (2001): 28f.

20   Jesus Christ as the Unifying Ecclesial Reality

1. John F. Thornton and Susan B. Varenne, *The Essential Pope Benedict XVI: His Central Writings and Speeches* (San Francisco: Harper, 2007), 57. Cf. Epiphanius, *PG* 43, 440–64.

2. Joseph Ratzinger, *Jesus of Nazareth: From the Baptism in the Jordan to the Transfiguration*, trans. Adrian Walker (New York: Doubleday, 2007), 47.

3. Ibid., 50.

4. Ibid., 55. Cf. Peter Stuhlmacher, *Biblische Theologie des Neuen Testaments*, vol. I (Göttingen: Vandenhoeck & Ruprecht, 1992), 67.

5. Ratzinger, *Jesus of Nazareth*, 59.

6. Ibid., 189. Cf. Joachim Jeremias, *The Parables of Jesus* (Philadelphia PA: John Knox, 1989), 17.

7. Ratzinger, *Jesus of Nazareth*, 141.

8. Joseph Ratzinger, *Introduction to Christianity* (San Francisco: Ignatius, 2004), 342.

9. Cf. Hans Urs von Balthasar, "Casta Meretrix," in *Explorations in Theology*, vol. 2, *Spouse of the Word* (San Francisco: Ignatius, 1991).

10. Ratzinger, *Introduction to Christianity*, 340.

11. Ibid., 345f.

12. One can only speculate to what degree the Jesuit theologian Otto Semmelroth's (1912–1979) groundbreaking research into the intimate connection between church and sacrament had informed Ratzinger. Cf. Otto Semmelroth, *Church and Sacrament* (Notre Dame, IN: Fides, 1965); and ibid., *The Church and Christian Belief* (Glen Rock, NJ: Paulist, 1966).

13. Joseph Ratzinger, "Le Pluralisme: Problème Posé à l'Eglise et à la Théologie," *Studia Moralia* 24 (1986): 299–318, at 317f. As translated by Nichols, *Benedict*, 289f.

14. Joseph Ratzinger, *Christian Brotherhood* (London: Burns & Oates, 2005).

15. Ibid., 8.

16. Ibid., 16.

17. Ibid., 44.

18. Cyprian of Carthage, *De Dominica Oratione*, ed. with French trans. by M. Réveillard, *Études d'Histoire et de Philosophie Religieuses*, vol. 58 (Paris: Cerf, 1964).

19. Cf. Frank J. Tobin, *Meister Eckhart: Thought and Language* (Philadelphia: University of Pennsylvania, 1986).

20. Ibid., 48f.

21. Karl Barth, *Church Dogmatics*, vol. II (Edinburgh: T & T Clark, 1977).

22. Ratzinger, *Christian Brotherhood*, 84f.

21   Christ and Freedom: Evangelization

1. Joseph Ratzinger, *The Nature and Mission of Theology: Approaches to Understanding Its Role in the Light of Present Controversy* (San Francisco: Ignatius, 1995), 123f.

2. Ibid., 9f.

3. Ibid., 123f.

4. Convinced of the futility of individual reason, Lamennais advocated *"raison générale"* or *"sens commun."* Apart from the Holy Spirit, tradition is for him the collective wisdom of humankind accumulated over time. The common consent of all generates infallibility. Félicité de Lamennais, *Essai sur l'Indifférence en Matière de Religion*, 4 vols., 1817–1823, (Paris : Turnachon-Molin et Seguin). Cf. its rejection esp. during Vatican I, DH 2751–56 and 2811–14.

5. "Die Kirche verurteilt hier das autoritäre System, das man ihr geben wollte." Andreas Wollbold, "Benedikt XVI. und die Katechese," *Münchener Theologische Zeitschrift* 56 (2005): 485–97, at 486.

6. Joseph Ratzinger, *Dogma und Verkündigung* (Munich: Wewel, 1977), 52.

7. Joseph Ratzinger, *Milestones: Memoirs 1927–1977* (San Francisco: Ignatius, 1998), 56f.

8. "...die Explikation des in der Schrift bezeugten Christusgeschehens in der Geschichte des Glaubens in der Kirche." Quoted from: Joseph Ratzinger, "Das Problem der Dogmengeschichte in der Sicht der katholischen Theologie," in *Arbeitsgemeinschaft für Forschung des Landes Nordrhein-Westfalen*, Geisteswissenschaften 139 (Cologne-Opladen: Bachem, 1966), 21.

9. Joseph Ratzinger, *Behold the Pierced One: An Approach to a Spiritual Christology* (San Francisco: Ignatius Press, 1986 [1984]), 34–37.

10. Joseph Ratzinger, *Der Gott Jesu Christi. Betrachtungen über den dreieinigen Gott* (Munich: Kösel, 1976), 33–55.

11. Joseph Ratzinger, "Der Heilige Geist als communion. Zum Verhältnis von Pneumatologie und Spiritualität bei Augustinus," in *Erfahrung des Heiligen Geistes*, ed. Claus Heitmann and Heribert Mühlen, 223–38, at 226 (Hamburg and Munich: Kösel, 1974).

12. Augustine *Epist.* *187*, c. 11, n. 33.

13. Petrus Canisius *Catechismus* (Latinus et Germanicus, Rome: Pontificia Universitas Gregoriana, 1933 [1554])—over 130 editions have since been issued.

14. Jacques-Bénigne Bossuet, *Exposition de la Doctrine de l'Église Catholique sur les Matières de Controverse* (Paris: Mabre-Cramoisy, 1671).

15. *Catechism of the Catholic Church* (Washington, DC: USCCB, 2006).

16. Andrea Bellandi, *Fede cristiana come "stare e comprendere." La giustificazione dei fondamenti della fede in Joseph Ratzinger* (Rome: Gregoriana, 1996). This is probably the most exhaustive study on Ratzinger's understanding of faith as an aspect of fundamental theology.

17. Ratzinger, *Dogma und Verkündigung*, 7. English: Ratzinger, *Dogma and Preaching* (Chicago: Franciscan Herald, n.d.).

18. Wollbold, "Benedikt XVI," 485–97, at 488.

19. Joseph Ratzinger, *Introduction to Christianity* (San Francisco: Ignatius, 2004), 41.

20. Joseph Ratzinger, "Transmission de la Foi et Sources de la Foi," *La Documentation Catholique*, no. 1847 (March 6, 1983): 260–67.

21. Gérard Cholvy and Yves-Marie Hilaire, eds., *Le Fait Religieux Aujourd'hui en France. Les Trente Dernières Années (1974–2004)* (Paris: Cerf, 2005), 52.

22. Cf. the critical article of G. Baum, "Vom Dörren und Keimen—was sich in der Katecheselandschaft zeigt," *Herder Korrespondenz* 52 (1998): 34–39, at 36.

23. In 2004, only 10 percent of children between ages 10 and 11 were able to correctly answer the question, "What is Pentecost?" In the same survey, 50 percent believed King Arthur, Ulysses, and Hercules were biblical figures. Cholvy and Hilaire, *Le Fait Religieux*, 52f.

24. Ferdinand Ebner, *Das Wort ist der Weg* (Vienna: Herder, 1949), 125.

25. Joseph Ratzinger and Christoph von Schönborn, *Introduction to the Catechism of the Catholic Church* (San Francisco: Ignatius, 1994).

26. Ludwig Ott, *Fundamentals of Catholic Dogma* (Rockford, IL: Tan, 1974).

27. "Striving to be the '*Servus servorum Dei*,'" in *L'Osservatore Romano*, no. 16 (April 22, 2005): 3–4.

28. Romano Guardini, *Religiöse Gestalten in Dostojewkis Werk, Studien über den Glauben* (Mainz/Paderborn: Matthias Grünewald/Schöningh, 1989 [1933]), 129–45.

29. Joseph Ratzinger, *Principles of Catholic Theology: Building Stones for a Fundamental Theology* (San Francisco: Ignatius, 1987 [1982]), 337.

30. Ibid., 338.

31. Joseph Ratzinger, "Evangelisierung, Katechese und Katechismus," *Theologie und Glaube* 84 (1994): 273–88, at 275f.

32. "Glauben ist Eintreten in das Anwesen Christi, in die anwesende Christuswirklichkeit, von der die Schrift zeugt, die aber die Schrift selbst nicht schon schlechterdings ist." Joseph Ratzinger, "Ein Versuch zur Frage des Traditionsbegriffs," in *Offenbarung und Überlieferung*, Quaestiones Disputatae 25, ed. Karl Rahner and Joseph Ratzinger (Freiburg i. Br.: Herder, 1965): 40.

33. Johann Adam Möhler, *Die Einheit in der Kirche*, ed. with commentary by Josef R. Geiselmann (Cologne and Olten: Bachem, 1957). In English: Johann Adam Möhler, "Unity in the Church or the Principle of Catholicism," in *The Spirit of the Church Fathers of the First Three Centuries* (Washington, DC: CUA, 1996). Cf. also Pierre Chaillet, SJ, ed., *L'Église est une: Hommage à Möhler* (Paris: Bloud & Gay, 1939). Serge Bolshakoff, *The Doctrine of the Unity of the Church in the Works of Khomyakov and Moehler* (London: Society for Promoting Christian Knowledge, 1946), 217–62. Harald Wagner, *Die eine Kirche und die vielen Kirchen: Ekklesiologie und Symbolik beim jungen Möhler, Beiträge zur ökumenischen Theologie*, vol. 16 (Munich: Schöningh, 1977).

34. "Denn die Möglichkeit, sich auf positive und fruchtbare Weise von kulturellen Zwängen, von 'Paradigmen' eines Zeitalters zu lösen und mit der Lösung von kulturellen Gestalten des Glaubens neue kulturelle Begegnung zu öffnen, hängt an dieser zentralen Erfahrung: Ich muß Gott in Christus so lebendig begegnet sein, dass ich meine eigene kulturelle Herkunft, alles was mir in meiner eigenen Geschichte wichtig war, 'wie Staub ansehen' kann (Phil 3,7)." Joseph Ratzinger, "Der Heilige Geist als communion," 280.

35. "...meditativen Umgang mit dem Wort der Liturgie...der—wie ich meine—der Schlüssel für den rechten Zugang zum Hören und Verkündigen des Wortes überhaupt ist, weil nur so über alle Information hinaus (die natürlich sehr wichtig) das Wort der Offenbarung zu unserer Form, zur gestaltgebenden Kraft unseres Lebens werden kann, die wieder Leben zu erzeugen

vermag." Joseph Ratzinger, *Brief an die Priester, Diakone und Mitarbeiter in der Seelsorge* (Munich: Erzdiözese München und Freising, 1982), 5.

36. Joseph Ratzinger, "Evangelisierung," 282.
37. Ibid., 279–82.
38. Ratzinger, *Principles of Catholic Theology*, 338.
39. Joseph Ratzinger and Vittorio Messori, *The Ratzinger Report: An Exclusive Interview on the State of the Church* (San Francisco: Ignatius, 1985), 73.
40. Ratzinger, *Principles of Catholic Theology*, 374.
41. Joseph Ratzinger, "Interview mit dem Präfekten der Glaubenskongregation zu einigen Fragen des Katechismus der Katholischen Kirche," *Münchener Theologische Zeitschrift* 45 (1994): 445–49, at 446.
42. Joseph Ratzinger, *Die Krise der Katechese und ihre Überwindung* (Einsiedeln: Johannes, 1983), 27.
43. Ibid., 23.
44. Ibid., 234.
45. Joseph Ratzinger, *The Nature and Mission of Theology: Approaches to Understanding Its Role in the Light of Present Controversy* (San Francisco: Ignatius, 1995), 104f.
46. Ratzinger, *Principles of Catholic Theology*, 334–38.
47. Ratzinger, *Die Krise*, 15.
48. "Homily of Cardinal Joseph Ratzinger," *L'Osservatore Romano*, no. 15 (April 13, 2005): 2f.
49. "Sie ist Sammlung der Menschen zum Volk Gottes hin, und diese schließt Reinigung, Bereitung für Gottes Willen ein." Erster Hirtenbrief von Erzbischof Joseph Ratzinger an die Gemeinden des Erzbistums, June 7, 1977, in *Amtsblatt für das Erzbistum München und Freising*, no. 8 (June 14, 1977): 258–63, at 261.
50. "Die Unverzichtbarkeit dieses Zusammenhangs ist auch von der Struktur der Meßfeier, her, also in der gottesdienstlichen Gestalt des eucharistischen Sakraments selbst völlig unübersehbar. Vor dem eigentlichen Wort- und Sakramentsgottesdienst steht der Bußakt, der sozusagen die Tür ins Heiligtum der Liturgie hinein ist: Nur durch die Umkehr hindurch, nur durch den Akt der des Heraustretens aus der Gewöhnung des Alltags führt der Weg in die Nähe des Herrn; nur so geschieht jenes 'Unterscheiden des Herrnleibes,' das Paulus den Korinthern mit Nachdruck auf die Seele bindet (1 Kor 11,28)," in "Der Erzbischof von München und Freising. An alle, die im Religionsunterricht in der Grundschule tätig sind," August 24, 1977, typed document in the Cathedral Library of Freising, archived as "Joseph Ratzinger, Briefe, Nr. 1."

22 Christian Brotherhood: Entering into Jesus Christ's Earthly Ineffability

1. John F. Thornton and Susan B. Varenne, *The Essential Pope Benedict XVI: His Central Writings and Speeches* (San Francisco: Harper, 2007), 133.
2. Ibid., 135.
3. Cyprian of Carthage, *De dom. Or.* 8, CSEL, III, 1 (Hartel), 271f.
4. Thornton and Varenne, *Pope Benedict*, 137.
5. Joseph Ratzinger, *Jesus of Nazareth: From the Baptism in the Jordan to the Transfiguration*, trans. Adrian Walker (New York: Doubleday, 2007), 69.
6. Jacob Neusner, *A Rabbi Talks with Jesus* (Montreal: McGill-Queen's University Press, 2000), 87f.
7. Ratzinger, *Jesus of Nazareth*, 115. Cf. Neusner, *A Rabbi Talks*, 68.
8. Ratzinger, *Jesus of Nazareth*, 116.
9. Ibid., 74.
10. Ibid., 80f.
11. Ibid., 95.
12. Traudl Wallbrecher, Ludwig Weimer, and Arnold Stötzl, eds., *30 Jahre Wegbegleitung, Papst Benedikt XVI und die Katholische Integrierte Gemeinde* (Bad Tölz: Urfeld, 2006), 84f.
13. Erik Peterson, *Der Brief an die Römer* (Würzburg: Echter, 1997).
14. Joseph Ratzinger, *Dogma und Verkündigung* (Munich: Wewel, 1977), 7.

Notes

15. Joseph Ratzinger, *Der Gott Jesu Christi, Betrachtungen über den Dreieinigen Gott* (Munich: Kösel, 1976), 21 as translated by Aidan Nichols, *The Thought of Benedict XVI: An Introduction to the Theology of Joseph Ratzinger* (New York: Burns & Oates, 2005), 190.
16. Joseph Ratzinger, *Glaube und Zukunft* (Munich: Kösel, 1970), 86.

23 The Transparency of Christ and Christians: The Liturgy

1. Joseph Ratzinger, *Principles of Catholic Theology: Building Stones for a Fundamental Theology* (San Francisco: Ignatius, 1987 [1982]), 53.
2. Joseph Ratzinger, *Milestones: Memoirs 1927–1977* (San Francisco: Ignatius, 1998), 19f.
3. Joseph Ratzinger, *The Feast of Faith: Approaches to a Theology of the Liturgy* (San Francisco: Ignatius, 1986), 37.
4. Ratzinger, *Milestones*, 132. Joseph Ratzinger, *Das neue Volk Gottes. Entwürfe zur Ekklesiologie* (Düsseldorf: Patmos, 1977), 267ff.
5. Translated as: Hans Urs von Balthasar, *Love Alone* (New York: Herder and Herder, 1963).
6. Joseph Ratzinger, *Introduction to Christianity* (San Francisco: Ignatius, 2004), 63–66.
7. Joseph Ratzinger, *The Sabbath of History* (Washington, DC: William G. Longdon, 2000), 10f.
8. Joseph Ratzinger, *Theologie der Liturgie. Die sakramentale Begründung christlicher Existenz* [Theology of Liturgy. The Sacramental Root of Christian Existence], in *Joseph Ratzinger: Gesammelte Schriften*, vol. 11, ed. Gerhard Ludwig Müller along with the Institut Papst Benedikt XVI, Regensburg: Rudolf Voderholzer, Christian Schaller, Gabriel Weiten (Freiburg i. Br.: Herder, 2008).
9. http://chiesa.espresso.repubblica.it/articolo/208933?eng=y (accessed March 17, 2009).
10. Georg Schwaiger, ed., *Christenleben im Wandel der Zeit* (Munich: Wewel, 1987), 488–98.
11. John F. Thornton and Susan B. Varenne, *The Essential Pope Benedict XVI: His Central Writings and Speeches* (San Francisco: Harper, 2007), 171f.
12. Augustine *De Civitate Dei*, X, 5.
13. Ibid., 6.
14. Ibid.
15. Thornton and Varenne, *Pope Benedict XVI*, 141–54, at 154.
16. Ibid., 173f.
17. Benedict XVI, *Encyclical Letter, Deus Caritas Est, to the Bishops, Priests, and Deacons, Men and Women Religious, and All the Lay Faithful on Christian Love* (December 25, 2005), 13.
18. Ratzinger, *Das neue Volk Gottes.*
19. Referring to, among others, the Corpus Christi antiphon, "*O Sacrum Convivium*," Eamon Duffy in "Benedict XVI and the Eucharist," *New Blackfriars* 88, no. 1014 (2007): 195–212 suggests Ratzinger understates the meal-character of the Eucharist.
20. Ratzinger, *Feast of Faith*, 38f.
21. Ratzinger, *Spirit of the Liturgy*, 78.
22. Ratzinger, *Principles of Catholic Theology*, 288f.
23. Joseph Ratzinger, *On the Way to Jesus Christ* (San Francisco: Ignatius, 2005), 7f.
24. Ibid., 9.
25. Ibid., 61.
26. Ibid., 63–65.
27. Ibid., 62.
28. Ibid., 8.
29. Ibid., 68.
30. Ibid., 69f.
31. Ibid., 72f.
32. Ibid., 75.
33. Ibid., 77.
34. Ibid., 126.
35. Ibid., 127.
36. Ibid., 128.
37. Ibid., 32.

38. Ibid., 36.
39. Ibid., 38–40.
40. Henri de Lubac, *Catholicism: Christ and the Common Destiny of Man* (San Francisco: Ignatius, 1988), 25.
41. Ibid., 71.
42. Ibid., 65–71.
43. Ibid., 101.
44. Henri de Lubac, *Corpus Mysticum: The Eucharist and the Church in the Middle Ages* (London: SCM-Canterbury, 2006), 26.
45. Henri de Lubac, *The Splendor of the Church* (San Francisco: Ignatius, 1986), 134. Italics added.
46. Ibid., 154.
47. Paul McPartlan, *The Eucharist Makes the Church: Henri de Lubac and John Zizioulas in Dialogue* (Edinburgh: T & T Clark, 1993), 20f.
48. Ratzinger in de Lubac, *Catholicism*, foreword, 12.
49. Joseph Ratzinger, *Pilgrim Fellowship: The Church as Communion* (San Francisco: Ignatius, 2005), 133.
50. Ratzinger, *Spirit of the Liturgy*, 7f.
51. Ibid., 23.
52. Hugo Rahner, *Man at Play* (New York: Herder and Herder, 1965 [originally published in 1948]).
53. Hanna-Barbara Gerl-Falkovitz, *Romano Guardini, 1885–1968. Leben und Werk* (Mainz: Matthias Grünewald, 1985), 194.
54. Romano Guardini, *Letters from Lake Como: Explorations in Technology and the Human Race* (Grand Rapids, MI: Eerdmans, 1994).
55. Benedict XVI, *Deus Caritas Est*, 14.
56. Ratzinger, *Feast of Faith*, 127f.
57. Joseph Ratzinger, *Theological Highlights of Vatican II* (New York: Paulist, 1966), 87.
58. Ratzinger, *Die Erste Sitzungsperiode des Zweiten Vatikanischen Konzils, Ein Rückblick* (Cologne: Bachem, 1963), 25ff.
59. Ratzinger, *Ergebnisse und Probleme der dritten Konzilsperiode* (Cologne: Bachem, 1965). Cf. Aidan Nichols, *The Thought of Benedict XVI: An Introduction to the Theology of Joseph Ratzinger* (New York: Burns & Oates, 2005), 96f.
60. Joseph Ratzinger and Vittorio Messori, *The Ratzinger Report: An Exclusive Interview on the State of the Church* (San Francisco: Ignatius, 1985), 126–9.
61. Joseph Ratzinger, "40 Jahre Konstitution über die heilige Liturgie. Rückblick und Vorblick," *Liturgisches Jahrbuch* 53 (2003): 209–21.
62. Ibid., 212.
63. Ratzinger, *Spirit of the Liturgy*, 24–34.
64. Ibid., 35ff.
65. Ibid., 29. Cf. Pierre Teilhard de Chardin, *Hymn of the Universe* (New York: Harper and Row, 1965). See also in this regard J. A. Lyons, *The Cosmic Christ in Origen and Teilhard de Chardin*, Oxford Theological Monographs (Oxford: Oxford University Press, 1982).
66. Romano Guardini, *The Spirit of the Liturgy: Readings in Liturgical Renewal* (New York: Crossroad, 1998). Arno Schilson, *Perspektiven theologischer Erneuerung* (Düsseldorf: Patmos, 1986).
67. "Whole" or "totality" are recurring motifs for Ratzinger.
68. Guardini, *Liturgy*, 141.
69. Ibid., 85–95.
70. The formula "primacy of the Logos over ethos" is a key to comprehending Ratzinger's critique of liberation theology.
71. Arno Schilson, "'Vom Geist der Liturgie' Versuch einer Relecture von Romano Guardinis Jahrhundertsschrift," *Liturgisches Jahrbuch* 51 (2001): 76–89.
72. Ratzinger, *Spirit of the Liturgy*, 7.
73. John L. Allen, *Cardinal Ratzinger: The Vatican's Enforcer of the Faith* (New York: Continuum, 2000), 73–75.
74. Ratzinger, *Feast of Faith*, 71.
75. Ratzinger, *Milestones*, 146ff.
76. Benedict XVI, "Apostolic Letter *Summum Pontificium*," *Origins* 37, no. 9 (July 7, 2007): 129–34.
77. Joseph Ratzinger, *God Is Near Us: The Eucharist, the Heart of Life* (San Francisco: Ignatius, 2003), 51.

78. Ratzinger, *Spirit of the Liturgy*, 31f. Gnosticism expresses this "liberation from finitude" in an exemplary manner. Every age is in danger of falling victim to it.
79. Ibid., 33.
80. Ibid., 34–50.
81. Ratzinger, *40 Jahre Konstitution*, 213f and 217.
82. Ratzinger, *Spirit of the Liturgy*, 47f.
83. Ibid., 49.
84. Ibid., 49 translates "reasonable service for God" for the original "*logosgemäße Gottesdienst*" in Joseph Ratzinger, *Der Geist der Liturgie* (Freiburg i. Br.: Herder, 2000), 41.
85. Ratzinger, *Spirit of the Liturgy*, 54.
86. Ibid., 62f.
87. Ratzinger, *God Is Near Us*, 29. Except in the Anaphora of Addai and Mari (part of the liturgy in the Syriac Church), where the words of institution are missing, but the Congregation for the Doctrine of Faith under Ratzinger assumed its intended presence.
88. The cardinal addressed the much contested issue of "*pro multis*" in ibid., 31–38. The issue has since been settled in the apostolic exhortation *Sacramentis Caritatis*.
89. Ibid., 39.
90. Hugo Rahner, *Symbole der Kirche: Ekklesiologie der Väter* (Salzburg: Müller, 1964).
91. Ratzinger, *God Is Near Us*, 43.
92. Ibid., 47.
93. Ibid., 78f.
94. Ratzinger, *Spirit of the Liturgy*, 43f. Ibid., *God Is Near Us*, 81.
95. Alcuin Reid, *The Organic Development of the Liturgy* (San Francisco: Ignatius, 2005).
96. Aidan Nichols, *A Pope and a Council on the Sacred Liturgy: Pope Pius XII's Mediator Dei and the Second Vatican Council's Sacrosanctum Concilium with a Comparative Study. "A Tale of Two Documents"* (Farnborough, England: St. Michael Abbey's Press, 2002).
97. Reid, *Organic Development of the Liturgy*, 11.
98. Ibid., 10.
99. Joseph Ratzinger, *A New Song for the Lord* (New York: Crossroad, 1996), 32.
100. Ratzinger, *Spirit of the Liturgy*, 185.
101. Benedict XVI, *Post-Synodal Apostolic Exhortation, Sacramentum Caritatis, to the Bishops, Clergy, Consecrated Persons, and the Lay Faithful on the Eucharist as the Source and Summit of the Church's Life and Mission* (February 22, 2007), 49.
102. Ratzinger, *Feast of Faith*, 18–25.
103. Ratzinger, *Report*, 130.
104. Joseph Ratzinger, Mitarbeiter der Wahrheit, Gedanken für jeden Tag, (Munich: Pfeiffer, 1979), 129f.
105. Ratzinger, *Feast of Faith*, 66f.
106. Ratzinger, *On the Way to Jesus Christ*, 111.
107. Ratzinger, *God Is Near Us*, 51.
108. Ibid., 50.
109. Ibid., 52f. (italics added).
110. Ratzinger, *Pilgrim Fellowship of Faith*, 93f.
111. Ratzinger, *Spirit of the Liturgy*, 87.
112. Ibid., 89.
113. Ratzinger, *Pilgrim Fellowship of Faith*, 94–120.
114. Ratzinger, *God Is Near Us*, 82f.
115. Ibid., 74–93.
116. Ratzinger, *Principles*, 33.
117. Ratzinger, *Feast of Faith*, 44f.
118. Here he is inspired by Jacques Monod, *Chance and Necessity: An Essay on the Natural Philosophy of Modern Biology* (London: Collins, 1972).
119. Ratzinger, *Feast of Faith*, 25.
120. Ibid.
121. Ibid., 30.
122. Cf. Joseph Ratzinger, "Von der Liturgie zur Christologie, Romano Guardinis theologischer Grundansatz und seine Aussagekraft," in *Wege zur Wahrheit. Die bleibende Bedeutung von Romano Guardini*, ed. Eugen Biser (Düsseldorf: Patmos, 1985).

123. William of St. Thierry *Epistola aurea* I. 4, 10. Cf. Joseph Ratzinger, *Der Gott Jesu Christi, Betrachtungen über den Dreieinigen Gott* (Munich: Kösel, 1976), 71. Nichols, *Benedict*, 194.

124. Ratzinger, *Feast of Faith*, 55.

125. Ratzinger, *Feast of Faith*, 142. Cf. Nichols, *Benedict*, 221.

126. Josef Andreas Jungmann, *The Mass of the Roman Rite: Its Origins and Development* (*Missarum Sollemnia*) (Westminster, MD: Christian Classics, 1986).

127. Josef Andreas Jungmann, in review of Otto Nussbaum, *Der Standort des Liturgen am christlichen Altar vor dem Jahr 1000* (Bonn:, 1965), in *Zeitschrift für Kirche und Theologie* 88 (1966): 445–50. Louis Bouyer, *Liturgy and Architecture* (Notre Dame, IN: Notre Dame University Press, 1967). Everett Diederich, "The Unfolding Presence of Christ in the Celebration of Mass," *Communio* (1978): 326–43. Erik Peterson, "Das Kreuz und die Gebetsrichtung nach Osten," in *Frühkirche, Judentum und Gnosis*, ed. Everett Diederich, 15–35 (Freiburg i. Br.: Herder, 1959). Aidan Nichols, *The Art of God Incarnate: Theology and Image in Christian Tradition* (New York: Paulist, 1980). Klaus Gamber, *Zum Herrn hin!*, Regensburg: Pustet, 1994. Uwe Michael Lang, *Conversi ad Dominum*, Einsiedeln: Johannes, 2003.

128. Ratzinger, *Feast of Faith*, 144, referencing Zechariah 12:10 and Revelation 1:7.

129. Duffy, "Benedict XVI and the Eucharist," 195–212, at 212.

130. Ratzinger, *Spirit of the Liturgy*, 77–80.

131. Benedict XVI, *Deus Caritas Est*, 13.

132. Ibid., 14.

133. Ratzinger, *God Is Near Us*, 121f. First emphasis added. One is able to proclaim that God does not eliminate suffering, but he is able to transform it. The homilist and preacher finds this existentially attested to by the saints. They have turned their hearts to the suffering brothers and sisters in the world. By sharing in God's passion for humanity, the homilist and preacher existentially acquire credibility amid cynicism and *l'ennui* (boredom).

24 Regensburg: Provocation or Jesus Christ as the Basis for Civilized Discourse? Jesus Christ as the Reconciler of Faith and Reason

1. Joseph Ratzinger/Benedikt XVI, *Der Gott des Glaubens und der Gott der Philosophen. Ein Beitrag zum Problem der theologia naturalis*, 2nd rev. ed., ed. Heino Sonnemans (Leutesdorf: Johannes-Verlag, 2005).

2. Joseph Ratzinger/Benedikt XVI, *Glaube—Wahrheit—Toleranz. Das Christentum und die Weltreligionen*, 4th ed. (Freiburg I. Br.: Herder, 2005), 137 and 139, respectively.

3. DH 302.

4. Rolf Busse and Hans Rott, "Bedarf die moderne Philosophie einer Ausweitung des wissenschaftlichen Vernunftbegriffs?" in *Die "Regensburger Vorlesung" Papst Benedikts XVI. im Dialog der Wissenschaften*, ed. Christoph Dohmen, 86–99 (Regensburg: Pattloch, 2007).

5. Markus Mühling, "Mut zur weite der Vernunft. Thesen zum Verhältnis von Vernunft, Glaube, der universitas scientiarum und zum Dialog der Kulturen aus reformatorischer Sicht," in ibid., 100–110.

6. Benedikt XVI, *Gott und die Vernunft. Aufruf zum Dialog der Kulturen* (Augsburg: Sankt Ulrich, 2007), 15.

7. Cf. Verweyen's report from a seminar in 1959–1960 with Ratzinger in Hansjürgen Verweyen, *Joseph Ratzinger—Benedikt XVI. Die Entwicklung seines Denkens* (Darmstadt: Wissenschaftliche Buchgesellschaft, 2007), 107.

8. Joseph Ratzinger, *Introduction to Christianity* (San Francisco: Ignatius, 2004), 314ff. Joseph Ratzinger, *Milestones: Memoirs 1927–1977* (San Francisco: Ignatius, 1998), 42. Cf. Joseph Ratzinger, "Wesen und Weisen der auctoritas im Werk des heiligen Bonaventura," in *Die Kirche und ihre Ämter und Stände. FG für Kardinal Joseph Frings zum Goldenen Priesterjubiläum*, ed. W. Corsten, 58–72 (Cologne: Bachem, 1960. See also his gentle criticism of Bonaventure in, Joseph Ratzinger, *Wesen und Auftrag der Theologie* (Einsiedeln: Johannes, 1993), 15f.

9. Joseph Ratzinger, *Principles of Catholic Theology: Building Stones for a Fundamental Theology* (San Francisco: Ignatius, 1987 [1982]), 170. Joseph Ratzinger, *Dogma und Verkündigung*

(Munich: Wewel, 1977), 209ff and 216f. Joseph Ratzinger, *Werte in Zeiten des Umbruchs. Die Herausforderung der Zukunft bestehen* (Freiburg I. Br.: Herder, 2005), 116.

10. Ratzinger, *Werte in Zeiten des Umbruchs*, 115ff.

11. Ratzinger, *Introduction to Christianity*, 54f.

12. Michael Schulz, "Wenn das Salz 'dumm' geworden ist," in *Der Glaube ist einfach, Aspekte der Theologie Papst Benedikts XVI*, ed. Gerhard Ludwig Müller, 19–53, at 44f (Regensburg: Pattloch, 2007).

25   Jesus Christ, the Definer and Personification of the Eschaton

1. Joseph Ratzinger, *Principles of Catholic Theology: Building Stones for a Fundamental Theology* (San Francisco: Ignatius, 1987 [1982]), 155f. Cf. Josef Pieper, *The End of Time: A Meditation on the Philosophy of History* (San Francisco: Ignatius, 1999). Hans Urs von Balthasar, *A Theology of History* (San Francisco: Ignatius, 1994).

2. Joseph Ratzinger, "Europe in the Crisis of Cultures," *Communio* (English edition) 32 (2005): 345–56, at 346f. Cf. Adolf von Harnack, *What Is Christianity? Lectures Delivered at the University of Berlin during the Winter Term 1899–1900*, trans. T. Bailey Saunders (London: SPCK, 1901) and Hans Küng, *Global Responsibility: In Search of a New World Ethic* (New York: Crossroad, 1991).

3. Immanuel Kant, *Critique of Pure Reason*, 2nd ed. (1787), B 46f. A 31.

4. Jürgen Moltmann, *Das Kommen Gottes. Christliche Eschatologie* (Gütersloh: Kaiser, 1995), 83.

5. Jürgen Moltmann, *Der Weg Jesu Christi. Christologie in messianischen Dimensionen.* (Munich: Kaiser, 1989), 285.

6. Ibid., 213. Ibid., *Das Kommen Gottes*, 252.

7. Gisbert Greshake, *Auferstehung der Toten. Ein Beitrag zur gegenwärtigen theologischen Diskussion über die Zukunft der Geschichte* (Essen: Ludgerus, 1969), 385. Cf. ibid., "Auferstehung im Tod. Ein 'parteiischer' Rückblick auf eine theologische Diskussion." *Theologie und Philosophie* 73 (1998): 538–57.

8. "Für den einzelnen Menschen bedeutet das, daß er im Tod nicht nur sein eigenes Eschaton erfährt, sondern zugleich das Eschaton der Welt und der gesamten Geschichte. Er erfährt im Durchschreiten des Todes nicht nur, dass sich nun seine ganze *individuelle* Geschichte vor Gott versammelt, sondern zugleich—durch tausend Fäden mit der eigenen Geschichte verknüpft—die Geschichte der Welt und aller Menschen. Man kann es auch so formulieren: Indem ein Mensch stirbt und eben so die Zeit hinter sich lässt, gelangt er an einen 'Punkt,' an dem die gesamte übrige Geschichte 'gleichzeitig' mit ihm an ihr Ende kommt, mag sie auch 'inzwischen' in der Dimension *irdischer* Zeit noch unendlich weite Wegstrecken zurückgelegt haben." Gerhard Lohfink, "Zur Möglichkeit christlicher Naherwartung," in *Naherwartung— Auferstehung—Unsterblichkeit. Untersuchungen zur christlichen Eschatologie*, 5th ed., by Gerhard Lohfink and Gisbert Greshake, 72 (Freiburg i. Br.: Herder, 1982).

9. Joseph Ratzinger, *Eschatology, Death and Eternal Life*, vol. 9 in *Dogmatic Theology*, ed. Johann Auer and Joseph Ratzinger (Washington, DC: Catholic University of America, 1988 [originally published in 1977]).

10. Joseph Ratzinger, "Heilsgeschichte und Eschatologie. Zur Frage nach dem Ansatz des theologischen Denkens," in *Theologie im Wandel. Festschrift zum 150 jährigen Bestehen der kath. theologischen Fakultät an der Universität Tübingen, 1817–1967* (Munich, 1967): 68–89.

11. Ratzinger, *Eschatology*, 50.

12. Joseph Ratzinger, *Politik und Erlösung: zum Verhältnis von Glaube, Rationalität und Irrationalem in der sogenannten Theologie der Befreiung. Rheinisch-Westfälischen Akademie der Wissenschaften, G 279* (Opladen: Westdeutscher Verlag, 1986), 20.

13. Joseph Ratzinger, "Damit Gott allein alles in allem sei," in *Kleines Credo für Verunsicherte*, ed. Norbert Kutschki and Jürgen Hoeren, 121–40 (Freiburg i. Br.: Herder, 1993).

14. Ratzinger, *Eschatology*, 46ff.

15. Joseph Ratzinger, *Eschatologie. Tod und ewiges Leben*, vol. 9 in *Kleine Katholische Dogmatik*, ed. Johann Auer and Joseph Ratzinger (Regensburg: Pustet, 1990 [originally published in 1977, 6th rev. ed. 2007]).

16. For an informative review of his eschatology, see Gerhard Nachtwei, *Dialogische Unsterblichkeit. Eine Untersuchung zu Joseph Ratzingers Eschatologie und Theologie* (Leipzig: St. Benno, 1986).

17. "Die These von der Auferstehung im Tod entmaterialisiert die Auferstehung; sie schließt ein, daß die reale Materie nicht am Vollendungsgeschehen teilhat." Ratzinger, *Eschatologie. Tod und ewiges Leben*, 198.

18. Ibid., 96.

19. "Das Netz der Mitmenschlichkeit ist zugleich auch ein Netz der Mitzeitlichkeit." Ibid., 151. Solidarity implies simultaneity.

20. Ibid., 152–54. Along with Origen in his seventh Homily on Leviticus, Ratzinger was stimulated by Henri de Lubac, *Glauben aus der Liebe* (Einsiedeln: Johannes, 1970), 368–73.

21. Ratzinger, *Eschatology*, 18.

22. Ibid., 6.

23. Ibid., 9.

24. Ibid., 19–45.

25. Ibid., 29.

26. Ibid., 34.

27. Oscar Cullmann, *Christus und die Zeit*, 3rd ed. (Zurich: Mohr, 1962). Ratzinger, *Eschatology*, 51–55.

28. Ratzinger, "Damit Gott alles in allem sei," 136.

29. Ratzinger, "Auferstehung des Fleisches," *Lexikon für Theologie und Kirche*, vol. II, 3rd ed. (Freiburg i. Br.: Herder, 1995), 1049ff. Ratzinger, *Introduction*, 292.

30. Joseph Ratzinger, "Jenseits des Todes," *Communio* 1 (1972): 231–44, at 234.

31. Joseph Ratzinger, "Eschatologie und Utopie," *Communio* 6 (1977): 97–110, at 98.

32. Ratzinger, "Jenseits des Todes," 241.

33. Ibid., 72–79.

34. Ibid., 130.

35. *Faith of Damasus*, related to the Athanasian Creed and formally attributed to Pope Damasus (366–384), but produced in fifth-century southern Gaul. DH 71f.

36. DH 525–41.

37. DH 1000–1002.

38. Ratzinger, "Jenseits des Todes", 136f.

39. Ibid., 174.

40. "The universe, matter, is as such conditioned by time. It is a process of becoming. This temporality of the universe, which knows being only in the form of becoming, has a certain direction, disclosed in the gradual construction of 'biosphere' and 'noosphere' from out of physical building blocks which it then proceeds to transcend." Ibid., 191.

41. Joseph Ratzinger, *Dogma und Verkündigung* (Munich: Wewel, 1977), 297–310.

42. Joseph Ratzinger, "Zwischen Tod und Auferstehung," *Communio* 9 (1980): 209–23, at 218.

43. Ibid., 195.

44. Ibid., 217.

45. Only in Appendix II to the English edition: ibid., 262.

46. Ibid., 217f.

47. Ratzinger, *Eschatology*, 150ff.

48. Ratzinger, "Eschatologie und Utopie," 97–110, at 109.

49. Ratzinger, *Introduction to Christianity*, 315–18.

50. Ibid., 234.

51. Ibid., 238.

52. Alexander Kissler, "Am Scheideweg, Benedikt XVI. und das Christentum des 21. Jahrhunderts," *Communio* 35 (2006): 622–36.

53. Jürgen Habermas, "Ein Bewusstsein von dem, was fehlt," February 10, 2007, *NZZ Online*, http://www.nzz.ch/2007/02/10/li/articleEVB7X.print.html (accessed February 11, 2007).

54. Adolf von Harnack, *What Is Christianity?* Cf. Karl-Heinz Neufeld, *Adolf Harnacks Konflikt mit der Kirche: Weg-Stationen zum 'Wesen des Christentums,'* Innsbrucker theologische Studien 4 (Innsbruck: Tyrolia, 1979).

55. Leo Baeck, *The Essence of Judaism* (New York: Schocken Books, 1961).

26   Mary: In Christ, the First Free Human Being

1. John F. Thornton and Susan B. Varenne, *The Essential Pope Benedict XVI: His Central Writings and Speeches* (San Francisco: Harper, 2007), 20.
2. Peter Seewald, *Benedict XVI: An Intimate Portrait* (San Francisco: Ignatius, 2008), 130.
3. Brennan Pursell, *Benedict of Bavaria: An Intimate Portrait of the Pope and His Homeland* (n.p.: Circle Press, 2008), 30
4. Hans Küng, *Christsein* (Munich and Zurich: Piper, 1974), 450–52.
5. Louis Bouyer, *Women in the Church* (San Francisco: Ignatius, 1979).
6. Joseph Ratzinger, "Zur Theologie der Ehe," *Theologie der Ehe*, ed. G. Krems, R. Mumm (Göttingen-Regensburg, 1969): 81–115.
7. Thornton and Varenne, *Pope Benedict XVI*, 288.
8. Hans Urs von Balthasar, "Umkehr im Neuen Testament," *Communio* 3 (1974): 481–91.
9. Erich Przywara, SJ, *Alter und Neuer Bund* (Vienna: Herold, 1956).
10. Thornton and Varenne, *Pope Benedict XVI*, 290.
11. Hans Urs von Balthasar, "Commentary to the Encyclical 'Redemptoris Mater,'" in Joseph Ratzinger, *Mary: God's Yes to Man* (San Francisco: Ignatius, 1988), 164.
12. Ratzinger, *Mary: God's Yes to Man*, 168.
13. Ibid., 172.
14. Ibid., 176.
15. Joseph Ratzinger, *Mary: The Church at the Source* (San Francisco: Ignatius, 1989), 83.
16. Ratzinger, *Daughter Zion* (San Francisco: Ignatius, 1983), 9.
17. Ibid., 24.
18. Ibid., 41.
19. Ibid., 46f.
20. Ibid., 48.
21. Ibid.
22. Ibid., 61.
23. Ibid., 65.
24. Ibid., 70.
25. Ibid., 81.
26. Joseph Ratzinger, "On the Position of Mariology and Marian Spirituality within the Totality of Faith and Theology," *The Church and Women: A Compendium* (San Francisco: Ignatius, 1988), 67–81, at 72.
27. Ratzinger, *Mary: The Church at the Source*, 121.
28. Ibid., 31.
29. Peter Pfister, ed., *Joseph Ratzinger und das Erzbistum München und Freising. Dokumente und Bilder aus kirchlichen Archiven, Beiträge und Erinnerungen, Schriften des Archivs des Erzbistums München und Freising, Band 10* (Regensburg: Schnell and Steiner, 2006), 171f.

Epilogue: Jesus Christ Offering the World Identity and Meaning

1. "Missa pro Eligendo Romano Pontifice," http://www.vatican.va (accessed December 4, 2008).
2. IBID.
3. "First Mass of His Holiness Pope Benedict XVI at the end of the Eucharistic Concelebration with the Cardinal Electors in the Sistine Chapel," http://www.vatican.va (accessed December 4, 2008).
4. First printed as: Joseph Ratzinger, *Der Gott des Glaubens und der Gott der Philosophen* (Munich: Steiner and Schnell, 1960), 13.
5. Richard of St. Victor *De Trinitate* III/1.
6. Also St. Thomas Aquinas never thought, for instance, that human rationality on its own could obtain the term, let alone understand, the Blessed Trinity.

7. Joseph Ratzinger, *Principles of Catholic Theology: Building Stones for a Fundamental Theology* (San Francisco: Ignatius, 1987 [1982]), 34ff.

8. Hans-Georg Gadamer, *Truth and Method*, 2nd rev. ed. (New York: Crossroad, 1989), 405–18.

9. Ratzinger, "The Regensburg Address," in *Ratzinger's Faith: The Theology of Pope Benedict XVI*, by Tracey Rowland, 174 (Oxford: Oxford University Press, 2008).

BIBLIOGRAPHY

Primary Sources—Joseph Ratzinger/ Pope Benedict XVI

Books

Abbruch und Aufbruch. Die Antwort des Glaubens auf die Krise der Werte. Eichstätter Hochschulreden 61. Munich: Minerva, 1988.

Behold the Pierced One: An Approach to a Spiritual Christology. San Francisco: Ignatius Press, 1986 (1984).

Brief an die Priester, Diakone und Mitarbeiter in der Seelsorge. Munich: Pfeiffer, 1982.

Christian Brotherhood. London: Burns & Oates, 2005.

"Damit Gott allein alles in allem sei." In *Kleines Credo für Verunsicherte.* Edited by Norbert Kutschki and Jürgen Hoeren. Freiburg i. Br.: Herder, 1993.

Daughter Zion. San Francisco: Ignatius, 1983.

Dogma und Verkündigung. Munich: Wewel, 1977.

Einführung in das Christentum. Munich: Kösel, 2000.

(With Karl Rahner) *The Episcopate and the Primacy.* New York: Herder and Herder, 1962.

Die Einheit der Nationen: Eine Vision der Kirchenväter. Salzburg-Munich: Pustet, 1971; repr. 2005.

Ergebnisse und Probleme der dritten Konzilsperiode. Cologne: Bachem, 1965.

Die Erste Sitzungsperiode des Zweiten Vatikanischen Konzils, Ein Rückblick. Cologne: Bachem, 1963.

Eschatologie. Tod und ewiges Leben. Vol. 9 of *Kleine Katholische Dogmatik.* Edited by Johann Auer and Joseph Ratzinger. Regensburg: Pustet, 1990. Originally published 1977, 6th rev. ed. 2007.

Eschatology, Death and Eternal Life. Vol. 9 of *Dogmatic Theology.* Edited by Johann Auer and Joseph Ratzinger. Washington, DC: Catholic University of America, 1988. Originally published 1977.

The Feast of Faith: Approaches to a Theology of the Liturgy. San Francisco: Ignatius, 1986.

Der Geist der Liturgie. Freiburg i. Br.: Herder, 2000.

Gesammelte Schriften, Vol. 2 , Offenbarungsverständnis und Geschichtstheologie Bonaventuras. Freiburg i. Br.: Herder, 2009. *Gesammelte Schriften, Vol. 5, Zeichen unter den Völkern: Schriften zur Ekklesiologie und Ökumene.* Freiburg i.br.: Herder, 2009.

Die Geschichtstheologie des heiligen Bonaventura. Munich: Schnell and Steiner, 1959. Repr., St. Ottilien: EOS, 1992. English: *The Theology of History in Saint Bonaventure.* Translated by Zachary Hayes. Chicago: Franciscan Herald, 1971.

Glaube—Wahrheit—Toleranz. Das Christentum und die Weltreligionen. 4th ed. Freiburg: Herder, 2005.

Glaube und Zukunft. Munich: Kösel, 1970.

God Is Near Us: The Eucharist, the Heart of Life. San Francisco: Ignatius, 2003.

Der Gott des Glaubens und der Gott der Philosophen. Ein Beitrag zum Problem der theologia naturalis. Munich: Schnell & Steiner, 1960.

Der Gott Jesu Christi, Betrachtungen über den Dreieinigen Gott. Munich: Kösel, 1976.

Gott und die Vernunft. Aufruf zum Dialog der Kulturen. Augsburg: Sankt Ulrich, 2007.

Gottes Projekt. Nachdenken über Schöpfung und Kirche. Regensburg: Pustet, 2009.

(With Christoph von Schönborn) *Introduction to the Catechism of the Catholic Church.* San Francisco: Ignatius, 1994.

Introduction to Christianity. San Francisco: Ignatius, 2004.

Jesus Christ: Today, Yesterday and Forever. Washington, DC: John Paul II Institute, 1990.

Jesus of Nazareth: From the Baptism in the Jordan to the Transfiguration. Translated by Adrian Walker. New York: Doubleday, 2007.

Kirche, Ökumene und Politik. Einsiedeln: Johannes, 1987. English: *Church, Ecumenism and Politics.* New York: Crossroad, 1988.

Die Krise der Katechese und ihre Überwindung. Einsiedeln: Johannes, 1983.

Das Konzil auf dem Weg. Rückblick auf die zweite Sitzungsperiode. Cologne: Bachem, 1964.

Die letzte Sitzungsperiode des Konzils. Cologne: Bachem, 1966.

Mary: Church at the Source, San Francisco: Ignatius, 1989.

Milestones: Memoirs 1927–1977. San Francisco: Ignatius, 1998.

Mitarbeiter der Wahrheit, München: Pfeiffer, 1979.

The Nature and Mission of Theology: Approaches to Understanding Its Role in the Light of Present Controversy. San Francisco: Ignatius, 1995.

Das neue Volk Gottes. Entwürfe zur Ekklesiologie. Düsseldorf: Patmos, 1977.

A New Song for the Lord. New York: Crossroad, 1996.

"On the Position of Mariology and Marian Spirituality within the Totality of Faith and Theology." *The Church and Women: A Compendium.* San Francisco: Ignatius, 1988.

On the Way to Jesus Christ. San Francisco: Ignatius, 2005.

Pilgrim Fellowship of Faith: The Church as Communion. San Francisco: Ignatius, 2005.

Politik und Erlösung: zum Verhältnis von Glaube, Rationalität und Irrationalem in der sogenannten Theologie der Befreiung. Rheinisch-Westfälischen Akademie der Wissenschaften, G 279. Opladen: Westdeutscher Verlag, 1986. *Principles of Catholic Theology: Building Stones for a Fundamental Theology.* San Francisco: Ignatius, 1987 (1982).

"Das Problem der Dogmengeschichte in der Sicht der katholischen Theologie." In *Arbeitsgemeinschaft für Forschung des Landes Nordrhein-Westfalen. Geisteswissenschaften* 139 (Cologne-Opladen: Westdeutscher Verlag, 1966).

(With Vittorio Messori) *The Ratzinger Report: An Exclusive Interview on the State of the Church.* San Francisco: Ignatius, 1985.

The Sabbath of History. Washington, DC: William G. Longdon, 2000.

Salt of the Earth: The Church at the End of the Millennium: An Interview with Peter Seewald. San Francisco: Ignatius, 1997 (1996).

The Spirit of the Liturgy. San Francisco: Ignatius, 2000.

Storia e Dogma. Milan: Jaca Books, 1971.

Theological Highlights of Vatican II. New York: Paulist, 1966.

Theologie der Liturgie. Die sakramentale Begründung christlicher Existenz [Theology of Liturgy. The Sacramental Root of Christian Existence]. Vol. 11 of *Joseph Ratzinger: Gesammelte Schriften.* Edited by Gerhard Ludwig Müller along with the Institut Papst Benedikt XVI. Regensburg: Rudolf Voderholzer, Christian Schaller, Gabriel Weiten. Freiburg i. Br.: Herder, 2008.

Truth and Tolerance: Christian Belief and World Religions. San Francisco: Ignatius, 2004.

Values in a Time of Upheaval. San Francisco: Ignatius, 2006.

"Ein Versuch zur Frage des Traditionsbegriffs." Edited by Karl Rahner and Joseph Ratzinger. *Offenbarung und Überlieferung. Quaestiones Disputatae* 25. Freiburg i. Br.: Herder, 1965.

Volk und Haus Gottes in Augustins Lehre von der Kirche. In: *Münchener Theologische Studien* II, 7. Munich: Karl Zink, 1954; repr. St. Ottilien: EOS, 1992.

Vom Wiederauffinden der Mitte. Freiburg i. Br.: Herder, 1997.

"Was bedeutet Jesus Christus für mich?" *Wer ist Jesus von Nazaret—für mich? 100 zeitgenössische Zeugnisse.* Edited by Heinrich Spaemann. Munich: Kösel, 1973.

Wort Gottes. Schrift—Tradition—Amt. Freiburg: Basel, Wien, 2005.

The Yes of Jesus Christ: Exercises in Faith, Hope, and Love. New York: Crossroad, 2005.

"Zur Frage nach Grundlagen und Weg der Exegese heute." Edited by Albert Gelin and Anton Vögtle. *Schriftauslegung im Widerstreit. Quaestiones Disputatae* 117. Freiburg i. Br.: Herder, 1989.

Articles

"40 Jahre Konstitution über die heilige Liturgie. Rückblick und Vorblick." *Liturgisches Jahrbuch* 53 (2003): 209–21.

"Assessment and Future Perspectives." Edited by Alcuin Reid. *Proceedings of the July 2001 Fontgombault Liturgical Conference.* (Farnborough: St. Michael's Abbey Press, 2003): 3–21.

"Buchstabe und Geist des Zweiten Vatikanischen Konzils in den Konzilsreden von Kardinal Frings." *Communio* 16 (1987): 251–65.

"Cardinal Frings's Speeches during the Second Vatican Council: Apropos A. Muggeridge's *The Desolate City.*" *Communio* 15 (1988): 130–47.

"Der Heilige Geist als communion. Zum Verhältnis von Pneumatologie und Spiritualität bei Augustinus." In *Erfahrung des Heiligen Geistes.* Edited by Claus Heitmann and Heribert Mühlen. (Hamburg and Munich: Kösel, 1974): 223–38.

"Der Katholizismus nach dem Konzil" (German Catholic Diet) *Auf Dein Wort hin.* 81. Deutscher Katholikentag, July 13–17, 1966, in Bamberg. (Paderborn: Schöningh, 1966): 245–64.

"Der Weltdienst der Kirche. Auswirkungen von *Gaudium et Spes* im letzten Jahrzehnt." *Zehn Jahre Vaticanum II.* Edited by Michael Seybold. (Regensburg, 1976): 36–53.

"Die Christologie im Spannungsfeld von altchristlicher Exegese und moderner Bibelauslegung." *Urbild und Abbild. FS Herbert Doms.* Edited by Johannes Tenzler. (Regensburg, 1972): 359–67.

"Die Stimme der Zeit—die Stimme Gottes. Michael Kardinal Faulhaber." *Christlicher Glaube und Europa. 12 Predigten* (Munich: Erzdiözese München und Freising, 1981): 128f.

"Eschatologie und Utopie." *Communio* 6 (1977): 97–110.

"Europe in the Crisis of Cultures." *Communio* 32 (2005): 345–56.

"Evangelisierung, Katechese und Katechismus." *Theologie und Glaube* 84 (1994): 273–88.

"Guardini on Christ in our Century." *Crisis* (June 1996): 14–19.

"Heil und Geschichte. Gesichtspunkte zur gegenwärtigen theologischen Diskussion des Problems der 'Heilsgeschichte.'" *Regensburger Universitätszeitung* 5 (1969): No.11, 2–7.

"Heilsgeschichte und Eschatologie. Zur Frage nach dem Ansatz des theologischen Denkens." *Theologie im Wandel. Festschrift zum 150 jährigen Bestehen der kath. theologischen Fakultät an der Universität Tübingen, 1817–1967.* (Munich: Wewel, 1967): 68–89.

"Homily for Luigi Giussani." *Communio* 31 (2004): 685–87.

"Ich glaube an Gott, den allmächtigen Vater." *Communio* 4 (1975): 10–18.

"Interview mit dem Präfekten der Glaubenskongregation zu einigen Fragen des Katechismus der Katholischen Kirche." *Münchener Theologische Zeitschrift* 45 (1994): 445–49.

"Jenseits des Todes." *Communio* 1 (1972): 231–44.

"Joseph Ratzinger Stellungnahme." *Zur Debatte* 34, no. 1 (2004): 5–7.

"Meditation and Progress." *Communio* 25 (1998): 325–39.

"Newman gehört zu den großen Lehrern der Kirche." In *John Henry Newman: Lover of Truth.* Edited by Margarete Strolz and Maria Binder, 141–6. Rome: Pontificia Universitas Urbaniana, 1991.

"Offenbarung—Schrift—Überlieferung, Ein Text des hl. Bonaventura und seine Bedeutung für die gegenwärtige Theologie." *Trierer Theologische Zeitschrift* 67 (1958): 13–27.

"Le Pluralisme: Problème Posé à l'Eglise et à la Théologie." *Studia Moralia* 24 (1986): 299–318.

"Sie ist Sammlung der Menschen zum Volk Gottes hin, und diese schließt Reinigung, Bereitung für Gottes Willen ein." Erster Hirtenbrief von Erzbischof Joseph Ratzinger an die Gemeinden des Erzbistums, June 7, 1977. In *Amtsblatt für das Erzbistum München und Freising,* no. 8 (June 14, 1977): 258–63.

"Stimme des Vertrauens. Kardinal Josef Frings auf dem Zweiten Vaticanum." In *Ortskirche im Dienst der Weltkirche. FS für die Kölner Kardinäle Erzbischof Joseph Höffner und Alt-Erzbischof Josef Frings.* Edited by Norbert Trippen and W. Mogge, 183–190. Cologne: Bachem, 1976.

"Von der Liturgie zur Christologie, Romano Guardinis theologischer Grundansatz und seine Aussagekraft." *Wege zur Wahrheit. Die bleibende Bedeutung von Romano Guardini.* Edited by Eugen Biser, 121–44, foreword 7. Düsseldorf: Patmos, 1985.

"Zum Fortgang der Ökumene. Brief an den Moderator dieses Heftes." *Theologische Quartalschrift* 166 (1986): 243–48.

"Zur Theologie der Ehe." *Theologie der Ehe.* Edited by G. Krems and R. Mumm, 81–115. Göttingen-Regensburg: Pustet, 1969.

"Zwischen Tod und Auferstehung." *Communio* 9 (1980): 209–23.

Secondary Sources

Adam, August. *The Primacy of Love.* Westminster, MD: Newman, 1958.

Adam, Karl. *Das Wesen des Katholizismus.* Düsseldorf: Schwann, 1928. English: *The Spirit of Catholicism.* London: Sheed and Ward, 1934.

Adorno, Theodor. *Minima Moralia: Reflexionen aus einem beschädigten Leben.* Berlin: Suhrkamp, 1951.

Afanasiev, Nicholas. *Trapeza Gospodnia (The Lord's Supper).* Paris: YMCA Press, 1952.

Allen, John L. *Cardinal Ratzinger: The Vatican's Enforcer of the Faith.* New York: Continuum, 2000.

———. "Ratzinger Credited with Saving Lutheran Pact." *National Catholic Reporter*, September 10, 1999.

Althaus, Paul. *Völker vor und nach Christus.* Leipzig: Deichert, 1937.

Baeck, Leo. *The Essence of Judaism.* New York: Schocken Books, 1961.

Balthasar, Hans Urs von. "Casta Meretrix." In *Explorations in Theology.* Vol. 2 of *Spouse of the Word.* San Francisco: Ignatius, 1991.

———. "Commentary to the Encyclical 'Redemptoris Mater.'" In Joseph Ratzinger, *Mary: God's Yes to Man.* San Francisco: Ignatius, 1988.

———. *The Glory of the Lord: A Theological Aesthetics V: The Realm of Metaphysics in the Modern Age.* Edinburgh: T & T Clark, 1991.

———. *Love Alone.* New York: Herder and Herder, 1963.

———. *The Theology of Henri de Lubac.* San Francisco: Ignatius, 1991.

———. *A Theology of History.* San Francisco: Ignatius, 1994.

———. "Umkehr im Neuen Testament." *Communio* 3 (1974): 481–91.

Bardazzi, Marco. *In the Vineyard of the Lord: The Life, Faith, and Teachings of Joseph Ratzinger, Pope Benedict XVI.* New York: Rizzoli, 2005.

Baronio, Cesare. *Scritti vari.* Rome: Athenaeum società editrice romana, 1911.

Barth, Karl. *Ad Limina Apostolorum.* Edinburgh: St. Andrew's Press, 1969.

———. *Church Dogmatics.* Vol. II. Edinburgh: T & T Clark, 1977.

Baum, G. "Vom Dörren und Keimen—was sich in der Katecheselandschaft zeigt." *Herder Korrespondenz* 52 (1998): 34–9.

Bellandi, Andrea. *Fede cristiana come "stare e comprendere." La giustificazione dei fondamenti della fede in Joseph Ratzinger.* Rome: Gregoriana, 1996.

Bloch, Ernst. *The Principle of Hope.* Cambridge, MA: MIT, 1986.

Bonaventure. *The Mind's Road to God.* Englewood Cliffs, NJ: Prentice Hall, 1953.

Bossuet, Jacques-Bénigne. *Exposition de la Doctrine de l'Église Catholique sur les Matières de Controverse.* Paris: Mabre-Cramoisy, 1671.

Bouyer, Louis. *Liturgy and Architecture.* Notre Dame, IN: Notre Dame University Press, 1967.

———. *Women in the Church.* San Francisco: Ignatius, 1979.

Buber, Martin. *Ich und Du.* Leipzig: Insel, 1923.

———. *Das Problem des Menschen.* Heidelberg: Lambert Schneider, 1948.

Bultmann, Rudolf. *The Gospel of John: A Commentary.* Oxford: Blackwell, 1971.

———. *The History of the Synoptic Tradition.* New York: Harper and Row, 1963.

———. *Urchristentum.* Zurich/Stuttgart: Artemis, 1954.

Busse, Rolf, and Hans Rott. "Bedarf die moderne Philosophie einer Ausweitung des wissenschaftlichen Vernunftbegriffs?" In *Die "Regensburger Vorlesung" Papst Benedikts XVI. im Dialog der Wissenschaften.* Edited by Christoph Dohmen. Regensburg: Pustet, 2007.

Canisius, Petrus. *Catechismus*. Latinus et Germanicus, Rome: Pontificia Universitas Gregoriana, 1933 (1554).

Casper, Bernhard. "Rosenzweig's Criticism of Buber's 'I and Thou.'" In *Martin Buber: A Centenary Volume*. Edited by Haim Gordon and Jochanan Bloch. New York: Ktav, 1984.

Cholvy, Gérard, and Yves-Marie Hilaire, eds. *Le Fait Religieux Aujourd'hui en France. Les Trente Dernières Années (1974–2004)*. Paris: Cerf, 2005.

Congar, Yves. "Erinnerungen an eine Episode auf dem II. Vatikanischen Konzil." *Glaube im Prozeß. Christsein nach dem II. Vatikanum. Für Karl Rahner*. Edited by Elmar Klinger and Klaus Wittstadt. Freiburg i. Br.: Herder, 1984.

———. *I Believe in the Holy Spirit*. New York: Crossroad, 2001.

———. *Mon Journal du Concile*. Vols. 1 and 2. Paris: Cerf, 2002.

———. *Report from Rome II*. London: G. Chapman, 1964.

Cullmann, Oscar. *Christus und die Zeit*. 3rd ed. Zurich: Evangelischer Verlag, 1962.

Daniélou, Jean. *The Bible and the Liturgy*. Notre Dame, IN: University of Notre Dame, 1956.

Delp, Alfred, SJ. *Facing Death*. London: Bloomsbury, 1962.

———. *Der Mensch und die Geschichte*. Nuremburg: Glock and Lutz, 1974.

Dent, Nicholas J. H. *Rousseau: An Introduction to His Psychological, Social, and Political Theory*. Oxford: Oxford University Press, 1988.

Diederich, Everett. "The Unfolding Presence of Christ in the Celebration of Mass." *Communio* 5 (1978): 326–43.

Duffy, Eamon. "Benedict XVI and the Eucharist." *New Blackfriars* 88, no. 1014 (March 2007): 195–212.

Dulles, Avery. "Benedict XVI: Interpreter of Vatican II." Laurence J. McGinley Lecture. New York: Fordham University, 2005.

Dürckheim, Maximilian Graf von, and Esther von Krosigk. *Worüber der Papst lacht*. Saarbrücken: VDM, 2005.

Ebner, Ferdinand. *Das Wort ist der Weg*. Vienna: Thomas Morus Presse, 1949.

Ericksen, Robert P. *Theologians under Hitler, Gerhard Kittel, Paul Althaus, and Emanuel Hirsch*. New Haven, CT and London: Yale University Press, 1985.

Evdokimov, Paul. *The Art of the Icon: A Theology of Beauty*. Redondo Beach, CA: Oakwood, 1990.

Ferreira, M. M. Jaime. *Doubt and Religious Commitment: The Role of the Will in Newman's Thought*. Oxford: Clarendon Press, 1980.

Fiorenza, Francis Schüssler. "From Theologian to Pope: A Personal View Back, Past the Public Portrayals." *Harvard Divinity Bulletin* 33 (2005): 56–62.

Forstner, Thomas. "Zeitzeugenberichte über die Freisinger und frühen Münchener Jahre Joseph Ratzingers (1945–1959)." In *Joseph Ratzinger und das Erzbistum München und Freising. Dokumente und Bilder aus kirchlichen Archiven, Beiträge und Erinnerungen, Schriften des Archivs des Erzbistums München und Freisin*, no. 10. Edited by Peter Pfister, 84–127. Regensburg: Schnell & Steiner, 2006.

Fries, Heinrich and Karl Rahner. *Einigung der Kirchen—reale Möglichkeit. Quaestiones Disputatae* 100. Freiburg i. Br.: Herder, 1983. English: *Unity of the Churches: An Actual Possibility*. New York: Continuum, 1985.

Frings, Josef. *Für die Menschen bestellt. Erinnerungen des Alterzbischofs von Köln*. Cologne: Bachem, 1973.

Gadamer, Hans-Georg. *Truth and Method*. 2nd rev. ed. New York: Crossroad, 1989.

Gelin, Albert. "La Question des 'Relectures' Bibliques à l'Intérieur d'une Tradition Vivante." *Sacra Pagina: Miscellanea Biblica I, Biblioteca Ephemeridum Theologicarum Lovaniensium* XII (Gembloux: Duculot, 1958).

Gerl-Falkovitz, Hanna-Barbara. *Romano Guardini, 1885–1968. Leben und Werk*. Mainz: Matthias Grünewald, 1985.

Greshake, Gisbert. "Auferstehung im Tod. Ein 'parteiischer' Rückblick auf eine theologische Diskussion." *Theologie und Philosophie* 73 (1998): 538–57.

———. *Auferstehung der Toten. Ein Beitrag zur gegenwärtigen theologischen Diskussion über die Zukunft der Geschichte*. Essen: Ludgerus, 1969.

Grillmeier, Alois. *Christ in Christian Tradition*. Louisville, KY: John Knox, 1975.

———. "Jesus von Nazaret—im Schatten des Gottessohnes?" In *Diskussion über Hans Küngs "Christsein."* By Hans Urs von Balthasar, 60–82. Mainz: Grünewald, 1976.

Guardini, Romano. *Auf dem Wege.* Mainz: Grünewald, 1923.

———. *Berichte über mein Leben.* Düsseldorf: Grünewald, 1984.

———. *Christentum und Kultur.* Mainz: Grünewald,1926.

———. *Letters from Lake Como: Explorations in Technology and the Human Race.* Grand Rapids, MI: Eerdmans, 1994.

———. *The Lord.* Washington, DC: Regnery, 2002.

———. *Die menschliche Wirklichkeit des Herrn. Beiträge zu einer Psychologie Jesu.* Mainz: Grünewald, 1999.

———. *Religiöse Gestalten in Dostojewskis Werk.* Mainz/Paderborn: Matthias Grünewald/Schöningh, 1989.

———. *Die religiöse Offenheit der Gegenwart.* Mainz: Grünewald, 1934.

———. *Sinn der Kirche: fünf Vorträge.* Mainz: Grünewald, 1922.

———. *The Spirit of the Liturgy: Readings in Liturgical Renewal.* New York: Crossroad, 1998.

———. *Unterscheidung des Christlichen.* Mainz: Grünewald, 1963.

———. *Das Wesen des Christentums—Die menschliche Wirklichkeit des Herrn. Beiträge zu einer Psychologie Jesu.* Mainz-Paderborn: Matthias Grünewald, 1991.

Habermas, Jürgen and Joseph Ratzinger. *Dialektik der Säkularisierung. Über Vernunft und Religion.* Freiburg i. Br.: Herder, 2005.

Häring, Hermann. *Theologie und Ideologie bei Joseph Ratzinger.* Düsseldorf: Patmos, 2001.

Harnack, Adolf von. *Lehrbuch der Dogmengeschichte.* Vol. I, 5th ed. Tübingen: Mohr, 1931.

———. *What Is Christianity? Lectures Delivered at the University of Berlin during the Winter Term 1899–1900.* Translated by T. Bailey Saunders. London: SPCK, 1901; also New York: Harper, 1957 edition.

Heidegger, Martin. *Identität und Differenz.* Pfullingen: Neske, 1957. English: *Identity and Difference.* Chicago: University of Chicago, 2002.

Heiler, Friedrich. *Der Katholizismus: seine Idee und Erscheinung.* Munich: Reinhardt, 1923.

Heisenberg, Werner. *Das Naturbild der heutigen Physik.* Hamburg: Rowohlt, 1955.

Hemming, Laurence Paul. *Benedict XVI: Fellow Worker for the Truth.* London: Burns & Oates, 2005.

Hengel, Martin. *Judaism and Hellenism: Studies in Their Encounter in Palestine during the Early Hellenistic Period.* Philadelphia, PA: Fortress Press, 1974.

———. *The Son of God: The Origin of Christology and the History of Jewish-Hellenistic Religion.* Philadelphia, PA: Fortress, 1976.

Hick, John. *An Interpretation of Religion: Human Responses to the Transcendent.* New Haven, CT: Yale University Press, 1989.

Hofmann, Fritz. *Der Kirchenbegriff des hl. Augustinus in seinen Grundlagen und seiner Entwicklung.* Munich: Hueber, 1933.

Jaffé, P. "Epistola ad Imperatorem Anastasium." In *Regesta Pontificium Romanorum ab Condita Ecclesia ad Annum post Christum Natum MCXCVIII.* 2nd ed. Edited by G. Wattenbach. Vols. I and II. Leipzig: Kersten, 1885–1888.

Jaspers, Karl. *The Great Philosophers.* Vol. 1. New York: Harcourt, Brace and World, 1962.

Jeremias, Joachim. *Die Gleichnisse Jesu.* Zurich: Zwingli Verlag, 1947.

———. *Neutestamentliche Theologie, Erster Teil: Die Verkündigung Jesu.* Gütersloh: Mohr, 1971.

Jülicher, Adolf. *Die Gleichnisreden Jesu.* Vols. 1 and 2. Tübingen: Mohr, 1886, 1899.

Jungmann, Josef Andreas. *The Mass of the Roman Rite: Its Origins and Development (Missarum Sollemnia).* Westminster, MD: Christian Classics, 1986.

Kaes, Dorothee. *Theologie im Anspruch von Geschichte und Wahrheit. Zur Hermeneutik Joseph Ratzingers.* St. Ottilien: EOS, 1997.

Kant, Immanuel. *Critique of Pure Reason.* 2nd ed. 1787.

Kasper, Walter. *Der Gott Jesu Christi.* Mainz: Grünewald, 1982.

———. Preface. *Johann Adam Möhler (1796–1838)—Kirchenvater der Moderne.* Edited by Harald Wagner. Paderborn: Bonifatius, 1996.

———. *Theology and Church.* London: SCM, 1989.

———. "Theorie und Praxis innerhalb einer theologia crucis." *Hochland* 62 (1970): 152–9.

———. "Das Verhältnis von Universalkirche und Ortskirche. Freundschaftliche Auseinandersetzung mit der Kritik von Joseph Kardinal Ratzinger." *Stimmen der Zeit* 218 (2000): 795–804.

Kempis, Stefan von. *Benedetto: die Biografie.* Leipzig: St. Benno, 2006.

Kerr, Fergus. *Twentieth Century Catholic Theologians: From Neo-scholasticism to Nuptial Mysticism.* London and Malden, MA: Blackwell, 2007.

Kierkegaard, Søren. *Practice in Christianity.* Princeton, NJ: Princeton University Press, 1991.

Kissler, Alexander. *Der Deutsche Papst, Benedikt XVI und seine schwierige Heimat.* Freiburg i. Br.: Herder, 2005.

———. "Am Scheideweg, Benedikt XVI. und das Christentum des 21. Jahrhunderts." *Communio* 35 (2006): 622–36.

Knoll, Alfons. "'Die Seele wieder finden'—Romano Guardini auf der Suche nach einer 'anderen' Theologie." In *Konservativ mit Blick nach vorn, Versuche zu Romano Guardini.* Edited by Arno Schilson. Würzburg: Echter, 1994.

Komonchak, Joseph A. "The Church in Crisis: Pope Benedict's Theological Vision." *Commonweal* (June 3, 2005).

Kornacker, Susanne. "Der junge Joseph Ratzinger und sein Bischof Michael Kardinal von Faulhaber." In *Joseph Ratzinger und das Erzbistum München und Freising, Dokumente und Bilder aus kirchlichen Archiven, Beiträge und Erinnerungen.* Edited by Peter Pfister. Regensburg: Schnell and Steiner, 2006.

Kreidler, Hans. *Eine Theologie des Lebens. Grundzüge im theologischen Denkens Karl Adams. Tübinger Theologische Studien 29.* Mainz: Grünewald, 1988.

Krieg, Robert A. *Karl Adam: Catholicism in German Culture.* Notre Dame, IN: University of Notre Dame Press, 1992.

———, ed. *Romano Guardini: A Precursor of Vatican II.* Notre Dame, IN and London: University of Notre Dame Press, 1997.

Kuld, Lothar. *Lerntheorie des Glaubens: religiöse Lehren und Lernen nach J. H. Newmans Phänomenologie des Glaubensaktes.* Sigmaringendorf: Regio-Verlag Glock u. Lutz, 1989.

Küng, Hans. *Christsein.* Munich and Zurich: Piper, 1974.

———. *Global Responsibility: In Search of a New World Ethic.* New York: Crossroad, 1991.

———. *Menschwerdung Gottes. Eine Einführung in Hegels theologisches Denken als Prolegomena zu einer künftigen Christologie.* Munich and Zurich: Piper, 1970.

Läpple, Alfred. *Benedikt XVI und seine Wurzeln, Was sein Leben und seinen Glauben prägte.* Augsburg: St. Ulrich, 2006.

Laurentin, René. *Comment Réconcilier l'Exégèse et la Foi.* Paris: O.E.IL., 1984.

Lohfink, Gerhard. *Braucht Gott die Kirche?* 4th ed. Freiburg i. Br.: Herder, 1999.

———. *Jesus and Community: The Social Dimensions of Faith.* New York: Paulist, 1984.

———. "Zur Möglichkeit christlicher Naherwartung." In *Naherwartung—Auferstehung—Unsterblichkeit. Untersuchungen zur christlichen Eschatologie.* 5th ed. By Gerhard Lohfink and Gisbert Greshake. Freiburg i. Br.: Herder, 1982.

Lohfink, Norbert. *Church Dreams: Talking against the Trend.* North Richland Hills, TX: Bibal, 2000.

De Lubac, Henri. *Catholicism: Christ and the Common Destiny of Man.* San Francisco: Ignatius, 1988.

———. *Corpus Mysticum: The Eucharist and the Church in the Middle Ages.* London: SCM-Canterbury, 2006.

———. *The Four Senses of Scripture.* Vols. 1 and 2. Grand Rapids, MI: Eerdmans, 1998, 2000.

———. *Glauben aus der Liebe.* Einsiedeln: Johannes, 1970.

———. *Die göttliche Offenbarung, Kommentar zum Vorwort und zum ersten Kapitel der dogmatischen Konstitution Dei Verbum des zweiten Vatikanischen Konzils.* Freiburg i. Br.: Herder, 2001.

———. *Meine Schriften im Rückblick.* Einsiedeln: Johannes, 1996.

———. *The Motherhood of the Church.* San Francisco: Ignatius, 1982.

———. "Nature and Grace." In *The Word in History: The St. Xavier Symposium.* Edited by T. Patrick Burke. London: Collins, 1966.

———. *The Splendor of the Church.* San Francisco: Ignatius, 1999.

Lyons, J. A. *The Cosmic Christ in Origen and Teilhard de Chardin.* Oxford Theological Monographs. Oxford: Oxford University Press, 1982.

Maier, Eugen. *Einigung in der Welt in Gott. Das Katholische bei Henri de Lubac.* Einsiedeln: Johannes, 1983.

McPartlan, Paul. *The Eucharist Makes the Church: Henri de Lubac and John Zizioulas in Dialogue.* Edinburgh: T & T Clark, 1993.

Meier, Hans. "Bayer und Weltbürger." In *Eine Theologie in der Nachfolge Petri: Papst Benedikt XVI.* Special issue of *Münchener Theologische Zeitschrift* 5 (2005): 498–504.

Mersch, Emil. *Le Corps Mystique du Christ. Etudes de Théologie Historique.* Louvain: Museum Lessianum 1936.

Möhler, Johann Adam. *Die Einheit in der Kirche.* Edited with commentary by Josef R. Geiselmann. Cologne and Olten: Bachem, 1957. English: Johann Adam Möhler. "Unity in the Church or the Principle of Catholicism." In *The Spirit of the Church Fathers of the First Three Centuries.* Washington, DC: CUA, 1996.

Monod, Jacques. *Chance and Necessity: An Essay on the Natural Philosophy of Modern Biology.* London: Collins, 1972.

Moltmann, Jürgen. *Das Kommen Gottes. Christliche Eschatologie.* Gütersloh: Kaiser, 1995.

———. *Trinität und Reich Gottes. Zur Gotteslehre.* Gütersloh: Mohr, 1980.

———. *Der Weg Jesu Christi. Christologie in messianischen Dimensionen.* Munich: Kaiser, 1989.

Mühling, Markus. "Mut zur weite der Vernunft. Thesen zum Verhältnis von Vernunft, Glaube, der universitas scientiarum und zum Dialog der Kulturen aus reformatorischer Sicht." *Die "Regensburger Vorlesung" Papst Benedikts XVI. im Dialog der Wissenschaften.* Edited by Christoph Dohmen. Regensburg: Pustet, 2007.

Müller, Gerhard Ludwig. "Exegese V. Exegese und Systematische Theologie." *Lexikon für Theologie und Kirche.* Vol. III, 3rd ed. Freiburg i. Br.: Herder, 1995.

Mußner, Franz. *Die johanneische Sehweise. Quaestiones Disputatae 28.* Freiburg i. Br.: Herder, 1965.

Neufeld, Karl H. *Die Brüder Rahner, Eine Biographie.* 2nd ed. Freiburg i. Br.: Herder, 2004.

Neusner, Jacob. *A Rabbi Talks with Jesus: An Intermillennial, Interfaith Exchange.* New York: Doubleday, 1993 and Montreal: McGill-Queen's University Press, 2000.

Newman, John Henry. *An Essay in Aid of a Grammar of Assent.* Notre Dame, IN: University of Notre Dame, 2001.

———. *An Essay on the Development of Christian Doctrine.* Notre Dame, IN: University of Notre Dame Press, 1989.

———. *The Via Media of the Anglican Church.* London: B.M Pickering, 1877.

Nichols, Aidan. *The Art of God Incarnate: Theology and Image in Christian Tradition.* New York: Paulist, 1980.

———. *Catholic Thought Since the Enlightenment.* London: Gracewing, 1998.

———. *A Pope and a Council on the Sacred Liturgy: Pope Pius XII's Mediator Dei and the Second Vatican Council's Sacrosanctum Concilium with a Comparative Study. "A Tale of Two Documents."* Farnborough, England: St. Michael Abbey's Press, 2002.

———. *The Thought of Benedict XVI: An Introduction to the Theology of Joseph Ratzinger.* New York: Burns & Oates, 2005.

O'Meara, Thomas F., OP. *Thomas Aquinas Theologian.* Notre Dame, IN and London: University of Notre Dame Press, 1999.

Ott, Ludwig. *Fundamentals of Catholic Dogma.* Rockford, IL: Tan, 1974.

Peddicord, Richard. *The Sacred Monster of Thomism: An Introduction to the Life and Legacy of Reginald Garrigou-Lagrange OP.* South Bend, IN: St. Augustine's Press, 2005.

Peters, Tiemo Rainer, and Claus Urban, eds. *The End of Time? The Provocation of Talking about God: Proceedings of a Meeting of Joseph Cardinal Ratzinger, Johann Baptist Metz, Jürgen Moltmann, and Eveline Goodman-Thau in Ahaus.* Mainz: Grünewald, 1999.

Peterson, Erik. *Der Brief an die Römer.* Würzburg: Echter, 1997.

———. *Frühkirche, Judentum und Gnosis, Studien und Untersuchungen.* Freiburg: Herder, 1959; repr. Darmstadt: Wissenschaftliche Buchgesellschaft, 1982.

———. "Das Kreuz und die Gebetsrichtung nach Osten." *Frühkirche, Judentum und Gnosis.* Edited by Everett Diederich. Freiburg i. Br.: Herder, 1959.

———. *Der Monotheismus als politisches Problem, Beiträge zur Geschichte der politischen Theologie im Imperium Romanum.* Leipzig: Hegner, 1935.

Pfister, Peter, ed. *Joseph Ratzinger und das Erzbistum München und Freising. Dokumente und Bilder aus kirchlichen Archiven, Beiträge und Erinnerungen, Schriften des Archivs des Erzbistums München und Freising, Band 10.* Regensburg: Schnell & Steiner, 2006.

Pieper, Josef. *Begeisterung und göttlicher Wahnsinn: über den platonischen Dialog "Phaidros."* Munich: Kösel, 1962.

———. *The End of Time: A Meditation on the Philosophy of History.* San Francisco: Ignatius, 1999.

Pompa, Leon. *Vico.* Cambridge: Cambridge University Press, 1975.

De la Potterie, Ignace. In the introduction to P. Toinet, *Pour une Théologie de l'Exégèse.* Paris: Cerf, 1983.

Przywara, Erich, SJ. *Alter und Neuer Bund.* Munich: Herold, 1956.

———. *Augustinus, die Gestalt als Gefüge.* Leipzig: Hegner, 1934.

Pursell, Brennan. *Benedict of Bavaria: An Intimate Portrait of the Pope and His Homeland.* n.p.: Circle Press, 2008.

Rahner, Hugo. *The Church: Readings in Theology.* New York: Kenedy, 1963.

———. *Man at Play.* New York: Herder and Herder, 1965.

———. *Symbole der Kirche: Ekklesiologie der Väter.* Salzburg: Müller, 1964.

Rahner, Karl. *Foundations of Christian Faith: An Introduction to the Idea of Christianity.* London: Darton, Longman and Todd, 1978.

———. *Grundkurs des Glaubens.* Freiburg i. Br.: Herder, 1976, 25.

———. *Hearer of the Word: Laying the Foundation for a Philosophy of Religion.* New York: Continuum, 1994.

———. *Kirche und Sakramente.* : Freiburg i. Br.: Herder, 1960.

———. *Mysterium Salutis.* Vol. 2, 317–420. Einsiedeln: Benzinger, 1967.

Reid, Alcuin. *The Organic Development of the Liturgy.* San Francisco: Ignatius, 2005.

Reuter, Hermann. *Augustinische Studien.* 2nd ed. Gotha: Perthes, 1887.

Ricoeur, Paul. *Hermeneutik und Psychoanalyse.* Munich: Kösel, 1974.

———. *Hermeneutik und Strukturalismus 1.* Munich: Kösel, 1973.

Riley, Patrick, ed. *The Cambridge Companion to Rousseau.* Cambridge: Cambridge University Press, 2001.

Rowland, Tracey. *Ratzinger's Faith: The Theology of Pope Benedict XVI.* Oxford: Oxford University Press, 2008.

Schillebeeckx, Eduard. *Christus, Sakrament der Gottesbegegnung.* Mainz: Grünewald, 1960.

Schilson, Arno. *Perspektiven theologischer Erneuerung.* Düsseldorf: Patmos, 1986.

———. "'Vom Geist der Liturgie' Versuch einer Relecture von Romano Guardinis Jahrhundertsschrift." *Liturgisches Jahrbuch* 51 (2001): 76–89.

Schleiermacher, Friedrich. *The Christian Faith.* Edinburgh: T & T Clark, 1928.

Schlier, Heinrich. *Die Zeit der Kirche.* Freiburg i. Br.: Herder, 1955.

Schmidbaur, Hans Christian. *Personarum Trinitatis. Die trinitarische Gotteslehre des hl. Thomas von Aquin.* St. Ottilien: EOS, 1993.

Schmidt, Kurt D., ed. *Die Bekenntnisse und grundsätzlichen Äußerungen zur Kirchenfrage.* Vol. 2. Göttingen: Vandenhoeck und Ruprecht, 1935.

Schnackenburg, Rudolf. *Jesus in the Gospels: A Biblical Christology.* Translated by O. C. Dean, Jr. Louisville, KY: Westminster John Knox Press, 1995.

Schreer, Werner, and Georg Stein, eds. "'Universal- und Ortskirche in einem.' Walter Kasper, Zur Theologie und Praxis des bischöflichen Amtes." *Auf neue Art Kirche sein. Wirklichkeiten— Herausforderung—Wendungen. FS Josef Homeyer.* Munich: Bernward bei Don Bosco, 1999, 32–48.

Schulz, Michael. "Wenn das Salz 'dumm' geworden ist." In *Der Glaube ist einfach, Aspekte der Theologie Papst Benedikts XVI.* Edited by Gerhard Ludwig Müller. Regensburg: Pustet, 2007.

Schwaiger, Georg, ed. *Christenleben im Wandel der Zeit.* Munich: Wewel, 1987.

Schweitzer, Albert. *Die Geschichte der Leben-Jesu-Forschung.* Tübingen: Mohr, 1913. English: *The Quest for the Historical Jesus: A Critical Study of its Progress from Reimarus to Wrede.* New York: Schirmer, 1968.

Seewald, Peter. *Benedict XVI: An Intimate Portrait.* San Francisco: Ignatius, 2008.

Semmelroth, Otto. *Church and Sacrament.* Notre Dame, IN: Fides, 1965.

———. *Die Kirche als Ursakrament.* 3rd ed. Frankfurt am Main: Knecht, 1963.

Siebenrock, Roman. *Wahrheit, Gewissen und Geschichte.* Sigmaringendorf: Regio-Verlag Glock und Lutz, 1996.

Sloterdijk, Peter. *Regeln für den Menschenpark. Ein Antwortschreiben zum Brief über den Humanismus.* Frankfurt am Main: Suhrkamp, 1999.

Söding, Thomas. "Die Lebendigkeit des Wortes Gottes. Das Verständnis der Offenbarung bei Joseph Ratzinger." Edited by Frank Meier-Hamidi and Ferdinand Schumacher. *Der Theologe Joseph Ratzinger, Quaestiones Disputatae* 222. Freiburg i. Br.: Herder, 2007.

———. "Die Seele der Theologie." *Communio* 35 (2006): 545–57.

Sohm, Rudolph. *Institutionen des römischen Rechts.* Hannover: Duncker & Humblot, 1883.

———. *Kirchenrecht.* Vols. I and II. Edited by E. Jacobi and O. Mayer. Munich: Duncker & Humblot, 1923 (1892).

———. *Verhältnis von Staat und Kirche, aus dem Begriff von Staat und Kirche entwickelt.* Darmstadt: Wissenschaftliche Buchgesellschaft, 1965 (1873).

———. *Wesen und Ursprung des Katholizismus.* Darmstadt: Wissenschaftliche Buchgesellschaft, 1967 (1909).

Söhngen, Gottlieb. *Die Einheit der Theologie, Gesammelte Abhandlungen, Aufsätze, Vorträge.* Munich: Karl Zink, 1952.

———. *Die katholische Theologie als Wissenschaft und Weisheit.* Paderborn: Winfried, 1932.

Soiron, Thaddaeus. *Der Sakramentale Mensch.* Freiburg i. Br.: Herder, 1949.

Soloviev, Vladimir. *The Antichrist.* Trans. W. J. Barnes and H. H. Haynes. Edinburgh: Floris Classics, 1982.

Spaemann, Robert. *Glück und Wohlwollen. Versuch über Ethik.* Stuttgart: Klett-Cotta, 1989.

———. "Philosophie als Lehre vom glücklichen Leben." In *Die Frage nach dem Glück.* Edited by Günther Bien. Stuttgart: Klett-Cotta, 1978.

Steinbüchel, Theodor. "Die personalistische Grundhaltung des christlichen Ethos." *Theologie und Glaube* 31 (1939).

Stuhlmacher, Peter. *Biblische Theologie des Neuen Testaments.* Vols. I and II. Göttingen: Vandenhoeck & Ruprecht, 1992, 1999.

———. *Von Verstehen des Neuen Testaments: Eine Hermeneutik.* Göttingen: Vandenhoeck & Ruprecht, 1986.

Szczesny, Gerhard. *Das Elend des Christentums oder Plädoyer für einen Humanismus ohne Gott.* Reinbek: Rohwolt, 1968.

———. *Die Zukunft des Unglaubens, Zeitgemäße Betrachtungen eines Nichtchristen.* Munich: List, 1972.

Teilhard de Chardin, Pierre. *Hymn of the Universe.* New York: Harper and Row, 1965.

Thornton, John F., and Susan B. Varenne. *The Essential Pope Benedict XVI: His Central Writings and Speeches.* San Francisco: Harper, 2007.

Tixeront, Joseph. *History of Dogmas.* Westminster, MD: Christian Classics, 1984 (1910).

Tobin, Frank J. *Meister Eckhart: Thought and Language.* Philadelphia: University of Pennsylvania, 1986.

Treffler, Guido. "Der Konzilstheologe Joseph Ratzinger im Spiegel der Konzilsakten des Münchener Erzbischofs Julius Kardinal Döpfner." In *Joseph Ratzinger und das Erzbistum München und Freising.* Edited by Peter Pfister. Regensburg: Schnell and Steiner, 2006.

Trippen, Norbert. *Josef Kardinal Frings (1887–1978).* Vol. 2. Paderborn: Schöningh, 2005.

Valente, Gianni. "The Difficult Years." *Thirty Days* 5 (2006): 42.

———. *Student, Professor, Papst. Joseph Ratzinger an der Universität.* Augsburg: St. Ulrich, 2009.

Verweyen, Hansjürgen. *Joseph Ratzinger—Benedikt XVI. Die Entwicklung seines Denkens.* Darmstadt: Wissenschaftliche Buchgesellschaft, 2007.

Vico, Giambattista. *The New Science (1725).* Ithaca, NY: Cornell University Press, 1984.

Voderholzer, Rudolf. "Schriftauslegung im Widerstreit, Joseph Ratzinger und die Exegese." In *Der Glaube ist einfach, Aspekte der Theologie Papst Benedikts XVI.* Edited by Gerhard Ludwig Müller. Regensburg: Pustet, 2007.

Voegelin, Eric. *The New Science of Politics: An Introduction.* Chicago: University of Chicago Press, 1952.

Vögtle, Anton. *Das Evangelium und die Evangelien.* Düsseldorf: Patmos, 1971.

Vorgrimler, Herbert, ed. *Commentary on the Documents of Vatican II.* Vols. I–IV. New York: Herder and Herder, 1969.

Wallbrecher, Traudl, Ludwig Weimer, and Arnold Stöltzl, eds. *30 Jahre Wegbegleitung, Joseph Ratzinger, Papst Benedikt XVI und die Katholische Integrierte Gemeinde.* Bad Tölz: Urfeld, 2006.

Weil, Simone. *Gravity and Grace.* London: Routledge and Kegan Paul, 1952.

Wilkens, Ulrich. *Theologie des Neuen Testaments.* Neukirchen-Vluyn: Neukirchener Verlag, 2005.

Winter, Michael. "In der Mitte der Kirche, Warum die Integrierte Gemeinde neu ins Blickfeld gerückt ist." *Herderkorrespondenz* 1, no.62, (2008).

Wollbold, Andreas. "Benedikt XVI. und die Katechese." *Münchener Theologische Zeitschrift* 56 (2005): 485–97.

Ziegenaus, Anton. *Die trinitarische Ausprägung der göttlichen Seinsfülle nach Marius Victorinus.* St. Ottilien: EOS, 1972.

Ziegler, A. K. "Pope Gelasius I and His Teaching on the Relation of Church and State." *Catholic Historical Review* 27 (1942): 412–37.

Zizioulas, Jean. *Being as Communion: Studies in Personhood and the Church.* London: Darton, Longman and Todd, 2004.

INDEX